THE DOCTRINE
OF THE ATONEMENT
ACCORDING TO THE APOSTLES

BY

GEORGE SMEATON

HENDRICKSON
PUBLISHERS
PEABODY, MASSACHUSETTS 01961-3473

THE DOCTRINE OF THE ATONEMENT
ACCORDING TO THE APOSTLES

Hendrickson Publishers, Inc. edition

ISBN: 0-913573-98-1

reprinted from the edition originally published in 1870

First printing — April, 1988

Printed in the United States of America

PREFACE.

THIS volume, delayed by other engagements much beyond my anticipations, is the sequel of the volume which appeared in 1868 on the sayings of Jesus in reference to the atonement, and completes my undertaking ; the object of which was to exhibit the entire New Testament teaching on the nature and fruits of Christ's death. I started with the conviction that we cannot attain a full view of the New Testament doctrine on the subject, except in a biblico-historical way ; and have abstained from the artificial construction to which systematic theology has recourse, as well as from merely subjective combinations. The work is rather biblical than formally dogmatic or polemical, and intended to embody positive truth according to the setting in which the doctrine is placed in the apostolic documents.

The doctrine of the atonement being a matter of pure revelation, all our information as to its nature must be drawn simply from the Scriptures ; and the sole inquiry for us is, in what, according to the Lord and His apostles, does the historic fact of the atonement objectively consist, and what are its constituent elements ? The object steadily kept in view has been to determine what saith the Scripture—according to rigid principles of grammatico-historical interpretation—without dislocating or wresting, so far as I am aware, a single expression from its true significance, and thus to run up the matter to authority. Then only do we listen to the word of God, and not to the speculations or wisdom of men. Nor can I allow that, when we expound Scripture by the laws of language, and think over again apostolic thoughts expressed in intelligible terms, we have, after all, but our own individual conception of Christianity. That modern evasion throws all loose, and makes everything uncertain. To affirm that, after the most diligent efforts to interpret Scripture, with a psychology resting on Christian experience, we have but our individual conception of it, is either to call in question that inspired book, or to make its statements, given forth in precise terms according to the laws of language and the laws of thought, an insoluble enigma. On the contrary, I hold that we can think the very thoughts of Christ and His apostles.

The design of this work is mainly to demonstrate, in the only way in which this is to be done, the pure biblical doctrine of the atonement. But polemical references are by no means withheld ; that is, applications, necessarily brief, of ascertained truth to germinant errors, especially to those subtle forms of error which, in an evangelical guise, and not seldom with exegetical appliances, tend wholly to subvert the elements of substitution and penal visitation, which constitute the very essence of the atonement. It is a remarkable fact that since the Reformation no article has been so much impugned in every variety of form. Till recently this was uniformly done by a class of men who had forfeited all claim to be regarded as either evangelical in sentiment or biblical in doctrine. Within recent memory, however, a new phenomenon has presented itself to the attention of Christendom—a sort of spiritual religion or mystic piety, whose watchword is, spiritual life, divine love, and moral redemption, by a great teacher and ideal man, and absolute forgiveness, as contrasted with everything forensic. It is a Christianity without an atonement ; avoiding, whether consciously or unconsciously, the offence of the cross, and bearing plain marks of the Rationalistic soil from which it sprung ; and it has found a wide response in every Protestant land.

The work here presented to the public was suggested by

this new phenomenon, especially by the somewhat bold attempt
which it has made to vindicate its claims by an exegetical
appeal to Scripture. I refer to attempts in this direction by
Menken,[1] Stier,[2] Klaiber,[3] and above all by Hofmann[4] of
Erlangen, who, in the use of a peculiar exegesis, have arrived
at results diametrically opposed to the views at which the
entire Christian church in the east and west arrived, during
eighteen centuries of her history. Schleiermacher, the great
champion and bulwark of this tendency, from reasons which
may be easily inferred, did not attempt to base these views on
exegetical investigation, but on Christian consciousness. This
phenomenon of a Christianity without an atonement, professedly
based on an exegetical foundation, seemed to call for such a
work as the present ; and in the course of it I have thoroughly
investigated the teaching of the Lord and His apostles. Much
as I value the creeds of the church, I do not appeal to them
but to Scripture testimony strictly interpreted.

How was this object to be best accomplished ? Two modes
presented themselves, and between them a choice was to be
made—that of taking up in succession the passages as they
occur in the apostolic writings, and that of digesting them
under a variety of topics—chapters, divisions, and sections.
To avoid the repetitions which seemed certain to be entailed
upon me by discussing the passages as they lie (*in situ*) in the
several books, and giving them such an amount of expansion
as would be necessary to make the expositions readable by the
Christian public as well as by erudite men, the second method
seemed absolutely necessary ; and in point of fact I started
on that principle. But I soon found it necessary to alter my
method, for the following reasons. The quotations were necessarily truncated and fragmentary. Different apostles must
contribute a portion of thought out of every variety of connec-

[1] See Menken's *Schriften*, 7 vols., 1858.
[2] Stier, *Andeut. für glaubiges Schriftverst. zweite Sammlung*, Leipz. 1828.
[3] Klaiber, *die N. T. Lehre von der Sünde und Erlösung*, Stuttgart 1836.
[4] Hofmann, *der Schriftbeweis*, second edition.

tion, and it was impossible to refer to the occasion in which
the words were originally used. The same passage or clause
which contributed one quota must be recalled for another expression or thought not always well adapted to the artificial
division for which it was assigned. Besides, it became all too
evident that this must inevitably prove a new form of dogmatic
theology; and instead of avoiding repetitions, would, though
in another way, make them tenfold greater. The other method,
I was satisfied, was the only one to be adopted. Nor was the
repetition so great as I anticipated;[1] for every text, even when
there did arise a certain sameness, had so much peculiar to
itself as to give it a freshness of its own.

I have appended in the notes a few references to the
numerous works which I have perused on this great theme,
and a historical outline at the end. No one has hitherto
traversed the whole field in this way, though numerous speci-
men-texts are discussed in dogmatic compends, polemical
treatises, biblical dogmatics, outlines of Pauline, Petrine, and
Johannine theology, not to mention commentaries; and in all
these not much of value has escaped my notice.

I have only to add, that personally it has been to me the
source of the greatest pleasure to pursue these investigations,
the result of which is now given to others. To Him whose
atoning death I have laboured to expound from His unerring
word, I commit the work now finished. May He be pleased
to accept the offering, and use it for the glory of His name.

GEORGE SMEATON.

EDINBURGH, *Oct.* 1870.

---

[1] On this point I may say with Athanasius: ἐπειδὴ γὰρ περὶ τῆς εὐδοκίας τοῦ
Θεοῦ λαλοῦμεν, διὰ τοῦτο τὸν αὐτὸν νοῦν διὰ πλειόνων ἑρμηνεύομεν, μὴ ἄρα τι παραλιμπάνειν
δόξωμεν, καὶ ἔγκλημα γένηται ὡς ἐνδεῶς εἰρηκόσι. Καὶ γὰρ βέλτιον ταυτολογίας μέμψιν
ὑποστῆσαι, ἢ παραλεῖψαί τι τῶν ὀφειλόντων γραφῆναι. (Athan. *de Incarnatione,* c.
20.)

CONTENTS.

—◆—

CHAPTER I.

CHAPTER II. .

CHAPTER III.

CHAPTER IV.

CHAPTER V.

APPENDIX.

INDICES.

"A RELIGION with a sacrifice, and a religion without a sacrifice, differ in the whole kind. The first respects the atonement of our past sins, and our daily infirmities: it respects God as the judge and avenger of wickedness, as well as the rewarder of those who diligently seek Him. The other is a kind of philosophical institution to train men up in the practice of piety and virtue. A religion without a sacrifice is at most but half as much as a religion with a sacrifice ; and that half wherein they agree of a quite different nature from each other. The practical part of religion is vastly altered by the belief or denial of the sacrifice and expiation of Christ's death."—*Sherlock's Vindication.*

—— " si l'on ôte de la religion Chrétienne la croix de Jésus Christ, c'est à dire la satisfaction pour nos péchés par sa mort, l'assemblage de tous ses autres enseignemens se dissout ; il n'y reste plus ni certitude de vérité ni solidité de consolation, de sorte que la propitiation de Jésus et l'expiation de nos offenses par son sang sont comme la clef de la voûte, sur laquelle toutes les autres pièces s'ajustent et reposent."—AMYRAUT, *Troisième Sermon.*

APOSTLES' SAYINGS ON THE ATONEMENT.

CHAPTER I.

THE PREPARATION OF THE APOSTLES, AND THE CIRCLE OF THEIR TESTIMONY.

SEC. I.—THE APOSTLES' TEACHING ON THE ATONEMENT BASED ON THAT OF THE LORD JESUS.

IN the previous volume I examined fully the doctrine of the atonement as taught by Christ Himself. I recalled the several scenes in which the Christ of God uttered from His own consciousness the absolute truth as to the scope, nature, and fruits of His vicarious death. I traced in what terms, pursuant to the suretyship which He had undertaken, He gave expression in different connections to the dedication and obedience of His life. How ample His teaching is on this particular theme, when it is all collected and classified, we had occasion to survey. We took a list of His sayings in their number, variety, and fulness, and saw that every benefit connected with His atonement was referred to by the Lord Himself; nay, certain aspects of the atonement, and especially those which relate to its divine side, or exhibit it as redounding to the glory of God, are with more simplicity and comprehensiveness portrayed by the Lord Himself than by any other speaker in any other portion of Scripture.

In the present volume I purpose to exhibit the doctrine of the atonement as taught by the apostles. This is necessary,

A

in order to give completeness to the New Testament testimony. The great peculiarity of their teaching, as compared with the other teaching of Scripture, is that they treat it as an accomplished fact; and this single circumstance accourts for all that is distinctive in the statements of the apostles as compared with the sayings of the Lord Jesus. They refer to it as an eternally valid fact, pregnant with consequences that abide for ever. They not only give prominence to all the blessings it procured, but delineate the spiritual sentiments, feelings, and experience which take their rise from it. They show how it colours the history and moulds the life of those who receive it, and are saved by it.

It deserves notice that the views of the apostles, after the atonement had become an accomplished fact, underwent the most memorable change. Long had they repelled the thought of Christ's death, which they clearly enough perceived must be the death-blow of all their Jewish dreams and theories. But when it actually arrived, and they looked back on the completed fact, approved and accepted at His resurrection, they were ushered into a new world of thought and feeling. Theirs was a transition from a Jewish to a Christian experience; that is, to one where the atonement was a completed transaction with saving efficacy. They passed over from prophecy to fulfilment, from promise to fact, from anticipation to reality, from the Old Testament Church into that of the New Testament, from the knowledge of Christ after the flesh to a new mode of knowledge (2 Cor. v. 16). To live over again that revolution of experience, or to transfer ourselves into it even in idea, is impossible; for none but the immediate followers of the Lord could adequately know it. But one point is clear. Faith now reposed on fact—divine fact—not only as the embodiment of divine thoughts, but as the accomplishment of all the prophetic announcements with which those who waited for the consolation of Israel were familiar. To use a familiar modern phrase, we have here THE CHRISTIAN CONSCIOUSNESS in its purest form

—in its normal condition.[1] If we have in the sayings of Jesus the consciousness of the God-man or of the Christ, we have in the testimony of the apostles what may be called the Christian consciousness in its highest perfection.

But it is in a much higher light than this that the apostles must be regarded. Besides uttering the Christian consciousness, they are the ORGANS OF CHRIST'S SELF-REVELATION to the Church. Their message, intended to be the complement of Christ's own teaching, is a revelation addressed to all men, and extending to all time. For this function they needed a special preparation of their own minds, which may be described as twofold : first, oral instruction, imparted directly by Christ's own lips subsequently to His resurrection ; secondly, a mediate and more continuous aid of the Comforter, to enable them to apply to all emergencies the truth given to them by their Lord. It was this twofold revelation that secured a full coincidence between the Lord's teaching and theirs. All that they said or wrote for after times was thus divine revelation, not less truly than if all had been personally spoken by their Lord. He undertook, in fact, the responsibility of their official teaching (Matt. x. 40). Their testimony was thus in the last degree important, both as they were eye-witnesses to matters of fact, and as they were organs of a revelation which consisted in the application and further development of Christ's teaching on all points, as well as on the great doctrine of the atonement.[2]

The memory of Christ's earthly ministry was vividly recalled, and fresh instruction communicated, by Him after His

---

[1] This phrase *Christian consciousness*, as at first used by Schleiermacher, presupposed living Christianity ; and its expression was found in all the creeds of Christendom. On these he based his *Glaubenslehre*, and not immediately on Scripture ; and on these he exercised his constructive talent, sometimes well, oftener waywardly. The Christian consciousness was surely purest in the apostles.

[2] Though we are not defenders of mechanical inspiration, we contend for something more than the modern theory, or the Quaker theory ; that is, we hold that we have in Scripture *unerring revelation* as well as the Christian consciousness.

resurrection from the dead ; and to both these points we must refer.

1. As they had previously occupied a unique relation to the Lord, and had seen Him in every variety of scene till He finished His work, it was one part of their commission to testify orally what they had seen and heard and handled of the Word of life (1 John i. 1–4), and also to embody their recollections in written records. The importance of such records, as we have elsewhere shown, for a just idea of the atonement cannot be over-estimated. While the commission was given to all the apostles to rehearse what they had seen and heard, some were made aware that they had the more special task assigned to them of composing a historical narrative of His life which should be for all time. So essential a part of apostolic testimony, in fact, did this element of narration constitute, that we cannot conceive of the founding and permanent duration of the Christian church without it ; and to aid them, the Comforter, the great Remembrancer, was promised, to recall to their minds an accurate outline of what the Lord did and taught (John xvi. 13). Acting upon their memory, the Holy Ghost resuscitated His express words and deeds, with all their circumstances and accessories, so far as this was necessary to exhibit His person or to manifest His atoning work. A supernatural power, capable of evoking the past from the tablets of memory, rendered all things back in their original vividness, and fixed them in their minds with a clearness with which a stranger could not intermeddle.

But the *fresh instruction* which they received from personal interviews with the Redeemer subsequently to the resurrection must next be noticed. This oral instruction received from the lips of the risen Lord is certain as to the matter of fact, and on many grounds was indispensably necessary. Nor was it limited to the eleven alone. Paul, too, received it at a later day, when he took rank among the apostles as one born out of due time. How far the oral instruction of the risen Re-

deemer extended, it may be difficult for us to say. Whether
or not it comprehended all the great articles of divine truth,
it certainly extended to the atonement (Luke xxiv. 25). This
was to be the substance and foundation of all their preaching,
and it was indispensably necessary for them to possess the
most accurate knowledge of it. One object, therefore, which
the Lord had in view during those forty days' sojourn with the
disciples after His resurrection, was to open their understandings in the course of these personal interviews, to apprehend
with all possible precision the nature of His death—its necessity, constituent elements, and efficacy; against which, in every
form, they had long entertained the most invincible prejudice.
He now made all things plain, showing that the Christ must
have suffered these things.

How they were introduced into the theology of the Old
Testament is specially worthy of notice. A due consideration
of this point serves to bring out one most important fact, viz.
that Christ's oral expositions are to be taken as THE MIDDLE
TERM, or as the connecting link between the Old Testament
records on the one hand, and the apostolic commentary on the
other. In a word, He was Himself the interpreter of Scripture, and of His own history, in the course of those oral communications. In the book of Acts, and in the epistles, we
find numerous interpretations of the prophecies, as well as of
the types and sacrifices which owe their origin to this source.
The evangelist Luke relates, that on the first resurrection-day,
upon the Emmaus road, in order to instruct the two disciples
with whom He entered into conversation, the Lord, beginning
at Moses and all the prophets, expounded in all the Scriptures
the things concerning Himself (Luke xxiv. 27); that is, He led
them to a full survey of the typology and of the prophetical
system of the Old Testament Scriptures. The same evening
He reviewed the whole subject not less fully in presence of the
eleven and other disciples, expounding to them how the Old
Testament Scriptures received their fulfilment in Himself, and

opening all that related to His death and resurrection. It is
interesting to notice the extent of that never forgotten commentary, on which the Comforter in all His further revelations
ever afterwards proceeded. The evangelist mentions that His
exposition extended to the LAW of Moses, to the PROPHETS, and
to the PSALMS. The allusion to the law of Moses recalls the
whole range of typical theology—the sacrifices, the priestly
institute, and the temple services. The allusion to the prophets
reminds us of the wide field of Messianic prophecy, from the
first promise in the garden of Eden to the last of the prophets. The allusion to the Psalms recalls those utterances
which were put beforehand into the mouth of the suffering
Messiah in a series of psalms in which the Lord Jesus found
Himself. He thus, in all these three divisions of Scripture,
supplied them with the key which served to unlock what had
never been so fully understood before in reference to His
atoning death.

These invaluable expositions, which may be called in
modern phrase the Lord's own system of hermeneutics, formed
the apostles to be interpreters of the Old Testament, directing
them where and how to find allusions to the suffering Messiah.
Hence the certainty and precision with which they ever afterwards proceeded to expound those holy oracles in all their
discourses. Although these comments from the lips of the
Messiah, who thereby showed how He found Himself in the
Old Testament, have not been preserved to us in a separate
form, they are doubtless to a large extent wrought into the
texture of Scripture; and under the apostles' allusions to the
Old Testament we may read the Lord's own commentary.
These expositions, whereby He opened their understandings to
understand the Scriptures, introduced the apostles into the true
significance of the Old Testament (Luke xxiv. 44), throwing
light on the two economies, and thus bringing in the authority
of Christ to direct them in all their future career. His sanction is thus given to the apostolic interpretation of the Jewish

rites; and we are warranted to say that we see the Lord's own commentary underlying that of the apostles, whether we find allusion to the types, or to the prophecies, or to the Psalms, in their sermons and epistles. These expositions made the apostles acquainted with the doctrine of the atonement, in its necessity and scope, in its constituent elements and saving results. The apostles received the fullest instruction from the lips of their risen Lord; and on this theme it appears that the instruction was subject to none of the reserves which checked their curiosity upon another occasion, when they would make inquiries as to points bearing on the future of His kingdom (Acts i. 7).

2. It must be further noticed that the apostles' doctrine, as set forth in their sermons and epistles, was but an expansion or further carrying out of the Lord's own teaching. What the apostles added was pre-eminently a testimony to the atonement as an accomplished fact, and to its efficacy in the relations of Christian life. They put the doctrine in its due position as the central article of Christianity. They assigned it the prominent place which it was henceforth to hold in the life of the Christian church. All this followed, but could not have preceded, the actual consummation of that redemption-work. Their great business was to represent it as finished for all time, as possessing an everlasting efficacy, and requiring no repetition. They constantly refer to the great truth, that Christ DIED ONCE, and that there is no more sacrifice for sins. For the doctrine on the subject of the atonement, however, the Lord Himself gave the keynote of all that the apostles subsequently added. The sayings of Jesus, in fact, contain the germ of all that they afterwards developed. So far did the Lord supply the outline which the apostles filled up, that I feel warranted to affirm the apostles' doctrine on this point was ALWAYS SUPPORTED by what had been furnished in the Lord's own teaching, and was constantly supplied from it. Though it may be described as a further development or expansion of

what was found in germ in the Lord's words, it was in reality not so much new truth, as the free and varied application of what they had already heard to the several phases of Christian experience, and to the germinant errors that arose in the different churches.

The apostles' doctrine on the atonement coincides accordingly at all points with the teaching of Jesus; and it was unerring revelation. It is the more necessary to advert to this, because many misapprehend the apostles' relation to the Lord. Thus, some have argued that, to restore Christianity to its original simplicity, nothing is more indispensably necessary than to abide exclusively by the sayings of Jesus.[1] This they advocate, because they assume that the truth has undergone a certain transmutation in the apostles' hands. Others, again, unduly magnify their mental peculiarities, till they regard them not as announcing the same truth with a peculiar type of mind, but as actually maintaining differences of doctrine. To these opinions, in all their modifications, we must emphatically oppose two considerations: (1) Their conscious relation to the great Teacher, and (2) His superintending care. On the one hand, men imbued as they were with reverence for Jesus, whom they worshipped with divine honours, and whom they were directed to hear (Matt. xvii. 5), were far too humble and self-denied to suppose for a moment that they could add any perfection to His doctrine. Far from thinking that they were wiser than He, or capable of adding one new ray to His self-revelation, they kept themselves within the limits of disciples, and merely built on His foundation. On the other hand, as

---

[1] At the end of last century a school of Rationalism arose, which sought to prove that the apostles accommodated themselves to the prejudices of the age, and deviated from the pure and simple teaching of Jesus. Priestley represented the same tendency in England. Two important works were written in reply to the theory of accommodation by the two Dutch professors Heringa and Lotze. In fact, the same theory has often reappeared. It was the Gnostic theory; it was the theory of the late Dr. Baur of Tübingen; and it still exists to a very large extent. On this ground, the attempt was made to explain away the Lord's atonement and deity as Pauline additions or corruptions.

they had a continuous revelation by the Spirit, who brought up to them the Lord's own words, and also the Old Testament record, as was expedient for the necessities of the churches, they were never left without the superintending care and guidance of Christ; and there was no disharmony between Him and them. Nay, it must be further added, that as divinely commissioned men, they had the same authority with their Lord, who fully identified Himself with them.

SEC. II.—GENERAL VIEW OF THE APOSTLES' TESTIMONY TO THE ATONEMENT.

The plan to be followed in this volume is furnished to our hand by the several books of the New Testament. The previous volume, limited to the sayings of Jesus, which we classified according to the elements and aspects of the truth which they peculiarly unfold, was meant to embrace the testimony supplied by the evangelists. The present volume, taking up the same theme where the Gospels end, is intended to unfold the apostles' testimony, and to give a full outline of what is contained upon this subject in their epistles to the churches. The only practicable mode of doing this is to take the several books, and to exhaust in order the testimony they contain. To this we have been led by the necessities of the case; for the attempt to reduce the whole to a few heads, by taking a fragment from one text and another fragment from another, was found to be so dislocating and artificial, as to satisfy us that the apostles' doctrine could not be displayed, except by taking the several apostles and their several epistles separately. We have thus to notice the testimony of a Peter, of a John, and of a Paul, as they refer to the atonement, in the order of the epistles given in the common editions of the New Testament; for the advantages supposed to be gained by following the chronological order of their composition, even if this point could be fully ascertained, would not, we think, countervail the inconvenience thereby occasioned to the general reader. We shall therefore follow the order of the epistles in the English Bible.

As the apostles interweave, however, many allusions to the types of the Mosaic law, and to the Psalms and prophecies of the Old Testament, we deem it necessary, without turning aside from our definite purpose of exhibiting the apostolic testimony, to set forth, at least in outline, the use to which those parts of Scripture are turned in the book of Acts and in the epistles. We shall prefix, therefore, a chapter on the ancient sacrifices, and another on the ancient prophecies, as adduced by the epistles. But before entering upon these, it will be necessary to give a general view of the apostles' testimony and preaching.

1. The apostles insist much on the dignity of the Lord's person, and on the connection between the INCARNATION and ATONEMENT. After Christ's resurrection, we find in the apostles a surprising increase of light on the subject of Christ's person, as Thomas' testimony proves (John xx. 28). They saw in a new manner the effect of the incarnation on His atoning work, and they expressed it with wondering delight, as is apparent whether we look at the book of Acts or at the epistles to the several churches. Thus, they speak of the Jews as killing the Prince of life (Acts iii. 15); of crucifying the Lord of glory (1 Cor. ii. 9); of the Son, the brightness of the Father's glory, and the express image of His person, and upholding all things by the word of His power, having by Himself purged our sins (Heb. i. 3).

The apostles, in all those passages where they describe the redemption-work of the Lord, ascribe to the Saviour the possession of a divine nature, sometimes more directly, at other times more by implication. But it is never difficult to apprehend their deep conviction of the presence of His deity in all His atoning work. They speak of it as a divine work, immediately accomplished by God Himself. Nor do they represent God as the author of it merely in the sense of originating or concerting the plan which the Mediator was commissioned and empowered to carry into execution: they speak of a divine person as the agent by whom the redemption-work was completed, and of His work as closely connected with His divine nature,—that is, the work of one who was very God. The apostles, under the guidance of the Spirit, apprehended His work of obedience during the years He had sojourned with them, as infinitely valuable, and His blood as infinitely precious, because emanating from the abasement of Him who was God over all; ascribing it not merely to a sinless man, but to the Son of God, and thus, in virtue of the union of the natures, possessing an all-sufficient value and validity. Their doctrine on the subject of Christ's incarnation was, that it took place in a historic person, and in one only; and that, according to the will of Him that sent Him, He comprehended in Himself a body, or a vast multitude.[1] It is everywhere set forth as their deepest conviction, that instead of being one among His fellows, Jesus was the representative head of a redeemed company, who find their propitiation, righteousness, and redemption in Him.

The apostles' doctrine, too, is to the effect that the Son of God in this great transaction was simply acting as the restorer of the lost, for there is no allusion to the incarnation as a natural process. They represent the historical appearance of the Son of God as CONDITIONED SOLELY BY SIN, and there is no warrant from anything in their language for giving it a double foundation.[2] The stupendous fact of man's redemption was an end worthy of such a cost, but the incarnation was not necessary

---

[1] Most of the errors on the atonement have arisen from the habit of reading the life of Jesus as the biography of an individual, not as that of the Surety for others—the second Adam. See Luther on Gal. iii. 13 in Latin.

[2] The modern theory of an incarnation irrespective of the fall has been already noticed in our former volume, *Sayings of Jesus* (Appendix, sec. vii.).

except on the supposition of redemption from sin. The incarnation and the cross are thus viewed as inseparable, but both as MEANS to an end, viz. the vindication of divine justice, the expiation of sin, the meritorious obedience to be rendered to the law. This is the *rationale* of the infinite condescension displayed in the incarnation and the cross. The apostles make no allusion to any other design. When we put together the apostolic testimony on this point, there are not a few texts which plainly announce that the design of the incarnation was only for the redemption of the lost, and that the atonement owes its value to the fact that it was the work of a divine person. Thus, it is said that Christ was made of a woman to redeem men (Gal. iv. 4); that He took part of our flesh and blood to destroy death (Heb. ii. 14); that He was manifested to destroy the works of the devil (1 John iii. 8); that He came into the world to save sinners (1 Tim. i. 15). To assign a different intention to the incarnation, is not only to be wise above what is written, but well-nigh a contradiction to the explicit statement of what is set forth as the only design known to the apostles.

2. The apostles' change of mind as to the cross, and their testimony to Christ crucified. Before we enter into the apostolic testimony in detail, two things at the outset demand more particular notice : the entire revolution of the apostles' own views as to the death of the cross, and their uniform testimony to it as their confidence and boast. They first of all discerned its significance for themselves; and then, knowing that the atonement is suited to the capacity of every class and every age, they gave the utmost prominence to this great article in all their preaching. As it is not in my plan to offer reflections either of a practical or speculative nature, but to pursue an exegetical inquiry in the way that seems to me the best suited to convey strictly biblical views of the atonement, it seems proper here to refer to both these points. The change upon their own minds will lead us to understand the prominent

place which the apostles gave to this article in all their preaching. A few remarks illustrative of their state of mind, and of
the method they pursued, will suffice.

They were brought to see a peculiar significance in the
mode of Christ's death, and that something more was to be
seen in the cross than if He had undergone any other death.
They comprehended the weighty reasons which rendered it
expedient and necessary, according to the divine wisdom, that
the Surety should die by a death which was accursed by God.
They were persuaded that it contained more than any other
mode of death; and accordingly we find them repeatedly
making mention of the cross, or of the tree, as carrying with it
a peculiar emphasis. Thus John, in referring to the Lord's
own words, tells us: " This He said, signifying what death He
should die" (John xii. 33; comp. viii. 28). Peter, again, both
in his sermons recorded in the book of Acts and in his epistle,
refers to the TREE on which He suffered and bore our sins
(1 Pet. ii. 24). Paul glories only in the cross of the Lord
(Gal. vi. 14). They saw that God's terrible curse, on account
of sin committed in Adam and in their own persons, lay on
Jesus, and that He was made a curse, of which the cross was
the symbol rather than the cause.

The apostles were led either by the promised Comforter,
the Spirit of truth, or by the Lord's oral teaching in His resurrection interviews, to the conviction that Jesus died an accursed
death, according to prophecy. This comes out in a passage,
the point of which it is important to apprehend: " Christ hath
redeemed us from the curse of the law, being made a CURSE
for us: for it is written, CURSED is every one that hangeth on
a tree" (Gal. iii. 13). That quotation from Moses contains an
intimation of the way in which Messiah was to die. Like the
passage adduced by our Lord Himself about the lifting up of
the brazen serpent on a pole, it shows that from the first it was
intended to be symbolical, prophetical, and typical. We shall
not enter into the question whether crucifixion was a Roman

punishment, and not at all a Jewish punishment;[1] for the point of the quotation is the suspending of a criminal on a tree, whether by a subsequent judicial act after death, or by the crucifixion while yet alive. That is the point of resemblance between the two cases. By the Mosaic law, that mode of punishment was inflicted upon great criminals, such as blasphemers and idolaters, the rebellious and seditious. When we compare the passage in Deuteronomy with the doctrine which Paul declares in connection with that passage, he plainly intends to prove that Christ was the curse-bearer in our room, and that this great truth was established by the subjoined sign. Christ was made a curse before being suspended on the tree: for God made Him to be sin for us (2 Cor. v. 21); and that hanging on the tree was but the public testimony[2] to the curse endured in our room. The cause of the curse was not the hanging on the tree, but the sin with which He was charged; and that mode of punishment exhibited that He was the object of God's holy displeasure, not indeed because He was suspended on the tree, but because He was the sin-bearer; and the punishment of the offences for which that ignominious punishment was allotted was then inflicted. Divine wisdom appointed that He who bore the sin of the world should be exposed as a curse; for the divine displeasure was thus more awfully displayed.

But why was this peculiar method adopted? Of all the

---

[1] Baronius, Lipsius, A. Schultens, and others, warmly and with great learning maintained that it is a mere rabbinical shift and evasion to deny that this mode of punishment was ever used in the Hebrew republic. The Jewish commentators allow only four forms of capital punishment, but deny that crucifixion was ever used, or that a living person ever was in any form suspended on a tree. The opposite view was held by the above-named authorities. The opinion that crucifixion was a Roman punishment was always the common view, and still is.

[2] The shallow comment, that Christ was made a curse merely in the sense that His enemies executed upon Him the cursed death of a malefactor, devised by the Socinians and repeated by the Rationalists, has been recently renewed by Hofmann. But if it was not His enemies, but God, that made Him a curse, there is no room for two opinions on the subject (Gal. iii. 13).

explanations propounded, the simplest is that given by Witsius and others, that sin came into the world by the wanton violation of the divine will in connection with the forbidden fruit. As the fatal sin which diffused the curse over the human race was connected with the forbidden tree, God wisely ordained that the second Adam should expiate sin by being suspended on a tree; and He appointed in the law such a symbol of the curse as reminds all men of the origin of the divine curse on the world.[1] He would not have the curse removed by any other means. This adequately explains the divine wisdom in the giving of such a law. And they who had a true knowledge of the way of atonement might find occasion from that symbol, as in the parallel case of the lifting up of the brazen serpent on the pole, or in the leading up of the sacrifices to the altar, to conclude that Messiah should one day be made a curse, and hang upon a tree; but that He should not continue long, for He should be taken down on the same day before sunset. Whether many apprehended all this in the prophetic type, or only a very few, is not the question. We who live in the times of accomplishment are taught that such a lesson was conveyed by it to us (1 Pet. i. 11, 12).

The apostles justly regarded the crucifixion as the deepest possible humiliation. It was the most ignominious of punishments, inflicted only on slaves and the lowest of the people; and if free men were at any time subjected to crucifixion for great crimes, such as robbery, high treason, or sedition, the sentence could not be executed till they were put into the category of slaves by degradation. Their liberty was taken from them by servile stripes and scourging, as was done to Christ.[2] However that crisis in Christ's history perplexed and saddened the apostles for a time, they no sooner discerned the deep underlying truth of the symbol than they triumphed and gloried in

---

[1] See Witsius *on the Creed*, Ex. xvi. 32.
[2] See Turretin. *de Satisf.* par. ii. 26; Witsius; Binnæus, *de Morte J. C.* lib. iii.

the deep abasement to which the Lord of glory had descended for them, enduring the cross and despising the shame. Their symbol was the cross; their boast was the cross: they could not live without it; they could not die without it. They set forth, wherever they went, that the types of the law had received their fulfilment in the cross, and that the Messiah had died in such a way that every one must necessarily perceive that the curse of the law was fulfilled upon Him in our room and stead.

3. The apostles uniformly testify that the cross was their confidence and boast, and lead us to regard the atonement as belonging to the main scope of revelation. Thus, when Paul describes the purport of his apostolic labours, he says, "We preach Christ crucified" (1 Cor. i. 23); and, besides, he calls the gospel the preaching of the cross, or more strictly rendered, "the word of the cross" (1 Cor. i. 18). We cannot allow that this means no more than the preaching of the pure moral code which Jesus taught, with only the accessory notion that it was confirmed by His death. Nor can the language with any greater reason be referred to Christ's example, as sealed by martyrdom. Such comments as these, which aim at evading the vicarious sacrifice, are a violence to language, and wholly inconsistent with the import of the terms. The substance of Christianity, and the preaching of it, could not be described in such a way, unless the cross of Christ, considered as a vicarious satisfaction, constituted its essential element, nay, its principal design. We have a further evidence of the same thing when the apostle adds, that the cross was a stumbling-block to one, and foolishness to another, of the nationalities among whom he laboured. Had the cross, however, been simply propounded as a confirmation of Christ's doctrine, it could not have been an offence. It would rather have tended, as in the case of Socrates, to win respect for the teacher and for His doctrine, that He had closed His career in attestation to His teaching by the endurance of a violent death.

But the doctrine of the cross, as a propitiation and as a way of salvation, was equally in collision with Jewish pride and Gentile wisdom. To the Jew it was a stumbling-block, partly because it took him up on the ground of a sinner, helpless and in need of reconciliation, partly because it summoned him to trust in the innocence of a suffering Surety, and not in his own righteousness. His expectation of a Messiah as a temporal prince was in proportion to his pharisaic self-righteousness, and probably an offshoot from it. He was offended at a suffering Messiah, both because it crossed his theory, and because it presupposed a guilt which was to be expiated in no other way. To the Greek, again, the preaching of the cross was foolishness, because it proceeded on the supposition, so repugnant to the mere disciple of human wisdom, the speculative admirer of notions and theories, that salvation was the principal design of God, and that this was the scope of Christianity when it preached a crucified Christ. The preaching of the apostles confronted both these tendencies; and amid all their opposition, far from losing confidence or feeling shame, they retreated to the ground that the preaching of the cross was the power of God and the wisdom of God to them that are called, and that it effected what all the resources of human wisdom could not effect (1 Cor. i. 24; Rom. i. 16).

4. Paul in a variety of ways declares that the atonement was the principal topic of his preaching. One of these testimonies is to this effect: "*I determined not to know anything among you, save Jesus Christ, and Him crucified*" (1 Cor. ii. 2). No one can doubt what is the import of this statement. When he "determined to know nothing among them, save Jesus Christ, and Him crucified," the import clearly is, that he preached, as his grand topic, the atonement of Christ, in all its bearings and fulness of application. The words intimate that he made the doctrine of the cross the principal matter of preaching; the other truths which he taught being either derived from it or connected with it. They were, in a word,

B

either postulates or corollaries; and whatever could not be connected with it, was made very subordinate or omitted. This had been done on purpose and from forethought. The apostle went to work according to a plan; and to this his fundamental principle he continued faithful in all his subsequent ministry.

In the same epistle we find another passage where he declares that THE GOSPEL which he had preached, which the Corinthians had received, and by which they were saved if they kept it in memory, was " *that Christ died for our sins, according to the Scriptures*" (1 Cor. xv. 3). Now, can this mean that Christ's death was preached as but a dissuasive from sin ? Does the apostle say that the death of Christ was preached merely as a means to free men from the bondage of moral corruption, either by the force of suasion or by the infusion of spiritual life ? By no means. Such a comment not only fails to exhaust the idea, but misses the proper sense of the words, " dying for our sins." That expression, wherever it occurs, bears reference to THE MERITORIOUS CAUSE OF HIS DEATH. In no case does it refer to future deliverance, but always to the expiation of past guilt. This is apparent in a passage which combines the two ideas we have now noticed, making the expiation of past guilt a means to a further end,— a means to future deliverance : "Who gave Himself for our sins, that (ὅπως) He might deliver us from this present evil world" (Gal. i. 4).

In the Epistle to the Galatians we have the most copious evidence of the value which Paul attached to the preaching of the atonement. His great object there is to show, that if the cross is either obscured or superseded, the gospel is no gospel. He pointedly condemns the views of the Judaizing teachers, who enforced on the Galatian churches the observance of the Mosaic law as necessary to salvation; showing that, in reality, it is another gospel where the cross is either concealed, or not presented as the sole ground of acceptance. These Judaizing zealots were men who, instead of directing their undivided attention to the atonement as the exclusive ground of salvation, and therefore as the great doctrine of the gospel, put circumcision and the rites of the Mosaic law in its place (Gal. v. 1–4); and the apostle asserts that there is no other gospel but where the cross of Christ occupies the principal place. They to whom he referred perverted the gospel of Christ (Gal. i. 7). Then he declares, in a tone of authority as well as of the deepest solemnity, " Though we or an angel from heaven preach any other gospel unto you than that which we have preached unto you, let him be accursed" (Gal i. 8); a statement which he repeats, partly to show that it was no utterance of human passion, partly to recall to memory what he seems to have first spoken in the course of his personal ministry. Were the atonement not the principal matter of the gospel, and the highest exhibition of the united wisdom, love, and faithfulness of God,—in a word, the greatest act of God in the universe,—that terrible anathema on its subverters would seem to us something inexplicable, if not intolerable. But the doom is justified by the nature of Christ's death, and by the great fact of the atonement.

The apostle, as he proceeds, takes every opportunity from the course of his argument, not only to warn the Galatian churches against the perverters of the gospel, but to show that the cross formed the burden of his own preaching. He observes that the men to whom he wrote the epistle were they " before whose eyes Jesus Christ had been evidently set forth, crucified among them" (Gal. iii. 1); in which expression he gives us a brief outline of his preaching. And he winds up the epistle by the announcement that, in his official capacity, as well as in his individual capacity as a Christian, he would not " glory, save in the cross of the Lord Jesus Christ" (Gal. vi. 14). This one foundation he adduces in opposition to all these false grounds,—the rites, the ceremonies, the legal observances, on which the others built their confidence. He would glory in nothing save in the cross ; and all legalism he denounces as enmity to " the cross of Christ" (Phil. iii. 18). The expression " *the cross of Christ*," in the sense in which the apostle uses it, denotes salvation by the propitiation of the cross, or by the dying obedience of a Surety made a curse in our room. And when we minutely examine the various epistles addressed to the churches, whether composed of Jews or Gentiles, we find that the atonement was preached to men in all states of mind, as the great message with which the apostles were charged, and as equally necessary to the established Christian and the anxious inquirer.

In one memorable passage which I shall subjoin, the Apostle Paul remarks that the preaching of the cross was the main scope of his ministry, and the very end for which he was specially appointed: " Who gave Himself a ransom for all, to be testified in due time. Whereunto I am ordained a preacher, and an apostle (I speak the truth in Christ, and lie not)" (1 Tim. ii. 6, 7). He there declares, with all the solemnity of an oath, that he not only preached the atonement as a divinely provided ransom for man's salvation, but that he was specially ordained as an apostle and preacher for this very service. The cross was thus to him and to all his successors the main burden of preaching, without which, indeed, the function of preaching would neither have any deep foundation nor possess any true significance.

To this great commission the apostles were to continue faithful. We find, accordingly, when we examine the first announcements of the gospel in any place, that they prefixed the narrative of Christ's humiliation, obedience, and resurrection ; that they proclaimed Him as the Christ ; and that they coupled with the narrative the message of present forgiveness and reconciliation. In preaching such a doctrine, they exposed themselves to the loss of reputation, to hardships and peril, to persecution and death. But they held on their way, undeterred and undaunted, assured that they were ordained to deliver such a message ; and they boldly fulfilled the charge, that the great truth, which was unspeakably dear to their own souls, might be made known to all nations and to all times.

5. The sacred writers uniformly put the remission of sins in close connection with the death of Christ as its procuring cause. Man's standing before God, whether viewed in the light of the forgiveness of sins, or in the light of acceptance, is always deduced from the death of Christ as the direct CAUSE. Of this the Lord Himself gave the first example, when He described His blood as shed for many for the remission of sins (Matt. xxvi. 28) ; and He commissioned His disciples to go everywhere preaching repentance and the forgiveness of sins in His name,—that is, to make these points the burden of their message, and to put forgiveness through His blood upon the foreground, among the very first things to be proclaimed. It was not in any circumstances to be kept in reserve, as if it could be viewed—as is the tendency in our day to view it— in the mere subordinate light of an adjunct to the possession of the spiritual life. We may warrantably infer that, as they preached this everywhere as their special message in all the world, or to every creature, they were not neglectful to point out, after their Lord's example, the direct causal connection between the forgiveness which they announced and the atoning blood which had been shed for this end. Wherever the apostles went, we find them faithful to this commission (Acts ii. 38, x. 43, xiii. 38). That the same peculiarity was a feature of their teaching in the several churches, will appear from a few passages in their epistles.

Eph. i. 7: "*In whom we have redemption through His blood, the forgiveness of sins.*"—The apostle in the last clause, which gives additional explanation, more fully defines the nature of redemption as an objective benefit; for the words cannot be interpreted of the uprooting of sin within. They who so explain the two terms are wide of the mark. It is objective benefits to which the apostle refers, and not an inner state of the heart. The forgiveness is the remission of punishment due

to us for sin, and put in direct connection with the blood of
Christ alone as its meritorious cause.

2 Cor. v. 19 : *"God was in Christ, reconciling the world unto
Himself, not imputing their trespasses unto them."*—The reconciliation is connected with the non-imputing of sin, another expression for forgiveness or the remission of punishment. The
connection between two things here stated is to be carefully
noted : God, in the great scheme of reconciliation, is described
as not imputing sin ; while Christ, in the capacity of surety, is
described as made sin, or bearing the imputation of sin (ver. 21).
Thus the imputation of sin to Him, and its non-imputation to
us, stand in close causal connection. The substitution of the
Son of God is thus the ground and the explanation of our forgiveness.

Rom. iii. 25 : *" To declare His righteousness for* [better, *on
account of*] *the remission of sins that are past."*—I adduce this
passage as conveying, when rightly understood, a most emphatic
illustration of the connection between Christ's dying obedience
and the remission of sins. The righteousness of God there
mentioned means, as will be proved below, according to the
common Pauline usage, the righteousness divinely provided for
the justification of sinners ; and the reason assigned for its
actual manifestation in the fulness of time is, that sins had,
during ages of forbearance prior to the coming of Christ, been
remitted on the ground of an atonement yet to come. The
atonement, or, as it is there called, the righteousness of God, was
ushered in by reason of, or on account of (διὰ with ac.), the
pardon which had been extended to multitudes in the former
ages. We thus see the inseparable connection between the
atoning obedience of Christ and the remission of sins,—between
the actual bringing in of the atonement and the previous forgiveness accorded to Old Testament believers. The clause shows
the direct connection between Christ's work and pardon. This
is the only sense that can be grammatically put upon the words,
and they show that without atonement there could have been

no remission of sins. That the saints before the coming of
Christ frequently speak of pardon as a present experience, and
extol the sweetness of the privilege, no one can doubt (Ps.
xxxii. 1; Mic. vii. 18); for the atonement, from its retrospective
character as the great fact in the world's history, was a sufficient
ground for dispensing pardon in the proper sense of the word,
being already before the divine mind as a reality. Objectively,
there was no difference as to the participation of actual pardon
before and after the atonement, though in point of inner liberty,
or the subjective realization of it, there could not but be a certain difference between men eagerly looking forward to the
great coming fact, and their laying hold of it as already accomplished. In that respect something was awanting (Heb. xi.
40). But the point which this text illustrates, and for which I
have adduced it, is the inseparable link between forgiveness
and atonement: it is a causal connection—an immediate connection without any further addition.

Rom. viii. 34: " *Who is he that condemneth? it is Christ that
died.*"—The argument there would not hold, unless merited condemnation were directly removed from us by the death of Christ,
without another cause in operation. Now forgiveness is exemption from condemnation, and it is ascribed exclusively to Christ's
death. The death of Christ alone is thus the direct and immediate cause of pardon.

This will help us to understand the significance of the
biblical terms by which forgiveness is described. They are
numerous, whether we look at the Old Testament or at the
New; and they presuppose atonement, as a few instances will
show.

Rom. iv. 7: " *Blessed are they whose iniquities are forgiven,
and whose sins are covered.*" " *Blessed is the man to whom the Lord
will not impute sin*" (Ps. xxxii. 1, 2).—There are two phrases
which are here alternated, as interchangeable expressions with
the commonly used term " forgiveness." The first, that of covering sins, intimates that they are covered from the Judge's eye,

so that if they are sought for, they are not to be found. This figurative expression is thought to be taken from the blood-sprinkled mercy-seat or covering of the ark which covered the tables of the law, and therefore the curse due to the people for their sins, though we need not be too curious to settle this point when no materials are at hand. The meaning is, that sins, as covered from the Judge, no more cry for vengeance, and there must be something to cover them; while the second phrase, the non-imputation of sin, denotes that it is not charged to our account,—that is, that our persons are no longer subjected to merited punishment (2 Sam. xix. 19 ; Lev. vii. 18).

Heb. x. 17 : "*And their sins and iniquities will I remember no more.*"—This expression describes the perfection of the forgiveness when Christ's one sacrifice was offered. A judge no more remembers sins when he does not remember them judicially, or when he ceases to act against them; and the language means that, on the ground of Christ's death, God remembers sin no more.

Col. ii. 13 : " *You, being dead in your sins, hath He quickened with Him, having forgiven you all trespasses.*" This passage distinctly shows that the idea attached to forgiveness involved deliverance from punishment: for the apostle says first that they were by sin subjected to death and punishment, and that the quickening in which they rejoiced was a consequence of forgiveness; which again was owing to the atonement of the cross, or to the blotting out of the handwriting of ordinances by nailing it to the cross.

The most frequently used expression in the Old Testament to denote forgiveness, is literally *to bear sin*[1] (Mic. vii. 18; Ex. xxxiv. 7; Num. xiv. 18; Josh. xxiv. 19). It appears not improbable that this phrase, so frequently used to describe pardon in the Old Testament, was borrowed from the sacrifices, perhaps from the scape-goat, led away by the hand of a fit man, and let go in the wilderness (Lev. xvi. 21). The iniquity

---

[1] See our former volume, *Sayings of Jesus*, sec. xiii. 1.

of the people was borne by these two goats, used on the day of atonement, being first expiated by the one, and then borne away by the other. And as the two were intended to convey but one idea, and are a mutual complement of each other, they gave a symbolical representation of the mode of taking away sin and merited punishment.[1] The unrighteousness of the covenant people was removed from the eyes of the Judge, and no more suitable expression could be employed to intimate the remission of sin. But however the expression is explained— and various explanations will continue to be given—it certainly implies to remit or forgive sin, so that it is no more punishable.

Thus, according to apostolic teaching, the acceptance of the sinner and the pardon of his sins—that is, the positive and negative side of the new relation into which we are admitted— is immediately connected with the cross. The one is called justification, and the other forgiveness; but they are both forensic terms, having reference to our personal relation to the moral Governor and Judge; and they are immediately connected with the cross, or with the atonement which vindicates the divine law. This assumes that in other respects no duty is left undone; that there is no sin of omission as well as no sin of commission: for these two sides of the question are the complement of each other—correlative truths; the one presupposing the other. And the person may be described either by the negative or positive side of the sentence.

SEC. III.—THE APOSTLES' EXPOSITION OF THE SACRIFICES AND TEMPLE SERVICES, AS SYMBOLICAL AND TYPICAL.

In this section I purpose to consider the apostles' elucidation of the atonement from the ancient sacrifices. The plan we are pursuing leads us into this field under the guidance

[1] See Prof. Lotze's explanation of the phrase *over de Vergeving*, p. 20.

of apostles; and as they lead the way, we do not place ourselves, therefore, under any arbitrary human theories. Nor
have we any occasion to fall in with the attempt to stand
merely on the ground which the reading of the Old Testament
supplies to our own minds, apart from the apostolic commentary; a presumptuous attempt which has invariably failed.
We survey the sacrificial economy with the light which the
apostles reflect upon it; and where they stop short, there we
also stop.

On the subject of sacrifice, there have been before the church
two artificially constructed systems. The TYPICAL system, run
out into a labyrinth of detail; and the SYMBOLICAL system,
which finds higher truth in all the multiplied ceremonies
appointed for the sacrifices. And to neither scheme does it
seem safe to surrender ourselves fully, since both err by over-
doing. It must be allowed that there is an amount of truth
in both, and that neither element is to be rejected. But on
either scheme, unless we have controlling landmarks, we may
soon get beyond divine ideas, and lose ourselves in human
fancies and ingenious analogies.

That which was called the TYPICAL theology was much in
favour a century ago. It had engaged the ingenuity of
Cocceius, Witsius, Vitringa, and Lampe; and in the hands
of these eminent men, and of others who followed them, much
precious truth was brought forth as the carrying out of apostolical ideas; but it was carried to such an extreme, that it
sunk in course of time under its own weight. It soon came to
be out of keeping with the great purpose of exegesis, the object
of which is to exhibit the substance of revelation in its origin,
progress, and proper import; and a reaction was the consequence on the part of all men of spiritual insight and taste.
It was overdone, and the mind made the natural and necessary
effort to regain its equilibrium.

The modern school differs from the former, by fixing attention rather on the SYMBOLICAL meaning of the sacrifices. This

system has for its object to find out the spiritual ideas underlying them. The symbol is with these writers the tangible
substratum to exhibit a higher truth, or to illustrate God's
method of dealing with sin and sinning men. There is important truth in this view, especially as it unfolds a useful
mode of instruction in reference to God the moral Governor,
to the guilt and defilement of sin, and to the method of
expiation. But it must be added that many writers in this
school go as far in the indulgence of a restless fancy as did
the typical school. This may fully be affirmed of the artificial system propounded by Bähr in a direction opposed to
the vicarious sacrifice. But the opposite system advocated by
Kurtz, Hengstenberg, Keil, and Kliefoth,[1] while powerfully
maintaining the vicarious character of the sacrifices, and starting from apostolical expositions, errs in like manner in not a
few respects by overdoing. The Mosaic law, with its precepts
and prohibitions, threats and penalties, is correctly portrayed
as uniting into a system the great ideas of divine holiness, of
the evil of sin, and the necessity of expiation, which were all
symbolically taught by sacrifice. But it cannot be denied that
the minute details are overdone. If it was a labyrinth of type
a century ago, it has in more recent times become a labyrinth
of symbol; and to neither system in detail can we commit
ourselves, more especially when we reflect that the same mode
of interpretation, if applied to the parables, a similar method
of instruction, would throw obscurity, not light, over those
simple ideas which they are intended to elucidate.

I shall here collect into a few particulars the general doctrine of sacrifice, and keep the whole within due limits.

---

[1] See Bähr, *Symbolik des mos. Cultus;* Kurtz, *das mosaische Opfer;* Hengsten-
berg, *Opfer der H. S.* 1858; Kliefoth, *ursprüngliche Gottesdienst. ordnung,* 1858;
Keil, *Opfer des A. B.* (*Zeitschrift für die gesammte Lutherische Theologie,*
1856-7). Besides these, Philippi's *Kirchliche Glaubenslehre,* iv. 1863, and
Doedes' articles (*Jaarboeken voor Wetenschapp. Theol.* 1846), deserve attention.
The reader will find in English an able discussion of the whole subject in Dr.
Fairbairn's *Typology,* and also in Arch. Magee *on the Atonement,* and Dr.
Pye Smith's *Priesthood and Sacrifice,* not to mention many popular expositions.

1. They were a mode of instruction on the way of approaching God, and were peculiarly suited to the human mind struggling with a sense of guilt; and they have furnished to the church of all times a vocabulary or nomenclature, without which men could not with sufficient precision have been able to hold intercourse with each other on the subject of the atonement.   It deserves special notice, that prophecy and sacrifices are always found together, and throw light upon each other ; and that they run in parallel lines through the entire Old Testament economy.   Nay, the sacrifices may be regarded as a sort of prophecy, or a guarantee to which the veracity of God was pledged; for the shadow must one day become a reality.   But it was furthermore necessary that the great fact to which they pointed should be distinctly announced in prophecy, and hence we find both together from the time of the first promise (Gen. iii. 15).   If, indeed, the reality had not been appointed to appear, the shadow or rude outline which was presented to the mind by the sacrifices would never have been exhibited.

To apprehend the sacrifices aright, they must also be considered as sacraments.   The terms sacrifice and sacrament formally differ indeed in this respect, that sacrifice denotes rather what is given to God, while sacrament points out what God gives to us.   But while this is not to be denied, they may meet in one and the same thing; and the sacramental character of sacrifices may be discerned very clearly in the whole antediluvian and patriarchal periods, when they were signs and seals to believing men, as sacraments are to us now.[1]   This, of course, takes for granted the divine origin of sacrifices, of which, it appears to me, there is very little room for doubt. But whatever view may be held on the primeval origin of sacrifices, there cannot be two opinions as to the fact that they had an expressly divine appointment in Israel; for even they who are of opinion that men, in the exercise of their own

[1] See Witsius to this effect, *de Econom. Fœd.* lib. iv. c. 7. 7.

reason, fell upon the device of offering animal sacrifices as a method of acceptable worship, acknowledge that upon the Jews they were divinely enjoined, with many explicit directions in detail. But the evidence for their divine appointment in primeval times seems quite conclusive, as a few words will prove.

The sacrifice of Abel is so described as to show that it must have been offered in compliance with divine appointment, and that it was not a mere will-worship (Col. ii. 23). It is said to have been acceptable to God—more acceptable than Cain's (Heb. xi. 4), because it was offered in faith—and to have been received with a divine testimony of approval, which we may suppose was given by the descent of consuming fire from heaven upon the sacrifice, in the same way as was vouchsafed on several later occasions (2 Chron. vii. 2). But that solemn testimony of acceptance would only have terrified the offerer, had he himself invented this mode of worship. The lightning shooting round the altar and consuming the victim, would have conveyed the impression of an angry God; and how could they have apprehended by this means that they were reconciled? How could they have known without some divine revelation that this consuming fire was a token of divine acceptance? When we consider that revelation began at the fall, and that God spoke with man, and conveyed His mind to him in the most condescending and paternal way, as appears from the Mosaic narrative of those times, we cannot suppose that the divine goodness and wisdom abandoned him to the caprice of his own mind in the matter and mode of worship. For this is at the best but will-worship and the commandment of man (Matt. xv. 9).

But, besides, we do not see that in the ordinary way of acquiring ideas there was anything to lead men to that mode of worship as peculiarly acceptable, or calculated to please God. The first mention of sacrifice does not convey the impression that it was a new invention in the time of Abel, but rather that it was a wonted mode of worship; and we may suppose it derived from Adam's custom. The two brothers were not likely to fall upon the device at one and the same time, or to show more inventiveness than Adam. That Adam, however conscious of a good intention, would be very slow to rely upon his own reason and judgment in the institution of divine worship, may be safely argued from the painful remembrance of what he had brought on himself and the world by the plausibilities of that which had seemed good, and pleasant, and desirable (Gen. iii. 6). But the sacrifice of a slain animal does not, apart from the divine thought deposited in it, seem peculiarly fitted to edify the mind, or to awaken filial trust and boldness. The conjecture that the first garments of Adam and Eve were the skins of animals offered in sacrifice, has not only nothing improbable in it, but everything in its favour. They would not naturally have fallen on the device of themselves. But if the sacrifice was divinely instituted, and if it was the channel of an important prophecy as to man's acceptance, this was highly natural. I may further add, that the divine origin of sacrifice is not a little confirmed by the fact, that before the flood the distinction between clean and unclean animals was quite familiar: and from this the natural conclusion is, that as the flesh of animals was not the common food of men till after the flood, this distinction is only to be explained by the divine direction as to the sort of animals that were to be used in sacrifice (Gen. viii. 20).

The doubts which have been expressed on the divine institution of sacrifice are various. By some they are urged in the interest of a theory adverse to the vicarious sacrifice of Christ. With others, who are entitled to the utmost respect as evangelical divines, the doubt arises from a different cause: it is urged that, had they been of divine appointment, Moses would not have omitted a matter of such importance.[1] But it must

---

[1] As to the origin of sacrifice, the generally received opinion is that of Athanasius and Eusebius (*Demonst. Evang.* lib. i. c. 10), that they were of divine

be remembered that Moses comprehends the history of about sixteen centuries in six or seven chapters, and seems to record the incident of Cain and Abel, where sacrifice is first brought under our notice, in the bosom of the primeval genealogy. To deduce a doubt from this circumstance is as unwarrantable as to question whether Adam had any daughters, because there is no mention of them in the Mosaic record.

2. The sacrifices were symbolical. Though this may be affirmed of all the bloody sacrifices from the beginning, it was specially true since the giving of the Mosaic law, when sacrifices were distributed into classes, and combined into a firmly compacted system, to be kept before the eyes of all Israel. The burnt-offering, that belonged to the primeval and patriarchal age, was now to be accompanied with many other forms of sacrifice; or, we may say, it branched out in the new arrangement into various classes or divisions. ALL THE BLOODY SACRIFICES WERE ATONING. Even those who allege that the first sacrifices were nothing but thankofferings, and erroneously maintain that all the sacrifices offered in the patriarchal times were of this nature, are obliged to admit that at the national organization of Israel as a covenant people there were sin-offerings destined for the expiation of certain sins. The Mosaic law multiplied the sacrifices, and divided them into different classes, all meant for different purposes. The

appointment. So Rivetus (*Gen.* c. 4), Cloppenburg (tom. i. p. 24, and *Select. Disp.* xviii.), Owen *on Hebrews*, Witsius, Heidegger, J. Wessel (*de origin. Sacrific.*), Stackhouse, Buddeus, Goodwin in his *Moses and Aaron*, Quensted (Par. iv. 1. 2, Ques. 8). On the other hand, many learned divines have thought that they may be referred to the light of nature, or to the sense of human wants. Of this opinion were Bellarmin, Grotius, Episcopius, Selden. Outram hesitated, and pronounced for neither side in a matter which he thought obscure. Mosheim held the former opinion as by far the most probable. Spencer (*de legibus Hebræor.*), who maintained that sacrifice was not derived from divine revelation, but from human reason, and an expression of love to God, is followed by Hengstenberg and very many of the German exegetes. Oehler (Herzog, *Real Enyclopädie*, article *Opfer*) tries to find some place for both elements, likening sacrifice to prayer. As to the divine institution of the Mosaic sacrifices there cannot be two opinions, nor does the evidence for the divine origin of primeval sacrifice seem to us doubtful.

design which the bloody sacrifices were meant to serve from
the first, however, and which they never ceased to serve, was
to maintain a conviction of man's guilt, and a dependence on
the forgiving grace of God by an atonement. They clearly
taught this truth in a symbolic form to the Jewish nation.
They showed that reconciliation could be effected in no other
way than by a satisfaction to divine justice. They pointed out
that the worshippers had in many ways offended God, and
were worthy of death; that they were to see in the sacrifices a
symbol of the inevitable divine punishment which had been
incurred; and that God made the animal victim serve as a
pledge that the punishment was borne by a substitute, and
that on this ground the offerer could again be taken into
favour. The sacrifices were meant to exhibit the indispensable
NECESSITY OF AN ATONEMENT by vicarious expiation.

Whatever variety of opinion prevails on some of the symbols, there are three conclusions to which all come with perfect
harmony who have in any manner apprehended the significance
of the sin-offering. It was, (1) a gracious institution which
God had appointed as the means by which the offended moral
Governor could be reconciled; (2) it was vicarious in its
character; (3) a satisfaction was effected by means of the
victim's death.

Here, before proceeding further, it is proper to inquire what
were the cases for which the Mosaic law appointed sacrifice?
The sacrifices were not for moral offences, such as murder,
adultery, or idolatry, but only for trespasses of a merely ceremonial nature; for involuntary oversights and sins of ignorance; and for those states of bodily defilement which had
been pronounced trespasses according to the laws which
separated Israel from other nations. In a word, they were
positive and arbitrary laws, for the violation of which positive
and arbitrary atonements could fully suffice: such as the prohibition to touch a dead body or to touch a grave; mere
offences against theocratic purity, as appears from the rites

appointed for the sin-offering (Lev. xii. 7, 8; Num. vi. 11). The sins for which the sacrifices were available were not, properly speaking, moral offences at all; for these the blood of bulls and goats could never take away[1] (Heb. x. 4). They were nothing but theocratic trespasses, which could be cancelled and absolutely remitted by the same positive authority by which the ceremonial rites were instituted. And on the great day of atonement the annual sacrifice was offered for the collective sins of the entire people during the course of the year, thus readjusting their relation as the theocratic people (Lev. xvi. 15; Heb. ix. 13).

Now the design of the Mosaic law was obvious. The sin-offering, whether we look at the more public expiation for the whole nation on the day of atonement, or at the more private expiation for the defilement of the individual, was instituted at the same time with the law, and in order to relieve the worshipper. The positive law and the positive atonement thus came into existence together. As God wished to develope among the children of Israel the idea of sin, and to make their consciences alive to the fact of sin, it was necessary to impose a long series of positive and arbitrary laws, which, it is said, were given to make the offence abound, or, as it is put in another epistle, added because of transgressions (Rom. v. 20; Gal. iii. 19). These laws, not being based on the moral nature of man, were but external, positive, and transitory. They might have been of another character, and they have now ceased.

It is not denied that these ceremonial offences might be connected in some mysterious way with the effects of sin, or with the roots of sin, in man's nature; but they were properly

---

[1] I totally dissent from the notion supported by Kurtz, Hengstenberg, Keil, Doedes, and others, which connects in some sense with these sacrifices the forgiveness of moral offences against God. That is emphatically denied by the apostle, as we shall find in the Epistle to the Hebrews (x. 1-4, ix. 9); and Philippi is warranted to repudiate it in the sternest manner as a superstition. The apostle has settled that question for us.

external and positive. The sin-offering was appointed to remove them; and the Mosaic worship found its centre-point
there. While the covenant which God made with Israel was
kept unbroken on the part of the worshipper, he could approach
by the burnt-offering, which was not meant for special sins so
much as for the general sinfulness attaching to every man. If
the covenant relation *was* broken, access was restored and a
reunion effected by means of the sin-offering—without which,
indeed, there was no remission—and it always carried expiation in its train. The Israelite was well aware, when he contracted ceremonial guilt, that he was out of covenant relation
to the God of Israel, and sundered from Him who could allow
no approach to His presence till the trespass was taken away.
The trespass produced separation between God and him, as
well as conscious estrangement and fear, and death must necessarily ensue as the wages of sin. The great thought brought
out in this symbolical way was, that GOD COULD NOT SACRIFICE
HIS HOLINESS TO HIS LOVE. But death having ensued as the
due punishment for sin in the animal sacrifice, the worshipper
had a present restoration into covenant fellowship. Here it
might be proper briefly to refer to the symbolical import of the
sacrificial actions; but as the same actions are also typical, we
may more fitly notice their symbolical and typical elements
together than apart.

Meanwhile we must add, that for the transgression of these
ceremonial laws many calamities were threatened, such as the
withdrawal of civil and ecclesiastical privileges. The sacrifices
were provided not for a wanton disobedience to the law, but
for involuntary trespass or unwitting neglect; and the offence
committed was cancelled by the mere fact of the sacrifice considered simply as an act done (*opus operatum*). In reference
to the symbolical character of the sacrifices, it may be proper,
before proceeding further, to obviate a series of misconceptions.

a. The sin-offerings were not for mere offences against the
state. They were not offered to man, but to God; not meant

to avert civil pains and penalties, but to expiate offences against the ceremonial law. Though God was the monarch of Israel, or theocratic King, yet a trespass against the sacrificial economy was always more than a misdemeanour against the state. The Most High was to be obeyed even in the enactment of arbitrary laws, and the punishment was due from the justice and truth of God. And when the worshipper brought the sacrifice of atonement, he was purged from all that defiled him : he had access to God; and the courts of the sanctuary were again thrown open to him.

b. Nor were the sacrifices a mere expression of penitence. For a defilement having been contracted, it could be removed only by sacrifice, and by the sprinkling which was connected with sacrifice,—a result following according to the connection of cause and effect. Not that repentance was excluded as an accompaniment of every approach to Jehovah in the way of worship ; but the sacrifice must neither be resolved into a mere expression of penitence, nor be viewed as effecting its purpose only so far as the penitent, contrite heart went along with it. This accompanying penitence could not fitly be said to apply to the day of atonement, when the collective sins of Israel were annually expiated and fully removed. To prove that the sin-offering atoned for sin, or cancelled it, simply by the deed done (*opere operato*), we have but to remember the mediating priest, and the laying on of the hand of the worshipper upon the victim's head, as a proof that the guilt was transferred vicariously. The effect of these propitiatory sacrifices was the remission of the threatened penalty, independently of the contrition and penitence which might in many cases, but did not in all cases, and certainly did not on the great day of atonement, uniformly and in every instance go along with them.

c. Nor were the sacrifices a mere renewal of homage to the theocratic King. Such a notion confounds the things that differ,—confounds the SIN-OFFERING with the FREE-WILL OFFER-

ING. The former had in it nothing of the character of a friendly feast, whether taken in its more public form as offered for the sins of the nation, or in its more private form as offered for the ceremonial trespasses of an individual (Lev. iv. 3–21); but was intended to transfer the offerer's guilt to the animal victim which was put in his place. The great thought contained in all the propitiatory sacrifices was, that the guilt which the worshipper had incurred was transferred to the sacrifice; and that by the death of the victim he was set free from merited punishment, and fully re-admitted into the divine favour. We must dismiss the notion that the sacrifices were but an act of homage to an invisible King, or a mere renewal of allegiance to Him.

The symbolical meaning of the sacrifices—that is, the higher truth which they conveyed—was precisely what we have mentioned. These offerings did not atone for moral trespass or spiritual guilt; and the Epistle to the Hebrews, in language the most explicit and unambiguous, denies to them any possible efficacy to take away sin, or to purge the conscience. They were gifts and sacrifices, says the apostle, which could not make the worshipper perfect as pertaining to the conscience, and were imposed only till the times of reformation (Heb. ix. 9, 10).

But to make their symbolical meaning more apparent, it must be added that something was actually done IN A LOWER SPHERE on the occasion of every sacrifice. They not only taught a truth, but in a certain lower sphere effected actual deliverance, and re-admitted the worshipper to a relation of nearness which, but for the sacrifice, would have been denied. It was a transaction which not only taught a truth, but actually showed that in point of fact remission of guilt was effected. With that idea God made His ancient people familiar. And however much it may be decried at present as a gross opinion or as a popular error, it was stamped on the Old Testament church. To make atonement by sacrifice meant, in the language of Scripture, to avert penalty incurred, and to procure remission of sin (Lev. iv. 20). By means of those sacrifices threatened punishments were removed, whether consisting in national calamities, or in the death of the transgressor, or in the withdrawal of civil and ecclesiastical privileges. But the true and proper atonement was not, and could not be, through these elements of the world. The true atonement was not by, with, or under them in any proper sense of the words; for they did not make the worshipper perfect as pertaining to the conscience, or remove from him the sense of sin (Heb. ix. 9).

Against this view, that the sacrifices had a symbolical import, and actually effected a certain result in a lower sphere, it is sometimes urged that they are described as referring more to sacred things than to persons, for they are represented as making atonement for the sanctuary (Lev. xvi. 16). But this is easy of explanation. From the fact that, according to divine appointment, the holy place and its furniture were to be sprinkled with blood, we are by no means to conclude that the place demanded the atonement, and not the people. The sanctuary was but an emblem of the way in which God inhabits His church, or dwells among His people. This was made very evident in the old economy ; and as the sins of the people tended to make the sanctuary unworthy to continue as the dwelling-place of God, the sprinkling of blood applied to it was meant to show that God, notwithstanding recurring transgressions, would continue to reside in it when He beheld the blood of atonement. Thus, it was the people that needed reconciliation, while the reference to the sanctuary conveyed an emphatic lesson as to the continued inhabitation of God among them. That the people needed the reconciliation and not the place, is proved by the fact that the ceremony was demanded for the transgressions of Israel (Lev. xvi. 16), and made atonement for the priests and all the people (ver. 33).

Thus sacrifices conveyed the most important truth in a symbolical form. But their very frequency and repetition argued insufficiency. The daily return of the same round of sacrifice proclaimed, as with a voice, their complete insufficiency ; which, indeed, many of the more enlightened in Israel clearly perceived. Hence we find that David (Ps. xl. 6 and li. 16), Asaph (Ps. l. 8), Micah (vi. 6), and Isaiah (i. 11), give a clear and striking testimony to the inadequacy of those sacrifices to effect in any measure a true and everlasting atonement for sin.

3. The sacrifices were from the first TYPICAL OF THE GREAT ATONEMENT. The relation between the two was the same that obtains between shadow and substance, picture and reality ; therefore not an accidental harmony, or comparison based upon ingenious analogies or far-fetched points of resemblance. The connection between the two was in the things themselves, not in the mind of the observer; nay, we may warrantably affirm that the language proper to the real atonement for sin was thrown back upon the type—not conversely.

The opposite theory of sacrifice which calls in question their typical import, and assigns to them no other function than that of teaching some general truths, may here be noticed before we proceed to the ritual. They who would overthrow the atoning work of Christ in every form, admit that the sacrifices taught religious ideas in a general way, but deny that they foreshadowed the propitiation for sin that was to come, or that they were a prophetic anticipation of it. Here all depends on the question: Was the peculiar similarity or correspondence which undoubtedly may be traced between the ancient sacrifices and the atonement of Christ of divine appointment, or was it a merely accidental matter ? Apart from express design on God's side, we could not adduce a sufficient proof of the typical nature of the sacrifices. That there was such a design, however, and that the one adumbrated and was intended to adumbrate the other, a few words will suffice to show. Here we simply ask, What say the apostles, the great interpreters of the old economy according to the mind of

Christ ? Do they speak of the sacrifices as typical, and furnishing a prophetical foreshadowing of the atonement ? The
matter might be decided from the Prophets and Psalms ; but
the plan we are pursuing leads us to inquire how far the
typical character of the sacrifices is affirmed in the sayings
and writings of apostles. It is not the question, how many
of the Jewish nation rose to such anticipations, nor what ideas
were entertained by the people generally. The question rather
is : Did the believing Israelite on good ground come to the
typical view of the sacrifices ; and especially did the apostles,
as men taught by Christ orally, and filled with the Spirit, lead
the Christian church so to view them ? It must be decided
by apostolic testimony whether the typical character of sacrifice
is in harmony with the divine appointment and true design of
sacrifice. And this is not left doubtful to any attentive reader
of the epistles.

  a. One obvious proof that the sacrifices were typical, and
meant to be so, may be drawn from the fact that they are
expressly called SHADOWS ; a more apt designation than any
other that could be chosen to set forth what we understand by
their typical character. The term "shadow," intimating as it
does a certain resemblance to the thing signified, implies that
what is so named has a dependence on that of which it is the
rude outline, but no existence apart from the substance. Thus
the various arrangements as to food and festivals are called a
"shadow" of things to come (Col. ii. 17). The priests are described as serving unto the pattern and "shadow" of heavenly
things (Heb. viii. 5). The law is said to have a "shadow" of
good things to come, and not the very image of the things—
that is, not the reality or substance (Heb. x. 1). The patterns
of the heavenly things purified with blood are contrasted with
the heavenly things themselves (Heb. ix. 23). In a word, the
shadowy is contrasted with the true in a great variety of points ;
and the phraseology employed to express the contrast calls up
before us type and antitype (John vi. 32 ; Heb. ix. 24).

b. Another proof is derived from the fact that the death of
Christ is expressly represented as an offering and a sacrifice
(Eph. v. 2). He is described as offering Himself (Heb. x. 14).
We must admit a coincidence between the sacrifices and the
death of Christ of such a nature as exists between the sign and
the thing signified, and that this is established by divine design.
The apostles found this resemblance in the things themselves.
They teach us to regard the sacrifices as a prophetic foreshadowing of what was future, and the Lord's atoning death as
the reality of which the sacrifice was the shadow. No one
gazed so much on the coincidence or correspondence between
the shadow and the reality as the apostles, intimating that they
considered the former dispensation as finding its accomplishment in Christ's death. Without this typical reference, the
ancient sacrifices would be nothing more than an antiquity.
To adduce an example, we find it said, " Christ our passover
is sacrificed for us " (1 Cor. v. 7). Here the coincidence between the two appears in every variety of view, historical as
well as doctrinal. Thus Jesus entered Jerusalem on the day
when the passover was separated, according to the requirements
of the Mosaic law for the sacrifice; and everything proclaims
an essential connection between it and Him. The passover,
again, was the foundation of the covenant with Israel, and
that which separated the church from the world; and the
coincidence between the typical and spiritual redemption is
apparent at a glance. The same thing was displayed in connection with the annual sin-offering on the great day of atonement, when the collective sins of the nation were annually
expiated. Christ's priestly act of sacrifice was the truth or
substance of that shadow, and its typical character will not be
called in question by any one who compares the antithesis in
which the apostle places them (Heb. ix. 7–14).

c. Another proof of the typical character of the sacrifices is
furnished by their transitory nature. They merged in the
reality, which could not have been the case had the institution

been other than typical. Being but a shadow, they could cease when the reality came. The church can now dispense with the sacrifices, as she has infinitely more in Christ's atonement than the shadowy economy of Israel could ever bestow. It is replaced by a better, and abrogated as insufficient to meet man's spiritual wants. The one everlasting sacrifice having been offered, the unprofitable outline of it disappears. But this could only be because the whole was typical.

The worshippers under the Mosaic law, priests and people, were in constant fear. It was an economy given with terrible accompaniments, and gendered to bondage (Heb. xii. 18). They were subject to numerous rules and duties, the violation of which in the least degree entailed guilt, defilement, and danger. Sometimes a trespass was followed by immediate death at the hand of God; at other times, if the offence was one to be atoned for, the punishment inflicted was separation from the congregation, and from the privilege of approach to God. They were put far off, and could not draw near; and to put away what separated between the worshipper and God, a propitiatory sacrifice, or, to use the special term, a sin-offering, was indispensably necessary; for without the shedding of blood was no remission even for the ceremonial defilement. This mode of governing the Israelitish community was a wise arrangement, and suited to the numerous laws divinely imposed on them. It intimated a method by which the worshipper, estranged from God and out of covenant standing, could be restored, and come before the inflexibly holy and yet merciful God. The penalty as well as the distance could be removed only by sacrifice.

The great thought, therefore, underlying the whole Mosaic economy was, that transgression violating the order of the universe must be visited with punishment. Death must follow, and no regrets could remove the guilt. The offender must die, without the possibility of living in fellowship with God, unless a sin-offering were presented to God to atone for the trespass, and remove it. Necessary punishment must ensue; and till a sacrifice was offered, the worshipper must necessarily be separated from God, and forbidden to approach Him. The idea of substitution prevails in all the sin-offerings. The defiled Israelite who had broken the law, or the offending nation, offering the sin-offering to put them on a right footing with the God of Israel, had a representation or figure of what they must have endured had not sacrifice intervened. The sacrifices proclaimed the absolute necessity of an atonement for sin, and they effected the deliverance by the deed done, not by inward feelings or altered conduct on the part of the worshipper.

But we shall better apprehend the import of sacrifices, and their united symbolical and typical significance, if we follow step by step the order of the ritual. It must be carefully noted, that in the private sin-offerings of the people the priest was present at the first three acts, but began his proper function only when the blood was to be received for the act of sprinkling. On the great annual day of atonement, however, the high priest, the representative of the nation, performed all the acts of the sacrifice. The ritual advanced according to the following successive steps.

1. The worshipper who had contracted guilt by any violation of the law for which a sin-offering was provided, was enjoined to bring a clean animal, without blemish, to the tabernacle of the congregation. The animal must be alive, as the arrangements involved the taking of its life. The act of presentation, as performed by a willing offerer, implied the voluntary character of the sacrifice. The presentation was to be upon the altar, to which, as erected on an elevation, the victim was to be brought up, just as the great antitype was lifted up upon the cross (1 Pet. ii. 24). To the perfection of the sacrifice, however, it was indispensable that the victim should be without defect or blemish. This is constantly alluded to by the sacred writers (1 Pet. i. 19 ; Heb. ix. 14). Now what did this intimate, in a typical point of view, but the sinlessness of Jesus, who must be righteous to stand for

the unrighteous, innocent to stand for the guilty? Did this convey anything further than the thought that the spotless holiness of Jesus was necessary as a condition or prerequisite for the oblation itself? It meant more. The holiness of Jesus was itself an essential element or ingredient in the atonement, considered as a satisfaction to justice, as a fulfilment of the law. One essential part[1] of the sacrifice was the perfect holiness and sinless purity of the Lord, who through the Eternal Spirit offered Himself without spot to God (Heb. ix. 14).

2. The next act of the ritual was THE LAYING ON OF THE HAND upon the victim's head. This symbolically intimated the communication of that which was ours, and therefore the transfer of our guilt, to the substitute, and it was accompanied on the day of atonement with the confession of sins (Lev. xvi. 21). This conclusively shows what was the meaning of the act, and this is not to be overthrown by fanciful theories. Thus Bähr, opposed in principle to the vicarious sacrifice, will have the action mean no more than this, that the animal belonged to the offerer, or that it was his property. Kurtz, again, will have it mean the devoting of the animal to death, forgetting that there must be a reason why it was visited with death. That reason is the imputation of sin, or the arrangement by which it was made sin, or made incorporated guilt. The laying on of the hand, at one time for one end and at another time for another, was a common action, meaning generally the communicating of something from one party to another. In the case before us it meant that the offerer put himself in a relation to the victim, or into a peculiar connection with it, so as to communicate to it his own guilt, or the nation's guilt, according to the private or public nature of the sacrifice; and after this ceremony the animal suffered death for the sin. The punishment followed, and this determines its

---

[1] See an interesting argument from this fact for the whole obedience of Christ, that is, for His active as well as passive obedience in justification, in reply to Sibrandus Lubbertus, who demanded a proof of it from the sacrifices, in Walæus, *Opera*, tom. ii. p. 420.

meaning. Though this is the only act of the ritual not expressly named in the New Testament, it comes before us under other turns of phrase. Thus, when Jesus was numbered with transgressors (Mark xv. 26), when He was sent in the likeness of sinful flesh (Rom. viii. 3), and made sin (2 Cor. v. 21), we have that which was denoted by this ritual act.

3. The next act was the immolation—the animal's death. The symbolical import of this is, that death is the wages of sin, and that sin and death stand related as cause and consequence. But further, the animal must die by the hand of the worshipper, and for an obvious reason. His was the sin laid upon the victim—his the death; and hence none but he who laid his hand on the animal's head was to kill it. In this part of the sacrificial ritual there was, on many grounds, a deep significance; and not least is the circumstance that there was a marked correspondence between this fact and the mode in which the Saviour died. The Lord was not to meet His death in any other way but by violence. The sinner's hand was to be the instrument of inflicting the death, even as the sinner's guilt was the meritorious cause, and the only assignable cause, why death could come to Him at all. Still further, the death was penal. This is to be strictly maintained; as the notion that the death was only in order to obtain the blood, or a mere means to an end, and without further significance, would perplex and unsettle the entire ritual. The death in itself was punitive, or the wages of sin. If not, what could the blood have accomplished? But on the principle that the imputation of guilt was signified by the laying on of hands, death followed as the necessary effect; for the worshipper owed death, and the infliction of it was penal.

This excludes the subjective theory, which has been contrived by the opponents of the vicarious satisfaction to explain the death of the victim. Thus Bähr, with those who follow in his tendency, will have it mean that the self-seeking life of man dies, and is replaced by a spiritual life devoted to God.

According to this notion, the death of the animal, in its symbolical meaning, teaches the mortification of sin, or that self must be sacrificed. On every ground this exposition is untenable. Not to mention that it is out of keeping with the ritual, according to which the animal died and continued dead, it takes for granted that a guilty man can, without any reparation, dedicate himself to God. But that cannot be, as he has no power to dispose of a forfeited life ; and without atonement, or covering for his soul, he cannot be dedicated to God. There is no possibility of this without expiation, for death is the wages of sin.

4. The next act in the sacrificial ritual was the SPRINKLING OF THE BLOOD. At this point the priest's activity commenced. He had been, up to this step in the ritual, present as a spectator, but he now steps in to take part in it. It was he who received the flowing blood of the animal, and who put it on the horns, or highest point, of the altar, and who poured it out at the bottom (Lev. iv. 25–34) ; an action which intimated that the meeting-place between God and His people was from top to bottom covered with blood, that the sins of the people were covered by an atonement, and that the worshippers were no more exposed to His frown. The blood received by the priest, and made his own, is regarded as the vicariously shed blood of the priest. Thus, in the ritual, we consider not the victim alone, but also the priest, without whom the sacrifice could not be duly offered ; and the action of receiving the blood had a peculiar significance. It signified that he made the blood his own. But besides the ablutions, vestments and other typical sanctifications shadowed forth the holiness and righteousness of the Antitype. What was done upon the victim was supposed to have been done upon the priest, who now became a party to the action. He appropriated the blood, which now passed for his own blood : for the priest's action began here.

The ritual advanced gradually till it reached this act of sprinkling, where we find sin expiated and divine wrath propitiated. But from the necessary imperfection of types, the idea was exhibited broken into parts, and in succession. The blood was brought to God, and made to cover sin. The sprinkling, whether performed at the horns of the altar or in the holy of holies, the meeting-place between God and His people, figured forth that the sin of the individual, or of the nation, though piled up as an heap, was now covered, and all cause of separation removed. Death had intervened; and the blood that had passed through death was now most holy, and had atoning power wherever it was sprinkled (Heb. xiii. 12). The sacrifice, regarded as a propitiation, culminated in the sprinkling of the blood, which is to be viewed as an element in the objective atonement, and not, as is too much the case, as the application of redemption. This appears on various grounds. Thus the priest's action began with the receiving of the blood for the act of sprinkling; and the priest's act, as typical mediator, being essential to propitiatory sacrifices, nothing more conclusively proved that the objective atonement consisted in the sprinkling. This still further appears when we consider the Antitype, and the point of the ritual at which the great High Priest sprinkled the mercy-seat.

5. The last act of the sacrificial ritual consisted in THE BURNING OF THE VICTIM. This is not properly a separate element, but only another side of the propitiation, though made distinct, owing to the imperfection of the type. We are not, however, to destroy the unity of the idea by sundering it from the other. The two things demanding explanation here are the fire and the sweet-smelling savour (Heb. xiii. 11; Eph. v. 2). As to the first, it was the holy fire which fell from heaven on Aaron's first sacrifice, and was never to be extinguished (Lev. v. 6, 7). Only the sacrifice which was consumed by this fire, and rose to heaven as a sweet-smelling savour, was really acceptable. As a type, this fire has been variously explained. Thus Michaelis viewed it as typical of eternal punishment after death. Oehler regards it as denoting the

divine holiness. Philippi takes it as the divine love, the unquenchable love of the Son of God. If it were fitting to consider this type as exhibiting any of the divine attributes, it would be necessary to combine the two latter opinions as equally essential to the atonement, and make it an emblem of God in the unity of His perfections. But a different explanation commends itself to my mind, and the rather because the fire was given to produce a further result (ver. 12), that sweet-smelling savour which is the positive element in the sacrifice. It seems to me rather to denote the Holy Ghost, whose agency and operations are in several passages set forth by this emblem (Matt. iii. 11; Acts ii. 3; Luke xii. 49), and through whom we are expressly told the Lord Jesus offered Himself without spot to God (Heb. ix. 14). When we see Him stedfastly setting His face to go to Jerusalem, fully bent on His high work, we see the fire[1] of the sacrifice already kindled, and the Eternal Spirit prompting Him and strengthening Him to consummate the work, by imbuing His soul with a zeal and ardour, a love and obedience, which never allowed His mind to cool till the sacrifice was consumed. As to the second point, the sweet-smelling savour, this figured forth the acceptable service, the perfect obedience of the Lord in the light of winning the divine favour. As the expiation of wrath was the negative side, so the sinless obedience is the positive. They are two aspects of one great deed, by which sin was expiated and divine favour won; incomplete when separate, all-sufficient when combined. The blood-sprinkling refers to vicarious suffering; the burning, with its sweet - smelling savour, refers to the vicarious fulfilling of the law.

There are yet two points to which we would briefly refer

---

[1] This interpretation was given by the Greek exegetes, Chrysostom, Œcumenius, Theophylact, in commenting on the words, "who through the Eternal Spirit offered Himself" (Heb. ix. 14). The same explanation is thus given by Witsius, *on the Creed*, Exercit. xxiii. sec. 22 : "Mysticus ignis qui est Spiritus Sanctus, sanctificans victimam et gratam præstans Deo. De sacro igne cœlitus delapso, vide Lev. ix. 23, 24."

in thus tracing the correspondence between the type and the Antitype, viz. (1) the action of the high priest in sprinkling the mercy-seat, and (2) the change effected by the typical ritual generally upon the relation of the worshippers to the God of Israel. We do not anticipate the separate texts which will come under our notice in discussing the Epistle to the Hebrews, but would lay a foundation for the expositions which will afterwards be necessary when we treat of the apostolic testimony, which largely takes a tincture from the ancient worship.

(1.) In directing attention to the sprinkling of the mercy-seat, it must be noticed that the tabernacle had two divisions, of which the one, termed the holy place, was allotted to the daily ministrations of the priests; while the other, termed the holiest of all, was entered only by the high priest once a year, not without blood (Heb. ix. 6, 7). The arrangement corresponded to the time then present, a period of imperfect atonement. Why the holy of holies continued shut, and was opened on the day of atonement only, when the high priest entered within the veil, is explained by the inefficacy of those sacrifices, which could not perfectly atone for sin (Heb. ix. 7–9). But what was the typical significance of that entrance, and what was the time when the great Antitype, the truth of that shadow, must be regarded as sprinkling the mercy-seat? When did the true High Priest enter within the veil? Was it at His death? or was it, as is commonly thought, when He ascended and sat down on the right hand of God? This is a most important question; and it is the more necessary to settle it, because, as we shall find in the Epistle to the Hebrews, one of the subtlest modes of evading the vicarious satisfaction is to transfer the atoning element to heaven, and to withdraw it from the finished work on the cross: and many, swayed by exegetical reasons, think that countenance is given to that opinion by the allusions in the Epistle to the Hebrews (Heb. ix. 24–26). The prevalent notion, that the entrance of the high priest into the holy of holies found its truth in Christ's triumphal entrance into heaven, may have some show of probability, but it is burdened by insuperable difficulties. To suppose, as we must do in that case, that Christ's priestly action began in heaven,—that is, that He sprinkled the mercy-seat, and completed the atonement only when He entered on the mediatorial exaltation or reward,—seems to confound everything. It does violence, we think, to all analogy between type and antitype. The resurrection of Jesus coinciding with the return of the high priest from the holiest of all, was designed to be an evidence that divine wrath was removed, and forgiveness obtained. The confusion of idea to which I have referred as very prevalent, arises from not sufficiently distinguishing between the high priest, properly so called, and the High Priest after the order of Melchizedek, or the Royal Priest on His mediatorial throne. A few words will suffice to prove that He entered within the veil and sprinkled the mercy-seat at the moment when He commended His spirit into His Father's hand. This is the most natural interpretation; and this corresponds to the ceremonies on the great day of atonement, to which express allusion is made in the Epistle to the Hebrews[1] (Heb. ix. 11–14).

a. The typical entrance within the veil took place immediately after the victim's death; the body being carried without the camp to be burned in a public place, and the blood being carried into the holiest of all to be sprinkled on the covering of the ark, as the propitiatory or mercy-seat. These closely connected acts in the ritual were so related, that the burning followed last in order. And as we know from the apostle that that typical action coincided with Christ's sacrifice without the gates of Jerusalem (Heb. xiii. 11), it would reverse

---

[1] As this will come before us in the Epistle to the Hebrews, I shall then refer to the literature of the subject, and to the hints and discussions in reference to it by Witsius, Honert, A. Schultens, and Lotze. They all assert this view in the strongest terms. Its truth seems evident on its own merits, apart from its importance as an argument against the Socinian denial of Christ's priesthood and sacrifice on earth.

the entire sacrificial system to interpret the sprinkling of the mercy-seat of what was done by Him forty days after His resurrection, when He ascended to heaven. Not only so: the apostle argues, too, in a way that excludes such a comment, saying, " Nor yet that He should offer Himself often, as the high priest entereth into the holy place every year with blood of others; for then must He often have suffered since the foundation of the world" (Heb. ix. 25, 26). On the supposition that Christ went into the holy of holies at the triumphant ascension to heaven, the apostle would not have so reasoned; for the statement is, that if Christ had often entered, He must have often suffered,—a consequence that would not follow on the supposition we impugn. Had He so pleased, there was nothing to prevent Him from repeating His entry, or of renewing His triumph before the inhabitants of heaven. But it follows on the supposition that our High Priest entered at the moment He poured out His blood upon the cross. The Jewish high priest entered in with the still reeking blood of atonement, and sprinkled the mercy-seat; and our great High Priest entered when He died, claiming the opening of heaven for Himself and all His seed, for He still acted as the High Priest when soul and body were separated. The resurrection, in the first instance a testimony that all was done that justice required, was properly a reward.

b. The truth of this interpretation appears, too, from the fear and solicitude of the people while the high priest was within the veil. The ceremony of the annual atonement was accompanied with a dread on the part of the congregation, lest the Holy One might not be reconciled, and lest the priest and people should be consumed. While that is out of keeping with the idea that the ascension is meant, it is parallel to the disciples' state of mind during those heavy hours which intervened between the Lord's death and resurrection. They continued in suspense and doubt, dejection and dread.

c. The other ceremonies of the day of atonement all point in the same direction. Thus, when the high priest entered into the holiest of all, the atonement was not yet completed, for this was procured or won by the sprinkling of blood on the propitiatory or mercy-seat. This far more naturally figures forth Christ's violent death, or the separation of His soul and body, than His triumphal entry into heaven. The other accessories prove the same thing. Thus, the high priest laid aside his golden ornaments, the stately robes he usually wore, and entered in linen raiment, pure, but devoid of ornament and pomp (Lev. xvi. 4); an attire which was designed to indicate lowly abasement, not triumph or glory.

d. Another fact not less significant may be noticed : the veil of the temple was, at the moment of Christ's death, rent from the top to the bottom. That memorable fact in the sphere of the supernatural was intended for a purpose worthy of such an interposition from the hand of God. It was the great typical arrangement in which all the rest culminated, and on which all leant. Jesus had cried, " It is finished ;" and this miraculous event put a divine imprimatur on it. It took place in the sphere of fact, and we may warrantably hold that then the true High Priest entered the true holiest of all with His own blood. At that moment the true sprinkling of the mercy-seat took place : the wrath of God was fully propitiated ; the reality of the shadows had come. I do not refer to the other things adumbrated. I only advert to the circumstance that we have here a most remarkable answer to the question, When did the High Priest sprinkle the mercy-seat ? (compare Heb. x. 20.)

(2.) We come now to the great change effected by the sacrifices on the worshipper's relation. The allusions to the Mosaic worship in this respect are numerous and varied, the entire New Testament being pervaded by sacrificial phraseology of this nature.

a. For the clearer exhibition of this, let it be noticed that the expressions " coming to God " and " drawing nigh to God "

denote the attitude of these worshippers (Heb. iv. 16, x. 1).[1]
The first result effected by sacrifice on the relation of the worshipper was the removal of the divine anger incurred by trespass. When we consult the Mosaic worship, we find that the
sin-offering averted a divine penalty. Jehovah sat as Judge to
visit the sins of the people : by means of sacrifice He reinstated
them in His favour. That was the fundamental thought taught
by means of outward ceremonies of positive institutions, and it
disciplined and trained the mind for what was spiritual. Laws
manifold and burdensome left the transgressor nothing to expect but threatened punishment, if sin was not expiated by
sacrifice. Jehovah showed mercy only by maintaining invio-
late His holiness, rectitude, and authority. The sacrifices were
intended to impress this truth on every heart. Thus the idea
presented to us by the entire worship of the old economy
was, that without shedding of blood is no remission (Heb.
ix. 22).

b. Another class of expressions comprehends typical allusions
which represent men's sins as a defilement, taint, or stain, by
means of which the Israelite was excluded from the sanctuary,
and from fellowship with those who trode the courts of the
Lord : he was obliged to live apart. Only when the defilement
was removed by the blood of sacrifice, or by a sprinkling with
the water of separation, which presupposed a sacrifice (Num.
xix. 13), could he be re-admitted to the services and fellowship
of the people of God.

Various terms are employed to represent this restoration to
privilege, such as these : to SPRINKLE, to PURGE or PURIFY, to
CLEANSE, to WASH, to SANCTIFY (1 Pet. i. 2 ; Heb. x. 2 ; Tit. ii. 14 ;
1 Cor. vi. 11; Heb. ii. 11). If an Israelite became unclean by
touching a dead body, he could not approach the sanctuary till
sprinkled according to the peculiar ritual divinely appointed

---

[1] The apostle designates Christian worshippers by a name descriptive of their
approach on the ground of sacrifice : τοὺς προσερχομένους (Heb. x. 1), or ἐγγὺς ἐν
τῷ αἵματι (Eph. ii. 13).

for his case. Then only could he be restored, and partake
of privileges. On the day of atonement, the entire nation, on
account of sin separating between God and them, stood aloof
from the tabernacle of the congregation (Lev. xvi. 17), and were
re-admitted only when the blood of atonement had sprinkled
the mercy-seat. They obtained anew their forfeited privileges.
The whole nation of Israel, purified or sanctified, was then
holy. A single worshipper was also holy when the defilement
which shut him out from the congregation was removed by
sprinkling : he was now recognised as holy. Those two words
sanctify and *purify* involve each other, and intimate not so
much inward renovation, as a free approach to God, and an un-
challenged standing before Him. This phraseology will come
before us in the numerous texts which we shall have occasion
to examine.

It only remains to notice one thing further. The apostles
put in a strong light the insufficiency and unprofitableness of
the Mosaic rites, while they bring out their symbolical and
typical meaning. They are described as weak and beggarly
elements (Gal. iv. 9) ; they could not effect the pardon of sin,
or perfect the conscience (Heb. x. 1–3) ; and they merged, as
only a type could merge, when the truth of all appeared—when
the Messiah came. The Jews were then discharged from their
burdensome ceremonial.

SEC. IV.—THE APOSTLES' REFERENCES TO PROPHECY ON THE SUBJECT OF THE ATONEMENT.

As we found it necessary to consider the apostles' treatment of the types, it is not less necessary to take up their
references to prophecy. And we enter the field of prophecy, as
it bears on the sufferings of the Messiah and the effects of His
death, in the same way, that is, only so far as the apostles
point out the way and determine the reference.

Many rules might be laid down for deciding on the Messianic references; but these we do not need to consider. Thus, if the substance of a prophecy is of such a nature that it cannot competently be applied to any other illustrious person, but can be fitly applied to the Messiah, we must understand it as referring directly to Him. The descriptions of suffering, for example, which pervade many parts of the ancient prophecies, and of the Psalms, are so peculiar and unique, that while they are proper in Christ's mouth (Ps. xxii. 1, lxix. 1), as a divine person stooping to vicarious punishment, and are to us in that light awakening and affecting in the utmost degree, they would be simply incongruous and absurd if spoken by any merely human being. Human sympathy would be outraged, and inevitably regard them as utterances which no man ever indulged in, and which no literature ever attempted in the case of mere men like ourselves. The minute description of any other man's sorrows, sufferings, and death would be intolerable, and viewed as either misplaced, or as making an exaction on human attention which mankind must resent. But in Christ all this is in keeping, whether we find the description in prophecy or history, in the Psalms which foretold His experience, or in the history of His utterances unveiled by the Gospels.

But another rule might be laid down in reference to the prophetic statements which describe the Messiah as divine. Wherever Jehovah, God of Israel, is set forth in the exercise of royal or judicial functions, as the Bridegroom of the church, or the Shepherd of the sheep; wherever theophanies occur, wherever allusions are made to His ransom, or to His power as a conqueror mighty to save (Isa. lxiii. 1); the allusion in all such cases is to the Messiah: and the apostles, in a natural and unforced way, adduce these passages as Messianic[1] (Heb. i. 8–14). Another fact deserves notice. The prophets take occasion to speak of the Messiah in connection with events and personages

---

[1] Delitzsch well illustrates these Messianic allusions, *Commentar zum Hebräer-br.* 1857, p. 28.

of their times, and especially with the oppressions, captivity, or threatened ruin to which the nation was often exposed, partly because they lived, as we do, on His incarnation; partly because promises of His coming, of His birth by a virgin (Isa. vii. 14), of His being a great light to a people sitting in darkness, of His birthplace, contained a guarantee that the nation was not to perish, and might comfort herself in these prospects. There was also advancing light. In the first period there was only a promise that humanity should get deliverance from the evil consequences which the tempter had caused (Gen. iii. 15). That was doubtless known to Abraham by tradition, but new light dawned with the promise that in his seed all the families of the earth should be blessed; and thus Christology constantly became amplified.

As we survey the prophecies of the atonement only with the aid of apostolic allusion and quotation, it is not necessary to discuss the question whether the Messianic element existed in the Old Testament church, and whether men waited for redemption in Israel, as Simeon was found waiting when He came. Paul declared that he preached none other things than those which the prophets and Moses said should come, that Christ should suffer and rise from the dead (Acts xxvi. 22). The apostles put prophecy on an equal footing with their own authority as eye-witnesses, and never ceased to take heed to it. The prophecies on the atonement were so explicit, that they did little more than adduce, expound, and apply them. We limit our inquiry to passages descriptive of the atonement; and even from these, to curtail their number, we select only those which are rather doctrinal than historical in their character. This narrows the range to those more explicit allusions which portray the humiliation of the Messiah in our room.

Nor shall I discuss the question whether the quotations are correctly applied; for I assume that that point is definitely settled by the authority of inspired men, and that they are not literary accommodations, such as are often made to give point to an idea by apt illustrations from poetry. They are direct predictions in every case, giving the scope of the various prophecies. I have nothing in common with the method of exposition too common at present, that interprets the Old Testament otherwise than the apostles did, and enters the field without their guidance, and irrespective of their authority. It is one thing when the expositor, confiding in the apostles' inspiration, reverently selects a view-point in the prophet's age in order to add to his faith knowledge. That is only exegetical fidelity; for he believes, and wishes to know. But it is another thing, and cannot be sufficiently reprobated, when the interpreter fosters a state of mind that will not be controlled by apostolical authority, and claims to have better hermeneutics, and greater skill in interpretation, than apostles. I will be no party to the presumption which that involves. To one standing within the pale of revelation, and deferring to inspired men, that exposition is foreclosed.

The quotations take for granted, that from Adam downward the person and atonement of Messiah were revealed in new aspects, and with greater definiteness, from age to age. The promise as to the seed of the woman was the all-important point to which the saints, through long intervening periods, looked forward as the hope of humanity; and as the church needed encouragement in dejection, or light in darkness, prophets were from time to time raised up to repeat assurances of His advent (Mic. v. 2; Zech. ix. 9); and many points were foretold connected with His manifestation, all containing new encouragement.

To these prophecies the apostles refer as divine oracles, not as guesses of truth. They do not quote them as if the words contained nothing but dim anticipations of an ideal righteous man, whose appearance might perchance one day prove a reality. To them Messianic revelations were the most certain of verities —divine oracles, thoughts of God conveyed to man, predictions emanating from the Holy Ghost. The hope of the Messiah was never extinguished; nor, while the order of prophets lasted, was the announcement ever obscure as to His advent as the seed of Abraham (Gen. xxii. 18), the son of David (Ps. cxxxii. 11): for that was the great fact with which all history travailed, and with which all the saints were acquainted—the centre-point of religious life, as it is to us now. In Anna we see the anticipation with which the most simple minds were filled—the sun to which every believing eye was turned.

Particular prophecies of a later time may be regarded as expanding earlier prophecies. The primeval gospel promised victory over Satan, and the removal of death, the doom brought on the world by yielding to the tempter. For a time this was sufficient, because it announced redemption from the enemy, and restoration to divine favour. Clearer intimations were next made to the patriarchs, till in David and Isaiah the outline of the atonement and the sufferings of Messiah is so clear that we seem to be reading history. The design and nature of His sufferings were explicitly declared. So necessary was this for the ancient believers, and for the church of after times, that without this outline they who lived before the advent could not have had correct ideas of the atonement, and we who live after it would have wanted the necessary criterion for deciding whether Jesus of Nazareth was He to whom prophecy referred.

The purpose we have in view in this section will be best served if we limit the inquiry to a few particular predictions which expressly set forth the doctrine of the atonement. We shall therefore first take up the references to those Messianic psalms which describe the atonement in its nature and fruits. I will not discuss the question how far the Messianic element pervades the book of Psalms, nor how far we are to extend this recognition beyond those which Christ and His apostles have indicated; for the plan we are pursuing leads us to accept the latter without question on the authority of apostles. But when parts of a psalm are quoted by inspired men as Messianic, we see no reason to question the Messianic

character of the entire psalm, if it betrays no obvious marks of
a colloquy or change of speakers. Another thing deserves
notice. These psalms enter into details of suffering experience, and adduce facts of a historical nature which would be
anomalous in any other setting, but are significant in connection with that extraordinary Person whose fortunes, even to the
minutest details, were worthy of being foretold. Those psalms,
read with the apostles' commentary, are in the last degree
important, as placing Christ's redemption-work in the most
striking light, and bringing out its essential elements.

Of the Messianic psalms adduced by the apostles, some are
put in connection with the atonement by the inspired commen-
tator, though they do not in so many words contain express
reference to the Lord's vicarious death. Thus, in one psalm
written to describe the dominion of the second Adam over the
works of God, the apostolic commentary bases the mediatorial
kingdom on His being made a little lower than the angels, and
suffering death (Ps. viii. 5; Heb. ii. 9). In another psalm we
are taught that the Messiah would burst the bands of death;
and His resurrection is put as a reward, in connection with the
obedience and humiliation of the Holy One (Ps. xvi. 8; Acts
ii. 25). In another psalm, the throne of the mediatorial King
is described as based upon a work of holy obedience during a
previous period, when He was approved as one who loved
righteousness and hated iniquity (Ps. xlv. 7; Heb. i. 8, 9).
Some, indeed, explain these words as referring to the love of
righteousness and hatred of iniquity which are now displayed
in the administration of His kingdom. But the order of the
thought and the logical particle, lead us to refer the terms
to the spotless righteousness which the Christ evinced in
His life and death, and which was rewarded with the crown
of glory and honour. The word which connects the work
with the reward—viz. the word THEREFORE [1]—can have no

---

[1] διὰ τοῦτο can only mean *because of this.* It cannot have the final sense, *in
eum finem.* See Noldius on the Hebrew phrase so used nearly 150 times.

meaning but to announce that the exaltation was the reward of the obedience : "*Therefore* God hath anointed Thee with the oil of gladness above Thy fellows." In another psalm, where the Lord's ascension is described, the words "Thou hast ascended up on high" are interpreted as presupposing that He descended first into the lower parts of the earth (Ps. lxviii. 18 ; Eph. iv. 8, 9). We see that all these Messianic psalms, according to the commentary of inspired apostles, presuppose and involve the atonement. They take for granted that the cross was the foundation of His mediatorial throne—that the abasement preceded the reward. In these psalms we come to the atonement in a less direct way. We shall limit our attention, therefore, to those which directly define the nature of the atonement, and select two for particular consideration.

1. Among the prophetic psalms which bring out the essential elements of the atonement, one of the most important is the fortieth Psalm, as quoted in the Epistle to the Hebrews: "When He cometh into the world, He saith, Sacrifice and offering Thou wouldest not, but a body hast Thou prepared me : in burnt-offerings and sacrifices for sin Thou hast had no pleasure: then said I, Lo, I come (in the volume of the book it is written of me) to do Thy will, O God; *yea, Thy law is within my heart*" (Ps. xl. 6 ; Heb. x. 5–7). The question, Who is the speaker ? is not answered by saying that David, the writer, speaks in the first person as an individual. This is settled by the authority of the apostle, who introduces Christ as uttering the words when He came into the world; and no difficulties of interpretation, no critical reasons, can be suffered to unsettle this decision. But that leaves room for another inquiry : May not David have uttered these words in some lower sense, in the typical character which he bore ? Now it may be conceded, that without sufficient reasons we are not to deny all allusion to himself on the part of the writer. But when the words are not only put into the lips of the Messiah by an inspired apostle, but are palpably out of keeping with anything that

David did, or ever could do, we are amply warranted to ascribe them to another speaker; and the fact that David was a prophet, and a type of the Messiah, enables us to apprehend that he might consciously merge the type in the antitype in certain portions of a psalm, or through an entire psalm. As there was nothing in David's history to which this language could possibly refer, we may apply the principle which Peter adduced in the book of Acts to determine the Messianic reference of another psalm (Acts ii. 29, 30) as follows:—To nothing in David's life could these words have applied: he must therefore have spoken them as a prophet, seeing himself in his greater offspring, or, more correctly still, have spoken them as from the lips of Him that was to come. Dropping the type in the antitype, David was in all such cases, from the beginning to the end of the psalm, little else than the medium of communication, or the amanuensis, though he does not formally announce in whose name he is speaking, or whose words they are. There is no trace whatever of any change of speaker, and therefore the whole must be taken as the connected discourse of the same person throughout the psalm.

The only thing fitted to raise a doubt is the complaint that his iniquities took hold upon him (ver. 12); but that difficulty entirely vanishes when we consider that the Messiah, as the surety and substitute of His people, could in this way fitly speak of the sins of His people, as they were imputed or charged to His account: He made them His. If God made Him to be sin for us, and if He was our sin in God's judgment and account, while still the beloved Son, He could be all this too in His own judgment as the surety. That was but the subjective recognition of an objective fact; and in so speaking, the Messiah only describes Himself as the true sin-offering or trespass-offering,[1] which, as we shall immediately see, is the principal thought of the passage. If we can call Him OUR RIGHTEOUSNESS

---

[1] See the celebrated Lampe's *Geheimniss des Gnadenbunds*, iii. 15. 2, where this is well elucidated.

(Jer. xxiii. 6), why may not He for a similar reason call Himself our sin? Hence it is not necessary to suppose, as some have done, a change of speakers where this allusion begins (ver. 12). Besides, that would be a violent break in the train of thought and in the connection of the two verses, as indicated by the logical particle *for* linking them together (vers. 11 and 12).

Plainly, the psalm has two divisions, of which the first describes in vivid language the speaker's deliverance from a horrible pit and miry clay. Then the effect of this is represented as tending to make many fear and trust in Jehovah; that is, to repent and be converted from heathenism, or from false religions to the worship of the true God (vers. 1–5). The second division, which is emphatically marked by the words *Then said I* (ver. 7), contrasts the absolute weakness and insufficiency of the Mosaic sacrifices with the Messiah's obedience and atoning work. That these words cannot be David's, appears at first sight from the fact that the speaker adduces His own obedience or finished work in contrast with the animal sacrifices, which are described as not pleasing to God, and as of no value except as types of what should come. This obedience to the Father's will and to the divine law on the part of the great speaker was destined to usher in a new economy (Heb. x. 9); and hence the words cannot in any sense, or with any application, be referred to David.

But let us limit our attention to the words of the quotation. First, there is an enumeration of the several Mosaic sacrifices, which are distributed into the bloody and the unbloody. That classification is indicated in the original by the terms here rendered " sacrifice and offering." Then follow the chief bloody sacrifices, which are further classified under these terms:—
" Burnt-offering and sin-offering Thou dost not require;" or, as it is rendered by the apostle, " In burnt-offerings and sacrifices for sin Thou hast had no pleasure." The meaning unquestionably is, that in the appointment of those sacrifices a further purpose was to be served, and that they were appointed to

continue but for a time, and then to take end.   Mere pictures
of something infinitely more important which was to come—
pledges and testimonies to what was yet future—they were
destined to cease as things of little value, or as things in which
God had no pleasure on their own account.   But on David and
on Israel they were binding till legitimately displaced by the
fulfilment.

Now, in contrast with the total insufficiency of the Mosaic
sacrifices, the speaker in the psalm says, " Mine ears hast
Thou opened."   Many commentators explain this phrase by
the provision in the law to meet the case of the Hebrew
servant choosing to remain in voluntary servitude rather
than accept his freedom, as he might do at the seventh
year of release; and this comment affords a very competent
sense.   Others explain it as denoting that the ear was purged
by God of all impediment, so as promptly to know and do God's
will.   A third class take the expression *ears* as a synecdoche
for the whole body, denoting that the ear was prompt to listen,
and the entire body prompt to obey.   I see no cause to deviate
from the idea of the Hebrew servant (Ex. xxi. 5); for one
common mode of announcing Christ was to represent Him as
the servant of God by way of eminence—the perfect servant,
the chosen servant, the righteous servant (Isa. xlii. 1, liii. 11).
Thus, in the psalm under our consideration, Messiah describes
Himself as coming to serve—coming in the humanity He had
assumed, to fulfil the law in the meanest servant-form.   It is
no objection to the allusion already noticed, that according to
the law, only the right ear of the Hebrew servant was pierced,
whereas the plural number occurs in the psalm; for this may
imply a greater perfection in the antitype than in the type.
But in reproducing the phrase for the New Testament church,
the apostle abandons the Hebrew allusion, and gives us the
same idea under another guise.   He translates it, " A body
hast Thou prepared me."   Writing with the same authority and
the same spirit of inspiration, the sacred writer is content to

reproduce the thought in a different form, giving us the sense. He intimates that a body was prepared, in which all the prompt obedience and perfect service we have referred to were to be carried out to their utmost perfection.

The next words put beforehand into the mouth of the Redeemer as He came into the world were as follows : " Lo, I am come (in the volume of the book it is written of me) to do Thy will, O God." In the psalm there is somewhat greater fulness in the expression : " *I delight to do Thy will, O my God : yea, Thy law is within my heart.*" The verses, in the connection in which they stand, show the inadequacy of sacrifices to meet the divine claims, and announce that Messiah was to come as the true priest and sacrifice—the substance of all those shadows. His obedience in a true humanity is thus placed in direct contrast with the burnt-offering and sin-offering, intimating that He came as the great personal moral sacrifice to do what they could not do, and to attain the divine design in its utmost perfection and fulness of meaning, such as they never could attain. Moreover, when He says, " Lo I come (in the volume of the book it is written of me) to do Thy will," the allusion is to the Father's decree, or to that eternal covenant or compact to which the mission of the Son into the world at every moment bore constant reference (John vi. 39). That the words warrant the supposition of an agreement or compact between the Father and the Son before the actual incarnation, can scarcely be doubtful to any one who ponders the words. They mean, " Lo, I come to execute what Thou requirest." The volume of the book, or the roll, seems to be the Mosaic law containing the references to the shadowy sacrifices, or better, perhaps, the promises of Scripture generally, because in all its prophecies as well as types it gave a pledge that He should come ; and the force of this statement is augmented by the apostle's subsequent interpretation of the words, as denoting that the passage bore reference to the offering of the body of Jesus Christ once for all (Heb. x. 10).

But it is added still more definitely, that He came to do GOD'S WILL, and to fulfil HIS LAW. There is a shade of difference between the two words here used—THY WILL, or good pleasure, and THY LAW—which is by no means to be overlooked. The first term, WILL, or good pleasure, expresses the infinitely loving will of God which led Him to plan our redemption, and it is a comprehensive enough term to embrace whatever belongs to the covenant between the Father and the Son. It means all God's will in reference to the redemption of the human race. When the Messiah, in coming into the world, announced that He "delighted" to do GOD'S WILL, the language sets forth the condescending love of Christ, His mingled obedience and love in our room. As to the term LAW, it designates that which is the transcript of God's nature, and the rule of human obedience. To have the law in the heart, is to have it written on the heart and engraven on the mind, so as to be ever before the memory and active in the soul (Jer. xxxi. 33). It comprehends all that God demands, and all that pleases Him, or the entire service of love which as creatures we owe to God. Nor is it necessary to exclude the law of sacrifices. When we put together the import of the passage, then, it conveys these truths: that God the Father formed the plan of redemption here called His WILL,[1] or good pleasure, and that the Son came into the world as the party resolved to execute it by His active and passive obedience, and as having the law in His heart (Heb. x. 9, 10).

But, it is asked, why may not David here speak of himself as a man arriving at the conviction that the sacrifices did not please God? Does he not, in the passage, seem to contrast moral obedience with ritual observances, so as to disparage the latter? That comment by no means exhausts the sense, and

---

[1] C. G. F. Walch, *de obedientia activa Christi*, p. 9, says: "Voluntas illa erat conditio pacti inter patrem filiumque initi." The apostle uses only one of the terms, viz. τὸ θέλημά σου, unless perhaps he intends to combine both in the one word.

it is every way unnatural, not to mention that it runs counter to the interpretation given by the inspired apostle. Besides, it is not true that God required no animal sacrifices at the hand of David as an Israelite; for God had imposed them, and He did not leave this matter to the worshipper's choice. In the absolute sense of the terms, they could not be described as wholly nugatory, or as not pleasing to God. But as they could not usher in any real atonement for sin, they did not correspond, in the proper sense of the term, to the divine good pleasure, or to the law of God, but only foreshadowed what was to come; and it was in this subordinate sense that they were depreciated, that is, in comparison of Christ's finished work. The language is not absolute, but relative. God required a moral obedience and a personal excellence, which were to culminate in offering one great personal and moral sacrifice for sins, which should have no repetition; and the Messiah came to offer that one sacrifice, the true sacrifice, once for all, and by so doing to fulfil the will of God according to the covenant.

II. The next prophecy to be noticed, and cognate to the former, is contained in the 110th Psalm: *The Lord sware, and will not repent, Thou art a priest for ever after the order of Melchizedek* (Ps. cx. 4; Heb. vii. 21). This is properly a coronation-psalm, composed probably on some of those occasions when the royal seer beheld in vision Messiah's ascension to His throne. It is quoted both by our Lord and His apostles as Messianic (Matt. xxii. 44; Acts ii. 32; Heb. i. 13). It certainly cannot allude to David; for, as our Lord says, David in spirit calls Him Lord. Besides, it is adduced by the apostles as the Father's salutation to Messiah at His ascension to the right hand. He is further described as a priest (Ps. cx. 4); for the priesthood was the foundation of the dominion,—the cross was the basis of the throne. The titles Prophet, Priest, and King, indicating distinct functions performed by the Messiah, are never confounded. Hence, when He is represented as a sacrificing priest, this language, in David's mouth,

E

can only mean that He should bring in the great offering or
sacrifice which was appointed to be the truth of all the sacrificial laws. It is sometimes alleged by eminent divines, that
Melchizedek was not a priest properly so called, because it is
not expressly said that he offered sacrifice, but merely that he
blessed Abraham. But the brief notice given of the historical
event in Genesis gives no warrant for such a conclusion, and
the title Priest expressly ascribed to him, we think, refutes it,
for there was no priest without a sacrifice.

The great proof of Christ's priesthood is based on this
passage. The apostle, in the Epistle to the Hebrews, very
copiously expounds and applies it. Thus, it is quoted, in the
first place, to show that our Lord did not arrogate to Himself
the office of the priesthood without a divine call (Heb. v. 6).
It is next adduced and fully expounded to show His great
superiority to the Aaronic priesthood (Heb. vii. 1–28). And
it deserves notice that the apostle, in following out the line of
thought presented to us in the psalm, describes Melchizedek's
personal dignity as a type by language derived from the Antitype, and true only of the Antitype,—a peculiarity, in fact,
applicable not to this case alone, but to all the types and
shadows. The distinctive qualities of the great Priest and
great propitiation are reflected back upon the shadow, not
conversely. And as Melchizedek united in his person regal
and priestly functions—a combination not permitted to the
Levitical economy—he was in this respect a memorable type
of Messiah.

Our object is not to discuss the disputed questions which
have been raised in connection with Melchizedek, but to
elucidate the prophecy in the light of the apostle's commentary.
We accept the simple and natural exposition which takes the
narrative in Genesis as the record of a historical event. But
the significance attaching to it consists less in the history than
in the typical and prophetical elements belonging to it. These
seem exclusively to have been before the Psalmist's mind,

and the apostle's mind, for the latter only developes what the Psalmist supplied. That which was concealed, as well as that which was expressed, had in an equal degree a typical significance. And this is the singular peculiarity which the Psalmist and apostle alike were taught by the Spirit of inspiration to trace in the narrative. Some have imagined that Melchizedek was a divine person—the Son of God.[1] I take him to have been a historical personage, the prince of Salem, a worshipper of the true God, who united in himself the double function of priest and king. On this supposition the whole significance of the type proceeds. The apostle fixes our attention upon the import of his name and place of residence, translating them for the Christian Hebrews. The fact that he renders them into Greek for readers already familiar with their meaning, leads us to the conclusion that he expressly intended their import to be typical (Heb. vii. 2). The peculiarities mainly insisted upon are these: that his descent was not traced in any family register; that he came upon the scene and passed away as if he had neither father nor mother, and in this respect was like Christ, who in His earthly nature had no earthly father, and in His other nature no mother; that he seemed to have neither beginning of days nor end of life; and that he was made like the Son of God, who was the true antitypical Priest to whom the shadow referred. These peculiarities are read off from the history of Melchizedek in Genesis, which the Spirit of inspiration directed Moses to compose in such a way as to let all this fully appear, whether Moses was aware of it or not. The one great peculiarity which that psalm of David taught the Hebrews was, that there was to be another Priest out of the Aaronic line, or the line of any priestly family; and the other point which the psalm emphatically taught them was, that this

---

[1] In D'Outrein, *de Sendbrief van Paulus aan de Hebreen*, this is powerfully advocated, and the other opinions are reviewed. See Riehm's admirable work, *Lehrbegriff des Hebräerbriefes*, 1858, p. 192, where all the points are well discussed, and the literature given.

Priest was to be the first and last of his kind (3–10). But the apostle, in applying the quotation, takes it up in its several parts, and elucidates it as his text. He unfolds at large the divine purpose and the reason for which Messiah was made a priest after the order of Melchizedek. Three points are here mentioned, which we shall briefly state, in order to pave the way for the testimony in which the whole culminates—that there is but one priest, and one oblation.

1. He proves that the mention of another priest in the psalm involved the abrogation of the Levitical priesthood (11–19). This result is spoken of as necessary: it is regarded as a legitimate deduction, the force of which is not to be questioned. The appointment of another priest argued that the Levitical priesthood had made nothing perfect, and required to be replaced by a better. But another consequence was involved: the change of the priesthood carried with it the change or revocation of the Mosaic law (ver. 12). The reason is obvious. The entire ceremonial law presupposed the Aaronic priesthood, to which it was adapted, and to which it had reference in every one of its arrangements. The alteration of the priesthood was the subversion of the law; for the foundation of it was removed with the removal of the priesthood. This is the first result that necessarily accompanied the appointment of another priest after the order of Melchizedek. The great thought is, that the first priesthood was essentially defective, and that the entrance of a new priest was coincident with the bringing in of a better hope.

2. As to the word of the oath, another part of the quotation, it is next commented on by the apostle (ver. 20). The fact of the oath not only points to the immutable decree which God made in regard to this priesthood, but argues a new economy with better provisions. The Aaronic priesthood, mutable, because appointed without an oath, ushered in an imperfect or merely typical covenant. The Melchizedek priesthood of Christ, unchangeable, because it was appointed with the oath of

God, ushered in a better covenant (vers. 20–22). The priest-hood was in both cases the foundation of the economy; the Sinaitic covenant standing upon the Aaronic priesthood, the new covenant standing upon the Melchizedek priesthood of Christ. The apostle's reasoning is peculiarly worthy of notice, because it is an argument from the less to the greater. The logical connection must be apprehended in the following way. The two elements of the comparison are marked by the phrase *how much*[1] in one verse (ver. 20), and by the corresponding *so much* of a subsequent verse (ver. 22). The intervening verse is merely parenthetical (ver. 21). The argument stands thus: *In as far* as He was made a priest by an oath, *by so much* is He the Mediator of a better covenant. The new covenant, of which Christ is the Priest, Surety, or Mediator—for these are nearly synonymous terms, though used in their peculiar connection with a distinctive shade of meaning—is so much better than the Sinaitic covenant, by how much the great High Priest of our profession was appointed by an oath; and the new covenant and priesthood are never to be changed, as nothing better can replace them. The law made nothing perfect: this covenant does so, because it is the introduction of the better hope.

3. The third point of superiority is deduced from the words, *a priest for ever* (ver. 23). Contrasted with the Aaronic high priests, Christ continues in office for ever. The Aaronic high priests were many, because they were not suffered to continue by reason of death: words which mean that they could not continue to officiate, or continue in office, because they were ever dying. When it is said, " They truly were *many* priests," the words do not mean that they were many simultaneously, but many as holding office successively, because it was ever passing from hand to hand. The contrast is between many priests, as temporary occupants of the office, or invested with it for a time, and the true Priest, invested with the office for

---

[1] καθ' ὅσον (ver. 20) and κατὰ τοσοῦτον point to two counterparts, as is now admitted by all good exegetes. See Kurtz, *Brief an die Hebräer*, 1869.

ever. And when it is said He has an unchangeable priesthood,. the phrase may be interpreted in a twofold way, as descriptive of what is inviolable, or of that which does not descend to another occupant (ver. 24). The apostle deduces a further result from the everlasting priesthood, when he connects it with the perfection of the kingdom of God, whether we look at the New Testament worshippers individually, or at the church collectively, in its onward progress to the winding up of all things. That eternal priesthood enables Him to save men perfectly, or to save them for ever ; that is, to rescue them from sin and all its evils (ver. 25).

The mention of the eternal priesthood next leads the apostle by a natural train of thought to that abasement by which it was acquired. The power of an endless life, though connected with His divine person, is the purchased reward of His atonement. And this brings him to view the prophecy as a testimony to the great sacrifice, or satisfaction to divine justice. The royalty presupposes the humiliation, the expiation of sin. Hence the apostle's commentary advances to the two facts on which the atonement rests—the great New Testament priesthood, and His one ever-valid sacrifice (vers. 26–28). Starting from the idea of the eternal priest, and with man's necessities full in view, the apostle says, *For such an high priest became us* (ver. 26). The use of the causal particle *for* leads our thoughts to the ever-living High Priest, and introduces the further idea of a sacrifice as the foundation of that royal priesthood. He must offer a sacrifice so complete and meritorious, as to require no repetition. The Melchizedek priesthood of Jesus takes for granted ONE SACRIFICE FOR SIN never to be repeated, one atonement of everlasting validity, needing no supplementary addition, and equally applicable to all men and to all stages of the history of the kingdom of God. When we inquire more particularly on what elements such a sacrifice depends, they are unfolded in the following order :—(1) He was a sinless Priest, who needed not, like the Jewish high priests, to offer first for

His own sins, and then for the people's; for He had no sins of His own (ver. 27). (2) He offered only once, one ever-valid sacrifice. (3) According to the word of the oath after the law, and superseding it, He was not a high priest having infirmity, but the Son of God, a divine person, giving to His one oblation an infinite value, adequate to all our wants and to all the claims of God (ver. 28). There was to be but one sacrifice for sins. This was the presupposition of the everlasting priesthood, and its basis; and our great High Priest continues in office for ever, because of its inexhaustible and eternal validity. That is the apostle's train of reasoning in his memorable commentary upon the Melchizedek priesthood of Christ. It is lucidly developed by him from the 110th Psalm, a text which is taken up and expounded part by part. He winds up the whole by saying, that the foundation of the royal priesthood is the ONE SACRIFICE of everlasting efficacy.

III. Of all the prophecies, however, which bring out the essential elements of the atonement, the clearest is the fifty-third chapter of Isaiah, which deserves to be called the classical passage. From this chapter we have several quotations. Thus Peter quotes the words, *who did no sin, neither was guile found in His mouth* (1 Pet. ii. 22); and another passage is immediately subjoined, *by whose stripes ye were healed* (ver. 24). Isaiah is called the Old Testament evangelist, from the vivid descriptions of Messiah's sufferings, atonement, and reward, given especially in this section (Isa. lii. 13–liii. 12). These verses must be read together; for the division of the chapter, as is generally admitted, is unhappy. The passage proves that in the prophet's days, by means of his own teaching and that of other prophets, there prevailed, at least among the spiritually-minded members of the Israelitish community, a persuasion that Messiah should come as a suffering substitute, and that His obedience and death should constitute the one cause of man's redemption. Among the Jews in the most ancient times, it was the uniform opinion that the Messiah was the subject of this prophecy. Only at a later day, when embarrassed by the constant appeals of the Christians to this chapter, as the fullest and most connected explanation of the nature of Christ's death, did they invent the theory of a double Messiah —one coming in abasement, and the other in glory. As that was felt to be a mere artifice or evasion, other commentators referred it to a single person, and especially to Josiah. In these comments several of our laxer exegetes have followed the Jews, proposing to refer the language to Hezekiah or Josiah, to Jeremiah or Ezekiel; while others refer it to the Jewish nation before or after the exile. These are all sorry shifts; theories which go to pieces, or are discovered to be preposterous, the moment they are actually applied to the chapter, and made a key to open it: for was Josiah or Jeremiah bruised for our iniquities? or, applying it to Israel, was Israel healed by their stripes? were they exalted and extolled, or made to see their seed after becoming a sacrifice for sin? Equally preposterous is it to refer the language to the state in the third person, and to the citizens in the first; for then we must take all this language as applicable to the state. The chapter has only to be read in its connection, to see the exclusive reference to the Messiah. The repeated quotations in the New Testament— no fewer than six in number—by the Lord and His apostles, leave not a shadow of doubt that it can refer to no other than to Christ (Mark xv. 28; Matt. viii. 17; Acts viii. 32; Rom. xv. 21; 1 Pet. ii. 22, 24). What can be produced to overthrow this conclusion? To maintain that, on this supposition, Isaiah must have intimated that he was about to sketch Messiah's sufferings, argues a misconception of prophecy, and amounts to a demand that he should narrate history. Read in the light of history, applied as a key to the interpretation of our Lord's sufferings, the coincidence is marvellous; showing that, seven centuries beforehand, the history of Jesus, with the design of His sufferings, were not only foretold, but foreappointed in the thoughts of God. Our design is simply to adduce from prophecy, under the guidance of the apostles, a testimony to the Redeemer's satisfaction; and as this chapter contains all the great points connected with the atonement, we shall best attain our object, not by a formal exposition of all the verses, but by collecting the great essential elements of the doctrine as here developed. And in this single chapter we have almost all its essential elements exhibited with precision.

The chapter occurs in a larger section or division, which contains a constantly recurring allusion to the Messiah as THE SERVANT OF THE LORD (Isa. xlii. 1–liii. 12). That Messiah is meant by that title, is put beyond question by Matthew's quotation (Matt. xii. 18). The title SERVANT brings before us one obedient to God, and supposed to walk by a rule prescribed for his direction; and in this case it points out the servant by way of eminence, who thought it not robbery to be equal to God, yet put on a servant's form, and was obedient unto death. It is what Christ said: "As the Father gave me commandment, so I do" (John xiv. 31). After referring to Him as sprinkling many nations, and receiving the homage of kings, the prophet makes a transition from believing Gentiles to unbelieving Jews. At the commencement of the fifty-third chapter a preacher is introduced, complaining, as we may suppose the apostles did at Pentecost, that so few of Israel believed the report. Then follows the description of Messiah's sufferings. We shall extract a series of views containing a full outline of the atonement.

1. We have a divine estimate of the Servant of the Lord. We find, first of all, God's approval of Him, and infinite complacency in Him, before we come to the description of men's rejection of Him. What He was in the eye of God, is first stated figuratively (ver. 2); and then in plain words, in a subsequent verse (ver. 9), He is described as a tender plant or scion from a dry ground, growing up before the face of God: for the expression *grow up before Him* cannot refer, as some will have it, to an unbeliever discrediting the report of the

gospel. The words describe the Father's estimate, representing
Christ as growing up from His birth the object of divine complacency, as a fair plant or grateful flower on which God's eye
rested with delight. The *dry ground* is not to be interpreted
of David's fallen house,[1]—an idea imported without warrant
from another passage (Isa. xi. 1), and giving only a reference
to the poverty of His condition in the eye of men. The reference is to humanity in general. On this barren waste,
where no rain fell, and no nourishment was supplied by the
soil, this tender and beautiful shoot grew up alone amid a
desert of scorching sand, and God's eye rested on Him with
approval and delight. A second passage teaches the same
truth : *He did no violence ;* or, as Peter renders it, *He did no
sin, neither was guile found in His mouth* (ver. 9 ; 1 Pet. ii. 22).
The allusion is to His spotless purity in thought, and word, and
action ; but may also refer to the false charges of treason and
blasphemy on which He was arraigned.

By way of contrast, the prophet notices the Jewish estimate of Christ, or the offence at a suffering Messiah (ver. 3).
According to their ideas, His sufferings were a punishment
inflicted on Him as a pretender ; and how was the offence
removed ? The answer is supplied by the sequel of the chapter,
and pronounces sentence on all erroneous theories of the atonement. The offence was not removed by the notion that He
was a great teacher, a function in which sufferings incur no
disgrace. Nor was it removed by regarding Him as the founder
of a rational religion taking the place of a ritual one. The
connection shows (vers. 4, 5) that it was removed by the discovery that those sufferings were vicarious in their nature,
and effected our redemption. But how does the fact that the
sufferings were vicarious remove the offence of a suffering
Messiah among Jews or Gentiles ? It takes for granted a

---

[1] So Bleek and most of the moderns. Nor do the older and profounder
commentaries of Cloppenburg, Cocceius, Vitringa, do justice to the meaning
here : their expositions of this expression are all too external.

knowledge of sin; and when a surety is discovered by men in this state of mind, misconceptions are removed, prejudices vanish, the offence ceases, externalism is exploded, and glorying in the cross begins.

2. The Messiah suffers on account of sin as the meritorious cause (vers. 4, 5). These verses teach us why He suffered. Israel had been taught to regard the corporeal evils or diseases with which they were smitten as the penal effects of sin (Deut. xxviii. 22). The desolations of the land were its sicknesses, while victory was its healing. Matthew refers the words of the prophet to bodily diseases considered as penal consequences of sin (Matt. viii. 17). The commentary of the evangelist so far accurately defines the meaning; for we must understand diseases both of mind and body as penal effects of sin. ONE corruption was diffused through mind and body; and when the Physician bore our sin, He equally brought help to both. Whether, therefore, we take the words in the more mental reference, or in the sense which Matthew puts upon them, the allusion is to the penal consequences of sin, which Christ bore as a burden.

The prophet proceeds, in more precise terms, to show that sin was the meritorious cause of all Messiah's sufferings: "He was wounded for our transgressions, He was bruised for our iniquities" (ver. 5). Expressions to this effect are so numerous, that no doubt can remain on the mind of an unbiassed reader, that in this description we have an innocent sufferer bearing penal consequences due to the sins of others. Equivalent expressions occur, such as the following:—"The Lord laid on Him," or caused to meet on Him, "the iniquities of us all" (ver. 6): "He shall bear their iniquities" (ver. 11): "He bare the sins of many" (ver. 12). The phrase *to bear sin*, as we sufficiently proved elsewhere, means to bear sin as a burden, or to bear its punishment. They who will see nothing in this chapter of a satisfaction for sin on the part of the Servant of God, admit only such sufferings as a faithful witness encounters in declaring his testimony amid the enemies of his message (comp. Col. i. 24). According to them, the Servant of the Lord, the Mediator of a revelation in word, was brought to death for His faithfulness, like the Baptist, in the fulfilment of His prophetical career. The latter, though one side of Messiah's sufferings, is only what He had in common with His servants; but it is a wholly different suffering to which allusion is made in this chapter. The sufferings here described do not belong to the discharge of His prophetical office at all: they belong to His priestly function; and the entire chapter is confined to them.

Some expositors,[1] who take exception to the view that our sins were the meritorious cause of the Messiah's sufferings, argue that the words in the fourth verse must bear the rendering: "He was wounded *by*, or *through*, our transgressions." On linguistic grounds, apart from the connection and the nearer parallelism, that rendering is admissible. But it is not demanded by the language, as appears from passages where the same phraseology is used: "Fools, *because of* their transgressions, and *because of* their iniquities, are afflicted" (Ps. cvii. 17); and certainly it is wholly out of harmony with the connection. The decision as to the rendering must be arrived at by referring to the entire verse and context. The next clause confutes that rendering: "The chastisement of our peace" (that is, the punishment which procures our peace with God) "was upon Him." The words mean, the divine punishment that we should have borne. Such an interpretation interferes, too, with the prophet's scope, and contradicts his words; and every unprejudiced reader comes to a different conclusion. The rendering, "He was crucified by our frowardness," in the sense that the Israelites committed a great sin, is so wide of the mark, and does such violence both to the nearer and remoter parallelism, as well as to the tenor of the prophet's thoughts, that we can only regard it as suggested by the warping influence of a theological tendency.

[1] So the old Socinians put it, and so do Bleek and others recently.

3. The Messiah is described as the substitute of others. He was not exposed to suffering indirectly or incidentally, but in a direct and immediate way, as our representative. This comes out expressly when it is said: *The chastisement of our peace* (that is, the punishment which procured our peace) *was upon Him* (ver. 5). The language means, according to a familiar mode of speech in the sacred books, that the punishment due to us was reckoned to His account. We shall not draw illustrations of this usage from common discourse between man and man, where it is not uncommon (Gen. xxvii. 13; Judg. xix. 20; Matt. xxvii. 25); for, in truth, it is competently used only when men are considered according to a divine constitution which God alone has authority to make. The chapter under consideration is so full of substitution, that this idea colours its whole contents. In human intercourse we see men acting vicariously—that is, taking upon them the obligations of others—and we apprehend the idea. And when the Servant of the Lord, without sin of His own (ver. 9), suffered for His people—when their transgressions were the cause of His punishment—when He put Himself under their collective sins to atone for them—it is evident that in all this He acted vicariously.

This vicarious position is still more evident from two other expressions, which may be briefly noticed. The first is: *The Lord hath laid on Him*—that is, caused to meet or converge on Him—*the iniquities of us all* (ver. 6). This passage intimates that Messiah came under the consequences of those iniquities with which men are chargeable, and bore them in order that the flock for which He suffered might escape unhurt, and be restored to the Shepherd and Bishop of souls. This shows vicarious action. The second expression is even more emphatic: *His soul shall be an offering for sin (asham)* (ver. 11). The term denotes a trespass-offering, as used of an animal sacrifice (Lev. v. 15; Ezek. xl. 39; 1 Sam. vi. 3); and the victim was so termed as if it were embodied sin, and must die in the room of the offerer, who was deserving of death according to the law. What had for ages been figuratively done in legal ceremonies, was to be carried out on the Messiah, as the great personal and moral trespass-offering of His church. The language signifies that the sins of His people met on Him; that He was made sin, and subjected to the responsibility which this entailed, not in a metaphorical sense, or after a sort, as the Socinians put it, but really, by proper imputation or transfer. He who was the sinless and righteous Servant of Jehovah (ver. 11), could have no connection with sin but by substitution. If He did not die as a vicarious trespass-offering, or as a voluntary sin-bearer, what possible link could subsist between His death and the sins of the apostolic age, or our sins at this remote distance of time? The idea of substitution is unmistakeable in the entire chapter.

4. Messiah's sufferings are announced as coming from God, and inflicted by a divine hand. To this it is the more imperative to advert, because modern thought concedes to the sufferings of Christ only the more indirect and external sorrows encountered in the prosecution of His prophetical office from the ungodly generation to whom He bore the divine message. A perusal of this chapter, however, conveys the impression that He suffered directly at the hand of God, or in the exercise of punitive justice. This is apparent from expressions which need no comment. When it is said, " The Lord laid on Him the iniquities of us all " (ver. 6), this does not mean that God permitted indignities to be inflicted on Him by men without any divine action, but that God caused them to descend. This is further taught by the antithesis in which the exaction of justice is connected with the affliction which He bore. " He was oppressed "—or, more strictly, He was demanded in the exercise of a divine exaction—" and He was afflicted " (ver. 7). We see on the one side the claim of offended justice, and on the other Messiah's agonies in responding to that demand. We have two parties in their

several actions: the Most High demanding punishment, and the Surety bearing it.

But expressions containing the same idea are multiplied. Thus, when it is said, "For the transgression of my people was He stricken" (ver. 8), the allusion is to the infliction of punishment at the hand of God in satisfying the demands of justice. Not only so: it is added, *It pleased the Lord to bruise Him* (ver. 10). These memorable words intimate that the Lord not only permitted this at the hand of man, but had pleasure or delight in it, as it bore on His declarative glory and man's salvation. These sufferings, not in themselves, but in their scope and consequences, gave satisfaction to the Most High, who could not otherwise have had delight in it; and the supreme Author of all these sufferings was Jehovah, by whom we must here understand God the Judge of all.

This declaration enables us to meet all the statements of a general kind opposed to the infliction of punitive justice or wrath in any form. The objection is thus put: The sufferings of an innocent person could be of no avail, and could not be pleasing to God, or angels, or men. The text obviates this objection in proper form, asserting directly the reverse; and we do not require to adduce other recondite grounds to show that Jehovah delighted in the atonement of Messiah. It is here announced that the Messiah was to bear the punishment of sin, as inflicted by the hand of God. With this it is impossible to harmonize the views of the recent theology opposed to the vicarious sacrifice, when it allows no suffering but such as came from the hand of man in His office as the great Teacher. The prophet, as we here perceive, long before His coming, foretold the opposite. As to the objection urged by the Socinians, that nothing can be more unjust than to punish the innocent, a far more difficult problem is, How could the Son of God suffer what He did, if He is not allowed to be a surety? With a full exemption from punishment, on the double ground that He was sinless man and Son of God, how

could the moral government of God allow any infliction in the
mere course of things ?   On the supposition of suretyship, all is
easy ; on the other supposition, all is inexplicable,—nay, such
an anomaly and incongruity in the moral government of God,
that we can more easily suppose the annihilation of all things
than its occurrence.

5. The fruits or consequences of Messiah's death are next
mentioned.   These are twofold.   One class of these has more
special reference to the mediatorial reward to be conferred on
Him, viz. the promises that He should see His seed, and
prolong His days, and divide the spoil with the strong,—
all included in His reward (vers. 10–12).   The other class of
consequences have special reference to the redemption of His
people, and to these I limit attention.   Isaiah announces the
work of the Lord Jesus as a priest giving His life a trespass-
offering for His people, and as the righteous servant justifying
many ; and to both these effects of His abasement we shall
briefly refer, by illustrating the two clauses where these allusions occur.

The first of these affirms that we have peace by His
chastisement, and healing by His stripes (ver. 5 ; 1 Pet. ii.
24).   The commentary of Peter, who quotes these last terms,
leaves no room to doubt that the prophet's words, rightly
understood, mean that the punishment, which brings peace
or procures reconciliation with God, was upon Him.   This
proof would fall to the ground, were we obliged to render,
as some propose, " The instruction of our peace was upon
Him."   But there is no warrant for putting on the words
this meaning (compare Deut. xi. 2 ; Job v. 17 ; Jer. xxx.
14 ; Prov. xiii. 24).   The word means chastisement,—a signification confirmed by the parallelism of the next clause,
according to the well-known rule of the Hebrews, to repeat
the thought with a peculiar modification.   According to this
parallelism, the word *chastisement* in the one clause is re-
echoed by the word *stripes* in the other ; and the allusion

in the context is not to instruction, but to vicarious suffering and wounds. The thought, as Peter quotes the words,
is, that the punishment of the Surety was the healing of His
people.

If language is left to express thought, these words beyond
doubt connect reconciliation and healing with the sufferings
of Messiah. As to this PEACE, it is reconciliation with God,
the effect of Messiah's suffering. That cannot be explained
away by those who regard reconciliation as the result of absolute love, apart from any intervention or atonement. The term
"healing" designates deliverance from sin, including pardon,
and every part of spiritual recovery. The stripes by which
that healing is effected, refer to the scourging inflicted by man's
hand, and to the far worse stripes inflicted by the hand of God,
of which the former were but the outward emblem; for we
must include, by what is called synecdoche, the entire sufferings as well as entire obedience of the Lord. The language
at first sight is paradoxical, and meant to evoke the reflection,
How can wounds or maladies be healed by stripes? How
can stripes inflicted on one be the healing of another? The
phraseology was intended to show that this could not be by
mere natural effect, or in the ordinary course of things, or by
mere moral motives. But the moment we recall the idea of
substitution or exchange of places, all is plain; for the wounds
of the vicarious Sufferer bring in their train, by the connection
of cause and effect, a true healing for every disease.

The next fruit to which I referred is: "By His KNOWLEDGE
shall my righteous Servant JUSTIFY many" (ver. 11). It is the
Father who speaks. How Messiah was the righteous servant
of the Father, will appear when we reflect that His obedience,
measured by the law, was the bringing in of that everlasting
righteousness on the ground of which men are pronounced
righteous at the tribunal of God; for the import of the word
"justify" intimates here and everywhere a judicial sentence
of acquittal and acceptance. But how is that effected by His

F

knowledge ? The words can only mean the knowledge by which He is known, not the knowledge which He possesses. For the chapter refers not to His prophetical, but to His priestly office. Men are justified by the knowledge of Him, which is the same as to be justified by faith.

SEC. V.—THE TESTIMONY TO THE ATONEMENT IN THE ACTS OF THE APOSTLES.

The book of Acts gives testimony to the atonement in a peculiar way : it contributes important aid as to the connection between the death of Christ and the remission of sins. We see that, in every place to which the apostles brought their message, they inculcated neither conditions nor meritorious preparations, but preached remission of sins, both among Jews and Gentiles, as an immediate gift to all who had susceptible minds. They declared in unambiguous terms that it was procured by the humiliation and death of the Son of God, and given by Him without reference to legal works in any form (Acts v. 31).

Not only so : the book of Acts displays in a historic form the results of preaching the atonement, or the important consequences of inculcating the necessity and practical bearings of this great doctrine. Considered in its structure, it seems to have been prepared on the principle of showing with what success the preaching of the cross was accompanied among all classes, whether they were Jews, Samaritans, or Gentiles; for apostolic preaching proclaimed present forgiveness to every inquirer.

Here it is necessary to anticipate a difficulty. Some allege that the apostles kept silence on the doctrine of the atonement, when they might have been expected to speak of it : others, not duly considering the scope of the book, find comparatively little allusion to the atonement. But two things are forgotten.

None of the discourses is reported at large; for the sacred writer is content to record the salient points or heads of discourse. And though several outlines of discourses are interwoven with the narrative, they are not given as full reports; but as specimens of their testimony, illustrations of the success with which it was crowned, or arguments which Jewish unbelief withstood. Moreover, the discourses given in the Acts of the Apostles are missionary or evangelistic addresses to men in no state of preparation or mood of mind to bear a dogmatic elucidation or a full exhibition of the doctrine. For the most part, there was not such common ground between the hearers and speakers as must be presupposed for a full exposition. The apostles addressed impatient or hostile hearers; and from the nature of the case, the doctrine could only to a limited extent be propounded to men so minded. But one thing is clear: remission of sins was presented to the hearers in its causal connection with Christ crucified, and preached in His name (Acts ii. 38, iii. 18, 19, xiii. 38). From the complexion of these discourses, the apostles must either have started from the great central idea of the Messiah, or brought their discourses round to this point. The first method may be traced whenever they preached to Jewish audiences (Acts ii. 25, 36).

Let us glance at the testimony of Peter and Paul, the two prominent persons in the book of Acts.

I. On the birthday of the Christian church, when the new economy began by a display of supernatural phenomena not less evident than was given at the founding of the Sinaitic covenant, Peter testified that prophecy was fulfilled (Acts ii. 36); and to the awakened multitude he commended not a mere teacher, nor a bare example, but the Messiah, in whom the remission of sins was to be found. Underlying the entire address, we find the ideas involved in the doctrine of the Messiah. The promise of the woman's seed, the conqueror over death, the servant of the Lord, the sin-bearing substitute,

were thoughts present to his own mind, and by allusion recalled to the minds of his hearers.

This removes a misconception into which many fall. They
who argue that the apostles, in speaking of the death of Jesus
to the Jews, merely referred to the fulfilment of prophecy without involving in the allusion any doctrine of atonement at
all, omit to notice the title of THE CHRIST used by these first
preachers as the official name. This appellation recalled the
Old Testament prophecies from the first promise downwards,
and the part which the Messiah was to act for man's salvation.
Hence, to awaken conscience, the apostles reiterated in Jewish
ears that Jesus was their Messiah; that all which was to be
effected by the Messiah—the atonement of sin and the realization of the types—was accomplished; and that forgiveness of
sins as won by His death was preached in His name. Some
hold that the apostles preached the death of Jesus as a fact,
decreed in the divine purpose and announced in ancient prophecies, merely to take away prejudices against a suffering
Messiah. But we have only to examine these discourses to
perceive how baseless is this comment. We find the primary
elements of the doctrine of the atonement, and must expound
the brief allusions in consistency first with the Lord's sayings,
and then with the rounded exhibition of the doctrine in the
epistles addressed to the churches. An analysis of any of
these discourses proves that the apostles were consistent with
themselves, and in harmony with their Lord.

a. To take Peter's sermon on the day of Pentecost by way
of illustration, we find the atonement exhibited in those aspects
which may be said to form its constituent elements: (1) SIN-
LESS PERFECTION; then (2) SIN-BEARING on the part of a God-
appointed Mediator; followed (3) by the divine ACCEPTANCE
OF HIS WORK. We may notice these in order, remembering
that in Luke's condensed report we have but the outline of
what was said.

1. The apostle refers to Jesus of Nazareth as a man ap-

proved of God, or accredited by miracles and signs and wonders which He did (ver. 22). He represents Him as the seed of David, the fruit of his loins according to the flesh (ver. 30); and then, in the quotation from the sixteenth Psalm, as the Holy One of God by eminence—THY HOLY ONE. He bore this appellation because the Father sanctified Him, and because He approved Himself as the holy servant of God. Sinless perfection comes to light in another expression found in the Messianic psalm cited by the apostle: "I have set the Lord always before me" (ver. 25); which could not be affirmed by David, nor by any mortal man: for none but the realized ideal of humanity, the perfect Servant of God, could declare that in all positions He had, without interruption, set the Lord always before Him. But it expressly depicts the obedience of the Messiah in action and in suffering—the copy and counterpart of the divine holiness; the servant of God breathing loyalty, subjection, and confidence to the utmost extent required of a creature in relation to the Creator.

2. He was delivered to punishment by the determinate counsel and foreknowledge of God (ver. 23). To understand this statement, we must recall the Lord's own saying, "The Son of man is delivered into the hands of sinners" (Matt. xxvi. 45), and also the prophetic announcements (Zech. xiii. 7; Isa. liii. 10). Peter intimates that God subjected Him to death, and that He was not properly overcome by His enemies,—that it was the will of God, His determinate counsel or plan, that Messiah should be delivered as a malefactor into the hands of men, and be put to death with the forms of justice. With all the possible modes of carrying out this great counsel before the divine mind, this peculiar plan had been selected. He might have been cut off, had God willed it, by holy hands and a holy ministry; but the Judge of all determined that it should be executed by the hands of the wicked and lawless. Or the Messiah might have been made the great moral sin-offering of the world by the immediate hand of God, without the inter-

vention of any human agency to put Him to death. But the counsel of God with infinite wisdom appointed otherwise, to the church's unspeakable advantage. Not only was the fact of Christ's death appointed, but the mode of it. The sinless Surety, taking our guilt, and placing Himself at the divine tribunal, was to be delivered in the guise of a malefactor into the hands of the wicked, and brought forth to be examined, sentenced, and condemned by a judicial tribunal, that it might be evident that He was innocent, and yet accounted guilty,— that is, that the punishment of the guilty passed over to the sinless Substitute. Had the transaction been in secret, we could not so fully have been assured of this exchange of places.

The statement here made, that God by a judicial act delivered Jesus into the hands of men, gives us a right conception of His vicarious death. That great transaction was the result of divine appointment, and had its validity on that account. On the one hand, if the ransom was to possess any value, it must be of God, and not against His will; for without divine appointment it could not have served the purpose. The judicial sentence by which He became the object of punishment, and was delivered into the hands of sinners, was carried into effect solely on the ground that He was already a sin-bearer in our stead by express covenant with the Father. He had a full exemption from penal infliction on the ground of two absolute securities—His perfect sinlessness, and His relation as the only begotten Son. He was secured in a perfect immunity from suffering of every kind; and He could be delivered over to penal visitation only with His own consent, and because He could resume His life which He condescended to resign. The delivery presupposes sin-bearing by suretyship or substitution; for how otherwise could He have been the object of punitive justice? How else could justice have touched Him? It could not by possibility have reached Him except on the ground that our sin was laid on Him as the Head and Representative of His people. But God delivered

Him over, as a judge delivers a malefactor to punishment, because their guilt was made His own.

This fact serves to obviate a double objection,—one of Jewish origin, another adduced by the modern theology. As to the Jewish objection: they to whom Peter primarily addressed the words, regarding Jesus as stricken, smitten of God, and afflicted, put their objection in this form: Had this man been sent of God, according to his own claims, He who commissioned him would have been able to deliver him from men's hands. But according to Peter's declaration, based on prophecy and on the divine counsel, all this was done by God's appointment; and the infliction was necessary for the divine glory and for man's salvation. A second objection is that of the modern theology, that Jesus endured sufferings only at the hand of man, and not at the hand of God, and that they are to be regarded as sufferings encountered in His prophetical function,—the same with those which good men always encounter in this sinful world by the uniform law of evil. They were inflicted by the hand of God, otherwise men could not have put forth their hands to touch Him. The theory we impugn represents the moral government of God as leaving all to random accident, as if the world were under no law nor control, as if everything could have happened to the Son of God which happens to sinful men. But the world is not such an unfathered and unregulated province as this theory takes for granted.

As to the mode of His death, Christ was to be tried and judged by men. The manner of His death, as well as the atoning death itself, were equally appointed in God's counsel and outlined in prophecy. Our Surety was accounted guilty, while personally sinless; and however Pilate pronounced Him without fault, and acquitted Him, there was another tribunal whose sentence was only registered at that earthly tribunal, and there, though personally innocent, He was in His capacity as Mediator by no means innocent. What He bore was in respect of man most unjust, but perfectly just in respect of

God. It is urged that He could not be the object of punitive visitation, for it would be unworthy of a sinless being to be treated as a sinner. The answer is obvious: He was not the object of divine punishment on His own account, or considered in His personal relation to His Father. But He sustained the person of sinful men, and bore their sin, as the prophets and apostles again and again repeat. The object of the Father's delight personally, He was the object of punitive justice as the representative of sinners. The question, therefore, comes to this: Was sin the proper object of punishment? Is this an innate belief or first principle in natural theology? The reason why it pleased the Lord to bruise Him was, that sin could not be discharged without punishment, on account of the insult or wrong done to the divine perfections. Thus the infliction was just in respect of God, who visited sin with its due recompense of reward. When He was arraigned at a human tribunal as a rebel and blasphemer, that was but an emblem of what we had merited at the hand of God, or of what the Surety actually endured in our stead as a satisfaction to divine justice. An invisible hand executed in an infinite measure those punishments of which we see the outward form in the arrest and bonds, the stripes and scourging, the condemnation and mockery, the shame and casting out of the camp, as well as in the expressions which fell from Him amid His desertion. What came from man, was but a feeble outline of what came from the hand of God. That outward punishment showed the chastisement and curse which God Himself was inflicting upon the Surety; for behind the visible tribunal and the visible infliction was hid something infinitely more formidable which He suffered immediately at the hand of God. There were visitations and desertions infinitely more severe than any stripes that were visible, when He was made to feel the turpitude and guilt of sin, and to realize His obligation to punishment, temporal and eternal. But it is not possible to conceive what He endured.

3. We said the apostle mentions the acceptance of Christ's work. He says of death, " It was not possible that He should be holden of it" (ver. 24) ; and when we consider why this was not possible, it is not a full answer to appeal, as is commonly done, to His omnipotence and divine life. The great reason was, that His soul had been made an offering for sin, a sweet-smelling savour, and that He must be discharged in judicial form. Death could reign only where sin was ; it could remain only where it had a certain right. A sinner whose guilt is undischarged may be held under death; but the Holy One of God could not long be held under its power. But to illustrate this loosing of the pains of death, the apostle quotes from a Messianic psalm containing an allusion to the disembodied state and resurrection of the Lord : " Thou wilt not leave my soul in hell" (that is, in Hades, the invisible world), " nor suffer Thy Holy One to see corruption" (Ps. xvi. 10). On comparing the psalm with Peter's commentary, we find the Messianic reference vindicated on a principle which can be applied to all similar passages (Acts ii. 29). We have an announcement that the human soul of the Messiah was for a time to be in a disembodied state, but that the body, the other element of His humanity, should see no corruption. The soul of Christ was to be in a state of separation from the body. There may be some difficulty in apprehending the Hebrew conception of the invisible world, and whether it was represented as a locality or a condition ; but there is no doubt that Hades was not simply equivalent to the grave : for an allusion is made to the grave in the previous verse, in the words, " My flesh also shall rest in hope" (Ps. xvi. 9). The soul was to be in the invisible world (*sheol*, ver. 10). There has been a vast variety of expositions on this passage, throwing a certain obscurity over a text in itself obvious enough. The Romanists represent the Lord's descent to hell, or its suburbs, as designed to deliver the spirits of the Old Testament saints. The Lutheran divines for a long time regarded the descent to

hell as intended to display the Redeemer's triumph over the
devils.[1] To avoid these speculations and human fancies, other
interpreters have gone to an opposite extreme, for which there
is as little warrant, representing the term *soul* as if it might
denote something else than the human soul of the Messiah.
Some take the clause as containing an allusion to His dead
body; others expound it of His person; others of His physical
life ; while the term Hades is commonly taken for the grave.
That is not to interpret words, but to insert opinions. No
justice is done to the word *soul,* unless we view it as the immortal principle of humanity, distinct from the body, and
capable of existing apart. The Messiah in the passage expresses His confidence that God would not leave His soul in
a disembodied state ; which is the consequence of carrying out
the curse inflicted on sin, and unwelcome to humanity, because
not the normal state of man. To this separation of the constituent elements of man's nature the Lord submitted as the
sin-bearing Surety of His people. And in the psalm He
virtually says : Thou wilt permit me to come forth as a conqueror from the disembodied state into which I entered,
and from the grave into which I descended, because the guilt
charged to my account has been deleted, and the necessity of
wrath removed, by my vicarious oblation.[2]

The desire here expressed for deliverance from Hades,

---

[1] To enumerate all the shades of opinion among the Lutherans on this point
would be tedious. A not uncommon view is, that our Lord went to preach to
the spirits in prison, and they plead the misunderstood text in Peter (1 Pet.
iii. 19). Aepinus, a Hamburg theologian of the sixteenth century, put the
extravagant construction on it, that Christ not only endured earthly penalties
here, but descended into the lower world, there to undergo hell-punishments
for men's sake ; a notion arguing a very material view of the Lord's substitution, and wholly uncountenanced by Scripture.

[2] See a learned note by Beza on this passage, proposing to interpret, *Thou
wilt not leave my body in the grave,* which cannot be received. Nor can we,
with Calvin and Cocceius, understand τὴν ψυχήν μου of the animal life, giving us
the meaning of *the state of death.* The word ψυχή must be taken for the *soul ;*
and the sense will be : Thou wilt not leave my soul in the disembodied state
which it was necessary for me to endure as the Surety *under the curse of the law.*
Albert Schultens conclusively argues for this sense.

coupled with the apostle's statement that God loosed the pains
of death, gives us to understand that, till the moment when
divine justice was declared to be fully satisfied, the human
soul of the Lord was in an unwelcome condition. And the
reason is obvious : though there is no ground for thinking that
there was further anguish or agony to be endured after He
said, " It is finished," and commended His spirit into His
Father's hands, yet, so long as the soul was in a disembodied
state, the two elements of man's nature, separated by death
and under the consequences of sin, continued to be shut out
from the full participation of premial life. These pains of
death were not yet annihilated. But the perfect sacrifice
satisfied justice, restored our forfeited right to the inheritance,
and loosed the cords of death.

From this explanation it appears that the human soul of
Jesus, though no more under penal suffering, nay, partaking
of rest, refreshment, and peace in paradise, was, while disembodied, in an unwelcome position, from which, as the psalm
indicates, He longed to be delivered, as the lingering consequences of sin, to this extent, still attaching to the person of
the God-man ; and therefore it was not fitting that so august
and glorious a person should long be held captive to the dominion of death, when the completed atonement restored our
right to life, and put Him, as our representative, in possession
of it. There was no path out of death but by a satisfaction to
the divine law, and the endurance of that punishment which
transgression had incurred. The right to life was first made
manifest to angels and men, when the Surety was brought from
the grave by the Judge of all the earth ; that is, justified as
the Surety (1 Tim. iii. 16). All who believe on Him, to the
end of time, perceive in this open recognition of His vicarious
work the annihilation of their guilt, the putting away of their
own sins—a fact presupposed in the transaction. The ground
on which Peter puts the resurrection of Christ is very significant : " God loosed the pains of death, *because* it was not

possible that He should be holden of it" (Acts ii. 24). When the apostle affirms that He could not possibly be holden of death, the question arises, Why? Was it simply, as some have put it, because there was an invincible power of the divine life in Him? or was it, as others put it, because the promise given to David must be fulfilled in his seed—because prophecy must be accomplished? These reasons presuppose another. The work being finished, the Judge showed that the satisfaction was complete; for the Redeemer could not abide in death, which reigns only in the sphere of unexpiated sin. Death can come only upon a sinner, or one subject to guilt. The deepest reason why the Lord could not be holden of death, was the complete expiation of sin.

It is not correct to say, as some have done, that we find no allusion here to the death of Jesus for the remission of sins, or that the doctrine of the Lord's sacrificial death, afterwards enforced as the apostle's principal idea, was not yet developed in Peter's mind.[1] To say that the expressions are indefinite and general, and that nothing is intimated in the general structure of these first discourses, or in their single expressions, from which we may infer the connection between the death of Jesus and the sinner's acceptance, is quite gratuitous. For though Peter refers to the atonement in a less direct way than in his epistles, it will be found, if we examine their structure, that the Messiahship of Jesus, with the implied fact of sin-bearing, set forth in Isaiah, was always prominent in these addresses. On the foreground we always find the crucified Messiah, and the message of forgiveness in close causal connection with it.

[1] Lechler, in his excellent work, *das apostolische Zeitalter*, 1857, p. 14, thinks that Peter in his discourses nowhere refers to the death of Christ as a saving fact. So, too, Schumann, ii. 460. Lutz and Usteri go much further, and say that there is no doctrine here as to the causal connection between Christ's death and forgiveness. Weiss, *der Petrinische Lehrbegriff*, p. 258, puts this connection in its true light, and concludes : " Damit aber ist Wenigstens indirect angedeutet, dass in dem Tode Christi die objective Ursache der Sündenvergebung liegt."

b. A similar discourse was afterwards delivered by Peter on the occasion of the miracle performed on the impotent man at the beautiful gate of the temple (Acts iii. 12). The atonement, though not very directly introduced, is there referred to in its elements. Jesus is (1) called THE HOLY ONE AND THE RIGHTEOUS (ver. 14); titles which must be understood as descriptive of the Surety of sinners, considered in His sinless holiness and perfect righteousness before God, and not as a mere declaration of His innocence from the charges on which He was condemned. To these (2) we must add another title, HIS SERVANT JESUS (vers. 13 and 26): for though the earlier Protestant interpreters were wont to translate these phrases, " His Son Jesus," " Thy hold child Jesus " (Acts iv. 27), as if they referred to His divine Sonship, recent interpreters more correctly regard it as the translation of the prophet's appellation, " The Servant of the Lord "[1] (Isa. xlii. 1, lii. 13). That this is the true rendering there is no room to doubt, because we find it applied in a much inferior sense to David and to the people of Israel (Acts iv. 25; Luke i. 54). As applied to the Lord, it meant that He was the servant of God by way of eminence, or in a unique sense, so called because He came down from heaven not to do His own will, but the will of Him that sent Him, and complied with all the duties and obligations which the Father imposed on Him as the surety of sinners. The conditions which the Father prescribed were promptly fulfilled, in all the various relations which man occupies to the moral Governor as a creature and as a sinner, to the utmost extent a sinless nature could render them, when He submitted to vicarious suffering for men's redemption. On the Father's side it was a true command, and on the part of the Righteous Servant it was a true obedience in the room of others.

---

[1] Nitzsch, Olshausen, and most recent interpreters, following them, so interpret τὸν παῖδα αὐτοῦ (ver. 13), and τὸν ἄγιον παῖδά σου (iv. 27). This will be evident to every one on comparing Matthew's rendering of Isa. xlii. 1 by ὁ παῖς μου ὃν ᾑρέτισα (Matt. xii. 18).

His whole life was spent in the service of God for sinners. He was the servant of God, not simply in the execution of His commission as a prophet, but especially in His fulfilment of the office of a surety in our room. Now all this succinctly describes the very essence of Christ's atoning work, and we cannot allow that Peter in this address says nothing on the doctrine of the atonement. When put on his defence before the council, the apostle declared that there was salvation in no other (iv. 10–12); that this is the one name, to the exclusion of every other; and that redemption stands connected with the name of Christ, considered as the Messiah, the abased, the crucified, and exalted.

c. I shall briefly refer to the mode in which the first disciples preached Christ. An examination of passages satisfies us that by this phrase we are to understand the preaching of Christ crucified, with the saving efficacy of His death. One interesting passage in confirmation of this view is the description of Philip's preaching to the eunuch, as given in the book of Acts (viii. 29). Commissioned by the Spirit to instruct the Abyssinian inquirer, he preached to him Jesus, in connection with Isaiah's description of the suffering Surety: he took for his text the passage which he found the inquirer wistfully perusing, but unable to comprehend (ver. 12),—the account of the sufferings of Messiah portrayed by the prophet (Isa. liii. 7, 8). Plainly a higher hand was guiding both, the one to peruse that prediction of the suffering Messiah, the other to base his instructions on the passage. Beginning at the same scripture, he preached to him Jesus; in other words, preached the vicarious sufferer and the atonement. We may say that the one grand topic of Christian instruction during their brief interview, when mysteriously brought together and as mysteriously separated, was the cross. Had the atonement not formed the theme of that first missionary address which led the inquirer to salvation, there was no meaning in referring to the passage of Isaiah, no link of connection between the two things.

II. The second principal person in the book of Acts is the Apostle Paul. His testimony to the atonement is so full and explicit in his various epistles, that it may seem superfluous to adduce a proof of it from his briefly reported sermons in the book of Acts. We see, however, that he held one uniform doctrine wherever he went; determined not to know anything among the Corinthians but Jesus Christ and Him crucified (1 Cor. ii. 2), repudiating with strong feelings of aversion among the Galatians the least degree of glorying save in the cross (Gal. vi. 14), and always consistent with himself in every place. We have a record in the book of Acts of two addresses of a missionary character by Paul,—one delivered in the Jewish synagogue at Antioch in Pisidia (Acts xiii. 15–41), a second delivered to the heathen philosophers of Athens (Acts xvii. 22–31),—not to mention others spoken before the Jewish authorities in his own defence. These discourses bring the hearers to the cross as the centre-point of his preaching, but by different paths. Besides these, we have an address of a different nature to the Ephesians assembled at Miletus.

a. The address to the Jews at Antioch in Pisidia was in its form and texture very similar to Peter's sermon on the day of Pentecost, for they were both addressed to Jews. The apostle describes Jesus as the seed of David and the Son of God (ver. 33), and makes an appeal to the fulfilment of prophecy to prove that Jesus the Christ died, was buried, and rose again from the dead, according to the Scriptures (vers. 30–38). He establishes the sinlessness of Jesus, when he shows that they found no cause of death in Him (ver. 28). He describes Him as raised up to Israel as a Saviour (ver. 23), and then sets forth that FORGIVENESS OF SINS WAS PREACHED IN HIS NAME (ver. 38). This language deserves attention, as it intimates that forgiveness was preached, not sold nor bartered; in other words, that pardon was proclaimed without conditions or terms, simply on the ground of the humiliation to which Jesus submitted on earth. He next announces that on the same foundation who-

ever believes is justified from all things from which he could
not have been absolved by the law of Moses. We may say
that the apostle there preaches the righteousness of faith, not
the righteousness of the law, in the same way as in his various
epistles. He affirms, in the same manner as in his Epistle to
the Romans, that what the law could not do, because it was
weak through the flesh, was attained through faith in Christ
(Rom. viii. 3).

b. In the other missionary discourse delivered to the Gentile
philosophers of Athens, the apostle proceeded in a different
way (Acts xviii. 22). He in the first instance went back to
the principles of natural religion, because in every discussion
the first requirement is to have some common ground; and
the principles of natural theology were the only data, the
only platform, where they could find common ground. He
first preaches God as Creator, Upholder, Disposer, and Judge,
though He was unknown as yet to them—the unknown God.
He next advanced to the resurrection of Jesus, in connection
with the announcement of the judgment; the fact of a judgment being stated as appointed for a given day, and to be
carried out by Jesus Christ (Acts xvii. 31). This brought
the apostle to the cross, or would have brought him, had
the mockery with which he was assailed not interrupted the
continuity of the discourse.

c. Besides these discourses of Paul, which from the occasion and the hearers were of a missionary character, there
is a memorable pastoral address to the elders of Ephesus
assembled at Miletus. Among other topics, the apostle adverts to the death of Christ as the great ransom-price by
which He purchased the church, and the foundation of all
His right of property in the church. Speaking to elders
long established in the faith, he urges them to diligence by
the consideration that the church was dear to them as the
purchased property of Christ—as bought at an infinite cost.
He speaks of the church as purchased by the Lord with

His own blood, and won by Him to be His property, thus:
"Take heed therefore unto yourselves, and to all the flock
over which the Holy Ghost has made you overseers, *to feed
the church of God, which He has purchased with His own
blood*" (Acts xx. 28). Here several points connected with
the atonement call for exposition. Though there is a variety
of reading,[1] the whole clause shows that special emphasis is
laid on the dignity of the person, and on the preciousness of
the ransom, by which the church was bought.

1. The church is described as blood-bought property. That
price is said to have made the church God's church, or Christ's
church, in consequence of which the people of God stand in
the closest and most tender relation to the Lord. They are
His by right of purchase, analogous to what in ancient times
was customary when slavery prevailed. The church is called
God's, or the Lord's, whether we look at the several members
or at the collective body, not simply because He rules it—for
in that sense the entire creation might be so called—but by
reason of purchase, and of the close relation in which He
stands to it. This comes out in numerous passages, which
explicitly declare that the redeemed are the Lord's, and not
their own, by right of purchase (1 Cor. vi. 20; Tit. ii. 14;
Rev. v. 9; Rom. xiv. 8, 9). By that thought the apostle
stimulated the elders of Ephesus to fidelity, vigilance, and
care in feeding the members of the church. They had been
purchased with blood; and since God had bought them with
the most astonishing price, that consideration was to animate

---

[1] The reading τὴν ἐκκλησίαν τοῦ Κυρίου is supported by A, C[1], D, E, and preferred by Griesb., Lach., Tisch. The common reading is supported by B, א,
and favourably regarded by Scholtz and Alford. A third variety, or combination of the two former, is, Κυρίου καὶ Θεοῦ, found in C[3], G, H. See a discussion
by Doedes (Teyler's *Godgeleerd Genootsch.* Deel. xxxiv. p. 434); also, Meteler-
Kamp's *Dissertatio Theologica de Pauli Oratione Valedictoria, l.c.* It seems
almost impossible to decide, if the decision is to turn solely on external grounds.
Hence Paul's phraseology elsewhere, THE CHURCH OF GOD, is thought by some to
incline the balance in favour of the *receptus* (see 1 Cor. i. 2, x. 32, xi. 16 and
22, xv. 9; 2 Cor. i. 1; Gal. i. 13; 1 Thess. ii. 14; 2 Thess. i. 4; 1 Tim. iii. 5
and 15).

the elders and overseers of the church to take the most tender interest in every member, and to evince the most vigilant care.

2. The price or ransom was *His own blood*. Whichever noun is the antecedent to which the pronoun refers, the allusion is plainly to the personal dignity of Him by whom the price was paid. Text critics are more favourably inclined than they have been for a century to the common reading, "The church of God, which He has purchased with His own blood," which, of course, would give an express and formal testimony to the value of the atonement, considered in the light of Christ's deity. But the other reading, if due weight is given to the words, proves the influence of the person upon the work of expiation ; and we are plainly taught that we cannot make Christ mediator in one nature to the exclusion of the other, nor ignore the action and influence of the divine nature in His work of atonement. We see that Christ, in His redeeming work, was not regarded as mere man, but as God-man; for the blood here mentioned is called *God's own*, or *the Lord's own*, showing that the humanity to which the blood belonged was personally united to Deity—not mere humanity, but God assuming humanity ; that is, a God-man paid the necessary price, and bought us to be His. So great a work could have been accomplished only in the flesh of Him in whom dwells all the fulness of the Godhead bodily ; and He so possessed humanity, that He could give it for others. In every mediatorial act, accordingly, we trace the concurrent action of two natures in one person ; and hence it is the act of the God-man. This is easily perceived in the phrase, *His own blood*.

3. Next let us consider who owns the church. Only a divine person can be her proprietor or possessor. This may be said to incline the balance still further in favour of the reading, "the church of God." Whoever redeems another from eternal death, naturally becomes the owner or pro-prietor of the party so redeemed. But none can properly

be possessor of another, his owner or his lord, but one who superadds to the payment of a price the further dignity of a nature essentially divine. Redemption, indeed, is a divine act as much as is creation. He who claims us as His property must necessarily be divine.

Thus we find the apostles, in the book of Acts, constantly referring in the first instance to the Lord's humiliation as the SERVANT of the Father in the execution of a commission given Him to do. We find, too, in connection with this —we may say, in causal connection with this—the proclamation of a present forgiveness of sins, without qualification or preparation in any form. The evasion to which some have recourse, that in all this the apostles meant to obviate the Jewish objection to a suffering Messiah, is often repeated, but without warrant. The atonement was not omitted in these missionary discourses, as is evident from the references to prophecy, and the identification of Jesus with the Messiah, which at once recalled the element of sin-bearing (Isa. liii. 5). This must be conceded, unless we proceed, on the principle of evacuation, to reduce the meaning of terms to a minimum,—a mode of interpretation wholly to be repudiated. Neither the death of Christ nor the resurrection were preached as bare historic facts, but in their meaning and significance. We cannot reduce the uniform testimony of the apostles to the announcement of mere historic facts, apart from the reason of Messiah's sufferings and death, or dissociate the significance attaching to the connection of the two.

We are warranted to conclude, when we take to our aid the unambiguous statements of the apostles, that they made the death of Christ, considered as an atonement and an eternally valid fact, the centre-point of their preaching. How far the atonement was expounded in those addresses, in its *rationale*, constituent elements, and effects, it may be difficult to say; for their communications were proportioned to the hearers' capacity. Many recondite truths connected with the atone-

ment, such as the priesthood of Christ, on which the Epistle
to the Hebrews dilates, the bearing of the atonement on the
divine moral government, the various results in regard to
man's relation to his Maker, the number and extent of the
blessings flowing from it, and the like, were doubtless to some
extent reserved, till a people were gathered to whom these
truths could be intelligible. But the remission of sins, and
the free acceptance of sinners through the death of Christ,
were unquestionably preached in the very first addresses which
the apostles delivered (Acts xiii. 38).

SEC. VI.—THE APOSTOLIC EPISTLES.

Next to the sayings of Jesus, the most important source
of information as to the atonement are the apostolic epistles
addressed to the churches. The apostles kept this truth
before the mind of their readers, as they did before the mind
of their hearers. As these epistles were not addressed to
mankind indiscriminately, but to companies of redeemed men
gathered together in several places, and are to be read as
primarily addressed to believers, the numerous explanations
they contain as to the Lord's atoning death, suffice to prove
that there is not a spiritual blessing which does not stand in
immediate or mediate connection with it, not a duty which
is not enforced by it as a motive. How wide the influence
of this great article is on doctrine and practice, at once appears
from the place which it occupies in the epistles. The entire
range of Scripture truth takes a tincture from it, and its influence is felt even where it may not be expressly named.

A study of those apostolic documents to which we now
come, will satisfy every reader that the atonement was, in the
apostolic scheme of doctrine, viewed as an accomplished fact,
eternally valid before God, and requiring no supplementary
addition. They describe it as finished once for all, without

the need of repetition. They refer to the fact, that by this truth the gospel is distinguished and exalted above all human wisdom. With the apostles this is the great fact in the world's history, the chief topic, the central truth from which they start, and to which they return. All the Pauline epistles, with the single exception of the simple Epistle to Philemon— a letter to a private individual—make express mention of the atonement as the most momentous fact that ever occurred in human history, and fraught with the most blessed results. A few remarks will show this.

To prove that the epistles represent the atonement as the great fact of revelation, we have only to recall the circumstance that it is called another gospel, if man's acceptance is made to hinge on anything besides the cross (Gal. i. 7). The apostles preached reconciliation as effected by the cross alone, though their message was in perpetual collision with Jewish legalism and Gentile philosophy (1 Cor. i. 23). That the doctrine of the cross belongs to those articles which are to be comprehended in the perpetual teaching of the church, is evident from the fact that the apostle urged the Corinthians to keep what had been delivered to them on the atonement as the principal topic of Christianity (1 Cor. xv. 1–4). The epistles show what constitutes the perpetual doctrine of the church; and the place which the atonement occupies in them is abundant evidence that it must ever be kept in the view of the redeemed, if the scope of many exhortations is not to be perverted, and the significance of many motives is not to be misapprehended.

The atonement is interwoven into the texture of the epistles to a remarkable degree; but we do not find it equally in all. It must never be forgotten that they are not treatises, but letters written for a definite purpose, and that they do not cease to bear the character and impress of that style of composition. They are not exhaustive discussions: only five of the apostles have left behind them epistolary documents destined for the edification of the church, some more full of matter, others more brief, but all in some important respects bearing upon doctrine and practice, according to the special service for which they were destined. The reason of the prominence given at one time to one truth, and at another time to another, can be explained upon the principle that all truth does not equally require to be taught at all times. The different epistles have their particular scope, and hence we find a certain variety; but all concur to one end. We could not expect every article in every epistle.

To allege, as has been done, from the silence of one or two of the smaller epistles, that their writers must have entertained a different doctrine, or a system of truth exclusive of the vicarious sacrifice of Christ, is a mode of arguing which mistakes their nature. On this principle, it might as well be alleged that the writer of more epistles than one must have changed his views, if he is not equally explicit on every point in every epistle. When the death of Christ has a prominent place in almost every epistle, and is seen from every point of the Christian system and inner life, these facts may prove how fundamental the atonement is.

An appeal has been made to the fact that there is a silence on the point in JAMES and JUDE. It used to be stoutly maintained by the class of writers opposed to the vicarious sacrifice, that such a view perverted the doctrine of Scripture, by expounding metaphorical and figurative language in a literal way, and that the atonement was not to be found in the Bible. But an impartial examination of Scripture doctrine silenced that objection. Next it was argued that two apostles are silent on it. The answer is obvious. As to the Epistle of Jude, which has been adduced as containing no allusion to the atonement, it is not correct so to represent it. Though in his brief epistle Jude does not mention in express terms the blood, sufferings, or death of Christ, he mentions the mercy of our Lord Jesus Christ unto eternal life (ver. 21),—language by which we understand all that the other apostles have directly taught in reference to His sacrifice. Besides, he appeals to the words spoken before by the apostles of our Lord Jesus Christ (ver. 17). As to the Epistle of James, its scope and teaching are of such a kind, that we cannot reasonably expect him to dilate upon fundamental doctrine. It is expressly ethical in its whole cast and structure. And it were as much aside from a due conception of its scope to look for a discussion of Christian doctrine, as it would be to require of a Christian divine, in the midst of a moral theme, to turn aside to settle doctrinal questions. The epistle has a special aim, from which the writer does not turn aside to expatiate on doctrinal topics.

Our task, in conducting a strict investigation into the teaching of the various epistles on the doctrine of the atonement, is to bring out the apostolic view of the doctrine; and our object is to appeal, on sound principles of interpretation, to the true meaning of the apostles' words. There is the greater need for this, when we observe that many, under the influence of what is styled modern thought, or growing thought, express decided dislike to juridical ideas, and will have no other redemption than a moral redemption, and no other view of God than that of absolute love.

After the full classification of the sayings of Jesus in the previous volume, it seems to be superfluous to give a further construction of the doctrine as an organic whole, or a full dogmatic synopsis of the apostolic outline, because this would be but a repetition of the same divisions, or at most a distribution of different texts under the same heads. We deem it enough to refer to that classification. A distribution of the apostles' sayings in the briefest possible outline might be given, however, under THREE divisions as follows: The first would contain the POSTULATES of the doctrine; the second would exhibit its NATURE and constituent elements; the third would delineate its EFFECTS.

1. Under the POSTULATES would be comprehended the

necessity of the atonement (Heb. ii. 10); the harmony of justice and love, or the concurrence of wrath against sin, and love to the sinning creature (1 John iv. 10); the influence of Christ's supreme deity in His work (Rom. viii. 3); the appointment of a mediator, surety, or high priest by a divine call (Heb. v. 5),—thus providing for the possibility of substitution.

2. Under the NATURE or constituent elements, would be classified Christ's sinlessness and sin-bearing, according to the twofold obligation lying on us (1 Pet. iii. 18; 2 Cor. v. 21); in other words, the active and passive obedience of the Lord, in His undeviating performance of the divine will (Heb. x. 9, 10),—thus effecting the ONE sacrifice for sin (Heb. x. 12).

3. Under the EFFECTS would be classified a great number of distinctly expressed[1] benefits, referring first to our relative position of acceptance or reception into favour, where we may enumerate, *a.* redemption, *b.* forgiveness, *c.* reconciliation, *d.* justification, directly flowing from the atonement: next, the privilege of approach in worship to a holy God in the capacity of a royal priesthood, where we may enumerate the sprinkling or purifying, washing, cleansing, or sanctifying of a holy people relatively: then the renovation of the nature, or the communication of spiritual life subjectively: then the new relation to the persons of the Godhead—to Christ, as His blood-bought property (1 Cor. vi. 20); to the Holy Ghost, as His temple (1 Cor. vi. 19); to the Father, as His people and children: then the new relationship to angelic beings, and to men of all nations: then the victory over Satan, the world, and death: then the liberation from an economy of ceremonies (Col. ii. 14):

---

[1] It is noteworthy that these EFFECTS of the atonement are very often mentioned by the apostles in a *telic* clause introduced by ἵνα, or more rarely ὅπως, and give us a glimpse into Christ's design or aim, or His Father's. They are apostolic delineations of Christ's intention, or the scope of His work.

then the elevating motives derived from the cross, with various other points relating to the efficacy of the sacrifice, and the danger of neglecting it.

But having made as complete a classification as we could of the Lord's sayings, it is superfluous to do it a second time.

CHAPTER II.

THE TESTIMONY TO THE ATONEMENT IN THE PAULINE EPISTLES.

SEC. VII.—THE EPISTLES OF PAUL ON THE RIGHTEOUSNESS OF GOD.

A S Peter is called the apostle of hope, and John of love, Paul may be called the apostle of faith, or more strictly, of the righteousness of faith. As a testimony to the atonement, the epistles of Paul will be found particularly full and copious; for there is not a phase of the doctrine which he does not develope and apply. If he did not, like the other apostles, enjoy the personal teaching of Jesus in the days of His flesh, he was by no means without direct communications from his Lord; for he was taught by the revelation of Jesus Christ (Gal. i. 12), and even caught up into paradise to hear unspeakable words (2 Cor. xii. 4). Apart from this, he was led by the Spirit into the import of the law and the prophets, and there found the truth which his nature needed, and which was all verified in the Lord's atoning death. He reproduces the doctrine in many new lights, from the objective truth opened up to him in the Old Testament, and from his own deep experimental acquaintance with Christ as the end of the law.

As to the order of conducting the inquiry, we purpose to take the epistles in the order in which they stand in the common editions of the Bible. The advantage obtained by following the chronological order in which the epistles are supposed to have been written—for there is by no means a

complete uniformity of opinion on their exact order—will not
compensate for the inconvenience of departing from the well-
known arrangement. And we abide by it the rather because
we can discover no trace of any development of Paul's views
from one stage to another: he was like himself from the
moment when he died to the law by the reception of Christ
(Rom. vii. 4, 9). Not that his epistles are all alike; but they
take their colour from the circumstances and prevalent sentiments in the various churches.

While the apostle makes use of all the terms employed by
the other writers, such as redemption, propitiation, peace, and
the like, descriptive of Christ's sacrificial death, there is one
peculiar to him, THE RIGHTEOUSNESS OF GOD, which very frequently occurs. Though announced in the prophets, and indirectly alluded to by Peter and John in their use of the
designation "the Righteous One," it is specially found in
Paul, who uses this abstract expression to describe the atonement in relation to divine law.

I purpose in this section to consider somewhat fully the
righteousness of God, and to group together the Pauline doctrine on the subject. Amid the manifold negations of the
times, it cannot be without its use to give a new grounding to
this important expression. That a great change has entered in
the mode of viewing the righteousness of God, compared with
the general recognition which it received in all the Protestant
churches, cannot be doubtful to any one who has watched the
changes of opinion on the subject of the atonement. This was
long the descriptive name for the material cause of a sinner's
acceptance with God. The task we impose on ourselves is
to ascertain the import of the phrase, "the righteousness of
God," and to define the place which it occupies in the Pauline
epistles; and we aim at an objective statement, embodying the
results of exegetical inquiry, more than a formal discussion of
the opinions which have appeared on the ecclesiastical field,
though we cannot omit all notice of recent views fundamentally

opposed to the proper meaning of the terms. We wish to go direct to the apostles, except where it is indispensably necessary to refer to recent obscuring theories. The task of reproducing apostolic doctrine in its true significance and organic connections, is becoming an urgent duty; and the part assigned to exegetical theology is to recall, as far as may be, not only single phrases, but the general outline of those truths by which the apostles, as the chosen organs of Christ's revelation, exhibited in the church the riches of divine grace as seen in the incarnate Word, and unfolded to them after His ascension.

An occasion for a full inquiry into the righteousness of God will be found also in the fact that a large class of minds betray a hesitancy which contrasts painfully with the liberty and boldness which marked the days of the apostles. This attaches to not a few who are truly occupied with the personal Redeemer and the contemplation of the divine Life, but stop short of defining the mode in which THE RIGHTEOUSNESS OF GOD stands related to LIFE in the Pauline scheme of doctrine. They evince little interest indeed as to the relation of these points to each other, seeking the fellowship of life with Christ without distinct ideas as to the indispensable conditions of this communion. Under the influence of what can only be called a mystic element, limiting the regard to Christ IN US, and failing to give prominence to Christ FOR US, they never breathe freely the liberty of the gospel. They have fallen under a scheme of doctrine which makes no distinction between the person and the nature, the standing of the man and the renovation of the heart, the objective and the subjective; and though correctly regarding the person of Christ as the centre-point of Christianity and the fountain of life, they do not know how Life stands related to Righteousness—a thought pervading the whole Pauline doctrine.

Our first inquiry must be to ascertain the precise import of the righteousness of God in the Pauline epistles, and the place it holds in them. A comparison of these epistles with one another shows that there are two divisions or classes, with their own marked peculiarity, according as the apostle has occasion to counteract a Jewish Legalism, or a tendency to an incipient Gnosticism, invading the Christian churches while he yet lived. To the pharisaic cast of thought, with its attachment to the works of the law, and the enforcement of legal ceremonies as necessary, allusion is made in the Epistles to the Galatians, Romans, and Philippians ; and there the righteousness of God is the central thought. To the oriental theosophy, with its claim to a higher wisdom, which put notions in the place of the personal Redeemer, allusion is made in the Epistles to the Ephesians and Colossians (Col. ii. 8). There the personal Christ, and the life found in Him, are the central thoughts. But even there LIFE is viewed as subsequent to, and dependent on, the atonement. To the former class of the Pauline epistles we direct our attention in this section. And our purpose is to notice the place which THE RIGHTEOUSNESS OF GOD holds in them ; for this phrase, as we shall find, is descriptive of the finished work of Christ, as approved at the divine tribunal, and the meritorious cause of our acceptance.

Throughout the doctrinal part of the Epistle to the Romans, the righteousness of God, as a descriptive name for the atonement, is the grand theme. The Epistle to the Galatians, again, is nothing else than an enforcement of the great truth, that to the close of the Christian's career, the righteousness of faith is the one plea valid before God ; and no second recommendation or condition, in the form of works, is of any avail (Gal. ii. 21, iii. 21, vi. 5). In the Epistles to the Corinthians we find the same theme in the same antithesis, with this difference only, that other points required attention in this church (1 Cor. i. 30 ; 2 Cor. iii. 9). But when the apostle contrasts the two economies, the law is called the ministry of condemnation, and the gospel the ministry of righteousness. In the Epistle to the Philippians we find Paul, when very near the close of his career, still counting all things but loss for this righteousness, and far from having outlived this thought, which coloured his ideas in prospect of approaching martyrdom (Phil. iii. 9). We find allusion to the righteousness of God also in the pastoral epistles (Tit. iii. 5–7).

Having seen how prevalent is the reference to the righteousness of God in the Pauline epistles, we have next to consider in what it consists. And here it will be necessary to obviate some misconceptions.

1. The phrase cannot be held to refer to the divine attribute of righteousness. Divine justice, reflected in the law, is indeed the rule or standard on which, in a definite sense, the righteousness of God is measured; but this righteousness is not the divine attribute itself. The expression is uniformly introduced in Scripture as descriptive of what is due from man, or as the ethical response on man's side to a divine claim. It is a name for that which Adam should have rendered, and not a divine perfection. Some faint colour seems to be lent to the idea that it may be the divine attribute by the apparent connection—though it is but apparent—between the two statements in two successive verses: "The righteousness of God is revealed in the gospel;" and, "The wrath of God is revealed from heaven against all ungodliness" (Rom. i. 17, 18). But the two statements, though placed in close juxtaposition, and apparently connected by a causal particle (γάρ), belong to two wholly different economies, and have nothing in common. The tacit thought is : All alike need the provision of the gospel, and must repair to it; FOR they have nothing to expect but a revelation of wrath on their own account. The mode of expounding this phrase by allusion to the divine attribute was in reality overcome at the Reformation. Luther tells us that, having long had a desire to understand the Epistle to the Romans, he was always stopped by the expression "the righteousness of God," which he understood as the divine attribute; but after long meditations, and spending days and nights in these thoughts, the nature of that righteousness which justifies

THE RIGHTEOUSNESS OF GOD.

us was discovered to him; upon which he felt himself born anew, and the whole Scriptures become quite a different thing. It is evident, indeed, that there can be no allusion to the divine attribute of justice, because this would furnish the idea of an incensed God, which is the purport of the law; whereas the provision is one of grace, displaying a reconciling and justifying God, which is the essence of the gospel. Besides, such an acceptation as that which we oppose would not adapt itself to the general phraseology of Scripture. Thus, in the memorable passage which represents Christ as made sin that we might be made the righteousness of God, it is evident that in no sense of the terms, and with no propriety of language, could it be said of the Christian that he is made the attribute of righteousness (2 Cor. v. 21). The fact, too, that it is commonly put in antithesis to our own righteousness (Phil. iii. 9), determines the significance of the expression to be something different from the divine attribute. The only part which the divine justice acts in this matter is, that it furnishes the rule or standard by which it is tried. When this righteousness is called a gift (Rom. v. 17), and said to be of God, or divinely provided, in contrast with that which is of the law and our own (Phil. iii. 9), the idea is, that for those who have no righteousness of their own this is the gracious provision of God.

Attempts have been made, however, to explain the phrase in a mystic way, by referring it to Christ's essential righteousness as a divine person. This notion, propounded by Osiander, and restored by some men of mystic tendencies, separates the one indivisible work of Christ into two parts, allowing pardon to be procured by Christ's atoning blood, but maintaining that righteousness is the communication of Christ's essential attribute. That argues a complete misconception of Christ's mediatorial work, which was meant to bring in what was due from man as a creature, and has everything in common with what the first man should have produced. The essential righteousness belongs to God as God, and to the Son of God as a divine

person. But the righteousness of which the apostle speaks is
that which was required from man as man, and which a Mediator, as our substitute, brought in to meet our wants; and
though this could be brought in only by a God-man, uniting
the two natures in one person, the whole is properly a created,
not an uncreated, a human, not a divine righteousness. The
supreme Lawgiver did not demand the essential righteousness
of God, but what was proper to a creature made in the likeness
and image of God.   And it consists in action, not in the mere
possession of a perfect nature.   Adam had the pure nature, but
failed in rendering the righteousness.   But neither is it mere
outward action or outward deed, but a perfect nature acting
itself out, or approving itself to the Lawgiver by a compliance
with the law in the sphere of tried obedience.[1]

We have only to examine the language of Scripture to see
that the righteousness of God of which Paul so often speaks is
not His essential righteousness: for God does not demand from
man His own essential righteousness, but that which is competent to a creature; and the righteousness of created beings
corresponds to the thought of God and the will of God, from
whom they derive their origin.   The creature's destiny is to
bear the impress of the divine perfections in its sphere.   Such
would have been Adam's righteousness had it been verified
(v. 12); that which the creature owes to the Creator, not that
which the Creator Himself possesses.   This will appear from
the general phraseology of Scripture (Rom. x. 3).

2. Another opinion, much more common than the former,
is that the righteousness of God denotes an inward righteousness, on the ground of which, whether it is already perfect or
not, God pronounces men righteous by a judicial sentence.
This is the interpretation given by Neander, Olshausen, and
others; and it is still accepted by not a few believing men in
various churches, though not to the same extent as formerly.

---

[1] See Thomasius' able discussion on the views of Osiander in his two Uni-
versity Lectures, *de obedientia Christi activa*, Erlangen 1846.

Lipsius,[1] in his treatise on the Pauline view of justification, contends that the word never refers merely to an objective relation, but always to an inward condition as well, sometimes delineated in its principle, and sometimes in its future perfection.   We must do these writers the justice to state, that by this they do not mean a justification by works.   While they interpret it as the inner righteousness which God works, and represent it as so pleasing to God, that on account of it He pronounces men righteous, though not yet completely perfect, they avoid the abyss of legalism, and lay stress on the faith which unites us to the person of Christ as the Life.   This view has everything in common with the doctrine of Augustine and the Jansenists on the same subject; drawing a distinction between a man's own righteousness (Phil. iii. 9), as undertaken in the exercise of his unaided powers, and that which is " of God," interpreted as meaning produced by divine grace.   This, they think, is the import of the expression "the righteousness of God."

But the antithesis between our own righteousness and that which is called the righteousness of God is different.   It is between that which is subjective (our own) and that which is objective (God's).   The opinion we are controverting, though different from legalism, and speaking of salvation by faith, is at variance with the Pauline doctrine, as will appear by two considerations.   (1.) The objective relation expressed by the term stands out in bold relief when we consider the peculiar antithesis between Christ made sin for us, and believers made the righteousness of God in Him (2 Cor. v. 21).   These words intimate that, in the same sense in which Christ was made sin—that is, objectively and by imputation—in that sense are His people made the righteousness of God.   Nor is the sense different in another passage, where the apostle contrasts the going about to establish a personal righteousness, and submitting to the righteousness of God (Rom. x. 3); or when he

[1] *Die Paulinische Rechtfertigungslehre*, von Dr. Lipsius, Leipzig 1853.

declares that he wishes to be found in Christ, not having his own righteousness, but the righteousness which is of God (Phil. iii. 9). It cannot be alleged that the antithesis in the latter passage is between works of nature and works of grace, works of law and works of faith. (2.) It obliterates the distinction between the person and the nature and the standing in the first or second Adam, with which the whole Scripture is replete. It confounds righteousness and life, which are ever carefully distinguished, the one being the way to the other. This is conclusive against the interpretation, if we would abide by the apostle's use of language, and not efface his express distinctions.

3. Another opinion is, that faith itself is counted as the Righteousness. There are various modifications of this opinion; but none of them supposes an objective righteousness of God that has been wrought out, and then revealed in the gospel; and in almost every case it throws the mind back on itself in a neonomian tendency.

a. To begin with that phase of it which is simply Arminian, or that has everything in common with Arminianism, the act of faith is made this righteousness. The answer is obvious: Faith, in that case, is transformed into a new law, whereas we are accepted without works of law. Besides, this theory assumes that God accepts an imperfect title for a perfect, by accommodating His right to man's inability; an interpretation which, if carried out to the full, is derogatory to the divine law, and fitted to explode the whole redemption-work of Christ. If the divine law can be relaxed by God's receding from His rights, why may He not recede to a yet larger degree, and wholly supersede the necessity of the incarnation and atonement ? The inflexible strictness and immutable claims of the divine law are taken for granted by the atonement. This view was advocated by Tittmann,[1] who

---

[1] See his treatise, *de obedientia Christi ex apostoli Pauli sententia*, appended to his Synonyms (p. 311). Nitzsch, in his *protestantische Beantwortung der*

remarks that Scripture does not teach that the righteousness of Christ is imputed to men, but that faith is counted for righteousness. Though this has some colour from the expression, "Faith is counted for righteousness," it loses this when the phrase is properly rendered. It should be rendered, "Faith is counted unto righteousness," expressing the result, and lends no countenance to the notion that a substitute is accepted for a perfect righteousness. The righteousness of God is made ours through faith as the means of reception (Rom. iii. 22). But, on the other theory, how can the sentence of the Judge have a sufficient ground? A method of acceptance, without a real righteousness which can be measured on the divine claims, neither meets the requirements of God's justice nor satisfies an awakened conscience.

b. A modification of the same view, decidedly in a neonomian tendency, though of a subtle nature, is proposed by an ingenious opponent of the vicarious sacrifice. It is alleged that Christianity makes known the absolute forgiveness of sin without atonement as its procuring cause, and that the belief of this offer is considered as righteousness. Faith is thus supposed to be God-pleasing conduct, and accepted as righteousness. When a man renders this obedience, his conduct is pleasing in God's sight, and reckoned for righteousness.[1] Apart from other considerations, this theory supposes not a real, but a merely putative righteousness; and thus the foundation of acceptance is completely undermined.

4. Another opinion prevalent, is to the effect that the righteousness of God denotes the state of being justified. Not to mention names in the last age, this view was held by Stuart of Andover, and Wieseler[2] on Galatians. The latter makes it

---

Symbolik Dr. Möhler, p. 139, adopts the same conclusion, and commends Tittmann's Essay.

[1] See Hofmann's *Schriftbeweis*, i. p. 649. This perverts the idea of faith. Instead of making faith simply receptive, he makes it conduct, or *verhalten*, getting a reward!

[2] *Commentar über den Brief an die Galater*, von Dr. Karl Wieseler, 1859. He

the state into which the justified are brought, or the condition of possessing justification. This view, though certainly nearer the truth than the others already mentioned, is faulty: first, because it is not the precise interpretation of the term righteousness; and next, because it transposes the order of biblical doctrines. Righteousness is represented in the Pauline scheme of doctrine as the basis, or material cause, of the sentence of justification, not conversely. So far, indeed, is this view correct, that it makes allusion to our relation Godward, not to moral conduct; but it fails to bring out the substantive character of the righteousness, as consisting in tried obedience. The term righteousness, as we shall see, does not in any passage mean the state of justification. If the state of justification does not proceed on an underlying righteousness as its basis, we are lost in the mists of uncertainty. The divine rectitude insists, and cannot but insist, on a true fulfilment of the divine law, and acquits on no other ground than on the presentation of an actual obedience. But, on this theory, what is assumed as the material cause of justification? No one can be justified, in the government of a righteous God, by a connivance at defects, or by being accounted what he is not by a mere make-believe. Scripture everywhere shows that God demands a real, substantive righteousness.

These are all baseless theories, and lead to the notion of an acceptilation, that is, to the reputing of one to be what he is not. A complete righteousness, objectively brought in, on these theories, exists no longer. If so, faith wants its security, and rests on no corresponding reality. We must now ascertain the precise meaning of the phrase against these modern comments, which to a large extent declare that faith is taken for the righteousness, without any underlying reality. They

_____

says, p. 177: "The act by which God δικαιοῖ the sinner Paul calls δικαίωσις (Rom. iv. 25, v. 18), and the state of possessing this δικαίωσις of God he calls δικαιοσύνη Θεοῦ, which therefore, like the δικαιοῦσθαι, comes from faith (Rom. i. 17)," etc. This is a complete confusion of ideas.

may be in keeping with modern notions as to Christ's atonement; but our aim is to investigate the biblical import of
the expression. Having canvassed the subject negatively, it
remains that we investigate it positively from the apostle's
words.

1. An analysis of the apostle's language suffices to show
that this righteousness is an actually accomplished fact; not
less a historical reality than sin, and as productive of results,
but in an opposite direction. These two terms throw light on
each other. That this righteousness is the finished work of
Christ, considered from the view-point of the divine approval,
may be proved from the fact that it is presented to us as the
great subject-matter of the gospel. It is said to be revealed
(Rom. i. 17), and the righteousness must exist if it is revealed.
The same thing may be argued from the title given to the
gospel as the ministry of righteousness (2 Cor. iii. 19) : for
how could an economy be instituted to proclaim what did not
exist ? When it is called the gift of righteousness (Rom. v. 17),
and described as a provision unto all and upon all them that
believe (Rom. iii. 22), we must conclude that it exists.

That the righteousness of God is an actual reality, is proved
by the twofold parallel which the apostle draws between sin
and righteousness, and between the death which is the result
of the one, and the life which is the equally certain result of
the other (Rom. i. 18–iii. 18, and Rom. v. 12–18). If we consider these counterparts, we shall find that the apostle places
sin and righteousness in marked antithesis. In entering on
the description of the prevalence of sin, he not only displays
the wants of mankind, but exhibits the two great counterparts
of sin and righteousness as equal realities,—the one as the
world's ruin, the other as its restoration. The one is a completed fact as well as the other. They are the only two great
events or facts in the world's history, and they confront each
other.

At this point we may consider the peculiar shade of mean-

ing which the phrase acquires when put in connection with
God.   Why is it designated GOD'S righteousness, or the
righteousness of God?   Modern interpreters generally understand that it is so called because God was its author, as Christ
is also called the Lamb of God because God was the provider
of the Lamb.   We regard it as only a briefer expression of what
is more fully described as the righteousness which is of God
(Phil. iii. 9).   The fact that the phrase is contrasted with our
own righteousness leads us to conclude that it means the
righteousness of which God is the author.   The interpretation
long given by the Lutheran divines, that it denotes a righteousness valid before God, is more a paraphrase[1] than a translation,
though a legitimate inference: for the righteousness will be
valid at God's tribunal, if He was its author.   But that is
rather a secondary idea involved in the other.

2. The manifestation of this righteousness as a historic
fact is next noticed: "Now the righteousness of God without
the law is manifested" (Rom. iii. 21).   This refers to its manifestation as a historic fact in the incarnation and finished work
of Christ.   The allusion is not so much to its revelation in the
gospel, as to the bringing in of the righteousness once for all
by Christ's manifestation in the flesh.   The language used by
the apostle shows that it is coincident with the person of
Christ, and found in Him.   It is one of those terms—and they
are various—descriptive of the obedience of Christ in the mani-
foldness of its aspects and effects.   The personal Redeemer
crucified is Himself the manifestation of the righteousness of
God; and though it was completed with His finished work
when He expired, and is not capable of addition, it is not to

---

[1] Luther's rendering of δικαιοσύνη Θεοῦ is, *Gerechtigkeit die vor Gott gilt*, or in
the Latin form, *justitia quæ valet apud Deum;* and Calvin goes in the same
direction, though admitting the force of the rendering, *justitia quæ a Deo nobis
donatur.*   Recent expositors pretty unanimously concur in viewing the phrase
as an instance of the *genitivus auctoris*, and regard this as the strict grammatical construction.   Fritzsche, in his exact philological commentary, tries to
vindicate Luther's rendering, but without success.   The appeal to Jas. i. 20 is
not in point.

be denied that His living through death was necessary to the perpetuity of this righteousness of God. It was valid at death, but it is found in the person of the Lord (1 John ii. 2). It is no transitory, past, or putative righteousness, but one actually in the world, and the only great reality in it; a righteousness for man, because the Lord Jesus, as very man, brought it into Humanity. And when the Judge beholds His Son clothed with our humanity, and presenting the righteousness of God, then follows the re-adjustment of man's relation to his Maker, the reunion of God and man.

But the apostle is careful to notice that this righteousness was witnessed by the law and the prophets (Rom. iii. 21). First, as to the law, the sacrifices had special reference to it; and whether we look at the temple or at its services, at its priesthood, or the sacrificial blood that flowed in streams from age to age, we find a testimony to this righteousness. The law, too, in its moral aspect held up a lofty standard, which found no corresponding reality in any human heart, but pointed forward to Him who should one day come, saying, "Thy law is within my heart" (Ps. xl.). It testified in both its elements adumbrating good things to come, and pointing out, at least when Israel was in their normal condition, the re-adjusted relation of man to his Maker. As to the prophets, moreover, their expressions as to this righteousness are often as precise as Paul's own words (Isa. xlv. 24, liv. 17, xlvi. 13). The apostle alludes to the testimony of the law and the prophets, to make it evident that this righteousness of God was no new, unheard-of doctrine, with which the church had no acquaintance in past ages; and in receiving it, men did not depart from Moses and the prophets, but embraced what had before been announced. It was no abrupt phenomenon, for which there had not been a preparation; for the Old Testament, in all its parts, bore testimony to the righteousness of God.

3. The standard of this righteousness is divine justice and the law of God. Righteousness in a creature is measured by

the standard of justice. There is a manifestation of justice in demanding the satisfaction, and then in preparing and accepting this righteousness of God: "That He might be just, and the justifier" (Rom. iii. 26).

But specially, the law is the standard of the righteousness; that is, the law considered as a definite expression of the justice of God. The idea of righteousness in a creature implies conformity to law: law is the sphere of righteousness, the element in which it moves. These two terms, law and righteousness, are correlatives, and suppose each other. To unfold the principle of law to which this righteousness of God goes back, we find the apostle delineating both sides,—the law considered in its violation, and then in its positive demand with its promise of life. The transgressor of the law was under its curse, and the Surety came under it (Gal. iii. 10). Again, it enforced its unalterable claim to do and live (Rom. x. 5), and Christ was made under it (Gal. iv. 4), and so became its end (Rom. x. 4). Thus He obtained its reward of debt, not only for Himself, but for all whom He represented. A comparison of numerous passages where the work of Christ is mentioned, leads us to the conclusion that the phrase "righteousness of God," wherever it occurs, involves a subjection to law as the rule of ethical rectitude. The law, as the transcript of God's nature, and the mould in which man's nature was formed, is immutable; and far from losing its authority by human inability, it ceased not to claim all that it ever claimed. The law to which the Lord subjected Himself, moreover, was THE LAW AS VIOLATED. The two aspects in which the apostle presents the law, not only to the Jews, who were dispensationally under it, but to the Gentiles, who were not, are these: (1) That it urges its inflexible claims to sinless obedience as the only way to life (Gal. iii. 12); and (2) that it comes armed with the curse incurred by its violation (Gal. iii. 10-13). That is the twofold demand of the law made upon every man. That is apostolic doctrine, however much at variance with modern theories, which all too superficially limit it to Israel; as if the law, in its true character, were not a republication of the primeval and eternal law, binding on man as man. The Lord was made under it in both respects for the production of this everlasting righteousness; and accordingly the work of Christ is described in its relation to the law. Thus, it is said that He was made under the law, and that the righteousness of the law is fulfilled in us (Rom. viii. 4); that Christ is the end of the law unto righteousness to every one that believeth (Rom. x. 4),—an expression presupposing the fulfilment which the law demanded, and could not but demand, till its end was reached. The additional words, "the end of the law *unto righteousness,*" leave us in no doubt that the realization of the law and its end are found in Christ.

4. As another constituent element of this righteousness, it must be added that it owed its origin to a God-man. It was a work to the production of which the twofold nature of the Redeemer was necessary. We have to trace the influence of Christ's deity in the bringing in of the everlasting righteousness (Dan. ix. 24). Though purely human in its essential character, it is the result of the concurrent action of both natures, and therefore of infinite value and eternal validity; and as He was under no obligation on His own account to obey, or to be under the law, or to be incarnate, His obedience is capable of being given away. Hence the constant reference to the divine Sonship when the fulfilment of the law is described (Gal. iv. 4; Rom. viii. 3). Without personal obligation of any kind, the Son of God, in assuming humanity, entered into all those duties which man was bound to discharge,— into the burdensome duties of an Israelite, and into manifold temptations and trials which His position as the sin-bearing substitute entailed. In short, He united a sinless humanity to Himself, that, by entering into every part of our obligation as creatures and sinners, He might bring in an everlasting righteousness. Till the law received its satisfaction in the

twofold respect already mentioned—that is, by obedience to precept and penalty—the Supreme Judge could take none into favour.

But this obedience of the God-man was ONE and indivisible. Though possessing a twofold aspect, it was one finished work. As man is under precept and penalty because he is the creature of God under the eternal law of obedience, and a sinner under condemnation, the surety obedience of the Lord must satisfy the law in both respects. Many expositors incorrectly sunder the two, or fix attention on the one to the exclusion of the other. Others acknowledge both, but unhappily make the two elements separately meritorious, losing sight of the link that binds Christ's deeds and sufferings together as one vicarious obedience. The latter class of divines ascribe forgiveness to the sufferings, and the right to everlasting life to the active obedience,—an unhappy separation, though countenanced by eminent names, and by no means to be vindicated. As it is the work of one Christ, it is one atoning obedience; and though we may, and must, distinguish the elements of which it consists, we may not disjoin them, for the two elements concur to form one obedience. That they cannot be separated appears from many considerations, and especially from this, that in every action there was a humiliation, and in every suffering an exercise of obedience. They both pervade every event in that wondrous life. They were not in exercise at different times, in different actions, and in successive hours: they meet in the same action and at the same time, over the entire life of Jesus, from the first moment of His humiliation to the last.

This atoning obedience extended over the entire life of the Lord, and was not limited to the few hours on the cross. It was but the verification of His sinless nature in various scenes of action and agony allotted to Him, but formed one obedience from first to last. That the element of obedience pervaded His entire life, and went into all His sufferings, sufficiently appears from numerous texts, which I shall not expound in this place (Rom. v. 19; Phil. ii. 8; Heb. v. 8). If we call up before our minds the usual division of human duty, according to the different relations which man occupies to God, himself, and his fellows, He learned obedience in them all; and with the augmented trials, as they thickened and deepened, His obedience was also augmented,—that is, was capable of increase, though always perfect. The spontaneous surrender of His life in such a substitution as that which He consented to occupy, called for an obedience that bore Him up amid inconceivable difficulties; and from the greatness of His person, it had a dignity and value which entitle it to be called infinite. The humanity He wore was made by Him an instrument which He used for the great purpose of bringing in the righteousness of God; or, to put the matter in a personal, concrete form, Christ Himself is the righteousness of God. The Son of God made flesh, and obedient in life and death, is our righteousness before God. Scripture knows of only ONE righteousness uniting God and men, and the world has never seen another.

5. It remains to be added, that the righteousness of God was IN OUR STEAD as well as for our benefit. It is the more necessary to establish the *vicarious* nature of this righteousness, because not a few in every community are ready to admit the vicarious suffering who are not willing to allow the vicarious obedience in the whole extent of human obligation; that is, they divide the two parts of the law, the penalty and precept, into two portions, regarding the vicarious suffering as alone capable of imputation. But the vicarious character attaching to the one obedience of the Lord is as plainly taught as the fact that it is a substantive reality; and when the apostle says, " We are made the righteousness of God in Him " (2 Cor. v. 21), he intimates that believers in Christ come to a realization of the fact that it was rendered in their room, and that they are one with Him in the whole transaction. The obedience of Christ realizes the lofty ideal or goal set before the human

race; and on this account it is the greatest event in the
world's history. He was acting for His people, and they
were representatively in Him. The entrance of Christ's sinless humanity, with the law in His heart, became the central
point of all time, to which previous ages looked forward, and
after ages look back. He was the living law, the personal
law,—an event with a far more important bearing than any
other that ever occurred. It was the world's new creation. It
is made ours not less truly than if we ourselves had rendered
it, IN CONSEQUENCE OF THE LEGAL ONENESS FORMED BETWEEN
US AND HIM. Not that in the Lord's experience the personal
was merged in the official, for He had not, and could not
have, any of those feelings which stand connected with personal guilt. He was always fully conscious of inward sinlessness when the sin-bearer and curse-bearer in our stead;
and in like manner the redeemed, amid all the security of
imputed righteousness, never cease to cherish personally the
feelings of conscious unworthiness and deep abasement. That
the vicarious character of the whole may appear, it is only
necessary to recall the words, " By the obedience of one shall
many be made righteous " (Rom. v. 19).

As an objection to this mode of interpreting the righteousness of faith, it is commonly urged that the apostle nowhere
uses the theological expression " the righteousness of Christ."
But when we examine the terms in which it is expressed, the
vicarious character of the righteousness is made the more evident. CHRIST HIMSELF IS OUR RIGHTEOUSNESS. The incarnate
Son, dying in our room, the realized ideal of what man was
made to be, is made of God unto us righteousness (1 Cor. i.
30), in such a sense that we are said to be made the righteousness of God in Him. This is more remarkable: we are made
all that Christ was ; He is the Lord our righteousness (Jer.
xxiii. 6), and we are made the righteousness of God in Him
(2 Cor. v. 21).

Having noticed what are the elements of this righteousness,

and proved that it is but another name for the Lord's atoning obedience, it remains for us to add, with all brevity, the way by which it is appropriated, and its immediate as well as ulterior consequences.

6. The relation of faith to the righteousness of God is, that faith is the hand by which it is received. The righteousness is in another person, in such a sense that it is merely received as a gift, irrespective of moral worth on the part of the receiver. Why is such a gift given to faith, and to no other mental act ? Partly because faith is the only way by which the soul goes out to rely on an object beyond itself, partly because faith is the most self-emptying act of the mind. By its very nature, it negatives everything but that righteousness which it receives. Faith is the receptive organ by which we lay hold of the right-eousness ; while the gospel, or word of God, is the medium of revealing it (Rom. i. 17). It is unto all and upon ALL THEM THAT BELIEVE (Rom. iii. 22).

7. The immediate effect of receiving the righteousness of God is the sentence of absolution, called the justification of our persons ; for it must be kept in mind that the man is justified, and not his works,—the person, not the nature. This sen-tence is complete at once, and capable of no addition ; and it has a twofold side,—the ABSOLVING of the man from any charge of guilt, and the pronouncing of him ABSOLUTELY RIGHTEOUS, because in the possession of this righteousness of God.

8. A further point demanding notice, is the relation in which the righteousness of God stands to LIFE. This all-im-portant point is very much the theological question of the age ; for the relation between these two things is much misappre-hended. The relation of this righteousness to the divine life which Christ came down from heaven to restore in a dead world, is the leading thought with all the apostles, as well as with the Lord Himself, and it is brought out with great pro-minence in the Pauline epistles (Gal. ii. 20 ; Rom. viii. 10). The relation between the two is simply this : RIGHTEOUSNESS

IS THE PRICE, AND LIFE IS THE REWARD. It is a relation intimated in the law, which was ordained to life, but was found to be unto death (Rom. vii. 10). The man who should do what it enjoined was to receive life in return (Rom. x. 5). Modern theology, at least of the German type, and as far as it is modified from that quarter, evinces little interest about the relation in which the two points, righteousness and life, stand to each other. But a misapprehension here disorganizes the whole gospel. And the mystic theology which merely seeks communion with God, and life in Him, through the incarnation, has no adequate idea of the conditions on which life is conferred. They seek to delineate the life as an absolute donation apart from righteousness, or an atoning sacrifice as its ground. They speak of Christ IN US, not of Christ FOR US. There is no life, however, but through a vicarious death. The important question of the age, and of all ages, is, How does life reach us? and the answer is, By a vicarious fulfilment of the law in precept and penalty; in other words, by an atonement.

SEC. VIII.—THE RECONCILIATION SET FORTH IN THE PAULINE EPISTLES.

I deem it necessary to notice this aspect of the atonement separately, though it comes before us in various texts. If the righteousness of God is the positive side of the Pauline doctrine of the atonement, reconciliation by the death of Christ is its negative side. This term is not, like many others bearing on the atonement, borrowed from the sacrificial ritual; for no connection can be traced between the two. It does not, as a term, recall either the priesthood or the sacrifices. Rather, we may say, the expression is taken from common life, and refers to a state of things where two parties, disunited by a quarrel or some cause of offence, are made friends by the adequate removal of the estrangement. This phase of the doctrine is peculiarly Pauline; and after the consideration given to the righteousness of God, it is the more needful to bring it out, because reconciliation proceeds on the fact of sin, and presupposes the displeasure and moral aversion of God to the sinner.

1. Reconciliation, denoting a NEW RELATION toward God, presupposes a state of alienation between God and man; that is, an alienation which was mutual. It was not exclusively on man's side, nor was it brought to a termination by a change of moral disposition on the part of man. It was mutual estrangement: on man's side by sin and enmity (Rom. viii. 7); on God's side by the wide gulf of separation which sin inevitably makes (Isa. lix. 2), and by the wrath which cometh upon the children of disobedience (Eph. v. 6). There was mutual hostility, in the proper sense of the word, between God and man: we, on the one side, were alienated and enemies in our minds by wicked works (Col. i. 21); and God, on the other side, was provoked to anger, and under the necessity of visiting man as the object of His wrath (Rom. v. 9).

2. The change of relation implied in the term reconciliation was effected by the atonement, the great fact intervening between divine wrath and the objects over whom the wrath impended. This is the objective ground of reconciliation, as the special word rendered *atonement* in one passage properly means (Rom. v. 11); it is the divinely provided fact which is received from God, and the ground of the new relation or favourable disposition of God toward us. It must be observed that we are said to be reconciled to God by the death of His Son as a divine person (Rom. v. 10), or reconciled in the body of His flesh through death (Col. i. 22). And the apostle's words, which further announce that we are saved from wrath through Christ, plainly intimate that reconciliation, in the proper sense, is by the work of Christ, not by our change of disposition (Rom. v. 9). The favour of God is won for us by the blood of Christ, otherwise we should have been given up to condemnation.

3. The apostle represents the reconciliation as ORIGINATING WITH GOD, who took the first step to bring it about. And this leads me to notice a marked difference between the two words PROPITIATION and RECONCILIATION. The former is applied to Christ as the great sacrifice, and the priest of His own sacrifice; the latter is applied to God as the originator of the reconciliation.[1] The Father is the Reconciler in the proper sense, for the benefit emanates from His love; and the mode by which it was accomplished was the non-imputing of our trespasses on the part of God, who was not a mere passive spectator, but an active party in all the reconciliation (2 Cor. v. 19). His love reconciled us, and His anger was pacified. The great fact interposed between His holy anger and our sin was the atoning work of Christ, provided in the exercise of compassion and love. The Lord's atonement effected the removal of these sins; by which means the anger of God was brought to an end. That is the apostle's doctrine, as will be evident from several texts which will come before us.

On the contrary, it is argued by the interpreters who have come under the influence of Socinianizing opinions, that the idea of reconciliation does not involve a new relation toward God, or restoration to divine favour. It is held that reconciliation does not indicate any change on God's side, but only a termination of enmity on man's side; that God is never called man's enemy; and that the New Testament never speaks of the reconciliation of God to man, but from the other side of the relation, of the reconciliation of man to God. The whole opposition to the doctrine is based on this mistaken view of the phraseology. Though Scripture describes reconciliation from our side, this can readily be explained. The reconciliation is a divine fact, originating in the love of God; but from its nature it presupposes a displeasure not to be averted but by satisfaction or atonement. The mere fact that reconcilia-

---

[1] See Morus' *Epitome*, p. 163, and *Dissertationes*, ii. p. 98 ; Storr, *Brief an die Hebräer*, p. 407.

tion is not absolute, but by the death of His Son (Rom. v. 10), proves that love is not the only element in the transaction, but that a new relation must be formed, or a transition effected from wrath to favour. This, too, is the uniform expression in the language of common life, which describes reconciliation from the side of the offending party. Thus, an offending subject is said to be reconciled to the prince or superior, whose displeasure had been incurred. That is the uniform phraseology. But the nature of the case involves a restoration to divine favour: for what is wanting in the case of those who were without reconciliation, and what is conferred by those who receive it, but the full removal of estrangement caused by some offence? And what do they possess who are reconciled to God, but the remission of sins, the removal of guilt, the restoration to a new relation, consisting in the participation of divine favour? There is a new relation on God's side, that of friendship consequent on forgiveness.[1]

But, it is asked, is not God immutable, the absolute Love? and how can He at once be regarded as loving and hating, as disposed to visit us with love, and yet estranged by our conduct to such a degree, that He cannot but treat us as under His wrath? To this the simple answer is: Scripture affirms both, and we must believe both. They well enough consist together, when we recall the twofold relation which man occupies to God, as a creature and as a sinner. God cherishes love to man, whether we think of man merely as he is the creature of God, or still further regard him as in a Surety, or in union with the beloved Son, according to that eternal covenant by which Christ and the redeemed come before God's eye as one. That man is an object of displeasure, is not less evident to one who knows ought of divine justice; for sins could not but provoke His anger, and bring down punitive visitation in the exercise of His moral government.

Nor is it strange that anger and love co-exist, when we

---

[1] See Philippi's *Kirchliche Glaubenslehre*, iv. p. 272. 1863.

duly distinguish according to the twofold relation already
noticed. We may trace the analogy to a far greater extent
than is commonly done between God, and man made in the
image of God. Thus, for example, David loved Absalom as
his son, and gave strict commands to spare him in the midst
of that rebellion which, on the highest moral grounds, must
needs be repressed with stern severity. We see the father,
and yet the righteous king, subjecting that wayward son to his
frown on several occasions, because he hated his wickedness,
and was provoked to deep displeasure. He loved him as his
son, but as a righteous governor mingled punishment with
mercy. In the same way, God loves His creatures; yet He
cannot but cherish just anger against sin, and against sinners
because of sin, as will be sufficiently evinced by the everlasting
punishment striking on all who are out of Christ. And this
can more easily be conceived, when we reflect that love and
wrath are in God an eternal, constant will, expressive of His
nature: love being ever active to do His creatures good, so
far as it is not obstructed; wrath being active, to visit sin with
punitive justice. The atonement is nothing else than a provision to effect the removal of those obstructions or impediments
which stood in the way of the full exercise of grace; and it
consists in the satisfaction to justice in every respect.

Thus God represents things and persons as they really are:
He does not act in any way at variance with His perfect knowledge of man's double relation as creatures and as sinners. In
so far as they perverted their rational and moral nature, they
forfeited His favour, and are guilty before Him; in so far as
they are His creatures, they are still the objects of His love.
But to put them in a new relation, which was possible only by
effecting the remission of sins, He made them by federal union
one with His beloved Son, sent into the world to occupy their
place, and made sin, as if He had become the very cause of the
alienation. When He treated Him as if He were the greatest
sinner, or as sin accumulated and personified, we see the reality

of the representative position which He occupied. And having provided the arrangement by which His perfections could be vindicated and His honour established, He puts men into a new relation — one of friendship and favour — the moment they receive the atonement (Rom. v. 11). They are made friends of enemies. The analogy from the mode of governing a human family throws light upon the whole transaction: for though we cannot in all respects compare God to man, we may infer God's mode of action from the action of man made in His likeness; otherwise we could not in many respects know God at all. Can a disobedient son enjoy the favour of a parent in the same way as a son who is a pattern of filial obedience? When the displeasure is exchanged for the opposite by the removal of the offence, then the father restores him to favour. But we must meet the objections to this biblical representation more in detail.

a. It is alleged that God is never called the enemy of man, or said to be made a friend of an enemy; and consequently that the term reconciliation does not intimate any change on God's side corresponding to a restoration to favour. The reasons why God is not called in Scripture our enemy are, that God is interested in His creatures on the ground of His relation as their Creator; that He cherishes mercy in His heart to the prodigal son; and that an eternal purpose was formed to reconcile them. We are to apprehend equally the heart of God and the government of God. Men living in sin cannot share in the divine favour; and reception into favour is undoubtedly involved in the idea of reconciliation.

b. It is held that we cannot adduce anything from biblical language to prove that reconciliation implies aught on God's side involving the idea of restoration to His favour. This is of easy answer. The apostle connects reconciliation with an objective fact; and one passage may be adduced here as itself conclusive[1] (Rom. v. 11). Paul teaches that we who were

---

[1] See Spener's *die Evangelische Glaubens-Gerechtigkeit*, p. 650.

enemies were reconciled,—a statement which plainly announces two conditions: one a relation of wrath; another a relation of favour, based upon the great historic fact of Christ's death. Not only so: he adds, we have NOW RECEIVED the atonement; that is, as the term signifies, have now received the objective ground of reconciliation; the meaning of which can only be, that we have NOW received a peculiar relation, or a reception into favour unknown before. He is speaking, not of a change of disposition on man's side, though that of course immediately ensues, but of a fact provided for us in the love of God. The term reconciliation may be said to comprehend what is mutual, because the alienation was mutual. The passage intimates something on God's side that carried in its train a restoration to His favour.

c. It is further pertinaciously argued, that the New Testament language contains no such expression as God's reconciliation to man. This, as has been already noticed, is not necessary; and the entire gospel is an indubitable proof of this. It is nowhere said, in any proclamation of the gospel among Jew or Gentile, that they must reconcile God to themselves; for it is God who is always represented, and in the most natural way, as reconciling men to Himself by Jesus Christ (2 Cor. v. 18–21). But how was this done? Not by granting absolute remission of sins, not by a simple cancelling of the trespasses committed by us; but solely by putting Christ, as a representative, in their place to do what they could not have done, and by inviting men upon the ground of that atonement to be reconciled to Himself in a mediator. The whole transaction shows two things—the love of God's heart, and the rectitude of His government. All who refuse the atonement are, from the necessity of the case, left standing on their own footing as sinners, and out of divine favour; whereas all who receive the atonement are reconciled. Every other mode of reconciliation is deceptive, unavailing before God, and incapable of affording any firm consolation, because it would remain always uncertain whether God could accept the reconciliation. But as it originates with God, and as God in Christ is the reconciler (2 Cor. v. 19), in the exercise of His prevenient grace, we have full certainty that it is acceptable. Certainly that which is of God must be acceptable to God.

Thus on man's side nothing further is required, than that he should enter into this relation of reconciliation by accepting the atonement as its ground or cause. Nothing was wanting on God's side of the transaction ; and the whole language bearing on this truth amounts to this, that God turns away His anger from, and shows favour to, all those for whom the atonement was offered.

We can thus, on biblical grounds, explode the whole Socinianizing arguments, which allege that reconciliation consists in a change of our hostile will and disposition toward God, and in that alone. Such an exposition, owing its origin to a foregone conclusion, does not satisfy the texts which put reconciliation in causal connection with the death of Christ (Rom. v. 10); with His blood; with the body of His flesh through death (Col. i. 22). That there is a change on man's side also is not denied ; for the reconciliation is MUTUAL, as the alienation was mutual. But the change on our side is to this extent distinguished from the other, that it emanates from what God has done.

SEC. IX.—THE TESTIMONY IN THE EPISTLE TO THE ROMANS.

The Epistle to the Romans, written from Corinth before Paul's journey to Jerusalem, which ended in his imprisonment (Acts xx. 2 ; Rom. xv. 25–xvi. 23), the most connected outline of Christian doctrine given us by the pen of inspiration, was intended to place the Christian's relation to God, or the article of justification, in its true light. Paul accordingly, in various passages, describes the doctrine of the atonement as the basis of the whole. The theme or proposition laid down at the beginning, and illustrated in the course of his reasoning, is contained in the quotation from Habakkuk, "The just shall live by faith," or, more accurately rendered, "The righteous by faith shall live" (Rom. i. 17). The three words contained in this brief sentence, taken up one by one—RIGHTEOUSNESS, FAITH, LIFE—may be viewed as separate headings to three principal sections of the epistle: the first being brought out in contrast with the great fact of universal sinfulness (Rom. i. 17–iii. 27); the second extending over the whole fourth chapter (iii. 27–iv. 25); and the third, setting forth premial life, fills the larger portion of the remaining doctrinal contents (v. 12–viii. 39). The apostle is thus led by the scope and structure of the epistle to give a full exposition of the atonement at all points. These passages will be taken up in order, and we shall consider to what they amount. Omitting matter foreign to our purpose, let us concentrate attention on passages and statements which definitely refer to the atonement.

I. The first passage to be noticed is the following: *Being justified freely by His grace, through the redemption that is in Christ Jesus: whom God hath set forth to be a propitiation through faith in His blood, to declare His righteousness for* [better, *on account of*] *the remission of sins that are past, through the forbearance of God; to declare, I say, at this time His righteousness; that He might be just, and the justifier of him that believeth in Jesus* (Rom. iii. 24–26). We have here a compendious statement of the elements which constitute the great article of justification: (1.) The grace of God as the source or impelling cause; (2.) The blood of Christ as the meritorious cause or ground on which the sentence proceeds; (3.) Faith as the receptive organ or instrumental cause; (4.) The harmonious exhibition of justice and grace as the final cause, or the end contemplated by the whole scheme (ver. 26). These different points, when combined, comprehend the entire elements of the doctrine or great privilege of justification. But we shall single out the atonement, as here presented to us, for special consideration. The passage is difficult from its condensation, but we hope to make it clear by a few comments.

(1.) We have first to notice the appellations under which the death of Christ is described in this passage. THREE several designations are here applied to it, and it becomes us to discover the peculiar shade of meaning attaching to each of the terms. One leading thought applicable to them all is, that they describe the ONE WORK of Christ in different lights, and from various points of view; for they are not to be treated as if they set forth three several works of Christ, separately meritorious. The redemption-work of Jesus was one, and the obedience one, though carried forward in a twofold sphere. As the work of Christ has manifold applications, according to the relations which man occupies to the captivity in which he is held, to divine wrath due to us for sin, or to the law under which he was made, it may be described under various names. But it is one atoning work, with manifold bearings.

Of these names the first is, THE REDEMPTION THAT IS IN CHRIST JESUS. This term, as here used, denotes the objective ground in Christ on account of which divine action takes place. It describes Him as the cause, or author, of the actual deliverance. Captivity under an enemy's power is of course presupposed, and also a ransom as the necessary price. Wherever the terms REDEEM or REDEMPTION are found in connection with the death, blood, or sufferings of Christ, the reference is sacrificial; and that supplementary expression contains an allusion to the ransom (Gal. iii. 13; 1 Pet. i. 19; Rev. v. 9). The close connection between the notion of a ransom and the allied idea of sacrifice is easily understood. But it may further be asked, What are we to understand by the phrase here used, "The redemption WHICH IS IN CHRIST JESUS?" The import is, that the ransom is found in His person, that He is personally the redemption of His people; for the ransom, or price, of our deliverance is found in Christ Himself. The expression cannot mean "by whom we have redemption," as some put it, nor "in fellowship with whom," as others choose rather to expound it; for the phrase could have the latter sense only if it could fitly stand alone, and give a competent meaning, separated from the verb (see 2 Cor. xii. 3). The expression, as here used, conveys the idea that the ransom, or means of redemption, is objectively found in Christ's person—The Crucified, and The Risen.[1] It does not give the idea that union to His person constitutes redemption, however true it is that we share in redemption only in this way. The passage means, that He is our meritorious redemption, our infinite ransom, in the objective sense, and that He will continue to be so while His living person endures (1 Cor. i. 30; Eph. i. 7). There the Judge beholds the church's redemption, and every time He looks on the person of Christ He sees our eternal ransom.

As to the presupposition implied in the word, it always takes for granted a captivity, and involves the payment of a ransom for deliverance. Passages may be adduced where the word seems used to convey the idea of simple deliverance, the accessory notion of a price being less upon the foreground; but it is never wholly awanting. In all cases it will be found that this phraseology is never without the idea of an equivalent, price, or consideration, whether more latent or more open to view, by which a deliverance is gained or a good is won. When the death or blood of the Lord is named in the phrase, there is no room for doubt that that is added as the ransom. The ransom secures deliverance FROM something, and redeems us to belong to another Master (Rev. v. 9; 1 Cor. vi. 20). They who have the redemption obtain liberation from the curse of the law (Gal. iii. 13), from wrath, from death, and him that has the power of death (Heb. ii. 14), and a transition to the proprietary rights of another owner, to whom they henceforward belong.

The second term here used is, A PROPITIATION IN HIS BLOOD.

---

[1] See an exposition of the phrase ἐν ᾧ ἔχομεν τὴν ἀπολύτρωσιν in Harless' *Commentary on Ephes.* (i. 7).

This expression is variously rendered : by many, as a propitiatory sacrifice; by an equal number, as the propitiatory or blood-sprinkled mercy-seat. In either way, it brings up the idea of divine anger appeased by the intervention of an economy involving a priesthood and sacrificial blood. Some minds will be swayed in the one direction, and others in the other. But in either case the sense amounts to this, that the blood of Christ pacifies, or propitiates, the justly kindled anger of the Most High; for there is a wrath against sin which finds an outlet in the infliction of punitive justice upon the sinner himself, if he stands on his own footing, or in the infliction of wrath upon the Mediator who comes into our place and under our obligations. The language here used, whatever the shade of meaning attached to it, involves the idea of appeasing God by sacrificial blood. This is self-evident from the whole phraseology of Scripture, and it cannot be explained away.

For various reasons we prefer the rendering PROPITIATORY,[1] or mercy-seat sprinkled with blood. This was the cover of the ark of the covenant, in which the law was deposited, and the annual ceremony of sprinkling it with blood was performed on the day of atonement. But all the ordinary sacrifices bore reference to it, and stood in some relation to it. This was, in a word, the centre-point of the entire Old Testament economy ; and the whole argument of the Epistle to the Hebrews may be said to be echoed in this allusion, or summed up in the pregnant clause before us. But, in particular, there is a great similarity between the present passage and the statement that Christ's death atoned for transgressions under the old covenant (Heb. ix. 15).

---

[1] This is the meaning of ἱλαστήριον in the Epistle to the Hebrews (ix. 5) ; and the Reformers, Luther, Calvin, and their successors, so expounded it. Afterwards it came to be regarded as the neuter of an adjective, and as denoting a sacrifice, some supplying θῦμα, others nothing. See a conclusive note by Philippi, in his *Commentary on Romans*, in behalf of the first view—*propitiatory*. Though opinion is pretty equally divided, the idea of propitiating God comes out in both.

The idea is, that Christ is "set forth" to view, or, as some
will have it, "fore-appointed"[1] from of old to be the reality of
that blood-sprinkled mercy-seat; and, to apprehend the force
of the allusion, we must go back to the symbolical and typical
meaning.   The symbolical import was the following:—The
ark contained the law, and the ark's covering or propitiatory
covered its curse, whenever it was sprinkled by the atoning
blood, as was the case from year to year; for, as the great day
of atonement returned, this imposing ceremonial was annually
repeated to cover sins from God's sight.   As to the typical
signification, it was a prefiguration of Him who was personally
to pacify the divine wrath, and therefore of that work of
Christ by which at the appointed time He should at once
fulfil the law and remove its curse.   It deserves to be noticed
that the phrase here used by the apostle conveys but one idea;
and hence, in the grammatical construing, we must read the
word PROPITIATORY in immediate connection with the words IN
HIS BLOOD.[2]   The idea is one; and, viewed in this way, we
must regard the words as meaning, Christ crucified the means
of pacifying the wrath of God.   On this account the mercy-
seat was considered as God's throne in the midst of His people,
where He showed Himself gracious, and communed with His
people (Ps. lxxx. 1).   Here, too, rested the symbol of the
divine presence, the glory of the Lord.   We thus reach the
conclusion that the central point in the old economy foreshadowed the true propitiatory; and thus, in language borrowed
from the ceremonial institutions, the apostle shows us that the
way of propitiation was the same from the beginning.   Hence,
as it is said, "Christ our passover is sacrificed for us;" so we
can say, "Christ our propitiatory is erected or set forth for us."

The third descriptive name for the atonement is the term

---

[1] Some make προέθετο *fore-appointed* (so Chrysost., Diodati, Willet).

[2] The usual phrase is, πίστις εἰς. We cannot construe πίστεως ἐν τῷ αἵματι,
for that is abnormal. Some put a comma after πίστεως: others read ἱλαστήριον
ἐν τῷ αἵματι together, giving one thought, viz. blood-sprinkled propitiatory,
which is better.

RIGHTEOUSNESS—"to declare HIS righteousness." The question to be settled, in the first place, is this: Have we here the well-known Pauline expression which we have considered already—"the righteousness of God?" Or are we under the necessity of regarding it as the divine attribute of righteousness? A right view of the connection between the two things here put together—the righteousness of God and the remission of sins—will satisfy us that we have the well-known Pauline phrase. But as many eminent expositors, swayed by the view which they take of the connection of the clauses, hold the expression to be descriptive of the attribute of justice, we must prove that the phrase occurs here in no other sense than in other passages where there is no ambiguity. If the apostle has used the expression "righteousness of God" throughout the context to describe the atoning work of Christ, how can he be supposed to alter the meaning of his own phrase within the compass of a single sentence?

Some argue that the expression must refer to the divine attribute of righteousness, as it paves the way, according to them, for the reference to retributive justice in the following verse (ver. 26). But it is not so: that is a mere semblance of argument. Nay, we should rather say that it wants all probability, because it would be a repetition, a tautology. But no reason can be given for departing from the ordinary meaning of the Pauline phrase. We must attach a uniform, consistent meaning to the use of terms, and regard it as designating the atoning work of the Lord.

But the righteousness is brought out in a new connection, which we must now endeavour to trace. The apostle had proved that between Jew and Gentile there is no difference, either in the ruin or in the remedy, and that the righteousness was for both alike. But now his thoughts revert to the saints of God who lived under the former dispensation, and to the retrospective bearing of the atonement as applicable to them not less than to those whose lot is cast in gospel times. If the blood-sprinkled mercy-seat was a prefiguration of the atonement, the finished work of Christ is considered as the accomplished fact, or actual manifestation of the righteousness which was required. The apostle therefore refers to the bringing in of the righteousness as a historic reality, as he had done in a previous verse (ver. 21).

This leads us to inquire, What is the connection between the righteousness of God thus understood, and the remission of sins that were past in the forbearance of God ? A correct appreciation of this will make the meaning plain. Paul plainly refers to the time that preceded the atonement, and describes it as an economy of forbearance, during which the punishment of sin was deferred, and yet the salvation based on the atonement extended to many. How could there be this remission of sins during that past economy ? The answer is supplied by the apostle : It was on the credit of what was ere long to be accomplished. That is the connection between the righteousness of God and the remission of sins here mentioned. There were millions who shared in the retrospective character of the atonement before Christ came in the flesh.

The connection of these two things will appear if we correctly translate the word that connects them together. The language will not bear the rendering given in the authorized version—FOR[1] THE REMISSION OF SINS. The Greek preposition, when so construed, never denotes the final cause, or the intention and design, for which a thing is done. Neither can it bear the rendering BY, or THROUGH, which others assign to it. It uniformly assigns the ground or reason on account of which a thing occurred, or an action was performed, denoting ON ACCOUNT OF. In the present case the preposition assigns the reason on account of which the past remission of sins for thousands of years took place, viz. the future atonement, which

---

[1] The proper force of διά with the accusative, *propter*, must be retained, denoting the ground or reason on account of which the thing, viz. the πάρισις, had been done.

in Paul's time had become a historic fact. The righteousness of God, or the atoning work by which men are saved, has been actually manifested in the fulness of time, because the sins of millions had in previous ages been passed over and remitted. Without the actual bringing in of the everlasting righteousness, and merely on the credit of it as about to be, they had received forgiveness, and been enrolled among the spirits of the just made perfect. But since they had received remission of sins, it was absolutely necessary to bring in the expiation as a historic fact, or to give it a positive accomplishment. The retrospective efficacy of the atonement is made clear. But these were but effects or consequences of a cause which could not be withheld.

As to the peculiarities of the remission of sins that was proper to the Old Testament, we need not too curiously inquire. Some have indulged their fancy and been misled. A class of divines, headed by Cocceius, preferred to view the remission which belonged to the Old Testament church more as a passing over than as a true forgiveness. They asked, How could it be a true forgiveness, when the cause was not yet present? And they thought such a distinction warranted by the apostle's expressions. But what difference there was between the saints of God in the Old and New Testament, was not in the objective remission, but in the inward consciousness of pardon and liberty. The difference was within. The apostle affirms the remission of sins under the former dispensation. And as that was possible only by the blood of atonement, since there could be no infringement of the divine justice or law, the righteousness of God must be actually brought in. Whether men regard the remission under the old economy in the light of a true forgiveness, which is the preferable view, or in that of a preterition, there can be no doubt of the retrospective efficacy of the atonement, and of the cancelling of the guilt of sin before Christ came in the flesh by means of the atonement. The relation of the two economies, then, is as follows: The bringing in of the righteousness was necessary on account of the previous remission. The apostle shows that there was a causal connection between the righteousness of God and the forgiveness of sins in all ages, that the cross was the great fact of all time, and that God had respect to it from the beginning. This is the only sense that the words will exegetically bear. Because the forgiveness was already given, there must be an actual satisfaction to divine justice, and an actual righteousness in the fulness of time.

Hence the three words which we have expounded—redemption, propitiatory, and righteousness—delineate the atonement in different points of view; the first from the view-point of man's captivity, the second from the view-point of divine wrath against sin, the third from that of the inalienable claims of the divine law. And this variety of names to describe the same great fact argues that, though the work of the Lord is one, it has manifold bearings—as numerous, indeed, as our necessities.

(2.) The design or final cause which God had in view in the whole matter of the atonement is next subjoined: *that He might be just, and the justifier* (ver. 26). The allusion is to the concurrence or harmony of these two perfections of God. The word JUST, applied to God, means that He asserts just claims and inflicts just punishment. It is a perversion of language to interpret the term as if it could mean anything else than justice in the ordinary acceptation of the word among men made in the image of God.[1] The contrast in which it is placed to divine forbearance, and the allusion to the propitiatory, allow no doubt as to its import. Justice seemed to slumber during that period of forbearance; now it is displayed.

But this determines the character of the atonement. Such language would be unmeaning, if it were not admitted that the atonement is in the proper sense of the word a satisfaction

---

[1] See Section vi. of the former volume, *The Sayings of Jesus.*

of divine justice. This single clause, therefore, fully warrants the expression in common use, notwithstanding all the objections which have been adduced against it as unfitting or unwarrantable. And when the apostle adds, " that He might be just, AND THE JUSTIFIER," he alludes to the fact that these two apparently conflicting perfections, justice and grace, meet in full harmony on the cross: justice suffers no violence, and grace has full outlet.

This enables us to form a right judgment as to all those theories which allow only one element in the atonement, and reduce all to love. When modern theology commits itself to this one-sided theory, it is clearly out of harmony with the Pauline theology. As to the attempts which are at present made in many quarters to subsume justice under love, they are all sorry evasions of biblical ideas. Thus, when it is alleged that God must already have been reconciled when He gave His Son, and that there could be no further need of satisfaction, this is a mere confusion of ideas,—the confounding of a moving cause and a meritorious cause; the former being love, the latter the work of the sinless Sin-bearer in our stead. Unexpiated sin would for ever have stood in the way of obtaining divine favour, as is sufficiently evinced by hundreds of passages.

The other arguments drawn from the relation of the Fatherhood of God—the universal Fatherhood, as it is indiscriminately called—are equally refuted by this passage. It is rather a relation which draws down wrath, and calls for a propitiation. Only when sin is expiated can proper Fatherhood begin; and as to the notion which some try to propagate, that sin is rather a disease than a crime, the answer is: No man believes, or can believe, that the moral Governor is indifferent to human conduct, to the moral actions of His creatures; for this is contradicted by man's moral nature as well as by Scripture (Rom. i. 32).

II. A passage of much weight, as deciding on the nature of the atonement, is as follows: *Who was delivered for* [better, *on account of*] *our offences, and was raised again for* [better, *on account of*] *our justification* (Rom. iv. 25). The apostle, after discussing the case of Abraham as a ruling instance in proof of justification by faith alone, proceeds at the close of the chapter to describe faith as it is exercised on its proper object. He uses a striking name or title of God when he describes Him as the Christ-raiser, and represents faith as exercised on God in this capacity; that is, on God as the source of the atonement, and the accepter of it at the hands of the Surety.

The first thing that summons our attention is, that OUR SIN is represented as THE CAUSE of Christ's death; and it is the more important to determine with precision in what sense this language must be taken, because the consideration of the cause of Christ's death is in some quarters much misapprehended, and in other cases much neglected, in the discussion of this question. For the most part, men have stopped short at the inquiry, What was God's aim and intention in the death of Christ? But in endeavouring to apprehend the course of God's procedure, we must distinguish between the divine intention and the cause in operation; and the present passage throws light on the entire question. A strict interpretation of the terms here used proves that our offences were the proper cause of Christ's death, and that His delivery to crucifixion is considered as the punishment of sin. It is not possible in words more emphatically to express the idea of a meritorious cause, than by joining together our offences and the Lord's sufferings by a preposition (διά with ac.) intimating a connection of cause and effect. If we are to expound by language, and not by foregone conclusions, this is the only meaning that the words will bear. As our offences were the meritorious cause of Christ's death, it follows that by His delivery He paid the penalty. The phrases, TO DIE FOR SINS, TO BE DELIVERED FOR SINS, denote that sin was the cause of Christ's death, and that the death was the due punishment.

The language in these two clauses implies Suretyship; and

they cannot otherwise be understood. We may enumerate a few expressions where the preposition used to intimate causal connection occurs in the same construction. Thus, when it is said, "Ye shall be hated of all men *for my name's sake*" (Matt. x. 22) ; "They withered away, *because* they had no deepness of earth" (Matt. xiii. 5) ; "*because* they had no root" (ver. 6) ; "when tribulation or persecution ariseth *because of* the word" (ver. 21) ; "*for the oath's sake*, and them who sat at meat with him" (xiv. 9) ; "when they could not come nigh Him *for* the press" (Mark ii. 4) ; "Barabbas, who *for* a certain sedition, and *for* murder, was cast into prison" (Luke xxiii. 19) ; "Many of the Samaritans believed on Him *for* the saying of the woman" (John iv. 39) ; "*for* fear of the Jews" (xix. 38) ; "*for which things' sake* the wrath of God cometh on the children of disobedience" (Eph. v. 6) ;—in these instances, and in others too numerous to name, the import is a causal connection, or a statement of cause and effect. When it is said that Jesus was delivered FOR our offences, the words bring out the connection between our offences and His sufferings, and prove that it is a causal connection, on the ground of substitution. There must have been a relation formed between Him and us, of such a kind that He and His people were federally one, representatively one, legally one in the eye of God. But for such a covenant relation, our sins could not by possibility have affected Him, nor brought Him to the cross.

But we have next to consider what is meant by His being DELIVERED. This was the effect or consequence, of which our offences were the cause. These sins had the effect of handing over the Surety to the penal consequences which overtook Him from the hand of God and from the hand of man. This will be best illustrated from the ordinary style of speech. Thus, when a man is said to suffer for his crimes, no one doubts what the meaning is ; and in like manner, when an innocent person suffers for our sins, or is delivered for our

K

offences, this means that he bears the punishment, though the
sin was not personally his, but assumed by a voluntary act.
How was Christ DELIVERED ?   The word means, that in visiting
the Surety with the punishment due to us for sin, the Judge
of all saw fit to deliver Him into the hand of sinners.   Behind
each part of the judicial action, traced in the arrest, trial, and
crucifixion of the Lord, we see what was going forward at the
divine tribunal.   The human bar was the exponent, so to speak,
or the visible counterpart, of the divine bar.   The divine appointment appears in it all ; for nought but this could make
Christ's death a ransom, or give it efficacy for man's salvation.
Pilate's bar, therefore, was the bar of God where Jesus was
exculpated and condemned : exculpated on the ground of personal innocence, condemned as occupying the position of the
sin-bearing Surety.

He was JUDICIALLY DELIVERED into the hand of men.   It
was not in a tumult of the people, nor in a secret corner, that
the Lord was to be cut off, but after an examination and inquiry with all the forms of law.   In fulfilment of prophecy
(Isa. liii. 8), He was placed before Pilate as our Surety, having
no personal guilt, but condemned for our guilt, that it might
not be charged against us.   And all that befell Him, however
unjust as regards men, was justly inflicted at the hand of God,
who, besides what meets our eye, sent invisible strokes and
penal inflictions to an inconceivable degree.   The whole scene
is easy of explanation on the principle of substitution.   The
Surety, offering to satisfy in our room, was brought before a
human bar, in which God, as it were, erected His tribunal
before Him,—arranging the transaction in such a way that all
mankind might, to the end of time, perceive that the Judge
found Him innocent, and yet pronounced His condemnation.
He on His part promptly and cordially submitted to suffering,
in obedience to His Father, who had given that power to Pilate
in reference to the Son of God.

The last clause of the verse brings out that Jesus WAS

RAISED AGAIN ON ACCOUNT OF OUR JUSTIFICATION. The preposition (διά with acc.) must have the same import[1] and be translated in the same way in both clauses. Though this is not done by commentators, nothing can justify us in attaching a different sense to the same word in two contrasted clauses: whatever it means in the one, it must mean in the other. It is here taught that the sins of believers caused the death of the Lord, and that the impetration of a righteousness which could be applied as the sole foundation of justification, and was actually accepted on the behalf of all to whom it was to be applied, was the cause of Christ's resurrection from the dead. Had one jot or tittle been awanting in His surety-work, the resurrection of Jesus could not have taken place.

But before passing from this text, it is necessary to obviate the misapprehensions[2] of its meaning that have been taken up in various quarters.

The language cannot mean that Christ was delivered to death that He might abolish sins. There are two forms of this mode of exposition: a lower one, to the effect that we might be withdrawn from evil by the argument or motive furnished by the turpitude of sin in condemning so much excellence; and a higher one, to the effect that the Risen One imparts a new life to abolish inward corruption. But the answer to both comments is, that the language cannot bear that final sense. It always denotes ON ACCOUNT OF, intimating the cause or reason on account of which a thing has taken place; and from this mean-

[1] The general consent with which exegetes allow διά to have a final or *telic* force in this verse and some others (*e.g.* John vi. 57; Rom. iii. 25; Gal. iv. 13) cannot be vindicated. A difficulty is not to be solved by changing the meaning of words. Buurt, *beshouwende Godgeleerdheit*, § 1100, and Klinkenberg, *de Bijbel Verklaerd*, 1791, are the only writers known to me who retain the proper force of διά in the second clause.

[2] A stronger word than misapprehensions might be used, for every conjecture has been tried to evade the simple sense of διὰ τὰ παραπτώματα by expositors opposed to substitution. The words will bear no other meaning than this, that *our sins were the cause*, the meritorious cause, of His death; and we cannot but see suretyship here.

ing we cannot deviate. To bring out the notion of abolishing future sin, other words must have been used, and some additional clause to make this sense apparent. The allusion is not to future, but to past and present sin.

A second mistranslation is, that He was delivered by men's sins, or by wicked hands. But human malice and crime are never indicated in this way, as will appear by a comparison of other passages (Acts ii. 23).

A third theory is to the effect that the sufferings of Christ were intended to remove the groundless fear of punishment. But such an exposition has no warrant from the terms here used; for it is not said that Christ was delivered because of our fears, but because of our sins. And as to the notion itself, it is enough to say that redemption can never be a deliverance from baseless fear, and an assurance of divine favour; for how could that harmonize with the stern menaces connected with impenitence and unbelief? It is a mischievous delusion that God does not punish sin.

The words mean that Christ sustained our punishment, and was delivered to condemnation, human and divine, in consequence of our offences, which were charged to Him, and spontaneously borne on the ground of a union between us and Him. But it is proper to add, as showing the foregone conclusions with which many come to the interpretation of this passage, that even if it were affirmed in the plainest and most unambiguous language that sin was the cause of Christ's sufferings, and that His death was the proper punishment inflicted on Him for human sin, the opponents of the vicarious satisfaction, by their own avowal, would turn away the point of the evidence. Socinus says expressly: Though the thing were said, not once, but many times, he would not believe it; for the thing cannot be, inasmuch as the doctrine contended for is contrary to reason. Hence their whole aim is to discover any other possible meaning. To meet that rationalistic mode of treating Scripture, there is only one way. We must plainly tell such disputants either to stand within the pale of Revelation, and be bound by its announcements, or stand outside its borders altogether. It will not do to accept a Revelation, and then reject the doctrines they dislike,—to take it, and yet refuse it, according to their arbitrary caprice. They cannot be allowed thus to expound the contents of the divine word. They must take it or go without it, for they cannot be allowed to argue on the sceptic's ground when they please.

III. Another passage on the atonement follows after a few verses : *For when we were yet without strength, in due time Christ died for the ungodly. For scarcely for a righteous one will one die ; yet peradventure for a good man some would even dare to die. But God commendeth His love toward us, in that, while we were yet sinners, Christ died for us. Much more then, being now justified by His blood, we shall be saved from wrath through Him. For if, when we were enemies, we were reconciled to God by the death of His Son ; much more, being reconciled, we shall be saved by His life* (Rom. v. 6–10). The apostle, having described the fruits of justification,—peace with God, access, standing in grace, and the hope of glory,—proceeds to show that the Christian's hope is not disappointed. Two *à fortiori* arguments are used, both introduced by a MUCH MORE, and drawn, the one from the two states of the man, and the other from the two states of Christ. From the two states of the man he argues, that if we were justified when sinners, much more shall we be saved from wrath when made friends (ver. 9). From the two states of Christ he argues, that if our reconciliation was effected by the death of God's Son as a thing vast, arduous, and wonderful, much more, as if no further legal difficulty were to be encountered, shall we be saved by His life (ver. 10). As the force of these arguments can be seen only by comparison with the guilt of our natural condition, he uses four descriptive terms to exhibit this. We were WITHOUT STRENGTH, that is, unable to comply with any duty or command (ver. 6); UNGODLY, that is, without God, and violating duty at every turn (ver. 8);

SINNERS, that is, held under the bonds of guilt, and by nature attached to sin; ENEMIES (ver. 10), that is, either passively objects of God's displeasure, as some take it, or actively enemies of God in our disposition; which latter is the preferable view.[1] These four designations are mentioned with a view to commend the freeness and greatness of the divine love.

We limit our attention to the question of the atonement as developed in this passage. When Christ is represented as dying FOR THE UNGODLY (ver. 6), the question is, Are we to regard[2] this as a transaction in our stead, or merely for our benefit? Undoubtedly the former. And, to impress the idea of Christ's vicarious position, the apostle borrows an illustration from common life. Thus: Scarcely for a righteous man will one die: I say righteous, for[3] perhaps for a good man—that is, a great benefactor—some one would even dare to die. But in the world's history it was never heard of, that one died for an enemy. Now the commendation of divine love is, that Christ died for enemies and sinners. The apostle, in supplying this illustration, intimates that we are to reason from the one to the other; and if Christ's death is to be taken in the sense in which the death of one for another is here portrayed, the obvious meaning is, that one gives his life in the room of another. The death of Christ, far transcending every example of human love, which hardly ever dreamt of laying down one's life for a friend, was a display of love for enemies. The terms, and the entire character of the transaction as here described, allow us to form no other conclusion than that the death of Christ was vicarious. We have an unmistakeable description of the character of Christ's death, and of what the church must hold it to have been. No one, certainly, can understand this

[1] ἐχθροὶ ὄντες : these words refer to man's disposition. The great truth, that Christ's death ended God's hostility to us, is quite consistent with this.
[2] See a valuable note in Meyer's Commentary on the import of ὑπέρ and περί, and his reference to passages.
[3] The γάρ in the second clause of ver. 7 is not to be rendered YET; it leans on the tacit thought which we have brought out.

language in the sense that He suffered to give us an example of virtue. The illustration and reasoning show that the allusion is to a vicarious death.

From the Lord's vicarious death two important consequences are derived, and it is considered as standing in close CAUSAL connection with them both.

1. The apostle declares that we are JUSTIFIED BY HIS BLOOD (ver. 9). This expression means, not only His bloody death, but His whole sinless obedience, culminating in that bloody sacrifice. It is a synecdoche; and the apostle intimates that the sole cause of justification is the atonement, not our virtue, not our amendments, not the termination of our enmity already mentioned, not even our faith, however important this is as the instrument of reception. By that atoning blood sin is deleted as if it had never been, and the man is accepted. The apostle in this passage is content to put cause and effect together, without explaining how the result was brought about, because this had already been done in express terms. Now, when we are said to be justified by His blood, the expression intimates that we are not only discharged from deserved punishment, but personally accepted. The death of Christ is put in causal connection with the justification of our persons; but this could not have been unless it were a vicarious death, and a vicarious obedience accepted by Him who pronounces the acquittal. The apostle deduces, too, an important inference. He assumes that Christ's death put sinners on a new footing, a new standing before God; in a word, that it rectified their relation. And then he argues: " If justified as sinners by His blood, much more shall we as friends be saved from wrath through Him." This is an argument from the stronger reason.

2. The apostle next declares that we are RECONCILED TO GOD BY THE DEATH OF HIS SON (ver. 10). This is a phrase alternated with being justified. The term reconciliation, as we have seen, presupposes alienation, displeasure, or enmity on the part of the moral Governor of the world, and intimates that He

has cemented with us a new relation of friendship. That the
change is caused by the death of Christ, is here expressly
stated. In the language of Paul, where we chiefly find the
use of this expression, God is never said to be reconciled: we
are said to be reconciled to God. And the reason is, that in
ordinary language the action of reconciliation is described from
the side of the offending party. A prince is not said to be
reconciled to an offending subject, though it is he who lays
aside his displeasure: the subject is said to be reconciled to
him, because the transaction takes its designation from the
party offending. The atonement was interposed by God between His righteous wrath and us men in such a way as to put
humanity on a new and friendly relationship to God. When
the apostle affirms that we are reconciled to God by the death
of His Son, he means that the death of Christ removed all the
impediments on God's side, so that His just anger was averted,
and His free favour turned toward us.

Many interpret reconciliation as if it meant that there
never was estrangement on God's side, but only on man's side ;
and, consequently, that it is completed the moment we lay
aside our aversion, and by a course of repentance and loyal
obedience show ourselves well affected towards God. That
is not the apostle's meaning, as is proved by the slightest
examination of his words. He sets forth the vicarious nature
of Christ's death, and deduces reconciliation from it by the
connection of cause and consequence, alternating the words
RECONCILE and JUSTIFY as phrases descriptive of the same change
of relation. If justification is a judicial act of God implying a
change of relation on His side as well as on ours, reconciliation
implies the same, as appears from the words: " If we, being
enemies, were reconciled to God by the death of His Son."
The emphasis of the clause lies on the words BEING ENEMIES,
and it affirms that we were reconciled when enemies. If so,
it is self-evident that reconciliation to God does not consist
merely in laying aside OUR enmity. For how, on such a theory,

could we be said to be reconciled to God when WE WERE ENEMIES ?

On the contrary, reconciliation is caused by something objective (ver. 12)—by the death of God's Son. The apostle teaches that the vicarious death of Christ was the ground of restoration to the divine favour. The argument in this second case, altogether like the former, takes for granted that, in consequence of Christ's death, we passed into a new relationship to God—one of favour. It is as follows: If such a change of relation took place in virtue of Christ's death, if we were reconciled to God by the death of His Son, much more shall we, being admitted into friendship, be saved by His life. This is an argument à fortiori, based on the two states of Christ, taken in connection with the new relation in which we stand. And the apostle could not have argued in this way, if there had been nothing objective effected by the death of Christ.

The words mean that we were taken into the new relationship, or restored to favour, by the death of God's Son. The apostle thus connects cause and consequence, without defining in what way and by what steps the result was won. He declares that God Himself was the author of reconciliation by the death of His Son, and that we receive it in the free exercise of His grace. He does not base his reasoning, however, on the moral change effected: he does not say, If God loved us when we had no spiritual affection toward Him, how much more will He save us when we have amended our disposition and changed our sentiments towards Him! That would not be in keeping with the train or scope of his reasoning. He fixes his eye on the altered objective relation effected by the death of Christ. But when God stands related to us as a Father, and not as an offended Judge, then an inward change ensues: confidence and delight in Him must be the consequence, the immediate fruit, of reconciliation. Hence, glorying is mentioned as the result of receiving the objective atonement; and the apostle declares: "We also joy [better, glory] in God through our Lord Jesus Christ, by whom we have now received the atonement "[1] (ver. 11).

To this, however, it is urged as an objection, that such a mode of viewing reconciliation makes us at once enemies and friends; and it is said, Can we regard God as both hating and loving us; as evincing displeasure, and concerting the means of taking us into favour? This difficulty vanishes when we come to see that love and wrath well enough consist together, because men are presented to His view both as the creatures of His hand, and as sinners, yet the objects of His grace. He had wrath and enmity against their sin, according to His holy nature and the inalienable claims of justice; but He had love to His creatures, and a disposition to do them good. And the atonement, as an arrangement interposed between divine wrath on the one hand, and the sinful human race on the other, was the removal of all the impediments that stood in the way of the divine love. The text shows that free love provided the atonement, but that men were ACTUALLY TAKEN INTO FAVOUR ONLY ON THE GROUND OF SATISFACTION.

IV. Another memorable passage on the atonement is the section in the fifth chapter, which institutes a comparison between the disobedience of the first man and the obedience of the second man (vers. 12–19). From this section two verses may specially be selected, as giving a forcible illustration of the satisfaction of Christ: *Therefore, as by the offence of one judgment came upon* [better, *it is to*] *all men to condemnation; even so by the righteousness of one the free gift came upon* [better, *it is to*] *all men to justification of life. For as by one man's disobedience many were made sinners; so by the obedience of one shall many be made righteous* (Rom. v. 18, 19). The principal point to which the apostle directs attention, and which met him at this part of his argument, was, How could the satisfaction of

---

[1] The word καταλλαγή is the objective fact of the atonement considered as effecting reconciliation, and received as a gift. Christ's act is said to reconcile.

ONE MAN avail for many? And he shows that it is not surprising to find the entire ground of our redemption in the work of one, when we go back to the original constitution given to the human family: for we are saved upon the same principle, and by a constitution altogether similar. Without anticipating the result, let us analyse the passage.

In drawing the parallel between the two representative men in whom the whole human race is found respectively, Paul says: " By one man sin entered into the world, and death by sin" (ver. 12). To forestall mistakes, we must observe that this language does not mean by one man as created, but by one man as sinning. That this is the import of the expression, is proved by the frequent repetition of the same words: by one that sinned (ver. 16); by one man's offence (ver. 17); by one man's disobedience (ver. 19). The apostle does not mean that sin entered in consequence of some flaw or defect in the primeval constitution of man's nature, as if he were but earthly or carnal when he came from the Creator's hand.[1] The words before us mean, one man as he committed sin.

Another point that must be correctly apprehended in order to obtain a right view of the whole is, What is the import of SIN here described as entering? The answer is, that it refers to Adam's sinning act. This is evident from the language which the apostle holds all through the section, and which is frequently alternated with other terms of similar import. This terrible phenomenon—SIN personified through this and the two following chapters as a potentate, tyrant, or power—is described as entering into the world, where it was before unknown. It had a commencement in the world, and subordinated all to its sway. But while Adam's first sin is specially meant, as is clear from all the various antitheses in which it here stands to the atoning work of Christ, we are not of course to dissever it from the sinful nature to which it adheres.

[1] Usteri, in his *Pauline Doctrine*, reproduces the Schleiermacher theology to this effect ; but it has no support in Paul nor in any text of Scripture.

The next term is DEATH, represented as the penal consequence of sin. Temporal death is, beyond all doubt, comprehended in the apostle's words ; for he elsewhere says, that in
Adam all die (1 Cor. xv. 22). On the other hand, the limitation of the meaning to temporal death is quite unwarrantable,
when the contrast obviously leads us to the most extensive
signification. This is confirmed by the language of the New
Testament generally, and by the Pauline phraseology particularly (Rom. i. 32, vi. 21). The term death must be taken
here, and in the Mosaic narrative, in the widest sense, comprehending all that misery which flows from our estrangement
from God—the antithesis of divine life.

Next, the apostle draws a parallel between the two representative men as follows : As by one man sin entered into the
world, and death by sin ; so by one man righteousness entered
into the world, and life by righteousness. Such would have
been the two counterpart members, had the parallel been formally completed at the point where the comparison began
(ver. 13). But the latter member is withheld, and we have
only a compensation for it in the words, THE FIGURE OF HIM
THAT WAS TO COME[1] (ver. 14). The full parallel is resumed, and
at length completed, further down in the context (ver. 18). But
before advancing to that verse, which fills up the parallel (ver.
18), the apostle states some points of disparity, in which there
is A MUCH MORE, a preponderance, again and again repeated,
as found on the side of Christ. It is a much more of potency
in the causes in operation (ver. 15), and a much more also in
the results produced in connection with such causes (vers.
16, 17). Having stated the general resemblance, and certain

---

[1] Calvin well says on this clause : *Hæc particula posita est vice alterius
membri.* We cannot suppose the sense suspended by the long parenthesis between the ὥσπερ of ver. 12 and the οὕτω of ver. 18, more especially as the apostle
introduces points of dissimilarity as well as points of correspondence. Plainly,
the comparison must be completed before the points of dissimilarity begin (at
ver. 15). The best exegetes find the counterpart member to ὥσπερ, as we have
done, in τύπος τοῦ μέλλοντος. (See an essay by Dr. Schmid, *Tübinger Zeitschrift,*
1831.)

points of dissimilarity, the apostle returns to the broad outlines of the parallel, and gives full and formal expression to it
(ver. 18) ; and the words indicate a conclusion drawn from the
whole previous statement.

But we forbear further commentary, as we have adduced
the passage only as a striking exhibition and proof of the
atonement. The apostle is anticipating the objection, How
could the obedience of one avail for millions ?—a difficulty that
must be met. The current notion among the Jews of old, and
among self-righteous men' at all times, is: If our own virtue
and works of the law do not pass for righteousness, how can
another man's avail, and especially how can it avail for countless numbers ? The apostle's reply is, that this is readily
understood when men take into account the peculiar constitution under which the Creator saw meet at first to place the
human family. The principle on which we are saved is the
same as was originally set before mankind. The way of justification by the obedience of another stands on a similar footing
to the way in which we fell : the principle is that of ONE FOR
MANY. As by the trespass or offence of one it is to all men to
condemnation, so by the righteousness of one—in other words,
by the approved and accepted obedience of one—it is to all
men to justification of life. Here two things are comprehended
as standing in connection with the atonement : (1) the justification of the man, that is, of the person in his relative standing ;
(2) the restoration of the nature by the donation of life. The
former paves the way for the latter. The life is premial life,
and follows as the consequence of righteousness, but is comprehensive both of spiritual and eternal life. This life follows
as the reward of righteousness, according to the principle set
forth in the law : " This do, and thou shalt live."

The second of the verses above quoted grounds the former
by furnishing additional explanation. The two clauses of the
one (ver. 18) may be connected with the two clauses of the
other respectively (ver. 19) ; and the grounding particle *for*

links them together in this way : " Therefore, as by the offence
of one judgment came upon all men to condemnation,—FOR by
one man's disobedience many were made sinners,—even so by
the righteousness of one the free gift came upon all men unto
justification of life; FOR by the obedience of one shall many
be made righteous." What is the obedience of one, by which
many are made or constituted righteous ? This may easily be
perceived from the counterpart disobedience by which many
are made sinners. It is not enough to say that the death of
Christ is so called because on His part it was a proper act of
love. Nor will it suffice to say that the atonement is so called
because suffering was imposed by the Father's command, and
responded to on Christ's part by an act of obedience. These
views make no room for the element of active obedience, as
not less necessary than the suffering. The words are plainly
descriptive of the entire obedience of Christ, active and passive.
This is evident from the fact that by means of it many are
constituted righteous, which can only be by the double element;
and it is further evident from the disobedience of Adam in the
opposite member. For if Adam's trespass contains two parts,—
an obligation violated and a guilt incurred,—and if the second
man must enter into both, since the divine justice could not
permit either to be relaxed or modified by one jot or tittle, it
follows that in that obedience of one man, which makes many
righteous, we must comprehend both these elements. His obedience thus included all that was required of man in innocence,
and all that was justly incurred by man in his state of guilt.

This great transaction was not by accident. The obedience
of one for many, and as making many righteous, was the true
and intended effect of Christ's incarnation—the great compensation set over against the fall of Adam. It is the result of a
constitution expressly parallel to that under which man was
made, and, like it, of a positive and sovereign character; and
it is here said to be the principle of ONE FOR MANY. Scripture
thus puts the disobedience of Adam in express antithesis to

the obedience of Christ. It speaks as if there had been but two men in the world into whose obedience or disobedience their entire seed enters. And indeed there have been but two representative men, and under the one or the other we are all comprehended. A comparison of the two, such as is here instituted, greatly conduces to the correct apprehension of the constitution which it pleased God, in the exercise of sovereign dominion, to give to the human race. These two truths shed reciprocal light on each other, and are set over against each other. For this there may be many reasons; but one reason, besides the vivid contrast, undoubtedly is to furnish the only analogy which can be produced. Nor can I forbear to say that it would have contributed not a little to the clearer understanding of the whole subject, had the Scripture method on this great theme been universally followed. Had the atonement and the fall been more put in this contrast, the light shed by this means on both would have been steadier and clearer, and many a prejudice would have been removed. Many who have doubts of the one, would have had their difficulties overborne or removed by the evidence of the other.

To all the cavils of human reason the answer is easy. It does not fall to us to justify that constitution given to the first man, and renewed in the second man. Nor does it become us too curiously to inquire into the reasons of such an appointment, when we call to mind that the sovereign will of God, holy, wise, just, and good, is reason enough. To give reasons, argues a pretension to knowledge which is not given to us. Let it suffice that it pleased God to constitute man in a public head, who was made in the image of God, and summoned to the test of obedience in the full maturity of all his powers, in the possession of a sinless nature, and with a full knowledge, doubtless, of his representative position. The constitution given to man differed from that which was given to angels, who must have been placed on their own individual footing, from the fact that they partly stood and partly fell.

More than anything else, this original constitution given to man throws light on the atonement. We are redeemed in the same way : the obedience of one is the righteousness of many. This calls for a twofold submission on our part—a submission to the DIVINE SOVEREIGNTY which gave the constitution to which we have referred, and a submission to the divine WORD, which here emphatically proclaims it as a certain truth. We must accept both. Thus sin enters by the first man, and spreads through the race, and death by sin. On the contrary, righteousness, or the atonement, enters by the second man, and is unto all and upon all them that believe ; and life is by righteousness. This is the Pauline parallel; and I have only to add that it would have been well if human writers, in their discussions on the subject, had been content to receive this divine constitution on God's authority as a truth, and with the heart-loyalty due to His sovereign dominion. The whole matter has been complicated and perplexed by laborious attempts to commend it to the natural reason of men; all of them sorry efforts to make men believers by reason, whereas faith must stand, not in the wisdom of man, but in the authority of God.

The testimony of this passage is conclusive as to the great fact that the atoning obedience of Christ puts us into the category of righteous ones, for so the words signify.[1] It was the obedience of the Son of God, however ; for not only are we here to recall the primeval constitution, but also the divine dignity of the Surety. Not that He obeyed in the divine nature, but He who did obey was a divine person—the Son of God ; and it must never be forgotten that He took our nature as a workman takes a tool or instrument to accomplish a certain end. This obedience to the law in all its parts He

---

[1] κατιστάθησαν, rendered in the English version *were made*, is stronger than the Greek word warrants : it means, "were put into the class or category of" sinners, and into the category of righteous ones. How ? By the representative action of one for many.

required not for Himself, but wrought it out for us, that it might at once have infinite value, and be made an absolute gift.

V. Another passage of great importance on the atonement is the section in the sixth chapter, which sets forth the conscious relation which the apostle says he occupied to Christ in His death: *What shall we say then? Shall we continue in sin, that grace may abound? God forbid. How shall we, that are dead* [better, *that died*] *to sin, live any longer therein? Know ye not, that so many of us as were baptized into Jesus Christ were baptized into His death? that like as Christ was raised up from the dead by the glory of the Father, even so we also should walk in newness of life. For if we have been planted together* [better, *co-planted*] *in the likeness of His death, we shall be also in the likeness of* [better, *we shall at the same time belong to*] *His resurrection: knowing this, that our old man is crucified with Him* [better, *co-crucified*], *that the body of sin might be destroyed, that henceforth we should not serve sin. For he that is dead is freed* [better, *is justified*] *from sin. Now, if we be dead with Christ, we believe that we shall also live with Him* (Rom. vi. 1–8). This memorable passage must be clearly understood, because the same language recurs in many of the Pauline epistles. We have therefore to inquire whether the expressions represent the death of Christ as vicarious, or whether they are to be explained according to a mystical interpretation, without reference to the idea of substitution.

To understand what is meant by DYING WITH CHRIST, we must apprehend the connection. The apostle, after describing our standing in the second Adam (v. 12–19), had added, that where sin abounded, grace much more abounded. Perceiving the objection that would be made to such a view of grace, the apostle says, " Shall we continue in sin, that grace may abound ?" and rejects the imputation with abhorrence. Not content with this, he proceeds to prove that this perversion could not ensue, for a reason which touches the deep elements

L

of God's moral government, and renders it impossible. What is the reason he assigns ? It is not the influence of a new class of motives which he brings out at the end of the chapter, but a solid ground in law. He argues from a fact—the great objective change of relation intimated by dying with Christ.

We have to inquire, then, what is intimated by those expressions on which he lays the greatest stress of his argument (ver. 12) : DYING WITH CHRIST, and DYING TO SIN, BURIED WITH CHRIST, CO-CRUCIFIED and CO-PLANTED [1] with Him. One text will serve as a key to the meaning, viz., " We thus judge, that if one died for all, then all died," for so the words must be translated (2 Cor. v. 14). There the apostle, it is obvious, uses these two expressions interchangeably : HE DIED FOR ALL, and ALL DIED IN HIM. He describes the same thing from two different points of view. The first of the two describes the vicarious death of Christ as an objective fact ; the second sets forth the same great transaction, in terms which intimate that we too are said to have done it. Thus we may either say, CHRIST DIED FOR US ; or say, WE DIED IN HIM. We may equally affirm He was crucified for us, or we were co-crucified with Him. This alternating phraseology, duly observed, makes all plain. But it must be fully apprehended that we have NOT TWO ACTS presented to us by the expression,—one on Christ's side, and another on ours, that is, an experience on our side parallel to His. We have but ONE PUBLIC REPRESENTATIVE, CORPORATE ACT PERFORMED BY THE SON OF GOD, in which we share as truly as if we had accomplished that atonement ourselves.

The mistakes committed in the interpretation of this chapter of the epistle—and they have come down from ancient times—are mainly due to the fact that the ideas of the fifth chapter have not been carried into the sixth. If we carry the thought supplied by the representative character of the two Adams from the one chapter into the other, the difficulty vanishes. Nay, the very same form of expression is

---

[1] The preposition in composition retains its force in συνιτάφημιν, συνισταυρώθη, etc.

found in the fifth chapter in the statement: " By ONE MAN SIN
ENTERED into the world, and death by sin; and so death passed
upon all men, FOR THAT ALL SINNED " (Rom. v. 12). The meaning is, all men sinned in the first man's act of sin; for that
public act was representative, and common to all his offspring.
There have been, in fact, but two men in the world, with the
two families of which they are the heads; there have been
but two public representatives. The idea of Christ's Suretyship, and the representation of His atonement as the act of
one for many, run through the entire section, with only this
peculiarity or difference as compared with other passages, that
here WE are described as doing what our representative did;
that is, the one corporate act is described from our share in
the transaction. But let us notice the expressions.

It is said WE DIED TO SIN (ver. 2). As this phrase is
very much misunderstood, its meaning must be ascertained.
It frequently occurs in the Pauline epistles in different forms,
and uniformly alludes not to an inward deliverance from sin,
but to the Christian's objective relation, or to his personal
standing before God in the vicarious work of Christ; it means
that we are legally dead to sin in Christ.[1] This is rendered
quite certain by two other expressions occurring in the section.
The first of these passages applies the same language to the
Lord Himself; for He is said to HAVE DIED TO SIN ONCE (ver.
10). Now the only sense in which the Sinless One can be
regarded as dying to sin, is that of dying to its guilt, or to the
condemning power which goes along with sin, and which must
run its course, wherever sin has been committed. He died to
the guilt or criminality of sin, when it was laid on Him; cer-

---

[1] This mode of interpretation indicated by J. Alting in his Commentary, is
comparatively recent, and has mainly been advocated by recent Dutch divines,
Klinkenberg, Heringa, Vinke. Haldane, in his Commentary on Romans, maintains it; but it is not yet admitted by the Germans. The old view advocated
by the Reformers and Puritans, failed by making the whole too much a subjective experience, or an inward renovation. The origin of the misinterpretation
must be traced to the separation of the sixth chapter from the fifth, as if a wholly
new subject began at Rom. vi. 1.

tainly He did not die to its indwelling power. The second of
these passages shows that this dying was the ground or meritorious cause of our justification: "He that is dead has been
justified (not FREED, as it is unhappily rendered in the English
version) from sin" (ver. 7). The justification of the Christian
is thus based on his co-dying with Christ; that is, we are said
to have died when Christ died, and to have done what Christ
did. The words undoubtedly mean a co-dying with Christ in
that one corporate representative deed; that is, they mean that
we were one with Christ in His obedience unto death, as we
were one with Adam in his disobedience. Christ's death to
sin belongs to us, and is as much ours as if we had borne the
penalty. And the justification by which our persons are forgiven and accepted, has no other foundation. It is noteworthy that the fifth chapter, from which this idea is carried
over, describes all this in the third person; whereas the sixth
chapter describes it in the first person, and from our own share
in it.

It is also said in this section, that OUR OLD MAN IS CRUCIFIED,
or co-crucified, with Him. The entire section of which this is
a part, is to be regarded not as hortatory, but as the simple
statement of fact; it does not set forth anything done by us,
but something done on our account, or for our sake, by a Surety,
in whose performance we participate. But, it may be asked,
may we not hold with the great body of expositors, from the
Reformation downwards, that these varied expressions designate
two separate classes of actions,—one done by Christ, and a
similar or parallel one by us,—and that the phraseology must be
taken in two different senses as used respecting Christ, and as
used respecting us? No; the expressions are not to be taken
in a proper sense as applied to Christ, and in a figurative sense
as applied to us. The acts are NOT TWO, BUT ONE, described
from two different points of view. There is not one crucifixion
on the part of Christ, and a second, parallel and similar but
different, crucifixion on the part of His people. There is but

one corporate act, as we noticed in the previous chapter,—the act of one for many.[1]

But what is the OLD MAN that is said to be co-crucified with the Lord ? Does not this refer to inward corruption ? Though commentators have long expounded it in this way with a sort of common consent, such an explanation is untenable, as it would make the expression synonymous with the next clause, and thus not only yield a bald tautology, but give an instance of inept reasoning ; for the one clause is made the ground or condition of the other. The old man is crucified, IN ORDER THAT the body of sin, or sin within us as an organic body, might be destroyed. Now there must be a difference between the two clauses, as the former is in order to attain the latter. The old man said to be crucified with Christ, is therefore our old personality, or Adamic standing, which is terminated that we may have a new relationship to God in the crucified Surety ; a privilege which lays the foundation also for the destruction of inherent corruption. But these two (ver. 12)—person and nature—are not to be confounded ; nor will the apostle's reasoning admit any comment which confounds them.[2]

But, to bring the matter more fully home to the mind of his readers, the apostle says WE WERE BAPTIZED INTO HIS DEATH (ver. 3). The Lord, in the historic outline of His death, is presented to us as laden with sin, and satisfying divine justice ; and baptism, as a symbolical representation, exhibits our connection with Him, or participation in that great corporate act which was in the room of all His people. We are supposed to have done what He did, and to have undergone what He underwent, to satisfy divine justice. The symbol

[1] The notion of two acts, similar but separate, has led commentators and practical writers into a labyrinth of mysticism, which cannot be put into intelligible words. See the modern German exegetes as examples.

[2] The want of this distinction is the source of most of the modern theological confusion. The Reformers drew the line between justification and sanctification. Later divines called the two the relative and real, the forensic and inherent. But whatever name is used for the objective and subjective, we must maintain this distinction, or confound everything.

of baptism showed this, and the apostle recalls the fact that it was a baptism into His death, an emblem of oneness with Christ, or fellowship with Him in His death to sin (ver. 10).

But when it is said that we were CO-PLANTED with Him IN THE LIKENESS of His death, it may be asked, does not this seem to run counter to all that has been said as to the one corporate representative act of Christ? If mention is made of the likeness of His death, does not this seem to intimate two acts,—one on Christ's side, and one on ours? Does not this take away our attention from the objective act of substitution, to something more mystical in human experience analogous to the work of Christ? By no means. It is one act and one atonement in the room of sinners to which all these terms refer. And the expression, "in the likeness of His death," seems to be an allusion to baptism as an emblem, likeness, or symbolical representation.[1] The connection of the two verses, we think, proves this.

But another thought to be noticed is, that the oneness with Jesus in His death, or the co-dying with Him, secured the ulterior end of life. The DEATH WAS THE PRICE OF THE LIFE. The one was the cause, the other was the unfailing reward or consequence. We must put these two in juxtaposition.

First, then, all the above-named expressions, and others similar to them, point to a discharge from a hard master. That master is SIN, which is described through these two chapters as a mighty potence, or tyrant, that entered into the world by one man, and reigned over the human race. This is more than a personification, more than a figure of speech, for the apostle is struggling to express a relation where human analogies break down. He has no term by which to describe it but the power of a potentate, or of a master, over his slave. By death this yoke is broken, according to the language of Job:

---

[1] J. Alting, in his valuable Commentary, proposes this exposition on Rom. vi. 5.

" There the wicked cease from troubling; and the servant is free from his master" (Job iii. 19). The apostle declares that not only was the death of Christ a substitution in our room, but that, in consequence of its being a definite and express substitution, we may be said to have done what He did. And, in virtue of our oneness with Him, we are discharged from sin as a master.

But THIS SECURES LIFE; for this life is the fruit, effect, or reward consequent on the former. If the Christian died with Christ, he will also live with Him, by a bond as sure as that which obtains between antecedent and consequent, between Christ's own death and resurrection. If we died with Him, we believe that we shall also live with Him (ver. 8). But if that is so,—if Christians live with Christ as surely as they died with Him,—it follows that their life can no longer be devoted to sin, but to God, as was the life of Christ. They have fellowship with the Lord in His RESURRECTION-LIFE, a participation of the same holy LIFE that the Lord lives in heaven, and cannot, therefore, surrender themselves to a course of sin.

Now this is the grand answer to the current cavil or objection to the doctrines of grace mentioned at the beginning of the chapter. The apostle, in refutation of it, appeals to the deepest principles in the moral government of God. He proves that Christ's vicarious death, for the satisfaction of divine justice, and for the annihilation of sin, opens a way for the entrance of a new reign of life. He makes it indubitably evident that Christ's own resurrection-life, which comes in to renovate and transform humanity, renders a life of sin, or a continuance in sin, impossible. MOTIVES may go far; and they, too, are called into exercise. But this is a sphere immensely elevated above the power of mere motives. THE LIFE OF CHRIST ENTERS TO RENEW MANKIND, AND TO SECURE HOLINESS.

VI. A further testimony, of much weight on the doctrine of the atonement, is as follows: *For what the law could not do, in*

*that it was weak through the flesh, God, sending His own Son in
the likeness of sinful flesh* [better, *in the likeness of the flesh of
sin*], *and for sin* [better, *as a sin-offering*] *condemned sin in the
flesh; that the righteousness of the law might be fulfilled in us,
who walk not after the flesh, but after the Spirit* (Rom. viii. 3).
The apostle had stated at the commencement of the chapter,
that, notwithstanding the indwelling sin which still adheres to
us, and which he described in the previous chapter (vii. 15–25),
there is no condemnation to the Christian; and then he subjoins the text under our notice as the ground of the non-
condemnation, and of the deliverance from the law of sin and
death.   The passage amounts to this, that there is NO CONDEM-
NATION, because SIN HAS BEEN CONDEMNED IN CHRIST'S FLESH,[1]
and the approved fulfilment of the law is laid to our account.
The following elements of the atonement come to light in this
passage :—

1. The source of the atonement is traced to God the Father
having a Son to send.   The language emphatically declares
that the whole atonement owed its origin to God as its source,
and that it must be read off from the act of the Father as
sending His Son to offer it.   It emanated from God as its
fountain; for it could not have been extorted from Him had
He not spontaneously devised and executed it.   And as He
was the source from whom it came, so was He the authority
by whom it was accepted as a complete satisfaction.   What
was prepared by God, must of necessity be acceptable to
Him.

2. The person by whom the redemption-work was finished,
was the eternal Son, His own Son, His proper Son.   This
title indicates not only filiation, but true and proper Godhead;
for He is the Son of God in a unique sense, not by adoption,
not by incarnation, not by resurrection, but by an eternal act
of generation, in consequence of which He is designated the

---

[1] The two expressions, οὐδὶν κατάκριμα and κατέκρινε τὴν ἁμαρτίαν, must be seen
together.

only-begotten Son. And the influence of the divine nature of the Lord on His whole atoning work is not obscurely indicated: it was the work of a divine person, and owed to this its boundless value and dignity. Thus the Lord Jesus, in his redemption-work, cannot be regarded as mere man, but as God-man, in whom both natures concurred at every step to the production of a joint result. The work is thus one, because the person is one. It was the deity of God's Son that gave, His redemption-work a value which is altogether infinite ; and, thus viewed, we find that it not only emanated from God, but was consummated by the workmanship of Him who was God.

3. The Son of God was sent in THE LIKENESS OF SINFUL FLESH ; that is, of the flesh[1] of sin. This expression must be carefully investigated, lest we should either err by overstatement, or come short of its meaning by defect of statement. It goes very deep, but we must be careful to fathom it. One thing is self-evident : the language must be understood as affirming the true incarnation of the Son of God, and as ascribing to Him a real humanity, in contrast with every Docetic or phantom theory of His becoming man. And further, the union of Godhead and manhood in the one person of the eternal Son carried with it this consequence, that it must needs be sinless humanity, inasmuch as the Son of God could not have united to Himself anything sinful. By the operation of the Holy Ghost, His humanity, which never for an instant existed apart from the divine person of the Son, was generated pure ; like sinful flesh indeed, but not sinful flesh. And this was secured by the fact, that though He took His flesh from Adam through the Virgin, He never was in Adam's covenant, but the second Adam, the restorer. He was a kinsman-Redeemer, to be within the pale of our humanity; but He neither derived any taint of mind or body by transmission from Adam, nor contracted any guilt for which He was personally responsible.

---

[1] ἐν ὁμοιώματι σαρκὸς ἁμαρτίας ; on which Chrysostom says, οὐδὲ γὰρ ἁμαρτωλὸν σάρκα εἶχεν.

The import of the expression we are considering is not exhausted, however, by the idea of a bare incarnation, or His becoming man. That, of course, lies at the foundation of the whole ; but there is a further thought, which cannot be excluded. The statement that He was sent in the likeness of sinful flesh, implies that between Him and other men no perceptible difference could be traced ; that as to personal appearance, in weakness and exhaustion, in infirmity and weariness, in sorrow and mortality, He was in all respects made like unto His brethren. The language intimates that He entered into the human family poor and despised, hungry and thirsty, subject to the ordinary toils of labour in an earthly calling, and to the fatigue consequent upon it ; a man of sorrows, and acquainted with grief ; not exempt from the fear of death nor from actual mortality. In short, He came within the circle of humanity, and into all that this entailed, so far as it could be experienced by One who was at once sinless man and the beloved Son of God. But several observations are here necessary to put this matter in its proper light, which is rarely, if ever, expounded with all the fulness and precision which are necessary.

a. We are not to consider the Lord as assuming this likeness to the flesh of sin in a mere arbitrary way, and without sufficient cause. It is not enough to say that He assumed this likeness to fallen humanity for no reason at all, or merely for the purpose of being like His brethren. Though His participation in our nature, in its sufferings and temptations, qualified Him to sympathize with us, and fitted Him to be a merciful and faithful High Priest (Heb. ii. 17), we are not warranted to conclude that this was all the reason for which He was sent in the likeness of sinful flesh. He was found in fashion as a man, and in the likeness of a sinful man, so that no difference could be discovered between His flesh, which was sinless, and that of other men, who are sinful.

b. We are not to regard the Lord as deriving those sinless infirmities by transmission from Adam or from His mother by the necessity of nature. They were by no means an inevitable accompaniment of the incarnation, or of wearing our humanity. Mortality, which some suppose to be all that is meant by the phrase under consideration, was not a necessary adjunct of assuming our humanity, any more than were the heaviness and agony, the sorrows and fainting, the tears, trials, and temptations, by which He was made like unto His brethren. They could not come upon Him in any other way than sin came upon Him. They came upon Him, not as a personal legacy by derivation or transmission from the first man, or from the fact of His entering into our world, but simply on the ground of His voluntary Suretyship. They were in His case the consequences and effects of sin, but of sin not His own, and merely borne by imputation. In other words, He was the curse-bearer because He was the sin-bearer.

c. We cannot regard sin as attaching to the earthly life of Christ. A certain class of crude divines, who know neither what they say nor whereof they affirm, have of late been asserting a modification of Irvingism, to the effect that sin belongs, so to speak, to that life in which Christ knew no sin, and that He has " done with sin in having done with the life to which sin belonged." [1] The great error of Irving, who maintained that our Lord assumed fallen flesh, was precisely similar. But from this it would follow that the mortality and sorrows, the temptations and trials to which He was subjected, fell upon Him by the necessity of nature, not by substitution or voluntary Suretyship. That supposition subverts the very principle of substitution, which takes for granted that a sinless person, with a complete exemption from sin and all its consequences, spontaneously entered into the position and responsi-

[1] In this crude style do many Plymouthists express themselves (see Darby's *Girdle of Truth*, p. 298 ; and M'Intosh, *Synopsis*, iii. p. 454) ; not apprehending that if Christ was personally in Adam's covenant, He could not have been a Mediator for others ; for He would not have been without personal guilt and corruption.

bilities of the sinner. The crude theory to which we have
referred, is contradicted by the entire provisions and arrangements of the incarnation. The Lord Jesus never was in Adam's
covenant, but came as the second Adam, the counterpart of
the first; and His entrance into humanity by the supernatural
conception, was meant to obviate the imputation of Adam's
first sin, as well as the transmission of any of its consequences
by the necessity of nature. He was PERSONALLY exempt, both
as the incarnate Son and as the second man, from all the guilt,
as well as from all the consequences connected with the guilt,
of the first Adam. He was within the human family as a
kinsman-Redeemer, and not outside its pale; but that was all
which His incarnation as such, or simply considered, properly
involved. To suppose that sin, or any of its consequences,
attached to the person of the Lord by the fact of assuming our
humanity or entering into human life, is a lamentable confusion
of idea. It perplexes and disorganizes everything; it confounds
things that differ.

The personal and the official in the life of Jesus must
always be distinguished. These can never be merged in each
other, without the most mischievous and fatal issues. The
personal relation is one thing, the official is another. The
former brings Christ before us as a divine person, and calls
attention to a sinless humanity,—that is, to a humanity according to its idea or normal condition; and if the mediation
on which He entered had not involved the propitiation for
sin as well as the obedience originally devolved on man as
man, the Lord Jesus would doubtless have appeared in a
noble humanity, in the same humanity, at least, as that which
Adam possessed before the fall. But this could not be on
account of the problem to be solved. At present, all I wish is
to show that, in our conceptions, the personal must be distinguished from the official. The personal relation of Jesus
possessed a full immunity from the imputation of guilt, and
from inherent taint in every form. The personal underlies the

official; and if we should suppose that sin attached in any sense to the person of the Lord, or to the human life in which He came, He would have been incapacitated for His work of mediation and vicarious obedience. There could have been no substitution in our room and stead.

This will enable us to understand the words, " in the likeness of sinful flesh." The expression points to the effects of which sin was the cause, but sin not His own. The consequences resulting from the imputation of sin to Jesus were such, that He was in all points made like the brethren, or sent in the likeness of the flesh of sin; that is, subject to suffering and mortality, as if there had been no difference between mankind and Him. And when we call to mind what we have elsewhere proved, that He was the sin-bearer from the moment of assuming our humanity, we have at hand a ready explanation of the otherwise inexplicable fact, that He came among men as if He were one of them, exposed to sorrow and temptation, suffering and death. His human nature never existed apart from personal union to the Son of God, nor apart from sin-bearing; and hence He appeared in the likeness of the flesh of sin, not by a mere arbitrary assimilation to us men, but because He bore in His own body the weight of imputed sin; a fact which gave rise by legitimate consequence to such results.

The apostle states that God, in preparing a body for Christ, sent Him in a humanity, not such as it was in a state of integrity, when it was beautiful and glorious, but in a form such as it now is, viz., as bearing the sad marks of sin. Thus no perceptible difference appeared between His nature and ours, not because precisely the same flesh was transmitted to Him that goes down from Adam to his posterity, but because He took upon Him, by voluntary Suretyship, that load of imputed guilt, which carried in its penal consequences all that He endured of abasement and heaviness, temptation, suffering, and mortality. It was still, however, officially assumed, not personally inherited. It was sin not His own; and it was a humiliation and a cruel crucifixion to which He submitted, not because He must, but because He was pleased so to do. In a word, He was so like the flesh of sin when found in fashion as a man, so tempted in all points like as we are, that no difference was perceptible to any eye. That humanity so abased, and suffering from the effects of sin, must have been a vast humiliation for such a person, may easily be supposed. Yet God sent His Son to wear humanity in such a form; and the reason of all this is immediately subjoined, as we have next to notice.

4. The words, FOR SIN, or, more correctly, SIN-OFFERING, connected with the words on which we have been commenting, convey this meaning, that He came in the likeness of sinful flesh because He was a sin-offering or a sin-bearer. The first Adam, ushered into a world without sin, was provided with a nobler body. The second Adam, immensely greater than he, came among men from another sphere, and showed Himself in the likeness of the flesh of sin, in meanness and abasement. Some limit the likeness of sinful flesh to this, that He was subject to suffering and death. But while these elements are unquestionably included as important ingredients, they are not all, nor do they exhaust the apostolic idea.

The expression, FOR SIN, is by some regarded as denoting that Christ was cruelly put to death, or treated with sinful malice and insult. But such a comment cannot be made even exegetically plausible; the words will not bear it. Another comment is to the effect that He was sent on account of sin, as the cause which weighed with God to send Him. The meaning, on this supposition, will be, that God intended to punish sin by means of Christ; and but for such a design, it might have been thought that He was visited with suffering without sufficient cause. This is a tenable comment. But of all the interpretations, by far the most natural is the mode of construing which refers the words to the sin-offering, or to an

THE EPISTLE TO THE ROMANS.

atoning sacrifice. In confirmation of this, we find the phrase
so used in the Epistle to the Hebrews[1] (Heb. x. 6), and in the
Septuagint version of Isaiah, where Christ's soul is said to be
given as an offering for sin (Isa. liii. 10), as well as in many
other places in the same version (Lev. iv. 35, v. 6, vi. 17).
The sense will be as follows:—By such a sacrifice for sin, the
sacrifice of His own body, though He owed nothing, and was
under no liability, He condemned sin in the flesh. As Christ
is elsewhere directly and by implication called a sacrifice, I do
not see that there ought to be any doubt whether this is the
meaning of the Pauline expression. Besides, on this explanation, everything will be found to fall into proper order in
the structure of the sentence, without any ellipsis or any word
to be supplied: it will be construed with what precedes, not
with what follows. The only objection that can be made to
this interpretation is, that the passage does not make mention
of Christ's death, but of His mission. But there can be no
objection on that ground: for we often find similar phrases in
connection with the propitiation of Christ, the sending being
for the sake of the death, and comprehending it (1 John iv.
9–10). We hold, then, that the expression denotes a propitiatory sacrifice, a sin-offering.

5. But it is added, that by this means God CONDEMNED SIN
IN THE FLESH. To apprehend the meaning of this phrase, it
must be noticed that sin is still personified, as it was in the
three previous chapters. The apostle speaks of sin entering
into the world, and reigning over the human family as a
potence, monarch, or cruel master (Rom. v. 12, 17), and as
exercising an authority, from which we are legitimately rescued
only by a death to sin (Rom. vi. 2). The reason of this peculiar
phraseology may be, that a distinction can be drawn between

---

[1] Περὶ ἁμαρτίας, sin-offering. Origen interpreted it piacular sacrifice. The
great Lutheran divines, for a time, also took this view of the phrase here,—
Melancthon, Chemnitz (Ex. Conc. Trid. i. 141), Balduin, Spener (die Evangelische Glaubens-gerechtigkeit, p. 600).

the man and the sin which enslaves him; God condemning the man, not as His workmanship, but as he has sin. Sin destroys the person, and being therefore much like a person, is capable of being personified. From the passage where he first spoke of its entrance (v. 12), up to this point, the apostle has been personifying sin; and hence we have no warrant to take the word SIN in any other acceptation in the passage before us. We must still regard SIN in this passage as the potentate that has held the human family under his power. But when Christ was sent by the Father to engage with this enemy, He overcame him, judged, and condemned him.

But we have next to notice how God CONDEMNED SIN. The same personification as was before used, is still continued. Sin is spoken of as a person judged at a higher tribunal, and righteously condemned. In consequence of this, he has no further claim to those over whom he had previously tyrannized, for they are now set free. No other signification can be attached to the word CONDEMNED but such as is identical with the meaning of the word in the first clause of the chapter; for the no-condemnation which believers enjoy, is based on the condemnation of sin, which was accomplished in the flesh of Christ.

The question, indeed, as to the flesh, in which sin is said to have been condemned, is variously answered by different interpreters. But the connection decides that the allusion is to the human flesh assumed by Christ; that is, to the same person of whom he had said that He was sent in the likeness of sinful flesh. The apostle plainly refers to the flesh of Christ, and intimates that God condemned sin on Him as the sinless sin-offering. He satisfied the divine claims, partly by His perfect obedience,—that is, by what the Son of God, as sent into the world, rendered in our room,—partly by bearing the curse of the law,—in a word, by SINLESS SIN-BEARING; which may be taken as the descriptive formula for the atonement. And in consequence of this vicarious work, sin was condemned in His flesh, and lost its power over us.

But there are two ways in which this allusion to the condemnation of sin has been expounded. Some less accurately explain the expression in a more subjective sense, viz. of abolishing, or eradicating sin.[1] That cannot be accepted as the meaning of the word, which has always a judicial idea. Hence, others more happily take the term in its proper meaning, as denoting that God judicially condemned sin in the flesh of Christ, when He offered Himself as a sin-offering. The term, wherever we find it, intimates a judicial sentence (Rom. ii. 1, v. 18). In short, it is a condemnation that frees us from condemnation, the sentence being executed on our Surety (Gal. iii. 13; 1 Pet. ii. 24). The language denotes that Jesus was visited with penal suffering, because He appeared before God only in the guise of our accumulated sin; not therefore as a private individual, but as a representative, sinless in Himself, but sin-covered, loved as the Son, but condemned as the sin-bearer, in virtue of that federal union between Him and His people, which lay at the foundation of the whole. Thus God condemned sin in His flesh, and in consequence of this there is no condemnation to us.

The apostle furthermore states all this as a result which the law could do nothing to effect. And as to the philological construing of the sentence, the first part of the verse may be fitly placed in apposition with the whole statement, in the following simple way: " A thing impossible [2] for the law, in that it was weak through the flesh."

6. The last point to be mentioned is, that Christ was made the sin-offering, and condemned sin in the flesh, for this further

---

[1] This subjective exposition, proposed by the Socinians, has latterly found support from many evangelical divines; but it cannot be vindicated, because κατέκρινε has a forensic meaning, and no example can be adduced to prove that it means to *abolish*, apart from a judicial sentence.

[2] There are three modes of construing the sentence. Luther resolved it, *What the law could not do, God did ;* Winer makes it an anakolouthon; Fritzsche, followed by Philippi, makes τὸ ἀδυνατὸν τοῦ νόμου, as apposition to the whole sentence, thus: *a thing* [*or, the thing*] *impossible for the law.* The last is the simplest, and most natural.

M

object, THAT THE RIGHTEOUSNESS OF THE LAW MIGHT BE FUL-
FILLED IN US. That is so like another expression of the same
apostle, that the two passages may fitly be compared for mutual
elucidation (2 Cor. v. 21). This expression cannot be referred
to any inward work of renovation; for no work or attainment of
ours can with any propriety of language be designated a "fulfilling of the righteousness of the law." The words, "the righteousness of the law," are descriptive of Christ's obedience as the work
of one for many (Rom. v. 18). This result is delineated as the
end contemplated by Christ's incarnation and atonement, and intimates that as He was made a sin-offering, so are we regarded as
fulfillers of the law. The one was with a view to the other (ἵνα).
And when the righteousness of the law is said to be fulfilled IN
US, the meaning is that it belongs to us, and is applied to us in
consequence of that union by which Christ abides in us, and we
in Him.[1] It is fulfilled in us, as if we had done it all ourselves.

VII. Another passage on the atonement is to this effect:
*If God be for us, who can be against us? He that spared not
His own Son, but delivered Him up for us all, how shall He not
with Him also freely give us all things? Who shall lay anything
to the charge of God's elect? It is God that justifieth; who is
he that condemneth? It is Christ that died, yea rather, that is
risen again, who is even at the right hand of God, who also maketh
intercession for us* (Rom. viii. 31–34). Here the apostle ex-
tols the privileges of those who are completely freed from
condemnation by the atonement. And when we analyze these
triumphant questions, which follow each other in rapid succession, we perceive that the atonement is a real transaction,
furnishing the fullest security for real persons. Beholding
enemies and opposition on every side, the apostle confidently
defies them, on the ground that God is for us (ver. 31). But
that challenge is based upon another statement which connects
the Christian's safety with the atonement (ver. 32).

---

[1] This is the exposition of the best Lutheran divines of the post-Reformation
age—Calovius, Spener, and others; of Jacomb, Brown of Wamphray, etc.

Before entering on the explanation of the clauses, it is necessary to define the import of the words, HIS OWN SON. These words carry with them the idea of a proper Son, of a Son according to divine relationship prior to His incarnation; and every one who reads the words without prepossession, and with a simple desire to find out the meaning of the writer, is naturally led to refer them to the divine Sonship. The apostle's expression is intended to bring out two things: on the one hand, the strong love-relation which the Father occupied to the person of the Mediator; and, on the other hand, the infinite dignity and value attaching to whatever was done by the Son of His love. Furthermore, to apprehend the thought here brought before us, and how the Son is said to be delivered, it must be noted that we cannot suppose the three divine persons in the Godhead without any natural order of being, of willing, and of working; for the Father is said to have given the Son, and evinced His infinite love by giving Him. We cannot suppose that the second person assumed our nature merely by compact or agreement, without any relation of natural order; for such a notion would be out of harmony with the entire language of Scripture, which always represents the Father as sending His Son, or the first person as giving the second.[1] The love to sinners discovered in redemption is thus seen in its first origin in the Father.

Next, the scope of the apostle's argument, and the nature of it, must be distinctly traced. It is an argument from the greater to the less; the same style of reasoning of which we have already had some striking examples in this epistle (Rom. v. 9, 10). The argument is, that He who gave the greater, will certainly give the less; that He whose love surmounts the greatest difficulties, will not be baffled by what comparatively is much less arduous. And He amplifies the infinite love of God to make the cogency of the reasoning the stronger and more forcible. When God gave His Son FOR US, the expression

[1] See Vitringa's Latin and Dutch replies to Roëllius on Christ's Sonship.

undoubtedly means that He gave Him for our good, for our advantage. But the inquiry still remains: In what sense, and with what peculiar force, are we to understand that the death of Christ was for our good? Was it so by example, doctrine, or instruction? or was it because He died a vicarious death when we should have died,—a punishment in the place of those who must otherwise have perished? That is a point to be decided by other elements and expressions that enter into the description of His death; and they have already been under our examination in other passages. The giving up of the Son of God, here referred to, certainly does not mean for our benefit, in a vague and indefinite sense; for the inference deduced from it, that all things will be conferred along with Christ, plainly refers to the idea of substitution. Did not many pious men in the Jewish nation give themselves for the good of their countrymen? Were not many prophets and righteous men slain? But of whom was it ever said that their sufferings were the means of all other blessings that were conferred on others? On the contrary, the blood of Abel and of all the martyrs rather cried for vengeance. But here it is said that WITH CHRIST CRUCIFIED all good things were conferred.

In this passage there is first a statement of fact, and then an argument founded upon it. It is the statement of fact exhibiting the source, nature, and scope of the atonement, with which we have to do. The great argument practically deduced from it, supplies an inexhaustible ground of confidence and expectation.

1. The first thing in the statement of fact is: " God SPARED NOT His own Son." This expression occurs several times[1] in the New Testament with an allusion to punishment. Thus it is said of the Jews, that God *spared not* the natural branches (Rom. xi. 21); of the angels that sinned, that God *spared them not*, but cast them down to hell (2 Pet. ii. 4); and of the old world, that God *spared not* the old world, but saved Noah

---

[1] See De Haas, *over Romeinen*, v. tot. viii. 1793.

(2 Pet. ii. 5). The expression, as applied to the Son of God, means that God did not withhold Him, the constituted surety of others, from the abasement and suffering which must needs be borne in the execution of His function, but dealt with Him according to strict justice. Though essentially a divine person, He is here considered as the Son of God assuming our nature with the sin and punishment which are properly ours. Hence, notwithstanding the infinite and eternal love with which He was regarded as the Son, and which never could be lowered or withdrawn, God spared Him not. He was at once loved and not spared, according to the twofold relation which belonged to Him, as the Son of God and as man's surety. There is nothing incongruous in this. He was, on the one hand, the object of love as the Son of God, and also as the sinless fulfiller of the law (John x. 17). But, on the other hand, He was the object of punitive visitation, and not spared, as the surety and the sin-bearer.

The words here used seem intended to recall the human analogy in the case of Abraham, and certainly suggest that it was a sort of violence to the Father-love of God when He spared Him not. What does this presuppose? It assumes that He would have spared His Son had He wished to execute upon us the punishment we had incurred. He would have spared His Son, and removed the cup of suffering from Him, had He not purposed to confer upon us all conceivable good. But, in love to us, He spared not His own Son. He removed not the cup from Him, that it might never be presented to us. This scripture connects the Christian's safety under divine protection with the fact that God spared not His own Son,—a phrase which implies that He spared not the Surety, that He might rescue us.

The second thing in the statement of fact is: "God DE-LIVERED[1] UP His Son." This is not precisely synonymous with the former, nor quite the same as the expression, "He gave

---

[1] See J. Alting on the passage, and his proof that this comprehends a delivering over by God to human violence.

His only-begotten Son" (John iii. 16); at least there is a shade of difference. In the phrase before us, there is the further idea that the supreme God delivered Him into the hands of men, to be treated as if in reality He were the malefactor which they represented Him to be. This delivery into the hands of sinners has already been explained by us (Acts ii. 23). Judas and the high priest, with the council, were concerned in it; but there was a hand above theirs, and there is nothing to prevent us seeing a principal and an instrumental cause. The unworthy instruments of this delivery only sought to gratify their malice; the just Judge acted righteously. Christ was tried and sentenced at a human tribunal, which was but the visible foreground of an invisible trial in which the righteous God was judging righteously, for human guilt was laid upon the person of the Substitute. For wise reasons, already noticed, God arranged the events of the atoning sacrifice in such a way that Christ was not to be cut off by the immediate hand of God, but by men who were His hand, and only gratified their malice against the representative of God. The human judge, who in the most unprecedented way absolved and yet condemned, declared Him faultless and yet passed sentenced against Him, represented in the transaction the Judge of all the earth, who regarded Christ in a similar way. The human judge could only pass a sentence that would affect His body; but another sentence from a higher tribunal took effect upon His soul, and brought home the wrath of God. And under this invisible infliction the Lord experienced agony and desertion; under this He poured forth His complaint, His strong crying and tears, and endured that penal death which rescues us from the second death.

A further statement is, that the Son of God was delivered up FOR US ALL. As we have already noticed the substitution underlying the passage, we do not need to return to this, and only further inquire for whom all this was done. They are special persons; but the apostle does not say for all, but for

US ALL. And when we ask who they were, the obvious answer is, that they were the believing men to whom Paul wrote, and who were joined with himself. They are the same persons in reference to whom the apostle said, " If God be for US, who can be against US ?" They are the same parties who are described all through the epistle, and specially designated in the context as the predestinated, the called and justified ; in a word, they are the true church of God, for whom Christ died. It cannot be said that God is FOR ALL AND EVERY ONE, since there are many who are without reconciliation, and have Him not as a protector and defender.[1]

2. If such is the statement of fact, the argument based upon it is in the highest degree important. It is a form of reasoning from the greater to the less—from the stupendous act of God in delivering up His Son, to the lesser blessings which go along with it and are appended to it,—thus : He who gave the greater, will not grudge or withhold the less. The passage, too, takes for granted that the death of Christ altered our relation, making us, of enemies, the friends of God and the objects of divine protection. The argument is : He that did all this for sinners, will not abandon us when friends ; He who gave the greater, will not grudge the less.

The only point further demanding notice is furnished by the striking antithesis : " Who is he that condemneth ? It is Christ that died, yea rather, that is risen again" (ver. 34). This challenge as to its import gives a thought of the same kind with what was considered above at the commencement of this chapter (Rom. viii. 1, 3). The non-condemnation of the elect—that is, of every one for whom Christ died—is here affirmed in the most emphatic way by this triumphant challenge. The justice of God was satisfied for them ; and the challenge is : Who can condemn one for whom He died ? In a word, everything concurs to proclaim aloud the vicarious

[1] The explanation of this class of texts is easy, if we consider that the apostle, under the US and WE, comprehends the redeemed church of Christ.

death of Christ for our redemption, and none can condemn them.

VIII. Other allusions to the atonement, though more indirect and less express in statement, occur in the Epistle to the Romans. Thus the apostle refers to the connection between the purchase of a people and Christ's dominion over them when he says, " For to this end Christ both died, and rose, and revived, that He might be Lord both of the dead and living" (Rom. xiv. 9). The special reference of the atonement, too, comes to light emphatically in the descriptive name for a Christian—" one for whom Christ died" [1] (Rom. xiv. 15). Another passage may be noticed, containing a quotation from a Messianic psalm : " The reproaches of them that reproached Thee fell upon me" (Rom. xv. 4 ; Ps. lxix. 9). The words contain an allusion to the atonement, from which the ethical precept is enforced, as in many other passages (2 Cor. viii. 9). It is not enough to say with some that the words describe Christ as deeply affected, from the zeal animating Him, with reproaches cast upon God ; nor to say that, from the intimate fellowship between Him and the Father, He endured all that was cast on the Father. Nor do the words set forth the punishment of blasphemers pronounced on Christ. They rather intimate that sins, bringing dishonour upon God, were in their guilt laid [2] on the Lord Jesus, or so imputed to Him that He bore them in His own body, as if He were guilty and men were innocent. Hence He did not please Himself ; and from this the apostle enforces conformity to His example (comp. 1 Pet. iii. 18).

---

[1] We shall consider this title of a Christian below, when we come to 1 Cor. viii. 11.

[2] Bengel, who apprehends this passage more profoundly than other commentators, thus expounds it. See also Hofmanni *demonstratio*, l.c.

SEC. X.—THE TESTIMONY IN THE FIRST EPISTLE TO THE CORINTHIANS.

During Paul's three years' residence at Ephesus, he learned that doctrinal and practical corruptions, calling for prompt correction, had crept into the recently founded church of Corinth, and he sent from Ephesus (1 Cor. xvi. 8) his first epistle, containing a solemn warning, and a call for the immediate exercise of discipline (1 Cor. v. 1–5). Peculiar corrections of various kinds were needed to bring back the disciples to their true position; and in dealing with these abuses, the apostle takes occasion to exhibit the bearings of the atonement in a great variety of lights applicable to their religious condition. He places these corruptions one by one in the light of Christ's redemption-work, and refutes them from that central truth.

I. When party-spirit and undue attachment to the individual peculiarities or gifts of human teachers were to be corrected, the apostle exhibits the absurdity and self-contradiction of indulging this spirit in the following way: *Was Paul crucified for you? or were ye baptized in the name of Paul?* (1 Cor. i. 13.) He shows the Corinthians that this was a tendency at once incongruous and misplaced in Christianity, because they did not owe their redemption to the ministers by whom they believed; that only One was the true master; and that His unique authority, to which too much deference could never be paid, was based on His redemption-work. Nothing more convincingly shows that the atonement was in its nature different from a martyr's testimony, and from all mere example or instruction, however this might be confirmed by exposure to peril, or by actually sealing the testimony with blood.

The phraseology here used, shows that the meaning conveyed by the expression, CHRIST WAS CRUCIFIED FOR US, is, that

He satisfied divine justice in our stead.   As an illustration, the apostle spoke of one man dying for another who was a righteous or good man (Rom. v. 7).   Yet, when Christ is said to have been crucified for us, the meaning is, that He by substitution bore our sins, and brought in eternal redemption.   This question, WAS PAUL CRUCIFIED FOR YOU? contrasting Paul's work with Christ's, shows that Christ's death was for a wholly different end than can be competently applied to one man's act for another.   We may be required to put life to hazard for the brethren, and to fill up what is behind of the sufferings of Christ (2 Tim. ii. 10; Col. i. 24); but in what sense?   Not as dying for their sins, but to confirm the truth of the gospel, and edify the church by a spectacle of stedfastness and constancy; for the Christian rather suffers, than exposes the church to danger.   But between sufferings belonging to confessors for the truth, and vicarious sufferings as a propitiation for sins, there is a world-wide distinction.[1]   There may be a certain similarity, but no identity, no equality.   The expression, "crucified for us," intimates something unique and incommunicable, belonging to the work performed by Him who was the one Mediator between God and man.   That substitution was competent to Him alone: He redeemed us from eternal death, and the curse of the law.   When believers suffer in Christ's cause, this is a filling up of what is behind of His buffetings from the hand of man, or the fury of Satan stirring up human instruments against those who are engaged in spreading His cause.   But the question, "Was Paul crucified for you?" intimates by contrast, that as to His atoning work, Christ's sufferings were unique, vicarious, and incommunicable.

II. The apostle places in the light of the atonement another aberration of the Corinthian church,—the undue admiration of

---

[1] Turretin, *de Satisfactione Christi*, p. 97, says happily against Socinus, who expounds the phrase as simply denoting that Christ's position was only that of priority: " Paulus non negat tantum prioritatem ordinis aut gradus, sed rem ipsam tollit tanquam alienam et soli Redemptori . . . propriam."

human eloquence, or the wisdom of words : *For Christ sent me not to baptize, but to preach the gospel : not with wisdom of words, lest the cross of Christ should be made of none effect. For the preaching of the cross is to them that perish foolishness ; but unto us who are saved it is the power of God* (1 Cor. i. 17, 18). Two points are here brought out in connection with the atonement : the simplicity which Paul used in preaching it; and the fact that the preaching of it is the power of God.

(1.) The reason for simplicity and abstaining from the wisdom of words was, lest the cross of Christ should be made of none effect. Paul neither gratified the Greek passion for eloquence, nor threw into his preaching any powerful rhetoric at his command, and of which these epistles contain several striking examples (1 Cor. xv.) ; and this he did, lest the gospel should lose its power, lest men should turn their attention from the cross to the words in which it was presented. He did not call in the aid of human philosophy, or the wisdom of words, to make an impression for the gospel, well aware that foreign matter or rhetorical refinement was only subversive of its efficacy, and that it was sufficiently powerful of itself to bring conviction and peace to a human conscience. He abstained from the wisdom of words, lest men should undervalue it, as if it had not power to touch a human heart, but needed eloquence to induce men to receive it. The honour would thus be given to the art, and not to the matter.[1]

(2.) The preaching of the cross was the power of God. This remarkable statement is put alongside of another—that it is to them that perish foolishness. The wise among the Corinthians—that is, philosophic minds attached to some of the famous schools of philosophy—held it was folly to represent the Son of God as dying on the cross; while to the Jews the cross was an offence, because it was, as they thought, incompatible with the pictures of the Messiah's everlasting reign given in the prophets. Paul declares, notwithstanding all this

---

[1] See Mosheim's *Erklärung* of the two epistles to the Corinthians.

Gentile and Jewish resistance, that he was determined to know nothing and to preach nothing but a suffering Messiah, exalted indeed to universal dominion, but whose kingdom was based upon His cross.

The preaching of the cross was called the power of God, because the announcement of Christ's atoning death, in its full outline, brought divine power upon the scene, the renewing of man's nature, the restoration of the divine image once possessed in paradise. The power here mentioned refers not to miraculous accompaniments of the gospel, nor to the omnipotence which brought about the fact of the atonement, but to the power of God displayed in converting and regenerating men where the cross was preached. The gospel continues to be the power of God as the instrument by which men dead in sin are raised to spiritual life. An almighty, supernatural power goes along with the word; but with what word, with what message? With the preaching of that cross, which was, and still is, to so many foolishness. This result is found to follow wherever preaching is connected with the GREAT FACTS OF CHRIST'S ABASEMENT AND ATONING SACRIFICE, as the provision of divine love for the guilty.[1] But only that gospel is the power of God which proclaims that the cross was the propitiation for sin, the sole ground of pardon. The proclamation of these great facts continues to produce, as it has always done, transforming results, which are referred to the power of God; for God inhabits that word which is based on the incarnation and the cross. It is the habitation of His power,—it is, as it were, His chariot; all the attributes of God surround it and adorn it (Heb. iv. 12); but let anything else be substituted for the cross, and preaching is denuded of its efficacy, and stripped of this power.

---

[1] Compare Rom. i. 17, where the gospel is called δύναμις Θεοῦ; and Heb. iv. 12, where the various attributes of God are connected with God's word. This fact, that the word and divine power are united together, is one of the most signal proofs that the atonement is accepted and ever valid, for it brings God's present power upon the scene.

III. Another passage in the same context, to correct the same state of mind, is as follows : *But of Him are ye in Christ Jesus, who of God is* [better, WAS] *made unto us wisdom, and righteousness, and sanctification, and redemption* (1 Cor. i. 30). The whole section in which these words are found, has Christ crucified for its theme. It is primarily intended to guard the Corinthians from the undue love of human eloquence ; it shows that men partake of Christ, not by the wisdom of words, but by the gift of God. Four terms are used to describe what the Christ as crucified becomes to His people,—viz., WISDOM, RIGHTEOUSNESS, SANCTIFICATION, and REDEMPTION. The distribution of them has often been too artificial and out of harmony with the context. Thus many regarded them as descriptive of the threefold office of Christ; wisdom being referred to His prophetical office, righteousness to the priestly office, and the two others to the kingly office.[1] That classification—a most unhappy one—proceeds on a mistake of the meaning. The apostle, throughout the context, is describing Christ crucified : he had called Him, a few verses before, the power of God, and the wisdom of God (1 Cor. i. 24); and in the verses immediately after this passage he declares the determination on which he had acted,—to know nothing among them save Jesus Christ, and Him crucified (1 Cor. ii. 2). Certainly, Christ crucified is the theme to which the four terms refer, and this suffices without more formal distribution.[2] The entire passage

[1] See the numerous Latin, Dutch, and German expositions of the Heidelberg Catechism, where this text is quoted, question 18. They adopt almost universally this distribution.

[2] Cocceius and his followers suppose that the words are put in a reversed order ; that *redemption*, though placed last, is the first in order, or the source ; and that from this flows next in order, the regenerating and *sanctifying* faith by which we are *justified*, till we arrive at the *wisdom of God*. That is more subtle than natural. L. Bos supposes a parenthesis, thus : (*who was made wisdom to us of God ;*) and takes the three words, *righteousness, sanctification*, and *redemption*, as designations of Christians, instead of saying, fully righteous, holy, and redeemed. Others have given different distributions. See Meyer's note, though defective, and Prof. A. Butler's sermon on this text.

thus refers to the priestly office of Christ, or to the benefits derived from His cross.

(1.) Christ was made[1] to us WISDOM. The meaning is, that He was the objective wisdom, in whom are hid all the treasures of wisdom and knowledge; and that He was so, as the Christ crucified. First the constitution of His person, and next His finished work, peculiarly adapted to meet the wants of man, and to harmonize the attributes of God in man's redemption, discover unsearchable wisdom. Christ crucified was the objective wisdom of God; and the apostle, in dilating on the theme, felt that, though it was disrelished by those who boasted of Greek culture, and an offence to the Jew, he was speaking wisdom among them that were perfect.

(2.) Christ was made to us RIGHTEOUSNESS. The previous elucidation of this term enables us to dispense with many remarks. Two things were necessary. On the one hand, we needed to be saved from the guilt of violating the divine law, and from treason against the Divine Majesty; and the righteousness indispensably necessary was found in the second Adam, who subjected Himself to our guilt, and transferred it to His innocent head. He made it His own by suretyship, confessing it in the name of all for whom He appeared, accounting for it to divine justice, submitting to the penalty, and drinking to the dregs the bitter cup filled with the curse of a broken law. We equally needed, on the other hand, His active obedience, which fulfilled the divine law, and brought in an everduring righteousness. And the Lord Jesus DID BOTH FOR US. He transferred our sins to Himself as if they were His own, and laid His merits to our account, as if we had rendered all His meritorious obedience in our own person. And to make all this available to countless millions, who were to stand in Him as mediator, surety, and kinsman, He was at once very man and very God.

---

[1] The English version, in rendering ἐγενήθη as a present, has rather obscured the allusion to Christ crucified as the theme.

(3.) Christ was made to us SANCTIFICATION. This term is closely connected with the former by two Greek particles,[1] which show that it is of the same nature, class, and order with the former. Hence it is evident that we must take the term in the only sense in which it can apply to Christ crucified, in the objective acceptation, for that which Christ has been made to us on the ground of His atoning sacrifice, viz. the introducer of sinners to God, the foundation of priestly privilege, the Author of their worship and boldness of approach. The same thought is brought out in the Lord's words, when He announced that He sanctified Himself for the sake of His disciples that they might be sanctified (John xvii. 19); and in the Epistle to the Hebrews, where it is said, "Both He that sanctifieth and they who are sanctified are all of one" (Heb. ii. 11). We must go back to the Jewish worshippers, and the severe prohibition against coming before God if not purified according to the preparation of the sanctuary; for persons defiled were without access, and debarred from fellowship with Jehovah and other worshippers. But, when sprinkled by the blood of sacrifices, they were readmitted to the worship. They were then a holy people. The blood of sacrifice was their sole ground of access. Even so, by means of the one ever valid sacrifice of Calvary, sinners excluded on account of sin have access in worship and boldness to approach a holy God. In that sense Christ crucified was made of God to us sanctification.

(4.) Christ was made of God to us REDEMPTION. The term is to be taken here in the strict sense, denoting that Christ was our objective redemption, who has bought us with a price. It means that He was, in His own person, our Redeemer and redemption. We shall not enlarge on this word, as it occurs again and again in different connections. It may here suffice to say that Christ is viewed as the objective ground of our

---

[1] The particles τε καὶ always unite things as related classes, and the emphasis is thrown on the first. (See Hartung on the Particles, and Hofmann's *Schriftbeweis;* Passow by Rost, and Hand on τε.)

deliverance from captivity by a valid ransom, and that His active and passive obedience redeemed His people from the penal consequences of their sins. Though many expositors prefer to take this term in the wide sense as referring to final deliverance at the resurrection, that is out of keeping with the context, which refers to Christ crucified. Besides, that acceptation requires some other terms to warrant it (Rom. viii. 23 ; Eph. iv. 30).

IV. The church is directed to purge out the leaven of sin by the consideration that Christ, our passover, was an atoning sacrifice : *Christ our passover is sacrificed for us : therefore let us keep the feast, not with old leaven, neither with the leaven of malice and wickedness; but with the unleavened bread of sincerity and truth* (1 Cor. v. 7, 8). The whole matter is put in an Old Testament guise : the New Testament times are compared with the passover feast, the Redeemer with the paschal lamb, the purification of the houses from every particle of leaven with the outward and inward holiness of the Christian church. The entire New Testament age, or, more strictly, the entire life of a Christian, is to be nothing else than a keeping of the feast of redemption, in the same way as the passover was the feast of deliverance from Egypt. Christ is presented to us as the antitype of the paschal lamb, and all is traced to His vicarious sacrifice. In noticing this peculiar phrase, SACRIFICED FOR US, it is to be observed that we have not only a distinct allusion to the fact that Christ was sacrificed in the only sense in which a victim could be offered,—that is, as a perfect lamb, and by divine appointment,—but that it was a transaction which, from the nature of the case, involved substitution.[1] When it was FOR US, the import is, that it was for our benefit, but only so because, according to the nature of the transaction, it was in our room and stead. Christ, by His

---

[1] Turretin, *de Satisfactione Christi* (p. 198), says happily : "Si mactari et offerri debuit victima super altari, nonne et ipse pro nobis ἐτύθη et peccata super lignum tulit ?" (1 Pet. ii. 24 ; 1 Cor. v. 7.)

death, was our deliverance, the true Paschal Lamb slain for us; an expression never used of any merely human teacher or benefactor. If applied to a Paul or Peter, who bore much and suffered much for the church, it would be felt to be in the highest degree incongruous and absurd. It can be used only of a sin-bearing substitute.

The apostle's words plainly take for granted that the passover was a proper sacrifice, and hence it is called the sacrifice of the Lord's passover (Ex. xii. 27). It was not a mere symbol of deliverance from Egypt, though connected with their captivity and freedom, but pointed to something special: it lay at the foundation of the separate standing of Israel and of their economy. The sprinkling of the blood on the lintels and door-posts preserved their first-born from the destroying angel on that night of woe to Egypt. The lamb was the sin-bearer; the worshipper, confessing guilt, and acknowledging that no personal innocence of his exempted him from the merited infliction of that divine wrath which the adjoining families experienced, ascribed all to divine grace and to the divinely-appointed passover. It must specially be noticed that paschal blood effected the church's separation from the world, and made Israel a kingdom of priests. The passover was the foundation-sacrifice which set apart the nation for God, and made them a holy people. It was the passover that drew a clear line of demarcation between the church and the world,—the one being under God's protection, while the other was left under divine wrath. And from age to age it was this sacrifice of the Lord's passover that kept up the distinction between Israel and the Gentiles, the church and the world. Israel by this means became a peculiar people, a holy nation. They came out and were separate, much in the same way, though with a marked complexional or national variety, as the church of God still stands apart from the world and was redeemed for this end.

But what were the later celebrations of the passover—the

N

repetitions of it in subsequent times? Were they merely commemorative? They were much more.[1] The subsequent repetitions of the passover were also sacrificial, and not a mere
memorial, as appears from the language used respecting it as
a standing institution in Israel (Ex. xxxiv. 25). The offering
of it as the Lord's sacrifice, and the taking of the blood to the
altar, prove it not to have been a mere commemoration of a
past fact in Egypt. Its annual effect was to continue what
had been begun—to keep Israel what they had been appointed
to be, the people of God. The repetition only repeated His
redeeming act. God was considered as sparing Israel anew
from the avenging angel, redeeming them from bondage, and
renewing their fellowship with Himself, till the true Passover
came that accomplished the types, and terminated them for
ever. The annual celebration of the passover preserved Israel
to be the people of God, for the first paschal sacrifice was
only the first of the series. We may illustrate the first and
the subsequent passovers by the analogy of creation and
preservation. The latter is a work of God no less than the
former, the continuation of what was once begun, but not
less requiring the present agency of God. And so important
was the passover to Israel, the covenant people, that it not
only made them a separate, peculiar, and holy nation, but
gave significance to all the other sin-offerings. No Jew might
neglect it, and no stranger had a part in it.

From this realization of the type in Christ crucified the
apostle deduces two things, to which we shall but advert.

1. The Christian church in general, and every individual
believer, are exhorted to keep the feast (ver. 8), and to keep
it, not once a year, but constantly. Our entire life is to be
the keeping of a redemption festival, the reality of which the
deliverance from Egypt was but a type. All our life, nay, the
entire period of the Christian church on earth, must be festival

---

[1] See Hengstenberg's excellent exposition on the passover in his work *on
Sacrifice*, and also on John i. 29 ; also Kliefoth.

days,—days of pleasantness and joy, because of the magnitude of those blessings which the atonement conferred on us; for the Son of God was sacrificed that we might keep the feast perpetually, and with festive joy.[1]

2. They ought to purge out the old leaven (ver. 7), that is, have no old leaven of malice and wickedness in the celebration of the feast (ver. 8). The apostle interprets the meaning of this arrangement, and exhorts the Corinthian church to the observance of it: to labour for sincerity and unfeigned purity, external and internal, to evince their redemption and separation from the world by a holy and blameless life. The image is peculiarly adapted to the matter which the apostle was enforcing — the holiness, internal and external, of the New Testament church.

V. Some licentious practices had crept into the Corinthian church demanding immediate correction; and it deserves notice that the apostle puts them in the light of Christ's atonement, exposing their hatefulness as inconsistent with the position of redeemed men: *What! know ye not that your body is the temple of the Holy Ghost which is in you, which ye have of God, and ye are not your own? For ye are* [better, *were*] *bought* [2] *with a price: therefore glorify God in your body* (1 Cor. vi. 19, 20). Three things are contained in this memorable passage, which is of the greatest value on the doctrine of the atonement: (1) The privilege that Christians are the temple of the Holy Ghost, and not unoccupied; (2) they are bought to be another's, and are not their own; (3) the fact of being bought supplies the most powerful motive for glorifying God. These three apostolic thoughts are thus put together as an argument: A Christian may not surrender himself to impurity, for this reason, that he has become the property of a new master, and is moreover under the influence of a new motive, prompting him to

---

[1] See Calvin's admirable Commentary; also Mosheim's.

[2] Here again the English version is unhappy in its use of a present tense for ἠγοράσθητι.

dedicate his life to a holy service. As our task, however, is to develope the doctrine of the atonement, we limit our attention to the scope at which we aim.

The apostle, in setting forth that we are not our own, announces that we are BOUGHT, and bought with a PRICE ($\tau\iota\mu\acute{\eta}$). Though we do not expressly find here the terms ransom and redemption, beyond question the same thought is presented to our minds. The several apostles, as we shall see, with the most perfect uniformity of teaching, compare our deliverance from guilt to a slave's deliverance from bondage by the payment of a costly price. The underlying thought is captivity, or a state of slavery, under which we are viewed as held; and five distinct ideas are unfolded in the apostles' phraseology wherever they touch this theme,—viz. the captive, the holder of the captive, the Redeemer, the price, the receiver of the price. But it is asked, Why was it not an absolute deliverance, when divine love was engaged in this great transaction? Why did not the God of love simply pronounce our liberation, without a ransom? No absolute deliverance of this nature is ever alluded to in Scripture. Nor was a liberation possible without a price or ransom, in consequence of the fact of sin, against which all the divine perfections were arrayed. The unspotted holiness, the inflexible justice and faithfulness of God, as well as the inviolable authority of His law, rendered the liberation of guilty men without a ransom simply impossible.

When mention is made of a price, and of Christians as bought with a price, the terms plainly enough display the nature, intention, and scope of Christ's death (comp. Apoc. v. 9). The Lord's delivery to death was the price by which we were bought. The allusion is to the well-known prevalent custom of classical times, with which the apostle was familiar, by which, on the payment of a price, a slave passed out of the hands of one master into the service of another. The apostle applies the same style to the Christian's deliverance, or redemption from one service to another. He does not here speak of

purchased blessings, but of purchased MEN. In like manner
Paul speaks of the church purchased with the blood of Christ
(Acts xx. 28). As to the price paid, it is elsewhere sufficiently
described, when it is represented as the act of Christ, who
gave His life a ransom for many, who gave Himself a ransom
for all to be testified in due time (Matt. xx. 28 ; 1 Tim. ii. 6).
If the death of Christ, or His obedience unto death, was the
price, it must be added that the party bought or purchased
are Christians, who in virtue of the ransom pass into another
service, and become the property of another owner: "Ye are
not your own."

To invalidate this conclusion, various evasions have been
proposed by those who object to the doctrine of Christ's substitution. Thus, the Socinians were wont to allege that the
expression meant no more than absolute deliverance, without
the intervention of any price or ransom. And to give the
greater colour to this theory, it was alleged that the words mean
no more than that we serve Christ, without taking any account of the fact that once we were not Christ's servants.[1] In
a word, they will admit only the metaphorical use of the term.
But they cannot prove this. When a word occurs in a proper
and in a metaphorical sense, it is obvious that in each case
we have to consider which signification is the most natural
and admissible. But primarily we must take a term in its
proper sense, till we are required on good grounds to admit the
figurative sense. Even were we to concede an occasional use
of the metaphorical sense of this term by inspired men, it
would not follow that in all the passages commonly adduced
for redemption by ransom, we are to call in the metaphorical
meaning. Besides, there are appended terms which decide
the question. We do not argue merely from the words, TO
REDEEM, TO BUY, but take in as further proof the subjoined
terms, "ransom," "the precious blood of Christ," and the like,
which amply prove, if anything can, that the deliverance was

[1] That is all that Crellius will see in it.

not simple or absolute, but on the ground of a payment made in our room and stead. In a word, our opinion as to the fact of its being a true and proper redemption is confirmed by texts like the present, which make mention of a price.

In the present instance we have not merely the word BOUGHT, but also the additional idea of a PRICE. Not only so: the apostle's mode of reasoning from the ransom is of such a nature as to prove that it was no figurative or metaphorical buying to which he referred. These two clauses, "And ye are not your own, FOR ye were bought with a price," are so linked together, that the latter is adduced as the ground or cause of the former. A price had been paid; and as the reason why we are not our own is that we were bought with a price, nothing could more convincingly prove that this is no figurative buying, no metaphorical ransom. On the contrary, the ransom or price paid for us makes us another's property, and not our own. To insist on the metaphorical sense in such a passage, even though it were philologically admissible elsewhere, would make Paul reason absurdly.

On this text we must take notice of a new and strange comment offered by certain modern writers, who, with many evangelical sentiments, unhappily deny Christ's satisfaction, or accounting to divine justice in our stead. Admitting the biblical terms RANSOM and PRICE, they expound them as something not given to God with a view to the satisfaction of His law and justice, but graciously conferred on man, the poor, the naked, and the destitute, from the eternal riches of divine mercy.[1] That theory is propounded by those who will see nothing but love and moral redemption in the atonement; but it is little better than a fallacious use of Scripture terms, denuding them of their significance. With them, redemption means not deliverance from guilt and wrath, but liberation from self-will, and a life of self; and this text is made to mean that Christ gave His

[1] So Klaiber, *die N.T. Lehre von der Sünde und Erlösung*, 1836, p. 456; and also R. Stier.

precious life merely to liberate us from selfishness, that is, to do
a work IN us, but not FOR us.   It confounds person and nature,
the objective and the subjective, the standing of the man relatively and the inner condition of the heart, and is inconsistent
with the language of the text, whether we take account of the
words or the reasoning.   The apostle affirms that we are not
our own, because a price was paid, that we might become the
property of another, as in ancient times a slave became another's
property by right of purchase.   And it is nothing but an abuse
of terms to reduce this to the idea of deliverance from self-will
or self-love.

The meaning of the passage will be evident from the following outline.   It presupposes captivity : it takes for granted
that in our natural condition we were sold under sin, exposed
to the curse, subject to Satan, according to the just judgment
of God, and that a ransom was necessary and fully paid ; not,
indeed, to Satan, who was but the executioner of God's justice,
but to God, our original owner, and the fountain of justice, to
whom we are by this means legitimately restored.   Though
God condones all sin to us, exacting no price AT OUR HANDS,
deliverance from captivity was not without an adequate price
paid by a Mediator in our stead.   We thus pass into the
ownership of Him by whom we are redeemed.   This, of course,
assumes THE DIVINE DIGNITY of the Redeemer ; for redemption,
to be His property, is competent only to one who is divine.
The redeemed of the Lord, once slaves under a hard tyrant,
become the possession of Him who paid their ransom-price.

The practical deduction from this is, that Christians have
no warrant or right to use their bodies as they please, because
they are the property of Christ, and their members the members
of Christ.   They may not abuse their bodies, because they are
not their own, but His who bought them ; and are therefore to
live according to the will and pleasure of Him by whom they
were redeemed.   The argument is irresistible.   Bought at an
infinite price from the hand of their enemies, they belong

rightfully to Him who paid their ransom-price ; and hence the apostle adds the exhortation to glorify God. It may here be added, that we have a twofold security for holiness, objective and subjective—a new proprietorship, and a new motive ; and therefore that it is a calumny when the adversaries of grace assert that redemption by an atonement opens a door to licentiousness.[1]

VI. Another abuse which had crept into the Corinthian church, was such an undue exercise of Christian liberty as put a stumbling-block in the way of brethren ; and it is exposed and corrected by being placed in the light of the atonement : *And through thy knowledge shall the weak brother perish, for whom Christ died ?* (1 Cor. viii. 11.) The same admonition on the same subject we found in another epistle (Rom. xiv. 15). The question was as to the eating of things offered in sacrifice to idols, or eating what the Jewish Christians deemed defiling. The freer Gentile Christians felt themselves at liberty to partake without restraint ; but evils arose from their reckless use of liberty. They grieved and hurt the consciences of their weaker brethren, by inducing them to take a liberty in which their conscience did not allow them. Hence the apostle's reproving challenge.

Here we shall consider the peculiar designation by which a Christian is named, and the ethical principle based upon it.

1. The designation of a Christian is, ONE FOR WHOM CHRIST DIED. This expression occurs in the proper sense, or in an acceptation appropriate to the thing. The sense in which Christ died for a redeemed man is unique. Though the expression may, in a certain sense, be used to denote what one man does for his fellow-men with a view to be serviceable, especially in propagating the Christian religion, and in founding the Christian church (Acts xv. 26 ; 2 Cor. xii. 15), still that is only in a very modified sense. It cannot be denied by any one acquainted with Scripture phraseology, that it was never said of any mortal man who made himself useful to others by

[1] See Arnold's Latin refutation of the Racovian Catechism.

toils or endurance, imprisonment, danger, or death, borne for
their good, that he suffered or died for them to the extent that
Christ is said to have suffered and died for His people. We
cannot understand the phrase, as applied to Christ, in the sense
that He suffered to give us an example, nor in the vague sense
that He suffered by exposing Himself to danger which might
or might not actually strike Him. He spontaneously put
Himself in our room and stead, to bear sin and encounter certain death as the due punishment of those whose place He
occupied. When the apostle reasons on the supposition of
what may take place in common life,—that one may by possibility suffer for another in a lower sense,—he gives us to
understand how he uses the preposition (Rom. v. 7). As Christ
Himself puts the matter, the most important part of the task
committed to Him consisted in this, that He laid down His
life for the sheep; and He connects with this the additional
explanation, that He was neither constrained by inevitable
necessity, nor mastered by His enemies' power. He laid down
His life of His own proper motion, as one having power to
do so, and at His Father's command; proceeding, as this command did, on the supposition that He had power to lay it down
(John x. 18). A Christian is thus one for whom Christ died.

2. The apostle next adduces a motive for the well-regu-
lated exercise of Christian liberty from the atoning death of
Christ. Christian duty in general is enforced by considerations derived from the cross. But the special duty here referred to—that of abstaining to offend or vex a Christian
brother by unduly standing upon the right of exercising Christian liberty—is inculcated by the constraining motive derived
from the death of Christ. The consideration of the costly
price by which Christ redeemed any Christian brother in particular, furnishes a specially cogent motive to limit Christian
liberty. He who puts another's spiritual welfare to hazard
by such a course, knows not the value of the ransom; and
the apostle exposes the selfish disregard of a brother's wel-

fare by the contrast furnished by the love of Christ, and by the value which the Lord put upon him. It is as if he said : Christ died for that brother, and put such value on him, that He did not grudge His abasement and agony to win him ; and will you not limit your liberty in such trivial things as meats and drinks, to rescue him from danger to which he will otherwise be exposed ? The antithesis between Christ's redeeming love and the selfish disregard of a brother, implied in such a course, is put in the most pointed way.

Before leaving this passage, it is necessary to obviate an Arminian comment. From the expressions here used, a false conclusion has been drawn as to the extent of Christ's death, and the security of those for whom He died. That is a false deduction springing from a wrong idea of the word " destroy," which does not here denote eternal destruction. It often means to hurt, to injure—the opposite of that which tends to the use of edifying. The apostle does not mean that one man destroys another ; for that is not competent to man, and is the sole prerogative of God, who can destroy soul and body. But one brother may put a stumbling-block in another's way, and by this means mar his peace, defile his conscience, and occasion weakness, trouble, and sorrow. The apostle does not mean actual perdition, as if any for whom the Saviour offered Himself a surety could finally be destroyed. How could they perish finally, when Christ had offered Himself an eternally valid sacrifice, expiating their sin, and satisfying all the claims of the law in their room and stead ? (John vi. 39.) They are kept not only by power, but by the security furnished by divine justice itself, to the salvation ready to be revealed.

The motive here supplied is, in an ethical point of view, of the strongest and most cogent. The apostle wishes to point out to those uncharitable asserters of liberty, that he whom they respected so little was not so viewed by Christ, but was so tenderly loved that the Lord had not disdained to die for him. He speaks of those who were made Christian brethren by that atoning death, and shows that, from the infinite price paid, we may estimate the value to be set on them. Hence the point of the admonition, not to offend them.

VII. The apostle, while correcting another abuse, in connection with the Lord's Supper, which had also crept into the Corinthian church, takes occasion to expound the meaning of the institution. He points out that it was a memorial of the Lord's death, and that they who celebrate it show the Lord's death till He come (1 Cor. xi. 23–27). He records the event as he had received it from the Lord Himself; for though some suppose the words mean that Paul received the account of the institution from the disciples who were present, that is plainly an inadequate commentary on the words. The terms imply, beyond doubt, a special communication, given by the Lord Himself, that Paul, in founding the churches, might act with as much confidence and as certain knowledge as the other apostles. When he adduces the very words of Christ uttered at the institution of the Supper, they are carefully distinguished from his own. Among other things peculiar to the Pauline account of the Supper, may be noticed the words, "This do in remembrance of me." The verb may be either in the indicative or imperative mood, but far more fitly in the latter, expressive of command. These words are given twice, nearly in the same form, first at the distribution of the bread, next at the giving of the cup; and Luke, as was to be expected from Paul's companion, also records the words in the same way.

But what did the Lord mean, when He bade the first disciples do this in remembrance of Him? The opponents of the atonement considered as a vicarious sacrifice, say the words merely direct us to remember His salutary doctrine, or His example, or His great commandment to love our fellow-men. That Paul apprehended the words in a different way, is evident from the comment which he gives: he affirms that we show forth, not His doctrines, not His example, but His death as an atoning sacrifice for sin (ver. 26).

Without dwelling on the sacramental elements and actions, let it suffice to say that they point to the one sacrifice of the cross. Thus, when the bread was given, He said, " This is my body,"—alluding to His entire humanity, in respect of the obedience which He rendered to His Father in the room of sinners. When the wine was given, He said, " This cup is the new covenant in my blood,"—alluding to the blood of sacrifice, by means of which the new covenant was formed. Though the former may be said to bring before the mind His whole suffering obedience generally, we cannot fail to see that the Supper came in room of the passover, and recalled the eating of the passover. But besides, a new covenant was to come in room of the Sinaitic covenant, and the Lord deemed it fitting to give an emblem of the blood of sacrifice, by means of which those heretofore aliens could be taken into a new covenant, as a holy people, and sit as guests, without danger or dread, at the Lord's table. They, in a word, by that sacrificial blood entered into a new covenant-standing, no longer shadowy or capable of dissolution, but perfect and inviolable.[1]

All this is recalled to memory by the constant celebration of the Supper, intended to be a perpetual institution and frequently repeated. The disciples commemorated His death, not as a thing indifferent, not as a historic incident having no direct bearing on present interests and experience, not as a mere confirmation of His doctrine, but as a true atonement. They were to have a memorial of Christ crucified, and His redeeming love, brought home to them by means of emblems vividly recalling to them the nature of His sacrifice, and furnishing food for the understanding and the heart. When they were directed to show His death till He come,—that is, when the death of Christ was made the ground of festive commemoration,—we see what an important and unique design lay at the foundation of His sufferings and death. These could

[1] See our previous volume, *Sayings of Jesus on the Atonement*, on Matt. xxvi. 28, where this connection is expounded at large.

be no other than vicarious—the actions of a substitute and surety.

The Lord's Supper, thus replete with significance, has maintained its ground in the church amid all the revolutions of time. The Lord did not leave it to the apostles to institute it after His departure, but regarded it as so important, that by His own authority, while yet present, He instituted it in the most solemn manner on the night of His betrayal, immediately before going out to the garden. The bread and wine, selected as emblems of His body and blood, were designed to imbue His disciples with the persuasion, (1) that His body was the true paschal sacrifice; and (2) that His blood was the true sacrificial blood by which the new covenant was constituted, more perfect by far than the covenant at Sinai. The elements were signs of a reality,—pledges in hand, that as surely as they took the sign, they by faith received the thing signified; for they were seals and pledges as well as signs. The covenant is founded simply on the blood shed for many, for the remission of sins, without any other element, whether in the form of intervening merit, or moral improvement, or services to be performed, as the procuring cause. The cup of thanksgiving was thus the participation of the blood of Christ, and the bread the participation of the body of Christ (1 Cor. x. 16).

The sacrament of the Supper loudly proclaims this great truth to all time, and all ages must hear it. Till the Lord come, His atoning death must be proclaimed with festive joy at the Supper, as often as it is deemed proper to celebrate it. Of how great importance must that truth be which Jesus so vividly portrayed, and the perpetual memory of which He so carefully secured! This shows what a rank and place belong to the atonement. It is the principal thing in the gospel; nay, it is the gospel. Take it out of the gospel, and it ceases to be the gospel.

VIII. In proceeding to correct another error, which had

reference to the resurrection of the body, the apostle takes occasion to describe the gospel which he preached, and to which he continued faithful: *For I delivered unto you first of all that which I also received, how that Christ died for our sins according to the Scriptures; and that He was buried, and that He rose again the third day according to the Scriptures* (1 Cor. xv. 3, 4). Paul had received the gospel which he preached, not from men, but by particular revelation from the Lord; and it was all based on the cross. The gospel which he had preached from the beginning, which the Corinthians had received, and by which they were saved if they continued faithful to it, was to the effect that Christ died for our sins according to the Scriptures, and that He rose again according to the Scriptures. Can this mean that Christ died for our sins merely in the sense of a moral redemption—that is, as freeing us from moral corruption? No. The words mean, that our sins causally put Him to death. But we must more narrowly consider the phraseology.

All depends on the proper import of the expression, DYING FOR OUR SINS. The Greek preposition here used is sometimes found in connection with persons who are the proper object of Christ's atonement (Luke xxii. 19; 1 Cor. v. 7; Rom. viii. 32; John x. 11; Rom. v. 6, 7); and in such a connection the expression has the signification of expiation for the good of another, or for his benefit, always presupposing a vicarious atonement. The preposition is also used to denote men's advantage in connection with the final cause, or the end designed (John vi. 51). But when construed with sins, as here, the expression can only mean that HIS DEATH was the DESERVED PUNISHMENT. We could not from the preposition alone draw the conclusion that the death of Christ was the consequence of our sins, or the punishment of our guilt, were there no further particulars in the passage to lead us to that thought. But when mention is made, as in the passage under consideration, of suffering and death, the meaning unquestion-

ably is, that our sins were the procuring cause of the suffering.   The words, beyond doubt, refer to our sins as the meritorious cause of Christ's death ; and the thought expressed is,
that the death of Christ was the punishment of sin.   Though
the preposition of itself has various shades, according to the
connection in which it stands, certain it is, that when the
death of Christ is put in connection with our sins, the strict
meaning can only be, that these sins were the cause of His
death, and that the sufferings were the punishment of our
guilt.

This will be more evident if we take in another phrase
connected with His resurrection : " If Christ be not raised,
your faith is vain : ye are yet in your sins" (1 Cor. xv. 17).
The reason of this connection is not obscure, if we apprehend
the suretyship involved in Christ's death; that He was a
public person, or Representative of His people both in His
death and in His resurrection ; that He died for our sins, in
the sense that He, by imputation or transfer, took them upon
Himself, making them His own, and submitting to the consequences they entailed.   If Christ had remained in death, it
would have been an argument that those sins laid on Him,
and spontaneously borne, had not been expiated by His death.
Had Christ not risen, we should not have been set free from
former sins : they would still have been put to our account.
The argument of the apostle amounts to this, that the scope
of the atonement, with its validity and efficacy, would all
have been neutralized, if the Surety, who went down to death
under the sins of His people, had not risen : we should yet
be in our sins.   When He rose, therefore, it was undeniable
evidence that our sins had been expiated by His death (compare Rom. iv. 25).

What objection is propounded to all this by the Socinian
party ?   It amounts on philological grounds to this, that the
Greek preposition denotes, not the meritorious cause, but the
final cause,—that is, that Christ died to remove future sin.   But

that is not to expound words, but to deposit foreign thoughts in the record; and our function as interpreters is to evolve the meaning of language, not to adapt it to our preconceived ideas. It is one thing to say that Christ died for sins which have already been committed, and the guilt of which must be borne, and another thing to say that He died to abolish future sins. The former idea is in Paul's words: the latter cannot be put into them without altering the record. The expression can mean nothing but the guilt of sin considered as the meritorious cause, or impelling cause, of the Lord's death. Grotius has well proved that the preposition, thus used, denotes the impelling cause[1] (see Rom. xv. 9; Eph. v. 20). When it is said, then, that Christ died for our sins, it means that He bore their punishment.

The Socinians will have some words supplied or understood —a device that cannot be endured. To show, however, that it is not simply a matter of interpretation with them, but a foregone conclusion, it may be mentioned that Socinus explicitly declared, that were the doctrine of vicarious sin-bearing, and the punishment of one for the sins of another, mentioned not once, but many times, in Scripture, he would not believe it, because it could not be. That open declaration is candid at least; but it is an appeal to reason, not to revelation, and an admission that Scripture is not made the ultimate judge, but only to be interpreted as seems best suited to confirm or dress out a preconceived hypothesis.

But taking the divine word as the ultimate authority, we may affirm that no language could more precisely express a meritorious cause than the words of the text. When our sins are connected with Christ's sufferings and death, the words bring out cause and effect. The words can be taken in no other sense than in that of the impelling or meritorious cause of the effect described. They mean that our sins—that is, the

---

[1] See the admirable discussion of the prepositions διά, περί, ὑπέρ, when construed with ἁμαρτία, in the first chapter of his work, *de Satisfactione Christi*.

guilt contracted by us—caused the suffering and death of the Lord; and words cannot more accurately express the idea.

SEC. XI.—THE SECOND EPISTLE TO THE CORINTHIANS.

The second epistle, written a short time after the first—at least after such an interval as enabled Titus to go to Corinth and to return to Paul—is somewhat different in tone, and alludes to the good effect produced by the admonitions which had been addressed to the Corinthian church. Titus had been sent to learn the impression made by the first epistle, and reported that some of the abuses had been corrected. The party divisions, however, were not suppressed; and Paul was under the necessity of continuing personal explanations, and also vindicating his authority against those who depreciated his commission, in comparison with that of the other apostles who had been trained in the Lord's society in the days of His flesh. The apostle, in the midst of these personal allusions, takes occasion to interweave several references to the atonement; and to these testimonies we must now come.

I. In referring to activity and labour in the discharge of his office, the apostle declares that he was constrained by his Lord's atoning love: *For the love of Christ constraineth us; because we thus judge, that if one died for all, then were all dead* [better, *then all died,* or *the all died*]: *and that He died for all, that they who live should not henceforth live unto themselves, but unto Him who died for them, and rose again* (2 Cor. v. 14, 15). The intense activity and zeal to which the apostle alluded in the previous verses are traced to their source—the redeeming love of Christ. And this leads him to dwell on the nature of the atonement, which is aright apprehended, according to the meaning of this passage, only when we duly discover the prominent place to be assigned to substitution. This is seen in the clause " one died for all," even when we render the Greek

o

preposition ($\dot{v}\pi\acute{\epsilon}\rho$) FOR THE BENEFIT OF. The idea of substitution, or exchange of places, underlies the thought, as we have
noticed already (Rom. v. 7). Besides, substitution or vicarious-
ness comes to light, beyond all question, in the logical deduction, THEN THE ALL DIED ;[1] for if all for whom the Lord died
are regarded as dying in His death, no doubt can exist as to
the fact of substitution : it is taken for granted as an undoubted
reality. The apostle speaks of us men exposed to death on
our own account, and worthy of condemnation ; and to rescue
us, a Surety or Deliverer steps forward, in the exercise of
boundless love, and dies in our stead. The language involves
substitution, and can be understood only on the supposition
that one dies in another's room. It is not the case of a hero
exposing himself to danger or death for the benefit of his
countrymen, nor the case of a friend dying for the benefit of
a friend, which the apostle tells us (Rom. v. 7) may peradventure occur in the world's history. None of these cases
comes up to what is indicated here ; for in such a case it would
never be affirmed that they for whom the death was undergone died in Him. We have to understand, in Christ's case,
federal unity and substitution.

1. What does the apostle mean by the word DIE, as thus
applied to us ? And how are WE said TO HAVE DIED in the
Lord's death ? One thing is self-evident : the apostle does not
use it in the first clause literally, and in the next clause metaphorically ; for, on such a supposition, the deduction made by
the apostle would not hold, and the expression would be unmeaning. He has before his eye the case of sinners doomed
to death, for whom a Surety offered Himself vicariously ; and
only in such a case can they for whom the Surety interposed

---

[1] Beza correctly lays stress on the article *oi* before $\pi\acute{a}\nu\tau\epsilon\varsigma$: "Illi omnes
mortui sunt." Our authorized version is always unhappy in its rendering of
$\dot{a}\pi\acute{\epsilon}\theta a\nu o\nu$, *were dead ;* for the meaning is, *all died.* This is admitted by all the
modern exegetes of note, though they too exclusively limit it to the SUBJECTIVE
REALIZATION in the faith of the individual (so Meyer). Plainly it is here referred to as an objective fact.

be said to have satisfied the law or borne the penalty. We take the word in the two clauses in precisely the same sense. It is the same phraseology, with the same import, which we found in the Epistle to the Romans, as descriptive of the ONE REPRESENTATIVE ACT OF CHRIST; which for the most part is set forth as rendered for us, but in a considerable number of passages is also spoken of as if we had personally done it (Rom. vi. 2). And the manner in which the two phrases are here alternated is worthy of notice. We may either say that CHRIST DIED FOR US, or that WE DIED WITH HIM. And the logical form of the verse explains the principle on which that alternating phraseology proceeds: "IF one died for all, THEN the all died." From this it is plain that we must take the word DIE, applied to Christ in the one clause, and applied to His people in the other clause, not only in the same sense, but as referring to the same act. The death here mentioned is not twofold, but numerically one; for we are not to regard Christ as performing one act, and ourselves as performing another parallel and similar to His. When we look at the general tenor of the apostle's doctrine, we find, on the one hand, that death is represented as the wages of sin; and, on the other, we see the great Surety undergoing the penalty in our room: and we are said to have died in Him, because HIS ACT WAS REPRESENTATIVELY OUR ACT. The atoning death of the Lord, on the ground of federal unity and substitution, was also our act; that is, was accepted as OUR ACT in Him.

2. The next inquiry has reference to the LIFE into which the Christian enters, and to the connection between the life and the death He died. What was meant by the apostle when speaking of them who live, or of the living ones, as the expression literally means (ver. 15)? No one who apprehends the Pauline phraseology as to the believer's dying with Christ, or crucifixion with Christ, can doubt that the life which follows is premial life, subsequent to the meritorious obedience which was rendered. It is life following a perfect fulfilment of the

divine law, and regarded as its reward. Very generally, expositors take this life as referring to the term of our human existence, or the natural life. But that is wide of the mark. The connection between the atonement and the life immediately subjoined, points, we think, to a causal connection, and thus leaves no doubt that the allusion is to spiritual or eternal life, which is elsewhere described as hid with Christ in God (Col. iii. 3). The living ones are such as enter into premial life, because the Surety fulfilled the law, and expiated sin in His death.

But it is intimated that this life is a dedicated life, not a life of self-seeking, after the flesh, or in the prosecution of what tends to our own profit, honour, or gratification. This life was secured by Christ's death, and promoted by His resurrection: for the concluding clause of the verses above quoted shows that Christ DIED FOR US, and that He rose again. And it is not said that He rose for us, but that He died for us; for there is a certain difference of meaning. The resurrection comes within the sphere of reward, and enabled Him to diffuse His life through His own people, redeemed to be His—for He underwent death with this express end in view, that He might win a people as His property—and replenish them with the divine life which He procured for them, and dispenses according to their needs. He thus induces them to live not to themselves, but to Him.

To return to the expression ONE DIED FOR ALL: no doubt can be entertained, either from the nature of the transaction, or from the logical inference already mentioned, that the phrase denotes the exchange or substitution of one for another. But we have still further to consider in what sense Christ is said to have DIED FOR ALL. Plainly, the allusion in the present case is of equal extent in both clauses. The all for whom He died are the same parties, and no other,[1] who are next said

---

[1] In the discussions on the extent of the atonement, this has been triumphantly proved by Owen, *Death of Death*, vol. x. p. 350 ; Honert, *de gratia Dei*

to have died in Him; that is, all who are regarded as expiating sin, and fulfilling the law in Him—the same men to whom the redemption is applied, and no wider circle, at least in the passage under consideration.

It may not be unfitting, before leaving this passage, to refer to two expositions of such expressions which cannot be accepted, and yet are widely diffused,—the Arminian or Lutheran comment, and the Amyraldist comment.

a. As to the Arminian tenet, it is to this effect: that Christ in a certain respect offered Himself a sacrifice sufficiently for all, and for every man in the same sense. They leave it uncertain whether they interpret the preposition as denoting FOR THE GOOD OF ALL, or IN THE ROOM OF ALL. They maintain that it was for all alike, without distinction and without exception. Taking hold of the wider or more general aspects in which some texts appear to present the atonement to the mind, they conclude that Christ was priest and victim for all mankind without exception, whether they believe or not, whether they are saved or not; that the sacrifice of Christ was not only infinitely precious, but offered with such a purpose both on the Father's side and on the Son's side, that it should be for all and every man. That this is an unscriptural comment, is evident from the fact that an accepted sacrifice obtained the remission of sins. And Christ dispenses to all for whom He died—that is, to all who become His people—the reward of His obedience, remission, regeneration, and final glory. The clear inference from such a comment would be universalism, or universal salvation, which the Scriptures emphatically repudiate. It will not do to distinguish between the purchase and the application of redemption, so as to affirm that they

---

non universali, p. 571; Jac. Trigland, *de Volunt. Dei et grat. univ.* p. 282; Turret. tom. ii. loc. 14, qu. 14, sec. 36. So long as men incorrectly translate ἀπέθανον *were dead*, as in the English version, they readily argue that the spiritual death of men is universal, and that the death of Christ is equally so. But when they correctly render, in the second clause, THEN THEY ALL DIED, that argument has no foundation.

are not of equal extent; for that amounts to disjunction and separation, vitiating the nature of the atonement as a vicarious transaction.

b. The Amyraldist theory, or that of the double reference, acknowledges a true substitution in THE ROOM AND STEAD of those who were given to Christ, and whose sins He actually bore, but asserts, moreover, that He died FOR THE ADVANTAGE OF the rest, though not in their stead.[1] In a word, this theory maintains a double reference; that is, that He died in the room of some, and for the good of the rest. According to this exposition, the biblical phrase, TO DIE FOR MEN, has not a uniform sense, but a different meaning in different passages. This we can by no means concede; for Christ is never said to die for men in any other sense than in the sense of substitution or exchange of places. He really entered into our place, and by so doing incurred our doom and responsibility; and we as truly enter into His place, and partake of His merits and reward. And a different mode of viewing the transaction is not to be found in Scripture.

That many who are not believers derive great advantages from Christ's atonement, is not denied. They enjoy an economy of forbearance, are freed from the pernicious errors and defilements of idolatry, and live among the people of God. But these blessings, manifold and various, do not warrant us to say that the Lord died for men in a double way, or with a double reference; that is, for some vicariously, and for others to give them only a temporary advantage. He died as a representative and surety; and whatever their representative Head did, they are regarded as having done, as this text proves. He not only died for them all, but THEY ALL DIED IN HIM.

II. Another important passage, defining the nature of the atonement, occurs a few verses afterwards in the same chapter: *And all things are of God, who hath reconciled us to Himself by*

---

[1] This theory is equally unbiblical and inconsistent,—a makeshift or accommodation scheme between two other opinions.

*Jesus Christ, and hath given to us the ministry of reconciliation;
to wit, that God was in Christ, reconciling the world unto Himself*
[better, *God was reconciling the world unto Himself in Christ*],
*not imputing their trespasses unto them; and hath committed
unto us the word of reconciliation* (2 Cor. v. 18, 19). The apostle
had mentioned that the new creature emanates from God, and
then assigned as its ground the atoning work of Christ. We
have first to notice the principal cause of the reconciliation:
"all is of God, who hath reconciled us." The allusion is to
the Father, to whom the Saviour was wont to refer all that He
did. We have to consider God as offended and provoked by
sin, and yet providing the reconciliation by which they who
had incurred His displeasure are restored to His favour. The
term RECONCILIATION, as we have elsewhere shown, implies
that in ourselves we were exposed to divine wrath, and that
a divine provision brought it to an end.

There is no force in the current objection, that God could
not entertain anger or hostility, when He so loved us, that He
sent His only-begotten Son to usher in the reconciliation.
Scripture affirms both; and, as we have already proved, they
can well consist together. That sins provoke the holy God, in
the exercise of His moral government, to righteous anger, is
an axiom or first principle with every one who has acquired
a rudimentary knowledge of God; for all men know that He
is no indifferent spectator of the moral actions of His creatures
(Rom. i. 32). He claims the exercise of vengeance as His
peculiar attribute, which He will have left in His own hand; and
He declares that He will repay (Rom. xii. 19). But He ceases
not to love His creatures as His workmanship; and He loves
them with a supperadded love, when, viewing the elect in His
Son, He loves them with the same love with which He loves His
Son. In Christ the wrath of God is appeased, but not by a relaxation of justice or a reduction of His claims. He cannot but
bear just anger against sin, and against the sinner on account
of sin, as is sufficiently proved by actual punishments inflicted.

The apostle intends to bring out the proper nature of re-conciliation, as is plain from the fact that he expressly mentions that God hath reconciled us to Himself by Jesus Christ. This shows, as an analysis of the language suffices to prove, that in effecting the reconciliation, God exercised His mercy not absolutely, and irrespective of a mediator; for participation in divine favour depends on the work of a Surety, whom God appointed as the way of access or channel by which His favour could be obtained. This is evident by a comparison of passages in the New Testament, where allusion is made to reconcilia-tion as a transition from wrath to favour, from hostility to friendship, from alienation to restored fellowship. That is the uniform import of the term; and however much mutual reconciliation is involved in the nature of the case, the term principally means reconciliation on the part of Him whose anger was incurred, and who could renew a friendly inter-course only on the ground of a satisfaction.

But it is argued by those who allow anger in God, only in the case of those who remain at last impenitent till the day of grace is past, that reconciliation means our favourable disposi-tion toward God. They put this view on several grounds, all which are equally baseless. Thus, they assert (1) that God is never called man's enemy; an argument as absurd as it would be to argue against punishment, on the ground that a human state or judicial tribunal is never called the enemy of the citi-zens, when the question is whether the authority of the law is to be executed against transgressors: for a human tribunal is but a reflection of the divine, and based on the same eternal principles of justice. They assert (2) that, in biblical lan-guage, reconciliation never indicates that anything is necessary on God's side before our reception into favour.[1] That, too, is

[1] Ritschl of Göttingen, in his *de ira Dei*, pp. 13–20, utterly misapprehends the doctrine, when he maintains that the doctrine of the wrath of God has nothing to do with the atonement. See a much better exposition by Weber, *vom Zorne Gottes*, p. 290. But even he stops short of the full biblical doctrine on the *ira Dei*.

contrary to the words before us : "who hath reconciled us to
Himself BY JESUS CHRIST." And the same thing appears in
the Epistle to the Romans, where, as we already pointed out,
it is affirmed that we were reconciled to God by the death of
His Son (Rom. v. 10). But (3) another assertion, as baseless
as the two former, is, that we cannot suppose such a thing as
the appeasing or pacifying of God's anger, because we nowhere
read in the New Testament of God's reconciliation to man.
But we have already proved that the term, as used in Scripture, is not equivalent to our being well affected toward God,
and imbued with a friendly disposition toward God, but
means that we are secured from His wrath (Rom. v. 9), and
can count on His favour and benefits (Rom. v. 1). In a word,
it is God's favour toward us, not our favourable disposition
toward God.[1]

This leads me to the use of the term, and to the definition
of it. The party whose affection has been won cannot be
determined from the nominative to the verb, nor from the
accusative case which follows the verb, but is ascertained
from the connection and the known position of the parties.
The restored favour of the offended party has an influence on
the other : they each come into a new position. Warrantably
we may either say that a person is reconciled to us, or that
we are reconciled to him. When the verb is found in the
passive, it either means to give up a quarrel on our side
(1 Cor. vii. 11), or to induce another to abate his anger and
terminate his just resentment against us (Matt. v. 24). In
the latter passage, the words, "Be reconciled to thy brother,"
do not mean, Be well disposed to thy brother—for that, in the
case adduced by the Lord, could have been done in the temple
—but, Leave thy gift ; go and induce thy brother, who has just
cause of resentment against thee, to return to a friendly disposition toward you. And this required a visit to the offended party.

[1] See a fine note of Calvin in his commentary on this passage, putting the
grace of God and the anger of God in striking juxtaposition.

In this sense the word occurs wherever allusion is made to
man's reconciliation to God. It does not mean our subjective
reconciliation to God, but God's objective reconciliation to
us ; and one of the most conclusive proofs of this occurs in a
passage already noticed: "We joy in God, through our Lord
Jesus Christ, by whom we have now received the atonement,"
or reconciliation (Rom. v. 11). There it is said to have been
received. An inward act of man is done, or performed; it
cannot be received : but there it is affirmed that we received
it. That the allusion is to the appeasing of God's anger,
clearly appears from the words which refer to Christ's death
as the meritorious cause of effecting peace (Rom. v. 10).

In the great transaction of reconciling sinners, God is an
active party: He reconciles us to Himself by Jesus Christ.
And what comes in between the love of God and His holy
anger ? Only one thing—the atonement—which harmonizes
both in our reconciliation to God. God Himself provided the
atonement as the means of reconciliation, and on this sole
ground of intercourse He receives us to favour. Not that men
laid down their opposition and sued for peace. The principal
cause is God, who provided reconciliation. Then, as to the procuring cause, Christ by His atonement meritoriously won the
favour of God for those who, but for this, would for ever have
been given up to divine wrath and condemnation. Reconciliation, then, is simply the removal of the separation and enmity
between God and the world. But we must notice the language
more minutely.

As to the method of construing the second of the two
verses (ver. 19), three modes are proposed, for reasons which
demand attention.

a. Some take the expression, "God was in Christ reconciling the world," as an allusion to Christ's divine nature.[1] Paul
is thus regarded as teaching that the Redeemer was not

---

[1] This was for a time the received exposition in the Lutheran Church. See
Wolfii *curæ.*

merely the instrument which God made use of in the work of redemption, but that He was also God Himself. Certainly reasons may be urged in behalf of this view from the structure of the language. Thus, it may be said, two representations are given in succession, which we may warrantably suppose are somewhat varied, and not a mere tautology. In the first, God is described as the author of the reconciliation, and Christ as the instrument by whom it was accomplished: "All things are of God, who hath reconciled us to Himself by Jesus Christ." And in the second it is said: "God was in Christ, reconciling the world unto Himself." Now, it is argued that, to avoid the flat repetition of one and the same thing, it is better to view the clause as referring to the higher nature of Christ. This interpretation considered the Redeemer not as a mere instrument, but as a divine person, capable of so great a work, and giving it a boundless value.

b. Another mode of construing is as follows: "God in Christ was reconciling the world." This is the mode of resolving the words generally received at present by the most eminent philological expounders.[1] This view is maintained chiefly because the following clause more precisely defines in what way the atonement was effected. The two points, then, are as follows: 1. A non-imputation of sin to us so far as the matter bears upon our relation toward God; 2. The atoning act considered as emanating not from man, but from God, or as God's own act in inward unity and fellowship with Christ. Undoubtedly this interpretation can be rendered highly probable, and gives a satisfactory sense.

c. Another mode seems to me even preferable, according to the translation above given: *God was reconciling the world unto Himself in Christ.* This does not construe the words IN CHRIST with the activity of the divine nature in the Lord Himself, nor with the Father's activity in providing the atonement, but in connection with the new relation into which

---

[1] ἦν καταλάσσων are thus taken together as a sort of emphatic imperfect.

mankind were brought, as they stood in Christ. The meaning will then be : God reconciled them in Christ, as He regarded them in Him, and comprehended them in union with His Son, according to His covenant and purpose. This seems to me the shade of meaning that properly belongs to the passage.

With regard to the other terms, are we to understand the word WORLD as descriptive of the human family ? In this general sense the word frequently occurs in the style of Paul and the other apostles (Rom. iii. 19 ; 1 Cor. i. 21). It is often used to indicate the unbelieving world, as contradistinguished from the church of God, because the great majority still continues alienated from the life of God. Here it does not mean the world of believers—a sense in which, so far as I know, it does not occur—but the world of mankind as one day standing out to view, including Jews and Gentiles alike.[1] From this, however, it by no means follows that all were actually reconciled. Our mode of construing IN CHRIST proves the opposite. And this is further confirmed by the clause which runs parallel with it : " not imputing their trespasses unto them." Thus the apostle speaks of an accomplished fact, finished once for all. But one or two points may still be separately noticed.

1. We are said to be reconciled IN CHRIST; an expression which at first sight seems to be equivalent to the phrase BY CHRIST, which occurs in the previous verse. But they do not coincide. The present phrase denotes something more : for the apostle's language is precise, representing Christ not only as the meritorious cause of reconciliation, which the phrase of the previous verse in such a connection usually means, but as the objective reconciliation. As in Him we have the objective redemption (Eph. i. 7), so in Him we have the objective reconciliation ; much in the same way as He is said to be made of God unto us righteousness and sanctification (1 Cor.

---

[1] Charnock (vol. ii. p. 212, folio edit.) says, strikingly : "God imputed a world of sins to Him, because He undertook for that world God had created by Him."

i. 30), or as He is called our peace (Eph. ii. 14). The apostle changes the preposition on purpose.

2. The reconciliation was effected by not imputing to us our trespasses (ver. 19). Opinion varies, indeed, as to the way in which the participial clause is to be resolved : some regarding the non-imputation of sin as the cause[1] of reconciliation ; others, less correctly, considering it as the effect. The latter is a mistaken view, and is opposed to the usage of a participial clause. Paul affirms that God reconciles the world by not imputing to men their trespasses. And the reconciliation, as to its mode, is effected in this twofold way : (1) by not imputing sin to us, and (2) by Christ becoming the sin-bearer (ver. 21) ; that is, the world is reconciled because sin was laid on Christ, and not imputed to us.

3. God is said to place those to whom sin is not imputed in a state of reconciliation TO HIMSELF. That means, that the atonement restores men to their right relation to law and order ; or, more definitely, to a friendly fellowship with a personal God. It is the removal of hostility. As redemption is a redemption to God in the sense that we are liberated from captivity to belong to God (Rev. v. 9 ; 1 Cor. vi. 19), so reconciliation is a reconciliation to God in the sense that we are restored to God so as to be His friends ; and the reconciliation supposes something mutual : for a mutual relation of this nature is essential to the thing, though not properly in the word.

Only one thing remains to be noticed. The words, " Be reconciled to God," which Paul adds as the burden of all preaching (v. 20), are equivalent to " Receive the atonement."

III. Another passage, subjoined to the former, and closely connected with it, points out most emphatically the mode of the atonement : *For He hath made Him to be sin for us who knew no sin, that we might be made the righteousness of God in*

---

[1] Thus Calvin well puts it. On linguistic grounds, too, this is required by the relation of the participle to the verb. See Winer, § 45.

Him (2 Cor. v. 21). The verse, connected by the grounding particle FOR with the previous passage descriptive of the message of reconciliation, assigns the ground on which that message rests. That is the force of the particle *for;* and the import is, that God made an exchange between us and Christ, of such a nature that He, the sinless, was treated as if He were the sinner—nay, as sin itself—that we might be made the righteousness of God.

Two statements are thus brought together, and lie near each other: the non-imputation of sin to those who are reconciled (ver. 19), and the fact that Christ was made sin. And these two statements involve each other. The reason or ground on which the non-imputation of sin proceeds, is the fact that Christ was made sin[1] (ver. 21). That is involved in the message of reconciliation. But these two points just mentioned, and lying at the foundation of preaching, incontrovertibly show that the end of Christ's coming was not to proclaim absolute forgiveness, but to usher in an expiation, or a work of atonement, on the ground of which that proclamation of forgiveness might be made. The connection between the atonement and the message, " Be reconciled to God," is thus clearly brought out. Apart from the atonement, preaching would have no foundation, would have no message to proclaim, and would be denuded of all the force accompanying it.

In exhibiting the contents of this pregnant text, I shall endeavour, with all brevity, to bring out its import under a few heads.

1. The source of the whole atonement is traced to GOD, who is said to HAVE MADE CHRIST what the text describes. And the expression raises our thoughts to that agreement, or covenant, according to which the Father appointed His own Son to assume our human nature and bear our guilt.

2. But a further idea, that of sinlessness, is brought out

---

[1] The connection between the μὴ λογιζόμενος ἁμαρτίαν, and Christ being made ἁμαρτία, has been generally noticed in former and recent times. See Charnock

in the words, WHO KNEW NO SIN. The expression is intended
to show that the sinless perfection of Jesus—that is, His
innocence and perfect obedience to the divine law—was the
foundation or presupposition of the entire work of expiation.
But in whose account was He judged sinless ? The Greek
phrase, which has a peculiar force attaching to it, which must
accurately be ascertained, contains an answer to that question.
The peculiar phrase, WHO KNEW NO SIN, is called by philologists the subjective negation, because wherever it is used it
denotes a negative estimate or judgment formed in the mind
of some party. And when we ask, By whom was the judgment formed in this case ? the conclusion to which we must
come is, that it either expresses Christ's own conscious estimate—and the subjective negation will, on this supposition,
set forth His own consciousness of perfect sinlessness—or
else that it expresses the Father's judgment formed of Him at
the divine tribunal. One thing is very evident : the terms and
context do not allow us to refer the phraseology to a mere
ordinary human estimate of Jesus. Most naturally, the party
whose judgment is introduced, and who regarded Him as sinless, is the same that was represented as making Him to be
sin for us—viz. GOD.[1] If we take this acceptation, as the
strict import of the Greek phrase leads us most naturally to
do, then Jesus was esteemed or judged by God as completely
faultless, and as never having had one feeling at variance with
the divine will and law. He did no sin. But the relation of
the two connected clauses is of such a kind as makes it clear
that sinlessness is equivalent to perfect obedience, for the
negative side implies the POSITIVE MODE OF PUTTING IT. He
was thus exempt from every fault, whether of omission or of
commission. And the ultimate aim of God in all this, was

---

and Owen, *passim;* Weber, p. 296. Vinke, *Leer van Jesus en de Apostel. aang.
Zijn Lijden,* p. 357.

[1] Winer, in his *Grammar,* says of μὴ γνόντα, § 55, 5 : "Geht auf die Vor-
stellung dessen der ihn zur ἁμαρτία macht, zurück."

not only to qualify Him for undertaking the task of sin-bearing, but also to pave the way for bringing in a vicarious righteousness. The statement therefore is, that He who was sinless in God's account—and only one immaculately perfect in every part of positive obedience could be so—was made sin.

3. This sinless one, judged in God's account as one who knew no sin, is next described as having been MADE SIN. The first inquiry is, What does this properly mean?

a. Many deem it best to take it as simply equivalent to a sin-offering; and, indeed, the Septuagint several times uses the original word to denote this sacrifice : for the sin-offering was regarded as incorporated sin or embodied guilt, viewed objectively and apart. Such an exposition affords a competent enough sense, and does not in fact alter the meaning.[1] But it deserves notice, in the first place, that throughout this entire passage the apostle makes no use of sacrificial language; and the term reconciliation is allowed on all hands to be taken from ordinary life, and not from the sacrificial ritual. Then it is evident that the apostle draws a contrast between two things,—between the personal sinlessness of Jesus, and His official position as made sin for us,—and that this contrast is lost by the sacrificial reference. But there is a further antithesis not less strong. Christ is represented as made sin for us, in the same way in which we are made the righteousness of God; that is, by a judicial act on the part of God, the moral Governor and Judge. This is unfavourable to our accepting the idea of a sin-offering. It would be quite unsuitable in the second clause, which affirms that we are made the righteousness of God, and therefore it cannot be admitted in the first. But for the connection, and the twofold antithesis now mentioned, the rendering " sin-offering " would be unobjectionable.

---

[1] The phrase is not περὶ ἁμαρτίας (Rom. viii. 3). Though this view has been held by eminent men, and been very common for three centuries, it must give place to the view that we have the ABSTRACT NOUN for the concrete.

The double antithesis seems to demand the abstract term SIN, as correctly rendered in the English authorized version.

b. Much less appropriate is another interpretation, MADE HIM A SINNER. Many excellent writers have explained the phrase in this way,[1] but it is plainly inappropriate. In the first place, no instance of that usage occurs in Scripture. Then there is a want of due precision evinced in the way of distinguishing things that differ by the propounders of this interpretation. If, indeed, care was taken to distinguish between the personal and the official, there would not be the same objection to the word. But the term SINNER is in all languages too much associated with the idea of personal demerit to be applied to Christ, and is out of keeping with the constant reference to His perfect innocence, and to His suffering as the just for the unjust, the holy for the unholy. The two ideas, always put together throughout the entire Scriptures in the delineation of the atonement—viz. SINLESSNESS and SIN-BEARING, or personal perfection and official liability to divine wrath —and which are repeated here, must ever be kept apart both in form and substance. It is therefore a mistake to make the term SIN equivalent to SINNER in the passage before us.

c. We abide by the abstract term SIN,[2] which, we may notice, is here used by the apostle with a peculiar force. What does it convey to Christian minds ? It affords this sense— that Christ was made the sin of His people by the imputation of their guilt to Him; for the sin not imputed to those who

---

[1] The Socinians expounded it in the sense that Christ was so reputed, "pro peccatore ab hominibus habitum." Grotius exposed this, *de Satisfactione,* p. 24. Then many sound divines, down to the Dutch writers at the beginning of this century, rendered ἁμαρτία by the concrete term SINNER, raising their regard to God's tribunal. But that is harsh. See Witsius' beautiful chapter in his *Irenicum* (ch. ii.), in which he shows against Crisp and his followers, that they had carried their phraseology much too far : they appealed to Luther's strong language, but went far beyond him. Chauncey, *Neonomianism Unmasked,* 1692, admirably holds the balance between extremes.

[2] ἁμαρτία, as an abstract noun, is without the article, which is common (1 John ii. 2, iv. 10). See Winer's *Grammar,* p. 109. See Doedes' exposition of this text, in his second article on the Atonement, *Jaarboeken,* 1846, p. 341.

are reconciled (ver. 19) is, as we had occasion to notice already, here said to be imputed to Christ, and in such a sense that He could be described as made sin. The words, strictly considered, therefore mean, that by God's appointment He was made sin, not in mere semblance, but in reality, not before men, but before God, on the great foundation of a federal unity between Him and His people. He was, as it were, the embodiment of sin or incorporated guilt; and we may well affirm that never was so much sin accumulated upon a single head. He was not made sin in a vague, indefinite, abstract way; but the very sins of which we are painfully conscious in the moment of conviction—that is, our own sins of nature and life—were laid on Him, or transferred from our head to His. He bore their burden; and this rendered it possible to visit Him with the recompense due to sin, and with its necessary punishment, which would otherwise have been impossible.

The true import of this memorable clause, then—which, along with some other texts, has always been considered as of paramount moment for determining the true nature of the atonement—is thus rendered apparent. It means that, by God's appointment, Christ was made the sins of all His people, and that He made them His as much as if He had been divinely constituted sin in the abstract, or as sin embodied; that they were transferred to His person by what is usually designated imputation, and charged to His account.[1] That was effected in such a way as clearly displayed the distinction between His personal and representative standing before God. While He was personally the object of the Father's everlasting love and complacency, He was officially guilty in our guilt. The paternal and the governmental on the part of God may easily be distinguished and viewed apart. He never was the object of the Father's loathing or aversion, even when forsaken. He never was, what the sinner inevitably is, abhorred, or abominable;

[1] See Charnock, vol. ii. p. 684; and especially Turretin, *de Satisfactione*, p. 117, where we have a luminous discussion against one-sided tendencies.

because a distinction could always be made between the only begotten Son, the righteous Servant, and the sin-bearing Substitute.

How He was made sin, will appear from the following description. While here among men—that is, from the incarnation to the cross—He was, by a divine act, made the sin-bearer in room of His people; and there never was a moment, from the assumption of our nature to the death on the tree, when He did not bear our sins .and appear guilty as the surety of His church. Nor was He guilty before men, but before God. And furthermore, it must specially be noticed that this was not legal fiction, but divine fact. A second consideration, necessary to the full comprehension of this great transaction, is, that it was not by any infusion within, but by objective imputation. And it carried with it consequences of a punitive character not less real and heavy than if the sin had been His own. He made it His own by His voluntary act.

Here it seems necessary to take notice of the evasion to which the opponents of the vicarious satisfaction usually have recourse. The objections are singularly similar, if not the same in words, whether we have regard to former or recent times. These passages are all explained away by the writers to whom we allude, as if they referred only to indignities endured at the hands of men. They reduce the statement made by the apostle in this verse to this, that the Lord received from the hands of men a treatment which wore the appearance of, and might have been construed as if it were, the treatment given to a sinner. But is there any indication that the words express mere semblance or appearance? The text does not affirm that He was reputed among men to be a sinner. It affirms that He was made sin; that God made Him so: and that plainly goes much further than to imply that He wore in man's esteem the appearance of being a criminal or a sinner. Plainly the allusion is not to what He received at the hands of man, or was reputed in man's judgment, but to what was laid on Him by God. By no construction of language can the words be made to denote afflictive treatment at the hands of men; for that would make Christ occupy no other than a martyr's place. The superadded words, "made sin FOR US," sufficiently explode that commentary; for the injurious treatment to which Jesus was subjected could never, without substitution, have been described as undergone FOR US. Who will affirm that the fact of men entertaining ill thoughts of Christ, and treating Him as if He were a sinner, could make Him stand "for us," or make Him reputed by God as made sin FOR US, in any true acceptation of the terms?

The import of the passage, then, amounts to this: Christ, the sinless One, the realized ideal of humanity, the embodiment of the divine law, wrapped Himself in His people's sin, and was constituted sin, by His Father's act and by His own, in such a manner that at the bar of God He was no longer innocent. Rather He was made the concentrated sin of the redeemed church, because found among sinners, federally united to them, and charged at the bar of God with all their sins.

This sin-bearing capacity of Jesus proceeds on several presuppositions,—a community of nature, and a federal relation between the Surety and those in whose behalf His work was undertaken. Without these no basis could have existed either for imputation or punishment; for penal suffering has its formal ground in guilt. So true is this, that it would be an anomaly, an incongruity, a moral impossibility, in the divine government to punish without guilt. Nay, it would be a subversion of justice. The scope of this entire statement, therefore, is, that the Lord Jesus was in the divine judgment regarded in no other light than as a surety; and that, being made sin according to the divine constitution, He was charged with guilt not less really than if it had been all His own. The entire life of Christ on earth, as delineated by the evangelists and described by the apostles, is indeed set forth as the

brightest exhibition of sinless perfection. But they add another feature—that of sin-bearing. The expression, THE SINLESS
SIN-BEARER, may be said aptly to describe His earthly career.
Certainly they who look merely at His innocence mistake the
gospel, if they do not overthrow it. He was not a sinless individual, as one of many, but A SINLESS SURETY OR MEDIATOR
IN OUR STEAD. And the text further states, that to exempt us
from the guilt of sin—or, in other words, that sin might no
more be imputed to us—the sinless One was "made sin for
us." This is, in theological nomenclature, correctly enough
termed the imputation of sin to Christ.

4. The end for which Christ was made sin was, THAT WE
MIGHT BE MADE THE RIGHTEOUSNESS OF GOD IN HIM. The
apostle again uses the abstract term, as in the previous clause.
We need not dwell on the phrase " the righteousness of God,"
which we already expounded at large. Let it suffice to say
that here the one clause of this verse explains the other. We
are made the righteousness of God in the same way in which
Christ was made sin. The antithesis of the two clauses is in
the highest degree important. They are both objective ; they
are both by imputation, not by infusion. We are, through
Christ's vicarious obedience, made the righteousness of God.
And this is found only in Him objectively, and as we are
united to Him by a living faith.[1]

IV. Another passage in the same epistle, containing the
same allusion to the exchange of places, is as follows : *For ye
know the grace of our Lord Jesus Christ, that though He was
rich, yet for our sakes He became poor, that ye through His
poverty might be rich* (2 Cor. viii. 9). The apostle's design was
to enforce liberality toward the poor saints for whom he was
making a contribution among the Gentile churches ; and he
presents to the mind of the Corinthians the most constraining
motive—the Lord's abasement to poverty for our sakes. There

---

[1] See the chapter on the Counter-imputations of Sin and Righteousness,
p. 198, in Rev. H. Martin's excellent work on the Atonement. Nisbet, 1870.

are three points to which the passage refers, and to which we shall make a brief allusion.

1. The clause "though He was rich" refers to His divine pre-existence, or to that which He possessed as the Creator and owner of all. In the form of God eternally rich, exempt from any want, and not needing even the external universe to fill up a blank or to complete His personal happiness, He lived in the eternal fellowship of His Father before the world was. We may say, that before the outward universe was called into being by His fiat, and when it existed only by possibility in Him, He was infinitely blessed in Himself; and the world was made to be an object on which His boundless fulness was to be lavished, but not to fill up an unsatisfied want in Him, personally considered.

2. He became POOR in the exercise of GRACE TO US. This refers to earthly abasement, to which He spontaneously came down for man's sake; and it is affirmed of the whole person of the God-man, on the principle that we speak of Him in the concrete by either of His natures.[1] The allusion is to the incarnate state of the Lord, when He became what He was not; for there was no change, and there could be none, upon His deity. But as He entered into a new sphere, and a new form of activity, Paul has in his eye the whole abased poor life of Christ; and the statement is, that as He lived on earth without property, goods, or comforts, such as other men enjoy, and had not where to lay His head, it was all for our sakes.

This was done not simply as a preliminary to His arrest and crucifixion—though the apostle says that, had they known Him, they would not have crucified the Lord of glory (1 Cor. ii. 8)—but as the penal consequence of sin all through life; for He was AT ONCE THE SIN-BEARER AND THE CURSE-BEARER AT EVERY STAGE OF HIS CAREER. Hence it was that He took poverty as He took other parts of our curse; and the design was to free us from the penal consequences of sin.

[1] See Zanchius, tom. iii. de Filii Dei Incarnatione, p. 278.

3. It was FOR OUR SAKES; that is, for the good of the Corinthians, and all Christians generally.   The meaning appears
from the last passage expounded by us.   The Lord made an
exchange of places with us.   The atoning element, though
commonly ascribed to the death of Christ, or to His blood
sacrificially viewed, takes in His entire sin-bearing life, and
His continuous abasement as the substitute of His people.
But it may be asked, Why is such emphasis here laid upon
His poverty?   The subject suggested it to the apostle's mind,
and the whole is placed in a strong antithesis.   We do not
need to view the separate parts of His suffering obedience as
separately meritorious, as if it served a good purpose to ascribe,
as some have done, pardon to His death, and acceptance to His
active obedience.   That serves no purpose but to complicate
the matter, and divide into fragments the one work of the
Lord.   The whole obedience together is meritorious; but it
may be seen in many lights, as a compensation or exchange.
It is competent, doubtless, on the warrant of such a passage, to
hold that the whole atoning obedience is applied in its unity
at every point, and with a phase adapted to every actual want
of the human heart.   But that is rather the application of the
vicarious work to the details of human necessity; and in this
way we may fitly affirm that He was abased to atone for pride,
poor to expiate the guilt of covetousness, hungry and thirsty
on account of that intemperate indulgence which has in all
ages conquered men from the eating of the forbidden fruit to
this hour.[1]   In the same manner, we may affirm that He was
abased that we might be exalted, a servant to set us free,
troubled that we might be comforted, tempted that we might
conquer, dishonoured that we may be glorified, and scourged
that by His stripes we might be healed.   The entire abasement of Christ, in the unity of His obedience, was for us; and

---

[1] See Polanus, *Syntagma Theologiæ*, p. 1237.   This exchange of places and
experience is specially brought out by Anselm, *Meditations concerning Redemption;* by Luther and Gerhard; and by Calvin, *Com. in harmoniam Matthæi.*

we do not need to seek a separate atoning element in every little detail.

As to our becoming RICH in consequence of Christ's work, that is His reward as purchased for us. It is not earthly riches, indeed; for this was neither the design of His atonement, nor the actual result, but the whole riches of His inheritance and kingdom.

SEC. XII.—THE EPISTLE TO THE GALATIANS.

This epistle furnishes a testimony to the atonement the more striking, because, contrasted with a legal tendency, setting it off like a foil. The apostle had twice visited Galatia (Gal. iv. 13; Acts xvi. 6, xviii. 23), and refers to his preaching of the atonement there when he says that Christ Jesus had been evidently set forth before their eyes as crucified (Gal. iii. 1). But within a short time after his last visit, a perilous corruption of doctrine had been introduced, through the artful representation of zealots for the law, who had succeeded in bringing over the Galatians to the opinion that the observance of Jewish rites was necessary to their acceptance with God.

The apostle's aim in the epistle was to counteract this legal spirit. It was not a question as to a few indifferent rites with which the Jews were familiar, and which they were not prepared as yet to abandon, but a question as to acceptance with God; for these ceremonies were considered as necessary for acquiring righteousness. In exposing this error, the apostle brought the Galatians to the atonement as the sole ground of man's acceptance, and one to which no addition could be made; and the whole argument went to prove, that they who substituted another ground of acceptance overthrew the foundation of Christianity. Hence his repeated appeals to the atonement at all the turns of his argument. In the very salutation with which the epistle opens, he interweaves an

allusion to the death of Christ as the one foundation of acceptance and redemption.

I. The first passage on the atonement is as follows: *Who
gave Himself for our sins, that He might deliver us from this
present evil world* (Gal. i. 4).   How much the apostle's mind
was possessed with this great truth, appears from the fact that
he starts with it, and intimates through the entire epistle that
nothing besides Christ crucified can stand as the foundation of
a sinner's acceptance.[1]   Three points may be noticed on this
verse.

1. The self-oblation of the Lord Jesus: WHO GAVE HIMSELF.
The expression occurs elsewhere, to intimate that He willingly
offered Himself (1 Tim. ii. 6; Tit. i. 14; Matt. xx. 28).   The
phrase which our Lord employs is of the same import: "I lay
down my life" (John x. 17).   Christ was not seized by the
hand of violence, but spontaneously offered Himself; a line of
thought followed out in the Epistle to the Hebrews.   Not
only did the Father provide the sacrifice, and deliver Him up
to death for us all (Rom. viii. 32): the Lord Jesus gave Himself by a priestly act.   The phrase indicates Christ's spontaneous priestly action in His death.[2]   This peculiar mode of
describing the atonement indicates that He was the priest of
His own sacrifice—the sacrificer and the victim in one.

2. The apostle's language affirms still more definitely, that
He gave Himself FOR OUR SINS.   The object was to lead the
Galatians into deeper views of the scope of Christ's atoning
death, and to rescue them from any hankering after legal
ceremonies that made the death of Christ superfluous.   The
expression indicates that there was a relation between Christ's
death and the sins of men; that our sins made it necessary as

---

[1] This verse exhibits the sum and substance of the epistle, and the purport
of the gospel.

[2] τοῦ δόντος ἑαυτόν.   In many passages, the *giving* of Christ, always to be
taken *sacrificially*, is ascribed to the Father exhibiting His covenant love.
Here it is described as Christ's own priestly act in compliance with the Father's
will.

the procuring and meritorious cause of His death. The reason why He gave Himself is here assigned. The same representation is given in many passages, whether we turn to the ancient prophecies (Isa. liii. 5), or to the statements explanatory of Christ's death in the epistles (Rom. iv. 25 ; 1 Cor. xv. 3 ; 1 Pet. iii. 18). Between the Lord's priestly oblation and our sins there was a relation so peculiar, that our sins and His death stood connected as cause and consequence. These sins were the cause of His death.[1]

It is necessary to bring out the import of this phraseology, because many explain it away. The expression cannot mean that He was cut off by human violence sinfully exercised. Such a comment cannot be engrafted on the clause : it is descriptive of the Lord's giving Himself by a spontaneous sacrifice. They were actual sins, which did not first exist or come to light when Christ was violently put to death. Nor were the sins limited to that age, or to violent men in Jerusalem ; for the apostle, comprehending himself and the Galatians, who had nothing to do with these acts of violence, says, "who gave Himself FOR OUR SINS." Nor do such phrases allude to the putting away of sin by future amendment ; for this very thing, as we shall see, is subjoined as the scope contemplated by the sacrifice. To make the clause under our consideration of the same import with the final clause, afterwards to be noticed, would be a flat tautology. Not only so : it would fasten on Paul's reasoning the absurdity of making the means and the end, the cause and effect, identical.

The expression means that He gave Himself on account of sin ; that His death stood in the same relation to sin as death uniformly does,—that is, that death was in His case, too, the wages of sin. And the consequence is as follows : If the Lord died for our sins, they whom He represented do not require to die for their own sins. If, in the moral government of God, our sins were the cause of Christ's death, there can be no

---

[1] See Matthies' *Erklärung*, and Windischmann here on περί and ὑπέρ.

second exaction of the penal consequences from us personally.
The result of a comparison of these phrases is, that Christ
occupied a vicarious position; that He died on our account
and for our benefit, but only so because He was our substitute
at the tribunal of God.

3. All this was done, THAT HE MIGHT DELIVER US FROM THIS
PRESENT EVIL WORLD. The final particle (ὅπως) brings before
us the divine purpose, or Christ's own aim in dying for our
sins—that ethical and sanctifying result to which we already
alluded. The fruits intended by the death of Christ are very
various—as numerous, indeed, as the effects of sin; some bearing on the acceptance of our persons, others on the renovation
of our natures: and the death of Christ stands in causal connection with both. But it deserves notice, that when life and
renewing are referred to as the results of His atonement, the
acceptance of the person is always presupposed; that is, the
person is accepted, and then the nature is sanctified. Though
the atonement stands in causal connection with both, the personal standing is first rectified, as the immediate result of the
Lord's death.[1]

This passage shows that, besides the acceptance of the
man, as the immediate effect of the Lord's death, a second
effect is by no means to be overlooked. Most expositors view
the clause as referring to the ethical design of the death of
Christ; but it is not the ethical effect in the form of motive,
but new spiritual life, or renewing in the spirit of our mind.
This is procured by the death of Christ, as well as the pardon
of guilt; and that, too, not on the mere ground of moral influence, but on a ground immeasurably deeper—on that of the
divine rectitude—and according to the deepest principles of
the moral government of God. It is the more necessary to

[1] The *telic* particle ὅπως is meant to show the sanctifying result contemplated
by Christ's atoning death, according to His own and His Father's *purpose*.
And on this it is the more necessary to lay emphasis, as the Schleiermacher
theology and the advocates of a moral redemption represent the vicarious sacrifice as outward and cold.

lay emphasis on this, that we may meet the cavil, all too current, that the doctrine of substitution is cold, external, and disconnected from spiritual life and ethical results.

II. Another passage, descriptive of the relation between Christ and His people in His atoning work, is as follows : *I am crucified with Christ; nevertheless* [better, *and*] *I live; yet not I, but Christ liveth in me; and the life which I now live in the flesh I live by the faith of the Son of God* [better, *in faith which is upon the Son of God*], *who loved me, and gave Himself for me. I do not frustrate the grace of God ; for if righteousness come by the law, then Christ is dead in vain* [better, *died without a cause*] (Gal. ii. 20, 21). The context forms part of that reproof addressed to Peter for his vacillation and timidity. Peter did not as an apostle teach amiss; but his concessions to the zealots, in ceasing to eat with the Gentiles, encouraged them. Paul accordingly exposed the dangerous principle. He shows that its real meaning implied that a Christian was not complete in the atoning death of Christ, but needed something more ; that, according to the Judaizing party, men in Christ, and depending on nothing beyond His finished work, had so imperfect a ground of acceptance, that they could be viewed only as sinners, or such as were without a full title (ver. 17); that they made Christ only what Moses had been—a minister of sin and condemnation (ver. 17); in a word, that all who sought righteousness by something supplementary to Christ, avowed that He was not a perfect Saviour.[1] He adds that, in the first in-

---

[1] These memorable words of Paul are expounded, for the most part, in a far too superficial way ; and this must be so, if we do not take in the element of Christ's substitution. The apostle argues, that to make anything supplementary to Christ's work, is to represent Him as an imperfect Saviour, as a mere Moses or minister of an imperfect dispensation. To superadd anything to Christ's work, is to subvert His priestly sacrifice, and make His economy like the Sinaitic economy, and Himself a "minister of sin." Melancthon (*Apolog. Confess.* Art. 3) happily says : "Paulus ait, si justificatus in Christo opus habet ut postea alibi quærat justitiam, *tribui Christo quod sit minister peccati* id est, quod non plene justificet." See, too, the old Lutheran commentators, especially Brentius and Hunnius, who apprehend the words more profoundly than the moderns.

stance, they had sought to be accepted in Christ without the works of the law, believing on Christ as all their title; but that now they built again what they had destroyed. By seeking a title through works, they did not stand on the atonement as the sole ground of acceptance, but viewed themselves as imperfect and guilty if they had not something in addition to the work of Christ. The apostle adds, that by the law he died to the law (ver. 19); and the statement can only mean, that the death to the law was grounded on his being crucified with Christ. The following points here demand notice :—

1. We are said to be CRUCIFIED WITH CHRIST, because, when one died for all, it was the same as if all died. This expression belongs to justification from sin, or to our partaking of the merit of Christ's death, and does not mean the putting away of sin by inward renovation; for if that were indicated by our being crucified with Christ, what would then be meant by our resurrection with Him? When the apostle speaks of dying with Christ, or of being crucified with Him, he does not first use it literally, and then metaphorically; nor describe two different acts, resembling each other—one in Christ's personal experience, and one in ours, some way similar. What is there in us that can bear a comparison with the bitter death of the cross, or be designated by the name? But it consists with reason and the nature of the thing to designate our partnership with Christ, or participation in His sufferings, by this phrase; because, when Christ was crucified in our room and stead, it was in the divine account the same as if we ourselves had been crucified for sin. The compound verb CO-CRUCIFIED intimates the partnership of many in the Lord's action; and the additional words, WITH CHRIST, imply that it was accomplished in Him, or along with Him.

A wholly unique relation subsisted between Christ and His people—a relation which can be apprehended only when we call to mind the original constitution given to the human family, according to which one acted for many; for in the same manner one representative man—a God-man—died for His church, and obeyed in stead of many (2 Cor. v. 14 ; Rom. v. 12–18). This expression, and the principle on which it is based, have already been elucidated. Hence God the Father viewed the entire redeemed church as if it were hanging with Him—that is, in Him—upon the cross ; for the action of the Surety was regarded as the act of those whom He represented.

The apostle presupposes, too, what he afterwards brings out, that the curse of the law was executed on Christ crucified ; that His crucifixion comprehended His sufferings, as well as all that positive fulfilment of the law by which He became obedient unto death. And when Paul here says that we are crucified with Christ, the sense is : We are viewed as suffering what He suffered, and as doing what He did. And thus, in virtue of His finished work, we enter into His federal reward.

2. The apostle no sooner mentions his co-crucifixion with Christ, than he subjoins, according to his wont, an allusion to the risen life, or premial life. The two are commonly put together, because it is life considered as the reward of fulfilling the law (Gal. iii. 12) ; and the meritorious cause of this life is Christ crucified for all whom He represented—the cause of life by His atonement. Had the Son of God not interposed, in the capacity of surety, offering Himself to fulfil the precepts and satisfy the penalty of the divine law in our room, this premial life could never have been bestowed on fallen men. But the death and life are put together, on the principle that they must be conjoined in our case not less than in the experience of the Lord Himself ; because we were one with Him in both conditions—in Him when suffering, and then as sharing in His reward.

As we had occasion already to refer to this resurrection-life, it is unnecessary to do more in this place than to point out its inseparable connection with the Lord's atoning death. It may suffice to say, that the fountain of this life is God, and that union to the Lord by the possession of the Spirit sustains it, as natural life is sustained by the union of soul and body. The apostle in this passage connects it so closely with Christ's own life, that he puts it as if it were a reproduction, or continued manifestation, of the life of Christ. It differs from the creation-life, or what may be called the primeval Adamic life, in this respect, that it is secured for ever on the ground of justice; a premial life—a life of confirmation after a period of probation has been successfully fulfilled—a life immutable, to be forfeited no more. This eternal life evinces its presence in the same way as natural life, by the operations, exercises, or activity of its spiritual faculties; and they who possess it hear the voice of the Son of God (John v. 25), understand the word (1 Cor. ii. 10–14), taste that the Lord is gracious (1 Pet. ii. 3), see with enlightened eyes (Eph. i. 18), and will to do good, though not always effecting what they would (Rom. vii. 19). In a word, they live as members of Christ, the ever-living Head, to such a degree, that they say, "Not I, but Christ liveth in me," that is, with a federal unity, but a distinct personality.

3. Next follows a delineation of the life of faith, that is, of life as exercised in faith upon its proper object. Speaking of life in its activity here below, the apostle says that it preeminently displays itself in faith on the Redeemer, as loving His people with a special love, and giving Himself for them by a special atonement. Obviously, that is not the language of faith for attaining justification, but the language of a man already justified, and glorying in a sense of acceptance and the experience of grace. The spiritual life of a Christian finds its activity on the same object to which the anxious inquirer first came for pardon, with this difference, that it is now accepted in its special destination: "who loved ME, and gave Himself for ME." This exhaustless theme has been summed up in three pregnant terms—*talis, tanta, tantillis.*[1]

a. The Redeemer is described as the Son of God; and we

[1] Hooker, of New England, uses this formula with much effect.

see from this, that the expiation of sin is not the work of a mere man, but the work of the God-man, as He is designated in connection with His atonement, by a relation peculiar to His divine nature. The error of the Church of Rome consisted in ascribing the atonement too exclusively to the action of the human nature, and in limiting the mediatorial activity to this side of His person. But the sacerdotal sacrifice was the action of the person, and hence we read that they crucified the Lord of glory (1 Cor. ii. 8). The terrible suffering was not experienced by the divine nature, and took effect on the humanity. But it was the Son of God who atoned. The God-man suffered; and the sacrifice consisted in this, that it was the spontaneous act of one more worthy than any creature, and offering what was His own,—an oblation of more value than a whole world of sinners.

b. As to the love of the Son of God, to which reference is also made, it is described in the past tense, because it culminated upon the cross. That was displayed by the greatness of His person, the meanness and unworthiness of the objects toward whom it was exercised, and the inconceivable abasement and suffering to which He descended. It was self-moving, and uncaused by ought without Himself. It was love self-originated: He loved us, because He would love us; and whether we look at His person and offices, or at the fact that it was exercised to a people given Him by the Father, we find much to excite reflection. It was the love of a God-man, at once divine and human,—the love of one who interposed between two disunited parties to reconcile them, who had compassion on the ignorant as a priest, and discharged their obligations as a surety.

c. The apostle adds, HE GAVE HIMSELF FOR ME. This conveys a sacrificial idea, whether God is described as giving His Son, or the Son is described as giving Himself. When we inquire what He gave, the answer contained in the apostle's statement is: He gave not some, nor all, the riches of creation, but Himself,—an oblation beyond comparison greater than all the works of His hands.

d. The love and sacrifice are equally described in their special destination; and the conclusion to be drawn is, that the atonement was provided for a definite class given in the Father's gift, and specially represented by the Son in the mediatorial capacity in which He condescended to act the part of a substitute and surety. The language would be absolutely unmeaning if this were not intended. A special love and definite atonement cannot be explained away, if words are to be interpreted in their natural sense.

The apostle does not speak of the first exercise of faith, or the faith of adherence cleaving to the general declarations of divine love; that is, the faith by which we are accepted. The apostle's words refer to what is special, and presuppose assurance. They describe faith on Christ as exercising a special love to us, and offering a special atonement for us, taken from the general mass of men. This appropriation of faith animated Paul through life, and is imbibed by all true Christians subsequently to the acceptance of their person; though faith first clings to the general invitations indiscriminately addressed to the hearers of the gospel.

4. Next follows a syllogistic argument to prove that Christ's death was superfluous,—a thing for which there was no occasion, if righteousness is connected in any measure with the observance of the law (ver. 21). The dispute was not whether men could be saved by the law without Christ, but whether the law was necessary by way of supplement; and the question which the apostle decides in the affirmative is, whether justifying righteousness is to be found in the atoning death of Christ alone. Both parties admitted the sacrificial death of the Lord. But the apostle maintained that the Lord's death was the truth of all the types of the law, the exclusive ground of acceptance, and the ever-valid righteousness before God. In Paul's phraseology, Christ's death comprehends all

He did and suffered. The argument, put in syllogistic form, is as follows:[1] If righteousness come by the law, Christ died without cause. But Christ did not die without cause; therefore righteousness is not by the law.

Such is the syllogism; and if the argument has any cogency, or language any significance, OUR RIGHTEOUSNESS, or TITLE to eternal life, is found exclusively in THE ATONING DEATH of Christ. Attention is principally to be fixed on the minor proposition; and in expounding it, it must be noticed that the word rendered IN VAIN, may be taken either as defining the cause or the effect, but in the present case as defining the cause thus: He died without occasion, or gratuitously, and without necessity, as the word is elsewhere used (John xv. 25).[2] But no one with adequate views of divine wisdom, or knowledge of the prophecies respecting the Messiah, will affirm that His mission, at so great a cost, was without a cause, or superfluous; for God would not allow His only Son to be abased and suffer a malefactor's death without a cause. But there was no fit or adequate cause for His atoning work, UNLESS RIGHTEOUSNESS COME BY HIS DEATH, and by no other channel. If the law could have accomplished ought, the apostle says that righteousness and life would both have been by the law (Gal. iii. 21; Rom. viii. 3).

The apostle's argument, if we would correctly apprehend it, is as follows: Either Christ died without an adequate occasion, or the fruit as well as the definite design of His death was to usher in an ever-valid title, or righteousness. This is the positive side of the atonement, considered as a deed. It presupposes the negative side, or the atonement as the carrying out of the penalty of death originally pronounced against sin. All must die, and God can have no intercourse with sinners

---

[1] εἰ γὰρ διὰ νόμου δικαιοσύνη, ἄρα, etc.—a syllogism of much weight—proves indubitably that our righteousness and Christ's death are coincident, and that nothing else enters in.

[2] The meaning of δωριάν is not *in vain*, as Grotius, Piscator, and Theophylact render it, but *gratuitously*, or without a reason.

till the cause of separation is taken out of the way, and death endured as the wages of sin. No other cause can be assigned for the Lord's death and the sufferings through which He passed. His death was indispensably necessary, and inflexibly demanded, if a righteousness was to be brought in.

The reason is obvious: Had the law been able to contribute any aid in this respect, the Son of God, of whom the apostle has been speaking, would not have come. The Lawgiver would have erected a covenant of works, or been content with the Sinai covenant, and so have dispensed with a new covenant and a new mediator. But as the law availed not, as it only witnessed to a righteousness which it could not introduce (Rom. iii. 21), the mission of Christ to this world, His incarnation and death, had for their object to bring in the everlasting righteousness which could not otherwise have been attained. But for this, there was no assignable cause for the Lord's death, which is here viewed as the culmination of His obedience: our sole righteousness is found in His obedience unto death.

What other cause can be named which does not either proceed upon a humanitarian conception of His person, or carry its own refutation with it? According to the Socinians, there was no necessity for Christ's death, such as the apostle assumes to be conceded upon all sides, even by those whose additions tended to undermine it. Why did He die according to the text? Not to seal and confirm the truth of His doctrine; for His doctrine was confirmed by miracles: not to teach us that we enter heaven by suffering, or to give us an example how to die; for martyrs could have done that without an incarnation: not to present to us, for the sustaining of our hope, a specimen of immortality and resurrection; for the word could hold forth that: but to bring in a justifying righteousness; and on any other supposition, He died without a cause.

III. We have next a passage descriptive of Christ made a

curse for us; and of all the texts bearing on the atonement, there is none more decisive as to its nature : *Christ hath redeemed us from the curse of the law, being made a curse for us : for it is written, Cursed is every one that hangeth on a tree : that the blessing of Abraham might come on the Gentiles through Jesus Christ* (Gal. iii. 13).   The context shows, that far from obtaining righteousness, the Galatians, by placing themselves on a legal footing (ver. 10), brought themselves under the curse. This is not the Levitical law, because it proposes life to those who fulfil it (ver. 12), and pronounces a curse on non-fulfilment (ver. 13).   The apostle's object is to bring out that the law awards a curse, not a reward, to those who place themselves on a footing of law ; and this is contrasted with eternal life, the promised reward.   For the correct apprehension of the atonement in its essential elements, we must strictly define this curse.   It is the divine sentence pronounced upon transgressors, comprehending in it the loss of God as its chief ingredient, separation from Him (Isa. lix. 2), and whatever positive infliction is further included.   The Old Testament phraseology, from which the language is derived, takes in all that doom and shame which are the consequences of violating the divine law (Gen. iii. 17–19 ; Deut. xxvii. 14–26).

The text may be compared with another, to which it bears a strong resemblance, where Christ is said to have been made sin (2 Cor. v. 21).   The abstract noun in both passages demands notice ; for an abstract noun describes Christ as the sin-bearer, and an abstract noun describes Him as the curse-bearer.   The Hebrews were wont to take nouns in the abstract instead of adjectives, when they wished to intimate that a thing was done in the highest conceivable measure or degree. The expression MADE SIN FOR US is more emphatic and full of meaning than if Paul had said, MADE HIM A SINNER.   It avoids, moreover, the misconception to which the latter term would have given rise, and allows us, according to the design of the passage, to distinguish between the personal and the official. In like manner, the expression BEING MADE A CURSE FOR US is more emphatic and significant than if he had said, BEING MADE ACCURSED ; while it enables us to distinguish between personal relation and official suretyship. The similarity between the two passages is obvious ; and the difference is, that the former describes the imputation of sin, while the latter sets forth the actual doom or infliction. The former describes the relation of sin to punishment, the latter the punishment itself.[1]

In this passage four points demand notice, and we shall advert to them as briefly as is compatible with the importance of so conclusive a passage : 1. What is the curse of the law ? 2. The liberation from it ; whether absolute, or by price. 3. The mode by which the redemption was effected : the ransom. 4. The blessing on the Gentiles in room of the curse.

1. The CURSE OF THE LAW does not mean temporal and civil punishments inflicted on Israel for the transgression of the judicial or ceremonial law. To interpret the expression in that way, is wholly to misapprehend its meaning. That there were such visitations, cannot be questioned by any one who has acquired a knowledge of the old dispensation (Deut. xxviii. 15 ff.). These were evidences or proofs by which the people were trained to apprehend the divine wrath against the transgressors of His commandments ; but it is a far deeper thought that is before the apostle's mind.[2] As the context indubitably proves, the contrast is between wrath and blessing, between condemnation and justification. Besides, the Galatians to whom he wrote were Gentiles, not Jews ; and it would have had no appropriateness, to bring before them an allusion to the dispensational peculiarities of Israel. The term CURSE, here used, comprehends the penal sanction of the moral law, and takes for granted that mankind generally, having the work of the law written on their hearts, and a law to themselves (Rom.

---

[1] See Cameron, *Opera*, p. 518 ; Lechler, *das apostolische Zeitalter*, p. 75.
[2] See Balduin's Latin Commentary on Paul's Epistles.

ii. 14), were not less liable to the curse than the Jews: they were both equally under the curse.

2. From that curse Christ redeemed us, or, more strictly, bought us out. The word is a compound verb, denoting to buy out from one condition to transfer us into another.[1] The question here arises, In what way, absolutely or by price? Plainly it is not an absolute deliverance, but one which is the result of purchase. No terms could more explicitly declare this; for the price or ransom is immediately subjoined, as in many other passages where reference is made to redemption (compare 1 Cor. vi. 20; 1 Pet. i. 18, 19). It was a true and real curse to which we were subjected: it is a true and real redemption into which we are ushered; and the price, too, by which it was effected—the intervention of the cross, or Christ made a curse for us—was a true and real price. The curse lay on Jew and Gentile equally; and the ransom which liberated us was the transfer of punishment, and an exchange of places between us and Christ. We could not have been redeemed from this obligation to the curse, involving as it did a reference to God as Lawgiver and Judge, had the cross been an expedient of an arbitrary nature, having nothing in common with the burden of the curse. That this is a commutation of persons, or deliverance by substitution, cannot be mistaken or denied.

3. The price or ransom paid for us was nothing else but the personal Redeemer, the Son of God condescending to be made A CURSE for us; a thought so vast and unfathomable, that though our minds grow familiar with the phraseology, we are for ever incapable of comprehending or fully surveying it. The ransom which liberated us was not His divine doctrine, nor His bright example of holiness left us to follow; for that would but throw humanity back upon its own resources, and could never be disjoined from dependence on works, or inner holiness. The

---

[1] ἐξηγόρασιν. The verb denotes *to obtain by price*, and the compound verb refers to the misery out of which we were ransomed (Quenstedt).

apostle thinks of the ransom in a far other way : he identifies it with the Lord's abasement and ignominious death as a vicarious satisfaction. He affirms that the price by which He discharged us from temporal and eternal penalty was His being made a curse for us by entering into our position before God. That is the meaning of the participial clause (compare 2 Cor. v. 19) : He was made the accumulated curse of His people, as if it were embodied in Him. God treated the sin-bearer as if He had been the sinner : that is, what the law awarded to us was visited upon Him ; and by that substitution our redemption was secured.[1]

This curse culminated in the wrath of God. And here I must take occasion to expose the unbiblical theory prevalent in a certain school of theologians at present, that the element of wrath did not enter into the atonement, and that Christ was in no sense the object of the wrath of God. It suffices to explode such a notion to direct attention to this single phrase, which conveys the opposite thought : Were not men under the wrath of God when they were under the curse ? (Gal. iii. 10 ; Eph. ii. 3.) And WHEN CHRIST WAS MADE A CURSE, was He not, in an official respect, of necessity the object of divine wrath ? The term used in the text has only to be alternated with the equivalent term, to convince any mind that the theory in question is no better than a neutralizing evasion, if not a contradiction, of Scripture. That curse was the penal sanction of the law with which we were burdened, and from which we must needs be redeemed ; and the words will bear no other comment.

---

[1] It would be tedious to refer to all the discussions on the import of this passage. The expositions are numerous, because it is decisive as to the nature of the atonement, and every one is summoned to examine it. Against the Socinians, see Arnold, Calovius, Hoornbeek, Turretin, Quenstedt, Oeder, Pictet, Stapfer. See the remarks of Owen on the Socinian views (vols. ix. x.), and Hurrion *on the Necessity of the Atonement ;* Seiler and Tissel on the atonement, both of the Grotian school ; and more recently Lotze, Keiser, and Vinke. The discussions of Weber, *vom Zorne Gottes ;* Keil (see above, p. 27) ; Thomasius (vol. iii. p. 73) ; Philippi, in the course of the discussions excited by Hofmann, deserve perusal.

This transfer of punishment from us to Him is convincingly established by the context and by the structure of the sentence; and there is not room for two opinions on the subject. That curse was manifested in the infliction of death in its full extent of meaning, according to the primeval sentence on our race (Gal. iii. 3–19). It consisted especially in the privation of God, and in the desertion, which extorted from Him many agonizing complaints; for the worst ingredient of the curse is the loss of God, or the absence and complete withdrawal of God from a human soul, made to be His habitation. That, in fact, is the bitterest element of eternal death; and through it the Surety was constrained to pass when made a curse for us. None but a divine person, indeed, was equal to the endurance; and none but a divine person could have engaged his heart to appear before God to encounter the curse (Jer. xxx. 21). A God-man was required to bear it, to reverse it, and transform it into a blessing (ver. 14).

We must notice, before proceeding further, the quotation from the Mosaic law. Paul adduces it to ground what had been said, and to prove that death by crucifixion was not only painful and ignominious, but expressive of a divine curse: "For it is written, Cursed is every one that hangeth on a tree" (Deut. xxi. 22, 23). To understand this quotation grounding the previous statement, it is necessary to consider whether the particular law to which the apostle refers was intended to be symbolical, typical, and prophetical in its import. Expositors, following the uniform testimony of rabbinical writers, are mostly of opinion that crucifixion, or the affixing of a living person by nails to a tree, and thus leaving him to expire by a slow and painful death, was a Gentile mode of punishment common among the Romans, but never in use among the Jewish people, while their institutions remained entire; and that the Mosaic law, in referring to the suspending of a criminal on a tree, had reference not to a living man, but to a dead body thus exposed to view till sunset,—after which the body was to be buried, not remaining all night upon the tree. On the other hand, Lipsius, Baronius,[1] and above all, Albert Schultens, contend with great learning that there is no good ground for the conclusion, that death by crucifixion was not in use in the times of the Hebrew commonwealth; and that the rabbinical writers in this instance, as in many others that might be named, discover a determination to wrest from the Christians such a remarkable type or typical prophecy of the crucified Messiah. Without entering into this controversy, let it suffice to say, that between hanging on a tree as described in the Mosaic law, and death by crucifixion, an obvious point of similarity exists, which no one can mistake. But besides the suspension,—the point of resemblance,—such a mode of death was not only ignominious in the sight of men, but meant to appear accursed in the sight of God: for the terms of the law are express to this effect. God, in His divine purpose, willed it to be so. As it was a positive appointment, it is not necessary to search for deeper reasons, least of all for fanciful analogies; though the opinion expressed by many eminent divines, that this mode of death recalled the manner in which sin entered into the world, and by which the curse was diffused over the human race, is not unwarrantable. Our first parents sinned by the forbidden tree, and God, it is thought, willed that the reversal of the curse by the second Adam should be by hanging on a tree, that it might suggest the origin of the curse. Whatever ground may exist for this opinion, it was according to the determinate counsel and foreknowledge of God that the curse should be expiated in no other way but by crucifixion or hanging on a tree.

But as to the special point, how the person hanging on a tree was accursed, there can be no doubt. It was a symbol, type, or prophecy. They who were thus punished were not accursed because they were hanged on a tree—a shallow comment which reduces it to nothing—but conversely, were hanged on a tree because they were accursed. It is necessary to lay stress on

[1] Casaubon replied to Baronius.

this, to forestall the notion that Paul, by applying this language to Christ, means nothing more than that there was an outward exposure and shame attaching to that mode of death. That is far from the apostle's meaning, and far from a right conception of the symbol. He was not made a curse by the mere fact that He hung on a tree; but conversely, He was suspended there because He was made a curse for us; and the mode of punishment was first instituted to represent the idea now stated.

The Lawgiver, when He proclaimed that law by Moses, intended it to be typical as well as symbolical, or more strictly a typical prophecy. It figured forth a great idea, which had only to be apprehended by the first preachers of Christianity, and has only to be apprehended still, to impel men under the most constraining motive to boast of the cross, to admire the cross, and to commend the cross as the power of God and wisdom of God. In the eyes of men, crucifixion was in the highest degree ignominious,—a servile punishment inflicted on the lowest scum of the people, when they expiated their crimes by death. On freemen it was never inflicted till they were degraded from their rank, and classified with slaves; and then it was awarded only for the worst crimes committed against civil order and law, property, religion, and government. The stigma attaching to such a death, accordingly, was the same as now attaches to one who expiates great crimes upon the gallows. This was the Gentile conception of such a death. But according to the Jewish law, it carried with it the further brand of being accursed in the sight of God; and the fact of dying such a death was doubtless one principal ground why the nation esteemed Christ stricken, smitten of God, and afflicted. The law made such a death emphatically an accursed one; and were they not to view it in that light? Accordingly, the common name for Jesus among the Jews to the present day, THE HANGED ONE, sufficiently shows how they think themselves entitled to regard the crucifixion.

In giving such a law by Moses, God meant it to be a typical prophecy, as well as symbolical of curse-bearing. In the same way, the lifting up of the brazen serpent on the pole was meant in the divine purpose to adumbrate the crucifixion, whether many or few saw beyond the figure to the Antitype. Among the forms of punishment mentioned in the law, that of hanging on a tree was pronounced accursed, because it figured forth the cross, and announced that the Messiah should one day hang upon a tree. The question is not, how many could decipher the symbol and the typical prophecy? but, was that in the divine intention? And the apostle's quotation of the passage in this connection is decisive in the affirmative. Both the symbol and the type are equally emphatic. The cross was the expression of an idea,—a sort of fact-painting, an evidence or exhibition that the person suspended on it was already accursed, or a curse in the sight of God. Not that the tree was the cause of the curse; for the accursed one was suspended on the tree. This was an outstanding public testimony to a fact, and in this case a testimony that the Lord was burdened with the world's curse, and weighed down under its overwhelming load.[1]

4. The CURSE-BEARING paved the way for THE BLESSING (ver. 14). These two are directly contrasted, and the one is in order to the other. The curse under which we laboured was removed, that the blessing might be imparted. The curse laid on the Lord opened the channel of communication for the reception of the blessing; out of that redemption from the curse of the law, flows the blessing which comes upon the Gentiles (ver. 14).

To all this exposition three objections are commonly urged by those who impugn the atonement as a substitution and satisfaction. And we must advert to them, though they are easy of refutation to any one who apprehends the sin-bearing office of the Lord. The same objections were propounded by

[1] See Turretin, *de Satisfactione*, p. 107.

the first Socinians three centuries ago, and they are reproduced and repeated by modern writers, with little change of
expression.

(1.) It is objected that the apostle, in speaking of liberation
from the curse of the law, had respect only to the Jews. This
is groundless. Paul refers to men, of whatever nation, who
were under the curse of the law, or under the wrath of God,
revealed from heaven against all ungodliness and unrighteousness of men (Rom. i. 18). What is the apostle's object in the
Epistle to the Romans but to prove this ? But, to confine ourselves to the text before us, he aims to show that they who are
redeemed share in the blessing, and that curse-bearing on the
part of Christ was with a view to the blessing which comes
on the Gentiles also (ver. 14). When the apostle says, " He
hath redeemed US," nothing can warrant us to conclude, with
Socinians and many modern exegetes, that he has in his eye
Jews more than Gentiles. No antithesis of nationality is
intended when the apostle says, " He hath redeemed us from
the curse of the law, that the blessing of Abraham might come
on the Gentiles." When the apostle, writing to Gentiles, names
himself as comprehended in the class of those who are sharers
in redemption, the terms US, or WE, or OUR, can never be applied to Jews alone. We do not find a single case where the
apostle, after his conversion, puts himself into the category of
the Jews, except where he alludes to his past; for his nationality, his Judaism, his former course, are all absorbed in the
new relation. And every supposed classification of himself
among the Jews should be otherwise explained. We do not
hesitate to lay down this canon. Besides, the most rudimentary
inquirer into the scope of the epistles is aware that they were
written to Christ's disciples, to redeemed men, or such as
professed to be so. Wherever the apostle, then, makes use of
this style of language, including himself in the class of men
to whom he speaks of doctrine, privilege, or duty, he writes
to Christ's disciples as such, but neither to Jews nor Gen-

tiles apart. Moreover, the Galatians to whom he wrote were Gentiles.[1]

It is a low comment of the Rationalists, that we are redeemed from the yoke of the Mosaic law. With that shallow interpretation many satisfy themselves,—supposing Paul to say that, so long as he was a Jew, he was subject to the Mosaic law, from which he was now redeemed ; or, as others expound it, exposed to the constant risk of falling under the terrible penalties of the law, but was now free. In refutation of this comment, it may suffice to say that, however applicable in other connections, it is here out of place ; for the passage does not affirm that Christ redeemed us from all obedience to the law, or from all relation to the law, but from its curse. The language is definite : it refers to the condemning sentence or punishment awarded by the law, whether we have regard to what is temporal or eternal. The meaning is, that Christ bought us out or redeemed us from the penalty ; the language having reference to the custom of redeeming a captive or slave by ransom. The figure was peculiarly appropriate.

(2.) A second objection by the opponents of vicarious satisfaction is, that Christ is not said to have borne the SAME CURSE, the same elements of penal visitation, under which those lie who are burdened with the curse of the law. They hold that it was different in kind ; and, in a word, that so far as Christ was concerned, it had not the nature of a curse, and contained nothing of penal infliction at the hand of God. They allow that He bore the suffering of the cross as inflicted by the hand of man, but admit no deeper element of punitive infliction at the hand of God. Their shallow comment is reduced to this, that, according to the law, the mode of death by crucifixion had a certain brand or stigma attached to it, not as an exponent of a deeper idéa, but simply as a name among men or in common estimation. Thus the mere name or fact of the crucifixion

[1] See Stillingfleet's *Sermons on Christ's Satisfaction,* and Th. Goodwin (v. p. 188).

is, according to them, all the curse. In support of this view, it has been ingeniously argued in modern times[1] that the apostle does not say of Christ, "being made THIS CURSE," which, it is allowed, would mean the curse of the law; and they allege that since it is said, "being made A curse for us," the interpretation which explains the clause of substitution and penal suffering must fall to the ground.

The question whether our curse was removed from us and laid on Christ, must be dealt with in a different way. We cannot but resent this interpretation as unfair—as an exegetical violence which the structure of the sentence will not endure. It is a deliberate attempt to explain away the simple and natural relation of the clauses. The apostle did not need to say, "being made THIS CURSE for us." Nay, it might have been liable to misapprehension, more especially as the quotation from the Mosaic law was to be immediately subjoined. But the Holy Ghost knows how to use the most appropriate words, and to put them in the clearest setting. First, mention is made of the curse of the law awarded to transgressors; next, it is announced that we were liberated or discharged from that curse; thirdly, putting cause and effect together, the apostle affirms that such a result was brought about by Christ becoming a curse for us. Words cannot more explicitly teach that HE WAS MADE OUR CURSE, and that the means of redemption was Christ's intervention as a curse-bearer. That is convincingly brought out in the passage; and we may affirm, in the words of Dr. South, who in one of his sallies remarks upon this text: "Scripture must be crucified as well as Christ, to give any other tolerable sense of the expressions."

But might it not be Paul's intention to say that Christ suffered what made HIM APPEAR AS ACCURSED? Might he not mean that Christ was represented to men as a curse, appearing

---

[1] See Hofmann's *Schriftbeweis:* he argues from the text in this way. Keil's reply to Hofmann (*Zeitschrift für die gesammte Lutherische Theologie,* 1857, p. 452) is most conclusive.

as if He were so, or so reputed in men's esteem? No: the statement would then be no longer an objective one. We are not so to weaken or reduce the import of the expressions. They set forth A REAL and not A SEEMING CONNECTION between sin-bearing and curse-bearing. All the menace or penal sanction of the law was discharged on the Lord as our substitute. And the passage brings out what Christ was IN GOD'S ACCOUNT and by God's appointment, not what He was in man's repute, and as He was treated by the hands of men. The absence of the definite article, or of the demonstrative pronoun THIS, does not warrant us to think of any other curse, or any modification or alteration of the specific curse incurred by us, and necessarily inflicted for the violation of the divine law. It is not to be rendered nor interpreted A CURSE LIKE THAT WHICH is pronounced by the law upon transgressors, and conveying merely the idea of similarity or resemblance. That were but another form of the metaphorical or figurative theory of the atonement, with which the Socinianizing opponents of substitution and satisfaction rest content. But we cannot stop short there. The entire connection proves that it is THE VERY CURSE OF THE BROKEN LAW, the very infliction impending over us, and struck by God's own hand, to which Paul refers. We are not to take the words as meaning that His enemies executed Him by a malefactor's death; for it was GOD Himself, and not His enemies, that made Him a curse.

(3.) The third objection is, that Christ could not be said to be a curse for us in the sense of undergoing THE VERY PENALTY IN OUR STEAD, because it was eternal death,—a doom which they allege He could not undergo, as He must rise again. That objection could not be propounded but by men who neither recognised the divine person of the Lord, nor apprehended the infinite value of His sufferings. But in point of dignity and value, the penal sufferings of such a person, though limited in duration, were equivalent to eternal punishment; for His divine nature had an influence on His sufferings, and put Him in a position such as no mere man could ever occupy. We find, accordingly, that Scripture in many passages fixes attention on His personal dignity, and deduces from it the unspeakable value of His sufferings (Acts xx. 28; 1 Cor. ii. 8; 1 John i. 7). Finite creatures could give no satisfaction, however lasting the duration of their sufferings; whereas the divine dignity of the Redeemer counterbalanced the duration of the curse. In intensive merit, it was thus a full equivalent to eternal death. And we may add that the endless punishment of the sinner would not be necessary, were he adequate to endure infinite wrath in combination with the other conditions which a satisfaction presupposes.

Christ's whole career was marked by vicarious curse-bearing; and we have to notice what it involved. Properly considered, the entire life of the Lord, from the manger to the cross, or rather to the grave, was a course of sinless curse-bearing, because a course of sin-bearing. He was visited with the penal consequences of sin, with its curse and wages, from the day when He entered into humanity by incarnation. Already we have proved at large that Christ, through His entire earthly history, was conscious of occupying the position of a sin-bearing substitute; and where sin was, there too the curse was, its inevitable accompaniment. The term CURSE expresses the penal sanction of the law; and when Christ is so designated, the import is, that the curse, following the violation of the law, was executed on Him. It has therefore everything in common with condemnation and wrath. We must, however, distinguish several things when we speak of Christ made a curse in our room and stead, lest no definite or correct idea should be formed of the language.

a. We must distinguish between the personal and the official in this mysterious transaction. Inconsiderate and revolting phraseology has been sometimes here employed by certain ill-balanced minds. God certainly did not view the Redeemer as the sinner must needs be viewed, when the latter comes under the full infliction of the divine curse. He did not regard Him personally in any other light than as His beloved Son, on whom He looked with infinite complacency, as at once His righteous Servant and His only Son. But as the surety of His people, the Lord descended into the lowest abyss of that curse which we had incurred, and tasted death, the penalty of sin, that we might never taste of it.

b. Nor was it only in His death that He was made a curse for us, though it culminated upon the cross; for the curse of God, the penal sanction of the divine law, was expressed in Christ's life as well as in His death. The outline or tenor of the curse, sketched in Genesis in the narrative of the fall and its doom, may be read off in every particular from the earthly history of the Lord. The labour, sorrow, and death denounced on man in that primeval curse, may be seen in Christ in every variety of form in which they could possibly attach to the incarnate Son. In toil and grief, in frailty and fainting, in hunger and thirst, in want and weariness, in bearing the likeness of sinful flesh, we can trace this curse-bearing—the unfailing attendant of sin-bearing. His earthly career was, in fact, pervaded by it at every step. Though He saw no corruption, either living or dead—for sickness or disease could not, as a personal quality, attach to the sinless One—He knew by sympathy, and in some mysterious way, too, by the miraculous healing of disease, what that part of the curse comprehended. His death was a curse-bearing death, involving all the elements of the second or eternal death, so far as the privative sense, the loss of God, is concerned—that heaviest part of a God-inflicted curse. Such a death alone could be an adequate equivalent for the curse of the law due to transgressors.

c. It is evidently identical with the curse awarded to the violators of the law. There is only one divine curse, and it is ours, but transferred to a Substitute who was exempt from it on every ground, whether we think of His divine dignity or sinless perfection. Whether, therefore, we consider the struc-

R

ture of this passage, or the nature of the transaction itself, we
find a full proof that it was vicarious curse-bearing; and all
the efforts made by the opponents of substitution to wrest this
passage from the church—and no means have been left unused
—are utterly futile. They are a complete failure if we abide
by Scripture, grammatically expounded, as our sole court of
appeal. The words can convey no other meaning but this,
that the Lord Jesus underwent the penalty we had merited,
and was treated as an accursed person in our stead, and so
freed us from the curse by vicariously bearing it.

IV. Another passage, parallel to the former, but with an
extension of the idea, is as follows: *When the fulness of the
time was come, God sent forth His Son, made of a woman, made
under the law, to redeem them that are under the law, that we
might receive the adoption of sons* (Gal. iv. 4). Redemption
from the curse of the law was the scope of the former passage;
redemption from the law itself, considered in its covenant form,
or as the condition of life, is the scope of this.

1. The fulness of time, at which the atonement was accomplished, is here noticed. It may suffice to say, that though
we cannot enumerate all the elements that entered into that
fulness, some are on the surface. A fact so stupendous was not
to be ushered in as an abrupt phenomenon, without a preparatory economy of type and prophecy, by means of which a
circle of ideas and a peculiar phraseology might be formed to
bring it home to men's minds, both before the incarnation and
after it. A sufficient reason must also appear why such a
provision was necessary; and this necessity required to be
historically displayed in the failure of human schemes. Not
only art and education, culture and civilisation, but divine law
itself, must be tried. They were tried, and found inadequate
to meet the case.

2. The sending forth of the Son of God is next mentioned
as the presupposition or foundation of the ransom. The expressions here used unambiguously affirm that the Son existed

as a divine person with God, and very God, before He came to be made of woman. He was sent, in the exercise of love, by the first person of the Godhead; and no one interpreting words as they stand, can permit himself to reduce them to the tame, flat sense that Jesus was but a man. Here He is marked out as divine. His mission, and the possession of the divine nature, were not precisely the ransom, but the presupposition of the ransom, giving it infinite value, and rendering it applicable to the wants of millions. But no ingredient of the penal sanction of the law, or of the positive obedience, could be dispensed with on that account. It was of necessity the work of a God-man, but true human suffering and obedience.

3. The next gradation as here stated was, that Christ WAS MADE OF WOMAN. It might pass without challenge on philological grounds, were we to translate the clause BORN OF WOMAN; though it cannot be disguised that the latter is preferred by many, in the interest of an erroneous tendency, viz. that they may escape from the doctrine of the supernatural conception of Jesus. The true rendering is, MADE OF WOMAN; and the language implies, that as the Son He had another mode of existence, but became something that He was not. The divine side of Christ's person has been already noticed: here Paul teaches with equal clearness His true humanity. The incarnation of the Lord is here presented to us as a divine fact, the deed of God the Father; elsewhere it is spoken of as the Redeemer's own act (2 Cor. viii. 9). By naming a human mother from whom the Lord derived His human nature, the apostle plainly meant to announce His true and perfect humanity, but in terms which fully coincide with the acknowledged fact of His being virgin-born. Christ's derivation of humanity from Adam through His mother is no small or unimportant matter in connection with His atonement: for His fraternity, as our kinsman Redeemer, absolutely depends upon the fact that He derived His humanity from the substance of His mother; and without this He would

neither possess the natural nor legal union with His people, which must lie at the foundation of His representative character. To be our GOEL or redeeming kinsman, the humanity with which He was invested could neither be brought from heaven, nor be immediately created by the Godhead, but derived, as ours is, from a human mother; with this difference, that the Lord's humanity never existed in Adam's covenant, to entail either guilt or taint upon Him personally. He must be within the pale of mankind, yet its second man, or second representative; personally exempt from every charge and from every defilement descending from the first man, but freely assuming guilt by a federal engagement in our stead. In a word, He took of man all that needed redemption, a true body and a reasonable soul, without any personal obligation devolving on Him by mere necessity of nature; for what obligation or responsibility could attach to the God-man, that is, to humanity assumed into personal union with the Eternal Son? His was real humanity, but sinless,—a body incorruptible, and a reasonable soul without a taint of imperfection; and this woman-born or virgin-born Redeemer, with no personal responsibilities derived from the first Adam, spontaneously engaged to assume them by consenting to be the second Adam.

4. The next thing mentioned in the text, and a further step, is: MADE UNDER THE LAW. This clause affirms that Christ was made under the law for the sake of those who were under the law, and therefore not on His own account or from any personal obligation. Had He been personally subject to it, then His obedience could only have availed to His personal release or discharge. But there was this difference between Christ and us, that we were born under the law by the condition of creaturehood, while He was spontaneously made under it for the ends of suretyship.

This clause demands special notice on another ground. It is affirmed in certain quarters, and especially by those who do not admit the evidence for Christ's active obedience, that

the apostle does not here name the ransom, but leaves it to
be sought in the previous passage relating to the curse (Gal. iii.
13). That is by no means the case; and an analysis of the
words may convince any one that the ransom or equivalent
is as definitely named as in the other passage. The statement
that Christ was made a curse refers to His passive obedience;
this statement, that He was made under the law, refers to His
active as well as suffering obedience, or to the fulfilling of the
law in action and suffering. The PRICE of redemption is therefore named, and it is nothing but His incarnation and subjection to the law. The opinion that reconciliation and redemption
are effected by the death of Christ, to the exclusion of His
active obedience, is thus in collision with this passage, and with
many other parts of Scripture (Rom. v. 19). When Christ was
made under the law, it was with a view to that meritorious
obedience by which we are accounted righteous, and treated as
righteous.[1]

The active obedience considered as our ransom, or a constituent element of the ransom, has encountered many futile
objections. Thus some oppose it on the general ground that
the law was not applicable to non-Jews, but confined to Israel.
But however some portions of the law might be limited to
Israel, the moral law, adapted to man as man, and the reflection of the divine nature, was but a republication of the
law of nature. It is preposterous to speak of this element,
the core and essence of the whole, as limited to Jews, when

[1] The opponents of Christ's active obedience considered as vicarious invariably shut their eyes to this fact. They call it an ecclesiastical conception, like Meyer; or adduce, like Piscator and his followers, grounds to prove
that Christ owed active obedience on His own account; or make faith a righteousness by acceptilation, like the Arminians. But the fact is proved by this
and similar texts, that Christ's subjection to the law was for our redemption.
All the great Lutheran divines of the Reformation age maintained without exception, that Christ owed no obedience on His own account, and their reasoning
cannot be refuted; for the law was not given to the human nature in the person
of the Son, till He spontaneously put Himself under it. See, too, in the
Reformed Church, Calvin, Danæus, Pareus, Amesius, Maccovius, who are of the
same opinion.

it was not arbitrary, but eternal, and must needs receive its fulfilment AS THE CONDITION OF LIFE (Gal. iii. 12). The obedience
to it was necessary alike for Gentiles and for Jews.

It is further alleged by modern exegetes, that the expression
MADE UNDER THE LAW means no more than to be born a Jew.
That is by no means the idea which the apostle expresses,
nor does such an interpretation reach the meaning. Christ's
mission and subjection to the law were in order to redeem us:
the one was the way to the other, as appears from the final
particle, which connects the last clause of the one verse (ver. 4)
with the first clause of the following verse (ver. 5). We cannot
translate " born a Jew,"[1] because the relation of the means to
the design would be absolutely imperceptible; whereas the
apostle, by the repetition of the same words, intends to make
it plain. Moreover, it must be noticed, that if we translate
the words " born a Jew" in the one verse (ver. 4), we must, on
all grounds of consistency, translate the same words in the
same way in the next verse (ver. 5). And what sense would
be conveyed by the clauses thus rendered, " born a Jew, to
redeem them that were born Jews,"—as if He came only to
redeem the Jews? Nor does the absurdity end there. The
next clause, also expressive of design, and introduced by a final
particle, introduces a wider reference when it says, " that we
might receive the adoption of sons." All this is natural and
obvious, when we apprehend that redemption by Christ's
atonement and obedience paves the way to the further blessing
of adoption. But on the other mode of interpretation, the
sequence of thought would be as follows: Christ was born a
Jew, to redeem them that were born Jews, that we (the Gentile
Galatians as well as Paul) might receive the adoption of sons.
The redemption of the Jews is made the cause of the adoption
of the Gentiles. That is so absurd, that it needs no remark.
But all is plain and significant when we take the words as

---

[1] Meyer, Bishop Ellicott, and others, unhappily expound the words in this
superficial way.

already expounded, and remember that the essential elements of the law were written on the conscience of the Gentiles (Rom. ii. 15).

In the Pauline epistles, where the expression UNDER THE LAW several times occurs, it is always equivalent to being subject to the law (Rom. iii. 19, vi. 14, 15; Gal. iv. 21, v. 18; 1 Cor. ix. 20). In all these passages the expression has one uniform sense : it denotes subjection to the law, with the accessory idea that it has something burdensome and oppressive. These several passages are not to be mingled and confounded. But one thing is evident: it is not a mere circumlocution for a Jew. The meaning is, that God sent His Son, made under the law, for the redemption of those who were under the law in all its breadth of meaning. Now Jews and Gentiles were equally under the law, as the condition of life, by the fact of creaturehood (Rom. ii. 14, iii. 9).

Two things are comprehended. The first is, that the Lord Jesus, when made under the law for our deliverance, must have fulfilled all its claims, according to the terms. And as we were bound, according to essential human relations, to the strictest obedience on the one hand, and to the endurance of the curse on the other—that is, to the precept and the penalty —the apostle affirms that both were fulfilled by Christ in our room (Gal. iii. 10, 12). That is the fulfilment of the law in the full sense of the term. The second point is, that whatever Christ rendered in this capacity was done as our substitute, and for the benefit of those who were under the law. The objection of those who impugn the element of active obedience as part of the Lord's atoning work is, that Christ was under obligation as man to obey for Himself, like every rational creature. The answer to this, as it was uniformly given by the Lutheran, and also by the best Reformed divines, on the ground of such passages as the present, was, that humanity was assumed by the Son of God into the unity of His person, to be an instrument or organ in His work; that it existed only in the person of the Son, and never apart from Him; that the law as such had no competent authority over the Son of God, who was Himself the lawgiver; that His human nature, also called the Son of God, was not under the law, but exempt from it in any covenant form; and therefore that He was made under the law, not because He had a human nature, but because He willed to be under it, to finish a work of obedience which might be given away to those who had none. This was meritorious obedience, and given to us as a donation.

5. The fruit or benefit derived from Christ's subjection to the law is our redemption and, at a second remove, our adoption. The two final clauses,[1] which refer to these two blessings as the fruit of Christ's ransom, may be co-ordinate, as some view them, or subordinated in this sense, that one paves the way for the other. Both clauses, however, refer without distinction to Jews and Gentiles. By the obedience of Christ both are equally redeemed: then follows the blessing of adoption, of which the further result is the sending forth of the Spirit of adoption into our hearts (ver. 6).

V. The apostle strikingly utters his view of the atonement, when he declares, in contrast to the errorists, who adhered to rites, ceremonies, and legal observances: *God forbid that I should glory, save in the cross of our Lord Jesus Christ, by whom* [better, *by which*] *the world is crucified unto me, and I unto the world* (Gal. vi. 14). From the fulness of his heart, as a man and apostle, he declares his attachment to the cross, that is, to Christ crucified as the only ground of acceptance, discarding all supplementary additions with holy zeal. He elsewhere affirms that boasting is excluded (Rom. iii. 27); but legal boasting is displaced, that glorying in the Lord, or glorying in Christ crucified, may begin (see 1 Cor. i. 30). Only two things demand notice here as bearing on our theme.

---

[1] The first ἵνα clause in ver. 5 shows that redemption was aimed at as the immediate effect of Christ's subjection to the law; the second ἵνα clause in the verse may be co-ordinated with the former (as Meyer views it), or be taken as a further end contemplated and subordinated to the first.

1. The cross, viewed as a propitiatory sacrifice, is described as the sole ground of a Christian's boast or glorying. The antithesis in which the words occur repudiates every other plea but the finished work of the cross, but also implies that there is a boasting in which the Christian can never go too far or indulge too frequently. He gloried in the cross as the expiation of sin, the fulfilment of the law, the cause of reconciliation, the ransom of the church, the propitiation for our sins, and the sacrificial blood which brings us near and keeps us near to God in worship.

2. The fruit of the atonement is a twofold crucifixion. The relative clause, commencing with BY WHOM, may either refer to the personal Saviour, according to the rendering of the English version, or to the cross, BY WHICH this result is gained. These two clauses denote the dissolution of relations between Paul and the world, effected by the cross. The first clause, THE WORLD IS CRUCIFIED TO ME, means that it became to him unwelcome, distasteful, undesirable, like a crucified person. It was nailed to the cross, whether we suppose the allusion is to the world's attractions or to its legal righteousness. In both respects it was crucified, and influenced him as little as a dead man or dead thing could do. But it is added, I AM CRUCIFIED TO THE WORLD. That clause is commonly interpreted, The world has cast me out, as no object of its favour, and as alien to it.[1] The two clauses will thus set forth respectively Paul's estimate of the world, and the world's estimate of him. This is the usual interpretation of the clauses, and amounts to this: that Paul looked on the world, from the view-point of the cross, as an object that no more commended itself to him; and that the world, conversely, accounted him as worthy of contempt, because he so strenuously commended and enforced the one grand object of a sinner's confidence,—namely, Christ crucified, to the Jews a stumbling-block, and to the Greeks foolishness.

[1] See Seidel and Struensee in their Commentaries on Galatians. De Wette makes the two clauses the same in meaning.

The latter part of this commentary does not seem so appropriate or adapted to the apostle's design. His object was not so much to describe what the world thought of him, as how he stood affected to the world. The second clause, AND I TO THE WORLD, seems rather to intimate that, by the potentiality inherent in the cross, in so far as it rectified his relation toward God, and brought in new life to his soul, he was dead to the world. If the former clause affirmed that the world, as surveyed from the cross in which he gloried, was as a dead and crucified object in his esteem, the present clause will rather set forth that HIS HEART WAS DEAD TO IT.[1] Another object had so won his heart, that his tastes, desires, and sympathies were, as it were, dead within him, so far as the world was concerned. He drew no confidence from the legal rites, which were but elements of the world in his esteem (Gal. iv. 3), and had no hankering or looking behind in reference to its allurements and attractions. He did not dally with the world, or maintain any relations with it, when he saw how alien it was to the aims and aspirations of one who gloried in Christ crucified, and who was himself crucified with his Lord (Gal. ii. 20). This latter thought, that the apostle was crucified with Christ, and therefore one who no longer sought his life in the world (Col. ii. 20), will enable us to apprehend the force of the expression. It is this : Paul was personally dead to the world, because by the cross he was the property of another,—one of the peculiar people or heritage that Christ had won by His atoning blood. Paul felt that he was OBJECTIVELY CRUCIFIED with Christ, and his INNER FEELINGS corresponded to the change. He no more sought that world, nor lived for it, than a dead man is attracted by its honours, pleasures, or emoluments ; and it was the cross that made the great revolution.

[1] See Albert Schultens' Dutch exposition of the Heidelberg Catechism. See also Dr. Owen on this passage.

SEC. XIII.—THE EPISTLE TO THE EPHESIANS.

The Epistle to the Ephesians and the Epistle to the Colossians have a close affinity to each other, as developing the Pauline Christology.[1] They put the atonement in contrast with an incipient Gnosticism, which substituted ideas or mere speculative knowledge for the realities of Christ's work. In some epistles, as in that to the Romans, Paul appears as the expounder of divine truth in its wide connections. In others —as in the Epistles to the Corinthians, Timothy, and Titus— he appears as the pastor, issuing counsels, admonitions, and directions. In these Epistles to the Ephesians and Colossians there is a certain reference to the oriental speculations then beginning to thrust themselves on the notice of the Christian church ; and Paul, in displaying his knowledge in the mystery of Christ (Eph. iii. 4), appears more as the prophet giving abundant fulness of spiritual revelations. The principal thought of these epistles is the personal Christ, the medium of divine communications, Head over all things to the church, uniting Jew and Gentile under Himself as their one Head, and the link connecting all things with God and with one another. On these points we have striking revelations, nowhere else so fully imparted.

Allusions to the atonement run through the Epistle to the Ephesians, even where no express statements are given as to its nature. Thus, in the reference to Christ's love, we cannot fail to see an underlying allusion to His atonement (Eph. iii. 18). When the thought is brought in, " Now, that He ascended, what is it but that He also descended first into the lower parts of the earth ?" we have an allusion to His atonement as the foundation of His throne (Eph. iv. 9). When mutual forgiveness is enforced by the consideration that God for Christ's sake

---

[1] See Lange, *Geschichte der Kirche*, in reply to Baur's remarks on Ephesians and Colossians.

hath forgiven us, that forgiveness is connected with the work of Christ (iv. 32). But omitting passages which assume the atonement rather than express it, we shall confine ourselves to those which are definite.

I. The first passage on the subject of the atonement is thus expressed : *In whom we have redemption through His blood, the forgiveness of sins, according to the riches of His grace* (Eph. i. 7). The apostle celebrates God's praise for spiritual blessings, for election in Christ, and for all contemplated by election (Eph. i. 3). When we analyze the structure of the sentence, he does not say BY WHOM,[1] as he usually does, to denote the meritorious cause, but IN WHOM. The words IN CHRIST sometimes mean union, when the words have an independent position, and can be taken apart (2 Cor. xii. 2). Here, however, the expression IN WHOM denotes in His person objectively, as the surety or ground of our salvation. For Christ is a public person, and we have redemption in a way similar and parallel to the condemnation which we have in Adam. In a word, redemption is set forth objectively in Christ's person, who of God is made to us redemption (1 Cor. i. 30). All the expressions coincide with this interpretation ; for it is not said that we ACQUIRE redemption, but that we HAVE IT in Him (ἔχομεν). The testimony of this passage may be taken up in the following points :—

1. The apostle not only mentions the redemption, but subjoins the ransom, viz. THE BLOOD of Him who had just been called the Beloved. This establishes the reality of both. The language is not a metaphor or similitude, according to the Socinian comment ; it means that we are redeemed by blood as a ransom. The original term denotes deliverance by a price ; and the obvious sense is, that we are redeemed from a REAL captivity, by a REAL, not a figurative ransom. The theory of a metaphor makes but a metaphorical salvation.

---

[1] See Harless' *Commentary on Ephesians,* on the formula here used, ἐν ᾧ ; and also Stier's remarks on the same phrase, *Auslegung des Briefes an die Epheser,* 1848.

As to the features of the doctrine as set forth by these expressions. The first and fundamental idea is, that man as a sinner has fallen under punitive justice, which holds him captive. The second thought is, that the ransom is Christ's vicarious death, or His blood considered as the reality of the ancient sacrifices, and procuring the full redemption which they but figured forth. He gave Himself a ransom to redeem His people (Matt. xx. 28; 1 Cor. vi. 20; 1 Tim. ii. 6); and this He effected by becoming their curse (Gal. iii. 13). A third idea is, that God, to whose justice the price was paid, secured the discharge or liberation of the captive. As the law was an institution for the maintenance of which justice watched, this decides a question more frequently adduced for polemical purposes than for any other object: To whom was the ransom paid—to God or to Satan? The answer is, Satan had nothing to do with it, being the mere jailor, nay, criminal himself. The ransom was paid to the punitive justice of God. The statement then is, that the personal Christ is of God made to us redemption, and that we have redemption IN HIM.

2. Forgiveness of sin is subjoined in an apposition-clause, as a convertible term. The redemption consists essentially in forgiveness; and the latter, in its grammatical connection, sets forth more precisely the import of the former. They are here adduced as equivalent and convertible. It is evident, in the first place, that a direct causal connection is affirmed between the blood of Christ and forgiveness of sins. The passage does not state that Christ's mission was to reveal an absolute forgiveness, and to seal His testimony by His death as a martyr. The two things are put in such connection, that the forgiveness can only be viewed as the direct and immediate result of the atoning death, as the blood of sacrifice in the old economy was the direct cause of forgiveness to the Jewish worshipper. Christ's blood alone, without any addition of ours, or works of law, had the effect of winning forgiveness or exemption from punishment.

But how are redemption and forgiveness made convertible terms ? Might we not rather expect to hear that the redemptive act of Christ was the cause of forgiveness ? Undoubtedly a connection of cause and effect is affirmed in the verse, as we have already noticed. But there is a sense in which the redemption of the one clause, and the forgiveness which explains it in the next clause, have an objective reality for us in Christ as a public person ; and this is the point of the expression. As was noticed above, there was a NON-IMPUTA-TION OF SIN to us at the time when Christ was made SIN for us (2 Cor. v. 19–21), and the two things went hand in hand. That non-imputation of sin to us was not a mere subsequent result of Christ's sacrifice, but in some sense an essential element of the Lord's redemptive act. It had an application to all for whom He died, and whose person He representatively sustained.

3. The passage further shows the consistency between Christ's atoning blood, the price of pardon, and the exercise of free grace.[1] Though it has been much urged that one of these elements must of necessity exclude the other, both are here affirmed, and perfectly consistent. Though not found together in human transactions, they are found in the moral government of God ; for the divine administration differs from that of man in this respect, that God's rights are inalienable. He could not recede from His rights even when He purposed to redeem and pardon, but vindicated them to the full ; and this single text meets all cavils against the consistency of these two things—complete satisfaction and free grace. While pardon, therefore, is to us a gratuitous gift, it was procured by the payment of a price.

II. Another testimony, having reference to the effect of Christ's death in reconciling Jew and Gentile to each other, because reconciling both to God, is contained in the next

[1] This passage is conclusive against Locke and others, who represent the ransom and the exercise of grace as incompatible.

chapter: *But now, in Christ Jesus, ye who sometimes* [better, *once*] *were far off are now made nigh by* [better, *in*] *the blood of Christ. For He is our peace, who hath made both one, and hath broken down the middle wall of partition between us; having abolished in His flesh the enmity, even the law of commandments contained in ordinances; for to make in Himself of twain one new man, so making peace; and that He might reconcile both unto God in one body by the cross, having slain the enmity thereby* [or, *in Himself*] (Eph. ii. 13–16). Throughout this chapter the apostle brings under our notice a twofold alienation and a twofold reconciliation, with a sketch of the method by which the disunion was brought to an end. On the one hand, there was from their birth a deep alienation of mankind from God (vers. 3, 12), along with a division between Jews and Gentiles. On the other hand, the apostle refers to the historic fact of Christ's atonement as a divinely instituted method by which men, disunited by mutual hostility, meet in a higher unity, and become one new man (ver. 15), one city of God (ver. 19), one temple or habitation of God (ver. 21). I shall endeavour, with all brevity, to set forth the testimony here given to the atonement in its nature and effects, omitting such points as do not directly bear upon the theme which engages our attention.

1. As to the nature of the atonement, the number and variety of expressions here used to connect it with Christ's person are full of significance, apart from the immediate occasion which called them forth. But the reason why such phrases are so copiously employed may probably be deduced from the fact, that the Gnostic speculations, the oppositions of science falsely so called, as the apostle elsewhere styles them, looked upon matter, and therefore upon our Lord's organized human body, with disfavour, and formed presumptuous theories of the divine nature and absolute Godhead apart from the person of the one Mediator between God and man. The apostle shows that reconciliation was effected by an outward fact in the body of Christ's flesh through death; whereas the Docetism to which

we have referred denied the corporeity of Christ, or ascribed to Him a phantom-body. We may enumerate a few of the expressions which the apostle uses, and are full of meaning, apart from any connection with their origin.

Thus the apostle connects the atonement with the personal Redeemer when he declares, in the first place, " HE is our peace," and describes the Lord as " slaying the enmity in Himself." Secondly, he shows that the atonement was connected with a true humanity or corporeity, endowed with a capacity of suffering and obedience, when he says, "that He might reconcile both IN ONE BODY :" for the allusion is to the procuring of redemption, not to its application ; and it is more natural to expound the phrase of CHRIST'S HUMAN BODY, than of His body the church. Thirdly, when the enmity is said to be abolished " in His flesh," the language refers, as in other passages, to the condition of abasement and penal curse-bearing, to which the atoning Lord spontaneously subjected Himself. Fourthly, when it is said, " that He might reconcile both THROUGH THE CROSS," the meaning is that the curse, of which the cross was the exponent, was borne and exhausted on the tree. Fifthly, the blood of Christ, the cause of bringing us near to God, is described as sacrificial blood (ver. 13). All these descriptive terms serve to prove that the atonement was the surrender of Himself to God in a true humanity.

But a further idea here is, that Christ stood as a public person—AS ONE FOR MANY. The representative character of the transaction cannot be mistaken ; for the redeemed church is here considered as found in Him who, according to covenant, bore their persons and occupied their place, and, as a responsible surety, represented them before God. He sustained their persons in His own body on the cross ; that is, He, as a public person, in one body, sustained, through life and in death, the responsibilities of those who are described as His church. In His one humanity, He represented all who had been given Him, and reconciled them on the cross. Thus all is run up to the person of Christ. The whole person atoned,—the humanity suffering, the deity giving it worth ; the action being that of the God-man. The entire person acted in the atonement as in every mediatorial act,—the humanity being obedient, and the deity giving infinite value to all He did.

2. As to the fruits of the atonement, of which several are mentioned in these verses, the first in order is NEARNESS TO GOD IN THE BLOOD OF CHRIST (ver. 13). It is by no means necessary to alter the force of the preposition : for the same expression is used by our Lord at the institution of the Supper, "This is the new covenant IN MY BLOOD" (1 Cor. xi. 25); intimating that Christ's atoning blood was the element, sphere, or medium IN WHICH the new covenant was formed, and in which, as it is here put, they who were far off are made nigh. The language refers to sacrificial blood, which put men in covenant with God. Thus Israel at Sinai was by the sprinkling of blood made the people of God, near to Him, and from year to year preserved in covenant by the blood sprinkled on the mercy-seat. The expression "far from God," or "far off," was a phrase in common use to designate the Gentiles (Isa. xlix. 1 ; Acts ii. 39); and the statement is, that the blood of atonement made those nigh who were far off, or put them in covenant relation to God, as members of a spiritual society of which Christ is the head.

3. As another fruit of the atonement, the title OUR PEACE is ascribed to Christ (ver. 14). Some interpret this as meaning the cause of our peace, or our peacemaker, which gives a competent sense. More precisely, however, the title refers to Christ as our peace or reconciliation objectively considered, and with regard to our relation toward God ; the present verse being a grounding statement, with the causal particle *for*, to show the foundation of our nearness. The primary import, according to the analogy of numerous passages, is, that Christ is objectively our peace,[1] as He is also called our righteousness

---

[1] So Zanchius in his *Commentary on Ephesians.* See Harless' remarks, *Commentar über den Brief Pauli an die Ephesier,* 1858.

and redemption (1 Cor. i. 30).   But while He is pre-eminently our peace toward God, He is also the ground and foundation of peace in every other relation; as, for instance, between man and man.

4. As another fruit of the atonement, an end was put to the Jewish law, considered as A PARTITION-WALL between Jew and Gentile.   The law was so called, either, as many think, from the wall or fence in the temple which shut out the Gentiles from the access which the Jewish worshippers enjoyed; or, as others think, from the fence by which one city or territory was walled off from another.   The ceremonial law given to Israel as a separate people, and of positive appointment, was capable of being removed when its purpose was served; being destined to continue only till the reality or true sacrifice which it foreshadowed should appear.   Accordingly the cross, in which the law found its accomplishment, put a period to the ceremonies.   They were not simply revoked, but fulfilled: the atonement of the cross terminated the ceremonies, the law of commandments contained in ordinances, for ever.

5. The atonement made JEW AND GENTILE ONE (ver. 15). Previously the Jews regarded the Gentiles as unclean, and the Gentiles on their side retaliated by every mark of contumely, branding the Jews as the common enemies of the human race. By means of the cross, they who previously were sundered met in a higher unity, on a platform above and beyond the causes of division; and as they stood on the same level of reconciliation, they became one new man in Christ (ver. 15), who reconciled them in one body by the cross (ver. 16).   The atonement terminated the alienation, placing men on a footing of equality before the throne of God; and this was effected really, not typically, by the cross, which gave to all nationalities the position of a people near to God, and made Jews and Gentiles one.

6. The explicit biblical expression for the effect of the atonement is reconciliation in all relations, as expressed in

these words: "That He might reconcile both unto God in one body by the cross, having slain the enmity in Himself" (ver. 16). This full description may be taken up in four points of inquiry.

a. Who are the parties reconciled? The answer is, God on the one side; and the twofold nationality, that is, Jews and Gentiles, on the other. Nothing can be more explicit than this declaration that Christ's coming was intended to reconcile two parties,—the one party being God, and the other party mankind; and the obvious presupposition is, that beforehand disunion existed between God and man. Now, according to Scripture, reconciliation was effected by the removal of sin, so far as it was the cause of arming divine indignation against us. It is often said, that from the very nature of God as love, with friendly sentiments toward men, it becomes us to think of reconciliation only on man's side. That is by no means the case; for God's procedure and mood of mind in a relative point of view have undergone a change in consequence of a great historical transaction, as is manifest from the fact that it is not simply said, "God has reconciled us," but, "God has reconciled us to Himself by Jesus Christ" (2 Cor. v. 18). The two things there combined are, that the world was reconciled TO HIMSELF, and that this was effected by the historic FACT of the atonement; and reconciliation to Himself implies that anger and punitive justice were removed by the atonement. The same thing is expressed in the verse under consideration. The acting party is Christ, who is said to reconcile both unto God. And when it is added that this was accomplished, not by an absolute pardon, but in one body and by the cross, we have the same allusion to the great historic fact of the atonement, as the ground on which the reconciliation was effected.

b. In whom was the reconciliation brought about? IN ONE BODY, that is, in Christ's body. Some prefer to expound this expression of the church, but it is every way better to explain it of the Lord's own body, because it is similar to the parallel passage in Colossians (Col. i. 22); and the allusion is plainly limited to the way of PROCURING reconciliation, not to the way of APPLYING it. The reconciliation was effected in one historic person, in one second man, the counterpart of the first man; and the church was reconciled in one for many, and therefore not by works of law or personal deeds which we have done.[1]

c. By what was the reconciliation accomplished? BY THE CROSS,—a great fact in the world's history, and the culminating point of Christ's obedience unto death. The question raised is, Was the cross an objective fact for God as well as for us men? Did it reconcile the church to God, as it weighed with God, or merely as it moves the human heart? The phrase shows that reconciliation rests on Christ's work, and consequently on a fact; and this objective fact was reconciling, not as it moved the human heart, or ushered in a new conduct on man's part, but as it introduced a new relation or standing in which men were placed before God.

d. By what method was the reconciliation accomplished? The answer is, HAVING SLAIN THE ENMITY IN HIS CROSS, or in HIMSELF; for the difference between the two modes of rendering the phrase is so small in point of meaning, that we may equally affirm, He slew the enmity in His cross, or, He slew the enmity in Himself as crucified. What enmity? Not the alienation between Jews and Gentiles, to which reference had been made in the previous verse, for it would be a mere tautology to repeat it here. Rather we must understand the expression as alluding to the mutual enmity between God and man extinguished by the cross.

As one passage personifying sin speaks of condemning it in Christ's flesh (Rom. viii. 3), so the enmity personified in the present passage is said to be slain; and the question is raised, How? During the days of His flesh, the Lord, by taking on

---

[1] The commentators are pretty equally divided in opinion, whether this phrase is to be taken for Christ's human body, that is, His incarnate person, or for His body the church. I decidedly prefer the former.

Him the sins of His people, as the cause of disunion and
enmity, suffered Himself to be treated as an object of divine
wrath, though in reality His beloved Son. On His person, the
object of eternal love, the sin of man and the wrath of God
came into collision as never had been seen since the world
began. The Lord experienced both to the utmost, and by so
doing annihilated the enmity for all whom He represented.
Whether we look at the one body of the Lord, or at His
activity, we see the sphere, the locality, the medium of reconciliation.

The substance of this testimony may be thus summed up.
The Lord Jesus reconciled Jews and Gentiles to each other, not
because He brought a good disposition to the disunited parties,
but because He procured for both free access to God (ver. 18):
He reconciled both to God by His cross. Did the atonement
turn toward men the favour of God, or was it but a manifestation of an already existing relation of love? Scripture uniformly declares, that while the provision emanated from the
love of the Father's heart, the atonement was the great historic
fact by which the enmity between God and man was objectively removed, and men made the objects of favour. Then
only was a friendly relation actually cemented.

III. Another passage is descriptive of the death of Christ
as a sacrifice, and enables us to trace His priestly action in
offering it: *Walk in love, as Christ also hath loved us, and hath
given* [better, *delivered*] *Himself an offering and a sacrifice to
God for a sweet-smelling savour* [or, *a sweet-smelling savour to
God*] (Eph. v. 2). In the context the apostle inculcates mutual
forgiveness from the example of God (Eph. iv. 32), and then
mutual love from that illustrious instance of love which the
Lord Jesus gave in His atoning death, represented as the offering of a sacrifice. Though the idea of sacrifice is nowhere
fully exhibited except in the Epistle to the Hebrews, the
expositor would do violence to the import of language were
he to deny that we have here an allusion to a priestly offering.

That Christ was a priest on earth, and offered an oblation before His ascension to His Father, appears from this easy analysis of the text:—Who offered?   Christ.   What did He offer?   Not something external, not the blood of others, but Himself.   For whom did He offer?   For us.   And in what manner was it accomplished?   As an offering and sacrifice. From these questions, furnishing a simple analysis of the passage, we may warrantably collect that Christ offered Himself as the one true, ever-valid sacrifice to which the shadows of the former economy pointed.   Nor is it necessary to supply any ellipsis in order to complete the sense; for the apostle's words explicitly affirm, in the form here presented to us, that the sacrifice was not something apart from the personal Christ, not some action to be imitated, but Christ delivering Himself for us.

Which class of the sacrifices was before the apostle's mind? Without doubt, the propitiatory sacrifices, and not the thank-offerings.   When we look at the two terms, it is thought by some that the first denotes an offering or sacrifice in general, and that the second, subjoined as elucidating the first, denotes a bloody sacrifice of a propitiatory character.   Others roundly affirm, much in the same way as did the Socinians of a former age, that the apostle had not the idea of an expiatory sacrifice[1] before his mind.   Partly from the terms descriptive of the sacrifice, partly because of the additional phrase, "for a sweet-smelling savour," they argue that the apostle refers to the free-will offerings; and the entire passage, thus interpreted, conveys nothing beyond the thought that Christ left us an example.   But while he represents the riches of Christ's love for our imitation, he had also before his mind the idea of an atoning sacrifice.

1. With regard to the terms here used, the first of the two, rendered OFFERING, may denote a free-will offering presented to

---

[1] Rückert on the passage, and Usteri (*Paulin Lehrbegriff*), make it an allusion to a free-will offering, not to a propitiatory sacrifice at all.

God in token of gratitude and homage, but is also descriptive of propitiatory sacrifices, as will appear from a few passages. Thus, in the Epistle to the Hebrews the term is used in the phrase, " Where forgiveness of these is, there is no more offering for sin" ($\pi\rho\sigma\phi\rho\grave{\alpha}$) (Heb. x. 18). In like manner, the writer avails himself of the same word when he represents the death of Christ as the ONE OFFERING which perfected for ever them that are sanctified (Heb. x. 14). There is no question, then, as to the application of the term to propitiatory sacrifices;[1] and as to the second word, " an offering and SACRIFICE" ($\theta\upsilon\sigma\acute{\iota}\alpha\nu$), nothing warrants us to limit the idea underlying it to a free-will gift, as the apostle several times uses it for a propitiatory sacrifice. Passages in the Epistle to the Hebrews put this usage beyond all doubt; as, for example, "who needeth not daily, as those high priests, TO OFFER UP SACRIFICE first for his own sins, and then for the people's" (Heb. vii. 27). And many other passages might be adduced (Heb. v. 1, viii. 3, ix. 9, 23, 26, x. 5, 11, 26).

2. The additional phrase, " for a sweet-smelling savour," has been adduced as an argument against the application of the terms to propitiatory sacrifices, because free-will offerings are often represented as a sweet-smelling savour to God; but we have only to examine the ritual, to be convinced that the expression was also applied to atoning sacrifices. It is the expression used in Genesis in connection with the burnt-offerings which Noah offered when he came out of the ark,— "The Lord smelled a sweet savour" (Gen. viii. 21); and it is used of the burnt-offering on which the worshipper was to put his hand (Lev. i. 4, 9). Nor was it limited to the burnt-offering, though frequently mentioned in that connection in the sacrificial ritual (Lev. i. 13, 17); for the expression is also employed in reference to the sin-offering, whether brought to expiate the offences of the individual worshipper (Lev. iv. 31), or offered annually for the collective sins of the nation on the

---

[1] See Vinke, *Leer van Jesus en de Apostel*, p. 371. 1837.

great day of atonement (Lev. xvi. 25). In the last-mentioned
text, the burning of the fat upon the altar was with a view to
produce the sweet-smelling savour.

A further question is, whether the language refers to the
burnt-offering or the sin-offering. It may without violence
be referred to either: for the argument of Alting, Witsius, and
Deyling, against the possibility of referring the passage to the
sin-offering, on the ground that the sin-offering is never represented as a sacrifice of a sweet-smelling savour, rests on a
mistake. Thus[1] Witsius maintains that only those sacrifices
are said to be of a sweet-smelling savour to which the addition
of oil and frankincense could be made (Lev. ii. 2–9), and that
these additions could not be made to the sin-offering (Lev. v.
11). That is not true in point of fact, as has already been
proved from Leviticus (Lev. iv. 31, xvi. 25); and there is nothing in the allusion to a sacrifice of sweet-smelling savour
that decides the question either way, as it is applied both to
the burnt-offering and to the sin-offering. In that respect
there was no difference. But the complexion of the language
inclines us, if it is duly considered, to refer the terms rather
to the burnt-offering than to the sin-offering; for when the
New Testament writer more specifically refers to the sin-
offering, the additional words, FOR SIN, are commonly subjoined (Rom. viii. 3; Heb. x. 18, 26). The conclusion to
which we are disposed to come is, that these terms, descriptive
of the Lord's sacrifice, do not so naturally express the specific
idea of the sin-offering, inasmuch as that additional formula
is neither appended nor indicated by the context.

The apostle seems to refer to the burnt-offering when he
affirms that Christ loved us, and delivered Himself for us.
This is confirmed by the fact that he emphatically alludes to
the love of the Offerer, and to the oblation or sacrifice con-

---

[1] See Witsius, *Miscell.* i. 410; Deyling, *Observat.* ss. i. 186; also Reland,
Antiq. p. 310. Rückert and Harless maintain the same reference to the sin-
offering.

sidered as an action done. Had the apostle been alluding to
the sin-offering, the idea of sin would in some way have been
prominent. Hence the words comprehend His entire earthly
activity, as one uninterrupted continuous sacrifice from first
to last, reaching its culmination in His cross. The typical
burnt-offering figured forth the dedication of the entire man,
with all His powers and faculties, or the perfect fulfilling of
the Father's will, and sanctifying of Himself for our sakes
(John xvii. 19), only accomplished when He said, " It is
finished." The dedication of the Lord during His earthly
career, till the obedience reached its climax on the cross, was
adumbrated by the burnt-offering as a sacrifice of sweet-smelling savour.[1] The type found its truth in the Lord's holy life
and obedience unto death; and therein He gave the New
Testament accomplishment to the Old Testament shadow.

This fact, that the death of Christ, as an atoning sacrifice,
was fragrant and well-pleasing to God, proves two things—
that the cross was not only a PROPITIATION of divine wrath,
but an ACCEPTABLE OBEDIENCE. Not only did it appease divine
wrath, it also converted God's relation into one of favour. It
was merit as well as expiation. The passage is so expressed
as to show that the Lord's death was an infinitely acceptable
deed; that sinlessness and sin-bearing were combined in His
sacrifice in such way, that while punishment was expiated, the
divine claims were all satisfied, and that sin did not in any
sense attach to the personal human life of Jesus of Nazareth.
The sacrifice was well-pleasing, because without blemish and
defect. Personally perfect, but officially the object of the
divine wrath by reason of sin-bearing, the Lord, by His
vicarious life and death, offered a sacrifice of a sweet-smelling
savour,—that is, acceptable to God in the utmost conceivable
degree. The cross displays wrath appeased, death endured,
punitive justice vindicated, but does not stop there, according

---

[1] See Keil's excellent discussion of this passage in this direction, *Zeitschrift
für die gesammte Lutherische Theologie*, iii. Heft, 1857.

to the too common representation of the atonement even by its advocates. It was also a law-magnifying obedience, the fulfilment of the condition under which man was originally placed, the purchase of life, the title to the inheritance; and the acceptableness of the Lord's atoning sacrifice was typified by the fragrance or sweet-smelling savour of the old burnt-offering (Lev. xvi. 17).

Some points may be established by this text against the long-repeated cavils and objections of the Socinianizing party. To these we shall advert.

1. This passage proves that Christ's death was coincident with His sacrifice. When the opponents of the atonement alleged, as they were wont to do, that the death of Christ did not belong to His sacrifice, but preceded it, and that the sacrifice was His action in heaven, their representation did not satisfy the apostle's testimony, which distinctly affirms that He offered Himself a sacrifice, and that He was a sacrifice when He delivered Himself. But if He was a true sacrifice on earth, He was also a true priest on earth, offering the oblation. We cannot transfer the sacrifice and priesthood to heaven, without flatly contradicting the apostle, or asserting that Christ's earthly work was but fragmentary, and to be completed in heaven. Let them show that Christ twice offered Himself, and that it was but an imperfect sacrifice He offered on earth, or reconcile their position with the explicit declaration that He was once offered to bear the sins of many (Heb. ix. 28).

2. There is no discrepancy between this statement and the doctrine of sacrifice contained in the Epistle to the Hebrews. The Socinians, accustomed to maintain that the Epistle to the Hebrews describes only a sacrifice offered in heaven, after the death of the cross was accomplished, allowed that the same representation was not given by all the sacred writers. And the answer to this is, that the Spirit of truth is no spirit of contradiction, or of yea and nay.

3. The same parties, by a violence of construction, would evade the evidence of this passage by reading the words, OFFERING AND SACRIFICE FOR A SWEET-SMELLING SAVOUR, apart from the verb GAVE, or delivered. Rending it from the construction which belongs to it, they read it as an illustration, or commendation, or exclamation: thus, "What a sacrifice was that to God!" That is not to interpret language, but to twist it to the reader's purpose and preconceived ideas. There is no warrant but in their own fancy for such a mode of punctuation. Of necessity, we must construe the verb GAVE with the word sacrifice: "who gave HIMSELF AN OFFERING and sacrifice." The passage announces that He delivered Himself, and points out the way by which it was done—by sacrifice.

4. A fourth objection, emanating from the same parties, is to the effect that the word DELIVERED (παρέδωκεν ἑαυτόν) is not the term commonly found in the Old Testament ritual to denote the presentation of the victim. But the reason is obvious: the animal victim was presented on the altar because it was passive, and did not spontaneously offer itself, whereas the Lord Jesus willingly offered Himself. And here it is important to remark, that the sacrifice, properly so called, was not the act of giving or delivering, but THE THING ITSELF DELIVERED: that was the acceptable sacrifice. This will be evident from a comparison of the passages which speak of money contributions, or of gifts, communicated as an acceptable sacrifice (Phil. iv. 18; Heb. xiii. 16). In these instances, it was not the act of sending or communicating, but the thing sent or imparted, that constituted the sacrifice. And in the case before us, it was not the act of delivering, but Christ Himself delivered, that was the acceptable sacrifice.

In fine, this passage proves that the delivery of Christ as a sacrifice for us much more than compensated for the wrong done, and removed the wrath that had been armed against us: it won for us divine favour. The death of Jesus not only satisfied divine justice, but altered God's attitude, or, as we would say in human relations, His mood of mind, to those who previously had been objects of His just displeasure. The effect of Noah's sacrifice, the words of which seem here to be recalled, was, that " God smelled a sweet savour, and said in His heart, I will not again curse the ground any more" (Gen. viii. 21) ; and, in like manner, the sacrifice of Christ awakened favour in God's heart, because it magnified the divine law in the most signal way. The purpose for which the apostle adduced this allusion to the atonement was, that we might cherish love like Christ. Not that the Ephesians could follow Christ in such a work as His, which was unique in its nature, and to be shared with none ; but we are exhorted to cultivate love in general, after the example of our atoning Lord.

IV. Another passage, describing the church as the special object of the atonement, and the Lord's death as containing in it the meritorious element of its own application, is as follows: *Husbands, love your wives, even as Christ also loved the church, and gave Himself* [better, *delivered Himself*] *for it; that He might sanctify and cleanse it* [better, *sanctify it, cleansing it*] *with the washing of water by the word* (Eph. v. 25–27). The apostle, while exhorting the Ephesians to the practice of conjugal duties, adduces the love of Christ in His relation to the church as the great example, and takes occasion, as the apostles usually do while enforcing moral duties by His example, to expatiate on His meritorious abasement and death. The testimony here given to the atonement may be noticed in a few obvious particulars.

1. The love which the apostle was led by His theme to delineate, is that of the great Bridegroom to the church. It is not a vague, indefinite affection, but special love; that is, a love to real persons, chosen from eternity, and redeemed in time, to be called and put among the children. He did not love the church purified, but for the sake of purifying it, and with an affection so intensely active, that His endeavours never cooled till He had redeemed His church, or bought her to be

His; and the love which purchased the church at the most costly price (Acts xx. 28), is as unchanging and inseparable as it is great (Rom. viii. 35).

2. The love already mentioned is next described as prompting Him to deliver Himself for the church. Two parties are mentioned—Christ on the one hand, and the church on the other; and as death confronted us, the Lord became the substitute in such a sense that He delivered Himself, first into the hands of punitive justice at the bar of God, and then into the hands of men, by whom, according to the determinate counsel and foreknowledge of God, the sentence was carried into effect. The expression DELIVERED naturally recalls the Lord's own saying, that He was delivered into the hands of men as an offering and a sacrifice to God.[1] This is the uniform meaning of the term, whether applied to the Father's action in GIVING UP THE SON, or to the Son's action in GIVING UP HIMSELF. And we have the historic fact in the Lord's action in Gethsemane, as we have the doctrinal delineation of its significance here. His giving of Himself was, in point of fact, the sacrifice for the purchase of the church, His bride. He offered Himself for the church when He gave Himself spontaneously into the hand of God, permitting Himself to be seized and bound, tried and mocked, sentenced and buffeted, at the hand of those whom God appointed to execute His purpose. It was no vague, uncertain, and accidental transaction, but one according to special covenant and sponsion for the good of that elect company, the church of redeemed men, who were given Him by name and bought with a price. It was a transaction so definite, that it procured the redemption of the church, and carried with it the meritorious element of its own imputation and application. He could not lose one for whom He died: the holy rectitude of the divine moral government absolutely forbade that. His death was the spontaneous surrender of Himself, when He could have warded off all His

[1] See Weber, *Vom Zorne Gottes ;* also Harless' commentary on the passage.

enemies' attacks against His life; for He had power to lay it down, and power to take it up again. And what did He give as the sacrifice? Not an external thing, not something nor all things possessed by Him, but HIMSELF, HIS INFINITELY PRECIOUS PERSON. And for whom? For His church, that it might be His blood-bought property, and so belong to the great Bridegroom.

3. The end contemplated by the Lord's death was, THAT HE MIGHT SANCTIFY the church. This is plainly proved by the particle of design which introduces the clause (ἵνα). As to sanctification here, we must determine whether it means dedication to God on the ground of atonement, or inward progressive purity. The former view must be accepted wherever holiness is immediately connected with the death of Christ. The passage has in it a conjugal reference; and the primary meaning is, that the church was set apart, or consecrated, to Him as His bride,—the uniform meaning of the term when connected with the atonement. This is the use of the word whenever mention is made of the Levitical worship and of sacrifices, which sanctified to the purifying of the flesh (Heb. ix. 13).[1] We are admitted into fellowship with God by means of Christ's atonement. Whether sufficient ground exists for Michaelis' remark, that the high priest in Israel was called the bridegroom of his people, is doubtful (Lev. xxi. 4). If well founded, we should fully understand why the sacred writers so frequently employ this figure.

Two terms are here used, so nearly synonymous, that it is difficult to define the precise shade of difference between them, when they describe the effect of Christ's atoning blood. I refer to the two verbs SANCTIFY and CLEANSE, common to all the apostles. It may be proper first to define the relation between the two clauses, considered separately, according to the translation which we gave above: " That He might sanctify it, cleansing it with the washing of water by the word." We regard the participle (καθαρίσας) as expressing simultaneous

---

[1] See above, on the Levitical sacrifices, at p. 52.

action; for this is necessary to the sense, and there is no necessity for translating the participle as intimating previous action,[1] introductory to the action of the verb. They coincide in time, and the participial clause conveys an explanation of a peculiar nature, which it is possible, we think, to apprehend. The first clause seems more especially to denote the objective standing of the worshipper, and his near approach to a holy God by the blood of atonement; whereas the participial clause seems to refer to the subjective consciousness or felt experience of the same privilege (Heb. ix. 14); or, as Winer puts it, the CLEANSING may denote something negative, and the word SANCTIFY something positive.

To understand this language, we must carry with us the import of the Jewish worship. The terms on which we are commenting refer to the removal of defilements, which excluded the worshipper from coming into the presence of a holy God, and prevented him from intercourse with his fellow-citizens. When the uncleanness was removed by sacrificial blood, or in the use of sprinkling according to the law, the excluded person was restored to the enjoyment of all the privileges secured to the people of God. In a word, he was HOLY, or SANCTIFIED. With regard to the CLEANSING added in the participial clause, it is so allied to the former, that the one may be said to include the other; and the thought will be, that by means of the CLEANSING, WASHING, or SPRINKLING of Christ's blood—for all these expressions, borrowed from the sacrificial ritual, are employed with little if any difference of meaning—sinners, previously excluded from access to a holy God by sin, are restored to fellowship, and consciously nigh (Eph. ii. 13). When it is said that Christ gave Himself for the church, that He might sanctify it, the meaning is, that He gave Himself to deliver us from estrangement, the consequence of sin, and to reinstate us men, once far off by sin, in the favour, friendship, and fellowship of a holy God.

---

[1] See Winer's *Grammar* on aorist participles.

4. The passage furthermore brings out the SPECIAL LOVE OF THE REDEEMER, and the efficacy of His atoning blood. His redeeming love was specially directed to the church as its proper object; for the language is so definite and precise as to leave no doubt that His love finds out all those to whom it is exercised.[1] Nor can the efficacious character of His redemption-work be called in question, if we do justice to the terms of the present passage, and 'others similar; for either we must assert that the atonement was efficacious to all for whom it was destined, or concede that Christ has been largely disappointed of His design. The two clauses of these verses, connected together by a final particle (ἵνα), exhibit the scope or design from which the Saviour acted in His whole redemption-work. The first of the verses (ver. 25) is so connected with the following, that they declare the end for which He acted, and the means of attaining it; and no one with reverent conceptions of the Father's commission or the Son's finished work, will admit that He failed of His purpose. It was an atonement that satisfied all the claims of God. And whether we look at the divine appointment, or at the intrinsic merit of the redemption, the work was of such a kind as to carry with it the ground of its own imputation and application. He will not lose one for whom He died; for He gave Himself for the church, a surety fulfilling every condition.

SEC. XIV.—THE EPISTLE TO THE PHILIPPIANS.

This epistle was written on the occasion of receiving a money contribution sent to the apostle, then a prisoner in Rome. The Philippians had formerly sent once and again to his necessity, and after an interval their care of him flourished again (Phil. iv. 10, 15). To relieve their anxiety

---

[1] See Ames' *Coronis ad Collationem Hagiensem*, 1650; and *Antisynodalia Scripta*.

about himself, he enters into details as to his history, taking occasion to warn them against the Judaizing party, which sought access to all the new planted churches, and exhorting them to mutual concord, joy in the Lord, and preparation for the Lord's coming. The scope of the epistle is rather practical than doctrinal. Hence the atonement is less referred to than in many other epistles. There are some less direct allusions, as when the apostle designates certain men enemies of the cross of Christ (Phil. iii. 18). This shows the place which the atonement occupies; for the Judaizers were dangerous, because they subverted salvation by the cross. The apostle, now very near his crown, says, too, that he counted all things but loss to win Christ, and to be found in Him, not having his own righteousness (Phil. iii. 8); proving that to the last he clung, as at the beginning, to the atonement or righteousness of God.

The only text in this epistle to which we shall direct special attention is the following :—*Let this mind be in you, which was also in Christ Jesus: who, being* [better, *existing*] *in the form of God, thought it not robbery to be equal with God; but made Himself of no reputation, and took upon Him* [better, *emptied Himself, taking*] *the form of a servant, and was made* [*being made*] *in the likeness of men; and being found in fashion as a man, He humbled Himself, and became obedient unto death, even the death of the cross. Wherefore God also hath highly exalted Him, and given Him a name which is above every name* (Phil. ii. 5–9). The apostle, exhorting the Philippians to mutual concord, and bidding them esteem others better than themselves, passes over, in the most natural way, to Christ's example as displayed in His entire humiliation on earth. Is it true, as some allege, that Paul gives no outline of redemption here, but limits himself to the history of Christ as it furnishes an example? That is not admissible here, nor in other parallel passages which bring out Christ's abasement. The atonement is often put

in the bosom of what is properly an ethical context (Eph. v. 2,
v. 25 ; 1 Pet. iii. 18).   Besides, the connection between the
humiliation and exaltation of Christ indubitably points to the
atonement and its reward (ver. 9).

1. The first thing to be determined is, whether the mention
of Christ existing in the form of God refers to His divine pre-
existence—to a state anterior to the incarnation ?   This must
be affirmed if we interpret by the force of terms ; and this
was the general interpretation among the Fathers and the
divines of the Reformed Church.[1]   Though many Lutheran
expositors, after Luther's example, laboured with all ingenuity to refer the terms to the incarnate Christ,—sometimes
appealing to the name " Christ Jesus " occurring immediately
before, sometimes asserting that the ethical precept of humility
which is enforced did not require any allusion to the pre-
incarnate state,—the comment cannot be made even plausible.
The apostle obviously describes Christ in His divine glory,
and then in the state of abasement.   The expression, BEING or
EXISTING (ὑπάρχων) IN THE FORM OF GOD, can be expounded
only of divine existence with the manifestation of divine glory.
There is no need for debating whether THE FORM OF GOD is
an expression denoting essence or nature ; for the whole phrase
taken together, WHO BEING or EXISTING IN THE FORM OF GOD,
leaves no room for doubt that we must here unite the attributes and their manifestation.[2]   We cannot reduce the expression to the mere accidents of the divine ; for there is a reference
to subsistence, and a thing does not exist in its accidents.   We
may fitly alternate this phrase, therefore, with another, which
fully covers it : " who, being the brightness of His glory, and
express image of His person " (Heb. i. 3).

Another clause, equally significant, as exhibiting the con-

---

[1] The Fathers appeal to this text against the Arians and Sabellians, and the
post-Reformation divines against the Unitarians.

[2] See a valuable patristic discussion on the meaning of μορφή in Zanchius
on Philippians ; also Maestricht's full exposition in his *Theoretico-practica
Theologia*, lib. v. cap. 9.

sciousness or sentiments of the only begotten Son in those relations which subsisted between Him and the Father, is subjoined : WHO THOUGHT IT NOT ROBBERY TO BE EQUAL WITH GOD. This announces what the Lord frequently declared in His own words, that, without arrogating what was not His own by divine right, He was conscious of entire equality with God, and that He thought this sentiment no transgression of His limits, nor invasion of another's rights. As to the mode of rendering adopted by many expositors in the last age, " who did not regard His equality with God as an object of solicitous desire," or " who did not esteem it an object to be caught at to be on a parity with God,"[1] it has ceased to have much interest, for it is a conjectural meaning put upon the term ROBBERY. It is contrary to the etymology of the word, which denotes the act of seizing ; and it loses the emphasis of the clause, which, as descriptive of conscious equality with God, was meant to show spontaneous abasement in the light of that divine relation of which He was fully aware. The former clause is an objective delineation of the divine dignity of the Son of God, while this clause is a subjective delineation of the same thing.

2. A second question to be determined is, Are we to assume two different gradations of humiliation,—one indicated by the words, HE EMPTIED HIMSELF (ver. 7), as we rendered them ; and another indicated by the terms, HE HUMBLED HIMSELF (ver. 8): that is, Have we two parts of the abasement of Jesus,—one more particularly referring to the incarnation, the other more expressly alluding to the sufferings which led Him to the cross ? That mode of exposition,

[1] I may specially refer to Dr. Pye Smith's discussion in favour of this rendering of ἁρπαγμός in his *Scripture Testimony*, vol. ii. pp. 365–406, as he gives the literature up to his day. See, too, Stuart's Letters to Channing. Meyer's note, however, is conclusive against that sense of ἁρπαγμός. Raebiger, *Christologia Paulina*, p. 77 (1852), contends for the passive sense of the word, against Meyer, and also Usteri, p. 309. (See also Tholuck's *disputatio* on this text, 1847.)

adopted by many, conveys the idea of a first and second humiliation: the first consisting in the abasement which led Him to become man; the second consisting in subjecting Himself to the death of the cross. We should thus have two gradations of humiliation delineated objectively; and the two verbs, HE EMPTIED HIMSELF, and HE HUMBLED HIMSELF, taken with the participial clauses which severally belong to them, the hinges of these two gradations. I have never been satisfied that this has been made good by any ingenuity of arrangement that has ever been applied to the passage. Another view is to apply to the historic life of Christ the same distinction which could be applied to His pre-historic life in the previous clauses. We should, on this principle, take the one as an objective delineation of the condition into which His condescending love brought Him down (ver. 7); and the other as descriptive of the conscious aim or subjective feeling with which He entered into that sphere (ver. 8). This latter view, we think, has much to recommend it on the ground of simplicity. The passage, thus viewed, has a remarkable resemblance to the parallel passage, in which Christ is represented as a son, yet learning obedience by the things He suffered (Heb. v. 8, 9). This interpretation fits in, too, most aptly to that lowliness of mind, for the enforcement of which the Lord's example was adduced.[1] We shall so expound it.

a. The objective condition of abasement, then, is thus expressed: " But He emptied Himself, taking the form of a servant, being made in the likeness of men." Of what did He empty Himself? He was emptied by becoming another, not by ceasing to be what He was; that is, He became man, whereas He was God; a servant, though He was a Lord; of rich, poor; of glorious, abased; of omnipotent, weak; of omnipresent, limited; not by ceasing to be what He was, but by becoming what He was not. As to the expressions which

---

[1] See some excellent comments in this direction by Lechler, *Apostolisches Zeitalter*, 1857, p. 58.

follow in the participial clauses, they are highly significant, whether we take them as co-ordinate or subordinate.

The first clause, which says that He took the form of a servant, sets forth spontaneous abasement as contrasted with the sin of Adam. Humiliation came in to expiate usurpation. If the first man aspired to be as God, the second man, who by inherent right was above all service, descended to a servant's position that He might expiate their sin who sought to be more than was appointed for them.[1] The expression "taking the form of a servant" is not synonymous with human nature simply, but takes in the further idea of an abased condition. The second participial clause, in which it is said that He was made in the likeness of men, lends no countenance to anything bordering on Docetic theories, as if He were a phantom form. On the contrary, the clause affirms that, while He is neither a mere man nor a sinful man, He was very man, with a true humanity in all respects like our own; nay, made in the likeness of men in the most abased form—the consequence of that sin-bearing and curse-bearing career through which He passed from His birth (see Rom. viii. 3). When it is added that He was found in fashion as a man—a clause subjoined partly to resume the two previous clauses, partly to prepare for the outline of obedience given in the following statement—the meaning is, that externally, in discourse and action, in behaviour and mode of life, He was found in fashion as a man.

b. The obedience of Jesus—that is, His subjective disposition in the given sphere already mentioned—is thus described : " He humbled Himself, and became obedient to death, even the death of the cross." The meaning seems to be, that in this condition He subjected Himself to the service which the sphere imposed upon Him ; that He neither assumed any of the glory that properly belonged to Him, nor disdained to move in the

---

[1] See Ernesti, *Studien und Kritiken,* 1848 (pp. 858-924), elucidating the passage from Gen. ii.

restraints, reproach, and pain which were its necessary accompaniments; and that He adapted Himself, as the meek and lowly One, to His position. The same expression is applied by Luke to denote inward sentiment or disposition: "He that humbleth himself shall be exalted" (Luke xiv. 11). He filled up with humility and obedience His allotted sphere, that is, the position of a servant, with all its obligations, as He had spontaneously assumed it (Matt. xx. 28). The obedience mentioned in this clause has express relation to the form of a servant mentioned in the previous verse. They are counterparts; the one the outward condition, the other the animating spirit corresponding to it. The form of a servant may be distinguished from the obedience of the servant, but they cannot be separated; as the outward and the inward,—the sphere, and the spirit pervading it.

3. We next notice the features of the obedience; and the first question is, To whom was the obedience rendered? Not to the Romans or Jews, as some have put it, but primarily to God, sustaining the character of Lawgiver and Judge. But the capacity in which He obeyed comes out in connection with His person. When this divine person TOOK the form of a servant, the language signifies that He took it into the unity of His person; and consequently, as the creator and preserver of His own humanity, He could not but be its master. This decides on the nature of His obedience. It was not personally necessary from any obligations devolving upon Him, but solely undertaken for others, and meant to be laid to their account, according to the covenant by which He acted[1] as the Lord's servant (Isa. xlii. 1). He disdained not to stoop to the curse as our sin-bearing surety, sinlessly obedient at every step (Matt. xx. 28).

Of this obedience the first prerequisite was, that it should

---

[1] See an excellent elucidation of this text by Th. Hall, Norton regis pastore, *de activa Christi obedientia*, p. 180, Frankf. 1658. Also Walch, *de obedientia Christi activa*, 1755, p. 16; and the old Lutheran divines.

be voluntary; and this is the point affirmed. A double act was necessary in this transaction : one on God's side, who, as the world's ruler, and as the party to be reconciled, appointed the sacrifice ; for without His authority the whole atoning work of Christ would have been without a basis : the other on the side of Christ, whose vicarious obedience could be rendered only by free choice. The very notion of involuntary suffering, or inevitable suffering, in a world where all was disordered, had no application to Him ;[1] for no one could take His life from Him, or inflict suffering without His consent.

But His abasement is first described as OBEDIENCE, then as obedience UNTO DEATH, and then as the death OF THE CROSS. The obedience was one from His birth to His death, though consisting of two several parts or elements; in other words, an active and passive obedience, as it is commonly called, or an obedience previous to His sufferings, and during them.[2] No one will exclude the suffering part of the obedience who ponders the words UNTO DEATH, that is, as far as death inclusive ; and no one will exclude the active obedience, or that of His life, if he does justice to this expression, which describes obedience extending to the borders of death, and running through it. Christ is represented as complying with the will of a superior, as descending to death natural and eternal, and as undergoing the ignominious cross, an emblem of the curse, that we might go free (Gal. iii. 13). The apostle comprehends the whole obedience of life and death : for he does not say that He was obedient in death, as if nothing more were imposed upon Him than to die. He united the obedience of life and death as equally vicarious.

4. Next follows the reward expressed in the words, " Wherefore God hath highly exalted Him" (ver. 9). The particle WHEREFORE is not a consecutive particle, but causal, defining

---

[1] This is the πρῶτον ψεῦδος of the modern theology on Christ's sufferings. See, e.g., Robertson of Brighton.

[2] See Hall's treatise mentioned above.

the relation of causality; and here it is the relation between work and reward. It was at one time made a theological question: Did Christ win a reward for Himself by His obedience, or was He wholly born for us when He was sent on His divine commission and died for us? Calvin took up the notion, that Christ merited nothing for Himself; but it has always been felt that we cannot do justice to this text unless we maintain that by His atoning sacrifice Christ merited the fulfilment of the conditional promise of the law: "Do this, and thou shalt live."[1] We must hold that He merited the reward for His people, and therefore for Himself as the surety-head of His people; and He received a name above every name, which seems to be, as Zanchius puts it, that of Son of God, though he was Son from eternity[2] (Heb. i. 5). And adoration must be paid to Him by all intelligences in heaven, and on earth, and under the earth (ver. 10).

SEC. XV.—THE EPISTLE TO THE COLOSSIANS.

This epistle puts the atonement in a peculiar light. It contains what the other epistles set forth as to the direct connection of the death of Christ with forgiveness, redemption, and reconciliation; but it introduces a new thought—the bearing of the atonement on other orders of being. The occasion of it explains this peculiarity. This epistle, written during Paul's imprisonment, about the same time with the Epistle to the Ephesians, had as its chief design to bring out the positive doctrine of Christ's person. Therefore it is a Christological epistle in its main contents. Various allusions are made to an

---

[1] See H. Alting's *Problemata Theologica*, where he discusses this point, p. 176. Calvin, Danæus, Pareus, took the negative, in opposition to the scholastics; Zanchius, Piscator, and F. Junius held the affirmative.

[2] "Secundum utramque naturam dedisse hoc nomen; hoc est toti mundo patefecisse quod totus iste Jesus crucifixus est filius Dei unigenitus."—ZANCHI. *in loc.*

erratic philosophy threatening to spoil the Colossians in many ways, to a worshipping of angels, an intruding into the unseen world, and an asceticism according to the commandments of men (Col. ii. 18); plain marks of an incipient Gnosticism, with its theory of emanations.   The doctrine of angels, or of a spirit-world, was opposed to the sole mediation of Christ, and intro-duced an intermediate order of beings between God and man. Paul puts the relation of angels to Christ in its true light, showing how they stood to the Son of God both in creation and redemption; and that the work of creation was effected by the same person who was the cause of redemption (Col. i. 15, 16).   As the first-born of every creature, or, more strictly, the first-begotten before every creature, all things are said to have been created IN Him, BY Him, and TO Him; the allusion being to the fact that the world owed its origin to Him, and was constituted IN HIM.   The apostle, in short, reverts to the origin of all things, and their standing in the Son, and then directs attention to a new point—the union under one common Head of redeemed men and elect angels (i. 20).   By proving that Christ is the one uniting bond of both, he supplanted the Gnostic theories; for there was no place for dependence on a spirit-world or other mediators.   We shall omit passages the same in terms with texts in the Epistle to the Ephesians (Col. i. 14, iii. 13), but must consider two passages which, while dis-playing the effect of the atonement on men, also set forth its effect on other orders of being.

I. The first is as follows : *It pleased the Father that in Him should all fulness dwell : and, having made peace through the blood of His cross, by Him to reconcile all things unto Himself; by Him, I say, whether they be things in earth or things in heaven.   And you, that were sometime alienated, and enemies in your mind by wicked works, yet now hath He reconciled in the body of His flesh through death, to present you holy, and unblame-able, and unreproveable in His sight* (Col. i. 19–22).   The apostle opens up a view of the atonement as embracing angelic intelligences as well as men. In the Epistle to the Ephesians the atonement was exhibited as uniting Jews and Gentiles in one family. Here its effect is seen in bringing together into one family and under one Head the entire universe of spiritual beings in earth and heaven.

To obviate the difficulty that suggests itself on this point, it may be proper to make one or two preliminary remarks. Besides the union which the creatures celestial and terrestrial enjoyed with their Creator in their normal state, they had a relation to each other as fellow-citizens in one vast city of God, however different in federal constitution, capacity, or service. Man's sin dissolved this union in both respects, separating us from God, and from those who once were fellow-citizens, but who, like loyal subjects at the outbreak of a rebellion, could henceforth have no relations with the rebels. The unfallen angels took part with God, and respected the sovereign rights of God. When man's relation to God was broken, his relation to the heavenly hosts was also terminated; and he had as little access to their society as to that of their God, to whom they remained loyal. God's will was no longer done in earth as it was in heaven, and the union of men and angels under one Monarch was at an end.

This must be taken into account, when we think of the atonement as restoring the relations of the fellow-citizens, because restoring the throne-rights of God. So wide was the effect of the propitiation, that all intelligences and relations in the empire of God felt its manifold fruits. The abasement of such a person—the Creator and bond of the universe, according to the divine idea—was so meritorious, that it not only brought back a peaceful union to this world, but restored the universe to friendly relations, by bringing all into a new relation to God in Christ. It may be difficult to set forth the relation of the atonement to the angelic world. And hence many, swayed by the unduly pressed parallelism of the Epistle to the Ephesians, explain these words either of the union of

the Jewish church with the Gentile, or of departed saints in
heaven and redeemed men on earth,—but without any colour
or warrant. The best interpreters, the Greek Fathers, Calvin,
Bengel, and all in every age who have cast the most penetrating glance into Scripture, expound the passage of the reconciliation of rational intelligences in earth and heaven.[1] And
notwithstanding the dogmatic difficulty suggested to every
mind by the fact that angelic beings were never at enmity
with God, this is the correct view. In one sense, the efficacy
of the atonement reaches to them, but in a different way from
the reconciliation of those alienated by sin. God reconciles
all things to Himself, celestial and terrestrial, and the angels
seem to have been confirmed by the Son of God. It is not
to be affirmed that Christ was the Mediator of angels, for the
language of Scripture is, that He is the Mediator between God
and men (1 Tim. ii. 5); but He is their Head, the uniting bond
of the universe, gathered up anew or recapitulated under Him
(Eph. i. 10). In the remarks of Calvin on this text, two
reasons are assigned why angels must be reconciled to God:
first, that they were creatures never beyond the hazard of falling
till confirmed by Christ; next, that their obedience had not
such perfection or righteousness as might suffice to a full
union with God, and therefore needed a reconciler. Whether
we take in the second element or not—for some may think it
tantamount to affirming that Christ was the Mediator of angels
—certainly the work of Christ had an influence felt through
all heaven. The reconciliation of sinful men stands on the
foreground; but it must be added, that the rent caused by sin
was repaired, and the heavenly hosts united with redeemed
men under a new Head and by a new bond, in virtue of that
atoning work which called forth wonder, praise, and joy among
thrones and dominions, principalities and powers, referred to

---

[1] See also Zanchius; Owen, *On the Person of Christ*, chapter on the recapi-
tulation of all things; and Goodwin, *On Ephesians*, ch. i. Ernesti looked with
disfavour on this interpretation, *Neue Theolog. Bibliothek.*

in the previous context (ver. 16).   But let us look more particularly at the terms.

1. The reconciliation is of God's good pleasure (ver. 19);
that is, is traced up to God's appointment.   Though the nominative to the verb PLEASED[1] is not expressed in the original,
we can supply no other than the term God or Father, as is
given in the authorized English version; for in the New Testament it is uniformly said, that it pleased the Father to send
the Son.   The Father formed the purpose of reconciling us,
and wished to be reconciled.   Hence He prepared what was
necessary, and provided for its execution; the ultimate reason
being, that God was so pleased.   As to the import of reconciliation, we have had occasion to notice again and again that
it intimates a restoration of friendship, the appeasing of divine
anger, and a new relation of favour.   Hostility lay on God's
side as well as man's side, whose rebellion provoked it; it was
a mutual estrangement; and reconciliation is in like manner
a change in the divine relation and mood of mind toward us,
as well as a change on our side toward God.

2. Reconciliation was not absolute, nor without mediation.
It was by a historic fact in the moral government of God.
Hence it is said: "HAVING MADE [better, MAKING] PEACE
THROUGH THE BLOOD OF HIS CROSS."   As to the relation of
these clauses, we must fix attention on the fact, that the
scheme of salvation, whether we take account of the incarnation (ver. 19) or of the atonement (ver. 20), emanated from
the divine good pleasure as the supreme source of all.   Next,
reconciliation intimates the removal of all existing estrangement between God and the world, taken in its widest sense.
For we must take the term "reconcile" here, not in a
new sense, but with a wider extension of meaning, viz. TO
UNITE BY RECONCILING.[2]   That underlying thought cannot be

---

[1] The natural construction, according to the analogy of other passages, is
Θεὸς εὐδόκησι.

[2] Attempts have been made to deny the proper force of ἀποκαταλλάσσειν
elsewhere, because of the shade of meaning attaching to it in this connection,

denied; for the atonement refers only to men in the proper acceptation of the term. But the application of the word in this connection is appropriate only when we take in the further idea of uniting the universe to God, and restoring the disturbed harmony. The making of peace referred to in the participial clause is specially noteworthy. The past tense in both clauses in the original shows that reconciliation and peacemaking were contemporaneous, — that they covered each other, and were accomplished once for all. (See Winer, *Gr.* § 45, *d.*)

The apostle next subjoins the material cause or means by which this peacemaking was effected: " by the blood of His cross." This was added to show that such a relation was not formed without a satisfaction for sins, though it is not more particularly mentioned how the Lord's death produced that effect. This is obvious from the tenor of Scripture, and from the two terms here used, " BLOOD OF THE CROSS :" the first suggesting a comparison between the Lord's death and the blood of sacrifice, familiar to all acquainted with the Old Testament worship ; the second recalling the penal character of the death, as that of a curse-bearing substitute. Paul laid such stress on these aspects of Christ's death—for he repeats the same, or a still more definite allusion, in the two following verses—because the Colossian errorists, in their speculative teaching, appear to have turned men's minds away from the Lord's curse-bearing humiliation to a mystic contemplation, and a spirit-world of angelic mediators.

3. A transition is next made to the case of the Colossians, formerly alienated, but now reconciled (Col. i. 20, 21). It is not necessary to repeat the explanation already given of the word RECONCILE. Beyond all question, it is used to intimate that men, once at enmity, are now restored to friendly relations. As this is the meaning in the reference to the Colos-

but in vain. That there is a true reconciliation to God on the part of men is beyond all question, however men may explain the further allusion to angelic beings.

sians, we may affirm that the word has the same signification in both verses, coupled by the particle *and* (vers. 20, 21). But we have specially to notice the means by which it was effected: "in the BODY of His FLESH through DEATH;" a remarkable combination of terms, announcing with singular brevity as many constituent elements in the atonement. First, the atonement was a great historic fact, or objective reality, accomplished in Christ's person once for all during His earthly sojourn; and the circumstance now mentioned is clearly marked, that no one might conclude it was effected apart from the person of the incarnate Son, described in the previous context, or that it stood in any way connected with what He did after His return to glory. Again, this pregnant passage alludes to His true corporeity,—an allusion directed against those Gnostic theories in Colosse, which breathed a false spiritualism, and looked unfavourably on matter in every form, and therefore on the true corporeity of the incarnate Son. Thirdly, the apostle mentions the body of HIS FLESH, which, as already mentioned, denotes, wherever it occurs in reference to Jesus,[1] that He carried about on earth a sin-bearing humanity, and therefore a weak, abased, and suffering humanity (see Rom. viii. 3). Last of all, the apostle, to complete the outline of the Lord's atoning sacrifice, mentioned death the wages of sin. When we put together all these elements, the apostle's testimony here amounts to this, that the atonement was consummated historically and once for all in the person of the incarnate, abased, and dying Surety; and it takes in His life, wound up by His death (vers. 20, 22).

4. The fruit or effect of the reconciliation is next added: "to present you holy, and unblameable, and unreproveable in His sight" [better, *before Him*]. The importance of this declaration appears on two grounds. We are taught, in the first place, that sanctification does not precede reconciliation, or lay the foundation of reconciliation, but follows it. They who put sanctification first confound everything, and mistake the rela-

---

[1] See our remarks above, on Rom. viii. 3.

tions of things as well as the entire aim and scope of Christianity: they can never ward off an all-desolating legalism.

But while the reconciliation is first in order, a second thought of vast importance is, that the atonement gives rise to sanctification at the next remove, and stands in causal connection with it. This passage, and others similar, prove that the atonement was the purchase not only of the rectified relation in which we stand before God, but of that consecration by which we are set apart for God, and also of the inner life and renovation by which we are presented faultless before Him. Such a passage as this proves that we must connect the communications of divine life with the atonement as the purchase of all. If, in an externalizing way, the atonement is dissociated from life and sanctification, or, on the other hand, if we regard the divine life as first in order, and independent of the blood of the cross, all things are dislocated. Reconciliation is first in order, but the holy and blameless life follows by necessary consequence.

Attempts have been made to make all these predicates, HOLY, UNBLAMEABLE, UNREPROVEABLE, have reference not to outwardly perceptible advances in the divine life, but to the relative standing of the Colossians before God; as the people of Israel, after the offered sacrifice on the day of atonement, were immediately regarded by God as holy.[1] The words, IN HIS SIGHT, or before Him, may, it is alleged, describe an immediate relation to God by the death of Christ. That would have been by no means an unwarrantable interpretation, had the epithet HOLY stood alone; and we may attach that sense to this epithet. But the other epithets refer to the inner sanctification of the spirit. The whole clause, indeed, bears so close a resemblance to a parallel one in Ephesians (Eph. v. 27), which mentions the presentation of a glorious church, that it seems natural to refer both to what is future.

II. Another text in this epistle, of a very comprehensive

[1] So Dalmer, in his commentary on Colossians, incorrectly.

character, puts forgiveness, the blotting out of the handwriting that was against us, and victory over Satan, in connection with the atonement: *And you, being dead in your sins and the un-circumcision of your flesh, hath He quickened together with Him, having forgiven you all trespasses; blotting out the handwriting of ordinances* [better, *contained in ordinances*, as at Eph. ii. 15] *that was against us, which was contrary to us, and took it out of the way, nailing it to His cross; and having spoiled* [or, *dis-armed*] *principalities and powers, He made a show of them openly, triumphing over them in it* (Col. ii. 13–15). The apostle, in the previous context, spoke of Christ as having all the fulness of the Godhead (ver. 9), as the Head of all princi-pality and power, and as the channel of spiritual life,—views fitted to exclude every rival, and to turn away attention from lower intelligences. Another point demands notice: the apostle first speaks to the Colossians as YOU (ver. 13), and then adopts a style common to him and them, when he says US (ver. 14). Some, commenting on the passage, conceive a transi-tion from the Gentile section to the Jewish Christian section of the church; and in conformity with this, explain the allusion to the handwriting of ordinances as a something that properly applied to them. But for this there is no warrant: no trace of such a design can be discovered. Nor is it in keeping with the apostle's manner when taking in others with himself; for in such cases the pronoun WE, occurring in the apostolic style, expresses the Christian sentiment common to him with others, irrespective of nationality. The following points demand attention in the structure of this passage, and in the arrange-ment of these successive participial clauses, which bring out what, in point of order, is previous to the quickening to spiri-tual life :—

1. The acting party, or the nominative in the grammatical structure of the sentence, is God, described as quickening, and on the ground of forgiveness (ver. 13). Spiritual life is con-nected with forgiveness, and presupposes forgiveness: the sins

of men must be forgiven before life could properly enter.[1] Forgiveness precedes, and premial life takes for granted that obstacles have been removed. Nay, applying the same principle to the Surety, the Lord could not have been quickened till we, for whom He died, were virtually and potentially discharged (see Rom. iv. 25).

2. Another clause shows that forgiveness presupposes the objective fact of blotting out the handwriting of ordinances, and nailing it to the cross (ver. 14). Opinions as to the import of this handwriting are various.

a. Thus, in the first place, some refer the expression simply to conscience, as containing an indictment against us; the opinion of Luther and Melancthon, and repeated by many with the addition of a more objective element—guilt. According to this comment, the indictment, or, which is the same thing, guilt, was deleted like a bond, and nailed to the cross, when God suspended His Son on the accursed tree. In other words, Christ was so identified with the handwriting, that He was considered as the personal guilt, and His crucifixion as the means of its extinction.[2] The cross annulled the bond or handwriting that was against us. From this and other passages (Gal. iii. 13; 1 Pet. ii. 24) it appears that He took guilt on Himself, and subjected Himself to that to which the handwriting bound us; that is, He did not subject Himself to what was nominal, and procured a nominal discharge, but offered a full equivalent. This plainly is the substance of the phrase.

b. Others more particularly refer the whole to the Mosaic law; and here again interpreters go into two divisions. One class refers the phrase to the ceremonial law, arguing that the ritual observances were symbols of deserved punishment, or a confession of guilt. There might be some reason for this limitation if there was any ground—which there is not—for the

[1] See Thomasius' remarks, *Christi Person und Werk,* iii. p. 109. In a word, spiritual life (συνεζωοποίησε) presupposes (1) pardon, (2) the blotting out of the χειρόγραφον, and (3) the triumph over Satan.

[2] See Keil's remarks, *Zeitschrift für Lutherische Theologie,* 1857, p. 457.

U

supposition that the apostle here distinguished between Jews
and Gentiles. But since the apostles, in their use of the pronoun WE or US in the course of their epistles, only express the
Christian consciousness, it is better to understand the term HAND-
WRITING of the Mosaic law generally,[1] that is, of the law as
a complete whole, consisting of moral and ceremonial elements.
The cross was meant to be the blotting out of the indictment ;
and the law, in one important aspect of it, because it was never
fulfilled, was but the creditor's bond, the indictment, the charge
which was presented against those who were bound to it, but
who failed at every point.

How was the handwriting nailed to the cross when the
Lord's body, and not the law, was nailed to the cross ? Christ's
body was no bond ; but as He was made sin, or bore our sins
on His own body to the tree, all was embodied in Him.[2] The
handwriting, the curse, the sin of His people, are identified
with Him ; and the language of exchange can be competently
applied to Him in the performance of that great work of procuring our discharge. And why was the bond nailed to the
cross ? The only answer that can be given is, that it might be
nullified. Any other interpretation is inadmissible, because out
of keeping with Paul's design. The meaning of the clause,
then, may be easily collected : it is simply this, that sin could
be forgiven only on the one condition that its guilt was expiated, and that not by the sinner, but by a surety in his stead.
Hence we elsewhere read, that God condemned sin in Christ's
flesh (Rom. viii. 3). The key to these deep thoughts is to be
found in the fact that Christ exchanged places with us ; and as
the obligations are now discharged, the demands of the law are
no longer capable of being presented to us, because they were
discharged by the Surety, who nailed them to His cross, and
is now far beyond their reach. The sins of Christ's people

---

[1] Some of the best expositors and divines take the χειρόγραφον for the ceremonial law, e.g. Calvin, Turretin, Pictet ; but it is a one-sided view.

[2] See Steiger on the passage.

were annihilated, extinguished, and blotted out, as if they had never been. In short, they are no longer on the Christian, because borne by Christ to the tree; and no longer on Him, because they have been so completely expiated, that the deleted bond may be seen on His crucified humanity as nailed to His cross.

3. A third clause, grounded at least in thought by what precedes, states that the cross was the victory which God celebrated over principalities and powers of darkness (ver. 15). The acting party in this clause, as in the others already noticed, is God; and the thought is, that by the atonement of the cross God stripped satanic principalities of their dominion, or disarmed them, as a victor does in the hour of victory. And as the verb in the original conveys the idea of doing an action for Himself, there is a perceptible allusion to His glory, and to the interests of His kingdom. They who refer the language to Jewish authorities are wide of the mark. Three terms are here used—SPOILING, SHOWING OPENLY, TRIUMPHING; all significant, but describing effects contemporaneous with His crucifixion. We do not interpret the clauses as delineating a triumph over the powers of darkness during Christ's separate or disembodied state, for that comment is excluded by the fact that the agent referred to in this verse is God, as in the previous clauses. Neither are we to suppose a leading of them in triumph through space after His resurrection; for the terms limit the allusion to the expiation effected on the cross. But it may be asked, How did the cross effect the results recounted in the three several clauses? I answer: Sin was the ground of Satan's dominion, the sphere of his power, and the secret of his strength; and no sooner was the guilt lying on us extinguished, than his throne was undermined, as Jesus Himself said (John xii. 31). When the guilt of sin was abolished, Satan's dominion over God's people was ended; for the ground of his authority was the law which had been violated, and the guilt which had been incurred. This points the way to the

right interpretation; for all the mistakes have arisen from not perceiving with sufficient clearness how the triumph could be celebrated on His cross.[1]   When we reflect that the power of Satan was based on sin and guilt, and that but for sin justice would not have surrendered mankind into his power, we perceive that the annihilation of man's guilt annihilated the sway of these powers of darkness over all the elect.   Though confident that the shameful death of crucifixion would undermine Christ's influence, they found, in the first place, that it overthrew their own; for the cross *spoiled* or disarmed the satanic powers by destroying sin.   Moreover, it put them to shame, by making a SHOW OF THEM OPENLY before the universe; for though the men at the cross did not understand the bearings of that stupendous fact, holy angels present at His death, as they had been present at His birth, took in its vast dimensions. Still further, the cross was a scene of TRIUMPH on the part of God, because Satan's empire received a defeat from which there was no recovery: it was on God's part at once a victory and a display of all God's attributes, to the irretrievable ruin, dismay, and confusion of satanic powers.

SEC. XVI.—THE EPISTLES TO THE THESSALONIANS.

These two epistles, the first of the Pauline epistles in order of time, were addressed to a church distinguished for brotherly love and the eager expectation of the Lord's coming.   Cradled in persecution, which first caused the apostle abruptly to depart from their city (Acts xvii. 1–10), and then made several of their number martyrs (1 Thess. ii. 14, iv. 13), they cherished an eager anticipation of the second advent.   In consequence of supposing it immediately at hand, some of them, however, neglected the duties of their worldly calling,—a perversion which required a corrective at the hand of Paul.   But as a

---

[1] See Steinhofer on Colossians, and De Moor's *Commentarius perpetuus in J. Marckii compend.*, expounding this passage.

congregation they stood firm in the truth, and did not, like some others, need anew to receive doctrinal directions as to the sole ground of acceptance.   Twice in these epistles Paul directly mentions the death of Christ ; and in four passages we discern a distinct allusion to the atonement.

I. Deliverance from the wrath of God is described as secured by the atonement in two several passages, which we shall notice one after the other.

a. The first of these is thus expressed : *Ye turned to God from idols, to serve the living and true God, and to wait for His Son from heaven, whom He raised from the dead, even Jesus, which delivered us from the wrath to come* [better, *who delivers us from the coming wrath*] (1 Thess. i. 9, 10).   Paul, distinguishing the Christians from the Gentiles, and also from the Jews, names these two features as descriptive of true believers : their serving the living and true God, and their waiting for God's Son from heaven. Deliverance from wrath, expressed in the present tense, because a present as well as a future possession, is directly ascribed to Jesus, who is also called the Son of God. The death of Jesus is not expressly named, but there is no reason to doubt that this thought underlies the statement. For, in the first place, the clause " whom He raised from the dead " implies both suretyship and the acceptance of His finished work; and, in the second place, the actual deliverance is here mentioned as a present and constant privilege, in terms which obviously imply that it was won or procured for us by His earthly abasement and sacrifice.

b. A second text, not less express on the same theme, is as follows : *For God hath not appointed us to wrath, but to obtain salvation by our Lord Jesus Christ, who died for us* (1 Thess. v. 9).   The words " who died for us " are linked to the other expression, " by our Lord Jesus Christ," according to a well-known rule of Greek grammar, that serves to lay emphasis on the idea connected by an already well-known relation[1] (*quippe*

---

[1] Χριστοῦ, τοῦ ἀποθανόντος.

qui). The meaning intended to be conveyed is, that the deliverance was based on the ground of Christ's vicarious death, and that on this account alone men are not appointed to wrath, their deserved doom, but to obtain salvation. The double privilege is connected with the Lord's death as the meritorious cause. Language demands that interpretation, and will bear no other (comp. Rom. v. 9).

The question of divine wrath is at present the great point in debate on the subject of the atonement. It is undermined in a great variety of views, and it seems proper, nay, necessary, to dwell on it somewhat more at large.[1] A few inquiries may here be raised and answered, that we may arrive at satisfactory conclusions as to this point—on which, in fact, the two schools of theology in our day are divided—whether Christ may competently be described as bearing the wrath of God.

1. Does a wrath of God exist, and in what does it consist? That there is a wrath of God, in respect of sin and against sin, is declared so frequently both in the Old and New Testament, that they who call the doctrine in question must deny the authority of a large portion of revelation. Wrath is the displeasure of the personal God, the moral Governor, against sin, and the moving cause of that punishment which He righteously inflicts. Some, indeed, will have it that the anger of God is but another name for punishment, and maintain that the translators of Scripture would have better expressed the meaning of the sacred writers had they rendered the term in this way; for they think of it as the cause put for the effect. But there is no warrant for that conclusion; and we cannot concede that the term WRATH is used to express

---

[1] The voluminous discussion recently excited in Germany, in connection with Hofmann's *Schriftbeweis*, turns on the point whether Christ bore the divine wrath, and whether God has wrath (ὀργή). He denies that Christ bore any wrath from the hand of God; and so did Menken, Klaiber, Stier, etc., not to mention the Schleiermacher school, much less advanced in evangelical views. See the review of the Hofmann controversy by Weizsäcker, *Jahrbücher für Deutsche Theologie;* and Kraussold's *Theologische Zeitfragen.*

only the punishment of sin, or the effect of God's displeasure (Rom. i. 18, ii. 5, iii. 5). It is no mere effect, apart from the inward affections of a personal God. Were there nothing further than an impersonal moral constitution of the world, or had God left the world to take its course, indifferent to good or evil in His creatures, according to the Epicurean conception of providence, one might speak of the results of evil irrespective of the moral nature and moral feelings of an intelligent agent. But the world is not ruled by fate, nor by one indifferent to the moral actions of men, but by the living, personal God, who regards all things in relation to Himself and His moral government, and who has a holy displeasure at moral evil. Without ought of the turbulent emotion found in us, and which betrays human weakness, the supreme Lawgiver, from the perfection of His nature, is ANGRY AT SIN, because it is a violation of His authority, and a wrong to His inviolable majesty. Though He cannot be injured, as men commonly understand the term injury, He may be wronged by the creature's refusal to acknowledge His divine authority. How can any have such mean conceptions of God, as to make Him an indifferent spectator of human affairs and conduct involving His own rights ? Can He look with equal indifference and equal satisfaction on piety and impiety, virtue and vice, wisdom and folly, the morally beautiful and the morally disordered ?

But may not wrath be in some sense reduced to love, or to a certain modification of divine love, as has often been asserted, and is maintained by a great number of divines in the present day ? We answer most emphatically, No. However men may perplex their minds in speculating on the divine attributes, by reducing them to one in their artificial theories, that conclusion to which I have adverted is contrary to the plain teaching of Scripture. Wrath is not to be subsumed under love, nor represented as either love-sorrow or the fire-zeal of love.[1] It is

---

[1] While Delitzsch and Weber come in substance to the view of a real exercise of wrath on sinners, and therefore on Christ their substitute, they both have a

not the feeling of offended love, nor divine sorrow at the creature's froward disobedience.   These are poor dreams of the
human mind speculating on God, without dependence on the
word of revelation, by which alone we can know Him.   It is
unbiblical to say, that a God who has wrath is not a God who
loves; but it is scarcely less so to affirm that God is angry because He loves.   Consistently carried out, these speculations
run counter to the forensic idea of satisfaction, and are at
variance with any due recognition of law, guilt, or punishment.
The objective reality of divine wrath, on the supposition of sin,
is an axiom or first principle in natural theology (Rom. i. 32),
as well as in the theology of revelation.   All speculations of an
opposite character ignore the fact and criminality of sin.

Wrath, in biblical phraseology, therefore, is an essential
mood of the divine mind in respect of sin; and were we to
deny the objective reality of divine wrath, we should be com-
pelled to weaken and dilute the meaning of all Scripture.   The
passages in which the term WRATH occurs amount to many
hundreds, many of which are so definite, that they, beyond all
doubt or controversy, bring before us what is essential to the
divine nature.   Thus, when God SWEARS IN HIS WRATH, that
is, swears by that essential attribute of His nature which leads
Him to hate and punish sin, no doubt can be entertained that
this is a quality or property of God (Ps. xcv. 11).   It is a perfection having its root in the moral excellence of the living
God : it is proportioned to men's conduct : and, in a word, it is
inseparable from the idea which we form, and must form, of
the activity of a personal God in regard to moral evil (Heb. iii.
11 ; Rom. ix. 22).[1]

Nor is it unworthy of God to represent Him by a phrase-

philosophy on the subject, drawn from a peculiar view of the attributes, which
leads them to speak of divine wrath as an anger of love. See Delitzsch's preface
to Weber's work, *Vom Zorne Gottes*. Philippi, Thomasius, and Keil are much
more pronounced.

[1] See this admirably established by Bartholomäi in an article in the *Jahrbücher für Deutsche Theologie*. See, too, Van Voorst on punitive justice (Dutch).

ology borrowed from human feelings: for this is no mere anthropomorphism, but a delineation of His real displeasure at sin. Hatred, in like manner, or a real aversion to sinners surrendering themselves to sinful courses, is ascribed to God; and it is not represented as a figure of speech: it is an amiable moral excellency (Rom. ix. 13 ; Rev. ii. 15). And there is no reason to repudiate this biblical idea—because it has its analogue in man—or to call the wrath of God a mere anthropomorphism; for the Bible always speaks of God's attributes in words borrowed from human qualities, which indeed, with the due distinctions drawn between the Creator and creatures made in His image, are common to both. What sort of excellence would it be in man, to be morally indifferent, and to have neither aversion nor anger at sin ? In a word, the idea of divine wrath prompting retribution for moral disobedience, is involved in our very idea of God as a personal God and moral governor : it is inseparable from the fact of sin ; it is presupposed in the atonement ; and it must be carried with us into any conception which is formed of future retribution.

2. Now the great question on which the atonement may be said to depend is, Did Christ bear this wrath of God, the chief element of which is the privation of God ? As this is affirmed or denied—and opinion in modern times has very much come to be divided into two schools upon the point— the real doctrine of the atonement is either maintained or denied. The objective reality of Christ's atoning work is found to consist in the propitiation of the divine wrath. That is evident from these plain texts of Scripture in Thessalonians, and from the statements that He was made sin (1 Cor. v. 21) ; that He was made a curse for us (Gal. iii. 13) ; and that we are saved from wrath through Him (Rom. v. 9).[1] This point is undoubted from the evidence of texts, and it is equally certain from the fact of substitution considered as a real transaction.

---

[1] Schott of Erlangen (*Römerbrief*) follows Hofmann in the exposition of such texts.

Either the Lord entered vicariously into our position, responsibility, and guilt, or He did not. If He did—as all the texts bearing upon the atonement abundantly evince—then He endured divine wrath, that is, the divine desertion, as the Mediator between God and man, subjecting Himself to all that had devolved upon humanity as the curse of sin. His substitution was not, indeed, identity. He could therefore be the object of the divine wrath in our place, while still the beloved Son and the sinless man. He was made sin while sinlessly perfect and accepted : He was made a curse while yet the faultless servant : He was the object of true punishment, and of all that goes to constitute true wrath, as He stood in our place to bear what was due to us for sin, while in Himself the Son of His love (Col. i. 13), and the approved and accepted second Adam, and never more the object of His approval than when He offered Himself for others (John x. 17). We draw the distinction between the personal and the official.

It only remains to add, that He who comes to Christ, and is found in Him, shall never see wrath. The whole divine wrath is legitimately removed by Christ, for Christ's work of atonement can never be thought of without the wrath of God. Our deliverance, too, is a present deliverance from wrath incurred : for there is no truth in the representation that divine wrath belongs to eschatology alone,[1] and is only for the rejectors of Christ.

II. A second text, referring to the disarming of death and the removal of its sting by the atonement, is as follows : *For if we believe that Jesus died and rose again, even so them also who sleep in Jesus* [better, *sleep through Jesus*] *will God bring with Him* (1 Thess. iv. 14). The passage was designed to comfort Christians mourning the loss of fellow-Christians ; and in doing

---

[1] Ritschl, in his Latin tractate *de ira Dei*, 1859, adopts the eschatological view of wrath. He transfers all wrath to the future, making it light only on the despisers of salvation ; but he will not allow it in connection with past and present SIN, or with the ATONEMENT. On the other side, see Harless on τίκνα φύσει ὀργῆς (Eph. ii. 3), and also Philippi.

this, Paul points to the relation in which they stood to Jesus.
Sometimes the words SLEEPING THROUGH JESUS have been
viewed as referring to the case of martyrs suffering for the
cause of Christ. But that mode of expression is quite unlike
the ordinary language of Scripture in speaking of suffering for
Christ. The apostle intends to present to the Thessalonians
a certain argument based on the atonement, thus : If we believe
that Jesus died for His people's sins, and rose again, then certain
results or effects are referred to as standing connected both
with His death and resurrection. First, as to the effect derived
from His death, THEY SLEEP THROUGH JESUS : then, as to His
resurrection, which means that He rose as the first-fruits of
them who sleep, God will bring His people WITH HIM.

The object we have in view leads us to examine only the
first of the two expressions, THEM THAT SLEEP THROUGH JESUS ;
for we must construe the words in this manner. The mode
of construing which certain interpreters adopt, of connecting
THROUGH JESUS with the verb SHALL BRING, labours under the
intolerable defect of virtually repeating the same thing a
second time : thus, " God will bring them through Jesus with
Him."[1] But we next inquire what is specially intimated by
the terms, " them that sleep through Jesus ?" This has often
been interpreted as intimating that believers retain in death
the union with Christ which they enjoy. Though that idea
underlies the terms, and cannot be separated from the clause,
a much closer connection with the atonement may be discerned
in the argumentative form with which the verse begins. Plainly,
the allusion is to something effected THROUGH JESUS, or by the
death of Christ, as the medium of redemption. It means that
death is to the Christian no longer a penalty, but a falling
asleep ; and this belongs to the Christian's death in whatever
form it may come, and with whatever accompaniments. The
expression " sleep IN Jesus," as it is put elsewhere (1 Cor. xv.
18 ; Rev. xiv. 13), or THROUGH Jesus, as it is put here, has

[1] ὁ Θεὸς τοὺς κοιμηθέντας διὰ τοῦ Ἰησοῦ ἄξει σὺν αὐτῷ.

reference to the body, not to the disembodied soul, which is understood to be with the Lord: it means that death is not accompanied with the curse, but deprived of its sting (1 Cor. xv. 56), and that the redeemed will rise out of it as from a sleep. The comfort which the apostle suggests, and the foundation of our confidence in the prospect of death, is the vicarious death of Jesus, His suretyship for His people.

III. Another passage in this epistle brings out in a striking way the life hid with Christ in God, as a further fruit of the atonement: *Who died for us, that, whether we wake or sleep, we should live together with Him* (1 Thess. v. 10). The immediately previous verse, as already noticed, had stated that Christians are not appointed to wrath, but to obtain salvation, that is, are appointed to acceptance on the ground of Christ's atoning sacrifice. The primary fruit of the atonement, undoubtedly, is the reconciliation of the man, the acceptance of his person. Though that is the direct and immediate consequence of the Lord's death, it is followed by another; and this second result is the renovation of the nature as well as the rectification of the personal relation. These two, person and nature, though both affected by the atonement—the one immediately, the other mediately — are not to be confounded together, nor opposed to each other. In reality, subordinates neither conflict with each other nor exclude each other. Christ died, in the first place, to deliver us from wrath (1 Thess. v. 9): He died, too, to make us partakers of His life (ver. 10).

The final clause brings out what the Lord expressly planned and intended by His propitiatory death: "That (ἵνα) we might live together with Him." In the expression, LIVE TOGETHER WITH HIM, the thought is, that the life of the church collective, and of individual Christians singly, is so hid with Christ, and bound up with Him, that they are NEVER FOR A MOMENT SUNDERED from Him, either in their earthly life or in their disembodied state. It is a general statement of which there are elsewhere many echoes or expressions (Col. iii. 3; Rom.

xiv. 9). Several thoughts may be said to be contained in the expression, as follows: He bought them to be His possession, or purchased flock; He died to be their Lord; and He aimed, by so dying, to give them a life like His own—a life together with Him. As to the expressions, WHETHER WE WAKE OR SLEEP, they are very variously interpreted. But we have no doubt that they refer to the Christian's life in the body, and to the Christian's life in the separate state (see 1 Thess. iv. 14). They are not here used figuratively for moral or spiritual conditions, as in the earlier section of the chapter, where WAKING and SLEEPING must be so understood (1 Thess. v. 6–8). The whole terms of this clause have generally, but needlessly, been limited to the time of the second advent, as if they merely intimated that at that moment the saints should live together with Christ, whether they were alive or fallen asleep. But there is no need for this limitation: they apply to all times: all this is as true now as it will be then.

SEC. XVII.—THE EPISTLES TO TIMOTHY.

The three epistles next in order, from their scope commonly called pastoral epistles, do not contain many testimonies to the atonement. As to the first epistle, it appears that on one occasion Paul left Timothy in Ephesus, to consolidate the doctrine of the large congregation there, when he went into Macedonia (1 Tim. i. 3). He hoped to return shortly, but despatched this epistle to his fellow-labourer, to direct him how to act in the house of God, the church of the living God (iii. 15). There were erratic tendencies already appearing in Ephesus, as we explained above in noticing the epistle to that church: a teaching of the law (i. 7), and a science falsely so called (vi. 20); in opposition to which Paul points out the way of salvation by grace (i. 14–17), and the Lord's manifestation in the flesh,—obvious allusions to the incarnation and atonement (iii. 16).

The second Epistle to Timothy was plainly written when Paul was on the verge of martyrdom (2 Tim. iv. 6), containing parting words of direction to his son in the faith, whose presence he requests in a time of trial. Allusions to the atonement are to be found in this epistle—obvious enough to any one reading for personal satisfaction, though not such as we would adduce to a gainsayer. Thus Paul speaks of the epiphany, or first advent of our Saviour Jesus Christ, who abolished death (2 Tim. i. 10). Again, the apostle uses language of which we have had many similar specimens already: "If we be dead with Him [better, died], we shall also live with Him" (Rom. vi. 1–12 ; 2 Cor. v. 14).

The only text to be particularly expounded is the following: *For there is one God, and one mediator between God and men, the man Christ Jesus; who gave Himself a ransom for all, to be testified* [literally, *the testimony*] *in due time. Whereunto I am ordained a preacher* (1 Tim. ii. 5–7). The apostle began with directions as to the church assemblies, directing that Christians in their worship should pray for all men, for kings and all in authority ; that is, for all ranks, conditions, and classes of men. The apostle was thus led by a natural transition to speak of the unity of God, and the one mediator between God and man.

1. As to this designation of Christ, it must be remembered that a MEDIATOR is one who comes between two contending parties to remove the cause of contention, and restore them to friendship. In this case, a mediator was one who stepped in between God as an offended Judge, and men as guilty sinners (vers. 3 and 4), to pacify God, and restore men to favour. In this sense, Jesus is called a mediator between God and men ; that is, men needing to be saved (ver. 4). And this mediator is not a mere teacher, not a moral reformer, not a mediator of intercession, but of reconciliation, who removes the cause of quarrel by making reparation for the wrong (see 1 John ii. 1, 2). That is the meaning in the text before us, as indubitably appears from the appended participial clause in the Greek,

which states that He was mediator, as He gave Himself a ransom for all.[1] The words are so definite, that they will not permit us to explain them, as saying that He became a mediator when He ascended; for the participial clause (relative clause in the English version) means that He was a mediator in giving Himself a ransom. He did not give Himself, and then become a mediator: He was a mediator on earth when He died and gave Himself.

Christ was a mediator, not as He acted the part of a messenger, or made known the divine will, but as He ushered in redemption. The nature of the office presupposed the inability of the sinner, and was distinctly announced in many passages (Jer. xxx. 21). The mediator must possess true humanity and true Godhead in one person; and the reason is obvious. He must be TRUE MAN, according to the obligations of those whom He represented before God, with a compassion for the erring (Heb. iv. 15), and a nature holy and undefiled, to obey and suffer (Heb. vii. 26). He must be TRUE GOD, not only to sustain the humanity, but to give His work a value equivalent to everlasting punishment, and make His obedience adequate to the wants of millions. Deity and humanity were united in one person for a work to which each nature contributed its part, with a concurrent action at every step. The theory that makes the Lord mediator in one nature, whether in the divine, as Osiander held, or in the human, as the Church of Rome and Stancarus put it, never commended itself to scriptural divines.

But if so, why does the apostle designate Christ THE MAN CHRIST JESUS? In many passages he describes Christ as a divine person; but in this passage, when speaking of the mediator, he appends the designation MAN, because he is about to speak of His sufferings and death. Another reason was, that among the Ephesians a certain inclination began to discover itself toward the Gnostic errors which sought the root of all evil in matter or corporeity, and

[1] μεσίτης ὁ δοὺς ἑαυτὸν ἀντίλυτρον.

thus naturally led them to the notion that our Lord had but a phantom body—a semblance of manhood. Paul therefore calls Him the MAN Christ Jesus. The Apostle John, too, at a later time referred to those who denied that Jesus Christ was come in the flesh (1 John iv. 2, 3). They undermined the death of the Son of God, and, with the death, the atonement as a satisfaction to justice. These theories are here exploded, first by the designation MAN, descriptive of the Lord's person; then by the names CHRIST JESUS, which prove that He was the Christ, the unique man. This is brought out when He is represented as one mediator between God and man; that is, one who interposed between two divided parties, and occupied the singular relation in the universe of mediating between God and the human family of all time. While very man, He was thus unique man, having no equal nor parallel.

2. But it is added, HE GAVE HIMSELF A RANSOM FOR ALL, meaning that the surrender of His life was the price or ransom by which He obtained men's deliverance from captivity. Every expression and word here has a deep significance, and they are nearly a repetition of Christ's own saying (Matt. xx. 28). The phrase HE GAVE HIMSELF has much force, indicating boundless love to us, and obedience to His Father; in a word, priestly action, the reality of the typical worship. He gave Himself, according to the divine decree, spontaneously or freely.

3. The word RANSOM denotes the price by which one is discharged from captivity, with the further thought, as it occurs here, that the Deliverer encounters something similar to the evil impending over him who is delivered, or such a ransom as is made by something given in exchange for another.[1] But are there in this transaction the criteria of a

[1] See Grotius, *de Satisfactione;* Hoornbeck; Calovius; Quenstedt; Stapfer; De Witte, *Voldoening;* Mosheim's *Commentary on Timothy;* Muntinghe, *Geschiedeniss,* vol. ix. note 96; and Weber, *Vom Zorne Gottes.*

real ransom, and all its constituent elements ? Yes. 1. We have captives to be redeemed,—men whose guilt or liability to bondage too plainly appears from the fact that they are under sin (Rom. iii. 9), under the curse of the law (Gal. iii. 13), in bondage to death, and to the fear of death (Heb. ii. 14). 2. The Redeemer is here called the mediator, by whom the price was paid. That Christ is so represented, there is no doubt (Rom. xi. 26; Gal. iii. 13). 3. The ransom is announced in the most unmistakeable terms by our Lord elsewhere (Matt. xx. 28), and by the apostle in this text, as consisting in the priestly action of giving Himself in our room. 4. The party receiving the ransom is God, considered as Lawgiver, Ruler, and Judge, whose property we were by creation-right, and whose property we become anew by redemption-right (Rev. v. 9). When we put these elements together,—the captive, the Redeemer, the ransom, the party who held the sinner till he received the necessary equivalent to the inflexible claims of His law, and who then takes them into a new endearing relation as His purchased property,—we have all the elements of a real transaction. It was not metaphorical, but real.

Against the above-mentioned outline of this great fact the most determined opposition has always been evinced by all who stand opposed to our Lord's vicarious life and sufferings. They challenge the doctrine on the ground of reason and rectitude; to which the reply is, that we abide by the authority of the divine word. Sometimes they venture to assert that no passage of Scripture can be adduced where it is said that Christ suffered all in our room and stead; and they interpret the words FOR US as intimating merely that He suffered for our good.[1] No one acquainted with the Greek language, and taking into account the composition of the word here used ($\dot{\alpha}\nu\tau\dot{\iota}\lambda\upsilon\tau\rho o\nu$), will assert that it does not naturally and competently convey the idea of a

---

[1] Stapfer, in his *Polemical Theology*, admirably meets this challenge.

ransom in the room of others. It cannot be conceded, that *to give Himself to death for others* means no more than to die in some vague, indefinite way for one's good. On the contrary, the clause contains a double evidence for vicarious atonement. We had, by the transgression of the divine law, become bound to punishment, and must on account of guilt have for ever passed into the captivity of Satan, death, and hell, had not Christ acted the part of mediator, as described in the text. But when one is cast into prison for his sins, and another redeems him from it by repairing the wrong and meeting his obligations, this was not only for his good merely, but also in his stead.

One principal argument against the death of Christ, viewed as a ransom from captivity, is to the effect that no party can be pointed out to whom the ransom could be paid. The answer to that objection is obvious to any one who rises to the primary source of authority—law and obligation. The ransom or satisfaction was paid to God (Eph. v. 2). In commercial matters, and cases involving payment in money, we may hold one style of language, with all its correlative terms and notions. In criminal law another style of thought is necessary: we rise to the fountain of justice. In the great transaction of satisfying God's punitive justice, and vindicating the divine majesty and the authoritative claims of law, we are brought directly to God Himself, as moral Governor and personal God, having rights from which He cannot recede, because they are inalienable. As sinners, men are guilty before God (Ps. li. 4; Rom. iii. 19); and hence the ransom must be primarily viewed as offered TO Him, and accepted BY Him (Rev. v. 9).

According to the crude opinion of some of the Fathers, the atonement was too much considered in relation to Satan. Some, following Origen, imagined that the ransom was paid to him because, in the loose mode of thinking which they permitted themselves to entertain, it was alleged that Satan had acquired a rightful claim to fallen humanity, such as God Himself must respect. That groundless notion, though it kept its place for a time, never carried general consent. It was at variance with the Christian sentiment; and the difficulties connected with the idea of offering a ransom to Satan, for a conquest sinfully acquired, were always felt by judicious divines of all centuries. They who perceived the necessity of a different mode of statement in the early centuries, connected the atonement with the original menace against sin, and represented it as a satisfaction to the divine veracity.[1]

Satan's relation to men held captive under his dominion was but subordinate. Sinful men were indeed in bondage to Satan, but his power was founded simply on the guilt of that sin in which he involved them, or on the right of conquest which he had effected. He was but the jailor, having no power over his captives except by God's authority, who left them under a just doom—under sin, death, and hell. But, in the proper acceptation of terms, men are guilty to God: against Him, and Him only, was sin committed (Ps. li. 4). The party to whom the ransom was paid is evident. When we look at the analogy of human law—that is, at man made in the image of God, and acting out his views of right and wrong in a sphere closely resembling the divine procedure—a satisfaction for the infraction of the law is never made to the inferior officer, but to the Supreme Majesty, the fountain of authority. To the jailor or executioner it falls merely to carry out the sentence of imprisonment or death upon the criminal. In this great transaction of which we treat, the ransom was not paid to the inferior officer, but to the fountain of authority—the Judge of all. The ransom or satisfaction was paid to God; for there was none besides Him or beyond Him. And His sovereign plan was to discharge the captives only on receiving the ransom of His Son's obedience and death.

One consideration, too much omitted in theories of the atonement, will put this matter in its true light. We must

---

[1] Athanasius speaks in this way—a recoil from Origen's theory.

distinguish between SIN ITSELF, and the consequences, temporal and eternal, corporeal and mental, inevitably flowing from it by the connection of cause and effect. The redemption-work of Christ cannot be viewed merely in relation to the consequences of sin, but in relation to sin itself. And we consider it in a biblical way only when we study it with a full recognition of the fact that infinite guilt renders an infinite satisfaction necessary, nay, absolutely indispensable.

Two things remain to be noticed : first, the sense in which we are to take the apostle's words, *a ransom* FOR ALL ; secondly, how we are to apprehend Paul's testimony in connection with it.

a. As to the expression " a ransom FOR ALL," the meaning may be collected from the context. It is not all men numerically, but all conditions, ranks, classes, and nationalities, without distinction. This is so evident, that if we follow the rule of interpreting by the context, no doubt can remain on any mind. At the commencement of the chapter the apostle mentioned all men; and immediately adds, as an explanation of this use of the expression, " kings and all in authority,"—a superfluous addition, if we apprehend the terms as denoting absolute universality. When the apostle directs Christians to pray for all men, the allusion is to be understood as pointing out ranks, conditions, and classes of men. This is evident, partly because they did not know all men numerically; partly because, among men in the wide sense, there are some for whom we are not to pray, viz. those who have sinned unto death (1 John v. 16). That the allusion is not to all men numerically, may be proved, too, from the announcement that God will have all men to be saved (ver. 14), which refers to ranks and conditions, not to individuals ; for God's will would be effectual on all men, if the other meaning were intended. Still further to show the sense in which Paul uses the expression ALL MEN, we may notice his mode of describing locality : " I will that men pray everywhere," literally, in every place (ver. 8); which clearly means WHEREVER they may be.

This examination of the immediate context makes it evident how we are to understand the expression "a ransom FOR ALL." We cannot put a different sense upon the terms than the apostle employs throughout the context; that is, all ranks, conditions, and classes of men.[1] He died for men of all conditions, high or low; for all nationalities, Jew and Gentile equally. But the text does not affirm that He gave Himself for all men numerically. The allusion is to all classes indiscriminately—the elect of every rank, and tribe, and people. More particularly, THE ALL for whom He gave Himself a ransom, were they for whom He acted as a mediator in atonement and intercession; THE ALL of whom it is said, God will have ALL men to be saved, and come to the knowledge of the truth (ver. 4); the class undoubtedly coincident and identical with the elect; THE ALL for whom the ransom was offered—and it is never ineffectual or inoperative; THE ALL who are ushered into actual liberty, because their sins were borne, their guilt expiated, their curse reversed, and of whom not one shall finally be lost, but all shall be raised up at the last day (John vi. 39). The passage was introduced in connection with prayer, and as a motive to prayer.

b. The second thing is, how we are to apprehend Paul's testimony: "To be testified in due time, to which I was appointed a preacher and an apostle."[2] The connection between the ransom and the testimony, between the atonement and the preaching of it, is most explicit, both here and elsewhere. The preaching is a testimony to the ransom, or to the cross: that is, the atonement was accomplished, and an office was instituted specially charged with the proclamation of this

---

[1] See Augustine, who expounds the passage in this way: also the anti-Arminian writers—Ames, *Coronis* and *Antisynodalia Scripta;* Trigland; Turretin; Honert, *de Gratia;* Brakel; De Moor's *Perpetuus Commentarius in Marckium.*

[2] τὸ μαρτύριον is in apposition to the previous statement of Christ's mediatorial work of expiation. Then the words εἰς ὃ ἐτέθην denote the destination of his office as a preacher.

great theme; and preaching has no other foundation or warrant, power or influence. In this passage, with the solemnity of an oath, Paul declares that this was the scope of his ministry. After speaking of the Redeemer, who gave Himself a ransom for all, to be testified in due time, he adds, "to which I was appointed a preacher." Paul, therefore, not only preached this truth of the vicarious sacrifice, but was called and commissioned to do so: HIS OFFICE WAS FOR THIS VERY END. To give the greater confirmation to what he said, he added—doubtless with his eye upon those who undervalued that great theme, the burden of his ministry—"I speak the truth in Christ, and lie not."

SEC. XVIII.—THE EPISTLE TO TITUS.

This pastoral epistle, in many respects like the Epistles to Timothy, but more condensed, was meant to direct Titus in a difficult service in the island of Crete, where Paul had recently laboured: churches were to be organized and supplied with elders, and Titus was left behind to set in order what was wanting. The epistle served as his credentials, and as a rule for his guidance. Though it is difficult to fix the date, as the missionary tour to which reference is made is not elsewhere recorded, it bears on its front the immediate purpose for which it was composed; viz. to direct Titus, and give a code of rules for all time as to the qualifications of elders, and the mode of enforcing doctrine and duty. After stating duties incumbent on every age, sex, and condition, the apostle ascends to divine grace as the constraining motive (Tit. ii. 11), referring also to the glorious appearing of our great God and Saviour. From this he passes over to the atonement. The last chapter contains an outline of justification, which doubtless refers to the previous sketch of the expiatory sufferings of the Lord.

The single passage on the atonement demanding notice is this: *Who gave Himself for us, that He might redeem us from all iniquity, and purify unto Himself a peculiar people, zealous of good works* (Tit. ii. 14). Almost every word in this pregnant passage is significant.

1. The relative pronoun WHO has for its antecedent the double title applied to Christ in connection with His second advent: "our great God and Saviour." Undoubtedly the allusion is to one and the same person; and every one reading the passage for the first time, in the original, naturally comes to this conclusion.[1] It is the glorious APPEARING of one person: the article is common to both titles; and the person so described is further pointed out as the same who gave Himself for us. What is intimated by connecting the atonement with His deity? It shows the close connection that obtains between them. The true Godhead of Christ was the element which gave infinite value to His sufferings. His atonement, though confined to a brief period, became at the divine tribunal a ransom, or an equivalent, adequate to the wants of millions, because the abasement of such a person had inestimable worth in God's sight. When He died, it was as if all died; and the sacrifice was so valuable as well as acceptable, that instead of the curse which had been merited, the richest blessings were bestowed.

2. The simple affirmation, WHO GAVE HIMSELF FOR US, indicates two things—priestly action and vicarious sacrifice. As to the priestly action, we see that He gave Himself spon-

---

[1] The Fathers, who felt the nicer shades of the Greek language more sensibly than modern scholars, take τοῦ μεγάλου Θεοῦ καὶ σωτῆρος ἡμῶν as *our great God and Saviour:* so Matthies and Mack among moderns. Of course Socinianism opposed this; and as it could be rendered otherwise, it was not urged as it might have been by modern exegetes. See remarks in favour of this rendering by Rambach and Ernesti, *Neue Theol. Bibliothek*, though the latter will not press it in controversy. But three arguments for it are conclusive : (1) the ἐπιφάνεια, which is proper to the second advent alone ; (2) the common article ; (3) the relative ὅς referring to one person. Winer does not allow this ; but he lived in no Trinitarian atmosphere.

taneously; for the language is really sacrificial, borrowed from
the Levitical worship. That defective typical economy, indeed, could not unite what were found in Christ—priest and
victim. It is noteworthy that the Father, in many passages,
is said to have given His Son; but when Christ is here and
elsewhere described as giving Himself, we have priestly action
exhibiting boundless love and voluntary obedience, and then
a suffering victim,—in His soul forfeiting the joy which was
properly His own, and in His body enduring the agony and
shame allotted to a public criminal. As to the vicarious
character of the action, this comes out in the words FOR US,
implying that when we should have been given up to the
wrath of God, the Surety permitted our sins to be charged to
Him. The same thing appears from other words of the sentence, which plainly imply that we were IN ALL INIQUITY, and
far from being God's property.[1] We cannot read the words
without the impression that they indicate substitution, or the
action of one going into another's place.

3. This brings us to the twofold aim or design which the
Redeemer had in view when He gave Himself for us. These
final particles expressive of intention ($\nu\alpha$) give us a glimpse
into the Redeemer's heart, and discover to us the purpose
which He cherished.

a. The first of the two ends here mentioned is: "that He
might redeem us from all iniquity." The verb REDEEM ($\lambda\upsilon\tau\rho\acute{\omega}$-
$\sigma\eta\tau\alpha\iota$), derived from the word denoting RANSOM, signifies a
buying from captivity by the payment of a price. This is
the primary signification of the word; and that this meaning
attaches to it here is clear, because the price is expressed in
the phrase, "who gave Himself for us." Wherever the price
is named, it is impossible to admit a metaphorical use of the
term.

That there are cases where the word is used in the meta-

---

[1] The $\mathring{\eta}\mu\tilde{\omega}\nu$ and $\pi\acute{\alpha}\sigma\eta\varsigma$ $\mathring{\alpha}\nu o\mu\acute{\iota}\alpha\varsigma$, put together, imply that they were $\mathring{\alpha}\nu o\mu o\iota$ for
whom He gave Himself.

phorical sense, may be admitted; but in such a usage the primary sense is presupposed. The strange argument used by the opponents of the Lord's ransom is, that we are to take the term in all cases in its secondary or figurative sense ; that is, as intimating deliverance absolutely conferred, and not on the ground of a ransom. In short, they would have the meta-phorical sense the uniform usage. That is simply inadmissible when the ransom or price is expressly named. When redemp-tion is named in connection with the incarnation, the blood, the death of Christ, it is absurd to say that we must take the word REDEEM for absolute deliverance. How does the matter stand ? A word primarily denoting deliverance by price is found along with the mention of ransom-price. It is impossible in such a case to say that this is the figurative or secondary signification : for that is contradicted by the words appended, indicating the ground on which the deliverance is effected. In short, we have cause and effect together in too many cases to allow the least shade of doubt as to the causal connection be-tween Christ's blood as the ransom-price and the redemption (1 Pet. i. 18 ; Rev. v. 9 ; Gal. iii. 13).

The question is not, whether the term "redemption" may be taken in the general sense of deliverance, but whether, when connected with the blood of Christ, it can be so taken. The words so placed naturally suggest the ransom-price on the ground of which redemption is effected. It is asked, Is not the word used for absolute deliverance in the case of the national deliverance of Israel from Egypt and Babylon (Mic. vi. 4), and in the case of corporeal deliverance where nothing touches the element of justice ? (Heb. xi. 35.) It may seem so. But even in such cases, according to the laws of language, more or less of the idea of compensation will be found (Eph. v. 16). Wherever allusion is made to the work of Christ, however, as the ransom which is taken into account, and which of necessity intervenes, the word occurs in its strictly philological import. The modern opponents of Christ's propitiatory death, after the example of the old Socinian, maintain that even in this case the word is to be accepted as denoting absolute deliverance; but they argue from foregone conclusions, without regard to the thought before them.

What does the apostle mean by ALL INIQUITY ? When he says ALL, he excludes nothing: he comprehends sin, original and actual, and announces that we are redeemed from the penalty and guilt of all sin, considered as transgression of the divine law. The meaning is, that Christ redeemed us from sin, considered as guilt and entailing the curse of the law. Our great God and Saviour transferred the curse to Himself. Free from personal guilt, He entered into the place of the guilty, and transferred their guilt to Himself, that we, in virtue of His sufferings, might be pronounced free of further obligation. His sufferings had the quality of a compensation, price, or ransom paid for a captive ; and this bloody ransom dissolved all connection between sin and our obligation to punishment, giving a right to liberty.

b. The second thing contemplated by the Lord in His death, was to PURIFY TO HIMSELF A PECULIAR PEOPLE. The two clauses, introduced by the same final particle (ἵνα), contain two different thoughts. The benefits expressed are equally connected with the cross. The idea conveyed by the term PURIFY is sacrificial. There are no fewer than six cognate terms — viz. PURIFY, SANCTIFY, SPRINKLE, SANCTIFY, WASH, CLEANSE — used by the apostles to point out the effect produced by sacrifice on those who were defiled by sin. The general sense attaching to them is this, that sinners, excluded by sin from a holy God, are freed from impurity and readmitted to fellowship with God by blood. That is the meaning of the term PURIFY in the passage now under consideration.

The counterpart of these things—redemption and purification—we find in Israel's typical history. Redemption from Egypt was followed by the Sinaitic covenant, where the same people were taken into a new standing, as a kingdom of priests, to be a peculiar people to Himself[1] (Deut. vii. 6). There is little doubt that Paul had his eye on that fact, and on the passages descriptive of it (Ex. xix. 5, 6). Christ's people, redeemed by the true paschal lamb, and then admitted to a new covenant, are a true counterpart of the figurative covenant people. The apostle finely alludes to the redemption from Egypt, and then to the entering into covenant with God at Sinai as a people sprinkled with blood, and henceforth near to Israel's holy God (Ex. xxiv. 8). The design of that redemption was the consecration or setting apart of the nation to be a people near to Him; and the immediate effect of Christ's redemption is to separate a people from the world, for holy service, or for priestly worship. And the designations here applied to them are striking. They are called A PECULIAR PEOPLE, which means HIS OWN people, with the accessory idea of being a peculiar treasure, precious, and kept with care[2] (Deut. xiv. 2, xxvi. 18). They are His treasure, held to be most precious.

Next, the additional designation, ZEALOUS OF GOOD WORKS, assumes that they are partakers of the spirit of holiness (Rom. i. 4), and of the sanctification of the Spirit (1 Pet. i. 2). This comprehends the sober, righteous, and godly life already mentioned (ver. 12), as becomes men inhabited by the Spirit of God. They bear fruit, and zealously labour to bear it, as the end of their redemption, and as is worthy of a dedicated people.

[1] See Vitringa's posthumous commentary on Titus (Dutch).

[2] See Witsius' interpretation of περιούσιος, and the references which he makes to the literature on it (de Fœdere, pp. 358, 410).

CHAPTER III.

THE TESTIMONY TO THE ATONEMENT CONTAINED IN THE EPISTLE TO THE HEBREWS.

WE arrange the testimony of the Epistle to the Hebrews under a separate chapter, because we deem it best to leave the inquiry open, whether the epistle is of Pauline origin. The difficult and much canvassed question as to the authorship of the epistle we leave untouched, whatever weight may attach to the arguments adduced by many eminent expositors for the opinion that it must be assigned to another writer than Paul—to Apollos, Barnabas, or Luke. This much is admitted on all sides, that it breathes the spirit of Paul, and corresponds with his well-known mode of putting truth. If it did not emanate direct from Paul, which we for our part have never seen cause to doubt, it emanated from one of his companions, as the statements on the person, offices, and sufferings of Christ, and on the effects of His atonement, are identical with what we find in Paul; with this difference, that we have a new nomenclature borrowed from the priesthood.

SEC. XIX.—THE EPISTLE TO THE HEBREWS.

As supplying materials for defining the doctrine of the atonement, this epistle is perhaps the most important of all, not excepting those to the Romans and Galatians. It has this peculiarity, that it brings out the doctrine under figures or types borrowed from the Jewish worship. The epistle brings before us a typical and preparatory institution, having a spiritual element under that which appealed to the senses, a heavenly underlying the earthly, an eternal under the transitory. The typical worship lost its standing significance with Christ's coming in the flesh, but the comparison was most important.

This epistle was manifestly written while the temple services were still standing, and to a class of Jewish Christians who were in the habit of attending them. From several causes, the Christian Jews in Palestine were exposed to the danger of falling away from the faith, and the writer arms them to resist the temptation, and hold fast their profession. One danger arose from the persecutions to which they were exposed; a second was owing to the attractions of an imposing ritual, and to the perpetual depreciation of Christianity, as compared with Judaism, which they were obliged to hear. The epistle accordingly sets forth the superiority of Christianity to Judaism in every respect, and especially in its priesthood. It sets forth the insufficiency of the old economy by a comparison of the two, and shows that Christianity had far greater and enduring blessings.[1] Against Christianity the common Jewish objection was, that the life of its founder terminated in an ignominious death; and the apostle shows that this was the way of bringing many sons to glory (Heb. ii. 10).

If we would apprehend the scope of the epistle, and its reasoning, it must be borne in mind that the demonstration is based on ideas current among those to whom it was written, as to the function of the high priest, and the nature of the sacrifices. The epistle gives us a continuous parallel between the shadow and the substance. Christ is not compared to every Jewish priest accomplishing the service of God in the daily ministration, but to the high priest in his call, his qualifications, and peculiar ministry, as he entered the holiest of all

---

[1] The literature on the Epistle to the Hebrews is very ample, and recently has been largely augmented. I may refer to Riehm's *Lehrbegriff des Hebräerbriefes;* Ebrard's, Delitzsch's, and Kurtz's commentaries; Thiersch's academical prelection; Reuss' translation and abridged outline; Van den Ham (Latin); Wieseler, etc.

on the great day of atonement; the object being to prove that the new economy is in all respects superior. To put this in the clearest light, the epistle runs a parallel between the peculiarities of the two dispensations. In what sense is the title High Priest applied to Christ?

1. Many divines, especially during the three last generations, have maintained that the doctrine of the threefold office of Christ is without warrant; that the titles Prophet, Priest, and King, heretofore understood as descriptive of distinct works of Christ, express but one and the same thing under a variety of nomenclature. That attempt to obliterate distinctions founded in the nature of things, as well as in the marked peculiarities of the old economy, is quite unwarrantable. The titles are never confounded as terms of the same import. They are not only distinct, but indicate a different work on the part of the Saviour. When Christ is represented as a prophet, He is compared to Moses; as a priest, He is compared to Aaron. The arguments used by eminent men, like Ernesti, Tittmann, Doederlein, and Schleiermacher, to efface the distinction, have by no means carried conviction.[1] The distinction is one that takes for granted a threefold want in humanity to which the offices correspond—ignorance, guilt, depravity. And the arrangements in Israel, as positive institutions before the eyes of men, corresponded to this threefold necessity. Thus the prophet was commissioned to speak in God's name to men; and Christ was so called, because He announced the way of salvation (Acts iii. 22; John iv. 19; John ix. 17). The king had authority to rule; and Christ was so called, because He was set over a kingdom, and ruling all for His church (John xviii. 37; Eph. i. 21). The priest was one who could approach God on behalf of man; and Christ was so called, because,

---

[1] This theory, to which Ernesti, Tittmann, and Doederlein unhappily lent their influence, is scarcely a legitimate growth of Protestantism, and more akin to Socinianism. A good refutation of it is furnished by Lotze in his *Hoogepriesterschap van J. C.* 1800. See also an admirable discussion of the point by Rev. Edward Irving, and Halyburton in his *Man's Recovery*.

according to the Father's appointment, He underwent death to atone for sin. The priesthood of Christ was the foundation of His other offices; without which, indeed, the other two offices could not possibly have existed. They presuppose the priesthood, and proceed upon it. When Christ is called a priest for ever, the expression does not mean that He perpetually offers sacrifice, but that His sacrifice, once offered, has perpetual efficacy, value, and validity. There are many objections, however, which it may here be proper to obviate.

a. Thus, it is alleged that the term priest may be understood as denoting MINISTER; and attempts have been made to establish this from the etymology of the Hebrew word (2 Sam. iii. 18, xx. 26). But in this case all does not depend on etymology, but on the acceptation in which the word is found. And when Christ is compared to the Aaronic high priest, there cannot be room for two opinions that the term is appropriated to a function which contains the two elements of oblation and intercession.

b. But it is argued, that when Jesus is compared with the Jewish high priest, this is on account of the disparity between the two; and that where a correspondence is intimated, the terms "blood" and "sacrifice" are metaphorically used. There is no warrant for this; on the contrary, we cannot read the fifth chapter (Heb. v. 4–7) without discovering a regular comparison between Aaron and Christ. The apostle's discussion of Christ's priesthood was as much fitted as it was intended to convince the Jewish Christians held under the spell of the ancient stately ritual, that Christ's priesthood was immensely superior. But that object could not have been attained unless he also established that it was similar and parallel—the truth of the shadow.

c. It is further argued, that when Paul represents Jesus as a high priest, he contemplates Him not in His state of humiliation, but in His present glorified state, as the procurer and dispenser of salvation. That Jesus was a high priest in the days

of His flesh, and offered the required sin-offering in His state
of humiliation, is a point brought out in the Epistle to the
Hebrews with such convincing evidence, that one must do
violence to language to escape this conclusion. Thus, He is
said to be a merciful and faithful HIGH PRIEST in things pertaining to God, TO MAKE ATONEMENT—for so the word should
be rendered[1]—for the sins of the people (Heb. ii. 17). Nay,
the passage to which an appeal is sometimes made in proof of
His becoming a priest only on entering the heavenly sanctuary
after His resurrection (Heb. ix. 12–15), is, when correctly understood, a speaking proof of the fact that He was already a priest
when He offered Himself on earth as the atoning sacrifice for
sins. He is contemplated by the apostle as the High Priest
after the order of Melchizedek, when He is set forth as dispensing salvation.

d. Again, it is argued that we are not to ascribe the impetration or procuring of salvation to the high-priesthood
alone. To this it is enough to say, that the three offices of
the Lord were closely connected together, and that we cannot
in our minds consider one without immediately recalling the
others ; but we are not on that account to confound them.
They are to be distinguished : they each designate a separate
work : they were titles of persons who were known in Israel
to be invested with different offices, involving different works.
This threefold distinction must be maintained in all biblical
dogmatics on the work of Christ; for it is founded in Scripture,
and the three designations are expressly named in the divine
word.   Nor are they ever confounded.

This doctrine of Christ's priesthood and sacrifice is everywhere admitted on the ground of Scripture evidence, wherever
men do not argue in the interest of a theory or tendency adverse to Christ's suretyship and substitution.   From explicit
language contained in this epistle, we are warranted to conclude that the Lord Jesus was a high priest on earth; that

---

[1] εἰς τὸ ἱλάσκεσθαι τὰς ἁμαρτίας.

He offered the sacrifice on earth ; and that the exercise of His priestly functions in heaven is not to win redemption, but only to apply it. Throughout the entire epistle the principal aim is to establish this fact, to point out the agreement between type and antitype, and to set forth the infinite superiority of Christ to the shadowy priesthood of the old economy. Several times it is affirmed that He is a priest, and obviously in a real, not in a figurative sense (Heb. ii. 17, viii. 1, iv. 14).

2. At the beginning of his discussion on this subject, the apostle intimates that Christ possessed all the necessary qualifications[1] of a priest. These are chiefly the following :—

(1.) Divine appointment (Heb. v. 5, 6). He did not assume it, or take it to Himself, without a divine commission or call. The passage which makes Christ similar to Aaron, on this ground, that He glorified not Himself to be made an high priest, is very emphatic. The quotation of the second Psalm, too, reminds us of the divine dignity and excellence of Christ as the ground of His everlasting priesthood ; and this discovers the force of the allusion to the Son (ver. 8). The meaning is, that Jesus had a divine commission ; that He was appointed by the Father because He was the Son ; and that He was thus possessed of all requisite qualifications for His office. The high-priesthood of Christ was based in the divine decree ; and He was invested with the dignity by the will and appointment of the Father, the fountain of all authority and law.

(2.) He must be able to sympathize with the condition of sinners (Heb. v. 1–8). The Lord, who was rich, having come within the circle of human experience, was made a merciful and faithful high priest, and qualified by personal experience for compassionately guiding our highest interests, as well as conducting our cause. The bond of brotherhood, the identity of suffering and sorrow, fitted Him to be touched with the feeling of our infirmities. He was made like unto His brethren (Heb. ii. 17) ; He suffered, that He might be in a position to

---

[1] See Riehm's *Lehrbegriff des Heb.*

succour them that are tempted (Heb. ii. 18); He was made in all respects like us, with the single exception of personal sinfulness (iv. 15); and He learned obedience by what He suffered (v. 8). The design of all this was, that He might be a compassionate and sympathizing high priest.

(3.) He must lay to heart the interests of His people, and maintain the cause of those for whom He acted the part of a priest. With this theme the Epistle to the Hebrews is occupied; and the writer proves that Christ during His life thus fulfilled the duties of a priest (Heb. v. 7–9). The priests were required faithfully to fulfil the task committed to them, offering gifts and sacrifices for sins, and interceding for the people by prayer; and in general, they actively promoted the interests and affairs of the covenant people before God. All this the Lord discharged, practising obedience, and faithfully executing the charge committed to Him. The obedience of the Lord consisted in undergoing death for the sins of humanity, as the apostle explains it (Heb. x. 5–10); and He was made perfect, that is, perfected for the mediatorial work and the Melchizedek-priesthood, by His acceptance and confirmation as the surety. Thus the everlasting High Priest, made King and Priest, can evermore promote man's cause with God; and all who obey Him are warranted to expect eternal salvation from Him, whereas the Levitical priesthood advanced the interests of the people only for a time.

3. As we noticed the qualifications of the high priest, we next consider his ministry on the great day of atonement—the culminating point of his service. This is at large explained in the Epistle to the Hebrews (Heb. ix. 1–7). Two divisions were marked out in the ancient sanctuary: one called the holy place, allotted to the daily ministrations of the priests as they accomplished the service of God; the other called the holiest of all, into which the high priest alone entered once every year, not without blood, which he offered for himself

and for the errors of the people (ver. 7). The arrangement announced that the time then present was a time of imperfect atonement; that the Jewish sacrifices could not fully atone, but effected a certain external deliverance from temporal punishment, and confirmed their religious privileges to the Jewish nation. The reason why the holiest of all remained constantly shut, and the high priest entered alone for a little time once every year, is to be sought in the insufficiency of the Old Testament sacrifices. The way was not yet open—that is, open without impediment—while the first tabernacle and the Old Testament worship still stood (vers. 8, 24).

The high priest entering on the great day of atonement with the blood of sacrifice, and sprinkling it on the mercy-seat or covering of the ark, was the representative of the people, appearing before God in their name, and presenting blood for their atonement. By that solemn act the protection of God was sought and secured for the nation; for the most important actions of the Jewish high priest consisted in slaying the victim, and carrying the blood into the holy of holies once every year. Now the question is raised, Was that entrance typical of Christ's entrance into heaven? That action of sprinkling the mercy-seat was undoubtedly atoning; and many too precipitately think we are driven to the conclusion that Christ was not a priest on earth, and that His oblation, properly so called, commenced in heaven after His ascension. The Socinians deny, on doctrinal grounds, the sacrifice on earth, transferring it to heaven; and the principal argument by which they maintain that Christ never was a priest on earth, is based on a misunderstood text of the epistle (Heb. viii. 4). We allow that the death of the victim, taken by itself, and apart from the priestly action of bringing in the blood to sprinkle the mercy-seat, was not considered as the full act of expiation.

But this leads me to ask, When did Christ, our High Priest, enter with His own blood? It may, we think, be

convincingly proved[1] that the entrance of our High Priest
to sprinkle the mercy-seat took place at the moment of His
death; that no moment of time intervened; and that the
rending of the veil indicated His entry.   In pouring out His
blood on the cross, and surrendering His spirit into the
Father's hands, the Lord must be considered as sprinkling
the mercy-seat and expiating sin.   While His lifeless body
was hanging on the cross, the mercy-seat was sprinkled; for
He was still acting as a high priest, even when the lifeless,
inanimate body was on the cross and in the tomb.   Even
then the personal union was not dissolved.   If the question
were, whether Christ could be regarded as sprinkling the
mercy-seat before He bowed His head and gave up the ghost,
we should certainly deny it.   But as the inquiry is, When did
the true High Priest sprinkle the mercy-seat?—which was a
propitiatory act in the course of averting wrath—we must emphatically answer, At the moment of death.   His resurrection
was a reward for service done; not expiation, not propitiation,
in any sense of the word.

   This may conclusively be established.   The heavenly tabernacle or temple was, so to speak, erected over the ark of the
covenant.   That throne, or mercy-seat, must be viewed as for
ever wet or moistened with atoning blood, sprinkled once for
all.   The common notion that our Lord's entry into the holiest
of all with the propitiatory blood corresponds to His triumphal
entry into heaven, however plausible it may seem to those
who read the ninth chapter of this epistle in a cursory way,
is burdened with insoluble difficulties.   Without adducing the
grounds already given at the beginning of this volume, let it
suffice to say that the entry was immediately subsequent to
the death of the sacrifice; that the action was still expiatory;
and that all Christ's appearances to the disciples during His

---

[1] See our remarks at p. 48, on the temple services.   Witsius seems to have
been the first who threw out this exposition; Schultens and Lotze contend for
it earnestly.

forty days' sojourn, were so far from entering into the work
of expiation, that they presupposed it. His salutations to
the disciples, announcing PEACE accomplished and brought in,
presuppose it. It is incongruous and absurd to hold, then,
that the sprinkling of the mercy-seat and the purifying of
the heavenly things (ver. 23) took place only after His ascension. We distinguish between the acts of abasement and the
state of reward on which He entered at His resurrection; between the priesthood as such, and the Melchizedek or royal
priesthood.

If we want a proof that the atonement was accepted, and
procured forgiveness of sins, this was proved by the Lord's
resurrection from the dead, corresponding as it did to the coming out of the high priest from the holiest of all to give the
priestly benediction to the people. From what has all that
confusion to which we have adverted arisen? Plainly from
the fact that the expositors we have been refuting did not sufficiently distinguish the peculiarities connected with the High
Priest after the order of Melchizedek. He was the Priest
after the order of Melchizedek when He ascended to His
mediatorial throne, and that is always distinguished in the
epistle from His appearing before God with His own blood.
But it will be asked, Does not the debated text already
mentioned (Heb. viii. 4) conflict with the above interpretation? By no means. Christ must needs bring His sacrifice
into the true tabernacle, the reality of the figure; and if He
were on earth—that is, if He were a common priest of the
visible Jewish order—He would be no priest of the true tabernacle.

4. Points of contrast as well as similarity may be traced in
the whole analogy here instituted between the Jewish high
priest and the great High Priest of our profession, and between
the sacrifices offered by both respectively; and to these we shall
refer in a few words.

(1.) To begin with the contrasted high priests, the law

made men high priests who had infirmity, whereas the word of the oath made the Son (Heb. ix. 28). The Jewish high priests, moreover, were required to offer for their own sins as well as for the sins of the people (Heb. v. 3); whereas our High Priest was holy, harmless, undefiled, and separate from sinners, and needed not but to offer for the sins of others (vii. 27). The Jewish high priest could not exercise his ministry in any other but a standing attitude, and as became a servant, on the annual return of the great day of atonement; whereas our great High Priest, after His one all-perfect sacrifice, sat down on the right hand of God, from henceforth expecting till His enemies be made His footstool (Heb. x. 11–13).

(2.) Next, as to the sacrifices offered respectively, the weakness and unprofitableness of the one stood vividly contrasted with the enduring efficacy of the other. The Jewish high priest was under the necessity of constantly repeating the same sacrifice year by year continually; whereas the Lord Jesus, by one sacrifice needing no repetition, perfectly atoned for sin, and brought salvation to all who obey Him (Heb. ix. 25). Another point deserving notice is: The Jewish sacrifices effected only an external purity and the removal of corporeal punishments, but did nothing, and could do nothing, to remove the burden of guilt, or still an accusing conscience (Heb. x. 1–3); whereas the one sacrifice of Christ effectually secured a full deliverance from punishment and from an evil conscience (Heb. x. 19–22). Nor, from the nature of the case, could the Jewish sacrifices accomplish more: for they consisted of the blood of calves and goats; whereas our High Priest offered Himself to God a sinless and perfect sacrifice[1] (Heb. ix. 14).

(3.) Another point of contrast is, that the Jewish sacrifices were only for men then living, and for cases of ceremonial de-

---

[1] I cannot too strongly object to the position of Hengstenberg, Kurtz, Kliefoth, and others, that the sacrifices were, in a certain sense, the means of imparting a true forgiveness. See Philippi's refutation of this in his *Kirchliche Glaubenslehre*, iv. pp. 260–290. This borders too closely on the old Socinian doctrine to be tolerable. See Calovius' *Socinismus profligatus*.

filement, procuring temporary and corporeal deliverance, but
without any retrospective or prospective influence beyond the
case for which they were offered; whereas Christ's sacrifice,
intended for all time, effected the expiation of all sin, whether
we have respect to those who looked forward to it from the old
economy, or to those who now look back to it as an accomplished fact (Heb. ix. 26). In a word, the Jewish sacrifices
were limited in their range, whether we take into account the
class of men to whom they were applicable, or the nature of
the trespass for which they could be offered. The offences for
which they were available were all ceremonial (Heb. ix. 10).
The sacrifice of Christ, on the contrary, procured the forgiveness of all sins, being divinely adapted to all sins. Besides, it
gave free access, well-grounded confidence, and liberty; whereas
the Jewish sacrifices neither cancelled sin properly so called,
nor gave boldness of access into the divine presence; for the
throne of grace was still unopened to sinners after all that the
Jewish sacrifices effected.

One design of the Epistle to the Hebrews was, to point out
the inseparable connection between the atonement and the
remission of sins, or the sprinkling of conscience (Heb. ix. 14,
x. 2, x. 22). The epistle does not deny forgiveness to Old
Testament saints who lived before the incarnation. It certainly denies that efficacy to animal sacrifices, and connects
the actual redemption which the Old Testament saints received
with the death of Christ; for the apostle speaks of the effect
of the atonement in cancelling sins under the old covenant
(Heb. ix. 15). A theory was propounded, indeed, by Cocceius
and his school, to the effect that the privilege enjoyed by the
Old Testament saints did not amount to full forgiveness, and
that it was but the condition of non-punishment, as the atonement had not been offered, and the effect cannot be without
the cause. There is no warrant for such a supposition in the
peculiarities of the dispensations. But the apostle declares
again and again that forgiveness was not by the type, and that

the blood of bulls and goats could not take away sins (Heb. x. 4) or purge the conscience (x. 2).

The comparison instituted between the Aaronic and Christ's priesthood, between the animal sacrifices and the sacrifice of the cross, had for its object to convince those Hebrew Christians that the Lord Jesus accomplished all that was figured forth by the Jewish high priest; that the old economy was defective (Heb. viii. 8); and that the ancient sacrifices could not make the worshipper perfect as pertaining to the conscience. They were therefore replaced by a better. When the epistle was written, the sacrificial rites, the priesthood, and the Sinaitic economy itself waxed old, and was ready to vanish away (Heb. viii. 13). It was, in fact, superseded and abandoned; and the Hebrew Christians were to see that they possessed infinitely more in Christ. No one need be surprised at the abrogation of the old economy, when we remember that it was but preparatory to the fulfilment, typical or shadowy, and inadequate to promote man's highest interests: it was but the scaffolding round the building.

The difference between the two high priests was immense. In the former, or superseded economy, the high priest was but a sinful mortal man, who offered first for his own sins and then for the sins of the people; and after accomplishing the sacrifice, he entered into the earthly tabernacle as a servant. In the former economy, too, the perpetually recurring sacrifices could effect no remission of sins: they brought no purification or pacification to the conscience; all being external, procuring social advantages, but not pleasing God. The everlasting High Priest offered Himself for all nations; a sacrifice that effected remission, that pacified the conscience, and required no repetition. No one having once confessed the Saviour should entertain a doubt as to the privilege and duty of holding fast his profession.

5. Before particularly examining the several texts bearing on the atonement, a few remarks seem necessary on the

peculiar nomenclature and phraseology in the epistle, borrowed from the Mosaic worship. The epistle, couched in the Old Testament style, assumes that the accomplishment of the types had arrived, and that the shadows had been merged in the reality. We have forensic terms in the Epistles to the Romans and Galatians; but in this epistle we have terms which relate to worship, and describe the ground of confidence before a holy God. The latter stands connected with the former, and presupposes the former. Acts of worship, or the priestly element, take for granted the acceptance of the person, and are the natural outcome of that state of acceptance before God. The germ of all, found in this epistle, may be traced in the language of the Mosaic ritual, and also in our Lord's own words. Thus we read of coming not to Mount Sinai, but to Mount Zion, with the distinctive features of the two economies (Heb. xii. 18–24); of the blood of the covenant, or, as it is also called, the everlasting covenant, recalling the transitory covenant which had passed away (Heb. x. 29, xiii. 20). The blood so often mentioned is sacrificial, as is evident to any one who considers the import of the expression, "The blood of sprinkling, that speaketh better things than that of Abel" (Heb. xii. 24). That sacrificial blood cries for mercy, warranting us to come, before God's throne with confidence; and that one passage is singly conclusive against current theories adverse to the vicarious sacrifice. For if Christ died only a martyr's death, as Abel died under the operation of the world's wickedness and by the hand of violence, His blood could only cry, like Abel's, for vengeance; whereas it cries with a far other voice. The one cried for judgment, the other cries for pardon and deliverance because a vicarious atonement. There are some terms, however, which demand more particular notice, such as the following:[1]—

    a. The apostle uses the words PURIFY or PURGE in several

---

[1] The reader may here consult Zechariä's *Biblical Theology*, Lotze *on the Priesthood of Jesus Christ*, and Riehm's *Lehrbegriff*.

passages (Heb. i. 3, ix. 14, x. 2). To apprehend their meaning, it must be borne in mind that they are borrowed from the Old Testament worship, and presuppose the relation of a sinner stained by defilement and excluded from fellowship, but re-admitted into fellowship with God and His people when delivered from the stain. Thus, at the beginning of the epistle, we read that the Son, HAVING BY HIMSELF PURGED, that is, having made a purification of, OUR SINS, sat down on the right hand of God (Heb. i. 3); language emphatically declaring that the atonement was Christ's own personal act, and a completed act before He ascended. It is sacrificial language: it points out the objective effect of Christ's atonement. It cannot be referred to inner renewing, because, as the past participle here shows, it was consummated before His ascension. He did not merely announce the purification in word; He effected it, as the terms of the expression prove, by His sole activity,—that is, within the sphere of His own personal action. In other words, the apostle declares that Christ effected a purification of sin by Himself; or, according to Levitical nomenclature, that He was at once priest and victim—priest to offer the sacrifice, and victim to bear the sin, here considered as a defilement that must be purged away.

Without entering into an elucidation of the various passages in the epistle which mention PURIFICATION, let it suffice to say that this term is sometimes used in a purely objective sense. Thus, in the Mosaic worship, the vessels of the sanctuary, and the tabernacle itself, were purified by sacrifices (Heb. ix. 22). In like manner, when the heavenly things themselves are said to have been purified by better sacrifices, the meaning is, that the Lord's death was a satisfaction to the divine justice and holiness, cancelling human sin (ver. 23). But there is a subjective side of this same truth : the purging of the conscience follows as the certain and necessary consequence of pardon by Christ's blood. It is the taking away of the sense of sin. But how ? The meaning is, that the conscience, once purged, no more feels that burdensome and oppressive consciousness of sin constantly carried about with us, till the mind apprehended the sin-bearing substitute. Not that the knowledge of ill-desert is taken away or forgotten, but the gnawing burden of uncancelled guilt ceases. This is the subjective side. We may say, then, that purification of sins by Christ's sacrifice consists objectively in the removal of accumulated guilt, and subjectively in the purging of conscience.

b. A second term is SANCTIFY, having the same sacrificial reference. We find it in our Lord's sayings, and in other books of Scripture (John xvii. 19 ; Eph. v. 26), and it is much allied to the term PURIFY ; nay, the one may be said to include the other. They agree in this, that sinners defiled by sin, and thus disqualified for fellowship with God in any act of worship, are restored to nearness and to the service of God as a royal priesthood. It is the more necessary to vindicate the sacrificial reference, or the setting apart of the redeemed as a dedicated people, because, in the ordinary use of religious terms, the idea of sanctification has unduly been limited to renovation by the Spirit. The term is borrowed from the Mosaic ritual, and the privilege which it indicates is based on the sacrifice of the cross.

It may seem that the two terms PURIFY and SANCTIFY are simply coincident, and cover each other at all points, because they refer to the temple service, and are equally based on the blood of sacrifice. But they have their peculiar shade of meaning. The primary meaning of the term SANCTIFY, is to set apart to God for a sacred use, to consecrate or dedicate, as Israel was separated from other people to serve Jehovah, and called HOLY, as they were set apart by the blood of sacrifice to be in covenant, a kingdom of priests ; and as such they dwelt apart, the Lord being in the midst of them. But other things, such as the altar, the temple, the feast-days, were also said to be sanctified, or consecrated things. In short, separation from the world and consecration to God, as results brought about by the blood of atonement, is the meaning of the word. Thus we understand the words, " Both He that sanctifieth, and they who are sanctified, are all of one" (Heb. ii. 11). There is thus a negative and positive idea attaching to the term. Hence it is wider and more comprehensive than the term PURIFY, which has more the negative signification. The sacrifice of Christ was the great redemption-act by which the people of God were at once and for ever emancipated from a life of estrangement, and brought into fellowship as a holy priesthood (Heb. x. 29). Of course, THE SPIRIT OF SANCTIFICATION follows as the natural and necessary consequence.

c. A third term is TO MAKE PERFECT, repeated in a considerable number of passages (Heb. vii. 11, 19, ix. 9, x. 1, x. 14, xi. 40, xii. 23). This word forms a marked feature in the scheme of thought propounded to us in the Epistle to the Hebrews. This is distinctive of the epistle. If the term RIGHTEOUSNESS may be regarded as the distinctive feature of the Epistle to the Romans, and the essential element in the forensic aspect of the atonement, the term MAKING PERFECT may be taken as the equally marked feature in the priestly element peculiar to the Epistle to the Hebrews. The one epistle brings out justification, and the other our priestly standing and priestly service; and the two terms above mentioned are the distinctive feature of each respectively.

Thus several passages, making special allusion to the inadequacy of the Levitical priesthood and Old Testament sacrifices, affirm that they did not give perfection to the worshipper (Heb. vii. 19, x. 1). All was unprofitable in this respect. On the contrary, the one sacrifice of Christ had this effect, as it was offered once for all, that IT PERFECTED FOR EVER THEM THAT ARE SANCTIFIED (Heb. x. 14). What does that convey? It plainly carries with it a negative and positive, an objective and subjective idea, as to the priestly relation in which the worshippers of the new economy appear before God.

The primary and proper meaning of the term is to complete a work; and the idea of perfecting a work, of course, varies according to the design or end of the work that has been undertaken. In connection with the atonement of Christ, it means to attain the end contemplated by the sacrifice; and in this peculiar application of the term to make the holy priesthood, the peculiar people, perfect for the purposes on account of which they were sanctified or set apart (Heb. x. 14). That was accomplished once for all by the cross (Heb. vii. 19, ix. 9, x. 1–4). The meaning therefore is, that Christ's atoning death effected what was necessary to bring us to perfection, or to the goal designed for us as a royal priesthood. It removed guilt, and made us, as a priesthood, positively acceptable in the sight of a holy God, who not only regards our persons in His Son, but considers our services, notwithstanding all our personal imperfection, as well-pleasing on His Son's account. The one offering of Christ puts us into perfect fellowship with God as a people near to Him. And, subjectively, we are MADE PERFECT as pertaining to the conscience, and begin on earth to serve the living God (Heb. ix. 14).

We come now to the examination of passages which contain more particular reference to the atonement. These are numerous and various.

I. One explicit passage as to the nature and necessity of Christ's atoning work is thus expressed: *But we see Jesus, who was made a little lower than the angels for the suffering of death, crowned with glory and honour; that He by the grace of God might taste death for every one* [better, *But Him who was for a little while made lower than the angels, even Jesus, we see crowned with glory and honour on account of the suffering of death, that He by the grace of God might taste death for every one*]. *For it became Him for whom are all things, and by whom are all things, in bringing many sons unto glory, to make the Captain of their salvation perfect through sufferings* (Heb. ii. 9, 10). The epistle, in meeting the objections to a suffering Messiah, proves from prophecy and the divine perfections that Jesus must needs be made lower than the angels, and perfected through sufferings. The final clause, THAT HE MIGHT TASTE DEATH, may either lean on the statement, He was made lower than the angels, or depend, as we have put it, on the previous words, " on account of the suffering of death." If we take the latter construction, it will mean that the *scope* of Christ's sufferings was to taste death for every one. The final clause will thus bring out the fact that the sufferings of Christ were in the divine purpose vicarious. The following points must here be noticed :—

1. The source of the atonement was divine grace : " that He by the grace of God ($\chi \acute{\alpha} \rho \iota \tau \iota\ \Theta \epsilon o \tilde{v}$) might taste death." The meaning of this clause is, that the grace of God was the reason why the Lord tasted death, being the source or origin from which salvation emanated. It was grace to us, in whose behalf the ransom was provided, but penal infliction so far as Christ was officially concerned. This intimates that unmerited grace prompted God to give His Son, and to transfer guilt to Him. In short, whatever was vicarious was of grace in a special sense. A penal death was the effect of justice; but to admit a Surety-substitution was of grace.

2. The death was vicarious. The expression "to die for one" carries with it the notion of substitution, as has already been established (Rom. v. 6, 7). Though ingenious arguments have been used to evade this conclusion, and though the Greek preposition has been forced to speak in favour of the anti-substitution theory, all is of no avail so long as the nature of the transaction implies the opposite. The sufferings and death of the Lord are everywhere represented to us as the sufferings of an innocent person in the room of the guilty. To show that the Lord's sufferings had a near connection with the doom of the guilty, it is said in express terms that He died for the ungodly (Rom. v. 6), the just for the unjust (1 Pet. iii. 18). For whom was this vicarious death undergone ? For every one. What does this imply ? The Greek expositors, for the most part, referred the phrase to the entire creation,—extend-

ing the influence of Christ's death beyond the pale of humanity to angelic intelligences. That, however, would be otherwise expressed, and would scarcely be in the singular neuter, as this interpretation assumes. The limitation must be first to humanity, and next to that totality which was given to Christ, —the same persons who are designated "the many sons" to be brought to glory (ver. 10), and the ALL who are sanctified (ver. 11). This cannot be adduced in favour of the supposed universal atonement, as the reference in the context is most express to those who were actually to be saved by Christ.[1]

3. This expression, TO TASTE DEATH, is a style of speech common to all languages, and found in classical as well as Hebrew writers, in the sense of undergoing the experience of a thing (Ps. xxxiv. 9 ; 1 Pet. ii. 3). Here the expression means to experience the bitter ingredients of death in their utmost intensity.[2] When the Lord is said to have tasted death for every one of the many sons whom He was bringing to glory, the meaning is, that He experienced what constituted eternal death.

Were there sufficient evidence to warrant the reading WITH-OUT GOD, which occurs in some of the Fathers, and is preferred by certain modern writers,[3] it would give the idea of death without God, or as forsaken by God. It has not, however, sufficient warrant. But separation from God in consequence of sin constitutes the penal element of death. The sting of death is sin (1 Cor. xv. 56) ; and as sin separated between man and God (Isa. lix. 2), death in the proper sense of the term is the separation of God from the soul. And in Christ's case we see the expression of His feelings under penal death or deser-tion by God, when He complained of soul-trouble, agony, and exceeding sorrow. We can trace in many portions of the

---

[1] See D'Outrein *on Hebrews;* and Honert, *de gratia universali an particulari.*

[2] See Steinhofer *on Hebrews.*

[3] χωρὶς Θεοῦ is Origen's reading ; and Thomasius, *Christi Person und Werk,* iii., looks on it with favour : so do several recent exegetes and editors. But it wants outward authority.

Lord's historic life how He wrestled with the terrors and bitter-
ness of penal death, that is, God's withdrawal from the human
soul created for God, and incapable of finding happiness or
rest but in Him. This is plainly perceptible in that unfathomable cry, "Why hast Thou forsaken me ?" To taste death is
to experience the loss of God, in itself an overwhelming visitation, apart from positive outward punishment. To the Lord
Jesus death did not come by accident or permission, or mere
violence at the hand of man, but as the divine condemnation
striking the Surety for human guilt. In Gethsemane, where we
see Him tasting the second death, no human hand was near, and
all came direct from the hand of God. But His essential filial
relation was not dissolved, nor the Father's eternal love removed.

4. The apostle adverts to the fact that Christ WAS PER-
FECTED through sufferings, and to the DIVINE FITNESS in God's
moral government that it should be so. We shall briefly
notice both these points (ver. 10).

a. As to the fact that Christ was PERFECTED through sufferings, this is represented as the sole way of bringing many sons
to glory. The older commentators were wont to interpret the
verb PERFECTED as equivalent to consecrated, and in one passage it is so rendered in the English Bible (Heb. vii. 28). The
inaccuracy, however, is apparent, because Christ was already
a priest on earth when He offered Himself. The word is, in
its primary import, TO PERFECT, contrasting commencement
with consummation, feebleness and maturity. All the passages in which the term is applied to Christ, describe Him
after His humiliation, or finished labour (Heb. ii. 10, v. 9). In
the present passage it refers to His state of glory, but with a
certain modification of idea. The two verses we quoted are
so linked together, that the former (ver. 9), describing the
Mediator as crowned with glory, is grounded by the latter[1]

---

[1] The force of the grounding γάρ must by no means be omitted if we would
correctly apprehend the connection, and yet difference, between τελειοῦν and
στεφανοῦν.

(ver. 10), which represents Him as perfected. What can this mean, but that Christ was crowned after His finished work, as Adam would have been on standing his probation? It is the state of perfection on the ground of accepted obedience, or of confirmation as the Head of a new humanity, the second Adam; and the title CAPTAIN OF SALVATION—that is, cause and primary possessor of salvation—is an additional proof of this.

But how does the bringing of many sons to glory stand connected with this perfecting of the second Adam, the leader of salvation? The many sons were IN and WITH the Lord brought objectively to His perfection. The participle, as here used, denotes simultaneous action (ἀγάγων), that the many sons were brought to glory in and with Him; for as it is said that we sinned in Adam (Rom. v. 12), and were crucified and died with Christ (Rom. vi. 6), so we obtained, or won with Christ, all that enters into His perfection and glory. He objectively introduced us to glory with Himself, and we are represented as objectively sitting on the throne with Him, or sitting in heavenly places (Eph. i. 3, ii. 6). Though some regard the participial clause as portraying the Son's action, it is better to view it as the Father's action, in bringing many sons to glory along with the suffering surety. They were given to Him, represented by Him, and introduced at the same time with Him, when He reached the goal.

b. We have also to notice the DIVINE FITNESS of such a method of salvation (ἔπρεπε). It might simply have been said, " It became God." But we have a circumlocution full of emphasis, describing God's relation to the universe in terms which speak of Him as the ultimate end, as well as the great first cause of all things. Why is this introduced? It is an adaptation to the Hebrew Christians, embarrassed by the taunts of unbelieving Jews, pointing with scorn to the ignominious execution of Jesus as incompatible with His Messiahship, according to the glowing terms of prophecy. Prophecy is quoted to establish the fact of His abasement lower than the angels. Next, this humiliation is represented as worthy of God, and as becoming God. That divine fitness is based on God's moral perfections, authority, and law; and this emphatically shows that there is no salvation without atonement, and that the expiation does not rest on God's absolute dominion or arbitrary good-pleasure. On the one hand, it would not have been becoming to abase His Son as a surety in our place, and to subject Him to ignominious treatment by men, and to the endurance of the second death at the hand of God, had salvation been possible in the exercise of absolute dominion or by absolute forgiveness. But it became God to act thus, since there was no salvation without atonement. As it was necessary to vindicate justice and maintain law, to punish sin, and assert the inalienable rights of God, it became God, or was worthy of God, to perfect the Lord by suffering; for He acts according to His attributes, which, indeed, could not be contravened, obscured, or ignored, without denying Himself.

II. The death of Christ is described as liberating us from the power of Satan and the fear of death: *Forasmuch then as the children are partakers of flesh and blood, He also Himself likewise* [or, *equally*] *took part of the same; that through death He might destroy* [better, *bring to nought*] *him that had the power of death, that is, the devil; and deliver them who through fear of death were all their lifetime subject to bondage* (Heb. ii. 14, 15). This passage shows that the scope of the incarnation and atonement was to deliver the children from the power of Satan and the fear of death. A few points here demand consideration.

1. When Christ is said to have become partaker of our nature, the expression carries with it the idea that He assumed humanity, with feelings, affections, and mental constitution every way the same as ours; without sin, indeed,—for that was no part of human nature in its normal state,—but in

nothing differing from the likeness of the flesh of sin so far as this approximation to us was consistent with sinlessness. Though not in Adam's covenant, nor personally subject to its responsibilities apart from His spontaneous undertaking, there was a divine fitness, or necessity, in putting on humanity like ours,—a humanity not mortal by the necessity of its being, but mortal[1] because of the free assumption of our guilt and obligations. He must have a suffering mortal nature for His official task. The language not obscurely shows that He possessed another mode of existence. Not to recall the proof furnished by the previous context, and by the title Son (Heb. i. 1–8), the fact that He took our flesh and blood implies His possession of a higher nature. A person is introduced mightier than the adversary who already overcame the human race and held them captive; for no mortal could vanquish one armed with the sting of death and the curse of the law.

The passage reminds us of the first promise (Gen. iii. 15). Nay, there seems to be an express parallel: the terms of the one seem to be a paraphrase or exposition of the other. The object in both is Satan, who by sin acquired the power of inflicting death on soul and body. The seed of the woman was mentioned in the one; the participator of flesh and blood is mentioned in the other. In the one, allusion is made to the head of the serpent; and in the other, to the devil as having the power of death. The first promise represents the Lord as bruising the serpent; the text before us represents Christ as destroying Satan, or bringing him to nought.[2] The one text is thus a paraphrase of the other, substituting the language of fulfilment for that of prediction.

2. The meritorious cause of victory, or the weapon used by Christ, was His vicarious death. The apostle does not use the expression HIS death; but from this no argument can be

---

[1] This is the sense of θνητός, as Athanasius and other fathers used it in reference to Christ: and Pearson also.

[2] See the older commentaries on the passage : Steinhofer *on Hebrews*; Rambach's, D'Outrein, etc.

drawn against His substitution. The pronoun was not required, as the apostle's object was to show that Christ overthrew the adversary by turning his weapons against himself, defeating him by that death which was the sphere and element of his power. How Christ's death was the means of victory is not formally expressed, but it can be gathered from other parts of the epistle. Two modes of explanation have been propounded,—that by the modern theology, a highly objectionable one, and that given with a general consent in the Church.

a. The explanation given by the modern theology is, that the death of Christ was the termination of that portion of His life subject to Satan's power, and was succeeded by an indissoluble life (Heb. vii. 16). The theory is, that Christ, the appointed source of spiritual life to the human race, sustained the utmost enmity of Satan in His death, which, however, formed but the transition to a higher life, the commencement of a new life to mankind. To this comment the obvious objection is that it contradicts the text. It ascribes the victory not to the atoning death, but to the resurrection-life of Christ. It does no justice to the words THROUGH DEATH.

b. The other comment, currently adopted in the Church of all times, is, that Christ through death—that is, THROUGH DEATH AS THE EXPIATION OF SIN—annulled Satan's power. The dominion of Satan owed its origin to sin, because offended justice adjudged the guilty to a captivity of which Satan was but the subordinate executioner or gaoler. In like manner, Satan's dominion was overthrown by the expiation of the cross, because the satisfaction of justice and the vindication of the divine rights effected man's deliverance, and made those who were slaves of Satan the property of a new master.

3. Next we notice the twofold end contemplated by the Lord's death, as brought out in the two final clauses,—the annulling of Satan's power, and the deliverance of believers from the fear of death.

(1) As to the annulling of Satan's power, this is in plain terms announced as the scope of Christ's death, for the cross decided the great question who should be the world's Lord. The final adjudication was then given; the judicial process as to the proprietory right was conclusively determined (John xii. 31; Col. ii. 15). The word rendered DESTROY ($\varkappa\alpha\tau\alpha\rho\gamma\epsilon\tilde{\imath}\nu$), which occurs twenty-five times in Paul's epistles, meaning to annul or to make void, intimates that Satan was denuded of his authority, not destroyed as to his being. Not without reason did Christ suffer death, since the victory to be achieved could not be won by mere power. But the question is raised, How had Satan the power of death? Not in the sense that he tempted men to sin, which was followed by death as its wages; not in the sense that Satan is the immediate executioner of death, inflicting it as it is a physical evil by his hand; for though this is a received Jewish doctrine, it is nowhere affirmed by our Lord or His apostles.[1] The devil is said to have had the power of death, as he wielded it to men's eternal ruin, and thus obtained entire possession of them. To fall under the power of death was to fall under the power of Satan, which extends to all who live without Christ, and die in sin. By death he gets them into his possession; and the annulling of Satan's power by means of death consisted especially in this, that such a power was taken away, death being no more at the devil's service, nor a weapon at his command against any for whom Christ died.

(2) A further deliverance naturally flowing from the death of Christ, and secured by it, is, that Christians are delivered from the fear of death. The apostle treats of the fear of death connected with an evil conscience, or that sense of the wrath of God from which Christians were delivered by the satisfaction of Christ; and it shows how miserable is life when the sting is not taken out of death by the blood of atonement.

This enables us to rebut the comment of the Cocceian

---

[1] See Riehm's *Lehrbegriff*, Tholuck and Delitzsch *on Hebrews*.

school, and for two centuries repeated in many quarters, that this language, describing bondage and the fear of death, is properly applicable to Jewish believers living under the Mosaic covenant. The words of the apostle, however, have their true significance when understood in general of liberation from the fear of penal death; and there is no warrant for limiting the terms to Israelites, as they are spoken generally, nor to temporal death, as they naturally comprehend whatever is included in the primeval curse on sin. It is a one-sided theory which refers the language to believers under the Old Testament;[1] for though they had not the same clear views which the Christian economy discloses, we cannot warrantably represent them as oppressed by the fear of death, as if still unforgiven and under the curse. The apostle, speaking generally, first of a condition without Christ, and then of a condition in Christ, affirms that through His death is removed whatever is formidable in death. The fear which arose from an accusing conscience was removed by the Lord's death.

III. Another passage in the same context thus introduces us to the priesthood of Christ : *Wherefore in all things it behoved Him to be made like unto His brethren, that He might be a merciful and faithful High Priest in things pertaining to God, to make reconciliation for* [better, *to atone for,* or *to make propitiation for*] *the sins of the people* (Heb. ii. 17). The principal object of the epistle is to enforce the priesthood of Christ, and this is the first announcement of it. We may take up this testimony in these few points.

1. It behoved Him to be made like His brethren in order to atone for sin. The terms of the passage are so constructed as to show beyond dispute that the atonement was the ulterior object for which Christ was prepared by this previous discipline. The priestly sentiment which prompted the atonement was nourished by all the objective elements of His call and unction,

---

[1] See a full refutation of the Cocceian theory by Leidekker in his *Vis Veritatis,* and Witsius' *De Fœdere.*

and also subjectively developed by the sympathy imbibed through life from the personal experience of living amid the sufferings and temptations of the human family subjected to the captivity of sin and Satan. He entered into this state of things, holy, harmless, undefiled, and separate from sinners, but so surrounded by the atmosphere of darkness and defilement, trial and temptations, that the true priestly disposition—compassion and the purpose to deliver mankind—was fostered at every step. That undoubtedly is the thought. It refers to what went before the atonement, and spurred Him to complete it. As He learned obedience by suffering (Heb. v. 8), so He learned priestly sympathy; fitted for the priestly action by having an identity of nature and temptation, sorrow and trial. The mercy and faithfulness thus acquired are everlastingly retained on high, but they are here mentioned in their origin as preparatory to the sacrifice which pacified God.

2. Christ was a priest on earth making atonement. The strictly grammatical force of the terms intimates[1] that He was a priest to atone for sins, or to propitiate God for sins. The apostle does not speak of what was done after the ascension, but of what was done during the entire period of His earthly life; and the import of the words allows no other interpretation. No one without a foregone conclusion could deduce from this, as the Socinians and others following them have done, that the priesthood of Christ commenced only after the ascension. While they argue that Christ suffered and died that He might be made a priest, who that reads with any attention does not see that the apostle affirms a different thing? It is

---

[1] The priest *εἰς τὸ ἱλάσκεσθαι*. See some excellent comments of Streso, in his Latin *conciones* on Hebrews, on the preparation of Christ as the priest. Modern commentators for the most part surrender this text to those who, in a semi-socinianizing way, transfer Christ's priesthood to heaven, and they are swayed by the words *ἱλέημων* and *πίστος*. But these predicates belonged to Him on earth as well as in heaven; and the *εἰς τὸ ἱλάσκεσθαι* puts it beyond doubt that He was a priest in atoning. Neither Turretin nor Quenstedt have done full justice to this emphatic phrase, *ἀρχιερεὺς . . . εἰς τὸ ἱλάσκεσθαι*, which is to my mind one of the most conclusive proofs of Christ being a priest in His death.

not said that He was made like His brethren that He might be made a priest, but that He might be a merciful and faithful[1] High Priest; for the experience of our sorrows, temptations, and sufferings formed Him to sympathy, and prompted Him to pursue His atoning work. The entire language of the New Testament writers proceeds on the supposition that Christ acted on earth as a priest. Thus He gave Himself a ransom (Matt. xx. 28). He gave Himself for us an offering and a sacrifice (Eph. v. 2). The death of Christ is represented as the passover sacrifice for us (1 Cor. v. 7). The purification of our sins was effected by sacrifice, as a past act before He ascended (Heb. i. 3). That Christ acted as a priest during His earthly career, and that He once for all consummated the sacrifice on the cross, because it required no addition or supplement, is, as we shall see, repeatedly affirmed in this epistle.

The confusion in the mind of those who call this in question may be traced to the way in which they interpret the types on the great day of atonement, and especially the import of carrying the blood into the holy of holies, as already explained. We only add here, that the action in the holy of holies depended for its efficacy not on the bare fact of the priest appearing before God, but on his presenting the blood of sacrifice offered for the sins of the people. Some colour might have existed for the theory of a priesthood begun in heaven, and a sacrifice in heaven, had the priest been directed merely to present himself in the holiest of all without any further provision for expiating sin ; but we have only to recall the action of the Jewish high priest at the door of the tabernacle of the congregation (Lev. xvi. 7), to see evidence that the blood of sacrifice was indispensably necessary to the validity of the priestly action within the vail; that he could not have entered without it ; and that it was presupposed in all that was subsequently done.

---

[1] The old anti-Socinian champions, Calovius, Arnold, Maresius, Hoornbeek, Œder, correctly lay the emphasis here.

3. The apostle mentions THE PEOPLE: who were they? Since the language of the epistle partakes of a Jewish tincture, and the parties to whom it was addressed were Christian Jews, are we to hold that those objects of the propitiation designated "the people" were men of Jewish descent? By no means. The phraseology is varied, but they are the same persons who are called in the context many sons (ver. 10), the seed of Abraham (ver. 16), His brethren (ver. 17). By far the most natural and appropriate exposition is that which regards them as those who form the one family of God, irrespective of Jewish or Gentile descent. They are such as have the faith of Abraham without reference to nationality.

4. The last point to be noticed is, that the Lord Jesus, in His capacity as our High Priest, propitiated God, or atoned for sin. He was the priest of His own sacrifice. The proper import of the term here rendered, TO MAKE RECONCILIATION, is to propitiate, to pacify an offended party, or to turn away wrath. This is the uniform use of the term in all the Greek poets, historians, and writers generally; and no classical scholar will doubt this. The Greek verb is construed with the accusative of the person whose anger is turned away, and it may appear anomalous that no person is here named whose wrath is pacified. The phrase "to propitiate sin" would be uncouth and devoid of meaning. The mode of resolving the phrase adopted by all the most eminent philologists who acknowledge the laws of language and the authority of usage is, that the expression must be used as meaning that CHRIST PROPITIATED GOD FOR OUR SINS.[1] This makes all plain; and it is according to the fixed meaning of the term. The Septuagint translators

---

[1] The best philological commentators—Grotius, Meyer, Kurtz (so too Philippi and Weber)—construe the phrase with a Θεόν understood: ἱλάσκεσθαι (Θεόν). Then the τὰς ἁμαρτίας is either construed with a supplied περὶ, or made the object clause: " as to sin." Some have proposed that ἱλάσκεσθαι should govern ἁμαρτίας, but it is absurd. Delitzsch, after Hofmann, makes this attempt, and brings in an argument from another language; but Philippi's answer to Delitzsch is conclusive: *Kirchliche Glaubenslehre*, iv. pp. 267–278.

adapted the term to revealed ideas, but could not change its import.

This leads me to notice a theory propounded by certain modern writers, to the effect that the Septuagint impressed a new meaning upon the word, and that from this source it passed over into the New Testament phraseology with an altered acceptation. We must deny both positions. The Alexandrine translators found terms ready to their hand, fixed and settled in their import, and they could not at discretion alter them if they wished to be intelligible. That they used the word under consideration in the sense of propitiating or appeasing an angry party, is evident from their translation of the passage where Jacob is said to have appeased Esau (Gen. xxxii. 20), and from the text where a wise man is said to pacify the king's wrath (Prov. xvi. 14). The term did not pass into the Septuagint with an altered meaning; and hence we dismiss as groundless the double theory, that the word does not occur in the New Testament in its proper Greek significance, and that the apostles needed no classical Greek vocabulary, as suitable words for the ideas which they developed from the Old Testament were already fixed by the peculiar style of the Septuagint. The Septuagint did much to fix the usage for the Greek-speaking Jews, but not to alter the meaning of Greek terms, which would have defeated the end of translation altogether. Hence they who would make this phrase mean no more than " to cover sin," and allege that it is a Hebrew thought expressed in Greek, are liable to the charge of altering the meaning of terms, or of bringing the primary or etymological meaning of a word in one language to control the fixed usage of another without either warrant or probability. That is all the more hazardous when carried out, as is generally done in this case, under the spell of a dogmatic bias,—that is, to lend countenance to the theory that the Scriptures do not predicate wrath of God.

The phrase should have been rendered here, TO ATONE FOR,

OR TO MAKE PROPITIATION FOR SINS. And the noun, used several times by John, strictly rendered, denotes "propitiation" (1 John ii. 2, iv. 10). The expression here used brings before us the idea of the great High Priest and the sacrifice,—that is, the reality of that sacrifice which was offered for the Jewish people on the great day of atonement presupposing divine anger on account of the sins of the people, and intimating that our High Priest, by the intervention of His sacrifice, pacified the wrath of God. The propitiation presupposes wrath, and would not have been propitiation without it; it would have been but semblance or appearance. Not that mankind, as God's workmanship, ceased to be the object of divine benevolence and affection; but the Scriptures abound in proofs of a wrath of God, by which He not only stood aloof from sin, but was prompted by His holy nature to act against it, till a change was effected in our relation toward God, and in God's relation toward us, by the great historic fact of atonement. The propitiation came in between human sin and divine wrath, appeasing that wrath, and winning for us the favour of God.

It may be noticed that the term here used in the original is different from the word elsewhere used by the Apostle Paul for RECONCILE[1] (Rom. v. 10; 2 Cor. v. 18). The difference between the two may be described as follows:—The term commonly used for RECONCILE has no reference to the old law, or to the priestly institute; it is taken from ordinary life, presupposing the existence of a quarrel or controversy, and intimating that friendship has been restored by putting the cause of quarrel out of the way. The Bible term intimates that those hindrances were removed which had obstructed friendly union between God and man; but there is no allusion to sacrifice as the means by which the reunion was effected. On the other hand, the term PROPITIATE here used puts the new

---

[1] Καταλλάσσιν and ίλάσκισθαι must be distinguished: the former is used of the Father, the latter of Christ. See Morus' remarks; also Lotze, Muntinghe, *Geschiedeniss.*

relation cemented in direct causal connection with the priest-hood and sacrifice. It is never applied to God as the acting party, but to Christ in His high-priestly function. Though God is commonly described as the Reconciler,—that is, as the author of the remedial economy or scheme of reconciliation (2 Cor. v. 18),—He is never said to propitiate, for the obvious reason that that would imply a third party. God Himself was the party whose anger was to be averted, and whose favourable regard was to be restored by the intervention of the priestly sacrifice. The difference between the two modes of expression, which at first sight seem to have much in common, mainly consists in this, that propitiation was the work of a priest coming in between man and God; whereas the act of re-conciliation, as affirmed of God, is the more general term, setting forth that God not only was the source of the restored friendship, but also planned and carried into execution the propitiation, or great intermediate provision by which the reconciliation was effected.

When we sum up the force of this memorable testimony, it affirms that Christ made a propitiation for the sins of the people, or, as it is also put, HIS people (Matt. i. 21), not by delivering them from intellectual error, not by merely con-verting them from evil ways for the future, but by a fact in history once for all, having a potentiality for all time. His work effected much more than the abolition of the typical economy, or the introduction of a new economy of truth con-firmed by His death. As the Jewish high priest brought the atonement for the people of the old economy once every year, so Christ, once for all, satisfied divine justice, and removed the penalty of sin by His historic oblation at Jerusalem as Priest and Sacrifice in one person. The term PROPITIATE means to appease God, or to avert His wrath by sacrifice; and the pas-sage is not to be interpreted of intercession in heaven, though that follows and leans on the sacrifice, but of the one propitia-tion or atonement of the cross.

IV. Another passage bearing on the High Priest's suffering obedience is in these terms : *Who in the days of His flesh, when He had offered up* [better, taking in the last words of the verse, *when He had from godly fear offered up*] *prayers and supplications, with strong crying and tears, unto Him that was able to save Him from death, and was heard (in that He feared), though He were a Son* [better, *though He was the Son*], *yet learned He obedience by the things which He suffered ; and being made perfect, He became the author of eternal salvation unto all them that obey Him* (Heb. v. 7–9). In the context we have several points of comparison between Christ and the Aaronic priesthood: His divine call to the priesthood ; His sympathy learned in a career of trial. A divine commission was so necessary for one who should act between God and man, that apart from other questions bearing on His ability for the task, the sovereign rights of God stood in the way of any one taking the office uncalled. The salient points of the passage are these:

1. The days of His flesh mean the whole time of His humiliation,—that period when He came among men as one of them, but still the Son of God, whose majesty was hid. As applied to Christ, the term FLESH intimates that He put on a true humanity, but a humanity under the weight of imputed guilt, with the curse that followed in its train,—a sinless, but sin-bearing humanity. It has everything in common with the Lord's own expression, "The Son of Man" (compare Rom. viii. 3, 1 Pet. iii. 18). The Lord felt the weakness of the flesh in His whole vicarious work, and though personally spotless, was, in virtue of taking our place, subjected to all that we are heir to. We do not, indeed, find in Him the personal consequences of sin, such as sickness and disease, but the consequences which could competently fall to the sinless substitute ; for He never was in Adam's covenant, but was Himself the second Adam. As He took flesh for an official purpose, He submitted to the consequences following in the train of sin-bearing—hunger and thirst, toil and fatigue in the sweat of

His brow, fear and sorrow, persecution and injustice, arrest and suffering, wounds and death: this period is called "the days of His flesh."

2. We must examine the phrase "in that He feared." Two modes of interpretation have divided commentators: the one rendering the term fear of consternation; the other rendering it the fear of reverence, "piety," or "godliness."

a. The first interpretation, which renders it the fear of consternation, or amazement, became current in the Reformed Church under the influence of Calvin, who adduced it as a proof of the doctrine that Christ endured in His soul the wrath of God for our soul's redemption. The Romanists, who limited Christ's sufferings to corporeal pains, exclaimed against this exposition as subversive of His deity, and called it blasphemous.[1] Beza, in an important note, replete with erudition and sound doctrine, on the great truth impugned, endeavours to prove that the term means fear in the sense of dread, adducing passages from the classics and the New Testament (Acts xxiii. 16). He declares that he will be hard to persuade that the Greek preposition allows the rendering "was heard for His reverence," as in the Vulgate. Bellarmine, while discussing the doctrinal question of Christ's soul-agony, renewed the grammatical as well as doctrinal objections against that exposition; and he was answered by Junius, Ames, Turretin,[2] and others. On account of the important doctrine which was raised, this interpretation came to prevail among Reformed divines. The peculiar and anomalous expression, "was heard from fear," as it literally means, was construed to signify the terminus from which He was rescued. And they were wont to defend this exposition by an appeal to the words of the psalm: "Thou hast heard me from the horns of the unicorns," —that is, hast heard and delivered me (Ps. xxii. 21). But that

---

[1] See an interesting statement of opinions on ἀπὸ τῆς εὐλαβείας in Fulke's *Defence of the English Translations of the Bible*, p. 322.

[2] F. Junius, *Animadvers. in Bellarm.* vol. ii. p. 585. Ames' *Bellarm. Enervatus*, tom i. p. 100. Turretin, *De Satisfactione*, p. 153.

is artificial, and a supplement put in by the interpreters. The passages, indeed, by which they proved that the term denotes consternation and amazement, only show that it was used for the cautious avoidance of evil, physical or religious,—a sense that naturally passes into that of reverence.

b. The other interpretation, viz. THE FEAR OF REVERENCE, is every way preferable. As the noun elsewhere means godly fear (Heb. xii. 28), and as the adjective is commonly used for devout (Luke ii. 25; Acts ii. 5, viii. 2), usage, as well as etymology, is certainly in its favour. Besides, the general consent of patristic expositors and the best modern exegetes may be mentioned as all in the same direction. There is one point urged by Beza and Turretin which has not been satisfactorily obviated,—viz., that the Greek preposition here used does not commonly mean " by reason of," and that where it is so used, as it is in several passages (Matt. xiii. 44; Luke xxi. 26, xxiv. 41; Acts xii. 14; John xxi. 6), it denotes the inner influence or motive by which an agent is actuated. So much does this seem to have weighed with Chrysostom, with his delicate appreciation of the Greek language, that while retaining the sense for which we contend, he strangely ascribed the reverence to the Father. The whole difficulty, however, on this score vanishes, when, as I have proposed, we construe the GODLY FEAR with both the preceding participles; for it then means that He poured out prayers in godly fear and was heard: " having FROM GODLY FEAR offered up prayers and supplications, and being heard."

3. The offering up of agonizing prayers is next mentioned. Here we notice at the outset the peculiar expression OFFERING UP PRAYERS, which a century ago was commonly expounded as a sacrificial term, and as meaning that the Lord's priestly prayers in some peculiar sense belonged to His sacrifice.[1] But prayers are not the satisfaction: the sacrifice was HIM-

---

[1] So D'Outrein, Rambach, and many of the older commentators, without cause, expound προσενέγκας.

SELF; and we have never been able to see any force in this exposition, whether the idea is taken singly or conjoined. Besides, to offer prayer was a familiar Jewish phrase. We dismiss this comment as a groundless piece of overdoing.

These prayers, accompanied with strong crying and tears, to Him who was able to save Him from death, imply the endurance of penal death. Did He fear the mere corporeal suffering which many a martyr has met with fortitude? Sinless nature no doubt shrinks from death, but it was something of a far other quality which gave rise to the agony and amazement which weighed so heavily on the Son of God,—viz., the second death, the full infliction of wrath at the hand of God for the sins, not of one man, but of the whole company of the elect. The curse of the law under which He spontaneously placed Himself struck the soul as well as the body (Gal. iii. 13). More was comprehended than bodily pain, as might be argued from the horror and recoil of the Redeemer from the cup which was to be drunk. Besides, corporeal sufferings would not have sufficed for men's redemption, for He redeemed the soul as well as the body (1 Cor. vi. 20): He assumed both soul and body; and He offered both in our room, as was necessary to expiate guilt incurred in both and by both. As the sin was principally committed by the soul, and the body was used as but its instrument, it will not suffice to say that the suffering was in the soul merely by sympathy: the converse was rather true.

Hence, while the Lord Jesus continued amid all His agony the object of divine love as the only-begotten of the Father, He endured all the curse, wrath, and infliction justly to be awarded to the sin He bore on His own body. Had He not experienced that God was angry, not indeed at Himself, but at our sins, He could not have been a deliverer; for there was no relaxation of the law, nor could be; nor was there any relaxation of the penalty. The agony of Christ read of from His human life in many scenes before He reached Gethsemane

and the cross, consisted primarily in the loss of God,—a privation which removed from Him the vision of God and the sense
of His presence : the subject of suffering was the entire human
nature of the Lord. Not that He ceased to be the beloved
Son, and actually loved. Not that the Lord, in His own consciousness, ceased to draw the distinction between His personal
and official relation to His Father; for His whole language
virtually avows His innocence and Sonship, and proceeds upon
the plea that the Father would either remove the cup or up-
hold Him : there was no despair and no distrust for an instant.
But though His trust was never for a moment interrupted, nor
succeeded by despair, He was wholly without that sensible
enjoyment which commonly flows from trust, and was subjected to an overwhelming pressure of heaviness and sorrow,
caused by the divine anger at sin, which the Surety must
necessarily undergo. Though the Surety was in Himself the
beloved Son, He was, as the sin-bearer, under the hiding of
His Father's face when He poured out these prayers with
strong crying and tears.

And the apostle adds, HE WAS HEARD. But the inquiry
arises, How ? When ? Did He not undergo death ? How was
He heard, when He appealed to Him who was able to save Him
from death, and yet was given up to death ? The solution
is easy. Whatever the Lord absolutely and unconditionally
asked, was absolutely and unconditionally granted. But what
He conditionally asked—that is, asked from natural affection,
or from a sensitive recoil from what seemed to His human
feelings overwhelming and intolerable, and rather a wish than
a definite volition—was answered in the way most necessary in
the circumstances. We are warranted to say, when we compare this passage with the scene of the soul-trouble and Gethsemane, that God heard Him, either by mitigating the terror,
or by nerving Him to bear it, or by strengthening Him by
means of the angel. His fear was lest He should sink and
be swallowed up of death, and He was heard and rescued.

4. The next statement requiring notice is, that Christ, notwithstanding His Sonship, learned obedience by suffering. The clause is properly participial, and literally rendered, THOUGH BEING THE SON:[1] it takes for granted the divine Sonship as anterior to His obedience, and not the fruit of His obedience. The language would otherwise be unmeaning; for it assumes that He who personally was above all obedience, was put in the position of learning obedience. This shows what was required to the right discharge of that active and suffering obedience which must needs be vicariously rendered to fulfil the task of Suretyship, and the greatness of Christ's redeeming love in obliging Himself to render obedience in the midst of such suffering. The following elements constituted that obedience:—

It was developed from a sinless nature, beginning with His birth and pervading His life, till He bowed His head upon the cross. Though taking flesh from Adam, His humanity was, by the overshadowing power of the Holy Ghost, generated pure in the act of personal union to the only begotten Son, and never existed apart. He was sinless in His nature, and in His history; holy for the unholy, pure to occupy the place of the impure; the realization of the divine law at every moment, and in every scene; the ideal of the law. When He learned obedience by suffering, the meaning is, that the obedience grew in extent, intensity, and force, by the pressure put upon it: the hotter the conflict, the more did inward submission unfold itself. Not that this argues previous defect, for in sinless creaturehood there is progress. Even in that which claims to be perfect there are degrees of advancement; and in Christ's case the obedience, always perfect, was not at first in its full development. We see in all living things growth, progress to maturity. In Gethsemane, and in His soul-desertion, His will was never turned aside from the

---

[1] καίπερ ὢν υἱός. See a good discussion on the proper force of this expression, in De Moor's *Comment. perpet.* i. p. 756.

straight path of prompt obedience even by superhuman trials, but held on its course, still learning obedience. Not suffering alone, but obedience in suffering the most overwhelming and unparalleled, constituted the second Adam's task.

5. The reward follows: " Being made perfect, He became the author of eternal salvation." The import of perfecting, as applied to Christ in this epistle, has already been explained (Heb. ii. 10). But we must rescue the expression from the superficial gloss that makes it exaltation as contrasted with humiliation. The seeming antithesis between the days of His flesh and this ulterior stage, may seem at first sight to give countenance to that idea; but there is something deeper in the connection,—viz. the link between learning obedience in the days of His flesh, and being perfected as the second man for the purposes of the mediatorial economy. The language takes for granted a period of probation assigned to the second Adam, followed by a state of confirmation, or state of mediatorial fitness for securing the final welfare of His people : it is the reward of an approved obedience. This is the deeper connection and the true meaning, as is evident from the fact that the perfecting stands related to His being the author of eternal salvation, the same link that we noticed above[1] (Heb. ii. 10). IIe was officially perfected for all the ends of His mediatorial undertaking. A further proof may be adduced. It was through this perfecting of the Surety that we are said to be perfected; that is, we are partakers of Him and one with Him in His approved obedience and accepted sacrifice (Heb. x. 14).

Thus perfected, Christ became THE AUTHOR OF eternal SALVATION. The humiliation ended with the weakness, temptation, suffering, and death peculiar to the days of His flesh. The Representative, acting in the name of a chosen people,

---

[1] I may refer to Riehm's *Lehrbegriff*, and Van den Ham's *Dissertatio Theologica*, 1847 ; also to Morus' remarks on the passage. The reference, however, to the Mediator as second Adam must be added to give completeness to the view.

not only reached the goal, but became the author of eternal salvation. This passage has almost everything in common with the passage already noticed '(Heb. ii. 10): it well-nigh repeats it. The chief difference is, that in the former passage He is called the captain or leader of salvation, the first in the order of possession; whereas in this passage He is called the meritorious cause, the author of salvation. It remains only to notice that the salvation is limited to a particular class who bear the designation OF THOSE WHO OBEY CHRIST. This may primarily refer to the obedience of faith,—that is, to the obedience which is apparent in the very act of believing (Rom. i. 5), but also takes in the obedience of life.

V. The next passage is specially important, as showing that the Lord Jesus on earth was at once priest and sacrifice: *Such an high priest became us, who is holy, harmless* [better, *such a high priest befitted us,—one holy, innocent*], *undefiled, separate from sinners, and made higher than the heavens; who needeth not daily, as those high priests, to offer up sacrifice, first for His own sins, and then for the people's: for this He did once, when He offered up Himself* (Heb. vii. 26, 27). Melchizedek's priesthood, according to the outline in Genesis, is represented in this chapter as typical; next, a passage in the Psalms, written long after the institution of the. Aaronic priesthood, promised a priest of another order (Ps. cx. 4); and the apostle argues that perfection could not be by the law, because the replacing of its priesthood was a plain proof of imperfection. The irrevocable oath was also a proof of a better covenant (Heb. vii. 20–22). Christ's priesthood was everlasting and unchangeable, while the other constantly passed from one dying man to another (ver. 24).

The words have the same meaning as the previous passage, which set forth the necessity of the atonement on the ground of justice (Heb. ii. 10). The expression SUCH ($\tau o \iota o \tilde{\upsilon} \tau o \varsigma$) AN HIGH PRIEST is referred by some to what precedes (vers. 1–25); but far more naturally it refers, as we have rendered it, to the following clause, "one holy, harmless, undefiled, and separate from sinners,"—the same expression that we have below (Heb. viii. 1). The various predicates of the high priest, immediately subjoined, are by no means to be interpreted as properties that belonged to Him exclusively after His ascension. The first four are descriptive of what He was on earth, when brought into contact, during the discharge of His office, with sin and sinners; and only because all this belonged to Him on earth, does He continue to be all this in heaven. When taken together, they affirm moral perfection in all its parts and degrees, describing it negatively as well as positively.[1] The epithet HOLY might seem at first sight to intimate the consecration by which He was set apart to God; and the suggestion has been made, May it not recall the title "Holiness to the Lord" on the mitre of the Aaronic high priest? But an examination of the Greek word here used at once satisfies us that not the holiness of dedication is intimated, but the holiness of inward conformity to the divine will—of moral and religious conduct. The second epithet, HARMLESS, or innocent, was understood by the translators of the English version, as it is by many modern expositors, as intimating that He was, in His intercourse among men, free from evil, malice, or injury. But according to its etymology it has a more extensive meaning: it means a nature free from every taint of evil or original sin. The third epithet, UNDEFILED, signifies that He contracted no defilement amid temptations which solicited Him on every side, and that, while always in contact with sin, He continued sinless, for the infection never spread to Him. The fourth epithet, or descriptive predicate, SEPARATE FROM SINNERS, means that He was the true Nazarite: His soul was as a star, and dwelt apart. Several modern interpreters, following in the wake of the old Socinians, who interpreted these predicates of Christ in heaven, suppose that it means separated from sinners by His exaltation,—that

---

[1] ὅσιος, ἄκακος, ἀμίαντος, κεχωρισμένος ἀπὸ τῶν ἁμαρτωλῶν.

is, by local distance; a low and one-sided view. The expression means that Christ, while living among sinners, and supposed to be of the common order of men, was infinitely apart from them in nature and character, in thought and deed, in words and principles, in motive and conduct. He was among them, not of them; nay, in a moral respect, infinitely separate. The fifth predicate, MADE HIGHER THAN THE HEAVENS, undoubtedly differs from the previous four in this, that it refers to His exaltation. The design is to show that our great High Priest must needs be made higher than the heavens, infinitely exalted above all, in order to bestow as well as win salvation. But no one, with any colour of reason, can allege that He was then only made a priest, or that He then only performed the principal part of the priestly function—the offering of sacrifice. The previous predicates of the high priest, as well as the subsequent verse, indisputably prove that He was acting as a priest on earth. And the design of the apostle in naming these predicates of our High Priest, was to prove that He was infinitely pleasing to God, that He was under no necessity to offer sacrifice for Himself, and that His offering had everlasting validity.

Next follows a comparison between the Jewish high priest in the annual sacrifice on the day of atonement, and our great High Priest in His sacrifice once offered (ver. 27). There is a point of similarity, such as obtains between type and antitype, but also a point of disparity, in as far as Christ's sacrifice was infinitely superior in validity and value. On the great day of atonement the Jewish high priest offered sacrifice first for his own sins, and then for the people's. The expression DAILY, applied to the Jewish high priest, has been variously expounded; some referring it to the annual return of the great day of atonement, when this part of the ritual was ever repeated; others referring it to the morning and evening sacrifice. As the latter was offered, not for the high priest nor the priests in general, but for the people, it is better to understand it as intimating that, on every occasion of offering for the sins of the people, he offered also for his own sins.

On the contrary, the sacrifice of Christ was unique. What, from the necessity of the case, was always separated in the Jewish ritual, was combined in Him. When He gave His life a ransom for many, He was the priest of His own sacrifice—priest and sacrifice in one. This is the first time in the course of the epistle that we find express mention of Christ as at once priest and victim, but it is repeated again and again. This distinguishes the sacrifice of Christ from the Old Testament sacrifices. They were external to the high priest, the blood being foreign to him, or, as it is rendered, the blood of others (Heb. ix. 25): they had no relation to his person, for the two were not identified. But Christ offered Himself; and He could do so as the Son of God, the possessor of a higher nature, who united a humanity to Himself, and was competent to dispose of it, as no mere creature could dispose of himself, because it had been assumed as an instrument for working out the eternal redemption of His people. In this our High Priest was absolutely unique. But what is the import of the clause, " For this He did once, when He offered up Himself?" As to the demonstrative pronoun THIS, it cannot refer to both the previous clauses, as setting forth that our High Priest offered a sacrifice for His own sins and then for the people's. It can refer only to the latter, as the strictly grammatical import of the singular THIS properly intimates. Besides, in no sense of the terms could Christ be said to offer for Himself. The whole predicates above noticed were specially adduced to show that no such thing existed, or was possible ; and the attempts to maintain the opposite, in the interest of overthrowing the vicarious sacrifice in ancient or modern times, are reckless assertions bordering upon the impious.[1]

It only remains that we notice that important word ONCE,

[1] Hofmann takes up this Socinian evasion, and asserts that the prayer in Gethsemane was in some sense a sacrifice offered for His own weakness. The

so often reiterated. The word, as applied to the sacrifice of
Christ, intimates that this great sacrifice was offered once for
all, and that it required, and indeed allows, no repetition (Heb.
ix. 26, x. 10). Thus, as high priest, Christ had something to
offer: He offered Himself as the perfect high priest, and the
perfect sin-offering, tasting death for every one in such a way
that henceforth there was no need of further sacrifice for sin.[1]

Before passing from this text, two questions canvassed by
theological writers demand an answer: 1. Was the Lord Jesus
in reality a priest on earth? and, 2. Was He acting as a priest
on the cross, and previously? We answer: The entire epistle
affirms both, and assumes both. So obvious is this to unbiassed readers, that it might seem an extraordinary incon-
sistency to admit the canonical authority of the epistle, and
explain away its testimony to both truths. But from the
days of the first Socinians to our own time, many attempts
have been made to establish this on two grounds: first, that
the term priest, as applied to Christ, is metaphorical; next,
that His priesthood began with His exaltation, and not before.
These views tend to overthrow the vicarious sacrifice of the
cross.

1. The allegation that Christ is called a priest metaphorically, without being a true and proper priest, is easily answered, if we admit that biblical terms and analogies must
be taken in their natural meaning. When we find a regular
comparison between Christ's priesthood and the Aaronic high-
priesthood, in regard to qualifications, the necessary call by
God, and sympathy to be exercised (Heb. v. 1–7), it is preposterous to allege that all this is compatible with the supposition of a mere metaphor.[2] When the Messiah is described

opponents of the vicarious sacrifice are indeed reduced to straits when it comes
to this! Christ's sinless nature is incompatible with every shade of such ideas.

[1] See Allinga *on the Satisfaction of Christ*.

[2] See Stillingfleet *on the Sufferings of Christ*, and the appended remarks in
reply to Crellius ; Leslie, *agt. Socinianism ;* and Chapman's *Defence*, vol. ii. ; also
Harmsen, *Over de Genœgdœning van J. C.*, 1806, pp. 315–327.

as invested with a priesthood according to a peculiar order, different from that of Aaron, and superseding it, this establishes the same fact. And it further appears, when it is announced that every priest was ordained to offer gifts and sacrifices, and that this man must have somewhat also to offer (Heb. viii. 3). Christ is thus a priest in the real acceptation of the term—the truth of what was typical. In a word, He is spoken of as a priest when raised up among men (Heb. vii. 11); when He came out of Judah (ver. 14); during the whole period comprehended in the days of His flesh (v. 7); during His contact with human society, when He was holy, harmless, undefiled, and separate from sinners.

2. The allegation that His priesthood began not on earth, but at His ascension, has only to be placed in the light of this epistle to be fully refuted. Its entire teaching proves that He acted as a priest during His whole humiliation, and that His death was a sacrifice (Eph. v. 2; Heb. ii. 17, v. 7). A few arguments may suffice to put this truth in its proper light, without anticipating what will come before us in the sequel.

a. The high priest under the law was not first constituted a priest when he entered the holiest of all: he had already, in his capacity as high priest, slain the sacrifice, the blood of which was carried within the veil. And, in like manner, Christ was already a priest when He gave Himself for His people. It was not, and could not be, a new sacrifice within the veil, when one part, and the principal part of it, was performed previous to His entry.

b. The passages which make mention of Christ's ONE oblation, or of His offering Himself ONCE, are conclusive as to the fact of His being a priest on earth; for that word ONCE cannot be understood of what is done in heaven. It must refer to His death as a historic fact, completed and finished here below. It is against all reason to affirm that the sacrifice was offered once, if it still continues; for the expression ONCE, or ONE OFFERING, plainly contrasts the completed sacrifice with the continuous intercession which evermore proceeds upon it. Nor does the epistle stop there: the analogy instituted between the fact that it was appointed to all men once to die, and the one atoning death of Christ (ix. 27), leaves us in no doubt that we must view that sacrifice as completed on the cross.

c. The priestly sacrifice which Christ offered is emphatically described as coincident with the Lord's death. The clearest proof of this is furnished in this epistle (Heb. ix. 26), when it is noticed that the Lord was under no necessity to offer Himself often, like the Jewish high priest, who had to offer a new sacrifice with every annual return of the great day of atonement, and enter with the blood of others. It declares that to offer Himself often would have been equivalent to a repeated suffering on the part of Christ; and therefore there can be no more conclusive proof that Christ was a priest[1] on earth, and that His sacrifice was consummated by His suffering during His humiliation.

VI. We come now to a section of considerable extent, treating copiously of the sacrifice of Christ, and of His priestly action as the truth of all that was done by the Jewish high priest on the great day of atonement (Heb. ix. 10–x. 22). To this passage a greater amount of attention is deservedly due, because the high priest's entrance into the holiest of all demands a fresh consideration. A general misapprehension as to its meaning has given an appearance of probability to the notion of a sacrifice or offering in heaven.

To bring out the outline of the apostle's thought, let it be noticed that the priestly function of Christ falls into two divisions, the earthly and the heavenly. The priestly function in heaven begins with His ascension; and the apostle lays special emphasis upon His work in heaven, for the obvious reason that He was refuting the current objection of the Jews at the time when the epistle was written—viz. that Christianity, as con-

[1] See Calovius, *Socinismus profligatus;* Turretin, *de Satisfactione;* Maresius, *Hydra Socinianismi.*

trasted with the still standing Jewish worship, had no visibly officiating high priest. The apostle reiterates, in many ways, that we HAVE A GREAT HIGH PRIEST, who has passed through space into the heavens, Jesus the Son of God (Heb. iv. 14); that the ministration of our High Priest was in the true tabernacle (viii. 3); that this ministry was preceded by a sacrifice of atonement before He ascended; that He offered Himself once; and that this one offering was accomplished in His state of abasement here below (Heb. vii. 27, viii. 3, ix. 14, ix. 28, x. 14).

A. At the beginning of the ninth chapter reference is made to the two compartments of the ancient tabernacle, and to the fact that the high priest entered the holy of holies once a year, not without blood. This arrangement, while it lasted, intimated a time of imperfect expiation. His entering not without blood on the day of atonement is called his offering (ver. 7); but this did not attain the proper end of sacrifice, which is to pacify the conscience (ver. 9). Only by forgiveness was the worshipper made perfect as pertaining to the conscience, and into this condition the Jewish rites could not transplant him. But Christ being come as an high priest, the apostle affirms two things: first, eternal redemption was effected by Him as an objective blessing; next, the purging of conscience followed as the subjective consciousness of deliverance (vers. 12, 14). Both are put in close connection with the blood of Christ as the sin-offering, and the apostle reasons from the one to the other in a striking way.

1. As to the eternal redemption, it is here, and everywhere else in Scripture, put as the effect of Christ's atoning blood. This deserves notice, because the common rendering conveys a harsh sense: " *having obtained* eternal redemption for us" (ver. 12). The participle with the verb in the past tense denotes simultaneous action as well as previous action, and here it is plainly simultaneous action. The rendering must be: "He entered in by His own blood once into the holy place, OBTAIN-

ING eternal redemption." Grammar and doctrine equally demand this, because the blood of sacrifice is uniformly spoken of as the cause of redemption (Eph. i. 7; 1 Pet. i. 19; Rev. v. 9). The participle, too, in the Greek aorist middle,[1] conveys the idea that Christ in His own person, or IN AND OF HIMSELF, without aid or instrumentality beyond His person, procured this redemption, which is also termed ETERNAL because possessed of everlasting validity.

But how did His entrance into the holiest of all by His own blood secure eternal redemption, and how is the language to be understood? Both inquiries will be satisfied when we ascertain the moment at which this entering took place. The usual interpretation affirms that it took place at the ascension. But that is burdened with insuperable difficulties. We are here taught that this entrance on the part of Christ was the counterpart or truth of what the high priest performed when He carried the blood into the holiest of all to atone for the sins of the collective congregation of Israel. Now, if that action of the Jewish high priest was atoning or expiatory, it plainly had no correspondence to anything done by our great Lord in heaven; for certainly everything atoning, in the proper sense of the term, was effected by what was done on earth, not by what was done in heaven. But if we carefully examine the sacrificial ritual, no doubt can exist that the sprinkling of blood in the holiest of all belonged to the expiation objectively considered. Atoning efficacy attached to the sprinkling of blood on the mercy-seat, and to the pouring out of blood at the altar. The text must be understood with reference to this : *without the shedding of blood* [or perhaps better, *the outpouring*[2] *of blood*] *is no remission* (Heb. ix. 22). Though, from the imperfection of the type, the two elements of priest and sacrifice

---

[1] λύτρωσιν εὑράμενος. (1) The aorist participle, I am fully persuaded, is here expressive of contemporaneous action; and (2) the middle voice implies Christ obtained the redemption *in and of Himself.* (See Winer and the commentators.)

[2] αἱματικχυσία. So De Wette, Tholuck, Doedes, and others; and I think correctly.

could not be combined in one, the proper meaning of this action was, that the priest was viewed as sprinkling his own blood upon the mercy-seat.

The entrance of our High Priest into the heavenly sanctuary may be considered as taking place at the moment of Christ's death, when He resigned His spirit to God, and His blood was poured forth upon the cross: then He appeared before His Father and Judge. All the ceremonies on the great day of atonement corresponded with this view, for the atonement for the people of Israel was not consummated till the sacrificial blood was sprinkled on the ark of the covenant. The figure therefore corresponds with the Lord's entrance into heaven immediately after His death, when soul and body were sundered, and not with the idea of a triumphant entrance into heaven, as it took place at His ascension, with all the jubilee belonging to a coronation day. In the type, everything assumes that the whole was completed on the atonement day. And Christ's resurrection on the third day, equivalent and parallel to the return of the high priest from the holy of holies, was a proof that He had entered with His own blood, and been accepted. The confusion which has arisen on this subject is owing to the fact that writers have not duly distinguished between the Aaronic priesthood and the Melchizedek priesthood.

The explanation above given carries with it an amount of evidence and appropriateness which contrast, to its advantage, with the other view, which only perplexes all who maintain it. When we look at the passage before us, other indications incline the balance in the same direction. Thus, the words " He entered by His own blood" plainly speak of a separation between soul and body. They cannot naturally be expounded in any other way. And a second expression may be taken as decisive, " He entered in ONCE ;" for in all the other passages where this word is used in connection with Christ's work, it is contrasted with the frequent repetition of the Old Testament

sacrifices (vii. 23).   It is always used as descriptive of something finished or completed, without the possibility of per-
petuating the action, or of adding to it (1 Pet. iii. 18).   The
expression is used by the apostles to distinguish the atonement as completed once for all, from the intercession, which
is continuous; and these two are never to be confounded
(Heb. ix. 25–27).   For the object contemplated, only one
entry was necessary, not to be repeated; and this expression,
therefore, is diametrically opposed to the view that the language of this verse refers to Christ's ascension to intercede;
for the offering of Himself a sacrifice was completed once
for all.

This explanation was first proposed by several eminent
Dutch divines about the middle of last century, who felt how
unsatisfactory was the common interpretation; but it never
received the currency or approval to which it was entitled.[1]
The more it is considered, the more does it commend itself,
and the more do evidences multiply in its favour.   A double
entry into heaven is indicated in these chapters,—the first at
the time of Christ's death, the second when He entered with
His risen body as the Melchizedek priest.   Aaron's priesthood

---

[1] This interpretation, so far as I have been able to trace its origin and progress, seems to have been first propounded by Witsius (de Œconomia federum,
lib. ii. cap. 6, sec. 9).   He says: "Monui fusioni sanguinis respondere sepa-
rationem animæ Christi a corpore, quæ est ruptura veli et fractio corporis ; sicut
illatio animæ in cœlum ad representandam Deo expiationem morte factam,
respondet illationi sanguinis in Sanctum sanctorum." Honert, on Heb. ix.,
contends that there is a double entry of Christ into heaven mentioned in this
chapter,—the first in a disembodied state (vers. 11, 12), the second after His
resurrection (vers. 24–28).   J. Honert, son of the former, in his Collect. Misc.
S., maintaining the same view, argues at large that the entrance of the high
priest on the day of atonement corresponded to the entrance of Christ's soul into
heaven at the moment of death, and that the Aaronic priesthood shadowed forth
the priesthood of Christ only up to the day of His resurrection.   Albert Schultens, in his Dutch commentary on the Heidelberg Catechism, and Prof. Lotze,
over het Hoogepriesterschap van J. C., 1800, earnestly contend for the same
view.   (See our previous explanatory remarks on the sacrifices, p. 49.)   De Moor,
Comment. perpet., combats this view as if it were maintained only by Honert, but
admits repeated entrances into the holiest of all on the day of atonement (pars
iv. p. 238).

does not seem to have typified anything beyond Christ's resurrection.

2. The other benefit, subjective in its nature, is the purging of conscience, adduced as a proof or evidence of the former (vers. 13, 14). The logical particle FOR gives a reason for the statement as follows: that which purges the conscience brings in eternal redemption. In proof of this, the apostle appeals to the types. And no one can evade the force of the statement by calling it a mere allusion to ancient rites: for we have an express comparison in which the atoning efficacy of Christ's death is always presupposed; and a contrast between the insufficiency of the Old Testament atonements effecting only an outward deliverance, and the all-sufficiency of Christ's atonement bringing in an everlasting deliverance.

The appeal is to two facts in the lower sphere of the ancient ritual of sacrifice. They effected something there, and a comparison is drawn between these merely outward effects and the spiritual effects produced by the death of Christ. I shall but briefly touch on these types, more especially as they were considered in a separate chapter. (1.) The apostle announces that the blood of bulls and goats sanctified to the purifying of the flesh. That is simply a repetition of what was said in the previous verse as to the ritual of the great day of atonement (ver. 12): the terms are in reality the same, and the allusion the same. The meaning is, that the death of the victims in the room of the guilty removed the threatened punishment by removing the defilement of the worshipper; and the Israelites, for whom the sacrifice was offered, were now sanctified, that is, pure and holy, and entitled to all the ecclesiastical and civil privileges of Israel. The apostle mentions (2) that the ASHES of the RED HEIFER, preserved for cases of ceremonial defilement, effected the same as the former (Num. xix. 1–18). This heifer, as well as the sin-offering that was offered on the day of atonement, was a sin-offering for the entire congregation; and its ashes, collected and dissolved in water, and sprinkled on the unclean, gave renewed access to the sanctuary, and to the fellowship of God's people. These were of old the great arrangements for restoring the defiled, so that they escaped death from a holy God.

On the imperfection of the ancient ceremonies this passage is most explicit. The apostle shows that they sanctified only to the purifying of the flesh, but not to the purging of the conscience. This was obvious from the nature of the case. The Mosaic law itself was far from ascribing any influence to rites and ceremonies in the way of removing moral guilt, though this passed current in the pharisaic schools of a later day. The law appointed sacrifices only for some involuntary states of body, or some inevitable violation of those positive laws by which Israel was separated by God from other nations. An investigation of the texts referring to these offences clearly shows this (Lev. xii. 7; Num. vi. 11, iv. 19; Lev. xv. 15, xiv. 2). In the case of persons contracting defilement—not to mention the sacred utensils, the ark, the tabernacle, the altar, which are also spoken of as receiving a purification by atonement—the defilement was merely ceremonial, and did not of itself touch the conscience except in virtue of a positive appointment. The person under ceremonial guilt, exposed to outward visitations of punishment, and even to death, if expiation was neglected, was not, properly speaking, morally guilty or defiled in conscience. His offence, though shutting him out from the sanctuary of the Lord and from the communion of His people, was more in the court of ecclesiastical polity than in the court of conscience, and carried with it, when punishment came, nothing beyond what was corporeal and temporal. The touching of a dead body, necessary in the event of death, or the entering a tent where a dead body was, though bringing ceremonial defilement and necessitating cleansing, was different from moral trespass. The atonements were of the same character, positive and outward in their effects. They did not cleanse the conscience, nor even enter into that inner circle bearing upon man's immediate personal relation to God: they restored him to the outward sanctuary, and to the outward worship with the people. But they did more; they also taught important things. They taught (1) that sacrifices were of grace on the part of God; (2) that they were vicarious; (3) that they were a satisfaction for the sins of the people. The true point of comparison on which this verse fixes our attention is, that while a certain effect was produced in a lower sphere by the ancient sacrifices, an everlasting effect was produced in a higher sphere by the blood of Christ; that they both accomplished the end designed, but that there was a "much more" in the latter case as contrasted with the former. This is the *tertium quid* of the comparison.

What did the sacrifices effect? They sanctified to the purifying of the flesh,—that is, cleansed the worshipper ceremonially; for it is better to say ceremonially than corporeally, as the latter word scarcely defines the result. They could effect nothing more, nor was more intended. They did not, and could not, make the worshipper perfect as pertaining to the conscience (Heb. ix. 9): they could not remove the conscience of sin, or the conscious knowledge of sin (x. 2): they could not put away sin as to the objective guilt (x. 4). The Jewish sacrifices could do none of these things, and never were intended to come into that inner circle where man, as a moral and responsible creature under a holy spiritual law, has to do as a guilty sinner with a righteous and holy God. But they were meant to do something in their true sphere: they put away ceremonial defilement, temporal punishment, and that exclusion from the sanctuary and the fellowship of God's people to which ceremonial defilement exposed them. The passage before us asserts this.

It must be noticed further, that the Epistle to the Hebrews is peculiarly clear and express on the inadequacy of the sacrifices to take away sins in any sense of the terms (x. 4). The opposite opinion, by whomsoever maintained, and with whatever modifications and caveats, is explicitly condemned. The question is not, whether sin was remitted to Old Testament saints waiting for the Messiah, the consolation of Israel, for that is not to be called in question, but whether these animal sacrifices gave remission. And we do not hesitate to say that the bare supposition of such a thing is to mistake the magnitude of sin. It would be a heathenish superstition: no enlightened conscience could believe it; and certainly the Bible never required any to suppose that moral guilt was removed by the blood of bulls and goats. No modification of the theory can make it tolerable in any form.

On the other side of the comparison, it remains to be noticed that there was not only a similarity, but A MUCH MORE, effected by the blood of Christ. In all such deductions throughout the epistle there is a something of agreement, and also a something of disparity (Heb. ii. 2, x. 28); for the superiority of the one dispensation above the other is infinite. The blood of Christ, the counterpart of the blood of the Jewish sacrifices, purges the consciences,—that is, takes away the sense of guilt, or the painful foreboding of merited punishment. And when we inquire by what means that was effected, it appears that it was not by doctrine, but by the blood of Christ sacrificially shed to put away the guilt of sin. We have thus a correspondence between the two sacrifices, but also A MUCH MORE in the way of pre-eminence, and the writer argues from the effect of the ancient sacrifices in their sphere to the greater efficacy of Christ's death. The comparison is important for ascertaining the nature and effect of Christ's death; for the point of comparison is this: the animal sacrifice of the old economy, substituted for the worshipper, effected something in the lower sphere, and the blood of Christ, vicariously shed, purifies our conscience from dead works.

B. The peculiar character of Christ's atoning sacrifice must also be considered: *How much more shall the blood of Christ, who through the Eternal Spirit offered Himself without spot to*

God, purge [better, *cleanse*] *your conscience from dead works, to serve the living God?* (ver. 14.) Here several points of moment are mentioned, bearing on the nature of the atonement as well as its effects. First, Christ is introduced as the sacrifice, for what He offered was HIMSELF; next, The context, as well as language here used, in which He is described as the OFFERER, represents Him as the priest; thirdly, The object to whom the sacrifice was offered was GOD. Plainly, the Lord is spoken of in these words as priest and sacrifice united.

1. That Christ is the sacrifice, in the true sense of the word, is unambiguously affirmed; and this Israelitish style decides the peculiar character of His death. It is noteworthy, that in all the peculiar arrangements of the Old Testament ritual, guilt was not permitted to rest on the individual, but was removed by a variety of atonements. The trespass, though but an infraction of a positive precept, could not be connived at, and the offerers acknowledged their own just desert in the death inflicted on the victims. They acknowledged, too, the vicarious character of the transaction. By this means, indeed, the idea of vicarious satisfaction, and the nomenclature connected with it, came to be naturalized in the church of God,—a palpable fact being necessary to support the idea. The whole fifty-third chapter of Isaiah forms properly the transition from the typical economy to that of the great moral and personal atonement. But, from the imperfection of types, the victim used in the old economy could only in a faint degree shadow forth the constituent elements of the great sacrifice. Thus the true vicarious sacrifice could only be a voluntary one; for as sin arose from the free choice of the sinner, it followed that the substitute could only be voluntary, and the sacrifice only such as was freely offered,—a feature which could not, from the nature of the case, be displayed in animal sacrifices brought by constraint to the altar. The free-will offering of Christ discovers the love from which all originated. A second defect in the old system was, that as there was no community of

nature, no essential connection obtained between those for whom the sacrifice was offered and the sacrifice itself, in the arbitrarily formed relation between man and animal sacrifices. A far other connection obtained between Christ and us: first, a community of nature, on the ground of which He was a kinsman; and then, a federal or legal union, on the ground of which we were brethren (Heb. ii. 17).

a. Three words are here used to exhibit the greatness of the sacrifice, and each of them may be said to add an element of value and dignity,—viz. THE CHRIST, WITHOUT SPOT, THROUGH THE ETERNAL SPIRIT. As to the first, it cannot be questioned that the blood of Messiah, or the Christ, has a special emphasis, because He was known to possess the highest dignity as the Son of God, the Angel of the Covenant (Mal. iii. 1), and the Mighty God (Isa. ix. 6). The apostle means that Christ was not only the high priest (ver. 11), but also the sacrifice (ver. 14). The blood of the Christ, as the expression means, denotes that the long-promised Messiah was sacrificially offered, and that His blood was the blood of the divinely commissioned God-man; and no deficiency could be supposed to attach, even in idea, to His sacrifice in the room of millions, as the infinite merits of the offerer were added to His work.

b. A second word, " offered WITHOUT SPOT," also taken from the sacrificial ritual, is meant to bring before us that Christ was not only in a negative point of view exempt from every conceivable defect, but in a positive point of view the possessor of perfect holiness, consisting in love to God and love to man, to the full measure of the human capacity. He acted in every scene, even when reviled and buffeted, so as never to betray what savoured of impatience, reluctance, or want of love in any part of His surety-obedience. The question has been raised, Was that exemption from defect in the piacular sacrifices a mere condition, a mere prerequisite in the way of preparation, or an element of the satisfaction, and shadowing forth the active obedience of Christ as vicarious not less than His death? The answer must be in the affirmative. The integrity and unspotted perfection of the sacrifice were indispensable, not as a mere prerequisite, but as an element of the sacrifice, and offered with it. Here the apostle not merely adduces the blood, but adds the offering of Himself without spot, as equal constituents in the sacrifice which purges the conscience.

c. A third expression, "through the Eternal Spirit," must be noticed. This has been interpreted of the divine nature of Christ by many,—especially since Beza expounded this, and several other texts containing an allusion to the Spirit, in this way (Rom. i. 4; 1 Tim. iii. 16; 1 Pet. iii. 18). But to that exposition there are insurmountable objections. This introduces an arbitrary nomenclature of man's invention.[1] It is more appropriate to expound it of the Holy Ghost than of the divine nature of the Son: for, in the first place, we have in the passage a priest, who is Christ; then a sacrifice, which is also Christ; then the Eternal Spirit, as the impelling power that animated Him from within to respond to the divine commission. The most eminent Greek exegetes, Witsius and others, correctly see in this expression an allusion to the fire by which the Levitical sacrifices were offered to God. Of this fire that came forth from the Lord, and fell from heaven on the victim, a historical account is given us in Scripture (Lev. ix. 23, 24): it was kept by divine appointment burning on the altar, and was never to go out (Lev. vi. 12). That sacred fire was a symbol of the Holy Ghost, who was often so represented (Acts ii. 3; Luke xii. 49; Dan. vii. 10); who perpetually fans the flame of divine love in the human heart, and renders all sacrifices acceptable (Rom. xv. 6). There is no force in the objection adduced in many quarters, to the effect that we cannot suppose it an allusion to the Holy Ghost, because that would imply that the value attaching to the Lord's sacrifice would thus be ascribed to the Holy Ghost, whereas it is always ascribed to

---

[1] It cannot be proved that τὸ πνεῦμα, used personally, ever means aught else than the third person of the Trinity.

the divine dignity of Christ's person. The answer to this is at hand. The Holy Spirit was the executive of all Christ's actions, internal and external; and those actions, peculiarly fragrant because of their holy spirituality, derived their worth, so far as intrinsic merit was concerned, from the fact that they were the actions of the Son. The meaning of the clause under consideration is, that the Holy Ghost, filling the Lord's humanity with unspeakable compassion, ardent zeal, fortitude, energy, and fervent love, impelled Him forward on His atoning work, and never suffered His mind to cool till the sacrifice was accomplished.

2. Christ was the priestly offerer as well as the sacrifice: "He offered Himself." With regard to this expression, it does not refer to a mediatorial work performed in heaven, but to what was completed once for all during His humiliation here on earth, or at the moment of death; and all the passages which make mention of an offering and sacrifice on the part of Christ have this sense (Eph. v. 2; Heb. vii. 27, viii. 4, ix. 14, ix. 28, x. 10, x. 12, x. 14). We may regard the expression before us as coincident with the phrase already mentioned, "By His own blood He entered in once into the holy place;" that is, if we explain both clauses as pointing to the completed act of atonement within the veil. A large class of eminent expositors, not Socinian in tendency, but perplexed by an erroneous interpretation of the entrance into the holiest of all, have given plausibility to the Socinian comment, that Christ's sacrifice was, in some modified sense, offered in heaven subsequently to His ascension. The Socinian view is unmixed error, leading men's minds away from the cross, and setting aside the vicarious work of suffering obedience. In the other case it amounts to this: that the sacrifice was completed in heaven, and that men are in some mystical way pardoned by Christ's resurrection-life, and not by His cross; a theory tending, in a subtle though little suspected way, to turn men's minds away from the atonement as the doctrine of the cross.

We deny that the present text, or any text representing Christ's death as an offering and sacrifice, can be so expounded.

The expression HE OFFERED HIMSELF, in the historical tense, refers not to an action in heaven, but to what was done on the cross. The appearing in the presence of God for us is said to be NOW, and is expressed by a different word (Heb. ix. 24). We have explained what was meant by entering the holy of holies, and proved that the slaying of the victim was only one element in the sacrifice, requiring to be followed by sprinkling the mercy-seat, as completing the expiation and the principal act of sacrifice. All this was done in humiliation, and at the moment of death, when Christ entered within the veil, still a high priest when disembodied. The rending of the veil attested the fact. The completion of the atonement was not reserved for the ascension to heaven, into which the Lord was to enter as His reward, not to complete His atoning work. The entire atonement was in humiliation (Lev. xvi. 6, 9 ; 1 Pet. iii. 18; 2 Cor. v. 21). And in reply to those who allege that the cross was but a violence inflicted, the answer is : It was a sacrifice, as it was His own voluntary choice (John x. 18 ; Heb. xii. 2).

3. The blood of the great sacrifice is next said to CLEANSE THE CONSCIENCE FROM DEAD WORKS, TO SERVE THE LIVING GOD. As we already found a more objective purification of the worshipper (Eph. v. 26 ; Tit. ii. 14), so we here find a subjective purification of the conscience from dead works. With regard to those DEAD WORKS, so called because they emanated from a soul alienated from the life of God, they may be viewed as including two different expositions. The commonly received interpretation makes them sinful works to be repented of (Heb. vi. 1), by which the conscience had been defiled; for these made the man unclean, guilty in judgment, and the object of divine wrath and condemnation. Modern expositors, for the most part, regard those dead works as the outward works of the law, by which the Jews, according to their pharisaic

errors, expected their justification before God. There is no
warrantable ground for opposing one of these opinions to the
other : they ought to be united, on this ground, that they are in
an equal degree phases or displays of that alienation from the
life of God, to which the atoning blood is here said to bring
us back.

This purifying of the conscience is specially the removal of
a sense of condemnation, and of the pollution caused by conscious guilt. A distinction must be drawn between that
cleansing, effected by the blood of sacrifice first taking effect
upon the person of the worshipper, and then upon his conscience, and that further renewing which frees him from the
inward power of sin. The one is by the cross, the other is by
the Spirit; and unquestionably it is the former to which our
attention is here directed. When conscience is cleansed, the
painful sense of unpardoned guilt ceases to agonize the mind :
it no more accuses or brings us into judgment before God's bar.
Conscience, as a court erected in the human breast, and pronouncing sentence in accordance with God's law, is pacified by
nothing which does not pacify the justice of God. The blood
of Christ does this, and nothing else can ; and for this end it
is not only laid to our account in the court of heaven, but
immediately applied to, or sprinkled on, the conscience.[1] The
blood of Christ, sacrificially offered, cleanses the conscience,
inasmuch as it conveys the most satisfactory evidence that it
was adapted to all the ends of divine justice, originating in the
appointment of God, and fitted to magnify His law. And the
effects of a purified or cleansed conscience will be seen in the
boldness of access, the peace, liberty, and hope, which Scripture
commonly connects with it (Rom. v. 1–3 ; Eph. ii. 18).

When a man receives the atonement, he has a sensible
peace and a well-grounded persuasion of exemption from guilt
and punishment, on the ground that if God had intended to

---

[1] See the admirable sermon of Fraser of Alness on this text, as found in his
works, appended to the explication of Rom. vi. and vii.

visit him with punishment, the Son of God would not have been put in a position to be punished in our stead. But a further difficulty is presented to the mind. As I cannot say that I never sinned, what can unmake that fact as if it had never been? Does not this memory abide as an everlasting stain in my conscience; and who can undo the past? Can even Omnipotence undo it? The only answer is: Omnipotence cannot; but the atonement can. And the explanation, as suggested by this passage, is as follows:—A judicial exchange of persons has been effected between Christ and sinners, by which they truly enter into each other's position. When the man accepts this provision, keeping in view the two sides of that personal exchange, he says: Sin does not attach to me, but to my Substitute, who took it upon Him by an act allowed at the divine tribunal. Punishment is not to strike on me, for He tasted death for every one of His people: and the good which the divine law required in its utmost conceivable perfection I have done; for what the Surety did, I did in Him, and His merits are transferred to me with the accompanying boon of the divine good pleasure. All this is effected in a way that for ever humbles and abases the man; but that which pacifies God pacifies the human conscience, the vicegerent of God. The purging of the conscience[1] is effected when we see that the law suffers no wrong, and the divine attributes no indignity.

This turns aside the Cocceian comment, which refers the language to the difference between the two economies. The founder of this school, an eminent expositor in many respects, adopted the notion that the fathers under the law were not in possession of a pacified conscience, which he thought a privilege of gospel times. He argued that the effect could not exist when the cause did not exist. But the easy answer is: The blood of Christ had retrospective as well as prospective effects. The apostle does not deny a cleansing of conscience

---

[1] See an excellent anonymous work, *die grosse Lehre vom Gewissen*, Leipz. 1769.

under the law in the case of those who waited for the consolation of Israel. Contrasting two things, he ascribes to the
one what he denies to the other. He is not speaking of
believers under the law and under the gospel, but of Hebrews
recently converted, who found in the blood of Christ a peace
vainly expected in the rites and ceremonies of Judaism. He
speaks of the same men in their previous and present condition.

4. As to SERVING THE LIVING GOD, this is the natural and
necessary result. The defilement of conscience hinders access;
the cleansing and perfecting of conscience facilitates access, and
emboldens the worshipper to draw near. The conscience either
bars or permits access to God. So long as sins are uncancelled,
exclusion from fellowship is continued, and the man has a
defiled or evil conscience. A cleansed conscience, attesting his
reception into the fellowship of God, enables and emboldens
him to serve the living God.

C. The apostle having named the ever-valid sacrifice of
Christ, is led by a natural transition of thought to refer to the
new covenant founded on it, and to the Mediator's action in
regard to it: *And for this cause He is the mediator of the new
testament* [better, *covenant*], *that by means of death, for the
redemption of* [better, *for redemption from*] *the transgressions
that were under the first testament* [*covenant*], *they which are
[have been] called might receive the promise of eternal inheritance*
(Heb. ix. 15). This verse begins a section on the subject of the
covenants, very variously expounded. It would draw us aside
from our purpose to enter into the conflicting views, though
they have an interest of their own. The apostle calls Jesus
Mediator (compare Heb. vii. 22, viii. 6, xii. 24), a designation
that has everything in common with that of High Priest,—
intimating one who has come under obligations for another,
and occupies his place. Each of the terms used—SURETY,
MEDIATOR, ADVOCATE, HIGH PRIEST—differing as they do from
each other only by a shade of meaning, brings before us Christ's
work as a whole, and represents Him as occupied with it on

earth, and still continuing to be occupied with it in heaven. When Christ is designated the Mediator of the new covenant, the expression denotes that He is the founder of a new alliance or fellowship between God and sinners, who previously were infinitely remote and alienated from each other.

1. This did not take effect merely upon men then living; for His vicarious death extended to transgressions under the first covenant, as well as to those who lived subsequently to the incarnation. The atonement, adequate to the sins of His people in all times, made His sacrifice infinitely superior to the shadowy economy it superseded. The apostle draws a contrast between the sacrifice on the great annual festival of atonement, with its shadowy expiation of ceremonial offering, as an effect in the lower sphere, available only for the past year and for men then living, and the atonement of Christ, which was for all sins of all times, and even for men long dead. His death, as is here stated, was an expiation for moral transgressions under the first covenant, and which had remained unexpiated, though remitted in the forbearance of God (Rom. iii. 25). On the ground of the previous proof as to the efficacy of Christ's sacrifice, the apostle declares that it was retrospective, and atoned for transgressions till then unexpiated. Christ's atonement cannot be conceived of except as a proper expiation, if we trace these two elements: it took the place of the Old Testament sacrifices, which were undoubtedly atonements in their own sphere; and it accomplished what they, from their insufficiency, could not accomplish. When we consider the expression, "redemption from the transgressions that were under the first covenant," and connect this result with the Mediator's death[1] as the meritorious cause, according to the express terms of this passage, we are taught that Christ's death removed the punishment of those transgressions which previously were unatoned for by any sacrifices. That conclusion is inevitable: the allusion is to actual sins, or moral trespasses,

---

[1] θανάτου γενομένου εἰς ἀπολύτρωσιν τῶν παραβάσεων.

committed under the old economy.   This thought is demanded, too, by the connection: a barrier was put by these transgressions in the way of access to the sanctuary.

2. This representation decides on the nature of Christ's atonement as a vicarious satisfaction.   If we place it alongside of the theory that makes Christ's death a confirmation of His doctrine, what influence on previous ages could the Mediator's death by any possibility exercise, considered as the confirmation of His doctrine ?   All that effect must, from the necessity of the case, be prospective, not retrospective.   But, considered as an expiation of transgressions, it could very well influence past as well as future ages.   If, again, with others, we view the death of Christ as fitted only to deliver men from slavish fear, we may ask by what figure of speech can the expression here used, " redemption from transgressions which were under the first covenant," be made to signify slavish fear of punishment ? It were a violence to language to torture it to such a sense.

VII. The nature of the atonement is illustrated by the comparison between Christ's one sacrifice and the annually repeated sacrifice of the Jewish high priest; and then, again, by death, considered as the common lot of men, and the propitiatory death of Christ: *But now once in the end of the world* [or, *world-ages*] *hath He appeared, to put away sin by the sacrifice of Himself.   And as it is appointed unto men once to die, but after this the judgment ; so Christ was once offered to bear the sins of many : and unto them that look for Him shall He appear the second time, without sin unto salvation* [better, *so Christ, being once offered to bear the sins of many, shall appear the second time without sin to them who wait for Him unto salvation*] (Heb. ix. 26–28).   The statement is, that Christ once appeared, in the end of the ages, to cancel or put away sin. How ?   By the sacrifice of Himself.   The expression TO PUT AWAY cannot mean to put away the idea of criminality or ill-desert ; nor can we refer it to the removal of corruption by His doctrine.   The apostle speaks of His sacrifice, not of His doctrine. And as He did not offer Himself often, the one sacrifice was adequate to cancel the sin committed from the beginning. The sufferings of Christ effected this, not as a magnanimous display of self-sacrifice, nor as a mere declaration of divine love; for that could only gain its end prospectively, not retrospectively. The simple meaning is, that Christ put away sin by the atonement. Though the expression is so general that it seems to comprehend the putting away the power of sin, the connection and allusion to sacrifice limit the meaning[1] to the cancelling of guilt.

The next comparison between the once inflicted penalty of death and the one atonement is equally significant (ver. 27). The expression ONCE TO DIE is not to be taken simply for the separation of soul and body, but for death penally considered; for of some we read that they went down alive into hell (Num. xvi. 30). The apostle speaks of death as the penal doom of sin, the word ONCE being the emphatic term; and the analogy between the two things is, that as there is one penal death impending over men, so Christ died once to remove their penalty. The Surety, adequate as He was to the task of assuming our responsibilities, and of entering into our condition, was thus appointed to die only once. But after death followed the judgment. Two things are in the comparison: first, man's dying once, having its counterpart in Christ's one sacrifice; then the second advent of the Lord, for the complete salvation of the redeemed, in place of judgment. By an appeal to man's history, the passage thus convincingly establishes that only one sacrifice for sins was necessary, and that Christ's one death sufficed for all time. The proof is drawn from the consideration that as nothing more was due in the history of man, so nothing more was in Christ's obligation. The comparison is based on the suretyship of the Lord, rendering Himself liable to man's obligations. The dying once, and the one

---

[1] Bleek and Delitzsch, without necessity, make εἰς ἀθέτησιν ἁμαρτίας so general as to denote also the annihilation of the dominion of sin.

offering for sin, are thus put together as counterparts, plainly
proving substitution, if anything can. Not only so: the one
sacrifice of Christ, represented as the counterpart of our penal
death, indisputably proves, against the Socinians, and all who
fall in with their theory, that Christ's sacrifice was on earth,
and not in heaven after His ascension. His one offering was
in death.

We must now more particularly discuss the import of the
clause, "so Christ was once offered to bear the sins of many"
(ver. 28). The passage is by universal consent regarded as a
quotation from Isaiah (Isa. liii. 12), conveying the idea of
vicarious sin-bearing; that is, of taking His people's sins on
Himself, and bearing the consequences to be inflicted on sinful
humanity in their stead. They who give another turn to the
expression, and arbitrarily allege that the verb is to be viewed
as denoting "to take away," are chiefly biassed by doctrinal
prejudices adverse to vicarious sin-bearing. The assertion has
been hazarded, that the epistle knows nothing of the formula
that "He bore our sins," but always speaks of taking them
away.[1] Others, however, having no objection to the doctrine
of sin-bearing, encounter a new difficulty, founded on the order
of events, as follows: The language is, "He was once offered
to bear sins," which at first sight seems to say that He was
offered in order to bear sins, and consequently that sin-bearing
is viewed as succeeding the offering properly so called. Hence
they think themselves shut up to the rendering, "to take away
sins;" for they argue that it cannot be said, "He was once
offered to bear sins," but conversely. That difficulty, however,
may easily be obviated. As the oblation is commonly put in
the Epistle to the Hebrews, it is represented as Christ's own
act: He is set forth as at once priest and victim; the obvious
meaning being, that the sin-bearer offered Himself. Accord-

---

[1] Thus Reuss rashly expresses himself: l'Epitre ne connait pas la formule
qu'il a PORTÉ nos péchés ; elle dit toujours qu'il les a ôtés (*Hist. de la Theol.
Chret.* ii.).

ingly, we find Him represented as a sacrificing priest offering Himself (Heb. ix. 14), and carrying His own blood into the holiest of all (ix. 25). But here the expression is used passively, describing God's action in the matter, not Christ's action as the high priest. And in this use of the phrase it embraces all that may be regarded as included in the mission, manifestation, and giving up of the Son of God. The phrase has thus a larger and wider sense when applied to God.

The same thing is evident from a comparison of this verse with a previous one (ver. 26). The intervening verse (ver. 27) does not break the connection: it is only the first member in a serious of parallels. There is one parallel between Christ's appearing once for all and His one offering: there is another between His putting away sin and His bearing sin. A marked correspondence obtains, and the words set forth the completeness of the atonement as offered once, and needing no repetition. The passage assumes that Christ willingly submitted to the ordinary penal law appointed to man; the whole clause having reference to the vicarious work of the servant of God mentioned in Isaiah (Isa. liii. 12). That the expression here used means TO BEAR SINS, may be established by two conclusive arguments,—the one based on the philological import of the term, and the other on the context.

1. The proper import of the expression TO BEAR THE SINS OF MANY, is to bear or carry them up: that is, to the cross, as some view it; or to lay them on His own person, as others prefer to view it. This is the shade of meaning which the verb expresses.[1] The idea of removal does not express the primary signification, and no instance can be adduced from the

---

[1] See Beza, and Grotius, *de Satisfactione*, p. 14. Afterwards, when Grotius' Commentary appeared, it was found that he had changed his interpretation into *auferre*, as many moderns render it, viz. Bleek, Lunemann, Hofmann. See an admirable discussion on the meaning of ἀναφέρειν ἀμαρτίας by Van Voorst in his *de Usu Verborum cum Præpositionibus Compositorum in N. T.* 1818, pp. 148–166, with a thorough refutation of Grotius' second thoughts. He proves that χωρὶς ἀμαρτίας and *auferre* would furnish no antithesis such as is plainly meant.

usage of language in proof of the meaning "to take away." An interpreter, therefore, who knows his function, will abide by the laws of language. This fact is decisive as to the import of the expression, and may be appealed to by those who maintain that the essence of the atonement consists in sinless sin-bearing on the part of the appointed Christ, the Son of God. The constituent element of expiation is sin-bearing, and not the mere removal of sin in the future, whether that may be effected by instruction or inward reformation. They who persist in assigning to the verb the signification of TAKING AWAY, have nothing but conjecture in their favour; and something better must be adduced as authority when the question is the meaning of a phrase and the aspect of a doctrine.

2. The same thing is proved by the context. The apostle, contrasting the two comings of the Lord, affirms that at His first coming He bore the sins of many, while at His second advent He will appear WITHOUT SIN. The phrase must mean, without vicarious sin-bearing, suggesting that at His first coming He was a sin-bearer. It cannot refer to personal sin, as He had none, nor to anything approaching to the notion of a fallen humanity. But while He was on earth, He was at once separate from sinners and made sin.

The expression "to bear the sins of many" intimates that Christ, in a certain sense, sustained the person of sinners. As a historic fact, running through all stages of the Lord's earthly life, this was the core of the atonement; and this aspect of it is the key to the entire doctrine. Sin-bearing was necessary to the propitiation as a presupposition or indispensable preliminary; and without it we encounter difficulties which find no solution. What light does Scripture throw upon it? It is the well-known Old Testament formula for being guilty, whether that may be personal or vicarious; and in numerous passages it conveys the idea of being guilty as contrasted with being guiltless (Num. v. 31). It may be personal guilt to which allusion is made; or, where the sins of others are said to be borne, it means to incur their guilt, to come under their obligation to punishment (Ezek. xviii. 19).

Between the general undertaking of suretyship and the actual infliction of the curse there lay an intermediate arrangement, by which the Lord Jesus occupied a positive relation to our penalty. This was sin-bearing or guilt, rendering it just that the moral Governor of the universe should exact the expiation. That the Lord Jesus assumed sin, and incurred a liability to punishment, when He came in the flesh and was found in fashion as a man, is to be affirmed on the strict interpretation of the language used by the apostles. They affirm that He BORE sin, and was MADE sin. Of the two expressions just mentioned, sin-bearing has reference to sin considered as a heavy burden, while the other means that the Lord, personally sinless, was made the embodiment of sin, or incorporated sin in an official point of view; for the personal and official are to be kept distinct, and in this matter sin-bearing is official, distinguished from what was properly personal. However various the nomenclature, no biblical phrase more precisely sets forth the essence of the atonement than sin-bearing.

VIII. So important for the apostle's purpose was the difference between the annual sacrifice of the Aaronic high priest and the one sacrifice of Christ, that an entire section of the tenth chapter is devoted to the exposition of it (Heb. x. 1–10). And much may be derived from this connected portion to explain the proper nature of the atonement. The points of similarity have been brought out; now we have to trace THE POINTS OF CONTRAST. Having proved in the last verses of the previous chapter that Christ's sacrifice could not be repeated, partly because that would carry with it repeated suffering, partly because it would be contrary to the analogy of man's own history, which appoints man to die once,—the Substitute acting only according to the obligations of the represented,— the apostle, at the tenth chapter, sets forth by contrast the sufficiency of Christ's one sacrifice. The imperfection of the sacrifices annually offered on the great day of atonement is put before us in the first four verses of the chapter. There are three distinct grounds mentioned by the apostle which conclusively prove the inadequacy of those sacrifices, each furnishing a point of contrast to the perfection of Christ's sacrifice.

1. The first contrast is derived from the fact that the ancient sacrifices were but a shadow, or rough outline, of good things to come, and not the things themselves ; or, as it is here expressed, not the very image of the things[1] (ver. 1). It might at first sight seem that the apostle contrasts two things which in different degrees represent the substance,—a rude sketch and a fully painted figure. But it is the shadow contrasted with the substance or reality. Now if these priestly sacrifices, the culminating points of the ancient worship, were but shadows or pictures, they obviously could not put the worshipper on a right footing with God. They could not perfect him, in the sense of justifying his person, and giving him a right, as a purified worshipper, to approach the living God. We may take in the subjective element of a purged conscience as included in the term PERFECT, as it is commonly employed, though it is as natural to take it in the objective sense (comp. ver. 14). According to the apostle, those unsubstantial shadows could not perfect the worshippers ; that is, could not satisfy the justice of God, and atone for sin, which was the great promise from the beginning.

2. A second reason for the inadequacy of the ancient sacrifices is taken from their annual repetition (vers. 2, 3). Whether we read the first clause interrogatively or not, the apostle emphatically declares, that had they availed to perfect the worshippers, that annual iteration would have been needless. They would have ceased or been superseded. The ground on which this is put is noteworthy : *For the worshippers, once purged* [or, *cleansed*], *should have had no more conscience of sins ;*

_____
[1] See Turretin, *de Satisfactione*, p. 239.

assuming that the purifying from sin has, as its effect, the removal of a guilty conscience. The perfect participle denotes something done once for all, describing the condition of those whose consciences have been purged. The opposite of this was the characteristic of the Old Testament worshippers, where no provision was made for the acceptance of their persons, but only for the cleansing of ceremonial trespasses, soon to become as numerous as before. The new covenant accepts the person, and perfects him as pertaining to the conscience. The apostle's argument is, that had their relation been perfected, an echo of it would have been heard subjectively in a pacified conscience. The conscience, already mentioned (Heb. ix. 14), is not mere consciousness, but consciousness alive to man's relation to God, and having God for its object, the consequence of which is a charge of guilt while man's relation remains unrectified. The worshippers under the law thus had a fresh remembrance of sins year by year, having neither personal acceptance nor a pacified conscience.

Here it is necessary to correct a piece of over-doing—a theory as to the imperfection of the Old Testament believers. From this passage it was argued by the Cocceian school, that if there was a conscience of sin, true peace of conscience could not be possessed. That by no means follows, as will be apparent to every one who apprehends the retrospective character of the Lord's death. The power to perfect the worshippers is denied to the law, and proved by the repetition of the same sacrifices, but is not denied to the efficacy of the great sacrifice by anticipation applied to believers under the old economy.[1] So far from detracting from the honour of Christ's sacrifice, this exhibits its vast potency, as not only adapted to ages that were to run after He came, but also possessing retrospective efficacy. A certain difference there was between believers under the Old Testament and under the New,—a difference

---

[1] See Rev. A. Bonar's elucidations of Leviticus; also Knobel, *Com. zu Leviticus*, 1852; and B. W. Newton's *Thoughts on Leviticus*.

neither to be denied nor ignored, but of a peculiar nature. They had a conscience of sin, not yet expiated, but one day to be fully expiated by the great sacrifice of Messiah. They were like us, yet with a shade of difference; that is, more in degree than in kind. They could have, and actually had, peace of conscience, as we have. But, according to their historical position, they had of necessity a peculiar experience, into which we cannot enter. Not the want of acceptance or pardon, not the fear that had torment; but a certain conscience of sin, such as we have not, that is, of sin as a something not actually atoned for—not yet expiated in fact. Hence, though sin had long ago been judicially forgiven, the spirits of the just seem to have been made perfect in this subjective sense, when the great fact of the atonement arrived (Heb. xi. 40, xii. 23); for this must have been imparted to them by a knowledge of the event, and an experience of its potency.

3. The third reason assigned for their inadequacy and imperfection is: *It is not possible that the blood of bulls and of goats should take away sins* (ver. 4); a reason derived from the necessity of the thing, whether we look at the nature of God, the nature of man, or the infinite demerit of sin. The atonement must be offered in man's nature, to satisfy the injured rights of God, which the blood of bulls and goats could not effect. The apostle pronounces it impossible, because the blood of irrational animals bore no proportion to the sins of rational beings, which could not be removed by any arbitrary arrangement. But why could not sins have been taken away by these Jewish sacrifices, if, as many allege, God cancels them without atonement? We see the necessity of an adequate satisfaction; for the impossibility is founded in the thing itself, and the appeal is to the divine justice and holiness.[1]

Having proved, from the necessity of the case, the inadequacy of animal sacrifices, the apostle next shows that, in point

---

[1] An argument is warrantably based on this statement for the absolute necessity of a satisfaction by Witsius, *de Fœdere*, p. 177, Vander Kemp, etc.

of fact, they were set aside as insufficient (Heb. x. 5–10); and a quotation is made from the book of Psalms, in which this was clearly announced (Ps. xl. 6–8). As we have already explained this passage, nothing further is necessary than to advert to the appended words of the apostle in introducing the quotation, and commenting upon it. He plainly considered the passage as an utterance of Christ when He came into the world: "Wherefore, when He cometh into the world, He saith, Sacrifice and offering Thou wouldest not" (ver. 5). The logical particle WHEREFORE intimates that, by reason of the imperfection of the Old Testament sacrifices, He came not to offer these fruitless sacrifices, but to do the will of God in their room. The quotation contrasts the imperfection of animal sacrifices with moral obedience and willing service: "Lo, I come to do Thy will, O God." In animal sacrifices God had no pleasure, because, though divinely appointed, they were inadequate to be the true sacrifice, which required moral obedience. This spiritual obedience looked beyond Old Testament times, and was realized only when Christ fulfilled the divine will. But it is added, there was the removal or taking away of the first thing mentioned in the quotation, that is, of animal sacrifices, that He might establish the second, that is, the doing God's will. The Mosaic worship, with its complicated system of sacrifices, was superseded by something better coming in its stead. And the apostle appends a commentary, the import of which must be brought out in a few particulars: *By which will* [better, *in which will*] *we are sanctified, through the offering of the body of Jesus Christ once* (Heb. x. 10).

1. What is meant by the expression, IN WHICH WILL? Can it intimate the ready will or promptitude of the Messiah to respond to the divine commission, and to carry it out? That cannot competently be maintained, because the preceding verse (ver. 9) expressed the divine will of THE FATHER purposing that Christ should be the personal sacrifice. Besides, the will here mentioned is distinguished by the terms employed from the

offering itself. The original word used in the Psalm gives the
idea of God's GOOD PLEASURE ; but the apostle renders it THY
WILL (τὸ θέλημά σου), a term wide enough to comprehend the
agreement or compact between the Father and the Son, and the
commandment which needed to be performed, that the issue
might correspond to the will of God. It is not the moral law
simply,—an idea added in the Psalm, though not quoted by
the apostle,—but all that was enjoined upon the Surety; and
the translation we have given—IN WHICH WILL—brings out
the sphere or element in which the great sacrifice was offered,
as well as the sphere in which we are sanctified.[1]

2. The ONE offering must be noticed. This point the
apostle repeatedly inculcates in the epistle, in proportion to its
importance. He will have attention paid to the one historic
fact of Christ's vicarious obedience and death. The word ONCE
excludes all repetition of Christ's sacrifice ; for it must be construed, as our translators have done, with the offering of the
Lord's body (comp. Heb. vii. 23, 24, ix. 24–28). The unity of
the sacrifice is further mentioned, as we shall see in the subsequent verses.

3. Christ's sacrifice consists in the offering of His body :
He is compared and contrasted with the annual sacrifice. The
term BODY denotes here His humanity ; for His soul as well as
His body was offered. This term is contrasted with the bodies
of animals burned on the altar ; for in the previous verses the
Psalm was quoted : " A body hast Thou prepared me." More
necessary is it to examine the force of the expression, " THE
OFFERING OF THE BODY OF JESUS CHRIST ONCE," because many—
with a modification of the Socinian theory, which transfers
Christ's sacrifice to His ascension to heaven—give but a half-
hearted adherence to the great truth that the Lord's sacrifice
was completed on the cross. That scheme of thought is refuted

---

[1] See Walch, *de Obedientia Christi Activa*, p. 8. Sebastian Schmid, on
Hebrews, says here : " Voluntas et lex Dei patris non tantum decalogus, seu
lex moralis est ; sed omnis Voluntas Dei circa redemptionem humani generis."

by this expression, which can only refer to the cross.   It could not be in the apostle's mind to affirm that Christ offered His body to God at the ascension; for the only ostensible plea on which men advocate an offering in heaven is, that, according to the typical economy, the blood was carried into the holiest of all, which they groundlessly conclude was done at His ascension. But He offered Himself when He bore our sins on His own body (1 Pet. ii. 24); and the sacrifice was completed at His death, and incapable of supplement or repetition.

4. We are said to be SANCTIFIED in this element of God's will, and by the one sacrifice of the Lord's body. How the worshippers were sanctified by sacrifice, has been noticed above. It is a relative, not inherent sanctification; for sacrifice put men on a right footing with God, covering their guilt, and calming conscience.   It is sacrificial phraseology, and not to be interpreted of moral amendment.

The previous statements, taken from the sacrificial phraseology, throw a steady light on the true design of Christ's obedience unto death.   They show that He is the truth of those shadows.   Though the New Testament writers, accustomed to the sacrificial style, do not wholly abandon it even when no express comparison is made between the sacrifices and the death of Christ, it was the very design of this epistle to bring out the typical relation; and we have had express testimony to the fact that the death of Christ was a sacrifice (vii. 27); that He offered a better sacrifice (ix. 23); that He put away sin by the sacrifice of Himself (ix. 26); that His sacrificially shed blood purges our consciences from dead works (ix. 14); and that the offering of His body sanctifies us, in the sense of dedicating us as a covenant people to God (x. 10). All these passages affirm that the death of Christ was a sacrifice, by which men are separated as a peculiar people for the worship of the living God: and it is important to see the thing signified in the symbol, the antitype in the type.   If the ancient sacrifices, as symbols in the lower sphere, freed the

worshipper from merited punishment, because guilt passed
over to the victim, the death of Christ in like manner, in a
higher sphere, not only displayed the punishment due to us
for sin, but effected the removal of our punishment.   It put us
in the position of a people near to God, a holy people, as Israel
were in a typical sense.   All this was brought about by sacrifice.   The Old Testament sacrifices occupied the place of those
who brought them, and who saw their sin and punishment
transferred ; and in the same way the death of Jesus was
vicarious, because He actually bore His people's punishment,
and restored them to favour and holy fellowship.   Nor does
this view convey ought unworthy of God.   The sacrifices did
not represent God as moved to mercy by the shedding of
blood, for they were provided in grace, and argue a gracious
plan by which all the attributes of God are magnified.

As to the remaining portion of this connected section, we
may content ourselves with merely touching the salient points
(vers. 11–14).   The apostle contrasts the action of the Jewish
high priest with Christ's official action.   The Hebrew Christians were somewhat troubled by Jewish cavils as to the non-
repetition of the atonement ; and the apostle, comparing the
two priesthoods, shows why no repetition of Christ's work was
necessary or possible.   Omitting the proof for the sufficiency
of Christ's finished work, from the great fact of His resurrection, let us notice a threefold antithesis : the first, between
every priest or high priest daily ministering, and this Man ;
the second, between the same repeated sacrifices and the one
sacrifice for sin ; the third, between the insufficiency of the
one and the all-sufficiency of the other.   What a vain parade
of language, if it were not meant that the atonement is to be
traced to the death of Christ, in the same way as the Israelites,
in a lower sphere, ascribed to the priestly sacrifices their de-
liverances from defilement!

One point to be determined is : How are we to construe the
expression FOR EVER in the verse, " But this man, after He had

offered one sacrifice for sin for ever, sat down on the right hand
of God?" (ver. 12.) Opinion is pretty equally divided on the
question whether the words FOR EVER are most fitly joined
with the "one sacrifice," denoting that it was eternally valid;
or with the following words, denoting that He sat down for
ever. On many accounts we greatly prefer the former; and the
repetition of the same expression further down, HE PERFECTED
FOR EVER (ver. 14), renders this highly probable, for the one is
the foundation of the other. Thus, "Christ offered one sacrifice
for sins FOR EVER," and this fact "perfected FOR EVER" those
who share in it.[1] The everlasting validity attaching to it was
due to this, that it was ONE sacrifice of infinite sufficiency, with
retrospective as well as prospective influence, and capable of
rectifying for ever man's relation to God. This text plainly
calls it "one sacrifice" (ver. 12), and views it as incapable of
being repeated. It is not represented as perpetually offered in
heaven. The antithesis between the two sacrifices and the two
priesthoods is very emphatic. The one high priest is represented
as daily ministering, and offering oftentimes the same sacrifices,
which could never take away sins; the other High Priest offers
one sacrifice for sins, and then sits down. No one interpreting
naturally will refer this one sacrifice to anything but the
finished work on the cross—the ground of His reward. The
oblation was on earth, and the intercession in heaven; the
oblation only once, and the intercession perpetual. The participial clause in the first part of the verse is meant to indicate
antecedent, not simultaneous action (ver. 12); and a similar
style of expression occurs at the beginning of the epistle (Heb.
i. 3).

The apostle is now led to subjoin a further statement of the
same thing in an aphoristic form: *For by one offering* (προσφορᾷ)
He hath perfected for ever them that are sanctified (ver. 14).

---

[1] This is the construing of Theophylact, Luther, Tholuck. The original
pointing also of the authorized English version was: "This man, after He had
offered one sacrifice for sins for ever, sat down."

This assigns the reason of the previous statement, as is evident from the causal or grounding particle *for*,—a reason based on the sufficiency of the sacrifice for all the purposes of man's salvation. Because it was so, the Surety sat down on His mediatorial throne, waiting for the final victory. As to the word OFFERING here used, it is of the same meaning with the previous term SACRIFICE (ver. 12), but more general. The same two terms are applied, but in a different order, to the death of Christ in another epistle (Eph. v. 2). When the apostle says, "by one offering,"[1] he plainly alludes to the previous expression, "through the *offering of the body* of Jesus Christ once" (ver. 10). As all the terms here used have been already considered, two remarks will suffice.

1. We have another emphatic reference to the one sacrifice. The importance of this point was great. It could not be placed in too great prominence, as will appear by recalling other passages to the same effect (Heb. vii. 27, ix. 26, 28). In this passage, after pointing out that the Levitical atonements culminated in the sin-offering which the high priest offered year by year continually, and the repetition of which argued imperfection, he shows that the Lord Jesus, by one offering, or by the offering of His body once (ver. 10), perfected for ever them that are sanctified. Before passing from this point, it may be noticed that the ONE sacrifice is a point of as great moment against Socinians and Romanists as it was against the ancient Jews of the apostle's age: it cannot be put in too great prominence. It is diametrically opposite to the Socinian notion of a sacrifice in heaven, or a perpetual oblation; for it is one thing to offer an oblation, and another to carry on perpetual intercession. It is diametrically opposed to all Romanist or semi-Romanist theories, which argue for a repetition of the sacrifice in the Lord's Supper. The Epistle to the Hebrews supplies a ready answer to sacerdotal assumptions of this sort.

---

[1] προσφορά might be construed as the nominative to τετελείωκεν, but not so naturally.

The repetition argues defect and imperfection. Not only so: for a renewal of the propitiatory sacrifice the apostle explicitly declares there must be fresh abasement on the part of Christ; renewed suffering; the shedding of blood, coupled with an accursed death (Heb. ix. 26). The reason of this was, that the sin-offering was vicarious.[1]

2. The one offering PERFECTED the saints. This was accomplished objectively when Christ died; for all the saints were represented in their Surety before the divine mind. When the one sacrifice is said to perfect them, the meaning is, that it effected full remission, a complete expiation; objectively securing personal acceptance, priestly standing, covenant nearness as a peculiar people; and subjectively securing the purging of conscience, or the making the worshippers perfect as pertaining to the conscience. What effected this? Not Christ's doctrine nor His example, but the offering of His body once.[2] These three terms, PERFECT, SANCTIFY, PURGE or purify, are terms of sacrificial import—relative terms bearing on the standing of the worshipper before God. They do not mean moral amendment.

Another point remains to be noticed in this connected outline, which compares Christ's official action and that of the high priest on the day of atonement: *A new and living way which He hath consecrated for us through the veil, that is to say, His flesh* (Heb. x. 19). How could the flesh of Christ be the veil which served to shut out the holiest of all from human access? The investigation of this fact opens up a chain of important truths. The antitype of the veil is expressly said to be the Lord's FLESH; and we have already seen that, when the term FLESH is so applied, it has the peculiar meaning of sin-bearing humanity. Thus we read of the days of His flesh

---

[1] See the striking discussion of Calovius in his *Socinismus profligatus:* "utrum Christi oblatio jugis sit" (p. 368).

[2] We may compare Heb. ii. 10: The redeemed were viewed as objectively in Christ, and all who are ἁγιαζόμενοι were objectively reconciled and perfected in that one sacrifice.

(Heb. v. 7); of knowing Christ after the flesh (2 Cor. v. 16). The sins of His people were by imputation laid on Him so long as He sojourned among men; and therefore His humanity, so long as it was uncrucified, was still a proof that the curse was not removed, nor sin abolished. By the VEIL we understand Christ's flesh burdened with our sins, and laden with all the curse which the law threatened against transgressors.[1] His flesh was rent, as the veil was rent, at His death, to open up to His people free access into the holiest of all. He entered, and they entered with Him, into a state of perfect rest and intimate fellowship with God. He entered within the veil at the moment the spirit was separated from the body; and through means of His surrendered life, we entered into the nearest communion with God. This was a new and living way, and it was, so to speak, signed and sealed by the historic fact of the rending of the temple veil (Matt. xxvii. 57). The entrance of Christ's soul into heaven, or paradise, at the moment of His death, as has been already shown, corresponded with the carrying of the blood into the holiest of all.

Hence we draw near with sprinkled consciences (x. 22). Christians are all said to have come to the blood of sprinkling (xii. 24). As the blood was the blood of victims, to which the guilt of the worshippers had been transferred, the sprinkling of it freed the Israelite from punishment and ceremonial defilement. The sprinkling of Christ's blood cancels all sin, and purifies the conscience for ever.

IX. We come now to a section which delineates the sacrificial institute and its typical import in a variety of lights: *We have an altar, whereof they have no right to eat who serve the tabernacle. For the bodies of those beasts, whose blood is brought into the sanctuary by the high priest for sin [or, as a sin-offering], are burned without the camp. Wherefore Jesus also, that*

---

[1] See Witsius, *de Fœdere*, ii. 6. 9 : "Caro Christi velum erat, aditum nobis intercludens. Quamdiu enim adhuc erat integra, indicium erat nondum aboliti peccati, nec sublatæ maledictionis."

He might sanctify the people with [better, *through*] *His own blood, suffered without the gate* (Heb. xiii. 10–12). The apostle draws a comparison between the old and new economy, and exhibits the danger of abiding by the shadow. They who served the tabernacle are they who adhered to the external rites of Judaism, and never penetrated into the inward gospel worship which Christianity has introduced. As contrasted with this, the apostle says, WE HAVE AN ALTAR. A few words will suffice to show the meaning. In the arrangements of the Mosaic worship there were two altars,—the brazen altar of burnt-offering in the court, and the altar of incense in the holy place. To the former the apostle's words clearly refer, according to a phraseology current among the Hebrews, of which we find an example in Malachi (Mal. i. 7): the altar is spoken of as a table furnished with bread.

1. A preliminary comment is necessary as to the meaning of the first of these verses (ver. 10), and whether it is to be taken in connection with the next verses. The altar is described as supplying food,—that is, the flesh of slain victims; and all who ministered in the tabernacle—that is, who were officially connected with its services—had a right to eat of it. Of some of the sacrifices the Israelites generally, the women and children, were allowed to partake; but the reference is specially to the priests, who, according to the law, had their appropriate portions assigned them from the sacrifices brought to the altar. They participated in the thank-offerings, and also in the sin-offerings offered by private individuals (Lev. vi. 16, vii. 5). But this was kept within strictly defined limits. Thus, no priest could eat of the altar in the case of the burnt-offerings: they were wholly to be consumed. Nor could they eat of the altar on the occasion of the public sin-offering on the day of atonement, to which frequent reference is made in this epistle, for no part of it was to be reserved (Lev. xvi. 27). All these were indications of imperfect atonement, and that the great sacrifice was yet to come. And this fact was significant;

like the entire institutions of the first covenant, an actual prophecy of the new covenant.

What altar does the apostle speak of as peculiar to Christianity, when he says, WE HAVE AN ALTAR? The Lutheran
writers, for the most part, understand the wood of the cross,
or the tree to which Peter refers (1 Pet. ii. 24). Others, especially patristic writers, understand the Lord's Supper; a view
which, when once allowed, had a tendency constantly to receive new elements, till another priesthood and sacrifice superseded the one priest and one sacrifice. Others say the altar
means the entire New Testament worship. The altar of which
the apostle speaks, is plainly that on which the Lord offered
His sacrifice; that is, the cross, viewed as the manifestation of
divine justice and holiness. That is our altar in the court of
the Lord's house: there God showed Himself reconciled; there
the Son of God was offered, and poured out His blood abundantly.[1] Of this altar Christians eat without reserve, receiving
the crucified Christ, and having fellowship with Him. On the
other hand, they who served the tabernacle, that is, they who
attached themselves to the rites and ceremonies of the old worship, when all was abrogated by Christ's atonement, preferring
the shadow to the substance, could not eat of the Christian's
altar, and had no right to it.

2. The apostle finds typical significance in the fact that
the bodies of the victims offered as a sin-offering were burned
without the camp. The slain animal was carried without the
camp, by reason of the defilement with which it was laden, and
for which it was rejected, or deserted, by God and man; and
Christ, covered with guilt and defilement, was led without the
gates of Jerusalem, and suspended on the accursed tree, between heaven and earth, as if unworthy of either. The apostle
is the best expounder of the secret meaning of the ceremonial
law; and the meaning of the word WHEREFORE is best elucidated by this interpretation—viz. that the type might be ful-

---

[1] See the Dutch commentators, e.g. D'Outrein, Bonnet, etc., on Hebrews.

filled.[1] That removal of the victims beyond the walls clearly intimated that they were unclean, because the guilt and punishment of the people were imputed to them. They were considered as polluted with the guilt of the people. Now, according to the true meaning of the type, Christ is compared to the ancient sacrifices, the sins of the people being imputed to Him. He was considered as a sinner, and obliged to bear the guilt, the shame, the penalty of others,[2] to suffer without the gate, that He might restore men to the favour and friendship of God. We do not need to insist upon details; but taking into account the point of comparison between type and antitype, we ask, Can these words by any violence be made to mean, as some will have it, that Christ dedicated the Jews to Christianity, or brought them from one profession to another? The comparison instituted between Christ and the ancient sacrifices, whose bodies were burned without the camp, would then be destitute of meaning.

3. Consider the BURNING of the sin-offerings, whose blood was brought by the high priest into the holy of holies on the day of atonement. The connection between the sprinkling of the mercy-seat and the burning of the bodies demands attention. They were both atoning. The act of burning was after the act of carrying the blood into the holiest of all, but how long after it may be difficult to ascertain. As the burning following the sprinkling of the mercy-seat was a type of Christ's suffering without the gate, we may warrantably affirm that this is another proof that the entrance into the holiest of all stood connected with His death, and not with His ascension. This confirms the interpretation already given. The burning, identified as it is with Christ's suffering, followed, and could not have preceded, the sprinkling of the mercy-seat (Lev. xvi. 27, 28).

[1] So Estius, as quoted by Bleek: "ut ille typus V. T. impleretur."

[2] See Albert Schultens' Dutch *Commentary on Heidelberg Catechism*, i. p. 217. Bähr labours in vain to explain away this idea in *Studien und Kritiken*, 1849, p. 936.

We cannot sunder the burning of the bodies of the victims, the second part of the sacrificial ritual, from the sprinkling of the blood, which was the first part; for then the unity of the whole would be destroyed. That the burning of the sacrifice may be correctly apprehended, it must be added that the reference is not to inward holiness, but to vicarious obedience in suffering. This is indisputably proved by the present passage, making it equivalent to the Lord's death without the gate. If the sprinkling of blood sets forth the vicarious endurance of the penalty, the act of burning fitly brings out that active obedience, or positive sinlessness, evinced amid all that was to be endured, which was an odour of sweet smell to the Holy One of Israel (Eph. v. 1). The union of suffering and sinlessness was a sweet-smelling savour. The imperfection of the type, requiring as it did successive acts to bring out what in reality was simultaneous, prevents us from clearly perceiving these two in their combination. Only one thing more must be noticed, viz. the meaning of the fire by which the bodies of the victims were consumed. Already it has been proved that this was intended to figure forth the Holy Ghost, which came down from heaven upon the sacrifice, as the fire from heaven often fell, rendering it acceptable and of sweet-smelling savour to God (see Heb. ix. 14). The burning was vicarious and atoning.

This enables us to meet the modern objection, that the burning of the bodies was not a religious act at all, and had nothing whatever to do[1] with atonement. The two things put together are thus a mere coincidence, without typical significance. But the answer to all this is obvious: the apostle affirms the opposite in terms the most express, for he asserts the typical relation between the two things, according to divine appointment. A typical relation obtains between the two, and they must have the same meaning. On the one hand, the

---

[1] So Hofmann permits himself to speak. See Keil's admirable reply, *Zeitschrift für Lutherische Theologie*, 1857, p. 463.

bodies of the beasts slain for burnt-offerings were burned
without the camp, because they were unclean in consequence
of the sins of the congregation being laid on them; and on
the other hand, Christ, the sinless One, accounted guilty, and
adjudged a criminal by man, was led forth without the gate to
suffer the penalty of death, according to the terms of the law
(Lev. xxiv. 14; Num. xv. 35; Deut. xvii. 5). This was ex-
pulsion from the covenant people.[1] As Caiaphas pronounced
a prophecy without knowing it, so, in condemning Christ to
a malefactor's death without the gate, they fulfilled, without
knowing or intending it, the typical import of the burning of
the bodies of the sin-offerings. According to the divine purpose, He must suffer as a malefactor without the gate, if He
was to suffer the penalty of human guilt. This, according to
the apostle, was the typical significance of that act of burning.

4. Christ's design was, " that He might sanctify the people
with His own blood." This is one of those many final clauses,
introduced by a final particle (ἵνα), which are intended to bring
out divine purpose, or Christ's own design in connection with
His death; and they give us a glimpse into Christ's heart.
In the present instance, the design contemplated by the Lord
in His death, is said to have been the sanctification of the
people—that is, of the people of God, the elect of God. Cast
out by men, and punished as the surety of the guilty, He was
all the while, as the sinless sin-bearer, offering a sacrifice so
acceptable, that He was securing the dedication and separation
of the people to God. This is the relative sanctification, not
the inherent : it is that which immediately results from sacrifice. The great day of atonement did this for Israel in a lower
sphere, cancelling the sins of the year, and setting apart the
people anew. The blood of Christ did it in the higher sphere
for all sins, and for ever.

X. The last passage referring to the atonement is the memorable prayer in which the apostle commends the Hebrew

---

[1] So Bähr happily describes it.

Christians to God: *Now the God of peace, that brought again from the dead our Lord Jesus, that great shepherd of the sheep, through* [literally, *in*] *the blood of the everlasting covenant, make you perfect in every good work to do His will* (Heb. xiii. 20). This passage recapitulates in the form of prayer the contents of the entire epistle, which was specially intended to set forth the nature of Christ's priesthood, and the new covenant of which He is the mediator.

1. A particular title of God, referring to the new relation in which He stands to mankind on the ground of the atonement, is presented in the invocation, "the God of peace." This designation, intimating reconciliation with God,[1] implies that hostility has ceased. When we trace the history of our race, we find that the friendship which man made with Satan caused enmity with God, and that the first proclamation of the gospel in Paradise, foretelling enmity between the serpent and the woman, included a way of peace with God. The ancient types and sacrifices, though inadequate to give this peace, prefigured it till Christ came. The invocation is addressed to the God of peace, once angry, but whose anger is turned away by the atonement, which appeased Him; for in vain would blessings be sought from an angry Judge without the means of reconciliation. But the prayer is offered without fear to a pacified God, who looks not at human amendments or repentance, at human sorrow, humiliation, or gifts presented to Him on the part of those whose personal standing was that of rebels and criminals, but at the sinless life and vicarious sufferings of His Son.

2. The next clause, referring to the resurrection of our Lord, shows that by this fact God is proved to be the God of peace. The resurrection is here ascribed to the Father, because in our redemption He was the source of the great provision, sending the Son and receiving the satisfaction from His hands. The first

---

[1] The phrase ὁ Θεὸς τῆς εἰρήνης cannot refer to peace between Christians themselves. Though De Wette, Lunemann, and Delitzsch so expound it, it is plainly insufficient.

proof of being pacified was given by openly releasing or discharging the Surety on the morning of His resurrection. The apostle deduces the argument that God is reconciled, and His anger turned away, from the historic fact of the resurrection, which proved, if anything could, that He is "the God of peace." The Lord Jesus, in his capacity of Surety, had entered into our obligations in every respect—into prison and judgment for us—and was brought again from the dead by Him who is the fountain of law and justice, because ample satisfaction and payment had been rendered. Had not this been so, God could not have discharged the Surety, and brought Him again from the dead; but He liberated all His people in such a way that Christ stands before our view as the evidence and attestation of their discharge : and hence the apostle in this prayer appeals to all the attributes of God, expecting a display of grace and power for the ends of men's salvation and the welfare of the church of God.

3. It is further added, that all this was IN, or with, THE BLOOD OF THE ETERNAL COVENANT. The dispute among expositors here is, whether to construe these words with the resurrection, intimating that Christ was raised in virtue of the blood of the covenant; or with the Shepherd of the sheep, conveying the sense that the function of the Shepherd is founded on the fact that He bought the sheep with His own blood. An equal number of expositors is found ranged on opposite sides of this point.[1] I am persuaded that the apostle meant to combine both thoughts, and that we are not to think of the resurrection apart from the great Shepherd's function, nor conversely. It is a diversity of view where none should exist, and where conflicting views may be united.

It only remains to notice that this covenant is described with the addition of the term BLOOD, which conveys the idea of sacrificial blood as that on which it is founded.[2]

---

[1] Bleek, De Wette, and Delitzsch construe the words ἐν αἵματι with ἀναγαγών; whereas Lunemann and others connect them with ποιμένα τὸν μέγαν.

[2] See our former volume, on Matt. xxvi. 28.

CHAPTER IV.

THE TESTIMONY OF THE APOSTLE PETER.

SEC. XX.—THE EPISTLES OF PETER.

WE come now to the testimony of Peter, whose activity in the first founding of the Christian church, as the most prominent man of action, was already noticed under the Acts of the Apostles. We here confine ourselves to his epistles. The first of these was addressed to the strangers of the *diaspora* (1 Pet. i. 1), a title which seems an allusion to a class of Jewish Christians rather than a metaphor for their pilgrim life. This at least is the conclusion to which exegetical inquiry in modern days has brought most minds, though the tendency for a long time was different. The words STRANGERS OF THE DISPERSION lead us to regard the epistle as addressed to Jewish believers, whether they originally belonged to the Jerusalem congregation, and went abroad on the errands of their calling, or more probably came under Christian influences on some of those occasions when they came up from Pontus, Galatia, Cappadocia, Asia, and Bithynia, and carried home the truth to be diffused among their Jewish countrymen. The districts named, with the exception of Galatia and Asia, are not precisely in the sphere of Paul's missionary tours. Though it is not our object to discuss the date of Peter's epistle, Weiss' conclusion is not improbable, that it was prior to Paul's residence in Ephesus (Acts xix. 1): certainly it bears all the marks of being composed at an early period of the Christian church.

Peter has been called the apostle of HOPE, as John is of love; and agreeably to this feature of character, the aspect in which he presents the atonement is pre-eminently deliverance from the effects of sin. Peter sustains the character of a witness of Christ's sufferings (1 Pet. v. 1); and his allusions to the blood, the stripes, and the death of Christ, show how fully he had outlived the state of mind which was offended at the idea of a suffering Messiah. The aspects of the Lord's history set on the foreground are the sufferings that were to come on Christ, and the glories that should follow—the themes which the prophets searched into (1 Pet. i. 11). Peter represents the gospel very much in the light of the fulfilment of prophecy, as James represents it in the light of the perfect law. Hence, in his vivid delineation of Christ from personal recollection, he passes from prophecy to his own testimony, blending the two together in the most natural way. He speaks as the eye-witness of the Lord's abasement, and the spectator of that interview on the holy mount when heavenly visitants conferred with Christ about His death, and animated Him in His suffering career (1 Pet. ii. 23; 2 Pet. i. 16). He reproduces the Lord's words, or the Baptist's, in several passages which describe the atonement; and in unambiguous terms brings out the different elements of the doctrine, the nature, and fruits of the Sacrifice.

I. At the commencement of the epistle, Christians are thus described: *Elect according to the foreknowledge of God the Father, through* [better, *in*] *sanctification of the Spirit, unto obedience and sprinkling of the blood of Jesus Christ* (1 Pet. i. 2). The words describe God's election from a threefold point of view: its source in divine foreknowledge; the mode in which it is carried out by sanctification of the Spirit; and the end contemplated, viz. obedience and sprinkling of the blood of Christ. The obedience here named is but another name for faith, or, more strictly, for that obedience of faith which submits to the righteousness of God.[1] An obedience follows faith; but this is the obedience of faith itself (Rom. i. 5; Acts

[1] See Gerhard *on Peter*; also Klinkenberg on the passage.

vi. 7). As God's commandment is to believe, so it becomes a paramount duty to obey, or submit to God's way of salvation (Rom. x. 3).

The next thing contemplated by the election of. Christians, and their separation by the Spirit from the common mass, was "the sprinkling of the blood of Jesus Christ." This sacrificial language receives its illustration from the ancient ritual. Whenever mention is made in the Old Testament of the sprinkling of blood or of ashes, the allusion is to the blood or ashes of victims to which the offerer's guilt was transferred: sprinkling made atonement for the parties spoken of, freeing them from guilt and punishment. That the expressions TO SPRINKLE, and to absolve from guilt, are coincident, may be seen from the passages where the language occurs (Ex. xxix. 21; Num. xix. 13; Ps. li. 7). If justice is to be done to the present passage, and others similar, we must represent the Lord Jesus as an atoning sacrifice, to which the sins and punishment of His people have been transferred; while, on the other side, His merits applied to them serve to expiate their guilt, and present them faultless before God. The words mean that Christ's blood makes atonement for the elect, and that they are chosen of God and separated by the Spirit for this end. An atoning death for sin always preceded, and was presupposed by, the sprinkling. The apostle represents the blood of Christ as sacrificial, a meaning which the word usually bears. This passage limits the sprinkling to persons, without noticing the other sprinkling, more objective in its character, applied to the altar of burnt-offering (Lev. i. 5), to the veil of the sanctuary (Lev. v. 6), and to the mercy-seat on the day of atonement (Lev. xvi. 14). In its application to persons we find two things included—a positive and a negative; the remission of sins, and a provision for securing access with boldness and confidence. Pardon, in a word, was only a pathway to the further privilege of a covenant relation, as in the case of Israel at Mount Sinai (Ex. xxiv. 8).

Possibly, as has been conjectured, Peter only reproduces the ideas which he had heard from the lips of his Lord at the institution of the Supper (Matt. xxvi. 28). The blood shed for many, or sprinkled, as some choose rather to view it, was not only for the remission of sins, but for the institution of the new covenant, replacing that of Sinai. The further idea of a covenant relation secured by the sprinkling of Christ's blood on those who are set apart as Christians, is warranted by Peter's words. Nor is that all: a continuous sprinkling of the blood of Christ to perpetuate that covenant standing, and to adjust the relation afresh when it is disturbed, is also involved in the terms. As the term is used in the Epistle to the Hebrews, sprinkling intimates an action which lies at the foundation of a covenant relation[1] (Heb. xii. 24, x. 22). Whether we look, then, at the words of Christ on the occasion of instituting the Supper, or at Israel's position at Mount Sinai, or at the close connection between the blood of sprinkling and the new covenant, as indicated in the Epistle to the Hebrews, we may safely conclude that the apostle alludes to the founding of a new covenant relation in Christ's blood. The death of Christ atones, and puts away sin; but not only so: it forms a positive covenant relation by which Christians, elected and set apart, become a people of God by the sprinkling of Christ's blood.

II. In a second reference to the death of Christ, Peter connects it with redemption, placing them together as cause and effect: *Ye were not redeemed with corruptible things, as silver and gold, from your vain conversation received by tradition from your fathers; but with the precious blood of Christ, as of a Lamb without blemish and without spot: who verily was foreordained before the foundation of the world* (1 Pet. i. 18, 19). This is an echo of the Lord's own words as to the giving of His life a ransom for many, with perhaps a further allusion to the Baptist's testimony to the Lamb of God. The words are put in

[1] See Weiss' *der Petrinische Lehrbegriff*, p. 271.

such a form and connection as to imply an obvious allusion to the first passover in Egypt, and the subsequent redemption. The apostles have made the doctrine of the atonement more perspicuous and striking by the copious use of this class of terms, which also recall the Old Testament history, where the same ideas are typically exhibited. We have already had occasion to find a sure basis for the exposition of the text before us, in the elucidation of similar passages in due course in the several epistles. The remarks already made on the word RANSOM, as used by our Lord (Matt. xx. 28), may here be recalled.

The primary meaning of the term *redeem* is to deliver from slavery, or captivity under the power of an enemy, by the payment of a ransom. This is the simple meaning of the word, and it precisely corresponds to the English verb *to ransom*, derived from its cognate noun in the very same way. If the Saxon term, indeed, were used instead of the term of Latin origin, it would be the exact equivalent, and not less emphatically convey to an English reader the idea of deliverance from captivity by the payment of a ransom; and we are not to abandon the proper sense while it is compatible with the case in hand. Under an evangelical garb we find, in modern times, a new mode of representing the party to whom the ransom is given, which is very wide of the mark. Thus Stier and Klaiber make use of the term only to explain away its significance. They allow that Christ gave His holy human life and shed His precious blood as a ransom, and they will allow the word, if we wish it, that He PAID the ransom. But when the question is raised, to whom was it paid, and by whom was it received, the divergence becomes apparent. They will not admit that it was offered to God, who, as they represent the matter, is to be viewed as eternally rich, and, whether considered as Love or as Justice, as having need of none. They hold that it was paid to us men, the poor and destitute. In other words, they do not allow that it was paid to God in our stead; for God dispenses an absolute pardon in the exercise of pure love by His Son, only slain in proclaiming this gracious message. They retain the name and neutralize the meaning, or make it a mere metaphor, excluding the idea of an equivalent or satisfaction to the divine law for our deliverance. They hold that, without any reparation to the law of God, men enter into union with Christ, who descended into humanity and lived a sinless human life, which is reproduced in us, His followers, by means of fellowship with Him. Only in this subjective way have His people any benefit from Christ, according to the theory. A change of nature is admitted, but no provision is made for the rectification of man's relation, or for his personal standing before God. The judicial element is discarded, and the claims of the divine law have no place. To this the ready answer is, that man is not merely a nature, but a person who must have a standing in law before the moral Governor of the universe; and the terms connected with man's legal relation are, without exception, connected with the ransom offered to God in our stead by Christ's obedience unto death.

But this leads me further to notice how the two ideas of RANSOM and SACRIFICE, by a natural and easy transition, pass into each other. However these ideas seem to differ, they do not diverge so widely when we attend to the biblical phraseology, as a few remarks will show. What was effected by the ancient sacrifices, was the removal of the threatened penalty. On some occasions the Israelites, stringently bound to provide a satisfaction, were under the necessity of paying a certain RANSOM, which occupied the place of a sacrifice; and this ransom, paid in money, was called an atonement, as it exempted them from punishment (Ex. xxx. 15). The man was considered as a captive or prisoner to a divine retribution, if this was not rendered, whether it required a ransom, properly so called, or a sacrifice. But in all cases the principal matter is the turning away of a threatened calamity by means of the satisfaction (Job xxxiii. 24; Ex. xxi. 30; Ps. xlix. 7). If we keep this in view, we can have no difficulty in perceiving how the death of Christ can be represented in either light, and how the one thought passes over into the other by an easy transition. His blood is thus a *ransom*, and the atonement accomplished by Him is a *redemption*.

This enables us to obviate the often-repeated objection, that these terms are pressed beyond their legitimate significance, and that we attend more to the figure under which the truth is represented than to the thing itself. It is not so: for we hold as strongly as those who make the objection, that this would run counter to all the rules of sound interpretation. But the term means something, and cannot be treated as if it were not employed, or could be ignored; and we must do justice to its import, if we would not incur the deserved blame of indulging in a mere capricious exposition of terms meant to be significant. The question to be determined is: In what sense is the death of Christ called a ransom? In what sense is the deliverance designated a redemption, and derived from the Mediator? And to answer this inquiry, the rules of sound interpretation require not only that we shall examine the import of the terms, but the passages where they are found, the connection of the context, and the appended words which put the ransom and deliverance in the relation of cause and effect.

The opponents of the vicarious satisfaction, when pressed by the consideration that the apostles bring out this causal connection, resort to the following evasion: They say the language may denote absolute liberation, as it comes to us by the proclamation of Christ, its great messenger, who confirmed His testimony by His death.[1] That is to make the allusion to Christ's death nugatory, when the proper import of the terms intimates something much beyond a preaching of unconditional, unpurchased pardon. It contains nothing less than the

---

[1] A strenuous attempt has been made to make good this point by Oltramaire on Rom. iii. 24, and in one of the Latin treatises recently issued at Leyden by Bok on ἀπολύτρωσις, but in vain.

connection of cause and effect, price and deliverance. The language of the apostles on the subject of the ransom and redemption is too express to allow any such evacuation of the meaning, any evasion of this nature. It cannot be expounded in any other sense than this, that the redemption is the direct immediate effect of the ransom or atonement offered. As a captive held in chains was set at liberty when the full ransom was paid, so are the people of Christ liberated by His death from guilt and punishment. If the death of Christ exercised no causal influence at all, if it was but a confirmation of the proclamation of absolute deliverance, why does the Holy Ghost uniformly ascribe to the blood of Christ the character of a ransom?

The question on doctrinal grounds touches the deepest truths; it touches the divine attributes, to which all such questions are and must be run up—the authority of the divine law, the immutable justice, holiness, and truth of God. But does it, as is alleged, more fully display divine love to set forth absolute deliverance? No: that is but indifference to human conduct, concession, indulgence, not love; and we say, with the poet Young, "A God all mercy is a God unjust."

The import of Peter's words may be easily collected. Their connection and significance may be thus stated: After an exhortation to walk in fear, the apostle adds, that the death of Christ, considered as a ransom, redeemed the believers, to whom he wrote, from their vain, ungodly conversation. He intimates that the blood of Christ—that is, the whole surety-obedience of Christ—won for them holiness as well as reconciliation; for it is Peter's manner, when touching on the death of Christ, to unite the atoning and sanctifying elements. The thought is, that a sanctified life has its ground and possibility in the fact of the objective redemption from guilt, or in the blood of Christ as the ransom.

The more necessary is it to advert to this, to obviate the conclusion that, because the death of Christ had in view this liberation from moral corruption, it could not be a satisfaction to the justice of God. These two things are not opposites, but related as primary and secondary. The primary design is atonement, and deliverance from a liability to eternal death. The secondary design, or that which is consequent on the attainment of the former, is this redemption or rescue from unholy conduct. The former is preparatory to the latter, and the connection may thus be stated: Forgiveness of sins is directly effected by the blood of Christ; the forgiveness of sin paves the way for, and secures, the gift of the Holy Ghost; and where the Holy Ghost is, men are delivered[1] from their former vain conduct, according to the spirit of the age and the traditions handed down to them.

The apostle, too, lays stress on the greatness and value of the ransom by which we are redeemed. He exhibits the blood of Christ as the ransom, when he connects the redemption and the blood by a relation of cause and effect. To make this apparent, he compares two different kinds of redemption: one by corruptible things, as silver and gold; the other by a ransom infinitely more costly. This contrast proves that the death of Christ is a true ransom, and that the comparison is not between a proper and a metaphorical redemption, but between one effected by silver and gold, and another brought about by no lower ransom than the blood of Christ. He names the price, and points to the result—deliverance in the first case from merited punishment, and in the second from vain conduct.

Christ's blood, the price of our redemption, and described as precious, suggests, by way of contrast, the blood of lower animals constituting the ransom in typical ages before the reality was ushered in. The point of the comparison, or that which both had in common, was the satisfaction necessary for the liberation. We have seen how naturally, in the phraseology of Israel, the terms ransom and sacrifice passed over into

---

[1] See Gess, *Jahrbücher für Deutsche Theologie*, 1857; also Lechler, *das apostolische Zeitalter*, p. 178; and Thomasius, *Christi person.* iii. p. 143.

each other, and came to be united on the ground that any one neglecting the ceremonial precepts became by that neglect a captive to the retributive government of God, and a sacrifice or ransom redeemed him. When the blood of Christ is here contrasted with the ransoms or sacrifices current in the ancient Israelitish community, the comparison must either intimate that our liberation stands in the same connection, or be inept and nugatory.

In addition to this, let the particle by which the apostle introduces the allusion to Christ as the unblemished and spotless Lamb be carefully noted: " AS of a Lamb." It is not the particle of comparison, but of explanation, expressing the reason why the blood of Christ was so infinitely precious. The original word rendered AS, or AS BEING (ὡς), serves frequently to intimate the truth of a thing, or such a quality as belongs to a person or economy. Many passages serve to show this (John i. 14 ; Matt. xxi. 26 ; 2 Pet. i. 3 ; Phil. ii. 8 ; 2 Cor. ii. 17, v. 20). The important thought is, that Christ's blood is not to be considered as that of a teacher confirming his doctrine by his death, or of a hero exposing himself for his country, but sacrificial blood, as of a spotless lamb, whether the allusion be to the passover in Egypt, which is probable from the further reference to redemption, or to the lamb of the daily sacrifice. Ransom and sacrifice are so closely allied, that the one idea, from the nature of the case, at once passes over into the other.

Thus His blood was sacrificially shed ; and it is further designated PRECIOUS, or of infinite value, from the fact that it was the sacrifice of a sinless person. To go back to the type, the Lamb must needs be without blemish and without spot (Ex. xii. 5 ; Lev. ix. 3): for the perfection of the animal was not a mere prerequisite or condition of the sacrifice ; rather it was an element of it, offered in and with the blood. And the sinless perfection of Jesus was not a mere indispensable prerequisite to the atonement, but an integral part of it. His blood, viewed as sacrificial, possessed infinite value, because it was the blood not merely of the best of men, but of the eternal Son of God, and adequate to meet the wants of countless millions of mankind.   The apostle connects the high value of the sacrifice with the absolutely sinless purity of Christ. But the subjoined words, referring to the eternal fore-appointment of Christ and the federal transactions of the Trinity, recall the dignity of the Lord as lending a divine value to the whole.   Not one element then, but several, enter into the infinite value of this precious blood.

The remoter effect of Christ's redeeming blood, as here stated, is moral renovation.   It has sanctifying efficacy, and prompts the Christian too, in the way of motive, to walk in fear (ver. 17).   But this presupposes the remission of sins, and the acceptance of our persons, as the immediate effect of the Lord's sacrifice.   The sacrifice conditions the sanctifying change, or spiritual renovation, which sets us free from our vain conversation according to the course of the world.   The apostle's words assume that the Lord's death effects the remission of sins, and then gives rise to a sanctification of life or moral renovation.

III. Another decisive passage as to the nature of the atonement occurs in the following chapter: *Who His own self bare our sins in His own body on* [better, *up to*] *the tree, that we, being dead to sins, should live unto righteousness: by whose stripes ye were healed* (1 Pet. ii. 24).   The apostle had addressed Christian slaves, a class of men who suffered deeply from the cruelty, caprice, and absolute power of heathen masters.   Animating them to patience, he pointed to Christ as the grand pattern, who, when reviled, reviled not again, but committed Himself to God, the righteous Judge (vers. 18–23).   The apostle does not stop short there, but adds, by a natural transition of thought, that Christ's sufferings were more than an example. He mentions two things : first, what Christ did for us in His sufferings and death ; secondly, for what end all was done. He shows how painful, and yet voluntary, were those sufferings, how innocent and elevated in their nature. First, when it is said that HE BORE OUR SINS in His body, the shade of meaning conveyed by the terms is, that He bore our sins as a heavy burden. This will appear by a few considerations drawn from the primary meaning of the verb, from the accessory words, and from the context.

a. As to the primary meaning of the verb (ἀναφέρειν), it denotes " to carry up," " to bear upwards." From that primary signification arises a secondary or metaphorical sense in the most natural way, viz. " to offer in sacrifice." No writer uses the Greek verb in any other way, as will appear to any one who institutes a strict inquiry. It is used in its primary signification, when it is said that the Israelites, at the exodus from Egypt, *brought up* the bones of Joseph (Josh. xxiv. 21) ; when David *brought up* the bones of Saul and Jonathan from Beth-shan (2 Sam. xxi. 13) ; when our Lord *brought up* the disciples to the Mount of Transfiguration (Matt. xvii. 1) ; when He was *carried up* to heaven at His own ascension (Luke xxiv. 51). In the secondary signification, naturally derived from the former, it denotes *to offer in sacrifice ;* the allusion being to the fact that the victim was carried up to the altar, which was always erected on a raised or elevated spot (Jas. ii. 21 ; Heb. vii. 27).

b. The accessory words to be next noticed supply another reason for abiding in this case by the primary signification of the word. Two expressions render it absolutely necessary to retain that signification; for the statement that He bore our sins IN HIS OWN BODY, and next, that He bore them UP TO THE TREE,[1] can be fitly interpreted only when we maintain the primary meaning.

c. The context was further mentioned, as requiring that the passage shall be understood of the bearing of sin as a heavy burden. A few words will show this. The apostle had ex-

---

[1] See Van Voorst, *de Usu Verborum cum Præpos. Compositorum in N. T. ;* also Grotius, *Annot. in N. T.*

horted Christian servants, by the Lord's example, to the patient
endurance of the injurious treatment to which they were exposed ; and the notion of bearing a burden is so plainly contained in the passage, that, without it, no natural connection
could obtain between the context and the clause under our
notice. A threefold view of Christ is given : the patient
sufferer who, when reviled, reviled not again; the faultless
sufferer, who did no sin ; and the vicarious sufferer, who bore
our sins in His own body. This makes it evident that we
must retain the primary meaning of the verb.

On these grounds, we deny the competency of the translation, " He took away our sins." To this rendering many in
former and recent times have given a preference, for various
reasons. By most of the supporters of this rendering the idea
attached to the phrase is, that of removing future sin by moral
amendment. But, not to mention other arguments against
that interpretation, let it suffice that this idea is intimated in
the last clause of the verse, when the apostle mentions the
ultimate end contemplated by the atonement; and to make
both clauses affirm the same moral reformation, would not only
be a tautology, but make a matter the reason of itself. That
is decisive against the rendering, " He took away our sins."
According to the other rendering, the atonement is represented
as conditioning moral renovation.

But even if such a rendering could be admitted, it would
not make for the opponents of the vicarious satisfaction. The
question would still recur, How were they THEN AND THERE
taken away ? The limitation of this removal, or taking away
of sin, to Christ's own body on the tree, would still lead to the
conclusion that this was accomplished eighteen centuries ago,
and therefore would be tantamount to the atonement of the
cross. The language is so environed and limited by the other
words, that they must be taken as affirming that sin was taken
away in His own body on the tree. Sin was thus taken away
by a fact in connection with Christ's cross, and this virtually

amounts to expiation. Peter's words refer all this to the cross ; and it is simply inconsistent with the apostle's design to affirm, as Socinians were wont to do, that this was but an intermediate stage in Christ's way to heaven, where sin was actually taken away. It will not do to say, as they said, that the cross does all this, as it persuades men to believe and lead a virtuous life, which is followed in due course by the taking away of sin. The words cannot be understood in that sense. They must be understood of a result effected in His own body.

This leads me to an explanation which finds favour with a class who feel that they must say something about Christ's connection with human sin, but are committed to a disavowal of Christ's vicarious sacrifice : they make Him bear sin in His own body, because He received the outburst of human malice and passion against Himself. That we are warranted to call a mere evasion; for it changes the terms, substituting for the sins which He bore, the idea of malicious men opposing Him, and acting out their sinful feelings against Him. The answer to this is, that it runs counter to the Old Testament phraseology on the subject of bearing sin ; that no instance can be adduced where the phrase TO BEAR SIN has such an acceptation ; that certainly it does not so occur in a passage from Lamentations sometimes adduced in this sense (Lam. v. 7); and that, had Peter's design been to express this idea, he would have used wholly different language, as may be seen by comparing what he did say in the book of Acts (Acts ii. 23, iii. 13).

After removing these false comments, it remains that we bring out the positive ideas contained in the verse. These are specially two—vicarious sin-bearing, and priestly action on the cross ; and to both these we must specially advert.

1. The words imply that Christ, by His own act as well as by God's appointment, bore our sins in His own body, connecting Himself with sinful humanity, and taking our sins in such a way as to incorporate them with Himself, or conjoin them with His own body. The quotation from Isaiah estab-

lishes this still more precisely. He made our sins His own, in such a way that they adhered to Him in the only sense in which they could adhere to the sinless humanity of the incarnate Son—by suretyship and imputation. That is brought out in the words, WHO HIS OWN SELF. He became personified guilt: it was made His by His own act and His Father's will. The words refer to the efficacy of His person in the atonement, showing so marked an antithesis between Himself and our sin, that no man without prejudice can fail to apprehend the idea of substitution and sin-bearing. When a physician makes use of means, we cannot say that he himself wrought the cure. But of Christ it is said that He Himself bore our sins, and expiated them by transferring our obligations to His own person. He made them His, and bore them, that their guilt might not be imputed to us.

2. Another idea is Christ's priestly action on the cross. The word here used stamps the character of a priestly action on this spontaneous offering of Christ. He carried our sins up to the tree; in other words, He carried up His own body, laden with our sins, to the tree. The language is so put, that we cannot exclude the sacrificial idea. To that tree the Lord, by His own spontaneous act, carried up our sins, incorporating them with Himself, and consummating the oblation by His priestly act. It does not matter whether we take the wood of the cross as His altar, with some of the best commentators both in the Reformed and Lutheran Church, or prefer, with others, to abstain from such a definition of the altar. One thing is obvious, the idea is sacrificial. But when we decide for the allusion to a priestly sacrifice, it by no means follows that we must necessarily interpret the word SINS here used as meant to denote sin-offering. The language in the plural cannot naturally admit that sense. Rather the apostle alludes to our countless sins, viewed as guilt. What does the apostle mean when he names Christ's "body" as bearing the sin? It is a synecdoche for the person. He does not mean that our Lord bore

sin in His body alone. This appears very evidently from the other phrase, "who His own self." The body in which the Lord bore our sins is only contrasted with animal sacrifices.

Nor is this text to be interpreted as teaching that Christ was the sin-bearer only during the hours when He hung on the cross,—a notion to which James Alting gave currency in Holland two centuries ago, and which has been revived among certain crude religionists in our own time.[1] Alting maintained that our Lord's sufferings were divided into those borne in His encounters with Satan, or such as were warlike, and those endured as a satisfaction for sin, limited to the three hours on the cross when the sun was darkened. That notion was repudiated by the best divines on all sides, who expressed their conviction that the whole previous life of Christ came within the range of sin-bearing. They who appeal to this text as lending countenance to the theory that sin-bearing was limited to the time of the crucifixion, draw their argument from the English version, in this case palpably defective. The text does not say that sin-bearing coincided with the time of Christ's suspension on the cross. Still less does it say that He did not come within this experience in the previous stages of His life. It intimates that He who bore our sins all through His earthly history, bore them up to the cross, to be finally and for ever expiated.

We do not hesitate to declare for the use of the biblical expression SIN-BEARING, in preference to all the artificial language which many would put in its place. Some, without weighing the advantages of abiding by the nomenclature of Scripture, choose rather to speak of our punishment than of our sins being laid on Christ. The import in substance amounts to the same thing. But why alter the biblical phrase *sin-bearing* for any other mode of speech? We forfeit precision, for without sin-bearing punishment could have no place. God

---

[1] The Plymouthists adduce this text for their notion that Christ bore sin only on the tree, but mistake the sense.

made our sins meet on the Surety, in such a way that, from the time of the incarnation till He gave up His spirit on the cross, He appeared with them at every moment. He appeared with them before the divine tribunal, and even confessed them to His Father (Ps. xl. 12, lxix. 5).

This of course assumes that in this great transaction, whether we call it sin-bearing or the imputation of sin, nothing is out of keeping with truth. Sins were not charged to Christ in such a sense that He was held to have personally done the deeds when He bore their guilt. No reasonable mind ever adopted a supposition so unwarrantable. The distinction was always drawn between the personal and the official in all the language used of the vicarious satisfaction; and had due regard been paid to this distinction, as is always done by intelligent expounders of the Scripture, much of the revolting language used by the opponents of the vicarious satisfaction, and many of the difficulties which they have conjured up, would have been forestalled and obviated. On the one hand, sin is so personal a thing, that it never ceases to be recalled as ours, as a source of humiliation, even when its guilt is cancelled; for we may say, with Milton, "Who can undo the past? not God Himself." On the other hand, sins were charged to Christ in such a sense that they were transferred to Him, as He sustained the person of the sinner; and thus they are no longer ours, but His, who, as the sinless surety, condescended to bear them in His own body to the tree. They are to the believing mind still the cause of humiliation, for it will be always true that we committed them; and we must say, These sins are ours. On the other hand, seeing them in the light of Christ's cross, we also say, These sins are no longer ours, in consequence of the expiation of the cross, and are extinguished or annihilated as if they had never been. The exchange of places explains all. This can be fully maintained in harmony with the truth of God. I only add, that Christ's bearing of our sins was meant to fill the whole horizon of the church's view, as if nothing

were seen between us and God but the Surety surrendering
Himself as the sin-bearer, and satisfying for sin.

3. The next thing to be noticed is the final cause or end
contemplated in the divine plan by the atonement: "that (ἵνα)
we, being dead to sin, might live unto righteousness." The two
clauses of the verse are connected by the particle of design
(ἵνα), so as to show that Christ's death aimed at moral renovation as well as pardon. And this, as we noticed above, is
decisive as to the strict connection between the atonement and
holiness.

This fact is established, whether we hold with some, that
Peter has his own phraseology and phase of thought, or hold
with others, that we have a mode of expression common to
Paul and Peter. The former view renders the words, "that
we, being FREED from sins, might live unto righteousness;" and
the sense is, that we are freed from the heavy guilt of sin, and
no more disquieted by it. That is the practical end kept in
view by those to whom the atonement is applied, and more
and more to be attained. The words may admit this interpretation, which is supported by many excellent expositors, but
not so naturally. The other view is, that we have a style of
thought common to Paul and Peter, meaning, according to the
translation of the authorized English version, that we died
with Christ in that atoning death. We shared so fully in that
one act of our Representative, that we suffered the punishment
of sin, and fulfilled the divine claims in Him, as truly as if
we had personally performed it all. This is preferable, and
does greater justice to the language: it retains the contrast
between death and life; it shows more forcibly in what way
the Christian died TO sin, and is discharged from its guilt.

The important thought, in a doctrinal point of view, is, that
the atonement procured a PREMIAL LIFE, or paved the way,
according to the divine aim, for a life of holy obedience. That
is described in the way of purchase rather than in the way of
human motive. This was the ulterior end for which the Lord

bore our sins in His own body. The expiation of sin, and the acceptance of our persons, contemplated that further object.

Sin is considered as a potentate, or master, exercising authority over a slave. Death liberates the slave; and when the penal infliction due to sin ran its course on the Surety, with whom we were one in the eye of God, we died to sin. His death and our death are not regarded as two separate acts, of which the one is like the other, but one and the same. To understand how the action of one may be for many, we have only to recall the first Adam: by one man sin entered into the world, and it was the act of one for many. According to apostolic language, we may either say, Christ died for us, to deliver our persons from guilt, and secure the renovation of our natures to newness of life; or, We obeyed when He obeyed, and died when He died in that one representative act, that, as the recipients of a new premial life, we may walk in holy obedience. The latter is preferable. We find it repeated in the Pauline epistles in various forms, and particularly in the phraseology that we were co-crucified with Christ in that one corporate surety-act.[1]

The doctrine contained in this important clause is, that only as sin is expiated and the sinner discharged, can a holy life begin; and that there is no way apart from this for the dedication of our lives to God. Discharged by the sin-bearing death of Christ from the captivity under which we were held, we are prepared for personal dedication, and a holy obedience to God different from the previous life of sin. This was the great end for which Christ bore our sins in His own body on the tree.

IV. We come now to a statement which, of all the passages, gives us the clearest description of substitution and vicarious punishment: *For Christ also hath once suffered for*

---

[1] See our remarks above on Rom. vi. 1–11, and on 2 Cor. v. 14. See Doedes, p. 327, who makes ἀπογινόμενοι not *dead*, but *sundered*, or *having done* with. See Weiss.

sins, the just for the unjust [better, *the righteous for the unrighteous*]*, that He might bring us to God, being put to death in
the flesh, but quickened by the Spirit* (1 Pet. iii. 18). This verse
is introduced as grounding the practical duty that Christians
must willingly suffer for righteousness' sake (vers. 14, 17). The
expressions may be an echo of similar terms used by the Lord
Himself on various occasions, combined with others derived
from Isaiah's prophecy. They teach, in unfigurative language,
that Christ, personally righteous, suffered punishment for sins
in room of the guilty. The apostle's object is to bring out that
the effect of the atonement is to bring back to God, or restore
to priestly nearness and priestly service, those who by sin had
been widely separated and estranged from Him.

1. The first thing mentioned is, that HE SUFFERED FOR SINS.
The meaning of the expression, which it is necessary accurately
to apprehend, is that sin was the cause or ground on account
of which He suffered. Had there been no sin in us, Christ
would not have been required to suffer. But because we were
guilty, or liable to punishment, He underwent the suffering.[1]
The meaning of the words, " He suffered for sins," is self-
evident from the language of ordinary life. Thus, in common
discourse, when we say of any one that he suffered for his sins,
the import is that he bore their punishment; and no other
sense can be put upon the words by any hearer or reader.
And, in like manner, when we read that Christ the righteous
suffered for sins, which are further mentioned as the sins of the
unrighteous, the import is, that the innocent took upon Himself the sins of others, and suffered the punishment which the
guilty should have endured. That is the natural and necessary
meaning. Lest it should be alleged there was no relation between the sufferings of Christ and those of guilty men, Peter
says, in terms the most precise, that He suffered for sins, and
for the guilty. Nor can any other interpretation of the words

---

[1] Doedes (*l.c.*) shows that Christ's death was made necessary by the sins of
the ἄδικοι.

be made even probable. They cannot, for example, mean that Christ died to turn men away from future sinning, for that could not be called suffering for sin. To bring out that sense, many additional words would be necessary, whether it were understood as a motive on the part of man, or as an influence on the part of God. The suffering is spoken of as caused by actual guilt, past and present sin, of which the Christian is already conscious. When Paul speaks of Christ giving Himself for our sins, and unites with this a further reference to a future amendment or deliverance from this present evil world, the two things are plainly distinguished from each other (Gal. i. 4). As little can the words refer to the sinful passions of men, or to the bitter hostility with which the Jews were animated when they crucified the Lord: that could not be called a suffering for sins. The allusion is to the actual guilt of men, which must be expiated by punishment. This is the result or full effect of what was already noticed,—the bearing of sin in His own body to the tree. Here we may take in the phrase, *being put to death in the flesh*. This peculiar style of language applied to Christ, denotes His abased, sin-bearing humanity (see Heb. v. 7), contrasted with the state in which He now is, and implies all the infirmities proper to humanity in this life, and which could be in Christ along with a perfect immunity from sin. The whole time of His humiliation, from the manger to the cross, is thus described (2 Cor. v. 16); and the phrase, "put to death in the flesh," has reference either to the sin-bearing condition of the Lord, or to the guilt and cursed death to which He was subjected.

2. The next thing requiring notice is the emphatic allusion to the Lord's sinlessness as the Righteous One by way of eminence, or the one Righteous Person as contradistinguished from all men as sinners: He suffered, THE RIGHTEOUS FOR THE UNRIGHTEOUS. The term RIGHTEOUS denotes one approved by God when tried by the standard of the law. The word intimates perfect sinlessness of nature, and a life adjusted to the idea of

man's normal relation toward God. When it is added that He suffered, the righteous for the unrighteous, the words imply, in connection with the previous allusion to sin, that He was the innocent for the guilty, the pure for the impure, the holy for the unholy, in all the steps to which, as the surety of sinners, He must needs subject Himself. His sufferings were not on His own account, nor from the mere course of events or laws of evil in a sinful world, but the result of substitution in the room of others. The nature of the transaction, and the marked antithesis, imply that the suffering was in the room of the guilty; and no unbiassed mind can peruse these words in their natural import, with the desire to know simply what is written, without arriving at this conclusion. The words, even with the utmost violence, cannot be made to yield any other meaning than that of vicarious suffering. What is wanted is a full recognition of the claims of the divine law, for the atonement was but a satisfaction to them in all their breadth and extent. The main position, to which every one must come who has right conceptions of the extent of the divine law and of its unbending claims, is, that Christ's satisfaction is perfectly identical with that which men should themselves have rendered; and in the atonement of Christ we are to read off the unalterable claims of the divine law. We must argue from man's obligations to the nature of the Lord's undertaking, and conversely from the latter to the former.

The penal suffering or passive obedience must come to its rights. The infliction or visitation He suffered could be nothing else than a retribution—a suffering FOR SINS, as here expressed —the wages of sin. The active obedience must also come to its rights; for many too exclusively fix attention on the death of Christ, without taking into account, as they ought to do in speaking of the necessity of a satisfaction to justice, the sinless nature and immaculate obedience of Him who is here called the Righteous One. Some make His sinlessness a mere condition or indispensable prerequisite to the atonement; but it is

more. Others maintain that Christ's active obedience was a
service which He, in common with every rational creature,
owed to God on His own account; but they forget that He
was under no obligation either to take flesh, or to fulfil what
He did fulfil in humanity on His own account. The active
obedience was an essential factor or constituent element in the
atonement.

3. Another thing calling for notice is the declaration that
Christ ONCE SUFFERED. By that expression the apostle does
not mean that all penal suffering was confined to one time—
to the hours when He was suspended on the cross. The expression intimates that He suffered once for all, so that there
was no more need to repeat the sacrifice, as in the case of the
Old Testament sacrifices. His one all-sufficient atonement has
everlasting validity, needing no repetition. The allusion is
plainly to a suffering which on the one hand pervaded the
whole tenor of His earthly history, and on the other reached
its culmination on the cross (Heb. ix. 25–28). It is the more
necessary to advert to the true meaning of the expression, as it
has been thought to lend countenance to the notion that the
vicarious sufferings of Christ were limited to the time of the
crucifixion. But the apostle's aim in the use of this expression, is to contrast the completeness of His suffering obedience,
which comprehends His whole life, with the notion that it
needed a repetition. Even the Jewish sacrifices were not done
at one moment, but presupposed many successive steps; and
our Lord's sacrifice took in His entire earthly course. And it is
said that He once suffered, to intimate that the atoning work
which satisfied the law of God and procured remission was
limited to His first advent, as contrasted with anything performed during His present mediatorial activity or at His
second advent. It was once, and only once, as contrasted
with the oft-repeated sacrifices of the old economy. The Lord's
atoning work required and admitted no repetition.

4. The end contemplated by the Lord's death is next

noticed: THAT HE MIGHT BRING US TO GOD. The death of Christ attains this end only as it procures the remission of sins, and so delivers us from the dividing element which separates between God and man. The great end for which the Lord died was to restore us to the divine communion—to friendly intercourse and priestly privilege, after a complete disunion. The peculiar shade of meaning ascribed to the expression is very variously given. Thus, some have regarded it more in the light of inward renovation and dedication, while others make it identical with reconciliation. A third class are of opinion that, while it includes the divine favour, it principally alludes to the possession of future blessedness and the life with God above. The expression may be taken in the latter comprehensive sense. But it seems specially to contain an allusion to the restoration of access or nearness to God, and the priestly privilege,[1] in which these feelings find their fullest scope. They have an open door of entrance—a deliverance from fear and the depressing sense of guilt, which previously shut them out from God, and prevented every activity or liberty of approach. They are now made nigh as priests, and can do everything as a priestly service (1 Pet. ii. 5, 9). This was the privilege faintly set forth, but never realized, by the separation of Israel.

But the words, while tracing this great privilege to the Saviour's sufferings as the meritorious cause, refer also in no obscure way to the activity of the risen Christ. By whom are Christians brought to God? By Christ, in His function of risen Mediator or great High Priest, the introducer,[2] whose action is here distinctly intimated after His redemption-work was completed. Whether we refer the language to Oriental court ceremonies, and suppose an allusion to the introduction

---

[1] Some, as Calvin, make the προσαγάγη refer to inward renewing. Weiss, *Petrin. Lehrbegriff*, correctly refers it to the Christian's priestly standing.

[2] There is frequent mention of Christ's introduction (προσαγωγή, Rom. v. 2, Eph. ii. 12). Comp. Calvin.

effected by the favourite or son of a monarch, or simply call in the idea of Christ as the way to the Father (John xiv. 6), and as our introducer, we cannot fail to notice the action of our risen Lord and Saviour: it is He who brings us to God.

V. Still another passage must be noticed, though closely connected with the former: *Forasmuch, then, as Christ hath suffered for us in the flesh, arm yourselves with the same mind; for he that hath suffered in the flesh hath ceased from sin* (1 Pet. iv. 1). Peter returns to the same theme, which he expresses in the same terms; and the obvious conclusion is, that we must take the allusion to Christ's sufferings in the same sense. There is nothing to warrant a different exposition of the words, as the apostle returns to the same thought, and, indeed, in a formal way recapitulates its substance after completing the intervening parenthesis (1 Pet. iii. 19–22). When he resumes his previous expressions, he can only refer to Christ's vicarious sufferings in the flesh. And he bids the Christians realize the fact, that in Christ's sufferings, as the representative or surety of all believers, they were co-crucified or co-sufferers. The language goes much beyond a mere allusion to Christ's example, carrying with it the notion of two separate and similar actions parallel to each other. This is but one.

Here, then, we have another instance in which Peter and Paul use nearly the same phraseology in speaking of our death to sin; and this so far from offering a difficulty, or inclining us to make a difference when there is none, is only what was to be expected (compare 1 Pet. ii. 24). Any other explanation is in the last degree unnatural. They who represent the expressions as alluding to what Christ encountered in His earthly life from wicked men, and explain the second clause of the believer suffering in Christ's cause and after His example, can produce nothing to satisfy the forcible terms here used as to ceasing from sin. To allege that the words mean only, that he who suffers in the cause of Christ has broken with sin, or testifies that he no more obeys the will of the world, is to evacuate words of their significance. It makes the whole clause unmeaning. The best expositors of the Patristic and Reformation schools have agreed to explain the expression, " He that has suffered in the flesh hath ceased from sin," in the Pauline sense of suffering or dying with Christ[1] (Rom. vi. 7). Thus the meaning of the expression will be, that we suffered as one person with Christ. Peter considers Christians as one person with Christ, as suffering when He suffered, and paying the last tribute to sin—their old master and tyrant—when we died with Christ. There are two modes of speaking in reference to the atonement, either of which presupposes and involves the other. We may either say, " Christ suffered for sins, the just for the unjust;" and then we describe the Surety as interposing between God and us: or we may say, "He that suffered in the flesh," or suffered in the Surety, or in that obedience unto death finished by Him as a public person, has been discharged from sin, or parted company with sin. The person who is regarded at the divine tribunal—as every believer is regarded—as a co-sufferer with Christ, or crucified with Christ (Gal. ii. 20), is absolved from sin, dead to sin. He is here described as having ceased from sin; that is, as one who has done with sin, and has no more connection with it as his master. This naturally flows from the representative capacity of Christ and His vicarious atonement. But how could such a thought be deduced from the sufferings of Christ, and how could we be regarded as suffering with Him, if He did not suffer in our room and stead? The apostles, when they connect our sanctification with the death of Christ, always presuppose His surety-satisfaction in our stead. This enables us to meet the only plausible objection to the interpretation now advanced, viz. that the word FLESH must be taken in two different senses in the two different clauses of this verse. By no means. It has the same sense in both, denoting Christ's representative suffering, and our act, considered as one with Him in God's account.

[1] Œcumenius says: ὁ παθὼν ἐν σαρκὶ ἀντὶ ὁ ἀποθανὼν (Rom. vi. 8).

The only further point to be noticed in the verse is, that the Christian must realize all this, and arm himself with the same mind. There is a divine fact; but it must be apprehended and felt, and the inward realization of that objective fact is the Christian's armour in the way of motive. He must apprehend his discharge from sin in Christ (Rom. vi. 11). And this forcibly proves how much, in the practical conduct of life, the apostle deduced all privileges and all motives from the fact of the atonement.

The SECOND EPISTLE OF PETER contains less express allusion to the atonement. Nor should this excite surprise, as it was directed against a class of gnostic errorists, imbued with an Antinomian spirit, and scoffers in regard to the second advent; and this gave a peculiar tone to the epistle; for the genuineness of which, notwithstanding all the doubts which many have expressed, the church has a satisfactory amount of evidence, external and internal. It bears to have been written by the aged Peter toward the close of his apostolic labours (2 Pet. i. 14).

The sole passage that bears reference to the atonement is the prophetic announcement of false teachers, who were to bring in heresies, *even denying the Lord that bought them* (2 Pet. ii. 1). The term Lord (δεσπότην) has special emphasis, denoting a Lord who rules over others with unlimited power. While ostensibly appearing to serve Christ, they in substance deny His dominion and atoning sacrifice, spreading views at variance with these fundamental doctrines. This passage, considered in the light of an efficacious atonement securing the redemption of the true church (Acts xx. 28), is not without its difficulties, and is variously expounded; being the passage, in fact, in which the Lutheran and Arminian polemical writers uniformly intrench themselves and defy assault. It cannot fairly be adduced as impugning the biblical doctrine of the special redemption of the elect (Eph. v. 25); and two explanations have been given by those who maintain that, according to Scripture, the atonement is at once special and efficacious. The first mode, not so satisfactory, holds there is no allusion to Christ's death; that there is no mention of Christ, but of a Master,— a word not elsewhere applied to Christ, and rather applicable to God; no allusion to Christ's blood, sufferings, and death, as the ransom; nor of deliverance from Satan and the bondage of sin; and that the whole must therefore be referred to the outward relation which the false teachers occupy to God, as employing them in His church. That exposition does no justice to the term BOUGHT. The comment of Piscator and of the Dutch annotations is much to be preferred, viz. that these false teachers are described according to their own profession and the judgment of charity. They gave themselves out as redeemed men, and were so accounted in the judgment of the church while they abode in her communion. This is simple and natural. The passage by no means affirms that any but the true church or the sheep of Christ are truly bought by atoning blood.

CHAPTER V.

THE TESTIMONY OF THE APOSTLE JOHN.

SEC. XXI.—THE EPISTLES OF JOHN.

JOHN was reserved, with his calm contemplative mind, to lay a new impress on the Christian church, already founded by the labours of Peter and Paul. The activity of John presupposes the labours of Paul, and takes for granted, too, that the conflict on the subject of the law has been terminated. The disciple whom Jesus loved, less a man of action than of intuition, seems to have received into himself all the impressions to be derived from the life and death of his Lord, and all the experience to be drawn from the first founding of the Christian church, in order to appear upon the field in due season, when the rest of the apostles had passed away, and errorists began to arise,—to encourage and edify the church by new elements. His writings were sent forth long after the other inspired documents.

The first Epistle of John, supposed by some to have been a companion document to his Gospel, recalls in many ways the Lord's own words. None of the apostles in a brief epistle more explicitly refers to the atonement; and a few peculiarities may be noticed.

a. John most copiously expatiates on the LOVE of God.. And it is worthy of remark that, of all the apostles, he most frequently used the term PROPITIATION, which takes for granted divine WRATH against sin. The one suggests and presupposes the other.

b. A second point that may be noticed is: John, in delineating the work of atonement, commonly connects the divine Sonship with the sacrifice—as was indeed to be expected from the high conceptions everywhere expressed of the personal dignity of Christ. Sometimes he does this in direct terms, sometimes more suggestively.

c. Nor can we fail to notice another peculiarity : he attaches himself closely to the Old Testament doctrine of sacrifice in alluding to the blood of Christ (1 John i. 7 ; Rev. i. 5). The greatest mistakes of expositors have arisen from not keeping in view the sacrificial vocabulary, and allusions to the ancient worship occurring in his style. Thus, he describes the Lord as coming not by water only, but by water and blood (1 John v. 6): in the Apocalypse he twenty-seven times designates the exalted Christ as THE LAMB, recalling His humiliation as the ground of the dominion ; and no one shows more clearly that forgiveness comes directly from the atonement, not from moral amendments. His type of doctrine is the following :—The Eternal Life has been manifested to bring back to men that life which lies in fellowship with God. Before that could be effected, the fountain of death, which lies in sin, must be removed; and the atonement enters as the provision which restores men to fellowship with Him who is LIFE and LIGHT as well as LOVE.

I. The first allusion to the atonement is in the first section : *If we walk in the light, as He is in the light, we have fellowship one with another, and the blood of Jesus Christ His Son cleanseth us from all sin* (1 John i. 7). The context amounts to this: God is light, and in Him is no defilement at all : if we claim to have fellowship with Him, and indulge in unholy conduct out of keeping with union to Him, we are false pretenders : only as we walk in the light have we fellowship with Him and each other. Here it recurs to the apostle that the Christian's walk in the light, far from reaching steady, unsinning fellowship, contracts ever recurring taints, for which a cleansing is to be provided. The last clause of the verse, which might be marked off by a colon, and begin with an *also*, thus announces this provision :

2 F

" Also the blood of Jesus Christ His Son cleanses us from all sin."[1] The usual mode of connecting the two clauses is the following: If we walk in the light, we receive cleansing or remission of sins by the continuous application of the blood of Christ;—an exposition which seems to run counter to the received biblical principle, that forgiveness precedes, and a holy walk is its fruit. The connection rather is as follows: Amid the recurring stains of the Christian life, the blood of Christ is ever needed and applied anew to RESTORE the fellowship which it at first procured. The present tense, CLEANSES, intimates that the blood daily cleanses, that the merits of the Lord are anew imputed, as sin is contracted and confessed.

1. The apostle describes this cleansing blood as the blood of GOD'S SON,—an addition having peculiar emphasis, as it is intended to exhibit the infinite value and efficacy of that blood. The title SON occurs in a higher sense than can be ascribed to any other being. It assigns a divine nature to Him, and, in such connections as the present, exhibits His redemption-work not merely as planned and approved by God, but wrought out, so far as atoning action is concerned, by the only-begotten and beloved Son. This imparts to Christ's atonement its infinite sufficiency and value, making it adequate to procure for men the remission of sins, how great and numerous soever, whether we think of individuals or of countless millions. On account of the personal union of the two natures, the blood is spoken of as the blood of the Son of God. Though the blood belongs to Him as Son of Mary, yet in virtue of the hypostatic union it is the blood of God's Son, and therefore possessed of all the value that the divine nature lends to it, and adequate to the expiation of human sin laid in the scales against it.

2. How is the blood of Christ said to CLEANSE US ? One thing is obvious, this cannot denote inward cleansing, or the renewing of the Holy Ghost, as it is a cleansing by the BLOOD of Christ; that is, by His blood sacrificially shed. Several

---

[1] See Muntinghe, *Geschiedenis*, x. 118, and note appended.

recent expositors of note have referred the language to inward cleansing from the power of sin, but a cursory examination of the passage suffices to refute that comment. The very terms refer to the sacrifices.[1] Then in no case are men here below cleansed from all sin, in the inward acceptation of the phrase. Besides, it would run counter to the very object which the apostle intends to teach—that we are cleansed notwithstanding daily recurring stains. He asserts a continuous cleansing by the blood of Christ, applied as necessity requires; and we cannot therefore expound this cleansing by referring to the mission of the Spirit, or inward spiritual life, when it is so definitely ascribed to the blood of Christ, considered, in the sacrificial sense, as sprinkled and applied to the guilty.

To understand this cleansing by blood, we may go back to the Old Testament ritual, and notice the great national cleansing of Israel. On the day of atonement, when the blood was brought into the holiest of all, and sprinkled on and before the mercy-seat, this action was regarded as the appointed means by which sin was removed. But not only was this action said to atone (Lev. xvi. 17), it was also said to cleanse the people (ver. 30). In the latter verse we find the two expressions conjoined as coincident or parallel: "On that day shall the priest make an atonement for you, to cleanse you, that ye may be clean from all your sins before the Lord." Evidently the expression " to cleanse you " does not mean inwardly to amend and renew, but to free from punishment incurred by sin, so as to put the worshipper on a right footing with God. Moses explains it, by making atonement, or removing the penalty threatened in the law. To obtain remission was the great design of the sacrificial blood. Could the whole nation be cleansed or improved in heart, so as to be clean from all their sins, by a mere external ceremony? From this passage

---

[1] Doedes (*Jaarboeken voor Weten. Theol.* 1846, p. 320) argues for this view, and adds as an argument, that ἀπὸ πάσης ἁμαρτίας means *from every sin* which is covered ; hence, he argues, it is not an allusion to progressive holiness.

it appears that the two expressions above mentioned amount to nearly the same thing; and this is the import of the phrase wherever cleansing is coupled with sacrificial blood according to the Jewish ritual.

To this, however, an objection is taken by Socinus and his followers, on the ground that inanimate things, needing no forgiveness, nor capable of receiving it, are also described in the Jewish ritual as purified and cleansed by blood. The objection is easily obviated. It argues a defective insight into the true nature of the sacrificial laws and the Mosaic code. The primary question is, What is meant when men are said to be cleansed by the blood of sacrifice ? We have seen that it implies deliverance from punishment, and restoration to the due position of a worshipper. Nor is the meaning different when the expression is applied to inanimate objects. The words of the law are: "He shall make an atonement for the holy place, because of the uncleanness of the children of Israel" (Lev. xvi. 16). The general notion of cleansing by blood is retained even here, as the following explanation will show. The nation was regarded as a sinful people before God; as having defiled the sanctuary of God, which was His habitation. The priests, as they approached the altar with the sacrifices, indicated that the Israelites coming before God with so many sins defiled the sanctuary; and the vessels as well as holy places were annually cleansed by atoning blood. But this was because of the uncleanness of the children of Israel. Thus, the sprinkling of blood on inanimate things removed divine punishments from the priests and the people. This is the meaning.

The expression, "the blood of Christ cleanses," intimates purifying from the defilement of sin, by which the believer was again made meet to appear as clean before the Lord. The blood of Christ is regarded as the truth or realization of all the ancient sprinkling or cleansing which restored the Israelite to his standing or right relation before God, when this was interrupted by ceremonial defilement. The word CLEANSE is to be taken, first in the sense of effecting forgiveness for sins committed, and then of uniting us to God anew (Heb. i. 3, ix. 14), as the Israelite was absolved and restored to God's friendship by sacrificial blood.

This further appears by what the apostle subjoins in the context. Thus it is said: "If we confess our sins, God is faithful and just TO FORGIVE us our sins, and TO CLEANSE us from all unrighteousness" (ver. 9). It is a peculiarity of John's style to use two expressions for the same thing, the positive and negative (ver. 5); sometimes a coincident expression, as in Hebrew poetry, that the one may elucidate the other. The two expressions, "to forgive us our sins," and "to cleanse us," are equivalent, or a slight advance of meaning is found in the latter phrase. The Epistle to the Hebrews, recalling sacrificial ideas, speaks of cleansing or purging the conscience by the blood of Christ, and then identifies the purging with remission (Heb. ix. 22).

Nor can the force of this conclusion be evaded by asserting that the allusion is to a cleansing from future sins. The apostle does not speak of sins not yet committed, but of sins already contracted and every day recurring. He cannot mean deliverance from sin by moral amendment, and motives drawn from that which Christ had to encounter among men. The context shows that no such attainment is made by any one; and that forgiveness and cleansing cover each other, and mutually explain each other. It is sacrificial blood that cleanses, sprinkles, and purifies the Christian disciple, by covering his sin, and enabling him to stand before God.[1]

A single glance at the Old Testament sacrificial ritual suffices to show that it was not the death, or bloody action of slaying the sacrifice, that possessed the sin-covering and cleansing power. The action with the blood—the priestly action which ensued—cleansed and purified. And the apostle,

---

[1] See Calvin on the passage ; also Grotius on καθαρίζειν, de Satisfactione.

in writing to Christians, assumes that, amid daily recurring stains, they shall have a fresh remission, and restoration to their privileges. As the transgressor under the law, becoming unclean, was excluded from an approach to God, so he had access restored, and a renewal of the privileges of God's people, the moment the blood was sprinkled. He was clean, and again in communion and favour. Precisely so is it with us: by Christ's blood we are forgiven and restored to fellowship.

II. Another passage is as follows: *We have an advocate with the Father, Jesus Christ the righteous; and He is the propitiation for our sins, and not for ours only, but also for the sins of the whole world* [better, without the supplementary words of our translators, *but also for the whole world*]. The apostle, exhorting believers not to sin, takes for granted daily sins, which would forfeit the divine favour were no provision made to remove their guilt. He directs their thoughts to the Advocate, or Helper, through whom divine anger is averted; and the ground of that intercession is next subjoined, viz. the twofold consideration that Jesus Christ is righteous, and that He is the propitiation for sins. These two descriptive names bring before us His vicarious work in its double aspect, reminding us that it is all identified with Christ Himself, a present as well as a past.

1. As to the epithet RIGHTEOUS, the contrast in which it stands to sin proves that it must denote innocent or sinless; that is, one approved as righteous when tried by the test of the divine law. It does not mean constant to His promises, as the Socinians expounded it, but the sinless One, or righteous Servant (Isa. liii. 11; 2 Cor. v. 21; 1 Pet. iii. 18; Heb. vii. 26), and intimates that for the sinning a sinless obedience is prepared. Wherever Scripture speaks of Christ's redeeming work, it generally shows us His personal righteousness underlying it, and that not as a mere preparation, but as an element of the propitiation. Only the righteous One could atone: only the righteous One could intercede.

2. Another term is: THE PROPITIATION FOR OUR SINS. Personally sinless, He must also be the propitiation. It will be necessary to elucidate the import of this term (ἱλασμός) from the usage of language. The uniform acceptation of the word in classical Greek, when applied to the Deity, is the means of appeasing God, or of averting His anger; and not a single instance to the contrary occurs in the whole Greek literature. As interpreters, therefore, our business is to abide by language, and not pervert it from its proper meaning. As this is the received import of the term in the language of Greece, without a trace of any other, we are bound to hold that it here intimates the means of averting divine anger for the sins of mankind, when Christ Himself is called our propitiation.[1] The expression intimates that this propitiation is found in His own person, apart from any work which man can render for himself. God had just grounds for inflicting punishment, just cause of anger; and the word means that by which God's anger is turned away, and man ceases to be the object of divine displeasure. It is interesting to find that the word occurs in the same sense in what is called Hellenistic Greek. It is the word in the Septuagint for the day of atonement (Lev. xxiii. 27); for the ram of atonement, whereby an atonement was made (Num. v. 8); and for the sin-offering (Ezek. xliv. 27). This fact explodes all other senses put upon the word by Socinian writers. If men will maintain another signification, they cannot do so as interpreters of language, but must appeal to theories and foregone conclusions of their own.

The expression *propitiation for our sins* takes for granted the WRATH OF GOD, a property often ascribed to Him in the Old and New Testament, and the moving cause of the punishment which He inflicts on sin. This anger has its seat in the bosom of God, or in His moral nature, and its measure is ac-

[1] See Stillingfleet *on the Death of Christ;* Chapman's *Defence,* on this word ἱλασμός; Morus, *in suam Epitomen,* ii. 91; also Stein, *de Satisfactione,* p. 270; Oeder *on Racov. Cat.* p. 821; Calov. p. 556.

cording to the conduct of His creatures. It is grounded in His essential holiness, as appears from the fact that God swears in His wrath (Heb. iii. 11); and it belongs to the idea of the personal God, the Creator and moral Governor, as He acts in history. He is no indifferent spectator of human conduct: He cannot look on sin and obedience, on vice and virtue, in the same light. Had we no other idea of God than the Epicurean notion, which represented Him as remote from human interests, or the pantheistic notion, which makes all things equally divine, we could not affirm that God had affections corresponding to anger or displeasure in regard to human conduct. But the Scriptures give us a different view, and speak of God's wrath as comprehending the following elements: aversion to sin; displeasure at the sinner; and the will or purpose to avenge it. It is impossible to assent to their opinion, who, with Koppe, maintain that this term applied to God means nothing more than punishment, and that the translators of the Scriptures should have rendered it by the latter word (1 Thess. i. 10). A full examination of biblical language may satisfy every one that the term WRATH never means the mere outward fact of punishment, apart from the affection of an acting party: it never means the mere effect (Rom. i. 18, ix. 22; 1 Thess. v. 9).

Man, made in the image of God, is capable of regarding sin and vice in a similar way. The Bible speaks of God in words borrowed from what is human; and, on the ground already stated, there is no reason to remove from our representation of God the idea of displeasure or wrath against sin,—that is, without the turbulent emotion which is associated with it in fallen natures. We find it in the sinless Saviour (Mark iii. 5). There is in God a displeasure at moral evil simply as such, which He regards as a violation of His supreme authority, and an injury offered to His majesty. Irrespective of the consequences which sin carries in its train, He regards Himself as wronged, even though His essential happiness is not invaded by any denial of His authority or withdrawal of His declarative glory, and is led by the perfection of His nature to regard the offender with anger, and to visit him with punitive justice. This wrath rests on man by nature (Eph. ii. 3). We may affirm that divine wrath is essential to our idea of God as the moral Governor, that it is essentially connected with the doctrine of sin, with the atonement, and with the doctrine of future retribution. It cannot be limited to the future, however, as some propose,[1] on the erroneous supposition that it strikes only the rejectors of salvation, and is but a modification of love, or the sorrow of love. It strikes on SIN AS SIN, in all its forms and degrees, and is far from being a mere phase of love. If men, however, represent the essence of God as consisting in love alone without other perfections, such as holiness and justice, they cannot ascribe anger to God in any Scripture acceptation of the term.

This brings us to the PROPITIATION which presupposes the wrath of God. It is revealed in its full depth and severity in the atonement of Christ, as sin-bearer, curse-bearer, and wrath-bearer. Considered in its objective significance, the atoning work of Christ is the propitiation of the divine wrath—the appeasing of God. The Lord Jesus is called the propitiation for our sins, to intimate that He is the author, the cause, or the means of averting the divine wrath. The word which the apostle employs, denotes in general terms the means of expiation, without naming His death, and without a closer definition of its sacrificial character. But whether we look at the cleansing blood, referred to in the previous context (1 John i. 7), or at the Hebrew style of thought which is introduced, according to which the only propitiation was by sacrifice, no doubt remains that the allusion is to the sin-offering. The apostle could not more unambiguously teach that what the sin-offering was under the old economy, Jesus is for the sins of His people. By Him the divine anger is averted, and forgiveness bestowed. The allusion, as in the Epistle to the

[1] So Ritschl, *de ira Dei.*

Hebrews, is to the priestly office of the Lord, and to His death, as the truth of the Mosaic sacrifices. The words affirm: What the propitiatory sacrifices were to Israel, when they expiated their sins and delivered them from punishment, that Christ is to the world at large.

Here we may answer three inquiries : (1.) Who is propitiated ? God, provoked to anger by the sins of men. It is not man who is described as propitiated to God, but conversely. (2.) By what was the propitiation effected ? By the whole active and passive obedience of the Lord. The fact that He who is the propitiation is described as Jesus Christ the righteous, emphatically shows that it was not personally needed for Himself. (3.) Was the work done a full satisfaction ? He is called THE PROPITIATION in the abstract, intimating that, by His sinless obedience as the righteous One, and by becoming the sin-bearer, and consequently the wrath-bearer, in our room, a full provision was made for making peace between God and man. The divine anger was averted, and merited punishment was removed.[1]

These expressions of the apostle plead so convincingly for the doctrine of the atonement in all its essential elements, that it is hard to see how any, admitting the authority of God's word, can be insensible to their force. Other explanations, especially those which deny the wrath of God, and culminate in the twofold objection that substitution and penal suffering are not to be supposed as possible, are in the last degree unnatural. Did Christ vicariously take on Himself the punishment of sin, or bear the wrath of God in our room ? is the principal point in modern discussions of the atonement; and this text unquestionably leads us to affirm that He did so. This is to be coupled, indeed, with the explanation that He was personally the Son of His love. But as our substitute, in His official capacity, He was the object of the divine wrath. This

---

[1] See Düsterdieck's commentary and philological discussion on ἱλασμός in this passage.

cannot be denied, if it was a real substitution, without maintaining that God is indifferent to good or evil. When Christ is explicitly called THE PROPITIATION FOR OUR SINS—that is, the sole cause, author, or means of our peace with God—the meaning is, that He appeased the divine anger by becoming a sacrifice in our room. What goes to strengthen the statement is, that the propitiation is connected with our sins, and confined to our sins ; that is, it is not only for MEN, but for their SINS.

The Socinian explanation was, that the language refers to the prevention of future sins by working holiness in men, or moral amendment. But there is no warrant for this exposition but in a foregone conclusion.[1] When was the prevention of future sin ever designated *a propitiation for sins?* They might much better affirm at once that the term denotes moral amendment. The language does not intimate that sins are to cease, but that divine WRATH is to cease.[2] That is the meaning of the word, and it can bear no other. The design of misinterpreting language, contrary to its true and genuine meaning, we do not presume to scan. But its tendency is to weaken the meaning of words, and of the things signified. The natural meaning of the language, confirmed by classical and Hellenistic usage, is, that Christ appeased the wrath of God by expiating sin.

But, further, the apostle extends the propitiation TO THE WHOLE WORLD—that is, to all times and places. In analyzing this language, we must notice that the phraseology furnishes a case of altered structures : it is not an instance of concise expression or breviloquence.[3] The first clause describes the work of Christ as a propitiation for our sins : the second clause describes it as for the whole world. The supplementary words, *for the sins of,* inserted in the authorized version, are an un-

---

[1] Grotius, in his annotations, holds that it means "to make sins to cease," whereas he before stated the very opposite, *de Satisfactione.* See Weiss, *der Johann. Lehrbegriff,* p. 162 ; also Fromman, *Johann. Lehrbegriff.*

[2] See Calovius' remarks, *Soc. prof.*

[3] See Winer's *Grammar,* where this is clearly and correctly put. So Doedes. It is περὶ ὅλου, not περὶ τῶν ὅλου.

warrantable addition, from which the translators should have been preserved, both by the structure and by the repetition of the Greek preposition. To apprehend the meaning, it must be remembered that the sinner as well as the sin is represented in Scripture as the object of the propitiation, and that it was wide enough to take in the whole world.

These words have been much canvassed, and often unwarrantably adduced, in the discussions bearing on the extent of the atonement. What was the apostle's primary object ? To comfort dejected Christians on the recurrence of sin in their experience. And he reminds them that they can appeal to Christ's intercession, which has its basis in His propitiation. The words plainly allude to the atonement as offered and applied— that is, to the actual expiation, which does not go beyond the number of believing recipients. It is a perversion of the language when this is made to teach the dogma of universal propitiation; or that the atonement was equally offered for all, whether they receive it or not, whether they acknowledge its adaptation to their case or not. The passage does not teach that Christ's propitiation has removed the divine anger in such a sense from all and every man. Nothing betokens that the apostle had others in his eye than believers out of every tribe and nation.

What, then, does he mean when he calls it a propitiation for the whole world ? He intimates that it was not for him and for those to whom he wrote alone, but for the redeemed of every period, place, and people — that is, prospectively and retrospectively. The apostle connects the intercession and propitiation in such a way as to show that Christ's work is applicable to all the redeemed who then lived, or had ever lived, or should ever live, wherever found in the nations of the earth, and in whatever age. This is the point of the distinction; it is not the distinction elsewhere expressed between Jew and Gentile.

III. Another passage replete with the sacrificial idea, or the idea of the sin-offering, is as follows: *And ye know that He was manifested to take away* [better, *to bear*] *our sins; and in Him is no sin* (1 John iii. 5). It is plain, whether we have regard to the style of language or to the context, that the apostle alludes to the great object of Christ's manifestation in the flesh. This should naturally lead us to some phase of His redemption-work, as is usual in such cases. The verse occurs, it is true, in a section which aims at enforcing a holy walk, and it was not unnatural on that account that expositors should be biassed in favour of the supposed allusion to inward holiness.[1] This drops the sacrificial allusion. The argument of those who refer the words to inward renovation by the Spirit, is derived from the context, where the apostle combats certain perverters of divine grace, probably Gnostics of an Antinomian tendency, perverted in principle and vicious in practice. But an argument from the context, however important as a principle in hermeneutics, is by no means sufficient to control the usage of language. A closer investigation will show that such an interpretation is untenable on many grounds; that the passage does not refer to holiness, but furnishes a dogmatic basis or grounding for the enforcement of holiness; that the language is sacrificial; and that had the apostle meant to show that Christ came to sanctify us from sin, the singular would have been used. The context is as follows:—The apostle begins a series of arguments against the perverters of the gospel, derived from the scope of Christ's mission. He reasons from the fact that Christ came to bear sin or expiate guilt. Hence it would follow that no quarter can be given to sin, nor allowance granted to it. Nor is that out of keeping with the further statement, that Christ was manifested to destroy the works of the devil (ver. 8).

Another mode of interpreting the passage is to render the phrase TO TAKE AWAY SINS, and refer it to the efficacy of

---

[1] Calvin and some of our best exegetes have fallen into this subjective interpretation on such mistaken grounds.

Christ's blood. It is thus equivalent, or nearly so, to the sprinkling of Christ's blood (1 John i. 7). This is so far correct, that it apprehends the sacrificial allusion, and brings out the idea of deliverance from punishment. It is so far correct, too, as it refers the language to actual sins, and contemplates guilt as removed by Christ's work. But it fails to trace the precise shade of meaning, which is the same as is contained in the Gospel of John, where Jesus is called the Lamb of God that bore the sin of the world (John i. 29); the same thought that Isaiah expresses in the well-known passage descriptive of sin-bearing (Isa. liii. 12).

The phrase means strictly TO BEAR SIN. This is the uniform signification, and it may be used either of personal guilt, or guilt borne by imputation. Nothing can warrant us to take the phrase in any other than in the Old Testament sense when applied to the sin-offering. The phrase is the well-known formula for incurring guilt, which may be either personal or vicarious, according to the connection. From this acceptation we are not to deviate, if we would defer to the laws of language.[1] This is the undoubted usage, as we have elsewhere proved. What are the sins? The form of expression, as well as the use of the plural number, suffices to prove that the sins are actual sins, past and present, for which a provision must be made; not future sins, to be prevented or forestalled by the force of motives or communications of the life-giving Spirit of God. They are actual sins; and the whole phrase shuts us up to the conclusion that the words signify the transfer of guilt to the Son of God as manifested to bear our sins.

But the sin-bearer must Himself be sinless; and to this element, uniformly brought out in some form in connection with the redemption-work of Christ, the subsequent clause makes reference. We have only to recall the Petrine language, or the words of John already expounded, to see how constantly

---

[1] See Storr, *Brief an die Hebräer*, p. 193; and Doedes, p. 318: αἴρειν with ἁμαρτίας means *to bear*, as we proved in the former vol. at large, p. 68.

these two integral parts of the atonement are united together. If we accept this as the connection, it will denote that He was sinless, to stand for the sinful; innocent, to occupy the place of the guilty.

As no small division of opinion prevails, however, as to the relation of the second clause to the first, and as this decides on its significance, we must put it in its proper light. Some argue that the second clause, *and in Him is no sin*, is the commencement of a new topic or argument, which is continued through the next verse. The present tense of the substantive verb, it is thought, thus receives its due force. Sinlessness is thus referred to Christ as He now is, not as He verified sinless perfection and learned obedience in the days of His flesh. But that deprives the clause of its emphasis, and gives the whole a flat, unmeaning turn. To refute this mode of construing, it is necessary to notice that, whenever Christ is described as without sin, as doing no sin, as separate from sinners, the expressions always imply a state of humiliation, in which He was brought in contact with sin and sinners. The allusion is to the period of testing His obedience. Such expressions are not applicable, in the proper sense, to the heavenly glory, where sin cannot enter, and where He is far removed from the range of sin, and contact with it.

Besides, the second clause is subordinate to the first. And in John's manner, though without a grounding particle or conjunction, it intimates the relation in which sinlessness stood to sin-bearing; making it apparent that the sin was not His own, that sinlessness underlay the imputation of others' sins. There is in the thought a certain causal relation; the second clause bringing into vivid view the sinless holiness of the Lord, and intimating that Christ was competent to bear the sins of others because He had none of His own. It expresses a reason. The whole verse, thus connected, denotes that, as the true ideal of humanity, and as One exempt from all sins, either of omission or of commission, He was in a position to clothe

Himself with human guilt.[1]   But why is the present tense.
used—" in Him IS no sin ? "   It may imply what the living
Lord is, as well as what He was, and shall ever be before God's
face, even as He is called Jesus Christ THE RIGHTEOUS (1 John
ii. 1).   He still stands before God's face with that approval,
recognition, or imprimatur which He received in the days of
His flesh, and by which He was qualified to be the sin-bearer.

This important text, rightly understood, brings these two
elements together, sinlessness and sin-bearing,—the two constituent parts of the atonement, viewed in that which is
essential to it.   The one would not avail without the other.
They are the counterpart of the two elements in the divine
law, as it comes with its precept and its curse; and at every
moment of Christ's earthly history both may be discovered.
They describe all that goes to constitute the Lord's earthly life
or manifestation, as it is here termed ; and they coincided at
every moment.   Only as His life at every stage came up to the
ideal standard, was He in a position to bear the sins of others.
But with sinless perfection, measured by the divine law, and
reflecting in the most perfect manner the divine image, He was
in a position, as the accepted substitute, to be the sin-bearer.

The apostle's phrase here and in his Gospel is the same as
Isaiah's : HE BORE SIN.   He could be the curse-bearer or wrath-
bearer only as He was the sin-bearer.   It was this that brought
penal suffering in its train.   The sum and substance of the
atonement, considered in its essential elements, apart from
all its accessories, is SINLESS SIN-BEARING ; that is, not mere
punishment without sin-bearing, but punishment following on
the sin-bearing, and endured by One who is at once sinless
man and Son of God.   To exempt us from sin the Son of
God was manifested.

We have only to add, that the transaction always proceeds

---

[1] Doedes happily says, "The phrase καὶ ἁμαρτία ἐν αὐτῷ οὐκ ἔστιν is added, to
show both that Christ did not bear His own sin, and that He was fitted to bear
the sins of others."

upon a community of nature, and a real relation between the Surety and those in whose behalf His work was undertaken. But when this was formed, Christ was no otherwise regarded in the divine judgment, and at the divine tribunal, than if He had incurred by His own act the guilt with which He was charged.

There are various passages in this epistle where allusion is made to the atonement in a less direct way, but so as to be easily perceptible (1 John ii. 12, iii. 16, v. 6). These we shall pass over, that we may concentrate attention on those which are obvious and not to be mistaken.

IV. The only passage which we shall further adduce is found in the memorable verses which bring together the love of God and the wrath of God, as displayed in the atonement: *God is love. In this was manifested the love of God toward us, because* [better, *that*] *God sent His only begotten Son into the world, that we might live through Him. Herein is love, not that we loved God, but that He loved us, and sent His Son to be the propitiation for our sins* (1 John iv. 9, 10). Without doubt, the apostle repeats, in nearly the same terms, what he had long ago heard from the lips of his Master, as is recorded in the Gospel (John iii. 16). He verifies his title as the disciple of love. Not content to direct the attention of his readers to the atonement, considered merely in its effects, he leads them back to its source in the divine love, giving us a glimpse of the father-heart of God—a discovery of God as the sum of love. He had already said of God, GOD IS LIGHT (1 John i. 5) ; now he twice repeats, GOD IS LOVE (vers. 8, 16),—a definition of His nature not to be reduced to the shallow signification that it merely intimates the loving will of God, or even that God is full of love. It describes the essence of God, His nature, and His name. The epistle emphatically delineates the Supreme Being as Light and Love ; and we need not be surprised that in this passage love and anger are so intimately connected in the atonement of our Lord, or that both are displayed. Nor is

2 G

the one incompatible with the other when we duly consider their proper object.

1. As to the love of God, many who are swayed more by a philosophical transcendentalism than by biblical representations, are apt to represent love as a mere human affection, and to maintain that it is applied to God only in a way of accommodation, or in its effects.[1] They call it an anthropomorphic representation of God. They do not ascribe to God a true and proper love. On the contrary, this passage represents God not merely as possessing love, but as BEING LOVE.

2. But next, the term PROPITIATION, which we have already expounded, intimates that man, the sinner, has come to be the object of divine WRATH, and that this can never be averted, unless a sacrifice comes between the divine wrath and human sin (Num. xvii. 11). The language of the apostle seems at first sight to intimate that the pacifying of the divine anger did not exclusively lie in Christ's death, but took in all that is comprehended in His mission; and so indeed it does (ver. 10). But it culminated in His death, and the phraseology has undoubted reference to the sin-offering, or the atoning sacrifices in general. As we have already asserted the presence of the divine anger in connection with the propitiatory sacrifice of Christ, it is only further necessary to add, that God was thereby not merely made placable, but was absolutely pacified to all in whose behalf it was offered.[2]

The testimony contained in this passage may be briefly exhibited in the following particulars :—

(1.) The holy love of God is described as providing the atonement. And the apostle, in connecting the love of God with sending the only begotten Son into the world, sets forth two things—the infinite greatness of the love (ver. 9),

---

[1] They say *effectum non affectum*, as if man was not made in God's image.

[2] See Calvin's very striking remarks on this passage: "Sed hic emergit quædam repugnantiæ species: nam si prius nos amabat Deus quam se Christus pro nobis in mortem offerret, quid nova reconciliatione opus fuit? quia interea nos Deo eramus hostes, iram ejus assidue provocando."

and its gratuituous nature as free, unmerited, and self-moving
(ver. 10). The incarnation of the only begotten Son was undoubtedly the greatest fact of the divine love; but it is never
disjoined from the deep abasement and vicarious sacrifice to
which it enabled the Son of God to descend. The greater
the distance between the divine and the human, the infinite
and finite, the greater the degree of love displayed in sending
the Son. The first ground of the atonement is thus the love of
God, and the greatness of the Son displays its infinite magnitude. But the apostle, secondly, sets forth how gratuitous and
undeserved is the love of God: "Not that we loved God, but
that He loved us." His design is to teach that the scheme of
redemption is of God, emanating from free, self-moving, infinite
love, and not a recompense for love first rendered on our part.

(2.) We find the twofold fruit or effect of the atonement
with which all the apostles make us familiar. The one is
objective, the other subjective; the one bears on the acceptance of our persons, the other on the renovation of our natures;
and the latter is here put first.

a. One fruit is, THAT WE MIGHT LIVE THROUGH HIM (ver. 9).
The life here mentioned is PREMIAL LIFE, and must be taken in
its utmost amplitude of meaning as comprehending spiritual
and eternal life. And when it is said "through Him," the
allusion is plainly to His merit and satisfaction. There may
be a tacit antithesis between death as the price, and life as the
reward.

b. A second fruit of the atonement is the acceptance of the
person or the restoration to favour, which is involved in the
phrase "propitiation for our sins" (ver. 10). This is properly
the first in order in God's moral government. The appeasing
of the divine anger, according to the Old Testament representation, was effected only by the intervention of an atoning
sacrifice, which is the shade of meaning attaching to these
terms; and this was the end for which the Son of God was
sent. By that sacrifice sin was cancelled, wrath removed, and

the person accepted as well as brought nigh to the life-giving God. Thus, the acceptance of the person was the means by which the life was procured: for no life was possible but by a sacrificial death. Life was attainable only by satisfying divine justice, which restored men to God as the life-giving and renewing God.

Thus the passage connects the atonement and its fruits with divine love as its source. And it is only necessary to add, that this is TRUE AND PROPER LOVE, as may be deduced from a strict interpretation of the terms. God not only possesses love: He IS love; that is, infinitely inclined to the communication of Himself for the happiness of His creatures. We must take the term LOVE in its proper sense when applied to God, and not evaporate it into a mere abstraction, as if affections were to be affirmed only of man, but not to be affirmed of God.

SEC. XXII.—THE TESTIMONY OF JOHN IN THE APOCALYPSE.

The Apocalypse may be considered as one of the latest books of the New Testament Canon, and composed long after the destruction of Jerusalem. In its scope and structure it is adapted to delineate the mediatorial dominion of Jesus, showing that all power is given to Him in heaven and in earth. While this comes out in connection with the prophetic outline of the fortunes of the church in all the course of time, Christ's official power is throughout exhibited as a dominion based on the atonement. It is as the Lamb that He prevails to open the book, and to loose the seven seals thereof (Rev. v.–vii.). The perpetual allusion indeed to the Lamb has no other object in view than to show that He was invested with this dominion as the reward of His abasement, and that the cross is the foundation of His throne.

The book is in this way naturally connected with the Gospel of John. They are thus found to emanate from the same writer: he who records the Baptist's testimony to the Lamb, and was himself a spectator of the sacrifice, links the Gospel and the Apocalypse together. We could not have explained the constant use of this title in the Apocalypse had there been no preparation for it (John i. 29, 36, xix. 33). But now it is not only natural, but highly significant. Christ is described as a Lamb as it had been slain, implying that He bore the tokens of having been a piacular victim (Rev. v. 6). His saints are called to the marriage supper of the Lamb (xix. 9). The redeemed follow the Lamb whithersoever He goeth (xiv. 4). They who have a right to the city of God, and are arrayed in white robes, have washed their robes in the blood of the Lamb (vii. 14); the Lamb opened the seals (vii. 1); the church is the bride, the Lamb's wife (xxi. 9); the city had no need of the sun, for the Lamb was the light thereof (xxi. 23); the conquerors sing the song of Moses and of the Lamb, extolling the holy strictness of the law and the dying obedience of the Saviour (xv. 3); and the united hymn of earth and of heaven—that is, of redeemed men and angels—was an anthem to the Lamb (v. 12). The whole book, in a word, is replete with the Lamb. But a few passages call for more special commentary.

I. The first passage on the atonement is as follows: *Unto Him that loved us, and washed us from our sins in His own blood, and hath made us kings and priests unto God and His Father; to Him be glory and dominion for ever and ever. Amen.* (Rev. i. 5.) After adducing a reference to the Redeemer's love in general, the apostle specially mentions the cleansing effect of His atoning blood. This WASHING is the same thing that is meant in the Epistle of John by the cleansing of His blood (1 John i. 7). The words teach the priestly dignity of Christ; for the priest's work was to sprinkle the sacrificial blood (Heb. ix. 22). The whole statement intimates that Jesus, in self-sacrificing love to the unworthy, offered Himself as the priest offered the sacrifices to atone for guilt, and thus washes our

sins away.   And the apostle, inflamed by the contemplation
of the love of Christ, closes with an ascription of praise.

An utter violence is done to the language, when it is said
that the blood of Christ must be understood as shed for the
confirmation of His testimony, and to assure us of the truth of
what He taught.   We may despair of discovering what words
mean, if we do not see that they contain the statement that the
blood of Christ washes His people from their sins.   How feeble
and unmeaning would they be, if they did not intimate that
Christ's vicarious death puts away sin, delivers us from punishment, and restores us to the near relationship from which sin
exiled the human family !   The phraseology is to be understood
by the sacrificial ceremonies of the Jewish worship, according
to which, one defiled by trespass was freed by the blood of
sacrifice from merited punishment and from estrangement, the
consequence of sin so long as it was unexpiated.

But why may not the allusion be to moral amendment or
inward holiness ?   So some expositors choose to view the expression.   But it may suffice to reply that the language is
figurative, and borrowed from the Mosaic ceremonies.   Wherever we find the phrase TO WASH FROM SIN, TO CLEANSE FROM
SIN, it never alludes to moral amendment, but to deliverance
from guilt, and the estrangement from God which sin has
caused.   Passages sometimes adduced in the acceptation of inward holiness are all incorrectly interpreted (1 Cor. vi. 11 ;
Tit. iii. 5 ; 1 John iii. 5 ; Ezek. xxxvi. 25), and are rightly
explained only when we take them in their sacrificial reference.   This is evident, if we consider any of the passages
where the sacred writers use this phrase (see Ps. li. 2, 7).   The
Psalmist twice prays that God would wash him or sprinkle
him from sin ; and what he means by the petition becomes
plain by the whole context, which contains a prayer for mercy.
In these passages (vers. 2, 7, 9), the WASHING, purging, or
cleansing for which he prays, is not an allusion to inward
holiness, but to sacrificial expiation, by which sin was atoned

for, and regarded as if it had never been. In that acceptation the apostle takes the phrase here.[1] To remove all doubt on this head, the addition of the term BLOOD, as sacrificial blood, intimates that it is not inward cleansing by renovation. We owe the washing here mentioned to the Saviour's bloody death.

Not content with alluding to the removal of guilt, the apostle mentions the further benefit of priestly dignity and service which Christians owe to the Lord's atoning death: "and hath made us kings and priests unto God." They are in virtue of His atonement made kings and priests, just as Israel was designated a kingdom of priests (Ex. xix. 6), because the Lord Jesus, in whom they stand, and to whom they are united, is invested with these offices. They have this honour now, and a higher measure of it in reversion. Their priestly standing before God intimates that they are emboldened to come nigh to God, and can daily approach Him, so that every action they perform may have a priestly character and be acceptable to God (1 Pet. ii. 5). Their sins are covered (1 John i. 2), and their active services are welcome, whether it be worship, fruit-fulness, or social activity in any form (Heb. xiii. 15; Rom. xii. 1; Col. iii. 17).

II. Another significant passage in reference to the atonement is the hymn of the four living creatures, and the four and twenty elders who fell down before the Lamb, and sung a new song, saying: *Thou art worthy to take the book, and to open the seals thereof: for Thou wast slain, and hast redeemed us to God by Thy blood, out of every kindred, and tongue, and people, and nation; and hast made us unto our God kings and priests: and we shall reign on the earth* (Rev. v. 9). They who sing this song are the redeemed from among men, represented as singing when the Lamb took the book out of the hand of Him that sat upon the throne. The inadequate commentary, that nothing

---

[1] They who interpret the λούσαντι of *moral amendment* appeal in vain to such passages as Ezek. xxxvi. 25–27, 1 John iii. 5, 1 Cor. v. 11, Tit. iii. 5; for the meaning in all these is washing from guilt by expiation.

more is meant than Christ's knowledge of the future fortunes
of the church and the mysteries of God's kingdom, can no
longer satisfy any mind: a further and a deeper idea must be
developed. The allusion was to the actual commencement of
the mediatorial kingdom and the carrying into execution of the
divine purposes, evoking that new song from the redeemed in
glory. The blessed in their heavenly glory unite before the
throne of the Lamb in this song of redemption. The language
of heaven cannot be measured by the feebleness of our expressions. But their words communicated to us in human
speech testify to the fact of the atonement as still the topic of
adoring contemplation. And if this is so, far from charging
their song, as some have done, with want of meaning or comprehension of the subject on which they dwell with so much
wonder, love, and gratitude, the part of those who are permitted to read it is rather to follow their example of humility
and triumph, as they recall the pit from which they were
rescued, and the glory to which they are raised.

1. The first thing expressed in this song is, that the Redeemer's kingdom over all was based on His atoning sacrifice.
He is extolled as worthy to receive this dominion, because He
was slain,—language proving that, though the possession of a
divine nature alone fitted Him for the exercise of so vast a
sway, its foundation was laid in His atoning death. It was
based on His passion, and on the fact that He bought a people
to be His.

2. Another thing which the redeemed mention in their
hymn of adoring love is the purchase of a people, and the
payment of a ransom, or adequate price: AND HAST REDEEMED
US TO GOD BY THY BLOOD. As they beheld the Redeemer in
His majesty and glory, they recalled the abasement to which
the Supreme Potentate had descended for us men and for our
salvation, borrowing their language, if not from the nail-prints
and spear-mark which He may still bear, at least from something which recalled His wounds and the death He underwent

in paying our ransom. Not only so: they describe themselves as REDEEMED TO GOD; the meaning of which is, that they have passed from one master to another, like those who were bought in classical times to be the servants of their purchaser. And the blood of Christ, regarded as blood sacrificially shed, or the blood of atonement, is described as the price or ransom by which they became the property of Christ and of God. The notion of guilt leading to captivity under the holy wrath of God, and the infliction of His justice, is presupposed. The sacrificial blood, and the further idea of a ransom paid to liberate men from bondage, are closely connected in many passages of Scripture, and easily suggest each other. It is only natural to find them together again in this passage. The ransom by which He that sitteth on the mediatorial throne bought them, was His own blood. And when they are said to be redeemed TO GOD, the words imply that He won them for Himself, or bought them to be God's, as slaves were bought with a price in ancient times to be the property of a new master—the obedient servants of him who paid the price for them. In this case they are bought TO BE FREE, but not to be WITHOUT A MASTER, or to be independent—which man, from his mental and moral constitution, can never be—but to be the Lord's: "Thou hast redeemed us TO GOD." The thought is, that He has bought us to be God's, to live to Him, and not to another or to ourselves. This idea, uttered consciously in the name of all the saved, implies that, as the blood-bought property of God, the ransomed of the Lord correspond to their name, and to the new ownership into which they have passed. The phrase has respect to the holy ends of man's redemption, being redeemed to God. They verify their title, or correspond to it, when they live to Him whose they are: they falsify it, or deny the Lord that bought them, by a course of disobedience.

Here, however, it is necessary to obviate the Socinian evasion. Many argue in modern days, as did the Socinians of old, that the word REDEEM is to be taken in the acceptation of

simple deliverance, without a price or ransom.   Such a comment is inadmissible, as the ransom is expressly named.   That
passages may be found, such as the figurative expression " redeeming the time," where a metaphorical use of the word
occurs, no one ever denied.   But whatever ground exists for
admitting such a use of the word where the notion of price is
scarcely perceptible, or but a shade of that meaning remains,
there can be none for attaching a metaphorical signification to
the term where the ransom is in so many words expressed.
When we are here said to be REDEEMED BY BLOOD, there cannot
be two opinions that we have a definite statement of the price
paid, as well as of the deliverance procured.

3. A further privilege won by redeeming blood, is the
dignity of being kings and priests to God.   This, too, is causally connected with the blood of the Redeemer; and, as here
expressed, it differs from the allusion to the same privilege in
the previous passage (Rev. i. 5) in this respect, that the former
is the earthly phase of the royal priesthood, while this is the
heavenly aspect of the same dignity.

4. The elders further mention in their song, that they shall
reign on the earth; that is, when renewed and delivered from
the bondage of corruption.   Of this privilege, too, the death of
the Lamb is the procuring cause; and hence they fully express
their adoring gratitude, announcing that the Lord's atoning
death was the ground on which the Lamb is counted worthy
to be the Mediatorial King to take the book and open the
seven seals, or, in other words, to execute the divine counsels.

Other allusions might be adduced from the Apocalypse of a
more figurative kind.   Thus the saints seen in glory are described as having " washed their robes, and made them white
in the blood of the Lamb" (Rev. vii. 14).   This language at
first sight appears strange, because affirming that their robes
were made *white* by blood, but is intelligible when we reflect
that it is an allusion to the acceptance of their persons, to
their priestly privilege and attire, as procured by the cross.

Another phrase, " redeemed from among men " (xiv. 4), recalls the deliverance from Egypt and the separation of the peculiar people. And if the reading which modern editors prefer is adopted in that verse, which describes the right to the tree of life (xxii. 14), " Blessed are they that have washed their robes," an important doctrine is stated.

We have thus proved against modern theories, that, according to the uniform teaching of the apostles, the atonement stands in causal connection with forgiveness. Many ends are effected by the Lord's death, but the remission of sins and the acceptance of our persons are the immediate fruits. We do not contend for any human phrase, and are willing to abandon current nomenclature for a better when it is pointed out; but the fact is attested by every apostle, that Christ's vicarious death alone, and without addition, effects the remission of our sins and our standing before God. This is of such importance, that it touches the security of the ground on which a Christian lives, and on which he can die. Let us survey it.

(1.) What is the import of the term forgiveness? No passage can be adduced where the idea of forgiveness is used by the apostles in any but the common acceptation familiar to every mind, lettered and unlettered, in every nation, viz. the remission of deserved punishment. Sin, as an offence against God, carries with it a reference to positive law as an expression of the divine nature and will, and the further thought that God in His capacity of Legislator threatened punishments, which He actually inflicts in his capacity of Judge, from love to His own perfections,—that is, from regard to Himself. Every mind has a sense of guilt or liability to deserved punishment,—a feeling which they try to remove, but which the atonement alone meets. There is no necessity for explaining guilt, because it is familiar to every nation where there is law and justice; an innate belief, which no man can shake off by all his elaborate speculations. Though some would make sin an infirmity rather than a fault, a calamity rather than a crime; though others would represent the Most High as infinitely loving, and repudiate divine anger as an unworthy Jewish conception, this is opposed to natural as well as revealed theology: for man, by the very constitution of his being, is so made, that he cannot but retain it among his innate convictions, that God visits sin with the punishment of death (Rom. i. 32).

According to biblical ideas as well as ordinary language, forgiveness means the remission of punishment. Where false ideas of forgiveness prevail, this must be traced to incorrect or superficial views of guilt; and wherever justice is done to the great truth of men's guilt, they entertain different views of the connection between forgiveness and the Lord's death. The theory of unconditional pardon, the great untruth of the modern theology, is opposed to natural as well as revealed theology, and at open war with every correct idea of moral government. Absolute pardon supposes that the punishment which we represent to ourselves as connected with evil actions in a moral kingdom, is removed. But guilt and demerit are not removed. The man failing to observe divine laws is still punishable or blameworthy. If nothing more were to come into consideration but the consequences of a sinful life, these might be removed by mere absolution. But if demerit comes from a violation of moral law, this would remain as much as ever, though physical evils were removed. But would God be then the source of ethics, ruling by moral laws? There would, according to the supposition, be no regard to moral conduct, and thus absolute pardon overthrows all moral laws. But our judgments as men are based on immutable moral principles, and the theory is opposed to natural theology.

(2.) The nature of the connection between the Lord's death and the remission of sins is immediate, and of the same kind with that which obtained in the Mosaic law between the death of the sacrifice and the forgiveness of the worshipper.

That it is a connection of the same nature, a few words will suffice to prove. On the day of atonement, the principal design of which was to offer a solemn sacrifice for the priests and people in their national capacity, forgiveness was procured by means of the sacrifice for the entire people. Now, was forgiveness only mediately the fruit of the sacrifice, as it presupposed an amendment? No; they received forgiveness directly in connection with the sacrifice, and irrespective of amendments subsequently made; and it is in the same way that we receive forgiveness from merited punishment by the death of Christ. Sin is put away as the direct consequence of Christ's death, previous to any amendments, as the Mosaic sacrifices, simply in the course of being offered, turned away the penalty threatened in the law. Forgiveness followed as the immediate effect of the atonement, the sacrifice in the sinner's place satisfying the law. This fact, of which there can be no doubt, was intended to regulate our conception as to the immediate connection between the death of Christ and pardon, and to supply a vocabulary which we might use. Our Lord Himself uttered this connection (Matt. xxvi. 28); the apostles repeated it.

But another inquiry presents itself: Granted that the connection between the death of Christ and remission of sins is immediate, are we to conceive of it only in a subjective sense? Are we to represent to our minds the sufferings and death of Christ as an event with which God has connected the forgiveness of sins, merely to meet a weighty moral necessity of our natures, that require an assurance of the forgiveness of sins? That notion, often propounded, also undermines the atonement, as it reduces it to the subordinate office of giving us a persuasion or assurance that forgiveness is received by this channel. It supposes that the change is all effected on man's side, who is suspicious and backward to trust, but that no change takes place on God's relation to sinners by means of the atonement. The pardon is still supposed to be absolute and unconditional, but conveyed through the dying Messenger to undo our suspicious distrust. If the matter stood thus, if all were only subjective, how could the Lord's death have any relation to those who lived before He came in the flesh?

When we use accurate language, the atonement will always be distinguished from forgiveness. The atonement is the act of Christ as Surety; forgiveness, the act of God as Judge. The atonement is therefore the foundation on which the acquittal of the sinner is based, the cause of which forgiveness is the effect. This deserves notice, the rather because the confounding of atonement and forgiveness may be called the chief source of those erroneous opinions, which allege that in New Testament times men are no longer to pray for pardon, because, as they express it, their sins were put away in one day. So far as the atonement is an act done once for all, and eternally valid before God, that is true. But it is not true, so far as forgiveness is considered as an act of God, in His judicial capacity, which is extended from time to time to every believer. It is self-evident that sin is not forgiven, and cannot be, before it is committed. Hence the remission of sins, as contradistinguished from the atonement, is a continuous act, and from time to time dispensed to the same persons.

The act of forgiveness has a positive as well as a negative side: it absolves one from the charge of violating the law, and pronounces him as having actually fulfilled it; the latter being its positive aspect. In forgiveness, the two sides come into view as the two elements or co-ordinate parts of the judicial sentence.

APPENDIX.

HISTORICAL SKETCH OF THE DOCTRINE OF THE ATONEMENT.

I PURPOSE in an Appendix, which must now be limited, to subjoin a historical outline of the doctrine in its salient points, from the apostolic age to the present time. As my object is not so much historical as dogmatic, this will lead me to be sparing of facts, dates, and personal allusions, having no particular reference to the atonement.

A new study of all the elements that enter into the systematic form which the doctrine assumed as a subject of thought, is one of the great necessities of our age. If it continues to be studied only in connection with modern tendencies that look askance on the positions which former centuries took up in reference to God's moral government, law, penal justice, and the necessity of vicarious satisfaction, only partial and perilous conclusions will be adopted. Next to the primary duty of establishing the doctrine on a biblical foundation, and securing for it an independent place beyond the fluctuations of opinion, attention is due to the historic course of the doctrine in its way to symbolic recognition, and the various elements that from time to time entered to vindicate its truth, or give it systematic form.

While the ultimate decision depends on the authority of Scripture, interpreted by sound rules and without wayward caprice, at this day it is useful and necessary to retrace the principal points of the older discussions. The importance of this will appear from the circumstance, that they who break loose from previous conclusions commonly drop some essential elements of the question. They throw the whole subject into the crucible again, as if it had never taken form before, notwithstanding the arguments employed for centuries by some of the greatest minds that ever acted their part in handling the doctrines of the church; not to mention that the creeds and confessions express the Christian consciousness of the church collective. The modern theories dismissing whatever has been adduced to prove the necessity, rationality, and inward consistency of the atonement, and proceeding as if these considerations had never occupied the minds of earnest thinkers, deny the forensic element. Instead of satisfaction to divine justice, we hear of moral redemption, or deliverance from the power of evil, with a tendency to discountenance and throw overboard the judicial side of Christianity altogether. One important inquiry, therefore, is, How did the Christian consciousness utter itself during eighteen centuries of past history? We find, when we make due allowance for erratic tendencies, either of individuals or of sects, through all this time, one harmonious testimony to divine justice and the judicial aspect of Christianity. This might be expected, indeed, from the uniformity of human conscience.

Not only so: historical investigation shows that, on the side of the advocates of vicarious satisfaction, some integral parts of truth are at one time more prominent, and at another time less so, while certain parts occasionally have been allowed to drop. As another ground, then, for reviewing the historic formation of the doctrine, it must be added that half-truths and one-sided views were sometimes advanced,—as, for instance, by Piscator, Grotius, and others; and certain elements of the question, to which the highest importance must justly be attached, have occasionally fallen into the background, and, if not denied, have at least disappeared. It cannot be unimportant to recall the grounding elements of the doctrine in a historical way.

1. We shall notice the testimony of the post-apostolic age to the atonement. The doctrine was held and taught, during the FIRST CENTURY of the Christian church, with great simplicity and purity, by the men who immediately succeeded the apostles. From the first, the doctrine of the atonement by the death of God's Son was a central article never impugned. The whole worship was based upon it. The first Christians, as is well known, commemorated the Lord's death in the Holy Supper every Lord's day; and from the peculiar theory which made the worship culminate in the Supper, the atonement was constantly before the mind of the worshippers. This gave colour to primitive theology. The atoning death of Christ was central and fundamental. This accounts for the fact that the atonement never was a subject of discussion among the early Christians, and consequently never came within those currents or controversies which gave precise symbolical expression to other topics. The doctrine was so fully recognised and accepted, that heresy durst not assail it, and only sought to undermine the articles which lay at its foundation. We must not suppose, then, that the primitive Christians had vague conceptions of the mode of deliverance from guilt, and of the way

of restoration to divine favour. No one can read the early
Fathers, without feeling that a deep conviction of the nature
and efficacy of Christ's atonement animated them with zeal in
all those discussions and debates which referred to Christ's
person. An error admitted there, tended at the next remove
to overthrow the redemption-work of the God-man; and they
felt that, if Christ was not very God and very man, an atonement was impossible.

The APOSTOLIC FATHERS speak much of this fundamental
article of Christianity. The authenticity of some of these
documents is disputed, and interpolations have crept into the
text of others; but they are beyond doubt monuments of the
post-apostolic age, bearing witness to the reality of Christ's
coming in the flesh, and to His sufferings, in opposition to
Docetism, with its representation of a phantom body and a
semblance of suffering (ἀληθῶς ἔπαθεν). The Apostolic Fathers
bring out different sides of Christ's atoning work, against Judaizing Ebionism on the one hand, and Gnosticism on the other.

CLEMENS ROMANUS' Letter to the Corinthians, the oldest
monument that has come down to us, and written, as all
authorities agree, before the close of the first century (A.D.
92–96), gives a clear testimony to the atonement. We have
in Clement this statement: "For the love that He bore toward
us, our Lord Jesus Christ gave His own blood for us by the
will of God—*His flesh for our flesh, His soul for our souls*"
(ch. 49). The statement asserts, against Docetism, that Christ
assumed whatever was to be redeemed. If, then, any part of
humanity was not assumed, neither was it redeemed. We see
in these words the idea of substitution, or vicarious satisfaction.
Deliverance, too, in body and soul, by His self-surrender in
both the elements of His humanity, is equally marked. And
the whole is traced to the WILL of God, or to divine appointment. Another passage is thus expressed: "Let us look stedfastly to the blood of Christ, and see how precious His blood
is in God's sight (τίμιον τῷ Θεῷ); which, being shed for our
salvation, has brought (ὑπήνεγκεν) the grace of repentance to
all the world" (ch. 7). Atonement by vicarious satisfaction is
plainly taught. But in whose eyes was the blood of Christ so
precious? In the eyes of God, who alone knew its value.
The redemptive-act, satisfying the claims or justice of God, is
further described as producing repentance,—viz. making room
for it, and procuring it. According to Clement's theology,
repentance presupposes the atonement as a divine fact. He
also calls the blood of Christ a ransom: "that by the BLOOD of
our Lord there should be REDEMPTION (λύτρωσις) to all that
2 H

believe and hope in God" (ch. 12). We have here the idea of substitution and deliverance by exchange of places.

The remark is sometimes hazarded, that Clement recognised in the death of Christ only a moral example,—a deed of humility and patience,—not a redemptive fact. That conclusion is drawn from the fact that Clement, after quoting the entire fifty-third chapter of Isaiah, adds: "You see, beloved, what the pattern is (τίς ὁ ὑπογραμμός) that has been given us" (ch. 16). But when he urges love, patience, and humility, by an appeal to the redemption-acts of Christ, that is only what Peter does in his epistle, and does not prove that Clemens had no right idea of the atonement. The atonement is the first and principal object: the example is the second. If it is a perversion of Scripture to interpret Christ's sufferings merely as an example, it is also a perversion not to make them an example at all.

Two monuments of the post-apostolic age, the genuineness of which is admitted by the best critical investigators—POLYCARP'S LETTER TO THE PHILIPPIANS, and the CIRCULAR LETTER OF THE CHURCH OF SMYRNA—deserve attention. Polycarp's letter, written on the occasion of excommunicating a presbyter and his wife for a dishonest administration of church funds, and breathing the spirit of the holy man, bases his exhortation on the fundamental truths of the Christian faith (ch. 1, 2). With regard to the Lord's death, he represents our sins as the procuring cause of it: "who suffered Himself to be brought even to death for our sins" (ch. 1). Of the Docetic opinions of his day he speaks with stern denunciation, like the Apostle John: "Whosoever does not confess His suffering (μαρτύριον) upon the cross, is of the devil" (ch. 7). No one can question Polycarp's distinct testimony to Christ's vicarious satisfaction, who ponders the following words (ch. 8): "Hold stedfastly to Him who is our hope and the earnest of our righteousness, who is Jesus Christ, who bore our sins in His own body on the tree; who did no sin, neither was guile found in His mouth, but suffered all for us (δι' ἡμᾶς), that we might live through Him." The addition made to the quotation from Peter shows how he understood the apostle, and the connection between the atonement and life. He alludes to those witnesses who preceded them, thus: "who loved not the present world, but Him who *died for us*, and was raised again by God for us" (ch. 9).

The Circular Epistle of the Church of Smyrna, prepared after Polycarp's death († 168), allowed to be genuine even by those who take exception to the passage which betrays the marvellous in its narrative of the flames, is very explicit. The atonement is represented as having a definite reference : "not considering that neither will it be possible for us ever to forsake Christ, *who suffered for the salvation of the saved* (τῶν σωζομένων) of the whole world, or to worship any other. For Him, indeed, as being the Son of God, we adore" (ch. 17). Here we observe the special destination of the atonement.

To the other documents of the post-apostolic age—the LETTER OF BARNABAS, the Shepherd of HERMAS, and the Epistles of IGNATIUS—I might next appeal; but I forbear, as their authenticity is questioned by some, and their integrity by others. They do not show equally pure doctrine, or equal balance of judgment on the part of the writers, though they belong probably to the first quarter of the second century. Barnabas' letter is too anti-Mosaic in tone to have emanated from the fellow-labourer of Paul, though containing valuable references to the death of Christ, and the ritual of sacrifice as typical of Him. The Shepherd of Hermas, evangelical in several respects, is extravagant and visionary in others. It refers in only one passage to atonement by the death of Christ (Sim. 6). The seven Letters of Ignatius († 116), all mentioned by Eusebius, seem to have been much interpolated. They who reduce the authentic letters to three, have still to confront the question of interpolation. The letters contain important anti-Docetic statements and striking allusions to Christ's death, and breathe much which probably emanated from the saintly Ignatius ; but I will not appeal to letters which are doubtful, and which exaggerate the difference between the Old and New Testament, so that readers feel themselves removed from the Pauline equipoise and sobriety.

The EPISTLE TO DIOGNETUS, the production of an unknown author about the middle of the second century, though some make it much earlier, is justly regarded as a patristic gem. It gives us one of the most striking delineations of the atonement in ecclesiastical antiquity. The passage, which I shall give in full, is as follows : "When the measure of our iniquity was filled up, and it was perfectly manifest that punishment and death awaited us as a reward, and the time came which God had fore-ordained for now manifesting His own goodness and power, because God's love, according to His abounding kindness, is unique, He neither hated nor rejected us, nor remembered our wickedness, but showed long-suffering and forbearance, saying,[1] 'He BORE our sins.' He Himself gave His

---

[1] λέγων is in the text of the Paris edition ; but whether it is retained, as it is by some editors, or rejected, as by others, it is absurd to say, as Bähr does, that ἀναδίξατο is ascribed to the Father.

own Son a RANSOM for us, the Holy for transgressors, the Innocent for the guilty, the Righteous for the unrighteous, the Incorruptible for the corruptible, the Immortal for the mortal;
for what else could cover our sins but His righteousness? In
what but in the Son of God alone could we, transgressors and
ungodly, be justified? O sweet EXCHANGE! O unsearchable
work! O beneficence beyond expectation! That the iniquity of
many should be HID IN ONE righteous person, and the righteousness of One should justify many transgressors!" (ch. 9.)
The idea of substitution, or exchange of places, the essential
element of the atonement, is explicitly expressed; and nothing
can be conceived more precise. We do not hesitate to assert
that this noble passage, reproducing the substance of St. Peter's
statement, is a proof that vicarious satisfaction was held by
the writer. It will not admit the idea of a mere moral redemption. Bähr,[1] however, with a special pleading, which suggests
important lessons on the ethics of quotation, argues against
this conclusion on many grounds, and especially because redemption by Christ is not deduced in the epistle from punitive
justice, but from the ineffably great love of God, and because
the phrase " He bore our sins," as he supposes, is ascribed to
the Father, and cannot be taken in the Anselmic sense. In
other words, Bähr compels a writer in the beginning of the
second century to think the theories and speak the words of
the mediating theology of Germany in the nineteenth century!
No special pleading of this nature can invalidate this testimony
to Christ's satisfaction in room of His people. If the meaning
of the terms RANSOM and SIN-BEARING is not doubtful in the
epistles of Paul and Peter, this must determine the sense here
to be attached to them.

We here add a few remarks generally on the Apostolic
Fathers, and the theology of the second century. 1. They,
with one accord, connect man's salvation with the death of
Christ, considered in the twofold light of a RANSOM and a
SACRIFICE,—terms that came with a divine impress on them,
and were used in the church from the beginning with the
same meaning. A ransom and a sacrifice, notwithstanding
their peculiar shade of difference, agree in this, that they involve intervention, substitution, and satisfaction from without;
and no man is warranted to efface the meaning which belongs
to them, as Bähr has ventured to do. 2. The idea of divine
justice, and the necessity of satisfying it in its penal and
preceptive aspect, underlies these statements. The Apostolic

_____
[1] *Die Lehre der Kirche vom Tode Christi in den ersten drei Jahrhunderten.*
Von K. Bähr.

Fathers and the author of the Epistle to Diognetus presuppose the forensic side of Christianity, viz. moral government, law, sin, penal infliction,—elements which are all fully recognised. Modern notions were unknown; and we may say the early church was secured against them by high conceptions of Christ's divine dignity, naturally leading men to an objective atonement.   3. They laid stress on Christ's sinlessness as part of His vicarious work; for voluntary service and moral perfection on the part of Christ are made prominent in the Epistle to Diognetus.   This side of the atonement, on which too many modern schools look with disfavour, is emphatically asserted by the Fathers of the second century.   4. They maintained the special reference of the atonement, and its unfailing efficacy, or the property of carrying with it the element of its own application.   The first is found in the Circular Letter of the Church of Smyrna.   The other comes to light in such statements as those of Clement, affirming that Christ's death procured the grace of repentance.

II. We come now to the period of the patristic theology. In the writers of the second century we find constant reference to the BLOOD OF CHRIST as the ground of redemption, not to His doctrine or example.   This is a peculiarity of JUSTIN MARTYR, who suffered under Marcus Aurelius († 161–8).   His chief productions, the first and second *Apology* in behalf of the persecuted Christians, and the *Dialogue with Trypho the Jew*, when we consider the nature of those compositions as meant for readers without the Christian church as well as within it, contain very express passages on Christ's atonement, more indeed than our space permits us to quote.   Deducting some overdone typical references, the testimony of this Father is very emphatic. At the end of the second *Apology* he thus expressed himself, without the fetters of theological nomenclature, which was not yet invented: "Next to God [the Father] we adore and love the Word of the unbegotten and ineffable God, because for our sakes He became man, that, being partaker of our sufferings, He might bring us healing" (ch. 13).   Deliverance from death is happily likened to deliverance in Egypt by means of the passover blood: "And as the blood of the passover saved those in Egypt, so shall the BLOOD of Christ SAVE FROM DEATH them that believe" (*Dial.* 111).   Victory over Satan is a marked feature of his theology.

From such explicit mention of the EFFECTS of Christ's death, we anticipate equal accuracy as to its NATURE; and we find it so.   His favourite mode of representing the atonement is that of a sacrifice ($\pi\rho\sigma\sigma\phi\rho\alpha$),—a view that recurs constantly, more frequently indeed than the cognate term RANSOM, though we see the two ideas merging into each other (*Dial.* 40, 111). Justin notices Christ's ACTIVE OBEDIENCE as an element in His vicarious work. Thus, by a typical allusion to Jacob's service, Justin argues that Christ served a service unto death for men of every description (*Dial.* 134). His doctrine of the atonement assumes its SPECIAL DESTINATION, and the RECEPTIVITY OF FAITH. As to its destination, modern investigation overlooks this aspect of early patristic theology; nay, some are ill-informed enough to suppose that this involves the insertion of conditions to be done on man's part. Justin regarded the atonement as specially destined for the church, or for Christ's people, describing it as a " sacrifice for all sinners who are willing to repent, and fast the fast that Isaiah speaks of " (*Dial.* 40).[1] Such expressions, which are often repeated, intimate a definite connection, and that our sins were the cause of Christ's suffering and death. As to the receptivity of FAITH, we find that in Justin's time the application of redemption was considered as depending, not on works, preparations, or ritual ordinances, but on faith simply as receptive. Thus, in the first *Apology*, he says that Christ became man by a virgin, according to the Father's will, for the salvation of them that believe in Him (τῶν πιστευόντων αὐτῷ, ch. 63); and this frequent phrase means, as in Scripture, that works are excluded, and that all hinges on faith alone. Later corruptions made something else necessary. Nor does he make the Eucharist other than commemorative,[2] and subsidiary to faith (εἰς ἀνάμνησιν τοῦ πάθους ὃν ἔπαθεν ὑπὲρ τῶν καθαιρομένων τὰς ψυχάς, ch. 41).

Attempts have recently been made by Bähr, Ritschl, and Pressensé, to turn aside Justin's testimony, and make him speak in favour of what is called a moral redemption, but in vain. Not to dwell on Ritschl's[3] remark, that Justin conditions the forgiveness of sin by repentance, obedience of works, and the sinless life of the baptized,—an utter mistake of his theological views,—let me advert to the plausible assertion of Bähr and Pressensé,[4] that Justin knew nothing of vicarious satisfaction to divine justice. This is an allegation based on his comment on the apostle's words, that Christ was "made a curse for us." This text Justin was the first among the Fathers to ex-

---

[1] So *Dial.* c. 134: δι' αἵματος καὶ μυστηρίου τοῦ σταυροῦ κτησάμενος αὐτούς.

[2] The attempts of Romanists to prove that Justin lends countenance to the eucharistic sacrifice are refuted by Höfling, *die Lehre vom Opfer*, 1857.

[3] Ritschl, *die Entstehung der Altkatholischen Kirche*, 1857.

[4] Pressensé, *Bulletin Theologique*, No. 1, 1867.

pound, raising a question which he did not succeed in solving. Referring to the Jewish cavil, that Christ was crucified as an enemy of God, and accursed, he maintained that Christ's death by crucifixion was analogous to another fact in Jewish history, viz. that God commanded Moses to prepare the brazen serpent, though He had told the nation that they were not to make an image of anything in heaven above or in the earth beneath, and proceeds as follows (*Dial.* 94, 95): " As God therefore ordered the image of the serpent to be made in brass, and was blameless, so is there in the law a curse against crucified men, BUT NO MORE CURSE (οὐκ ἔτι δή) AGAINST THE CHRIST OF GOD, by whom He saves all those who did things worthy of the curse. For, according to the law of Moses, the whole human race will be found subject to the curse: ' Cursed is every one that continueth not in the things which are written in the book of the law to do them.' No one has perfectly fulfilled the law: you [Jews] will not venture to deny this: some have kept the commandments more, and others less. If they who are under the law are manifestly under the curse because they have not kept all things, shall not all the Gentiles much rather be under the curse, who are idolaters, youth-corrupters, and perpetrators of other enormities? If, then, the Father of the universe purposed that His Christ, for the sake of men of every tribe, should TAKE UPON HIM THE CURSES OF ALL, knowing that He would raise Him up again when He was crucified and dead, why do you speak of Him who undertook to suffer these things according to the Father's will, as if [or, on the supposition that] He was accursed, and not rather bewail yourselves? For if His Father, if He Himself brought it to pass, that He SUFFERED THESE THINGS FOR THE HUMAN RACE, you certainly did not do it as obeying the will of God. And let none of you say: If the Father willed that He should suffer these things that the human race might be healed by His stripes, we have done nothing amiss."

Justin did not successfully solve the difficulty which he raised, but he made the honest effort, with his mind plainly imbued with the doctrine of satisfaction. To any one who puts the two statements together this is evident: for, on the one hand, he says that there is NO MORE CURSE TO THE CHRIST of God,—that is, it does not properly extend to Him; and, on the other, that CHRIST TOOK UPON HIM THE CURSES OF ALL. Similar statements are repeated, to the effect that Christ was not accursed. The two affirmations are easy of explanation, if we distinguish the direct and indirect, the personal and official, which Justin, however, does not pause to do. No one, when maintaining that the Lord took the curse upon Him, ever spoke as if Christ were to be represented as the direct object of the curse. Justin does not expressly say, that in His death Christ directly bore THE PENAL INFLICTION of the curse from the hand of God; but neither does he, in the style of shallow modern theories, limit the curse to what was inflicted by wicked men. His comment, imperfect though it is, amounts to this, that in some sense Christ took on Himself the curse, atoning for our sin and removing our curse; and that Israel were the wicked instruments of carrying it out. Plainly, vicarious satisfaction is involved in the statement.[1]

Thus, at the earliest time, the essential elements of the atonement were held with full conviction, and it was accepted as the great saving fact before discussions and debates arose as to its nature. Christ's deity did not become an article of belief with the ecclesiastical confession of it at the Council of Nice; and in like manner the atonement, kept before the view of the church in the weekly Eucharist, had always been from the beginning the great central truth of Christianity.

We come now to IRENÆUS, Bishop of Lyons and Vienne, who suffered in the persecution under Septimius Severus (✝ A.D. 202). In him the doctrine of the atonement reached a development beyond which no advance was made for a very long period. Nay, it receded from Irenæus' view-point, much to its disadvantage. We do not hesitate to say, that Irenæus apprehended the doctrine more profoundly than any patristic writer whose works have come down to us. So definite, indeed, is his outline of the atonement, that we might almost make a transition from him to Anselm, without feeling any great gap in the development. So long a vista before us reminds me to curtail quotations as much as possible, and avoid repeating from other writers what has already been exhibited in those who preceded. This sketch might be amplified indefinitely; but we cannot, in the limits at our disposal, give an exhaustive statement, and shall restrict ourselves to the landmarks of history, or new phases of opinion, whether an advance or deviation.

With Irenæus the doctrine entered on a new or second stage. He exhibits its positive side; regarding it as a provision indispensably necessary, according to his ideal of humanity. He speaks of the death of Christ as a ransom (v. 1), and as a sacrifice (iv. 20), connecting the remission of sins with it, as do all the previous writers. Irenæus, however, developes

[1] Semisch denies the element of substitution here; Dorner, *On the Person of Christ*, more correctly, maintains it.

the doctrine of the atonement from TWO APOSTOLIC THOUGHTS in a way not expressly done before. The FIRST of these is, that Jesus was the SECOND ADAM. From this point of view he surveys the entire field, showing that the disobedience of the first man entailed the forfeiture of all things, bringing with it death, rejection, and subjection to Satan; while the counterpart obedience of the second Man reversed all this, and brought with it the opposite blessings. The expositions of Irenæus have this Pauline thought constantly in view (Rom. v. 12–19). Conse-quently these elucidations have a completeness and a positive character, which serve to show how necessary the atonement was, according to Irenæus, from the very idea of man. He connects the unity of the represented and the representative, after the Pauline style of description (Rom. vi. 1–11), when he expresses himself thus: " In the first man WE sinned, not keeping the commandment; but in the second Adam WE were reconciled, BECOMING obedient unto death: for we were debtors to no other but to Him whose commandment we had transgressed at the beginning" (v. 16. 3). This great thought, introduced into the subject of the atonement, gives Irenæus' view a breadth and elevation far beyond all the statements of his predecessors. He considered Christ's entire obedience from the incarnation to the crucifixion as the vicarious work of the second Adam entering into the position of the first. This, therefore, is, according to him, the constituent element of the atonement. Speaking of the Mediator, Irenæus says: " He united man to God; for un-less man had conquered the enemy of man, the adversary would not righteously have been conquered. Again, had not God gifted (ἐδωρήσατο) salvation to us, we should not securely possess it. And unless man were united to God, he could not have been partaker of incorruption. For it was necessary that the Mediator between God and men should, by His peculiar affinity with both, bring both to friendship and concord, and at once present man to God, and manifest God to men" (iii. 18. 7). Irenæus, in a very profound way, views the second Adam as entering into man's place, and accomplishing all that was necessary to propitiate God, and redeem man from the tempter. The great fact of satisfaction by substitution, though neither of these terms actually occurs, is thus described: " the Lord having ransomed us (λυτρωσαμένου) by His own blood, and given His soul for (ὑπέρ) our souls, and His own flesh for (ἀντί) our flesh" (v. 1). We have in these terms an explicit description of a ransom paid by the Lord in His own person, without addition or aid from external sources; and the several elements of our nature are thus made constituent parts of the ransom. No man without arbitrary caprice can construe the language otherwise. Not only so : we find Irenæus explicitly asserting that Christ was a high priest on earth, as He fulfilled the divine law[1] (iv. 8).

The SECOND apostolic thought with which Irenæus' mind was imbued, and from which his whole theology takes its peculiar tincture, was that Christ, for the overthrow of Satan, became partaker of the same flesh and blood with us (Heb. ii. 14). To this deep conviction he was particularly conducted by the gnostic theories of his age. His views of redemption from Satan are more copiously developed than by any previous writer. But there is no ground for the assertion sometimes hazarded, that Irenæus maintained the notion that the ransom was paid to Satan. No statement to that effect is found in his writings, though he strongly maintains that man's deliverance from Satan was effected in a way of justice; that is, by that which rendered it right for a just God to liberate us. Irenæus proves (v. 1. 1 ; 21. 1–3 ; iii. 18. 2. 7) that man, by complying with the tempter, fell under his power. His liberation was impossible for sinful men ; and as little could God liberate him but in conformity with His immutable rectitude. Man must conquer his deceiver in a way of rectitude, and revoke his dis-obedience (*solvere, replasmare*) by a free obedience. As man was incompetent for this, the Logos became incarnate for this end (iii. 18). Irenæus vehemently insists on the identity of the Lord's flesh with ours, but in terms which expressly make room for the maintenance of Christ's absolute sinlessness in contrast with our defilement (v. 14. 3). Thus, referring to the apostle's statement that we are reconciled in the body of His flesh, Irenæus says : " Righteous flesh reconciled that flesh which was held captive in sin, and put it on a friendly footing toward God" (v. 14. 2). After making the distinction already noticed, he adds : " If any one ascribes to the Lord another substance of flesh, the word of reconciliation will no longer last for him ; for that which was once at enmity is reconciled. But if the Lord took *flesh of a different substance,* it is no longer that which had been made an enemy by transgression that is reconciled to God. But now the Lord has reconciled man to God the Father by fellowship with Himself" (iii. 14. 3). He views the obedience of the second man as the ground of accept-ance, cleansing, victory, and LIFE (iv. 10. 2).

---

[1] Non enim solvebat sed adimplebat legem summi sacerdotis opera perficiens, *propitians* pro hominibus *Deum* et emundans leprosos (iv. 8). This profound allusion by Irenæus to the fulfilling of the law shows that he in part anticipated what the Reformers displayed.

Not to adduce other passages, we call attention to the fact that Irenæus, one of the profoundest minds of all antiquity, in a thoroughly biblical way took in all the previous development, and assimilated it, but made a great advance upon it. He penetrated more fully into the Pauline thoughts, and it would have been well had no distracting theories subsequently come in to draw the church aside from the ground he occupied.

CLEMENS of Alexandria did nothing to advance the doctrine of the atonement, and refers to it only incidentally, though with a full appreciation of its value. We advance to his more distinguished pupil ORIGEN, whose vast influence, mixed indeed, and subject to many deductions, was felt for many ages († A.D. 254). This remarkable man speaks in one character when he utters the simple faith of the Christian, and in another when he presents himself to us as the speculative divine. He has interwoven into his works as many allusions to the atonement, and with as deep a sense of its importance, as are to be found in almost any writer. The fact of SIN-BEARING, and the infinite ACCEPTABLENESS of the sacrifice, are everywhere described with singular freshness. Thus, in his *Homilies on Leviticus*, Origen says : " He who was made in the likeness of men, and found in fashion as a man, doubtless for sin which He had taken from us, *because He bore our sins*, offered a young bullock without blemish—that is, an undefiled flesh—as a sacrifice to God " (Hom. 3). Speaking of the acceptableness of the offering because He did no sin, he adds : " What was so acceptable as the sacrifice of Christ, who offered Himself to God ?" (Hom. Lev. 1.) In his *Commentary on John* he often mentions sin-bearing. Thus he says, on John xii. 50 : " God the Word, the truth, the wisdom, and the righteousness, did not die : for the image of the invisible God, the first-born of every creature, was incapable of death. But this Man died for the people, the purest of all creatures, who bore our sins and infirmities, inasmuch as He was able (ἅτε δυνάμενος) *to take upon Himself the sin of the whole world, to destroy, consume, and delete it :* for He did no sin, neither was guile found in His mouth. Nor did He know sin ; and for this reason I think Paul spoke thus : ' He made Him to be sin for us, who knew no sin, that we might be made the righteousness of God in Him :' for, said he, He made Him to be sin, though He knew no sin, by His taking on Him the sins of all, though He sinned not Himself; and by becoming, if we must boldly say so, much more than His apostles, the filth of the earth, and the offscouring of all things unto this day." As to the necessity of the atonement, Origen says : " Had there been no sin, it would not have been necessary for the Son of God to become the Lamb, nor would He have needed to appear in the flesh to be immolated, but would have remained what He was in the beginning—God the Word. But as sin entered into this world, and the necessity of sin demands propitiation, and propitiation is not effected but by sacrifice, it was necessary that a sacrifice for sin should be provided " (Hom. on Num. xxiv. 1). Perhaps none of the Fathers did more than Origen to exhibit and circulate this great central thought of VICARIOUS SIN-BEARING.

The cognate idea of the vicarious *bearing of punishment* is not less prominent in Origen. Nothing can be more express than Origen's language as to Christ's sin-bearing and curse-bearing in His capacity of substitute; and his wide influence circulated these precious thoughts, in a dogmatic form, more fully throughout the Greek Church than had ever been done before. Nor was this ever afterwards counteracted. Further, he urges that the atonement rendered God propitious (see on Rom. iii. 23). He shows, on Leviticus, that Christ, both priest and sacrifice, accomplished in fact what the types foreshadowed and foretold.

But there is another side of Origen's theology on the atonement, so faulty and mischievous, that, were we to adjust the balance between his services and demerits, we should almost be at a loss to say whether he more established the truth or undermined it. When he comes to ground the doctrine and portray the effects of the atonement, he discovers a faulty theology, an ill-balanced judgment, and great temerity. Some of the best elements of Irenæus' exposition, especially the great thought that the atonement was the obedience of the second Adam, fall into the background, or are altogether dropped. Not only so; the indispensable necessity of the atonement, involved in Irenæus' first principle, becomes but a RELATIVE necessity. This could not be otherwise, when we reflect on two peculiarities of Origen's theology,—his view of justice, and his view of punishment. As to his view of justice, though it is more definite and biblical than the Platonic theory expressed by Clemens Alexandrinus, it is still in the highest degree defective. He makes it a form of manifesting GOODNESS, another side of goodness. He does not speak of the atonement as the equipoise of justice and goodness, but in the same style with Bonaventura, Grotius, and the semi-philosophic theories of after ages. He sometimes, indeed, strongly speaks of the love of God as exercised in no arbitrary way, but through the channel of justice ; but his avowed principle as to justice is in the last degree faulty, though he is often, happily, inconsistent with himself ; and this appears especially in the way in which he speaks of Gethsemane, and the cup which Christ, as the vicarious sin-bearer, of necessity must drink (*Com. on Matt.*). Origen's notion that punishment is disciplinary and corrective, must be noticed as a further flaw which tended to sap and undermine biblical doctrine. These philosophizing speculations were corrected in himself, however, by the deep piety and biblical study which were the element of his life, but were still hurtful to the church.

There were other speculations of Origen, however, which were doctrinally and practically mischievous.

1. One was the wayward theory which he engrafted on the admirable statements of Irenæus as to the victory over Satan. Origen's baseless fancy was that the RANSOM WAS PAID TO SATAN ; that Satan demanded the soul of Jesus, the most precious thing that ever was ; and that God, from love to us, delivered Him, or, more strictly, that the Logos gave up His human soul to Satan. This was a foolish fancy ; and our only wonder is that it was ever accepted by others, and dressed up by such able men as Gregory of Nyssa, and other followers of Origen in the Greek Church, and then transferred as a discovery to the Western Church. According to Origen's theory, Satan had legitimate authority to hold men in the domain of death, but forfeited that right as soon as he brought it to bear against a sinless man. He held that, by a certain artifice practised on the adversary, Jesus, who could not long have been holden of him, was for a time surrendered up, that Satan might be misled into an abuse of his authority—legitimate only within a given sphere—and forfeit his right altogether. This preposterous notion, unbiblical in itself, and a complete misconception of God, the prime fountain of law and justice, and also of Satan, a mere subordinate official, is not really worthy of a grave refutation. To state is to refute it. The apostles leave us in no doubt that the ransom or sacrifice was offered to God (Rev. v. 9 ; Eph. v. 2).

2. It was another error of Origen, that he extended the efficacy of the atonement to all the universe. Up to this time the Fathers, as we have already noticed, spoke of the atonement as efficacious for the church, and destined for the church. Nor did they perplex themselves and others with fruitless and insoluble problems as to the bearing of the atonement on the class outside. The blood of Christ was the full and adequate ransom for the church, and there, with spiritual wisdom, they stopped. Origen, however, speculated on its possible applications ; and not content with saying what it could by possibility be con-

ceived as capable of accomplishing had God so willed, he extended its actual range to the whole universe, maintaining that all creatures, and even devils, shared in its redemptive power. He made it co-extensive with creation, the stars, angels, and man; engrafting upon it the theory of the restoration of all things. This may show the high value which Origen attached to the atonement as the achievement of the God-man; but it was a mischievous perversion of biblical doctrine.

3. Another error of Origen, which he did not mean to put in opposition to the atonement, but too soon came to neutralize the doctrine of the cross in after ages, was that he began to speak of forgiveness by good works; and this evil leaven soon spread.

In the fourth century, to which we now come, the greatest name is ATHANASIUS, whose services in defence of Christ's deity have rather hid his contributions to the doctrine of the atonement († A.D. 373). But no man, in the whole compass of patristic theology, with the exception of Irenæus, rendered more important service in connection with this doctrine. His theory, superior to Origen's, and not liable to so many deductions, seasonably met the wants of men repelled by the notion that the ransom was paid to Satan. Two treatises of Athanasius—*On the Incarnation*[1] *of the Logos*, and the *Orations against the Arians*, especially the former—contain a digest of his opinions on the atonement. I shall give a brief outline of his theory, with a notice of its merits and defects.

Athanasius does not start, as Irenæus and Anselm do, from SIN ITSELF, but from ITS EFFECTS; but he has a profound view of death as the wages of sin. The theory, traced to its fundamental principle, though it is not based on the deepest foundation, is the EQUIPOISE OF GOD'S VERACITY AND LOVE. A few passages will exhibit this. The death threatened at the beginning as the penalty of sin, consists in estrangement from God, the principle of life ($\alpha\dot{v}\tau o\zeta\omega\dot{\eta}$); and the problem to be solved was this: The divine veracity threatening death as the inevitable penalty of sin must be maintained, while divine goodness could not allow the creatures of God to fall into annihilation: "God would not have been TRUE, if, after saying that we should die, man had not died. On the other hand, it was not befitting that rational beings, once created and partakers of His Logos, should perish, and through corruption return to non-being.

---

[1] Though this book is adduced under different titles by subsequent writers, it was never doubted that it was a genuine work of Athanasius. I am surprised to see M. Pozzy, in his effective reply to Pressensé, speaking of it as a work *attribué à Athanase*," and adding, "D'après l'auteur quel qu'il soit de ce Libre." Ample quotations from it as Athanasius' work by Theodoret (see third Dialogue, entitled ἀπαθής) put its authenticity beyond doubt.

For it was not WORTHY OF GOD'S GOODNESS, that creatures made by Him should be destroyed because of the fraud practised on men by the devil" (de Incar. ch. 6). He then proceeds to show that none but the Logos was competent to renew all, to suffer for all, to intercede for all (ch. 7); and thus forcibly describes the mode of the incarnation with a view to the atonement: "Taking a body from us similar to ours, because we were all subject to the corruption of death, He offered it to the Father, delivering it to death, in the exercise of the highest love, in the room of all, that, since all died in Him, the law as to man's corruption might be dissolved, inasmuch as its power was exhausted in the Lord's body, and had no more place against men in the same body" (ch. 8). The two elements of veracity and love are exhibited in the same way in the Orations against the Arians (Or. i. 44, ii. 14), where he argues that it was unworthy of God to let His workmanship perish, and His love would not permit it.

He gave prominence to the Lord's vicarious death, as the actual fulfilment of the threatened penalty. No more explicit statement of substitution can be expressed, than when he speaks of death, the common lot of man, as a universal principle holding the race in captivity, and of Christ assuming a body to die this death in the room of others, allowing it to assail and hold Him under its power: "Since it was necessary that the debt of all (τὸ ὀφειλόμενον παρὰ πάντων) should be paid,—for, as I said before, all were subject to death, and this was the main reason of the incarnation,—therefore, after manifesting His deity by miracles, He at last offered the sacrifice for all, surrendered His own temple to death in the room of all, that on the one hand He might discharge and free all from the old transgression, and on the other evince Himself superior to death, exhibiting His own incorruptible body as the first-fruits of the general resurrection" (ch. 20). He adds that, the common Saviour of all having died for us, we who are believers in Christ no longer die as of old according to the threat of the law : for such a judicial sentence has ceased[1] (20, 21).

[1] That the quotations from the Fathers are by no means unimportant, Priestley showed when he actually had the confidence to appeal to patristic theology to countenance his Socinian opinions. A crushing reply was given by three Dutch writers—Velingius, Segaar, and Gavel—1787, in one thick volume, and by Bishop Horsley. For those who have not the Fathers, I may refer to the quotations given by GROTIUS, Stein, and Seiler, at the end of their works on Christ's Satisfaction ; by Thomasius, Christi Person und Werk, p. 157 ; Philippi, Glaubenslehre, p. 48 ; Shedd, History of Doctrine ; Pozzy, Histoire du Dogma de la Redemption, 1868. But second-hand references are always unsatisfactory ; and all who have access to the Fathers themselves will find that a belief in Christ's expiation was part of the Christian consciousness of all ages.

These passages clearly evince Athanasius' views as to the mode in which death was overthrown, and this paved the way for the communication of life by Christ's resurrection.   He shows that Death was annihilated by invading this body, and that life flowed in; that martyrs trample on death, and that women and children can triumph over him.   The doctrine of Athanasius is, that the Logos, to destroy death and remove the curse, took a mortal body (*θνητόν*); meaning MORTAL not by the law of its being, but in the sense of being capable of undergoing death.

While Athanasius asserted the elements of the doctrine already mentioned with great power, and gained general recognition for them in the Greek Church, his theory has defects which it is proper to mention.   1. He did not, with Irenæus and Anselm, put the atonement in RELATION TO SIN ITSELF, but surveyed it in connection with THE CONSEQUENCES of sin.   He fixed on death, and sees the atonement as its destruction; giving an important contribution so far as he goes, but stopping short at man's liberation from the penal consequences of sin, and not referring to the reparation of the divine honour.   2. Athanasius did not put the necessity of the atonement on its true foundation: with him, as with Origen, it is only a relative necessity.   Thus he says: " God could have simply spoken, and destroyed the curse without any incarnation at all.   But it is necessary to consider what is profitable for men, and not reckon in all things what it was possible for God to do" (3d Orat. against the Arians).   However much these statements were approved among the Fathers, and even by Calvin, they were unsatisfactory, and found to be no bulwark against Socinianism.   3. In Athanasius' theory the positive element of vicarious obedience, and the position of the second Adam under the law, were not allowed to come to their rights.   It acknowledges the curse, and sees a provision for its removal: but it leaves untouched the positive demand or inflexible claim of the law, which the entrance of sin neither revoked nor modified.[1]

One thing demands notice in connection with the development of the early patristic doctrine of the atonement: the discussions on the dignity of Christ's person exercised an im-

---

[1] See Dr. Baur's *Christliche Lehre von der Versöhnung*, Tübingen 1838,—a work of great learning and historical research.   Of his impartiality and competence I had a higher opinion sixteen years ago, when I first perused the book, than further study will permit me to express now.   Not that he intends to be unfair.   He states the views of different writers as honestly as can be expected from a man who had no belief in the historic fact of the atonement; but all too plainly he sees many things with a jaundiced eye.   The main use of the book is to prompt and direct independent research.

portant influence of a favourable kind. The Fathers first argued from the work of redemption to the necessity of a divine Redeemer. Afterwards, when the Council of Nice gave ecclesiastical sanction to the doctrine of the Lord's deity, they set forth the infinite value of His person as essential to His vicarious work. Throughout the fourth century, and still more so after the rise of Nestorianism in the fifth century, we find the Fathers maintaining with one voice that Christ's sufferings were of infinite value, in virtue of the union of the divine and human natures in His one person. His divine dignity, they argued, put Him in a position such as a mere man could never occupy, conferring infinite value on His SACRIFICE or RANSOM,—the two terms by which they designated the death of Christ. This truth, though held from the beginning, was now brought out prominently. Finite creatures, it was shown, could not have brought a sacrifice of infinite value; but when a divine Redeemer undertook it, His infinite dignity brought it to a successful issue. A brief notice of the views of the great divines who adorned the Greek Church during the fourth and fifth centuries will fully exhibit this.

EUSEBIUS of Cæsarea, surnamed the friend of Pamphilus († A.D. 340), and a member of the Nicene Council, though giving a reluctant consent to the distinctive expressions of its creed, brings out with precision the main elements of the atonement. Without multiplying quotations, a few passages from Eusebius will sufficiently prove this. Thus he says (*Demonstratio Evangelica*, book x.): "Certainly the Lamb of God, who beareth the sin of the world, was made a curse for us, whom God made sin for us, though He knew no sin, delivering Him as a substitute for the life (ἀντίψυχον) of us all, that we might be made the righteousness of God in Him." Then, two or three sentences afterwards, he puts this question: "But how does He make our sins His own, and how is He said to bear our iniquities?" In answering this, Eusebius bases his remarks on the saying of Paul, that we are the body of Christ, and thus proceeds: "As, when one member suffers, all the members suffer with it; so, when many members suffer and sin, He also, on grounds of sympathy—since it pleased Him, who is the Word of God, to take the form of a servant and to be united to the common tabernacle of us all—takes upon Himself the sorrows of the suffering members, and makes our diseases His own, and suffers grief and trouble for us all, according to the laws of philanthropy; and that Lamb of God, not only by doing these things, but by being punished for us (ὑπὲρ ἡμῶν κολασθείς), and enduring the retribution (τιμωρίαν) which He did not owe, but which we owed by reason of the multitude of our offences, became to us the author (αἴτιος) of the forgiveness of sins, as He bore death for us, and transferred to Himself the stripes, insults, and dishonours due to us, and drew upon Himself the curse merited by us, being made a curse for us. And what else was this but giving life for life (καὶ τί γὰρ ἄλλο ἢ ἀντίψυχον)? Hence the oracle, speaking in our person, says, ' By His stripes we are healed.'"[1]

One of the most pleasing and practical writers of the fourth century is CYRILL of Jerusalem († A.D. 386), whose sermons on the Creed (Catacheses), though bearing to have been delivered as extemporary expositions, contain much precious, well-expressed truth. In his discourse on the words CRUCIFIED AND BURIED, Cyrill refers to the atonement in terms nearly similar to those of Athanasius, laying stress on the divine dignity of Christ: "And do not wonder if the whole world was ransomed (ἐλυτρώθη); for He was *not a mere man*, but the only-begotten Son of God. Yet the sin of one man Adam prevailed to bring death upon the world. But if, by the offence of one, death entered the world as a king, how shall not life much more reign by the righteousness of one ?" (13. 2.)

Then, towards the close of the same discourse, Cyrill expresses himself to this effect: "We were by reason of sin God's enemies, and God appointed that the sinner should die. One of two things, therefore, must happen: either God must maintain His veracity (ἀληθεύοντα), must cut off all, or in His philanthropy revoke the sentence. But behold the wisdom of God! He at once maintained the truth of the sentence, and gave effect to His philanthropy. Christ took sins in His own body to the tree, that through His death we might die to sins and live to righteousness. It was no insignificant one (μικρός) that died for us : it was not an animal victim (πρόβατον αἰσθητόν) : it was not a mere man: it was no mere angel: but God incarnate. The guilt of sinners was not so great as the righteousness of Him who died for us. We did not sin to such an extent as He accomplished righteousness; who laid down His life for us,—laid it down when He pleased, and took it again when He pleased " (*Cat.* 13. 33). The outline of the atonement given by this judicious thinker, though severely practical and disinclined to speculation, bears a certain affinity to that given by the equally practical Chrysostom.

The three Cappadocians, allied by friendship and culture— BASIL, GREGORY of Nyssa, and GREGORY of Nazianzus—did not

[1] Book x. of Eusebius' *Demonstratio* is full of similar statements. See especially his comment on the twenty-second Psalm.

advance beyond the views of Origen. Basil and his younger brother Gregory Nyssen were but reproducers of Origen's opinions on this subject. Gregory Nazianzen repudiated the notion of a ransom paid to Satan, but in other respects adhered to the peculiarities of Origen's doctrine on the atonement; but all three evince the importance of the Lord's divine person as an essential prerequisite to the ransom.

BASIL († A.D. 379) brings out his views on the atonement in his homily on the forty-ninth Psalm (vers. 7, 8),—a rather conflicting combination of two things—the persuasion[1] of Satan and the propitiation of God (ἐξίλασμα τῷ Θεῷ). Thus he says: "Do not seek a brother for redemption, but one who exceeds your nature—not a mere man, but a God-man (ἄνθρωπον Θεόν)— Jesus Christ, who alone is able to make a propitiation to God for us all." Then, after a few sentences, he adds: "But one thing was found that was equivalent (ἀντάξιον) to all men, and given for the price of our soul's redemption—the holy and precious blood of our Lord Jesus Christ, which He poured out for us all" (sec. 4).

GREGORY Nyssen, more of a systematic divine than his brother, attempted an exposition of the deeper grounds of the atonement, so far as was consistent with the views of his master Origen. Raising the question why God did not denude Satan of his possession by simple power, he shows that the divine GOODNESS, WISDOM, JUSTICE, and POWER were all equally to be displayed, if the redemption of mankind was to be worthy of God. In his *Catechetical Oration* (ch. 15–26) he expatiates on the exercise of God's perfections, while we see in the background the idea of the deception or artifice which he supposes practised upon Satan. He says (ch. 24): "Goodness is apprehended in the choice to save that which was lost; wisdom and righteousness are displayed in the mode of our salvation; and power in His being made in the likeness and fashion of men, according to the meanness of our nature, and in the hope (ἐλπισθῆναι, i.e. on Satan's side) that He could, after the similitude of men, be held captive by death." Gregory widens the circle of the divine attributes called into exercise, as compared with his master Origen, who chiefly referred to the divine justice. He firmly held the GREAT FACT of the atonement, though theories are interspersed; and the atonement stands out as the great saving fact for mankind. Thus, in his elaborate work against Eunomius, the able champion of Arianism, Gregory rebuts an argument derived from Christ's

---

[1] Basil speaks of the devil being persuaded (πεισθείς) by a ransom of equal value to consent to the exchange.

obedience in the following terms (lib. ii.):—" He became obedient for our sakes, when He was at once MADE SIN AND A CURSE by reason of the divine plan in our behalf; not being such by nature, but made this by loving-kindness." No one can fail to see how closely he connected Christ's deity and atonement, recognising in the fullest manner the fact of the atonement, its nature, and consequences.

Gregory Nazianzen (✝ A.D. 389), the attached friend of Basil, differed from the theory of Origen in one point. He repudiated the doctrine to which the two last-mentioned Fathers attached themselves, viz. that a ransom must be paid to the enemy of mankind, such as the possessor of the captives demanded. Thus, in his forty-fifth Oration, delivered in the year 385, he rejects it as an audacious thought (φεῦ τῆς ὕβρεως): " We have to examine a doctrine neglected by many, but by me diligently investigated. To whom was the blood for us [offered], and for what reason was the great and precious (περιβόητον) blood of God, at once high priest and victim, shed? For we were held in bondage by the wicked one, sold under sin, receiving pleasure in return for vice. But if the ransom (λύτρον) does not belong to any other party but to him who holds the captive, I ask, to whom was this paid, and for what cause? If it is paid to the evil one (fie upon the audacity!)— if the robber not only receives a ransom from God, but receives God Himself as a ransom, and such exorbitant wages for his tyranny as the reason why it is just to spare us —. But if it is paid to the Father, then, *first*, how was it so? for we were not held in bondage by Him; and *secondly*, what is the reason that the Father was pleased with the blood of the Only-begotten, whereas He did not receive Isaac, offered by his father, but exchanged the sacrifice, substituting a ram for a rational victim? It is manifest that the Father receives it, not *that He either demanded it or needed it* (!), but by reason of the divine scheme of salvation, and because man needed to be sanctified by the humanity of God, that He Himself might deliver us, overcoming the tyrant by force, and bringing us back to Himself by His Son as Mediator" (ch. 22). Gregory Nazianzen abides by the other conclusions of Origen as to overreaching Satan; a preposterous theory, which had a strange fascination for many of the Fathers in the East and West.

CHRYSOSTOM (✝ A.D. 407), distinguished for his eloquence and the fervour of his piety, gives us positive biblical doctrine, without any theories or speculations beyond what the absolute necessity of the case required. He was a biblical divine, with an instinctive recoil from speculations which he seems to have felt would be exploded by a wider survey of the relations of truth. The doctrine developed by this great man is singularly balanced, because for the most part traced out from apostolical ideas, and an expansion of them doctrinally and practically. We make a few extracts from his Commentaries, or more properly Homilies, on the Pauline Epistles. Referring to the benefits conferred through Christ as a divine Saviour, Chrysostom remarks (Com. on Rom. v. 17): "For Christ has paid far more than we owed—as much more as a boundless ocean compared with a drop of water. Doubt not therefore, O man, when you see such a wealth of benefits; nor inquire how that spark of death and sin can be extinguished, when such a sea of blessings is let in upon it." Few commentators in any age have apprehended more profoundly than Chrysostom the great mutual exchange of places between Christ and His people, according to which He was made our sin, and we His righteousness. On this point, which may be called the core of the atonement, the statements of Chrysostom deserve special consideration. Thus, in commenting on the passage in Corinthians (2 Cor. v. 21), in connection with the previous context, he says: "Reflect how great a thing it was to give His Son for those who insulted Him. But now He has accomplished great things, and, besides, permitted Him who did nothing amiss to BE PUNISHED (κολασθῆναι) FOR OFFENDERS. But he (the apostle) did not merely say this, but affirmed what is much more than this: He made Him to be sin who knew no sin, who was absolute righteousness (αὐτοδικαιοσύνην); that is, left Him to be condemned as a sinner, to die as accursed: for cursed is every one that hangeth on a tree." Then, after a few sentences, he refers to the apostle's words as follows: "He [the apostle] says, He made the Righteous One a sinner, that He might make the sinners righteous. Nay, he not only said this, but what is a much greater thing; for he did not affirm the concrete (ἕξιν), but the abstract itself (ποιότητα). He did not say, He made Him a sinner, but sin." It appears, too, that the positive element of Christ's obedience entered into Chrysostom's theology. Thus he says (Hom. on Rom. x. 4): "Do not fear, then, as if you transgressed the law when you came to faith; for you transgress it when, by reason of it, you do not believe on Christ. When you have believed on Him, YOU HAVE FULFILLED IT, AND DONE MUCH MORE THAN IT COMMANDED: for you have received a far greater righteousness."

The last great movement within the pale of the Greek Church, which contributed powerfully to develope the doctrine of the atonement, was the NESTORIAN CONTROVERSY. In

opposing the division or separation of the natures of Christ,
the church saw how fatal Nestorianism would soon prove to
the atonement; and in proportion as the church teachers laid
emphasis on the UNITY OF THE PERSON, and asserted that Jesus
was the Son of God incarnate, in the same proportion did they
attach infinite value to His work of atonement. It was the act
of the person, not of a mere man.

Among the teachers whose influence was most felt in this
direction, CYRILL of Alexandria († A.D. 444) was prominent. He
constantly raises the objection to Nestorius' views, that Christ's
atoning death owed its validity to the fact that He who suffered
in our stead was the divine Logos, and that His blood was the
blood of God's Son; and he asserts that it would have been
no equivalent had Jesus been a mere man. But His ransom
suffices to meet the wants of all mankind. Let me adduce a
specimen of the mode in which he brought this truth to bear
on the atonement. Thus, in his second *Oration de recta fide*
(sec. 7), Cyrill says on Gal. iii. **13** : "The law having pronounced him accursed who is in transgression and sin, He
who knew no sin—that is, Christ—has been subjected to
judgment, bearing an unjust sentence, and *suffering what was
due to those under the curse*, that He who was EQUIVALENT TO
THE UNIVERSE (ὁ τῶν ὅλων ἀντάξιος), dying for all, might discharge all from the charges of disobedience, and purchase all
that is under heaven with His own blood. Therefore one
would not have been an equivalent for all, had he been a
mere man. But if He is considered as God incarnate, and
suffering in His own flesh, the entire creation is small in comparison; and the death of one flesh is sufficient for the ransom
of the human race (τῆς ὑπ᾽ οὐρανον), for it belonged to the Logos
(ἰδία τοῦ λόγου), begotten of God the Father." Many similar
passages occur in Cyrill (see Cyr. on John i. 29, and reply to
Julian, lib. 9).

THEODORET, the contemporary of Cyrill, does not give such
express testimonies to this aspect of truth, as might indeed have
been expected from his Antiochian tendencies. We find the old
doctrine of Origen as to the defeat of Satan combined with the
reference to death on which Athanasius dwelt; but he lays
emphasis on substitution and curse-bearing as much as Cyrill.
In his tenth Oration on Providence, Theodoret eloquently dilates on Christ our substitute, and represents the Saviour as
addressing Satan subsequently to the crucifixion, and previous
to His resurrection: "You have been taken (ἑάλως), O wicked
one, and snared in your own toils." He challenges him to
point out a flaw in His life or heart; bids him withdraw from

his authority and desist from his tyranny, and says that He will deliver all from death, using righteous mercy (ἐλέω δικαίω).

After the age of Cyrill and Theodoret, little fresh thought was exercised within the pale of the Greek Church on the doctrine of the atonement. The thinking of previous ages was handed down, but never reduced to a unity. But the doctrine of vicarious sacrifice was the received view throughout the flourishing period of that church for five centuries. Man's captivity and his ransom by a representative were never questioned, even when the ransom was supposed to have been paid to the enemy of the human race. The elements were all there, though not fused into a unity; and John Damascene, the dogmatic divine (✝ 750), gathered up the thinking, but did not go beyond Athanasius' views. When we said that the elements were all received, we meant to add that the Greek Fathers did not ground the atonement sufficiently in the absolute necessity of satisfying divine justice. With them it was a positive arrangement, suited to man's wants, and worthy of God, not an absolute necessity on the supposition of man's salvation. From the time of Origen, whose philosophy of justice was too plainly derived from Clemens Alexandrinus, all the great Fathers of the Greek Church were much less decided than Irenæus in regarding the atonement in the light of SIN ITSELF, and more inclined to connect it merely with the CONSEQUENCES of sin. They speak of the atonement as if God had been pleased to appoint this positive provision for man's salvation. Origen, Athanasius, Gregory Nazianzen, Gregory Nyssen, Theodoret, all assert that it was positive, not based on a deeper necessity than man's welfare and God's free choice. Statements, it is true, occur in Cyrill of Jerusalem and Chrysostom, which, if fully thought out, would have led them, and it may be did lead them, to occupy the deeper ground of Irenæus, with whom Chrysostom at least had much in common. But as a school of theology, the Greek Church, while firmly maintaining the fact of the atonement, stopped short at what has been called its relative necessity. We shall see that the Confessions of the Reformation took better ground. The indecision on the part of the Greek theologians arose from the circumstance that they recoiled from a definition which seemed to interfere with the absolute dominion and unconditional freedom of God. But they did not give full justice to the forensic and ethical aspect of the question in the divine moral government in connection with the FACT OF SIN.

Our notice of the LATIN FATHERS may be much more succinct. They add nothing, in fact, to the outline of the doctrine furnished by the Fathers of the Greek Church; nay, sometimes, as in the case of Origen's theory, imported what might much better have been left behind. It would be a tedious repetition to adduce large extracts from their works, when they are quite similar to those already given. The death of Christ was viewed as a RANSOM and a SACRIFICE: the modern notion of moral redemption and absolute pardon, irrespective of expiation, was utterly unknown.

TERTULLIAN († A.D. 220), contemporary with Origen, but formed by earlier writers, assails the gnostic phantom-theory of Christ's humanity. He treats it as subversive of the atonement, because a phantom could not suffer. Thus, in his work against Marcion, he says: " Christ's death, the entire weight and fruit of the Christian name, is denied; the death which the apostle so strongly asserts as certainly real, making it the very foundation of the gospel and of our salvation, and of his own preaching" (book iii. ch. 8). The Latin word SATISFACTION, it is commonly said, was first applied by Tertullian to the atonement, though Bähr casts a doubt upon this, on the ground that the term SATISFY was used for a voluntary submission to the discipline of the church. He does not deny, however, that this juristic term found its way into the nomenclature of the Western Church from Tertullian, an eminent jurist before his conversion. CYPRIAN (A.D. 250), who had many things in common with Tertullian, is as explicit on vicarious sin-bearing. Thus he says: "Christ bore us all (*nos omnes portabat*), who also bore (*portabat*) our sins;" language proceeding on the assumption that Christ sustained our persons as a surety, and incurred our responsibilities (Epistle 63).

AMBROSE († A.D. 397), a man of Greek culture, speaks of Christ's atonement as a payment or ransom, as emphatically as Origen, who was in no small measure his master: "He owed nothing, but paid for all, as He Himself bears witness, saying, Then I restored what I took not away" (*Lib. de Tob.* 10). Again, in his elucidations of Genesis, he speaks in a style recalling the Epistle to Diognetus and Irenæus: " God, therefore, took flesh that He might abolish the curse of sinful flesh, and was made a curse for us, that the blessing might swallow up the curse, sinlessness sin, benevolence condemnation, and life death. For He underwent death that the sentence might be fulfilled, that A SATISFACTION might be made (*satisfierit*)" (ch. 7).

When we come to AUGUSTIN († A.D. 430), the greatest Western teacher, the same doctrine of sin-bearing and satisfaction by a sinless surety is explicitly asserted. We are, no doubt, surprised that so little is said by him on the subject of the atonement, compared with its prominence in Scripture and in the theology of the Reformation. But that may be explained by the fact that the church recognised the truth, and that the Supper kept it before men's minds. Besides, polemical discussions had never called substitution in question. Augustin expresses himself thus, on John (Tract 41): "We are reconciled only by the taking away of sin, which is the separating medium. But the Mediator is the Reconciler. Therefore, that the wall of separation might be taken down, the Mediator came, and the Priest Himself was made a sacrifice." In his exposition of Ps. xcv. he says: "Men were held captive under the devil, and served devils, but were redeemed from captivity. For they could sell themselves, but they could not redeem themselves. The Redeemer came and gave the price, shed His blood, and bought the world. Do you ask what He bought? See what He gave, and find what He bought. The blood of Christ is the price: what is of so great worth? What, but the whole world? What, but all nations?" In speaking of Christ's priestly oblation, Augustin lays emphasis on the incarnation, regarded as a something taken from our humanity: "Our Priest received from us what He might offer for us, for He took flesh from us: in that very flesh He was made a victim, a burnt-offering, a sacrifice" (on Ps. cxxix.). In perusing Augustin, we are at times made to feel, as we feel in the perusal of the Greek Fathers generally, that the elements of the question, though recognised, are not yet fused into a unity, nor so practical as they ought to be. Augustin's view looks like a modified Origenism on the atonement. Thus, in his work on the Trinity, he says: "What is the righteousness by which the devil was conquered? What, but the righteousness of Jesus Christ? And how was he conquered? Because, though he found nothing worthy in Him of death, he yet killed Him; and certainly it is just that the debtors whom he held should be liberated when they believe in Him whom he slew without any obligation to die" (book xiii. ch. 12–15). In the same strain, speaking of death, Augustin says: "Death could be overcome only by death; therefore Christ suffered death, that an UNJUST DEATH might overcome just death, and might deliver them that were justly guilty, while He was *unjustly* slain for them" (Serm. li.). He starts from the correct view, that man is liberated from Satan's dominion by means of a ransom or atoning death offered to God; but, to our surprise, comes in the course of his discussion to what seems tantamount to the doctrine of a ransom offered to Satan. But it is obviously more a mistake in manner and expression than in doctrine. He plainly means that the ransom was displayed and exhibited to Satan rather than offered to him. He seems, indeed, to vacillate or to go over from one mode of representing the matter to another. But in reality he was much more on Athanasius' ground than Origen's; and his language may be interpreted as meaning only a display or representation to Satan, so that the enemy must acknowledge the rectitude of the liberation of believers. Augustin had all the elements of the doctrine, though a certain reference to Satanic injustice, as in the case of the Greek Fathers, intercepted his view to some degree (see our remarks on Acts ii. 23).

In this historical outline our aim is to trace with all brevity the development of the doctrine of the atonement in history, and to exhibit its successive phases; and we therefore next advert to the most marked aspect which it assumed in the West. The discussions of Augustin on divine grace were not without a special influence. It was now definitely represented as offered for the elect or redeemed church. Not that this originated with Augustin, or was peculiar to the West; for the Greek Fathers, as we have already noticed, bring out the same element. But it was polemically maintained in the West against Pelagian and semi-Pelagian views. Prosper, the friend of Augustin, first contended in a definite form for special redemption, that is, for a specific ransom for the elect of God. But long before his time we find echoes of the same thing. Thus Cyprian, in his treatise addressed to Demetrianus, says: "Christ imparts this grace. He gives this gift of His mercy, by subduing death with the trophy of His cross, by *redeeming the believer* with the price of His blood" (*redimendo credentem*). Ambrose, too, in a definite way, speaks of a certain totality constituted by the people of God as taken by themselves: "God's people," says he, "have their own fulness. For there is reckoned to be a certain *special universality* in the elect and fore-ordained, distinguished from the generality of all; so that the whole world seems to be delivered from the whole world, and all men taken out of all men" (*ad Gratianum*). Augustin, whose views of special grace are well known, distinguishes in the same way with Ambrose between two totalities—a world at enmity with God, and a world which is reconciled. Thus, in commenting on 1 John ii. 2 (A.D. 416), he says: "The whole world, then, is the church, and the whole world hates the church. The world, then, hates the world: that which is at enmity hates the reconciled, the condemned the saved, the defiled the cleansed. But that world which God reconciles to Himself in Christ, and is saved by Christ, and which has all sin forgiven by Christ, is elected out of the world which is at enmity, condemned, and defiled. For out of that mass which is entirely ruined in Adam, are formed vessels of mercy, in which is the world belonging to the reconciliation" (Tract 87 on John).

PROSPER, in his correspondence with Augustin, referring to a class of men of semi-Pelagian sentiments, complains: "They would affirm that our Lord Christ died for all mankind, and that no man is excepted from the redemption of His blood." Without referring to Prosper's verses (de ingratis), we find him in different passages of his works declaring explicitly the doctrine of special redemption. Thus he says (A.D. 440): "He was not crucified in Christ who is not a member of the body of Christ. When the Saviour, then, is said to be crucified for the redemption of the whole world by reason of the true assumption of human nature, He may nevertheless be said to be crucified for those only to whom His death was made available" (resp. ad Cap. Gal. c. 9). In another work Prosper thus defines the special reference : " The propriety in redemption doubtless belongs to them from whom the prince of this world is cast out. The death of Christ was not so expended for the human race, that they also belonged to His redemption who were never to be regenerated" (resp. obj. Vincen. 1). The school of Augustin, while its salutary influence pervaded the Western Church, uniformly proceeded on the supposition that Christ's atonement was offered for a chosen people given by the Father to the Son. The notion that the atonement was for mankind indiscriminately was unknown. They explained the terms which express universality, by accepting the language as descriptive of a definite self-contained whole, terminated in itself. They speak of that totality as a compact body, designated in Scripture THE ALL or THE MANY; and undoubtedly this explanation is in some passages appropriate. The great names of Western Christendom for a considerable time confessed to Augustin's and Prosper's views on particular redemption, as emphatically as the Synod of Dort long afterwards. Four centuries after Augustin's death, however, Godschalk (A.D. 847) encountered persecution and imprisonment for asserting the very opinions which Augustinian theology had triumphantly vindicated. The age was then no longer capable of maintaining the sovereignty of grace amid the current legalism. Isolated witnesses indeed appeared, such as Remigius at Lyons and the Council at Valence (A.D. 855), to do what in them lay to maintain the truth and protect its oppressed champion. But they could not turn the tide.

Here we may fully notice the principal defects attaching to the patristic theology as an exhibition of the doctrine of the atonement. The essential elements of the doctrine are all found in the Greek and Latin Fathers. Certainly they had not the remotest conception of the modern theory of moral redemption and absolute remission, however they philosophized on possibilities. They all maintained the fact of the atonement. It must be confessed, however, that important desiderata and neutralizing influences came in to mar the effects which it was fitted to produce; and three principal defects or misleading tendencies may be mentioned.

1. The patristic theology, considered as a whole, directed attention more to the bearing of the atonement on men as captives under Satan and death, than to its bearing on the divine rights. It was too exclusively considered in connection with the consequences of sin, and too little WITH SIN ITSELF. Irenæus was an exception. He apprehended the propitiation for sin, we think, more profoundly than any of the Fathers. He described it as a manifestation of divine goodness and righteousness, but held that it was the obedience of the second Adam, entering by appointment into the position of the first, that Satan might justly be overcome (3. 20). All the others took lower ground. Hence patristic theology, as a whole, surveyed the atonement in relation to man, but did not insist on its absolute necessity as seen in connection with the rights of God. Athanasius makes the atonement a satisfaction of the primeval menace against sin, but in such a way as argues that he had no idea of anything beyond a relative necessity. All the eminent Fathers of the Eastern as well as Western Church—Origen, Athanasius, Gregory Nazianzen, Augustin, and Theodoret — expressly declare that God, in the exercise of His free-will‘ and absolute dominion, could have redeemed men from their captivity without atonement. Augustin speaks of innumerable other ways which the Almighty might have adopted to deliver us (*de Trin.* lib. xiii. c. 16). Theodoret, in his Orations against the Greeks, maintains that it would have been easy for Christ to deliver men by His mere will, but adds: " He would not display His power, but the righteousness of His divine administration " (Orat. vi.). To the same purpose John of Damascus, the dogmatic divine of the Eastern Church, says: " All is in His power. He could by His almighty power rescue men from the captivity of the devil; but the latter would have had ground for accusing God," etc. (i. 3, c. 18). While they argued for the absolute dominion of God, they united to set forth that the actual method of redemption selected was adapted to man's necessities, and worthy of God. In short, it was a speculation in which they indulged, as later divines also did, without sufficient ground; for

they separated God's free-will from the moral perfections of His nature—rectitude, wisdom, and goodness. This speculation, which we find resuscitated after the Reformation, assumed too much. It was not a question of mere power, for God always acts in character. Patristic theology, in short, did not give the atonement the deep grounding which it must of necessity receive. Hence the later divines, who merely aimed to revive patristic thought, naturally went no further than the relative necessity of the atonement, and asserted that God chose this way because it seemed good in His sight.

2. We notice another marked defect in patristic theology, which began at a very early age, viz. the theory of the remission of sins subsequent to conversion, by prayers, alms, good works, and penitential exercises. This unscriptural notion lost sight of explicit statements which ascribe forgiveness after conversion as well as before it to the blood of Christ alone (1 John i. 7, ii. 2). This was one of the most mischievous mistakes of the ancient church. It began at an early period. We find it in Origen, and earlier; for Clemens of Alexandria expresses himself in this perilous way: Christ's blood was supposed to atone for sins committed before conversion, and to secure remission; but after conversion or baptism something else was required— good works and satisfactions. Certain terms originally applied to the discipline of the church, such as SATISFACTION and the like, came in process of time to be applied to God, as if some satisfaction was to be made by the Christian. This tended to neutralize the atonement, and to cast it into the shade. The comparatively limited allusion to the cross in the patristic literature, as compared with the Reformation age, must strike every one. This is the reason: and Augustin, the great champion of grace in its INWARD operations, was here as wide of the mark as any of the others. The forgiveness of sins after conversion was, according to him, ascribed in no small measure to good works, prayers, alms, and fasts. Numerous passages of this nature might be produced from his works.[1] He explains his sentiments on this point at large in the epistle addressed to Macedonius (Ep. liii.). His doctrine was, that in baptism previous sins are forgiven, but that sins committed afterwards are, to a large extent, expiated also by sacrifices of mercy. That unscriptural and mischievous position is found in the Fathers before the times of Augustin. That it tended to intercept the

---

[1] Of many passages that might be adduced, I give the following: "Non enim sufficit mores in melius commutare, et a factis malis recedere ; nisi etiam de his quæ facta sunt *satisfiat Deo* per pœnitentiæ dolorem, per humilitatis gemitum per contriti cordis sacrificium, co-operantibus eleemosynis" (tom. v. p. 950, edit. con. S. Maur).

benefit of the atonement, and to neutralize its effects, needs no proof. The notion descended to the Church of Rome, where we find it in all its force to this day. The Reformation swept it away.

3. A third neutralizing influence was the doctrine of the eucharistic sacrifice, which came to light about the middle of the third century. Cyprian, the first of the Fathers who speaks of the blood of Christ in this doubtful way, expressed the thought that Christ offered Himself a sacrifice at the institution of the Supper (Letter 63). The Fathers used the term SACRIFICE in the general sense, that everything given to God may be biblically called a sacrifice. It was an unhappy application of the word when the Supper came to be so designated; for a sacrifice and sacrament are different, — the former implying what is OFFERED BY US, the latter implying what is GIVEN TO US. Properly viewed, the Lord's Supper is not a sacrifice, but a sacrament, as all the Reformers correctly represented it. Cyprian's use of this unhappy term soon found access everywhere; but it had nothing in common with the perversion of later days. The Fathers meant only a commemoration of Christ's sacrifice, when speaking of Christ's body and blood as present in the Supper as a victim and propitiatory sacrifice. They meant nothing more than to set forth by symbolical language what was the reality to which the sacramental symbols pointed, and what were the effects of Christ's propitiation. In process of time that style ceased to be hyperbole, and came in between the worshipper and the atonement of the cross. The emblem more and more threatened to supersede the reality : sacraments were made the means of applying the atonement; and gradually became a substitute for it, till the remedial scheme was identified with sacraments.

III. We come now to *medieval doctrine*. The true theory of the atonement, not in full development, but in its fundamental principles, or in that which gives it systematic form, was propounded by ANSELM, well termed by one the Grotius and Leibnitz of his age, and by another Wolf and Augustin united. Any correct view of the medieval period will always place Anselm at the fountainhead. He stands between two epochs, inheriting the one, moulding the other. Our present object is to discuss the merits of his theory of the atonement. At the time when he taught theology at the monastery of Bec, of which he was prior (A.D. 1063–1093), many minds, literate and illiterate, had a desire to obtain an explanation on dogmatic grounds of the nature of the atonement, to meet speculative wants, not unlike the theories of our own day. Anselm himself was quite dissatisfied with the current modes of explanation that had descended from the patristic theology, for no attempt had been made to demonstrate on solid grounds the inward necessity of the atonement.

A remedy was necessary, more especially as the speculative tendencies were beginning to develope themselves on all sides. The doctrine of the atonement had long occupied Anselm's mind. He was solicited to give his solution of the difficulties then widely discussed; and none was more importunate than a favourite pupil, Boso, who had come to him engulphed in theological difficulties. Anselm's work took the form of a dialogue between him and Boso, and was entitled, CUR DEUS HOMO, describing the reasons why none but God incarnate was competent to the work of propitiation. It must be translated, WHY A GOD-MAN? The treatise consists of two parts, of which the first was prepared after his translation to the See of Canterbury (1093); and it was finished by its author in the summer of 1098, during his exile from England, at a country-seat in Campania. It has, during nearly eight centuries, directed and influenced opinion in the most remarkable way on the subject of the atonement. As a large quotation was inserted in the former volume, there is the less necessity for multiplying extracts from the treatise, and it will suffice briefly to notice its scope and merits.

Anselm dismisses the defective representations of the patristic theology, especially the theory that a satisfaction was made to the legitimate claims of Satan (i. 7). He sees in the actual dominion of Satan the righteous sentence of God, and the well-deserved doom of mankind, but repudiates any legitimate claim on the part of the adversary to receive a satisfaction. Anselm goes back to THE IDEA OF SIN, and sketches a theory of the atonement, of which we may say that it took in all the scattered parts of truth found in the previous discussions, but made an immense advance on them, as it put the atonement in connection with the MAGNITUDE OF GUILT. This was an important advance on the patristic theology generally, which surveyed the atonement only in the light of our captivity, or from the view-point supplied by THE EFFECTS of sin. The fundamental thoughts of Anselm are the following :—Sin is nothing else but not rendering to God His due. He who does not render to God this due honour, withdraws from God what is His, and dishonours God ; and this is to commit sin. Every sinner must repay the honour which he took from God, and restore it. This is the satisfaction which every sinner must make to God (lib. i. ch. 11). Referring to divine justice, which is de-

scribed as nothing but God Himself, Anselm asserts : There is
nothing which it is more just for God to maintain than the
honour of His majesty (ch. 13); and he adds : It is indispensably necessary that every sin should be followed either by
satisfaction or punishment (ch. 15). And as to the satisfaction, Anselm's position is : Man cannot receive what God purposed to bestow on him without RESTORING the whole of what
he took away from God (ch. 23). He brings out, in the most
emphatic way, that God alone was in a position to render this,
and consequently that He must perform it as GOD-MAN, which
evinces the necessity of the incarnation. From this circumstance the satisfaction possessed infinite value, not only com-
pensating for human guilt, but completely restoring the injured
or insulted honour of God.

The influence of this treatise on subsequent centuries is
mainly due to the fact that it gave such a happy statement
of the INDISPENSABLE NECESSITY of satisfaction. The ampler
statements of the Reformers as to the constituent elements of
the atonement did not subvert in any degree this unanswer-
able proof of its indispensable necessity, but fitted in to it without any incongruity. The theory has defects, as we shall see ;
but in respect of the great demonstration which it furnishes as
to the necessity of satisfaction, the work is as seasonable and
valuable as when it first appeared. The peculiar distinction
belonging to Anselm's theory, contrasted with·all that preceded
it, and with most theories that succeeded it to this day, was,
that he viewed the atonement in connection with SIN AS SUCH,
and not merely in connection with the consequences of sin.
He based his argument on the magnitude and enormity of
sin (*nondum considerasti quanti ponderis sit peccatum*, i. 21).
The infinite evil of sin is the great thought that at once con-
fronts us at the commencement of the treatise. The patristic
theology, especially in the Athanasian type and doctrine, had
been wont to connect the atonement with the original threat
against sin, and viewed the penalty as the result of the divine
veracity. Anselm viewed the necessity of the atonement far
more profoundly than any of the Fathers, not even excepting
Irenæus, though he wants elements which the latter enforced.
The elements of the atonement, as we have seen, existed in the
church in an isolated form, but needed to be fused and molten
together by one who could apprehend it in its inward necessity ; and this Anselm performed.

With regard to the distribution of matter introduced into
the treatise, it is as follows :—After the first preliminary chapters, he demonstrates the absolute necessity of satisfaction as a

condition of forgiveness (i. 11–19).   This FIRST division of the work may be called the enunciation of the problem.   He establishes the necessity of the atonement on grounds which have only to be stated to constrain the assent of every spiritual mind imbued with any adequate apprehension of the creature's relation to its Maker.   He puts this necessity on the ground that God's rights must be restored, and His honour repaired; and that to pronounce pardon without reparation would violate God's declarative glory.   Then, in what may be called the SECOND division of the treatise, Anselm shows that unaided man is incompetent to restore God's honour, and that this very inability is criminal (i. 20–24).   After this he proceeds in the second book to establish what may be called the THIRD point of his argument, that only a divine person or God-man was competent to make the satisfaction that repairs God's injured honour (ii. 1–22).   This is followed by a brief outline of the events of Christ's historic life, considered as essential requisites to the solution of the problem, which was in harmony with God's perfections, as well as with the dictates of enlightened reason.

We have thus put together the integral parts of the theory. Anselm may be said to stand alone in all antiquity in the clear enunciation of the problem that was to be solved on behalf of humanity.   As to the positive elements or actual fulfilment of the divine claims, the theology of the Reformation far exceeded all that this treatise contains,—nay, in this respect, superseded it.   But, in the statement of the NECESSITY of satisfaction, Anselm has never been surpassed, and in this respect the treatise is still invaluable.   The *Theodicœa* of Anselm is replete with those lofty conceptions of God's excellency and claims with which we are brought in contact in Augustin and Edwards— minds of the same family; and we feel that nothing but divine teaching, united to great holiness and intimate communion with God, could have put him in possession of such views of SIN. Assuming the existence of sin as an experimental fact, he regards it as an infraction of the divine rights, a spoliation of that declarative glory for which the universe exists, and a disorder or criminal rebellion in the moral universe.   His discussion commences with the relation which the moral Governor occupies to sin, showing that sin is a fact for which provision must be made in God's moral government,—a disharmony that must be reduced to order.   The atonement is not with him as with Grotius, a governmental display before the universe; nor a merely positive device, which waives the essential claims of justice and offers but the semblance of satisfaction.   On the contrary, the satisfaction, according to Anselm, is grounded on deep inward necessity, and is a provision for SIN, and not merely for its CONSEQUENCES. He particularly excels in exhibiting the necessity of satisfaction for such a tremendous disorder and evil as sin, or of punishment as the only other alternative. Compared with other theories before or since his day as to the ground of the atonement, this outline is immensely more commanding, and better fortified by evidence. He knows no court but that of God Himself, and the harmony of His attributes. In this great transaction there is no human nor angelic public before which God makes a governmental display : His public is Himself, or His own perfections, which are inviolable.

As I dislike the modern mode of representing another man's views by a mere artificial construction from a reviewer's point of view, without sufficient extracts, I would request the reader's perusal of the passages at large, extracted from this treatise in our former volume, as they serve to exhibit Anselm's views in their natural order (pp. 383–398). Let me now enter on a critical estimate of the merits of this treatise.

No work perhaps on the atonement ever encountered such determined opposition at the hand of modern Rationalism, and not less so from the champions of that new theory which is termed *moral redemption,* opposed to the juristic view of theology. When Anselm declares that God can no more fail to maintain His honour and justice than He can lie, they denounce him as giving a representation of God as if He were an implacable and vindictive tyrant. In spite of all these characteristic denunciations of modern Rationalism, this theory for eight centuries has given repose and comfort to the most earnest minds of all churches : it was accepted by every Protestant church, and, we think, God will not let it die. The reason of the opposition it has encountered may in large measure be traced to the fact that it establishes the perfect rationality of the atonement as a satisfaction to divine justice. Rationalism, with its reasons of a low order, is here met on its own ground, and disarmed by reasons to which no spiritual mind takes exception. Enlightened Christian rationality is brought face to face with natural reason ; grounds are assigned for an atonement sufficient to commend it to every one alive to the fact of sin as a disorder in the universe ; and the reasons to which Anselm appeals in opposition to the exceptions of which Rationalism avails itself, are based on inward necessity in the moral government of God. It is not difficult, perhaps, to explain why Rationalism has so keenly opposed this demonstration. Rationalism arrogates all reason demanding a WHY and wherefore for every truth ; and it here encounters reasons more than it has ever answered.

Starting from the fact of SIN which must be expiated, Anselm, as the preface purports, undertakes to prove by necessary reasons apart from the historical Christ (*remoto Christo*), that man could not be saved without such a satisfaction as a God-man alone was competent to offer. As it is a demonstration conducted against a certain phase of speculative unbelief, he proceeds on common grounds in reason. What gave the treatise its importance, was his conception of sin as an infinite evil, arguing a singularly realizing view of God. God, he maintains, is wronged by sin, and His rights taken away (*aufert Deo quod suum est*) ; and the Creator owes it to Himself to vindicate His declarative glory, and secure the honour due to Him as the personal God. This is the central point of Anselm's theory,—one of those elements too much displaced by subsequent speculations. Frequently Anselm's critics have not apprehended it. But it is comprehensive enough to take in all the more definite statements as to the divine law furnished by the Reformation theology. Some disparage the notion of restoring the divine honour as an outward view-point of abstract reflection ; and it has been said that the mode adopted by the Protestant Church, of referring Christ's work to the divine law, is more practical, living, and experimental. But, in point of fact, these two modes of representation do not exclude each other : Anselm's principle comprehends the other. The one is from the view-point of Christian experience ; the other from the view-point of the divine right.

The inward necessity of the atonement, on the supposition of pardon, was evinced by Anselm as had never been exhibited before. He put it in a new light when he based his theory on the great truth that man was made to honour God by a pure nature and sinless obedience ; and that the restoration of this honour to the full, nay, to a larger degree, is a tribute or claim which the Supreme Justice owes to Himself. Anselm starts from God's declarative glory,—a conception not only biblical in its import, but necessary in an experimental point of view, and comprehending under it all the more definite statements subsequently made in the church on the subject of imputed righteousness. There is a biblical foundation for the position that the divine honour was taken away, and must needs be restored as an indispensable condition for forgiveness : for the apostle plainly exhibits it in his statement of redemption. He connects the glory of God with sin and satisfaction.[1] Nor could conscience be satisfied with any method of atonement not securing the divine honour, but involving a mere connivance at defects.

This shows that, far from propounding mere abstract reflection as the guiding principle of his theory, as has been alleged, Anselm derived it from the centre of biblical and experimental truth. Against the tenor of his theory it has been argued that man cannot be said to give to God, or to take away from Him. That would be true, were it a question as to man's rebellion tending to the prejudice of God's ESSENTIAL blessedness. But it is a question of His declarative glory, and of His relation to the world, existing only to bring back to Him a revenue of praise. All this Anselm puts in a form arguing the deepest views of God's personal relations to the universe.

A certain surprise is justly occasioned by the fact that he makes no express mention of THE LAW, which must always be taken in as the standard of obedience. Whether that arose from the fact that he had undertaken to argue on grounds of reason, or to avoid the supposition of a law standing above God, or because he thought it best to run up the whole question to the relations immediately occupied by the personal God to the world, and without a true conception of which neither sin nor punishment can be adequately apprehended, it is difficult to determine. But he does not treat of SIN, of PUNISHMENT, and of the WILL of the Supreme, in the impersonal way in which these points are often viewed in discussions of this nature. The Supreme Justice is, according to Anselm, God Himself (*Suprema Justitia non est aliud quam ipse Deus*, i. 13). From this view of the intimate relation which the personal God occupies to the world, Anselm describes sin as an infinite evil—an infraction of divine right—a spoliation of the divine honour, of which God cannot be deprived; for either men spontaneously comply with the preceptive will of God, or fall under His punitive will,—the latter being an exaction of the

---

[1] See Rom. iii. 23 : "*For they all* [sic] *sinned and come short of the glory of God.*" What is the GLORY OF GOD here ? Of four different views given by exegetes, we decidedly prefer that exposition which involves the idea of RENDERING TO GOD HIS HONOUR. Without adducing the other opinions, let it suffice to say that the old Lutheran expositors, Chemnitzius, Flacius, Seb. Schmid, Calovius, and also J. Alting, among the reformed, as well as Rückert and Olshausen more recently, interpret the δόξα τοῦ Θεοῦ of a glory originally imparted to men, but lost—viz. the divine image. That is nearer the truth than any of the other three interpretations (viz. 1. future glory ; 2. the commendation of God ; 3. glorying before God). But, instead of limiting it to the *divine image*, we must extend the idea to all the declarative glory to be rendered to the Creator by a pure nature and God-glorifying obedience ; and, taken in this sense, there is a complete correspondence between the want of the δόξα and the provision of δικαιοσύνη : they are counterparts to each other. (Comp., too, John xvii. 4.)

divine honour from the sinner against his will, and in some sort a satisfaction; and from this, says Anselm, a sinner can no more flee than he can flee from the circumambient heaven, which he recedes from at one point only to approach it at another. But we should misapprehend his view of sin were we to conclude that he regarded it as a mere transient act—the mere time-act, so to speak, of a creature on one occasion transgressing the will of God. Rather, sin is the perpetual contrariety of a nature which is enmity against God (*nequaquam potest velle mentiri voluntas, nisi in qua corrupta est veritas*, i. 12). This demonstration of the necessity of satisfaction was a new epoch in the history of the doctrine; and it connects Anselm's name with the atonement much in the same way as Athanasius' name is recalled in connection with the proof of Christ's deity, or Augustin's with the doctrines of efficacious grace, or Luther's with justification by faith alone.

Another objection to this theory is, that Anselm gives prominence to divine justice at the expense of divine love. This is wholly without foundation, and can be adduced only by those who will see nothing in the Divine Being but love. Unquestionably LOVE is the source of the atonement; for when God spared not His own Son, that delivery of Christ can be regarded in no other light than as a manifestation of sovereign, self-moving love. But Anselm demonstrates the necessity of satisfaction to shut men up to unmerited love, which is nowhere called in question, but presupposed as the originating element of the whole satisfaction. But the greater the obstacle surmounted, and the greater the price paid, the greater obviously is the love. A reference to Anselm's work shows that he comprehended in his exhibition of justice not only what was punitive, but all that the Divine Being owed to Himself. He shows that the necessity demanding the incarnation and humiliation of the Son of God for the restoration of the divine honour, was nothing but the demand of justice; but that, instead of obscuring divine love, this only magnified and exalted it, for love is commended by the greatness of the satisfaction. And we find Anselm winding up his demonstration by expressly placing mercy and justice in harmonious concert.

The relation of this theory to later modes of representation, and especially to that of the Reformation theology, which supplemented it, is worthy of notice. The difference between the two corresponds to the peculiar elements of the two schools of theology. Anselm is less happy in filling up his outline than in defining the boundary lines of that necessity which could not be modified. He has, however, laid down principles of such general application as comprehend the ampler positive doctrine supplied by the Reformation, and even necessitated in a manner a better exposition of the truth than he himself had supplied. He fails to fill up his own outline.

An objection has been made to the general character of the reasoning. But for this there is no foundation, for he brings enlightened reason to disarm the prejudices of natural reason, and introduces a higher rationality. Starting from the infinite guilt of sin as his view-point, he exhibits the adaptation of the divine economy to the wants of fallen nature—the true *rationale* of every gospel doctrine.

Three points of difference, however, may be traced between this admirable treatise and the Reformation theology, and these we shall briefly notice.

1. Anselm, following out a speculation derived from Augustin, embarrassed the question by an unnecessary reference to the fall of angels. He argued that the number of fallen angels must be compensated by an equal number, perhaps a greater number, of redeemed men. The introduction of this speculation, which can neither be affirmed nor denied, as it is beyond the circle of our knowledge, mars the symmetry of Anselm's work (lib. i. 16–18). But it is a mere episode, which may be separated from the theory itself; and the Reformation theology happily disembarrassed the question of all reference to the fall of angels, and limited the scope of the atonement to man alone.

2. A second point of difference, to which it is necessary to refer, is, that the active and passive obedience of Christ was never correctly stated in any of the explanations furnished by Anselm in connection with the atonement. A further expansion of truth was reserved for the Reformation, by penetrating more deeply into the nature of the divine law than was ever discovered to the great scholastic. What his theory wanted, indeed, was a full recognition of the claims of THE DIVINE LAW, and of the atonement as a satisfaction of these claims in all their breadth and extent. Anselm, on the contrary, stopped short at an indefinite equivalent, content to forego all more explicit statement. He contemplated the work of Christ in concrete connection with His divine person, and concluded that on this account it was an ample reparation of the divine honour.

The theory of Anselm may be said in one respect to make provision for the active and suffering obedience of Christ; and in another respect, from the cause assigned, to allow neither of these elements to come to their rights. He seems to have been deterred, in common with much of the patristic theology, which he inherited, from fully adopting the conclusion that Christ made an exchange of places with us under the law, to the extent that He entered unreservedly and without exception into all the obligations of His people. He drew too wide a distinction between punishment and satisfaction, as if they had nothing in common. He considers the death of Christ only as a voluntary deed. In defining satisfaction he did not inquire what is included in the obligation, nor read off the satisfaction from the claims of the divine law, of which it is but the fulfilment. The SUFFERING OBEDIENCE does not come to its rights in Anselm's theory, though he held that the satisfaction involved the spontaneous offering up of Christ's life. The reason of this was, that he considered the indefinite equivalent an ample reparation of the divine honour. Nor does the ACTIVE OBEDIENCE of Christ come to its rights in Anselm's theory. Some provision was undoubtedly made for the active obedience, as an indispensable prerequisite ; but it was not fully developed. He fixed attention too exclusively upon the death of Christ, without taking into account the life of the Lord Jesus, as we should have expected from his delineation of the necessity of satisfaction. But, not guided by the more correct views of divine law to which the church arrived in the days of the Reformation, Anselm stopped short at an indefinite satisfaction, which he saw in connection with the God-man surrendering Himself to death. He regarded this as a compensation for the divine honour, without analysing it in detail. He did not occupy that point of view which alone could lead him to give due prominence to the elements of active and passive obedience ; and without deeming more precision necessary, he held that the surrender of life by a divine person was of worth and dignity sufficient to countervail the evil of sin, and make full reparation to the divine honour.

3. We must add a third point of difference. The Reformation theology on the doctrine of the atonement starts from man's personal relation to Christ by justifying faith. It was anthropological. Man's consciousness of guilt, derived from apprehending his position under the law, coupled with the conviction that the law must be fulfilled by a mediator bearing the penalty and complying with the positive requirement, was the view-point of the Reformation theology. Anselm's is rather systematic. He omitted the experimental application of the atonement, and confined himself to the objective side. The Reformers looked at it from another view-point—from the subjective side of union to God in Christ by justifying faith. But in Anselm's MEDITATIONS the doctrine of exchange is

brought out in an experimental way, with scarcely less clearness than by Luther himself, and in a manner which presupposes that the application of the atonement is by faith alone.
His views of the infinite evil of sin are expressed from his own
consciousness ; and though he says little of the application of
the atonement by faith alone as the receptive hand, no one can
read Anselm without the conviction that this truth underlies
all he says, though it was reserved to the Reformation age to
find full expression for it.

The immediate cause of the vast influence exercised by
Anselm's treatise was due to the statement of the absolute
necessity of the satisfaction, more than to the exposition of
its essential elements. He laid the formation for all the
subsequent grounding of the doctrine; and the advances made
at the Reformation did not subvert the foundation laid, but
fitted into it without incongruity.

On the views of medieval writers after Anselm it is unnecessary to dwell at large. Their speculations, with the
single exception of Aquinas, did not tend to advance the
knowledge of the doctrine; and without being aware of any
abrupt transition, we might pass from Anselm to the Reformers. Anselm, in his atonement-theory, stood very much
alone. The far-reaching consequences of his views were not
discerned. We hear no more, it is true, of a ransom paid to
the devil; that whole theory now disappeared. But what was
done subsequently was rather a return to patristic views of the
relative necessity of the atonement; and during the course of
four centuries, in which scholasticism had full play, excepting
a few patches from Anselm, elements of a neutralizing or negative character went on increasing. A few notices will suffice,
for our object is rather to point out the stages and landmarks
of the history of the doctrine, than to accumulate individual
opinions.

ABELARD, sympathizing neither with the holiness of Anselm's
life nor the soundness of his doctrinal opinions, was a direct
antithesis in every respect. He has been of late more canvassed than he deserves. Eloquent, logical, but ethically lax,
he has been well termed the precursor of modern Rationalism.
His views of redemption were the logical result of his Pelagian
view of sin. He allowed only sinful deeds, but no sinful
nature, and no representative position of the first man, or any
imputation of his sin : views naturally leading him to deny the
necessity of satisfaction. He represented pardon as absolute,
without regard to a mediator's work. His shallow view of sin
disjointed everything. Hence, according to him, reconcilia-

tion was all on man's side ; and God's anger needed not to be appeased, but man's.   This was but the prelude of modern Rationalism.   The well-known BERNARD, deeply offended by Abelard's audacity, controverted his views with all the energy of his character, but did nothing to advance the doctrine.   He held that sin could not be forgiven without a satisfaction, but did not insist on its absolute necessity.   In a word, Bernard took up Augustin's ground, which was a modification of the theory of Origen.   PETER LOMBARD, *magister Sententiarum,* whose compend was long classical in the Western Church, furnished a compilation of sayings from the Fathers, digested into system. He reproduced the indefinite type of the patristic theology, after Anselm had overthrown its insecure positions ; and was little influenced by either Anselm or Abelard, though he discovers marks of living in a period when the old form was in process of dissolution.   His starting-point was the notion of merit (*Lib. Senten.* iii. 18) ; and he held that Christ merited for Himself and for us,—for Himself by His humility, love, righteousness, and other virtues, which He exercised from His conception ; and for us by His sufferings.   Lombard's *Book of Sentences* became the text-book on which teachers and writers commented for many centuries, and we thus see the ideas current on the atonement in Western Christendom.   There was much uncertainty and vacillation in his views.   He held that we are justified by the love which redemption awakens in us in return (*et per hoc,* says he, *justificamur*).

Three scholastic divines plainly exhibit the influence of Anselm's theory : HUGO *a Sancto Victore,* ALEXANDER HALESIUS, and BONAVENTURA.   They cannot be said, however, to have rendered any service in the further elucidation of the doctrine.

HUGO OF ST. VICTOR makes some approach to the distinction between the active and suffering obedience of Christ (*Sacr.* c. 4). He speaks of Christ discharging man's obligation to the Father by His birth, and expiating man's guilt by His death (*reatum hominis*),—a crude statement of the two constituent elements of the atonement ; but, had they been taken in earnest, and carried out, the germ of a fuller development was there.   He discovers plain marks of Anselm's influence, though not asserting the absolute necessity of the atonement.   It might, he alleges, have been effected in a different way, though this was most appropriate on many grounds stated.   The necessity of the incarnation for the atonement appears, according to him, from the fact that man must offer a reparation to God for his apostasy, and suffer an adequate punishment as a satisfaction for the indignity.

ALEXANDER OF HALES adhered to Anselm still more closely than the former, adducing frequently the words of Anselm. Hales lays down the position that, according to divine justice, sin is never remitted without punishment (*Summa*, iii. 16. 3, 4) ; and he distinguishes, like Lombard, between merit and satis- faction, affirming that Christ merited glorification for HIMSELF, and FOR US the cancelling of guilt. There is, however, the usual confusion which we everywhere encounter in this period from the neutralizing elements of good works.

For BONAVENTURA'S views, let me refer to Shedd's excellent outline. He came under the influence of Anselm's opinions. Bonaventura acknowledged that God, equally merciful and righteous, revealed these two divine attributes in their harmony and equipoise. He did not affirm the absolute necessity of satisfaction, though, like the Fathers, he acknowledged that, of all the possible modes, this was the most appropriate. These writers were afraid of invading the free-will or absolute power of God, when they might have thought out the matter to an end, and seen that it is not a mere question of omnipotence, but one involving God's moral perfections ; and we can, with Anselm, affirm the absolute necessity, on the same ground on which we affirm that He cannot lie.

The Thomist and Scotist opinions fill up the remainder of the Scholastic period.

THOMAS AQUINAS, the great systematic divine of medieval times, exercised considerable influence in connection with the doctrine of the atonement. He is represented by Lutheran divines, such as Thomasius and Philippi, as contributing nothing of value. We cannot concede this ; but his services lay chiefly in a sphere to which Lutheran divines discover no favourable inclination,—viz. the special destination of the atonement.

Having much in common with Anselm, he differs from him in maintaining that the satisfaction was wholly of free-will on the part of God, and that justice is based on the positive will of God. He will not allow that satisfaction was of abso- lute necessity, though the most appropriate means for the end. As to the elements of the satisfaction, two points may be termed peculiar to him. (1.) As to the suffering, he is not content merely to name the death of Christ : he shows that He encoun- tered human suffering for men of all tribes and all ranks, in mind and body, in honour and estate ; and that the amount of pain which He endured was the greatest that could be borne in this present state (*Quest*. 46. 4–7). But he adds, that what contributed to make it an adequate satisfaction, was the greatness of His love, the dignity of His person as God-man, and the magnitude of His sorrow.   One noteworthy position was, that the Redeemer's obedience was a fulfilment of the moral precepts of love to God and man, as well as of what was properly cere-monial; and this suffering obedience was free and voluntary. (2.) Another peculiarity of Thomas' doctrine was, that the Lord's satisfaction was superabounding,—that is, exceeding the requirement.   Though this position was afterwards sadly per-verted to the purposes of superstition, yet, as put by Aquinas himself, it expressed what was often uttered by orthodox divines, such as Quenstedt and Dannhauer, in the Lutheran Church.   (3.) There is another point to which great value at-taches : he demonstrates that the atonement was made for the church.   Substitution in the room of others was based by Aquinas on the position that there was an organic unity between Christ the Head and the church His body.   He con-ceives of Christ as the Head of a mystic body—viz. the church of redeemed men—and sets forth this great truth in a manner worthy of a disciple of Augustin.   "The whole church," says he, "which is the mystic body of Christ, is accounted as one person with its Head, which is Christ" (*Summa Th. Q.* 8).   The analogy between the head as the ruling part, the seat of the senses, and the source of the entire movements of the members, is consistently carried out.   Christ comprehends in Himself the whole company of redeemed men through all time ; and, by this conjunction between Christ and His church, all that the Head performed redounds to the advantage of the members. Aquinas maintained and carried out this position to its legiti-mate consequences in respect of the Lord's sufferings, so far as they fall under the idea of merit.   Satisfaction was destined for all believers, and belongs to them as His members (*Quest.* 48. 2).   His sufferings won the forgiveness of sins and the remission of punishment (*Art.* 3).

The importance of this contribution to the doctrine of the atonement, will not be questioned by any one who takes its dimensions.   It has always been accepted, from Aquinas' days down to the present time, by every advocate of substitution in its special reference, as the only tenable explanation.   This presupposes not a vague, indefinite, hap-hazard relation, but an actual oneness of a peculiar nature between Christ and the people of God.   Suretyship presupposes this relation ; imputa-tion proceeds upon it : the penalty which Christ endured could not otherwise have been inflicted ; and they for whom this was done naturally share in the benefit, or receive what was des-tined for them.

Aquinas conceived of Christ as the Head of His mystic body, and not as the mere Head of humanity. The objection urged against this position by the above-named Lutheran theologians, is that it puts to hazard the importance and value of redemption, by limiting its compass. The theory proceeded on the Augustinian doctrine of election; and, so far from undermining the value of the atonement, it secures its efficacy to the church of redeemed men; and this is in harmony with all biblical statements. What the atonement was to unsaved men we spare to inquire; but Scripture proclaims that the death of Christ redeemed the church. By this mode Aquinas explained two things. First, he met the cavil that only the guilty, and not the innocent, should satisfy : his answer was, that the Head and members are one mystic person (*Quest.* 48. *a.* 2). And, next, he explained the transfer of the merits of Christ's sufferings to the redeemed.

The last of the Scholastics to whom we refer as a moulder of opinion, was DUNS SCOTUS, a great speculative and dialectic mind, but lacking spiritual elements to regulate thought in divine things. He occupied very much the same relation to Aquinas as did Abelard to Anselm.

Notwithstanding his acknowledged mental power, the theory of Scotus was superficial. Properly speaking, he has no atonement at all. This ceases to cause surprise when we apprehend his Pelagian view of sin. He denied the infinite evil of sin (*peccatum a se formaliter est actus finitus*). He consequently impugned the infinite merit of Christ, describing it as belonging only to His human nature. Scotus' view of the atonement differs only by a shade from the absolute redemption or absolute forgiveness of modern Rationalism.

Scotus' theory reduces man's redemption to a mere acceptilation on the part of God. God was pleased to account Christ's work as a fit medium of salvation by an act of acceptance (*acceptatio divina*). He denied the necessity of satisfaction, and would overthrow the theory of Anselm, which he examined more fully than any other of the scholastic writers. So shallow are his views of what was necessary to satisfy the claims of God, that he asserts : A good angel or a good man was competent to render satisfaction; and he does not deny the possibility of a man satisfying for himself. A mere man, by a meritorious act of love, could have offered the satisfaction, according to Scotus, for he viewed it as depending wholly on divine acceptance.

The superabounding satisfaction (*Christi passio non solum sufficiens, sed etiam* SUPERABUNDANS SATISFACTIO) was the point of discussion between the Thomists and the Scotists. The Thomist position as to the infinite merit of Christ's satisfaction received ecclesiastical sanction in 1343; but it was perverted to lend sanction to the figment of a treasury of merits at the disposal of the church.

After Aquinas the confusion in the church as to the atonement became extreme, Scotus' followers tending largely to complicate opinion. An exception may be made in favour of Gerson, who knew how to distinguish mercy and justice, and to harmonize them in the atonement; and also in favour of medieval mystics, such as Tauler and Wessel. The latter is supposed to have approached to the definition of Christ's work as an active and suffering obedience; at least he uses terms almost equivalent (*satisfaciendo* and *satispatiendo*). But we cannot open the later Scholastics without feeling that they are wholly away from Bible ground. They agitate questions of grace and merit, satisfaction and redemption, guilt and punishment, which are but a tangled skein of nomenclature. They are on a wide sea of legalism, remedial sacraments, and philosophical terminology, confounding objective and subjective—the work of Christ and the work of man. William Occam, in his *Commentary on Peter Lombard's Compend.*, omits the atonement altogether.

IV. We come now to the REFORMATION PERIOD, which brought back theology to its true centre. The great question of that age turned on the justification of the sinner; and the atonement therefore, as the material cause of justification, was the turning-point of the whole discussions. The atonement was now set upon a candlestick to give light to all the house. The merit and satisfaction of works were wholly removed from the ground of man's justification; deep views of the INFINITE GUILT OF SIN, as seen in the light of the divine law, were diffused; and the sole mediatorship of Christ was fully recognised. The Reformation, turning on these points, began in Luther's own heart, and may be traced in his memorable experience before it became the great moving force in the world's history. The deep consciousness of guilt, derived from vividly apprehending his position under the law, coupled with the conviction that the law must needs be fulfilled, shut him up to the ONE MEDIATOR between God and man, presented in the gospel as bearing the penalty, and complying with the positive requirement, of the law. This was Luther's view-point personally, and this was the view-point of the Reformation theology. Previous theories wanted a full recognition of THE CLAIMS OF THE DIVINE LAW, and of the atonement as a satisfaction of these claims in all their extent; and this became the element in which the theology of the Reformation moved, and by which all other truth was coloured. On the subject of the atonement, the divines of the Reformation period were in the habit of arguing from man's obligations to the nature of Christ's undertaking, and then conversely from the latter to the former. Their main position, to which they were conducted by deeper views of THE EXTENT OF THE LAW, and of its unbending claims, was, that Christ's satisfaction was perfectly identical with that which men should themselves have rendered; and in the atonement they read off the unalterable claims of the divine law.

A brief sketch of the doctrine of the Reformation, for obvious reasons, may suffice. Every theological reader may safely be presumed to have an adequate acquaintance with the views of at least some of the Reformers—Luther, Melanchthon, Calvin, Knox, or Cranmer. Besides, all the symbolic books, articles, confessions, and catechisms of the Protestant churches, whether Lutheran or Reformed, contain a full expression of the Reformation doctrine. Without exception, it is the common doctrine of all evangelical churches. Every Protestant church embraced the Reformation doctrine on this point as THE ULTIMATE TRUTH. They held it as the adequate expression of biblical doctrine, in the same way as they all accepted the Nicene-Constantinopolitan doctrine of the Trinity, and the doctrine of Christ's person, ratified at Chalcedon, and many of them the Augustinian doctrine of grace, as the ultimate truth on these different topics. As there is such a general recognition of the doctrine of the Reformation on the subject of the atonement in all the churches, it would be superfluous to give a detailed outline of what is generally known. The sound elements in the development of previous centuries were all combined into a unity, and placed in a new setting or connection. The doubtful and neutralizing elements, interfering with the meritorious ground of acceptance, were thrown off; and the question was canvassed in an experimental interest, from which everything extraneous was of necessity removed.

We begin with a brief survey of Luther's opinions. No man since Paul's days seems to have ever apprehended so profoundly the great fact of the Mediator's substitution, or His bearing of imputed sin, in the room of others whom He was commissioned to represent. Luther makes it the most real exchange of persons and places between the Son of God on the one hand, and sinful man on the other; though always giving it to be understood that the substitution was a relative exchange, but not identity. His language sometimes seems extreme, but it is that of a man who had to bend opinion in another direction; and accordingly he reiterated and enforced the great truth with all the energy of language, by metaphor and similitude, and a dramatizing representation of the transaction. Thus, in his commentary on Gal. iii. 13, where we have a condensed view of his opinions on the atonement, he represents Christ as transferring our sins to Himself, and expounds the confession of sin in two Messianic psalms (Ps. xl. 1, and lxix. 5) as the utterances of Christ sustaining the persons of sinners and bearing their sins (*voces non innocentis sed patientis Christi*). He denounces the Sophists of his day, who separated Christ from sins and sinners, and proposed Him to mankind merely as an example; "whereby," says he, "they make Him useless." To show how Christ's suretyship was understood by him, the Father is represented as saying to His only-begotten Son: "Be Thou Peter the denier, Paul the persecutor, blasphemer, and injurious, David the adulterer, the sinner who ate of the fruit in paradise; in short, be Thou the person (*tu sis persona*) that committed the sins of all men; therefore, consider how you may pay and satisfy for them. Then comes the law and says: I find Him a sinner, and such a sinner as has taken on Himself the sins of all men; and I see no sin besides but in Him: therefore, let Him die on the cross" (*Luth. Oper.* tom. iv. p. 91). A few passages afterwards we find the following memorable passage: "The sole way of evading the curse is to believe and say with sure confidence: Thou, O Christ, art my sin and curse; or rather, I am Thy sin, Thy curse, Thy death, Thy wrath of God, Thy hell; Thou art, on the contrary, my righteousness," etc. (p. 95). It may safely be conceded that, when Luther permits himself, as Calvin also does (see Calvin on Gal. iii. 13), to call Christ a sinner, and the greatest of sinners, this is language rather to be avoided than imitated, for it grates on the Christian sensibilities. It has no Scripture warrant; and we must always distinguish, in thought and phrase, between what is relative and real, between the legal and the moral. But this style of speech, which in Luther's energetic description cannot be misunderstood, may show the reckless assertion to which those men commit themselves who would represent Luther as holding similar sentiments with those who deny vicarious satisfaction. He is the absolute antithesis of this.

Another point must be noticed. Under the influence of views derived from that doctrine of exchange, Luther never disjoins Christ's actions from His sufferings,—that is, His vicarious obedience from His death. He takes in both. To this point I the rather refer, because it is common among the writers who object to the element of active obedience in Christ's atonement, and call it an ecclesiastical notion, to allege that it formed no part of Luther's testimony, but was a mere subsequent addition, dating from the composition of the *Concordiæ Formula.* That is very far from being a correct view of the Reformation doctrine; and to me it is matter of no small surprise that writers, pretending to any accurate acquaintance with Luther's works, either in Latin or German, could entertain a moment's doubt of this fact. In a remarkable sermon on Gal. iv. 1–8 (vol. vii. p. 438, Erlangen edition of his German works) Luther speaks explicitly on the point. After remarking that no man can fulfil the law unless he is free from the law, and not under it (p. 265), and that Christ fulfilled the law spontaneously, and not by necessity or constraint, he goes on to say (p. 470): "But, that we may the better perceive how Christ acted under the law, we are to understand that He put Himself under it in a twofold way. *First, under the works of the law:* He permitted Himself to be circumcised, and sacrifices and purifications to be made for Him in the temple: He was subject to His father and mother, and the like: and yet was under no obligation; for He was a Lord above all laws. . . . . . *Secondly, He put Himself under the punishment and agony of the law spontaneously:* Not only did He perform the works to which He was not bound, but He spontaneously and innocently suffered the penalty which the law threatens and pronounces upon those who do not keep it." (Luther adds, after a few sentences, *Uns, uns hat er's zu gute gethan, nicht zu seiner Nothdurft*). In like manner, he elsewhere says (xv. p. 59): "When the law comes and accuses thee for not keeping it, point to Christ and say: 'Yonder is the Man who has fulfilled it, to whom I cling, *who fulfilled it, imparted His fulfilment to me;* and it must be silent.'"

Not less explicit is Melanchthon in many passages of his works, and quotations might be multiplied to this effect from his *Apology for the Augsburg Confession,* his *Loci Communes,* and *Commentaries.* Equally express is the language of Calvin, whether we consult his *Institutes* (book ii. ch. 17), the *Geneva Catechism,* or his *Commentary on the New Testament.* Chemnitz and his coadjutors, who composed the *Concordiæ Formula,* expressed the definite doctrine of the Reformation, when they set forth that the ACTIVE AND PASSIVE OBEDIENCE of Christ were equally vicarious and equally essential. This was no new theory nor addition. Protestant doctrine, alike in the Lutheran and Reformed churches, with a wonderful harmony, set forth that the entire human life of Christ, consisting of the elements of suffering and obedience, constituted the atonement according to the twofold relation which man, as a creature and as a sinner, occupies to the divine law; and that they were equally indispensable.

We need not adduce the other points of the Reformation doctrine at any length. As to the importance of Christ's divine person for the production of the atonement, it was in full accord with the patristic theology. All depended, according to Luther's exposition, on the fact that the Substitute was the only-begotten Son. He illustrates this doctrine by the case of two scales, in one of which are weighed our sins, with the wrath of God due to them; and in the other the expiatory sufferings, not of a mere man, but of the God-man (*Dei passio Dei mors, Dei sanguis*). A happy coincidence obtained between the two Protestant churches in this and in almost every point bearing on the atonement. In the Lutheran Church the doctrine of the atonement was, for about a century, discussed under the topic of Justification as its sole meritorious ground. The merit of works was swept away; and faith was made simply receptive. Thus it was elucidated by Chemnitz, Gerhard, and Hutter, till Calovius, by introducing the systematic method, departed from the topical treatment of doctrine. In the Reformed Church Calvin had, from the first, appended the discussion of the atonement to the person and office of Christ.

From the first the Lutheran Church never faltered as to the ABSOLUTE NECESSITY of a satisfaction for sin. Nor did the speculative question whether salvation was possible without atonement, and which was too lightly conceded by the patristic theology, ever find favour within her pale. This was the natural result of the profound views entertained by Luther on the infinite evil of sin, and on the inflexible claims of the divine law, as well as on the severity of divine wrath. On this point Luther writes in the spirit of Anselm, though it does not appear that he was acquainted with Anselm's works. He repudiates, with the utmost aversion, the notion of men being pardoned by absolute omnipotence. Thus he says (vol. vii. p. 298, Erlang ed.): " There are some, especially among the recent high scholastics, who affirm, Forgiveness of sins and justification of grace, lies absolutely in the divine imputation; that is, in God's accounting it enough that he to whom God imputes or does not impute sin should thereby be justified or not justified from his sins, as Ps. xxxii. 2, and Rom. iv. 7, 8, seem to them to say—' Blessed is the man to whom God imputeth not sin.' Were this true, the entire New Testament is already nothing,

and to no purpose; and Christ has laboured foolishly and use-
lessly in dying for sin. God thus exhibited, without necessity,
a mere sham fight and juggle, since He might, without the
sufferings of Christ, have forgiven sin, and not imputed it; and
thus another faith might have justified and saved us than faith
in Christ, viz. his sins, who relied on this gratuitous mercy of
God, would not have been imputed. Against this hateful and
terrible notion and error, the holy apostle is wont to direct
faith perpetually to Jesus Christ; and so frequently does he
name Jesus Christ, that it is a marvel how any one can be
unaware of the necessary cause." Whenever Luther adverts
to the idea that God might have adopted another mode of redemption, he does this to assign reason its limits. He says
he too could refine and speculate before God, but that he will
simply believe, and follow His word. No eminent divine, in
fact, in the Lutheran Church, till the rise of Rationalism, expressed himself with indecision on this point.

The same thing cannot be affirmed of the Reformed Church,
where we find for a considerable time a tendency to adopt the
language of Augustin. Thus Calvin, in his *Institutes* (ii. 12. 1),
and in his *Commentary* (John xv. 13), permits himself to speak
of the possibility of redemption in an absolute way, and to use
language directly the reverse of what would have been employed by Anselm and Luther. Similar language is found in
Zanchius and Musculus, as well as in various other Reformed
divines. Vossius, in vindicating Grotius' statements to this
effect, against the strictures of Ravensperger, adduces quotations from a large number of Reformed writers; and a leaven
of this description lingered among many Reformed divines,
down to the time of Twisse and Rutherford, who both shared
in this opinion. But greater caution was imposed by the
rise and spread of Socinianism, which unquestionably was
aided by these undue concessions, and was able to appeal to
them. At a later time, however, the two Protestant churches
everywhere avowed the same principle as to the ABSOLUTE
NECESSITY of a satisfaction, in order to the salvation of sinful
men (see Owen's *Vindication of Divine Justice*).

In another point the advantage decidedly lay with the
Reformed Church. While the Lutherans spoke loosely of the
universality of expiation, without limiting the destination of
the ransom by its efficacy, the Reformed divines more correctly
asserted and vindicated the special reference of the atonement.
This was from the first a characteristic of the Reformed Church
—a necessary result of the Augustinian views of grace with
which it was imbued. Calvin put it in the form in which it

had descended and was discussed in the schools: "SUFFICIENTLY for the whole world, but EFFICIENTLY only for the elect" (Calvin on 1 John ii. 2). The Reformed Church maintained that the efficacy of Christ's merits bore special reference to the elect. This impress was stamped upon the church from its first origin, and to this view she may be said to have continued generally faithful. The Lutheran Church always held the universal element, without formulating it.

The historical outline of the doctrine of the atonement, which we have thus far sketched from the Apostolic age to the Reformation, proves that, in every phase of what can warrantably be termed ecclesiastical doctrine in the Eastern or Western Church, the death of Christ was uniformly viewed as standing in the closest relation to man's salvation. The sincere investigators of the divine word were always persuaded that the remission of sins stood directly connected with the Lord's death, however much might be the influence of Christ's teaching, example, and constant care of the human family. But a further inquiry arose: What was the nature of that connection, or could it be precisely ascertained? We have seen, whether we turn to the patristic theology, to the comparatively mixed or philosophical theology of the Middle Ages, or to the more biblical theology of the Reformation, that every century agreed with one consent in the conclusion that there was a connection between Christ's death and the remission of sins; and that the connection was one of cause and effect, whether they speak of ransom and deliverance, of sacrifice and exemption from punishment, or of merit and reward. The single exception of the rationalistic Abelard is scarce worthy of notice. HERE, THEN, WE HAVE THE CHURCH-CONSCIOUSNESS OF CHRISTENDOM, if anything deserves that name. Though opinions of a neutralizing tendency undoubtedly were fostered in the East and West, yet the doctrine of the causal connection between Christ's death and pardon—in other words, the expiation of sin by His blood—was not denied at any period either by the Greek or Romish Church. This harmony of Christian conviction and doctrine is not to be ignored or undervalued.

We have brought down the history of the doctrine to the Reformation, at which time it may be said to have stood forth in meridian brightness and full-orbed development. At that date nothing interposed between the sinner and the atonement —no merit of works—no preparation by ecclesiastic rites; the application of it was by faith alone. The Reformation doctrine was, that the atonement alone saves, and that it is received by faith alone. Christ's twofold work of active and passive obedience was set forth as something merely to be received by faith for the remission of sin.

As true doctrine, however, is invariably followed by error as its shadow, that exhibition of the ultimate truth on this great article could not be expected to be preserved for any length of time untarnished and unclouded. The atonement was made central, and offered for men's reception, without preparations or conditions, in the purest form in which it had ever been presented since the Apostolic age; but before the century closed negations arose on every side, viz. Socinianism, the rejection of the vicarious active obedience, Grotianism, Arminianism, and the like.

As to SOCINIANISM, it is not necessary, after the historic sketch given in the previous volume, to enumerate its peculiarities; and the cognate views of the present day adverse to the vicarious satisfaction, which, with Christian elements not to be denied, are unquestionably Socinianizing in their theory of Christ's death. These were pretty fully exhibited and brought down to recent times in the previous volume. In this historical outline I deem it best to avoid that class of opinions, and to limit myself to other theories, which, though deviating from Reformation doctrine in certain points, yet agree in ascribing to the death of Christ the remission of sins, the acceptance of our persons, and our redemption from the curse. This leads us into a different class of theories, and among writers more pronounced in doctrinal opinions, and approaching nearer to the truth. The great question which divided the schools of theology after the appearance of Socinianism, and divides the modern thinkers of the German type from the class commonly regarded as evangelical and biblical, is, *whether remission of sins is an absolute gift*, or obtained by the death of Christ as its meritorious PURCHASE? The theory of absolute pardon, which represents Christ as preaching but not procuring pardon—the great untruth of the modern theology, as contrasted with the general Christian consciousness—we delineated historically already. We have described it also dogmatically, as subversive of all moral laws, and opposed to natural as well as revealed theology. But to enter more into detail as to the peculiar views of this class of writers, though it might have its interest, would be but a repetition or enlargement of what has been done already.

1. The first negation which obscured the full-orbed doctrine of the Reformation, was the rejection of the element of Christ's active obedience. This error assailed the Protestant Church in three different quarters, and was particularly injurious, leaving behind it a leaven never fully purged out to this day.

Osiander of Königsberg, in his treatise on Justification, 1550, immediately after Luther's death, attacked the distinctive principle of Protestantism, by denying that justification was to be regarded as a forensic act on the ground of Christ's righteousness. He allowed that mankind obtain pardon and redemption from the curse of the law through the blood of Christ, but divided between pardon and justification in such a way as to make the former relative and the latter inherent; and he charged the Lutheran teachers with ignorance and indecision, inasmuch as they could not state or define what Christ's righteousness involved. This challenge to the Protestant Church to become self-conscious led to definition. Not only Flacius Illyricus, Brentius, and others in the Lutheran Church, but Calvin also, in replying to Osiander, explicitly combined the active and passive obedience of Christ as equally vicarious. They taught that Christ's one complete obedience was comprehended both in His actions and sufferings, and that the matter of our redemption consisted of both. Flacius Illyricus sets forth that Christ, as perfectly obedient to the law, did and suffered all that the law required of us, and imputed to us His whole obedience as our righteousness. This controversy, which shook the Lutheran Church in an extraordinary way, led the way to clearer definition as contained in the *Concordiæ Formula*. It was maintained that sin consists in omission as well as commission, and that remission of sin necessarily involves not only the removal of guilt, but the imputation of righteousness. Their conclusion was, that the divine law must be perfectly obeyed by a mediator; and they defined this righteousness sometimes as satisfaction AND obedience, and at other times as Christ's OBEDIENCE IN LIFE AND IN DEATH.

Another tendency originated by Piscator in the Reformed Church, divided between Christ's active and passive obedience, hitherto regarded as equally belonging to His vicarious work. Piscator maintained that the active obedience was necessary for Christ Himself as man, and that only the passive obedience was imputed to His people. The same theory, probably suggested by a Socinian taunt (of a *nimisfactio*), was propounded by Karg, a Lutheran divine, but soon recanted. It was earnestly maintained by Piscator, and spread in all directions from him. It was taken up in the French Church by Cameron, Cappel, Blondel, and La Placette; in the Palatinate by Pareus and Scultetus; in Holland by Wendelinus, Henry and James Alting, father and son; and the mischievous leaven continues to work in many churches to this day. It could exist only in connection with a semi-Nestorian view of Christ's person, and defective views of man's double obligation as a creature and a sinner, which is not to be expressed in the formula, obey OR suffer, but obey AND suffer. Piscator admitted that, as a qualification for the work of redemption, or indispensable condition, Christ's active obedience was presupposed; but he denied that it was vicarious or imputed.[1] These views were condemned by the National Synod of Gap, and by several French Synods, from 1603 to 1612. The theory continued to spread, and tended to undermine the great fact of substitution, at least in the definite sense that whatever was in man's obligation formed part of the Redeemer's suretyship. It is not necessary to adduce arguments in refutation of this theory, as we have, in the discussions of this volume and of the former, asserted from Scripture directly the reverse. It would be a mere repetition to restate the biblical truth that perfect obedience according to God's legislative authority, constitutes our sole ground or title to life.

2. The theory of Grotius, which comes next in order, menaced the integrity of the doctrine of the atonement in another way. His well-known work, *The Defence of the Catholic Faith on the Satisfaction of Christ against Faustus Socinus* (A.D. 1617), was hailed by the most eminent divines, and translated into various languages. It was made the basis of Stillingfleet's work on the sufferings of Christ. When fully examined, however, in the light of the Reformation doctrine, and read according to its avowed principle, it is found to surrender almost as much as it retained. Differing from the theory of Duns Scotus in maintaining that Christ's sufferings were of infinite value on account of the dignity of His person, it yet decidedly approached his views in maintaining an acceptilation theory. The argument of Grotius proceeded on the supposition that the divine claims were relaxed, that God exercised His dispensing authority, and might have dispensed

---

[1] Our great epic poet far more correctly writes :—

"—— Nor can this be
But by fulfilling all which thou didst want,
Obedience to the law of God imposed
On penalty of death, and *suffering death,*
The penalty to thy transgression due,
And due to theirs which out of thine shall grow :
So only can high justice rest appeased.
The *law* of God exact He shall *fulfil,*
Both by obedience and by love ; though love
Alone fulfil the law : thy punishment
He shall endure."

—*P.L.* xii. 395.

with any satisfaction, had He so pleased. It is sometimes called THE ACCEPTILATION THEORY—implying that the creditor remits the debt without payment or compensation; and it is sometimes called THE GOVERNMENTAL THEORY, because God is considered only as a regent who adopted a certain wise measure in the way of punitive example, to impress His subjects with a necessary respect for law and authority. That may be used as a rough illustration, but not as a theory of the atonement.

The theory was not based on a satisfaction of divine justice, for he allowed that God might have left sin to go unpunished; nor was the atonement regarded as effected by entering into man's responsibilities in their full extent, so that we can reason from what man owed to what Christ rendered. Grotius reduced it to a mere expedient or measure of government. He started in his inquiry from the question of PUNISHMENT, as if the infliction of punishment—a mere consequence of sin—were all that was essentially involved. To bring down the question into a yet lower region, he based punishment on purely positive law or arbitrary appointment, which, being subject to no higher law, might by possibility relax the obligations, remit the sanctions, and remove the consequences.[1] Grotius retains the actual satisfaction; and herein lies the service which he rendered, and which the church gratefully accepted. His conclusions on the atonement, however valuable so far as they are a statement of fact, suppose no inward necessity in the divine government for such a costly provision. They are thus very different from Anselm's. The latter starts, not from a punitive example, arbitrary and capable of being dispensed with, but from SIN as a violation of the divine honour, a disharmony in God's universe, and DEMANDING punishment as well·as reparation.

On this account, Grotius' theory could not counteract the Socinian views, because he gave up the main elements of the ecclesiastical doctrine—the indispensable necessity of satisfaction to divine justice, and of the complete fulfilment of man's obligations, in precept and in penalty. His views of sin were shallow. He did not regard the personal God as sustaining by its commission any wrong which the wisdom of the Moral Governor could not undo by a mere punitive example. What does a punitive example amount to in connection with human guilt? It means no more than that a certain expedient was

---

[1] Milton, the theologian poet, far more accurately puts it thus :—

" Die he or justice must ; unless for him
Some other able, and as willing, pay
The rigid satisfaction, death for death."—*P.L.* iii. 210.

adopted to DETER FROM SIN IN FUTURE, or to influence other orders of being in the universe. The guilt of past sin was thus not affected by the atonement in the way in which the church argued. Nor does the theory maintain the inward link between sin and punishment, far less explain how the punitive justice of God could approach such a person. FOR THIS IS THE PROBLEM. If the death of Christ stands only as an example for the future, then its necessity was not based in the divine nature. It was the most inappropriate possible, because the punishment of the innocent could not deter the guilty. Plainly, Grotius smuggled in the notion of a punitive example for the true theory of satisfaction. Justice must be done to Grotius, however, as compared with Socinianism; for, though he acted unfairly by the truth, and adopted a mediating policy, yet he still connects remission of sins with the atoning death of Christ.

The Grotian theory has been largely accepted in America under the name of the governmental theory. Hopkinsianism was one phase of it; and it is sometimes designated the New England theory, or the New School theory. We repudiate in the strongest terms the designation lately given to it—THE EDWARDEAN THEORY[1] of the atonement—because the honoured name of Edwards, one of the greatest in church history, is not to be identified with a theory of which not even the germs can fairly be deduced from his writings. We could exhibit illustrations from the President's writings of almost every position we have advanced in this volume; and mere stray expressions occurring in his writings are not to be fitted in to the crude outline of the governmental scheme, from which his whole mode of thought diverged. No writer more fully describes Christ as entering into all the obligations of His people, both as to active and passive obedience. The Hopkinsian or governmental scheme, repudiating imputation in the proper sense, reduces the atonement from the high ground of a propitiation to the level of an empty pageant, however imposing, or a governmental display[2] for the good of other orders of creation. It is a scheme which connects the death of Christ with some imaginary public justice, not with the divine nature and perfections; as if God Himself

---

[1] See a thick volume entitled *The Atonement*—discourses and treatises by Edwards, Smalley, Maxey, Emmons, Griffin, Burge, and others, with a preface by Professor Park: Boston, 1859. This is one of the ablest defences of the Grotian theory; but we have right and reason to object to Professor Park's title, "The Edwardean Theory of the Atonement." Whatever were the views of Edwards' son is of little moment comparatively.

[2] Dr. Jenkyn on the Extent of the Atonement (*English Congregationalist*, 1842), reproduces the Grotian theory, and makes it universal. He calls the atonement "an honourable ground or medium for expressing mercy."

were not His own public, the only august public worthy of regard in this great transaction. According to the Grotian or Hopkinsian theory, the atonement is fit to impress the creation of God, but is not necessary in respect of the divine attributes.

3. Next followed the theory of ARMINIUS and the Arminian type of theology—a tendency starting from the notion of universal grace, and allowing no special reference to the elect. It deviated widely from biblical doctrine, and infected all the Reformed churches at one period or another of their history. Though different in kind from Socinianism, because it still maintained a causal connection between the death of Christ and pardon, it yet departed very far from the proper idea of substitution and strict views of divine justice. The assertion of universal atonement without suretyship in any true sense of the term, led by necessary consequence to a new view of the nature of the atonement, when the theory found it necessary to complete itself. The Arminians, in their second distinctive article, maintained that Christ, according to the Father's purpose and His own, died for all and every man alike: that He made God placable and man salvable, but did not actually procure reconciliation for any. They held that He merely removed the obstacle on the side of divine justice, and acquired power for God to form a new covenant with all mankind. It was a theory which took in almost all the negative elements already mentioned, and, under the guise of enlarging Christ's merits, tended only to undermine and diminish them. A few considerations will prove this against the representations of the Arminians.

(1.) They denuded the atonement of any efficacy, denying that it carried with it the element of its application. They did not shrink from the avowal that the ransom might have been paid, and yet applied to none in consequence of intervening unbelief; nay, that Christ's atonement, though not actually applied to any individual, would still have been complete in all its parts. A gulf was thus drawn between the procuring of redemption and the application of it, as if these were not of equal extent and breadth. The application was thus suspended on man's free will, and humanity was thrown back on its own resources, or on such aid as all equally receive, to apply the redemption for themselves.

(2.) They held, as appears from the transactions of the Synod of Dort, that the end of Christ's death was to acquire a new right, on the ground of which God might make a new covenant with mankind; and that this new covenant consisted in this, that God accepts faith as an imperfect obedience. How this menaced the atonement is obvious. A relaxation of the law was assumed, and the immutable claims of God were supposed to be reduced. This shows that it became a question as to the nature of the atonement, as well as its extent.

(3.) They held that Christ, by His satisfaction, did not secure redemption for any individual, or merit the faith by which the atonement should be effectually applied. They would not admit that the atonement carried with it the ground of its own application. If we compare Arminian views with biblical teaching on the subject of satisfaction, we soon find that they can no more be harmonized than light and darkness ; for, according to apostolic teaching, the deliverance follows the ransom. Thus the whole doctrine was put to hazard. It was held that the death of Christ only made God capable of re-conciliation, while the actual reconciliation was left to men themselves working out their own salvation.

The Synod of Dort, though much decried, was a noble bulwark of divine truth. It set forth that the death of the Son of God was of infinite intrinsic value, *and abundantly sufficient to expiate the sins of the whole world*. And after declaring that the death of Christ derived its value from the fact that He was not only a true and perfectly holy man, but the only-begotten Son of God, it is added: " That many who are called by the gospel do not repent or believe in Christ, but perish in unbelief, is not from the defect or insufficiency of Christ's sacrifice on the cross, but from their own fault." The admirably put statements of this great Synod, equal as it was to any of the ancient Councils, deserve special attention. It asserted sufficiency in respect of intrinsic potency and value. But while asserting this, and coupling it with human responsibility, the Synod maintained at the same time that, in respect of proper destination and efficacy, it was not universal, but appointed for certain definite persons whom God freely chose from eternity. As to the proper scope of Christ's atonement, it was asserted that He died as Mediator of the elect alone, to procure reconciliation for them, and also to apply it. The sum of the matter, as stated by the Synod, was, that the merits of Christ, considered in them-selves, were of infinite value, or amply sufficient for all, but of efficacious validity for the elect alone. Why all men are not saved is not due to any deficiency in Christ's merits—for He would not have needed to do or suffer more than He has done for the salvation of millions more,—but must be traced to the purpose of God appointing who should be partakers of His merits. These truths are not inconsistent with each other: the intrinsic value of the atonement did not affect the extent of its saving efficacy, as a general of an army, capable of delivering many captives, may receive from his prince a command only to deliver some; or a physician, having the means of healing many, may apply the cure to a limited number. This was the position which the church maintained against Arminianism.

About the time of the Synod of Dort, when the theological mind of the age was intensely turned to the doctrines of grace, THE FEDERAL THEOLOGY, as it was called, was propounded, and contributed more powerfully than any other influence to promote the sound doctrine of the atonement. We are told that Luther anticipated that some pious and learned man would arise to elucidate the doctrine of the covenant of God and its various economies. Bullinger first broke ground on this topic in his book on the Covenant. Olevianus and Cloppenburg followed, the latter discussing the subject pretty copiously in his third *Disputation on the New Covenant of Grace and its Surety* (A.D. 1622). But it was reserved for Cocceius, in his famous *Treatise on the Covenant* (A.D. 1648), to supply the key which served to unlock the mystery of the covenant of grace. After him a whole cloud of witnesses in England, Scotland, and Holland supplied further elucidation of it. It formed one of the distinctive peculiarities of the Puritan theology; and as a scheme of thought developed by Witsius, Strong, Petto, Owen, and others, it combined into a whole and in an organic way the entire doctrines of sovereign special grace.

Nothing tended more to establish the true doctrine of the atonement, because it brought out the counterpart relation of the first and second Adam, and the work of the great Surety, as read off from the obligations of the first man. It grounded the legal conjunction between us and Christ, and the suretyship, the substitution and imputation into which Jesus entered. Scripture shows a covenant or compact formed between God as the source of law, and His own Son as head of the elect, whom He represented. The Arminian scheme broke upon it as a wave on the rock. That system directed the most strenuous efforts against it, but in vain. No direct covenant could be immediately made between God and man; a surety alone was adequate to bring the Creator and the sinner together. The Father made the claim of full obedience upon His Son, and the Son now claims the fulfilment of the stipulations.[1] Thus, the whole was

---

[1] Thus Milton, in the true spirit of the federal theology, represents the Son as saying :—

> " Behold me, then ; me for him, life for life
> I offer ; on me let all Thine anger fall ;
> Account me man ; I for his sake will leave
> Thy bosom, and this glory, next to Thee,

removed from the region of the vague and indefinite by the idea of special destination. Not only so ; it exploded the Arminian notion that faith was the proper condition of the covenant. That first principle of the Arminian scheme—a legal element throwing men back on themselves—was obviated by the federal theology, which showed that the conditions were all fulfilled by the Mediator of the covenant, as the very end of His incarnation, and that it is pure grace to us. If the Mediator fulfilled the conditions, they cannot be a second time required without undermining the unity between the Surety and His seed. Christ's atonement was thus the fulfilment of the federal conditions. The Father, who in every part of this great transaction was at once the Lawgiver and the Fountain of the covenant, insisted on the full performance of the law, and yet provided the surety, who was made under the law in the proper sense of the term. It was a true command on God's side, and a true obedience on Christ's side. He stood in our covenant, which was the law of works ; that is, the law in its precept and in its curse.

4. Next in order we must notice the theory which emanated from the divines of Saumur, which has been called the AMYRALDIST THEORY. It was a revolt from the position maintained at the Synod of Dort, under the guise of an explanation ; for the propounders of the theory would not allow that they were out of harmony with its decrees. Not content to affirm, with the canons of Dort, that the intrinsic value of Christ's atonement was infinite, and capable, had God so pleased, of being extended to all mankind, they maintained that, along with a sufficiency of value, there was a certain destination of Christ's death, on the part of God and of the Mediator, to the whole human race. This theory owed its origin to Cameron, a learned but restless Scotchman, Professor of Theology at Saumur. He propounded the theory of hypothetic universalism ; that is, that God wills the salvation of all men, on condition of faith, and that Christ's death was for all men, on condition of faith. Cameron declares that Christ died for no man simply, but on condition that we who are of the world should be delivered from the world, and engrafted into Christ

> Truly put off, and for him early die,
> Well pleased : on me let death wreak all his rage ;
> Under his gloomy power I shall not long
> Lie vanquished : Thou hast given me to possess
> Life in myself for ever : by Thee I live,
> Though now to death I yield, and am his due,
> All that of me can die."
> —*P.L.* iii. 236.

by true faith (*Opusc. Miscell.* p. 533).   This system, adopted by a distinguished class of pupils, Amyraud, Testard, Cappellus, and Placæus, widely leavened and corrupted the Reformed Church of France.   Amyraldus digested it into system in his *Treatise on Predestination* (A.D. 1634), and in various publications.   It was controverted by Rivetus (*Op.* iii. p. 830), and F. Spanheim in his *Exercitations on Universal Grace.*

When we examine the theory minutely, it will not hang together.   Its advocates speak of a UNIVERSAL DECREE, in which God was supposed to have given Christ as a Mediator for the whole human race; and of a SPECIAL DECREE, in which God, foreseeing that no one would believe in his unaided strength, was supposed to have elected some to receive the gift of faith. Unquestionably it differs from the Arminian positions in this respect, that the faith was not referred to man's free will, but was supposed to be derived from God's free grace.   The theory acknowledged the sovereign election of God, according to His good pleasure.   But it laboured under the defect of supposing a double and a conflicting decree; that is, a general decree, in which He was said to will the salvation of all, and a special decree, in which He was said to will the salvation of the elect. To Christ also it ascribed a twofold and discordant aim, viz. to satisfy for all men, and to satisfy merely for the elect.   As a reconciling system, and an incoherent one, it aimed to harmonize the passages of Scripture, which at one time seem to extend Christ's merits to the world, and at another to limit them to the church; not to mention that God is supposed to be disappointed in His purpose.

The various writers of this school are very far from uniformity in their explanations of the theory.   Some write that Christ died for all men, on the condition of faith; others that Christ opened a way to salvation for all believers, and that His redemption was twofold; others that He offered Himself equally for all.   Thus Amyraud expresses himself in his *Treatise on Predestination* (ch. 7): " The sacrifice which Jesus Christ offered was EQUALLY FOR ALL ; and the salvation which He received from His Father, in the sanctification of the spirit and the glorification of the body, was destined equally for all— provided the necessary disposition for receiving it were equal." The National Synod of the Reformed Churches of France, which met at Alençon in 1637, at which Amyraud and Testard gave explanations in harmony with the canons of Dort, was satisfied, but at the same time decreed that in future they should abstain from the statement that Christ died equally for all, because that expression EQUALLY had been formerly, and might be again, a stone of stumbling to many. Not only so; the entire theory of Amyraldus labours under two defects, which indeed are very closely connected with each other. It denied, along with Piscator, the element of Christ's active obedience; and the atonement was never described as carrying with it its own application. On the contrary, this was secured by another mode, as follows : Christ died for all, on condition of faith; and man being incapable of this, God, by ANOTHER DECREE, purposed to give faith to some.

This peculiarity distinguishes Amyraldism, unfavourably to it, from another theory with which it has sometimes been confounded—viz. that presented to the Synod of Dort by the five English deputies,[1] of whom the most eminent theologian was Davenant, one of the greatest names that adorn the English Church. When we examine their statement to the Synod (*judicium*), we find, what seems at first sight the same double reference, Christ's death for the elect, and then His death for the world at large. But the only point to which the Synod of Dort attached importance was unambiguously uttered. They said that Christ died for the elect according to the love and intention of God the Father and of Christ, that He might actually obtain, and infallibly bestow, remission of sins and eternal salvation; and that faith and perseverance are given to these elect persons out of the same love, *by and on account of (per et propter) the merit* and intercession of Christ. This draws a wide line of demarcation[2] between the theology of Davenant, or of the Church of England, and that of Amyraldus, which insisted on a view of the atonement which, on the one hand, did not contain the element of its own application, and, on the other, continued to hold that Christ's death was equally for all. The celebrated Baxter has been often unfairly claimed as an Amyraldist. We will not defend all his positions in his controversy with Owen, when handling the doctrine of the atonement, yet an injustice is done to this truly great man when he is represented as an advocate of the Universalist theory. These words of Baxter made it as plain as did the Synod of Dort that

---

[1] *Acta Synodi : Judicia Theologorum Exterorum*, p. 78.

[2] The works of Polhill (A.D. 1677) reproduced Amyraldism in England in the sense now described. He sometimes seems to approach Davenant, but his view is different, and to be distinguished from Davenant's theory. Dr. Wardlaw, in his work on the atonement, fluctuating between Grotianism and Amyraldism, goes no further than to say " that the atonement is a great moral vindication of the divine character, and especially of the divine righteousness, *not binding God to pardon any*, but rendering it honourable to His perfections and government, should He so will it, to pardon all " (p. 71). Andrew Fuller, sometimes claimed as not a strict Calvinist, with much more correctness represents the atonement as securing its own application.

the atonement merited its own application: "He whose sufferings were primarily *satisfaction* for *sin*, were secondarily *meritorious* of the means to bring men to the intended end; that is,
of the Word and Spirit by which Christ causeth sinners to
believe; so that faith is a fruit of the death of Christ in a
remote or secondary sense" (*Cathol. Theol.* p. 69).

5. We further notice a class of theories which limited the
duration of Christ's expiatory sufferings to the period when He
hung on the cross. The opinion of all Protestant divines up
till the time of James Alting, was that the Lord's sufferings
from His birth to His death were vicarious. He propounded
the notion that proper satisfaction was limited to the sufferings
undergone during the three hours when darkness covered the
land at the crucifixion. He divided the Lord's sufferings into
two kinds,—those which were vicarious and bore a surety-
character limited to the time of His suspension on the cross,
and those which were undergone in the conflict with Satan.
This limitation to a few hours evacuated it of its true character,
as the denial of Christ's active obedience weakened the doctrine
of substitution on the other side. The true doctrine is, that as
the active obedience was a vicarious fulfilment of our obligations from His birth to His death, so His passive obedience
was a vicarious satisfaction from the manger to the cross. The
same theory is propounded in the crude theology of the Ply-
mouth Brethren. Thus Mr. Mackintosh says: "We are not to
regard the cross of Christ as a mere circumstance in the life
of sin-bearing. It was the grand and only scene of sin-bearing:
'His own self bare our sins in His own body on the tree'
(1 Pet. ii. 24). He did not bear them anywhere else. He did
not bear them in the manger, nor in the wilderness, nor in the
garden, but ONLY ON THE TREE. He never had aught to say to
sin, save on the cross." Biblical theology is the very opposite
of this extract, as we have proved throughout.

What were the arguments by which Alting laboured to
defend such a position? He argued from the statement that
"Christ ONCE suffered;" a phrase which cannot bear the sense
put upon it, but denies the repetition of His atonement. He
argued, too, that previous to the crucifixion Christ received
tokens of divine favour—nay, several audible voices from
heaven,—and that the wrath of God was borne only on the
tree. We have proved the opposite at large. It is matter of
wonder that one so eminent as a divine should put these two
in collision. There were intervening moments of comfort all
through His curse-bearing life, and even on the tree. This
theory is opposed to just views of substitution; for Christ's

entire suffering obedience was the discharge of His one mediatorial work, and essentially connected with the servant-form
which He bore. To ground the theory on the fact that darkness covered the face of the world, is a baseless fancy.

Scripture makes it evident that all Christ's sufferings were
the work of a surety, and expiatory. This appears from the
fact that He was sinless; and it would have been inconsistent
with the divine perfections to inflict suffering on Him unless
He occupied the place of the surety: for agony and suffering
could not have assailed a sinless being on any other ground.
Besides, the Scriptures expressly affirm that by His stripes we
are healed (1 Pet. ii. 24).

6. I might further mention a theory propounded by Roëll,
that Christ's atonement did not *satisfy for temporal death*. But
it was limited to Holland, triumphantly refuted by Vitringa, and
generally repudiated.

I shall not further pursue this historical sketch. No further
modifications of the Reformation doctrine, at least of much
moment, occurred till the church encountered the first rise of
Rationalism, after the middle of last century. It is noteworthy
that the assault began at the very point where the Reformation theology had completed itself—viz. by denying the active
obedience of Christ[1] and His entering into all His people's obligations. We deem it needless, however, to enter on Rationalistic theories which run counter to expiation in any form,
inasmuch as this was pretty fully done in the former volume;
and the present outline was intended to delineate that other
class of theories which continued to maintain the causal connection between the death of Christ and the remission of sins.
Let me sum up this outline, which cannot be further enlarged,
with the following couplet of Voetius, which succinctly states
the various elements which enter into Christ's atoning work :—

"Propitians, purgans, redimens, ut victima sponsor,
Salvavit sic jura Dei verumque requirunt."

[1] This was done by Töllner in his work *Der Thätige Gehorsam Jesu Christi*,
1768.

INDICES.

———

I.—THE PASSAGES EXPOUNDED.

II.—SUBJECTS.

III.—GREEK WORDS SPECIALLY NOTICED.

THE END.